CU00959975

THE HUMAN IN COMMAND

THE HUMAN IN COMMAND
EXPLORING THE MODERN MILITARY EXPERIENCE

UB
212
.H 86
2000
c.2

Edited by

Carol McCann

and

Ross Pigeau

Defence and Civil Institute of Environmental Medicine
Toronto, Ontario, Canada

Kluwer Academic / Plenum Publishers
New York, Boston, Dordrecht, London, Moscow

Library of Congress Cataloging-in-Publication Data

The human in command: exploring the modern military experience/edited by Carol McCann and Ross Pigeau
    p. cm.
    Proceedings of a NATO RTO workshop held June 8–12, 1998, in Kingston, Jamaica.
    Includes bibliographical references and index.
    ISBN 0-306-46366-0
    1. Command and control systems—Congresses.   2. Command of troops—Congresses.   I. McCann, Carol. II. Pigeau, Ross.

UB212.H86 2000
355.3'3041—dc21   99-089695

Proceedings of a NATO RTO Workshop on The Human in Command, held June 8–12, 1998, in Kingston, Jamaica

ISBN: 0-306-46366-0

© 2000 Kluwer Academic/Plenum Publishers, New York
233 Spring Street, New York, New York 10013

http://www.wkap.nl/

10 9 8 7 6 5 4 3 2 1

A C.I.P. record for this book is available from the Library of Congress.

All rights reserved

No part of this book may be reproduced, stored in a retrieval system, or transmitted in any form or by any means, electronic, mechanical, photocopying, microfilming, recording, or otherwise, without written permission from the Publisher

Printed in the United States of America

FOREWORD

MAJOR-GENERAL M. K. JEFFERY

Command, and indeed the *human* in command, has always been key to military operations. The complexity and tempo of modern operations make this statement even more true today than in the past. However, both the military and the research communities have tended to treat command and control (C^2) from a limited perspective. For too long, command and control have been considered as if they were a single concept, with control often dominating our study. Indeed, in many cases we have divorced operational C^2 from the military institution itself, resulting in disconnects and inefficiencies. Then, in an attempt to overcome these self-inflicted deficiencies, we have pursued the Holy Grail of technology, hoping that it would solve our C^2 problems. Only now, as we start to realize technology's costs and limitations, are we looking critically at C^2. This book attempts to take such a look.

The contributions that make up this book are the product of a June 1998 NATO (North Atlantic Treaty Organization) workshop called *The Human in Command*. Far from being purely an academic exercise, this gathering brought together military leaders and civilian scientists to discuss C^2's central pragmatic and conceptual issues—its assumptions, its practices, and its organization. Indeed, in recent years there has been mounting evidence that both our society and its military institutions are facing organizational crises. In the introduction to her 1992 book *Leadership and the New Science*, Margaret Wheatley eloquently expresses the widely shared bewilderment and concern about this problem:

> I am not alone in wondering why organizations aren't working well. Many of us are troubled by questions that haunt our work. Why do so many organizations feel dead? Why do projects take so long, develop ever-greater complexity, yet so often fail to achieve any truly significant results? Why does progress, when it appears, so often come from unexpected places, or as a result of surprises or serendipitous events that our planning had not considered? Why does change itself, that event we're all supposed to be "managing," keep drowning us, relentlessly reducing any sense of mastery we might possess? And why have our expectations for success diminished to the point that often

MAJOR-GENERAL M. K. JEFFERY • *1st Canadian Division, P.O. Box 17000, Station Forces, Kingston, Ontario, Canada K7K 7B4*

the best we hope for is staying power and patience to endure the disruptive forces that
appear unpredictably in the organizations where we work? (p. 1)

Militaries around the world are living, on a daily basis, with the failings of our
current approaches to command and control. The basic organizational models used
by military forces have not changed in more than a century. Although the demands
and complexity of operations have changed significantly during that time, our organizations have responded only by becoming larger and more bureaucratic. New
technology has been thrown haphazardly at these old organizations in the hope that
this approach would solve their problems. But it hasn't. As a result, every organization has found C^2 increasingly difficult, demanding untold energy just to keep
those organizations functioning. This situation is unacceptable—if for no other
reason than that our organizations are literally running out of energy.

Recently, the militaries have started questioning C^2's underlying models. But in
my view, we must go further. We must rethink the entire paradigm. We must develop
new concepts that balance the needs of the operation with those of the organization, and balance the need for technology with the need for human flexibility. Before
we can meet these challenges, many issues must be addressed and many tough questions answered. I offer here only a few examples:

- Militaries claim a desire for mission-oriented command and control, but is
  this goal achievable? Western societies have developed very centralized
  organizational structures that promise high levels of control. In some ways,
  such structures are politically and militarily attractive. But can our cultures
  tolerate decentralized C^2 philosophies—philosophies that encourage independent thought and action?

- How can we maximize the performance of people in our organizations? We
  often say that the human is the most vital component in any system. But do
  our military structures and operational concepts—many of which are quite
  old—bring out the best in our personnel? Do they foster motivation and
  prudent risk-taking?

- Are the demands placed on the human in C^2 systems realistic and sustain-
  able? As we load more work, more stress, and more information onto our
  people, are we sufficiently sensitive to their limits? Do we expend reasonable effort in adapting technology to the human, rather than expecting the
  human to adapt to technology?

- Is our concept of command and control suitable for all operational environments? Does it address the full spectrum of operations, from disaster
  relief to peacekeeping to warfighting? Militaries have always believed that
  organizing and training for war prepares them for all other eventualities. Is
  this belief still realistic? And if so, is it practical, or should we look at implementing multiple approaches to command and control—approaches that
  more closely match operational needs?

- What are the human limits to command in the technological age? Command
  is a personal matter, requiring the development and maintenance of trust

with subordinates. For example, there may be no replacement for the firm hand of reassurance on the shoulder of a junior team member. Does our ever-increasing reliance on technology jeopardize this essential human aspect of command?

- Inevitably, military operations are also moral affairs, requiring delicate and difficult ethical judgments. How do we ensure that those judgments are properly considered and carried out? How do we avoid relinquishing to technology the responsibility for making those judgments?

These and many other questions must be answered if we are to master command and control in the new era.

This book represents an excellent first step toward bringing the military, scientific, and academic communities together to address C²'s fundamental concepts. Given the topic's complexity, as well as the relatively narrow focus of many of its experts (military and civilian alike), this book should go a long way toward challenging our assumptions and charting a logical way forward. The fresh perspectives offered here can begin to empower us to resolve our problems and regain a measure of control in this chaotic era. Finally, this book makes clear that whatever concepts we do develop, we must ensure that the human remains in command.

REFERENCE

Wheatley, M. J. (1992). *Leadership and the New Science.* San Francisco, CA: Berrett-Koehler.

ACKNOWLEDGMENTS

This book is the product of much care and effort by a number of talented people. Our initial idea of bringing together military leaders with research scientists to discuss issues in command would soon have died had we not received encouragement and help from several key individuals.

We are indebted to Major-General Mike Jeffery and Brigadier-General Jan Arp for hosting the NATO Human in Command Workshop at the Canadian Land Forces Command and Staff College, Fort Frontenac, Kingston. The workshop was held under the auspices of NATO's Research and Technology Organization. During the workshop, Major Richard Vos and his staff provided outstanding administrative and logistics support, making our task immeasurably easier. We would also like to thank Lieutenant-Colonel Peter Kramers, Canadian Forces liaison officer at the Combined Arms Center, Fort Leavenworth, Kansas, for encouraging senior military commanders to participate in the workshop.

Here at our own establishment, the Defence and Civil Institute of Environmental Medicine in Toronto, we are indebted to Andrea Hawton, Siobhan Lydon, Joe Baranski, and Megan Thompson for helping organize the workshop and for giving us the moral support to finish the long process of editing; to Heather Devine for helping with the many details of manuscript preparation, especially the figures; and to Stewart Harrison, the DCIEM librarian, always quick to assist us in finding some obscure reference or out-of-print book. Finally, we would especially like to thank Riça Night for her thorough review of the chapters and her diligent copyediting of the manuscript.

CAROL MCCANN
ROSS PIGEAU

CONTENTS

THE HUMAN IN COMMAND

CHAPTER 1

THE HUMAN IN COMMAND
A Brief Introduction

ROSS PIGEAU and CAROL McCANN

> If you know the enemy and know yourself, you need not fear the result of a hundred battles. If you know yourself but not the enemy, for every victory gained you will also suffer a defeat. If you know neither the enemy nor yourself, you will succumb in every battle.
> —SUN TZU, *The Art of War* (circa 490 BC/1910, pp. 24–25)

1. WHY THIS BOOK?

The impetus for this book is simple: to outline, discuss, and emphasize the uniquely human dimension of military command.

In a world replete with natural disasters, regional conflicts, and geopolitical tensions, modern militaries are tasked to carry out a range of missions that require a broad array of skills. Among these skills, the ability to capitalize on technology is often touted as the most important. The media regularly show pictures of military sensors, warcraft, and impressive computer systems. Indeed, images of precision bombing strikes during the 1991 Gulf War, and during the 1999 conflict in Kosovo, have become the icons of Western military might. But in reality, such operations are not nearly as straightforward and tidy as they first seem. Militaries, after all, are made up of ordinary individuals—individuals with varying strengths, weaknesses, stamina, and frailties—who must deal with extraordinary circumstances. During their careers, military personnel behold the tragic extremes of the human condition: famine, war, death, destruction, and disease. And witnessing such calamities induces feelings of anger, fear, fatigue, and despair. Yet through it all, they are expected to perform. They are expected to carry out the mission.

ROSS PIGEAU and CAROL McCANN • *Defence and Civil Institute of Environmental Medicine, 1133 Sheppard Avenue West, Toronto, Ontario, Canada M3M 3B9*

The Human in Command: Exploring the Modern Military Experience, edited by McCann and Pigeau, Kluwer Academic/Plenum Publishers, New York, 2000.

Ironically, the scientific community understands the physics of flight, the chemistry of explosives, and the metallurgy of armour without understanding nearly as well the psychology of leadership, the sociology of group behaviour, or the cognitive basis of decision making. And this knowledge gap prevails despite the fact that human behaviour and conflict have existed for much longer than airplanes, explosives, and tanks. This book, like the workshop on which it is based,[1] attempts to redress that imbalance by bringing together operational commanders and behavioural scientists to identify and explore human command issues.

The book's central assumption is that the world's militaries exist first and foremost to resolve *human* conflict. Since in many cases, human conflict can be resolved only through human intervention, militaries are a nation's instrument of last resort for interceding, for imposing control. Therefore, it is worth delving into the types of human conflict that militaries are tasked to resolve—if only to appreciate the uniquely human dimensions and challenges involved in military command.

2. A DRAMATICALLY DIFFERENT MODEL OF HUMAN CONFLICT

When military personnel speak of a "spectrum of conflict" in world affairs, they usually have in mind a unidimensional continuum anchored on one end by less violent operations (for example, humanitarian aid and disaster relief) and on the other by all-out war. Peacekeeping and peace support operations occupy spots somewhere in the middle. While militaries may find this model useful in planning their operations and allocating their resources, it fails to adequately capture the broad range of conflicts that humans—and, by implication, militaries—can become embroiled in.

It might prove more instructive to consider the classifications of human conflict found in drama. Drama, after all, deals almost exclusively with human conflict, as many great historical works of fiction—Tolstoy's *War and Peace*, Hemingway's *The Old Man and the Sea*, Shakespeare's *Hamlet*, and Hugo's *Les Misérables* among them—attest. Drama theory distinguishes three classes of human conflict: person-versus-person, person-versus-Nature, and person-versus-self.

- *Person-versus-person conflicts* are every military's fundamental *raison d'être*. Militaries exist primarily to protect (and sometimes to extend) a nation's sovereignty. Whether doing so entails minor skirmishes or nuclear war, sovereignty is asserted through person-versus-person conflict. Such conflicts are therefore an unavoidable aspect of military life, and they can induce tremendous stress in commanders, despite the purported justness of the cause or the humanitarian validity of the operation. Some contributors to this book discuss the character and nature of those stresses, as well as the

---

[1] This book is based on the edited proceedings of the NATO (North Atlantic Treaty Organization) Human in Command Workshop June 8–12, 1998, at the Canadian Land Forces Command and Staff College, Fort Frontenac, Kingston, Ontario.

strategies that commanders must use to deal effectively with them (both for themselves and for their subordinates).

- *Person-versus-Nature conflicts* encompass not only all instances in which humans are threatened by natural disasters, but also all human attempts to control Nature through clever inventions, through the application of science, or even through sheer physical prowess. In many countries, the military embodies the nation's broadest capability for facing Nature's challenges. Militaries are routinely required to perform in extremes of heat and cold, from the stratosphere to the ocean's depth, while carrying with them both the means for their own survival and the means for imposing their will. In many ways, those militaries that best control (or account for) Nature have an advantage when it comes to achieving operational success—whether success requires being able to predict changes in the weather, travel faster, shoot farther, or communicate more quickly. While person-versus-person conflicts often provide the impetus for military action (and are also one of the most common results of such action), person-versus-Nature conflicts more often occur during the process of military engagement itself. Each combat maneuver, air sortie, or naval campaign requires either explicit or implicit knowledge of the physical terrain, the laws of physics, or the principles of hydrodynamics. Such knowledge can be gained either through experience or through scientific investigation. Command must therefore take account of technological advancements and be prepared to use them effectively. Command must also be prepared to assist when attempts at controlling (or predicting) Nature fail: in disaster relief, search-and-rescue operations, and humanitarian aid.

- *Person-versus-self conflicts* cause the first two types of human conflict—as important as they seem—to pale in comparison. Humans appear unique among animals in spending significant amounts of time engaged in self-reflection. According to Adler (1985), Plato reasoned that consciousness is a state that entails being aware of something—of the world, of others—but more importantly (for humans), it entails being aware of one's self. Self-reflection creates human identity, and identity allows each of us to speculate on our wants, our desires, our strengths, and our weaknesses. When these wants and desires become inconsistent with self-perception, person-versus-self conflicts ensue. Humans experiencing such conflicts question their motives, their place in society, and sometimes even their role in the universe.

Great commanders, we believe, realize that person-versus-self conflict is the single biggest factor in determining a military mission's success or failure. Equipment is useless without personnel who believe in the cause and are motivated to achieve the goals that will further it. Commanders must understand that self-doubt, poor discipline, low morale, and a weak ethos arc symptoms of person-versus-self conflicts. Such conflicts surface predominantly during times of adversity—a family member's death, a natural catastrophe, or perhaps a serious social injustice. Such times challenge complacency in both self and society. Person-versus-self conflicts therefore arise inevitably from the first two types of human conflict, and militaries are particularly susceptible to them. For example, military personnel experience society's worst and most disturbing person-versus-person conflicts (extreme violence, war, genocide). And in providing aid to civil powers during earthquakes, floods, and famines, military personnel also face many of the most severe person-versus-Nature conflicts. No other organization exposes its members to a more varied and more extensive array of human adversity. As a result, no single group of individuals has more occasion to experience profound person-versus-self conflicts. Indeed, under such circumstances it would be unnatural if average armed forces members did *not* suffer from such conflicts. How could they not question their morals, their cultural values, even their humanity? And how does such questioning affect performance, both during and after an operation? Command must acknowledge these issues in order to guard against the pitfalls of person-versus-self conflicts and minimize their negative effects. Much of this book is devoted to describing and discussing the nature of such conflicts in military culture.

3. WHAT TO EXPECT FROM THIS BOOK

The following chapters represent some of the most current operational experience and scientific thought regarding military command: personal testimonials from senior officers about leadership; treatises on and descriptions of new concepts related to command theory; and empirical findings from experimental studies in operational settings. Throughout, the contributors challenge both the military and the research communities to reaffirm command's importance by devoting more resources, research, and training to this area.

The book is divided into two parts. Part 1, "The Command Experience," begins with *personal* descriptions of command's difficulties and complexities (Chapters 2 to 7). Senior military officers from four nations share their insights into and their conclusions about their personal command experiences. Part 1 ends with *conceptual* discussions by military officers (and by an Australian Federal Police commander) concerning such key aspects of command as leadership, intent, tempo, and decentralization (Chapters 8 to 11).

Part 2, "The Science of Command," presents scientific attempts to define and study command. It begins by continuing where Part 1 left off, with *conceptual* treatments of command—although here the approach is more scientific (Chapters 12 to 15). These contributors attempt to reconceptualize command and control, to develop practical ways of thinking during command, and to question the generalizability of the mission command philosophy. The next section (Chapters 16 to 18) explores three *methodological* considerations for studying command: dynamic decision making; methods for assessing the effectiveness of multiforce command; and event-based performance tools for training. Part 2 ends with contributors offering *empirical* evidence from studies investigating a wide range of command issues: communicating intent; the breakdown of military discipline; assessing morale and cohesion; experiencing and coping with stress; training; and analyzing command behaviour (Chapters 19 to 25).

In the book's closing chapter, "Research Challenges for the Human in Command," we synthesize the issues and questions that workshop participants raised during the evening discussion sessions and during the question periods that followed the presentations. This chapter provides guideposts for future research as well as a framework for discussing the entire topic.

4. INTO THE DARKNESS

There is irony in this book. Although command's psychological and social-psychological importance has been recognized since at least 490 BC (as the Sun Tzu quotation that opens this introduction illustrates), very few researchers have investigated the topic scientifically. The axiom "Only humans command" seems to have suffered the fate of many axioms: its self-evident nature conceals its fundamental truth. Few have deduced the organizational, psychological, and technological implications of this essential principle. Although much has been written about the "art of command" and the "science of control," too often the literature pays only cursory attention to command (acknowledging its importance, but using its fuzziness as a justification for virtually ignoring it otherwise). We do not deny that there is much of art in command, just as there is much of art in all well-expressed and well-performed enterprises (including science), but acknowledging this fact in no way diminishes the importance of studying command scientifically. The art in command merely renders it difficult and puzzling as a subject for scientific inquiry—one with complexity and mystery that match most of the human sciences, but one that will yield great potential rewards.

The problem brings to mind the old joke about the drunk who loses a set of keys in a dark alley but looks for them under a lamppost "because the light is better there." We maintain that both the military and the research communities have behaved like that drunk. They have devoted too much time and too many resources to the known (applying technology) and the doable (applying standard procedures and established paradigms), while enjoying the relative comfort and safety of bright lampposts (scientific traditions, military rules and regulations). We maintain that the answers to the problems faced by humans in command lie elsewhere—outside that pool of light. They lie in the darkness of the three types of human dramatic conflict—particularly person-versus-self conflict. They lie in the gloom and murkiness of human behaviour.

We offer this book as a lantern for exploring that darkness. Illuminated by the experience of senior military officers and fuelled by the strength of diverse scientific disciplines, let us set out together and search for the lost keys to command.

5. REFERENCES

Adler, M. J. (1985). *Ten philosophical mistakes.* New York: Macmillan.
Sun Tzu. (1910). *Sun Tzu on the art of war: The oldest military treatise in the world* (L. Giles, Trans.). London, U.K.: Luzac. (Original work published circa 490 BC)

Part I

The Command Experience

CHAPTER 2

THE NATURE OF COMMAND

LIEUTENANT-GENERAL R. R. CRABBE

1. INTRODUCTION

When I was asked about a year ago if I would be interested in participating in this workshop, I jumped at the chance, because I feel that command is such a very fundamental issue in the profession of arms. I, for one, feel that the human element and human presence will always play a very significant role on the battlefield and will have a direct influence on the outcome of future conflict in war and in operations short of war. Humans will always play the most significant role in war and in combat.

In 1966, a young infantry lieutenant was wrapping up a week-long period of training at Camp Sarcee in Alberta, Canada, with a 10-mile (16 km) route march with his platoon of about 30 soldiers. The fact that he had not seen the company commander all week created a somewhat conflicting feeling. But on balance, the young lieutenant was disappointed, because he was proud of his accomplishments and there had been times throughout the week when he would have appreciated some guidance. The company commander, with the sergeant-major, did show up in his jeep at about the 6-mile (10 km) point; without getting out of the vehicle, he complained loudly and angrily that the pace was too slow. Both had obviously been drinking.

This young lieutenant later (in 1983) found himself serving as the commanding officer (CO) of an infantry battalion in Wainwright, Alberta. Three weeks into a seven-week concentration, he had seen the brigade commander once—in the officers' mess in camp. When the CO had been beckoned to a meeting with the brigade commander to discuss, of all things, the suspension of one of his soldiers from the upcoming hockey league, not a word had been mentioned about tactics or doctrine or tempo or training. The only real appearance of the brigade commander occurred

LIEUTENANT-GENERAL R. R. CRABBE • *Deputy Chief of the Defence Staff, Department of National Defence, Ottawa, Ontario, Canada K1A 0K2*

The Human in Command: Exploring the Modern Military Experience,
edited by McCann and Pigeau, Kluwer Academic/Plenum Publishers, New York, 2000.

during the final live-fire battle group exercise—when he hovered high overhead in his helicopter. Following the gut-slugging three-hour assault, the troops were gathered for a debrief. The lieutenant-colonel and the subunit commanders made a few points regarding tactics, battle procedure, coordination, and so on, and congratulated the troops on a job very well done. When the brigade commander was asked to comment, his only utterance was a question that he posed rhetorically to the 300 or 400 gathered soldiers: Why did you attack into the sun? The young CO very simply and quickly explained that the tactical situation dictated that the attack be conducted from west to east. The officers and noncommissioned officers shuddered when the brigade commander nervously asked—again rhetorically—whether they had ever read about the Japanese pilots' cardinal rule, about never attacking into the sun. Then he hopped into his helicopter and headed back to the officers' mess.

I was that young lieutenant, and later that CO. And I recount these two incidents because for me they illustrate examples of poor command. Not just a lack of leadership, not just a lack of presence, not just a lack of influence, but indeed a dereliction in duty by commanders who should have known better—or perhaps did, but chose not to execute their responsibilities. In both cases, they had established and enunciated the objectives that were to be achieved; yet both, in my view, failed miserably at doing so. In these examples, command was not executed. There were no examples exerted of what I will later describe to be the *essence* of command.

2. THE MEANING OF COMMAND

We have all, no doubt, wrestled with the real meaning of command and its inevitable comparison with and differentiation from leadership, management, authority, responsibility, and accountability. The *Concise Oxford Dictionary* provides several definitions for command—among them the following: as a verb, "give command to or order" and "have authority over or control of"; and as a noun, "the exercise or tenure of authority, [especially] . . . military." The North Atlantic Treaty Organization (NATO) definition of command (the noun) is "authority vested in an individual . . . for the direction, coordination and control of military forces" (NATO, 1988). NATO also defines command as an order given by a commander.

One cannot argue with the theme of authority when speaking of command. Indeed, command, in Canadian terms, is derived from the National Defence Act. Without legal and constitutional backing, commands that are issued—especially those dealing in terms of human lives—would be weak and totally ineffective at best. Command does entail the authority to issue orders and, in the ultimate sense, the authority to place soldiers in harm's way—in essence, ordering them to put their lives on the line. In a military context, then, command would take on an extremely onerous tone if it were simply related to authority. It is this ultimate sacrifice and the fact that we are dealing in terms of human lives that separate military command from civilian command or authority.

We are all too well aware from recent events in our Canadian military— although not in the context of the ultimate sacrifice—of the very direct relationship between command and responsibility. A precept of command is that commanders are responsible, are responsible, are *responsible*, for their orders, direction, and action (or inaction) if and when action is necessary. They have a responsibility to make decisions and issue orders. They have the authority—the right or legal basis—to issue orders, and they must be held accountable for their decisions. But as we saw and heard during the Somalia Inquiry[1] on probably too many occasions, accountability was not viewed as extending to the actions or inaction of subordinates receiving those orders. Clearly, it does. Hence, command entails the authority for direction and issuing orders, but it also includes responsibility and accountability for the orders issued—and, I would add, for orders not issued.

With regard to leadership and management, these are both inherent in command. One cannot command in the military unless one has the capacity to decide on the allocation of resources needed to execute an order, and then, having done so, to influence subordinates to collectively achieve the mission. While these two requirements vary considerably with the level of command—and, indeed, many will argue the context of both under varying circumstances—I contend that these elements are essential ingredients of command. Like so many United Nations commanders before me, I was continually frustrated in the former Yugoslavia because I had little or no control over U.N. resources, and was not allowed to change the ways of doing business, despite the archaic and outdated modus operandi of the United Nations in this regard. These limitations severely restricted my ability (and that of the force's commander) to command.

What, therefore, is command?

- To command is to direct and to do so with authority.

- In a military sense, to command is to think and make sound judgments and decisions, often without all the facts or necessary information.

- To command in war is to commit young Canadians to battles from which they may not return alive or may return permanently maimed, incapacitated, or disfigured. It is to be responsible for taking lives and saving lives.

- To command in peace and war is to establish moral standards and direct how soldiers, sailors, and airmen will conduct themselves toward each other and toward society as a whole. The commander, in other words, sets the standards and enforces them.

- To command is to think, decide, act, establish standards, and exert influence.

- In the end, a military commander must be able to bring military forces to bear on the enemy on behalf of the state. He or she cannot do so without possessing the essential ingredients of command.

To describe an effective military commander, we must go well beyond leadership, management, and responsibility in issuing orders. Command is much more than

---

[1] The Commission of Inquiry into the Deployment of Canadian Forces to Somalia (Canada, 1997).

authority. Commanders must be fighters—they must have the will to win. This incorporates taking calculated risks, being innovative, being daring and bold when called for, and seeing the mission through to its end. Commanders must be leaders: they must be able to influence human behaviour in a collective manner in order to achieve the mission. They must be tacticians: able to understand, and apply flexibly on the battlefield, the doctrine and principles of war. They must be thinkers: without brainpower, they cannot be decisive, they cannot motivate, and they cannot react to changing circumstances. Given the very nature of the battlefield—the unknown, the fog of war, the lack of information on which to base decisions—commanders must be able to think clearly, based on experience, and make those "gut feel" decisions calmly and accurately, when necessary. They must be disciplinarians, for discipline is at the heart of all we do and how well we do it as a cohesive, well-oiled military unit. Lastly, in order to command, military commanders must be examples of fine moral character. Honesty, loyalty, and integrity are indispensable values without which no commander can survive for long. They are the cornerstones of command.

3. EFFECTIVE COMMAND IN ACTION

Let me try to illustrate some of these tenets of command with examples. You may be aware that during his trial in Nova Scotia following World War II, Kurt Meyer commented on Canadian commanders and their centralized, meticulous, detailed staff work and planning. Once an operation had commenced, however, Canadians were extremely hesitant to exploit German vulnerabilities or successes, because they felt that another session of detailed staff work was required before launching on to the next objective. This plodding, rather unimaginative approach smacked of a lack of initiative. The contrast, during the Cold War, was the German Army's *spearfunkt*: reliance on initiative and creativity to get to the objective. As a German commander once said to me, "Give me my boundaries, objectives, and timings, and let me get on with the job." I was always fascinated with this approach, and I am pleased that the Canadian Army has adopted a similar approach with the principle of maneuver warfare.

As I alluded to earlier, plans rarely unfold as expected on the battlefield. Commanders must expect the unexpected, and be sufficiently flexible to react accordingly. History is replete with examples of the "best laid plans of mice and men" having gone quite badly awry. Let me give you an unhistorical anecdote. During a winter exercise with the U.S. forces in Alaska, I was commanding a battalion and was to attack and seize the only hill feature in the area. For several reasons, I reluctantly planned to attack across 5 miles (8 km) of open country on foot to seize key objectives. I dispatched my recce platoon under darkness on snowshoes to define the enemy, only to determine that the key features were unoccupied. I had received intelligence reports indicating that the enemy was one to two hours away; if I could get to the high feature immediately, I could grab it without a fight and, in the process, totally dominate the surrounding area. I asked for and got permission from the brigade commander to advance the H-hour, decided to totally change my plan, and very quickly issued new orders that called for making a "mad dash" with two companies mounted on snowmobiles, the few armoured personnel carriers we had, and two helicopters, rather than having my people snowshoe across the open ground for 5 miles (8 km). We did so, seizing the objectives without a shot being fired—and in the process, totally upsetting the U.S. commander's timetable and objectives for the exercise. Indeed, a very irate U.S. two-star flew in by helicopter and ordered me back so that the exercise could proceed as planned. I told him absolutely not! To further illustrate this point of flexibility or creativity, the U.S. enemy force insisted, time after time, on attacking up the river valley—even though each attack resulted in more casualties. Had there been some creativity on the part of the enemy force commander, he could have made it an interesting battle. Instead, he played right into our hands, and suffered the consequences.

Looking at it from another angle, I believe it is essential on the battlefield that subordinates have a clear and unequivocal understanding of what the commander wants to accomplish. This can be achieved only by the human touch. This is often referred to as getting inside the commander's mind, understanding the commander's intent, or simply having a grasp of the concept by which the commander intended to accomplish the mission. If the plan does not unfold as the details may have dictated (and it seldom does), then the subordinates have a framework of understanding on which to base their actions and decisions. In army parlance, this is the "concept of operations" or "general outline" paragraph of the operations order. In my opinion, this is the most important part of any orders issued. When I've been on the receiving end, I have always admired commanders who could stand up to a map with confidence and explain, in conceptual terms, how they intended to achieve the mission. Equally, I have been dismayed by those who had to read this vital part of orders, or worse still, have a member of the staff do it for them. If there is ever a time for the human touch and an opportunity to motivate, initiate, and create, surely it is the personal involvement of the commander in influencing his or her subordinates and spurring them on to fight and win. It is, after all, the commander's plan—and if that commander cannot explain it simply and logically, it is doomed to fail. This is truly personal command in its truest form, when troops are about to be committed to battle. It is a responsibility of command to create the plan, explain or communicate it, and then execute and oversee its implementation, always with the aim of winning and of doing so with the fewest casualties possible.

If there is one characteristic of command that I believe must be ever present, it is the will to get the job done, to see an action through to its successful conclusion, to be resolute. The ability to overcome obstacles and impediments and get to the objective, to remain focused on the mission, is one that one could translate into reliability—not necessarily in the sense of strictly following orders, but rather in the sense of intelligently interpreting the mission or action, and then ensuring that impediments do not become showstoppers. This is true whether in combat or in a peacetime headquarters setting.

One of the most frustrating elements of service in the United Nations Protection Force (UNPROFOR) was dealing with sector and area commanders who were, in some cases, completely inept at carrying the mission through. Due to a lack of resolution—sometimes combined with incompetence—one side or the other got away time and time again with ceasefire violations, unacceptable actions, and even humiliating the troops. These events steadily chipped away at the U.N. force's resolve to maintain the peace or achieve the overall mission. In one particular incident, the Croat Special Police had established an observation post and checkpoint that was clearly inside the Zone of Separation. This got the Serbs in the area most upset—not just because of the overt encroachment, but also because the local U.N. commander did not resolve the issue, instead allowing the situation to drag on and on. Despite being ordered to show strong resolve, and virtually being told how to do it, the U.N. sector commander could not muster enough wherewithal to act resolutely. He was totally unreliable. This particular incident proved to be one of the U.N. force's downfalls, in my view, in achieving a peaceful resolution in that sector—resulting, in the end, in hundreds of dead Serbs.

On the positive side, the Canadian troops were totally reliable in getting the job done. I recall, on many occasions, the battle group in Croatia and Bosnia being challenged by all sides to test the Canadian resolve. Violations of the Zone of Separation, freedom of movement, and ceasefires were met with immediate and appropriate responses. This tough-minded approach in prevailing over obstacles, impediments, and frustrations is what I concluded, after a year in the former Yugoslavia, distinguished the good peacekeepers and enforcers from the bad. This does not imply a "damn the torpedoes, full speed ahead" approach, but rather, as I mentioned earlier, an intelligent application of tactics, analysis of the situation, consideration of all factors, and the resolute pursuit of mission accomplishment.

As an aside, I would quickly add that the personal influence and involvement of the commander in these circumstances is often the crucial factor. The term *command presence* conjures up images of General George S. Patton, General Joseph Stilwell, and Field Marshal Erwin Rommel—all successful commanders in their own right. It's interesting that we do not refer to *leadership* presence: while the exertion of influence is obvious, our emphasis is instead on the application of the commander's knowledge, on his or her desire to motivate, and above all, on the need to press on to accomplish the mission. Influence, not interference, is the key. It is a "feel" for the battle and the battlefield that can be achieved only by being there. The human element is very much in play. When I think back on my experience, the best officers, warrant officers, and noncommissioned officers were those on whom I could rely to get the job done—to overcome obstacles, to persevere—and who showed a lot of resolve, through personal presence and involvement, in mission achievement. I admire Barbara Tuchman's (1981) description of this prevailing characteristic and requirement of command in her book *Practicing History*: "the determination to win through, whether in the worst circumstance merely to survive or . . . to complete the mission, but, whatever the circumstance, to prevail" (p. 277).

Finally, let me say a few words about the commander as moralist. Certainly, as I said earlier, we have had plenty of opportunity to examine this issue recently within the Canadian Forces. One of the primary responsibilities of a commander is to establish and maintain a moral climate within his or her command. This can be achieved in several ways, depending on the level of command, but regardless of the method, commanders at every level must set and maintain the standards. They must enunciate clearly their views and attitudes on professional attributes, discipline, and the boundaries of professional conduct. But most important, they must practise what they preach. They must "walk the talk." As I mentioned previously, we have seen several failures in command lately, and unfortunately, these failures have been synonymous with failure in morality. How can we expect authority to be taken seriously if the person in authority does not exhibit moral behaviour? Put another way, it is incongruous that a commander who is a fraud, a thief, a bigot, or a drunk, or who is disloyal or dishonest, be vested with the authority to commit troops under an unlimited liability to battle. Those who have failed in this way will surely fail in battle, for such failures chew away at the very essence of cohesiveness, teamwork, trust, and reliability. A moral atmosphere with clear lines in the sand is essential in a military environment. The commander at any level has the duty and responsibility to enunciate this, insist on it, and above all, practise it.

When I was in the former Yugoslavia, I found myself in precarious situations from time to time, but never more so than when I attempted to deal with a deeply rooted moral issue involving a contingent in one of the sectors in Croatia where the aim was, in simplistic terms, to maintain peace between the Croatian and Serb forces. One of the battalions in that sector was stealing gas from the U.N. forces, running a prostitute ring, and stealing and reselling cars—among other things. Toward the latter part of my tour, they had become operationally corrupt—that is, they were falsifying reports, allowing gross violations to occur, and totally favouring the Serb side. Without getting into the details, in my attempt to deal with this situation I received two death threats that I am convinced originated from that contingent. What was most disturbing through all this was the total involvement of the contingent commanders, from the top down. While the Serbs may have accepted such practices as representing "business as usual," the Croats did *not*; in the end, the latter completely lost faith in the contingent's and the U.N. force's ability to deal with this entire issue. We were faced with a situation where the senior commander had the morals of a snake, allowed these practices to be perpetuated, and, from all reports, encouraged such action. The moral atmosphere in that particular sector was directly responsible for mission failure.

4. THE FUTURE OF COMMAND

In summary, let me just say a few words about the future. It is accepted that there will be—and indeed we are now seeing—a proliferation of information systems and information available to commanders. Commanders have immediate access to their bosses and their bosses' bosses. Intelligence from all sources can be fed in and analyzed very quickly by an intelligence centre. This continual barrage of information and intelligence can and will influence command. The tendency will be to remain in a more static location to do so. This location will usually be well behind the lines. As I mentioned earlier, command presence is far too important to allow this to happen. The resoluteness of command must not be allowed to wane.

One could argue—with some degree of correctness—that the lethal capability that exists on the battlefield, in the hands of a very few individuals, will dynamically change the structure of military organizations, and technology will take over where formed bodies of soldiers, sailors, and airmen were once required. A soldier with a laser designator and radio set can direct weapons of mass destruction to targets. Why, therefore, is command presence still going to be necessary on the future battlefield? To influence, direct, decide, and think—just as commanders must do now. I would suggest as well that devolution of authority will occur and may even *need* to occur to allow commanders to react, to be innovative and creative, and to take advantage of vulnerabilities in the enemy's disposition. This fast-paced, quickly evolving, and ever-changing battlefield will call up other changes, but I believe devolution will be one of them.

There are many other challenges to command today, many driven by social changes and legislation. I suppose we could have an entire seminar on that alone. Suffice it to say that we must continue to rise to the new demands that these challenges bring. The human element in command will always be essential to success, and central to saving the lives of our subordinates in the accomplishment of the mission.

REFERENCES

Canada. (1997). *Dishonoured legacy: The lessons of the Somalia affair—Report of the Commission of Inquiry into the Deployment of Canadian Forces to Somalia.* Ottawa: Commission of Inquiry into the Deployment of Canadian Forces to Somalia [Somalia Inquiry].

NATO (North Atlantic Treaty Organization). (1988). *Glossary of Terms and Definitions* (STANAG AAP-6(R)). Brussels, Belgium: NATO.

Tuchman, B. W. (1981). *Practicing history: Selected essays.* New York: Knopf.

CHAPTER 3

THE HUMAN IN COMMAND
A Personal View

BRIGADIER GENERAL (RETIRED) STANLEY CHERRIE

1. INTRODUCTION

When I was asked to participate in the NATO (North Atlantic Treaty Organization) Human in Command Workshop, I was extremely flattered; but after the initial glow wore off, I realized that I was not the most widely read student in the art of command—despite my own command experience and my 33 years of service under some outstanding commanders. So I started by doing some reading. I soon realized that much of what had been written closely matched my personal opinions about the critical importance of the human in command. This article draws on the insights about command offered by these references, but relies mostly on my own experiences in the U.S. Army. In particular, I'll use incidents from my two Vietnam tours (1967/68, when I served as a helicopter gunship pilot; and 1971, when I commanded an Armored Cavalry troop) to highlight one of the most important aspects of command: the commander's will.

I'll also describe the characteristics that I believe successful commanders must have (and some that they shouldn't have), as well as the approaches they should use for ensuring successful command. Crabbe (this volume, Chapter 2) also raises several concepts that I think are important—for example, those of *will*, *intent*, and *command philosophy*. I'll begin with a few references to the literature, and then offer some doctrinal definitions, comparing and contrasting them with my personal definitions, to ensure a common reference base for the discussion. I'll describe, from my own experience, the positive and negative attributes of commanders, after which

BRIGADIER GENERAL (RETIRED) STANLEY CHERRIE • Cubic Applications, Inc., 426 Delaware, Suite C-3, Leavenworth, Kansas, USA 66048

The Human in Command: Exploring the Modern Military Experience, edited by McCann and Pigeau, Kluwer Academic/Plenum Publishers, New York, 2000.

I'll comment on command philosophy, emphasizing the importance of communicating intent, and on the commander's will. I'll touch briefly on the environment's influence on command, including the relationship between the commander on the ground and the national headquarters, and the influence of the media. Finally, I'll suggest how researchers and academics might help those of us in command and leadership roles to better prepare ourselves either for war or for operations other than war.

2. SOME USEFUL RESOURCES

One of the first documents I came across in reviewing the topic of command was the August 1985 issue of *Military Review*, the U.S. Army's professional journal. Its cover depicts the command decision-making process supported by an entire panoply of technology: crewless aerial vehicles linked by satellite to the commander's suite of digital command and control devices, Joint Surveillance Target Acquisition Radar feeds converging in the same suite, and individual vehicles deployed with their own situational awareness consoles. But all this technology would be useless without the person in the centre of the picture: a battle-hardened senior commander, who will, in the end, be called upon to make a decision. I could not have designed a better way to illustrate my position that the human is the most important element in command.

The next reference I found was a pamphlet produced by the U.S. Army Training and Doctrine Command shortly after the war in the Persian Gulf (United States, 1992). It summarizes the results of a postoperation survey that the Army conducted in an attempt to understand why it had been successful in the Gulf. Immediately after the war, the Army sent teams to the region to interview commanders at every echelon, from battalion to corps. Commanders at each level were asked the same 14 questions, including why they felt *they* had been successful, what they felt *they* had done well, and what they felt *they* had done poorly. Their responses yielded some interesting observations on the importance of the commander's presence, how the commander relates to the members of his or her unit, and how that relationship influences the unit's success.

A third source that I relied on heavily in preparing this presentation is "Battle Command: A Commander's Perspective," a *Military Review* article by my mentor, General (Retired) Frederick M. Franks (1996). I met Franks in the summer of 1971, when he and I both found ourselves on the amputee ward in Valley Forge General Hospital,[1] where we were each recovering from combat wounds received in Vietnam. Subsequently, we served together in the 11th Armored Cavalry Regiment, and then at the United States Army Command and General Staff College. Most recently, I served as G-3 operations officer when Franks led the attack on the Forces Command of Iraq's Republican Guard during the Gulf War. His abilities during that operation provide a fine exemplar of the traits I consider vital for commanders.

---

[1] Located in Phoenixville, Pennsylvania, this hospital is contiguous to a famous Revolutionary War winter encampment.

Another useful source of command insight was written by my colleague, friend, and all-around hero Colonel Greg Fontenot (1995), who chronicled his observations as a battalion commander preparing his troops to go to war. Among other things, Fontenot discusses where and how he positioned himself when communicating with his troops and some of the ways he captured their attention to ensure that he could suitably imprint the information he wanted to transmit. This document is an ideal primer for commanders who must prepare their troops for combat.

3. SOME DOCTRINAL DEFINITIONS

Now, let's try to pinpoint what the term *command* means. The U.S. Army's leadership manual (United States, 1987) defines command as "the means by which the commander's vision is imparted to his organization." The manual goes on to state that leadership is the guts or the toughness that allows a commander to make sure that the mission is accomplished over time. When asked for my definition of command, I generally reply that it's the method or methods used by commanders to inflict their will on their subordinates. Perhaps "inflict" is too harsh a word— "impart" also captures the notion—but the point is to get across the idea that "This is what I want done!" Critical for rounding out this view of command is the commander's leadership style. Is the commander an encouraging leader ("Come on, guys and gals, let's go!") or a screamer ("You are going to do this or else!")? One facet of command leadership involves the way the commander's staff is employed. In one method, the commander issues guidance; staff members then work up some products or options from which the commander then chooses, based on his or her experience and competence. In a different method—often used in the U.S. Army— the commander conveys to the staff exactly what he or she wants done, by when, and how; the staff then simply execute these instructions. I've seen each of these methods work well—and not so well. Another factor is the amount of control a commander exerts once an operation is launched. Some commanders micromanage. Others use the mission orders approach—that is, they just frame the issue and set certain parameters; then once the mission is launched, they let their subordinates handle it, with periodic updates provided to the commander. I subscribe to the latter method.

4. ATTRIBUTES OF COMMANDERS

I'd like to mention some of the key characteristics of senior commanders with whom I have served.[2] First, every one of these commanders, without exception, had *vision*. They could all look at a complex problem and know, intuitively, exactly what needed to be done and how to get from point A to point B. Sometimes this quality caused problems—for example, when the boss already knew what he wanted, but the staff

---

[2] Hereafter, when I use the term *senior commander*, I am referring to divisional commanders (major generals) and higher.

came up with a different course of action. Second, every senior commander in my experience was also very intelligent and, as a corollary, very competent. All were at the top of their own fields: aviators knew aviation tactics in detail; armoured officers knew gunnery and maneuver; and so on. Intelligence and competence go hand in hand. Third, all had a capacity for working that bordered on being surreal. People around them often wondered whether these officers came from another world— they never, ever, seemed to tire or slow down. Each had both mental and physical stamina that were far above the norm. I've also seen that kind of stamina in certain successful football coaches—for example, Vince Lombardi (perhaps that's why he did so well). Fourth, a strong sense of mission awareness is yet another characteristic that I have observed in all senior leaders. They all knew exactly what the mission was and, by golly, they were going to get it done at any cost. Last but not least, each had immense self-confidence. Some were a little brasher than others, but underneath the bravado, there was a strong sense of "I know what I am doing, and I believe it's right."

These are the positive traits. But in my experience, there's a dark side to the senior commander's profile, and these negative attributes must also be acknowledged. For instance, with one notable exception, all the senior leaders with whom I have worked were, unfortunately, short on "caring skills." They all *believed* that they were caring, but they didn't in fact go the extra mile to do things for their subordinates—particularly the officers closest to them. Being a "people person" takes a tremendous amount of effort; often, the high degree of mission zeal that commanders believe is demanded of them seems to overshadow the importance of taking care of their own people.

Another less-than-desirable trait of many senior commanders is an obsession with perfection. In pursuit of this goal, some commanders fill every available minute with endless fine-tuning and double-checking. The impact of such demands on staff officers is criminal. They are continually robbed of badly needed rest and time with their families. "Perfection is the arch-enemy of 'good enough'": though military personnel often hear—and even repeat—this admonition or a similar one, many commanders have a distinct problem in behaving accordingly. I think that the problem lies with the phrase "good enough." Some may see it as describing a person whose standards are lower than theirs, or who cares less about important matters than they do. Perhaps the research community can show us that "good enough" people can also be very successful.

Related to this problem of perfectionism is the fact that the majority of the senior leaders in the U.S. Army are unwilling to handle situations involving risk. We claim to be an institution that is willing to accept risk, but my assessment is that we don't have any risk-takers at all in the U.S. Army. My concern about the inability of commanders to accept prudent risk seems to be shared by our chief of staff, who, during a recent senior leaders' conference, personally requested that the Combat Training Centers develop scenarios to exercise our senior commanders in the handling of risk. Worse than an inability to handle risk, however, is the abdication of responsibility for controversial issues. I have actually seen leaders who structure their methods for planning and conducting operations so as to erect protective "firewalls" between themselves and any issue known to be risky or controversial.

This tactic permits them what, in the back rooms, is jokingly termed *plausible deniability*.

Finally, micromanagement is rife among the majority of senior leaders with whom I have served. Decisions that ought to be made at very low levels now demand the attention of a four-star general. A prime example of this phenomenon occurred in January 1996, when the U.S. 1st Armored Division was crossing the Sava River into Bosnia–Herzegovina.[3] The weather was terrible, and the setup of base camps had not been completed: cold-weather injuries were a definite danger. The CINC (commander in chief), a four-star general, prohibited U.S. soldiers from entering Bosnia until they had a warm, dry place to sleep. (This decision, in my opinion, severely hampered Task Force Eagle's ability to accomplish the tasks set out for it by the General Framework for the Agreement for Peace that had been signed in Dayton.) For my money, handling the risk of frostbite is the responsibility of squad and platoon leaders, not of a CINC.

In my opinion, the above traits—both positive and negative—characterize the typical senior commander. I suspect that the profile may appear a bit negatively skewed, but I feel obliged to tell you the bad as well as the good.

5. COMMAND PHILOSOPHY

On many occasions in my career, I have been asked to describe my command philosophy. My stock answer is "I'm not a philosopher—I'm a combat leader!" But in preparing for this workshop, I struggled to put on paper what I have been living my whole career—and the task was much harder than I had expected. I finally concluded that command is 75 percent automatic: you have your troops and your mission, and, as a common U.S. television ad says, you "just do it." I'll try nonetheless to describe my philosophy for good command.

One of the most important words in my civilian and military life has been *team*. I think that all good senior leaders consider themselves part of a team. Although they are aware that they have been given the leadership role based on their proficiency, competence, and ability, good leaders also know that they are not above the team—not better than the other members. The team captain is also a member of the organization! Units led by a commander who feels significantly unlike and better than the other team members are rarely high-performance units.

I consider myself a participative leader. I like to get involved. I've always tried to surround myself with intelligent, diligent people—the kind I can trust to do what's right when no one's looking. Trust is essential between a commander and his or her staff. Trust also implies listening to the staff members' ideas, even when the course of action being recommended differs from the commander's own. A wise commander remembers that today's staff officers have been given much more extensive staff schooling than most commanders ever receive. Commanders who hear out the ideas of their staff show recognition of the time and effort that the staff have devoted to producing a solution—one that just may be better than the commander's own!

---

[3] Officially the Federal Republic of Bosnia and Herzegovina; hereafter generally referred to as Bosnia.

Another essential for successful command is visibility. Commanders absolutely must be *seen* by their troops. Some commanders believe that they can achieve visibility by helicopter, because they can cover tremendous distances and can visit countless places. For example, during one day in Bosnia, the commanding general typically "visited" half a dozen or so units by helicopter. He touched down on six or eight mountaintops; at each, he was greeted by colonels and staff officers, sat in big leather chairs, had coffee and goodies, and was given briefing slides and maps—and then he was off to the next unit. On a day like that, the boss was a mile wide but less than an inch deep: he hadn't really "seen"—or been seen by—his command. He had indeed visited the units, but how could he have a real feel for what was going on there without talking to the soldiers he led? Mobility doesn't automatically mean visibility. A commander must be *with* the soldiers, must invest time with them, must eat and sleep inside their perimeter. This approach is the only way to get what the Germans call *fingerspitzengefühl*, or the feeling in your fingertips that allows you to know really what's going on.

Another prerequisite for successful command is approachability. I'm not talking about being approachable by one's own staff—but by the ordinary soldier. Good command involves really being with the soldiers. The troops need to feel that when they say something, the commander listens—and that he or she truly hears what they are saying. Real battle commanders know that having a reputation for being approachable is key, since soldiers' perceptions of command are critically important to the unit's success. Two days before we crossed the berm in Saudi Arabia and attacked Iraq, General Franks, the VII Corps commander, was out in his armoured command vehicle, talking with the soldiers. He was a little nervous about doing so, since he knew that he'd soon be committing them to combat. As he was explaining to the troops that we had wargamed the upcoming breach maneuver to ensure that we would always have the maximum advantage, a young specialist soldier stopped him in mid-sentence and said, "General, you don't have to talk to us like that. We trust you!" Now that's reputation! No higher accolade can be paid to a commander than to have a young soldier far down in the ranks affirm trust in the commander's leadership. And that can happen only if command is approachable.

Good command, however, involves more than simple approachability. Commanders should also be encouraging—for example, patting people on the back when they have done a good job (as well as giving them a swift kick when they deserve one). Encouragement can be quite low-key and personal. In the United States, for instance, we have a wonderful TV ad that shows a young hockey goalie missing an easy save. After the match, the coach walks the youngster the length of the rink and offers him a Life Saver candy. One of my former commanders used to take me on many of these "Life Saver walks"; I learned a lot in the process. I was reassured and encouraged to know that the chain of command was tolerant enough to let me make mistakes and then try again.

Finally, a good commander is always focused on what the unit is doing and on what's good for the soldiers. Such focus can be very hard to accomplish nowadays, however. The "Monday-morning quarterbacking," for example, that results from CNN-style coverage of military actions often causes today's commanders to focus more on how their actions will play in the media than on how the operation should actually be conducted. This factor is having a serious effect on command, but it is here to stay: our commanders must therefore learn to cope with it.

6. THE IMPORTANCE OF COMMUNICATING INTENT

No discussion of command would be complete without considering the importance of *commander's intent* and its influence on the way a unit acts and fights. Definitions of commander's intent abound, but here's my take on the term's meaning: "a clearly articulated written statement issued by the commander through which that commander imparts his or her vision to subordinates. The statement gives guidance, sets limits, and articulates the desired end state of mission in recognizable terms."

The statement of intent must be *written*, so that subordinates can refer to it at any time during the operation. A concise statement of intent shows that the commander has thought through the operation and has distilled the relevant concepts succinctly. In addition to existing in written form, the intent must also be articulated and issued personally, not simply sent out in the mail. Good commanders ensure that the statement of intent travels all the way down the chain of command, so that everyone in the unit knows exactly what the boss wants done. This knowledge then allows them to continue to operate even in the absence of further guidance. Just as important as the commander's written statement of intent, though, are the more subtle aspects of his or her intent—aspects that are continuously imparted in a variety of ways, including field training exercises, command post exercises, after-action reviews, drills and rehearsals, and many, many other activities.

During the Gulf War, General Franks would leave the command post at first light in his helicopter for face-to-face meetings with each of his division and regimental commanders. He constantly reiterated his intent to them. If he modified it in any way, his aide would contact me via satellite communications; I would enter the revision into the computer as part of the daily electronic fragmentary order that was published each evening. In this way, Franks was able to keep his front-line commanders constantly up to date on what he wanted them to do, based on the current situation. A unit that knows its commander, and that has learned to interpret the various forms of that commander's intent, exhibits more initiative and performs better than a unit that must always be issued orders before it can act.

7. THE COMMANDER'S WILL

The commander's *will* can make or break a unit, especially in times of stress. The following forceful passage from John Keegan's 1976 book *The Face of Battle* has stayed with me for my entire career:

> Once conditions become difficult, as they must when much is at stake, things no longer run like a well-oiled machine. The machine itself begins to resist, and the commander needs tremendous willpower to overcome the resistance. . . . [I]t is the impact of the ebbing of moral and physical strength, of the heart-rending spectacle of the dead and

wounded, that the commander has to withstand, first in himself, and then in all those who, directly or indirectly, have entrusted him with their thoughts and feelings, hopes and fears. . . . As each man's strength gives out, as it no longer responds to his will, the inertia of the whole gradually comes to rest on the commander's will alone. The ardor of his spirit *must* rekindle the flame of purpose in all others; his inward fire must revive their hope. Only to the extent that he can do this will he retain his hold on his men and keep control. Once that hold is lost, once his own courage can no longer revive the courage of his men, the mass will drag him down to the brutish world where danger is shirked and shame is unknown.

Powerful stuff! In essence, Keegan says that one person—the commander—is the spark, the stimulus, and the strength that can turn the impossible into the possible and save the day. The commander must be the stabilizing influence—the steady breeze that keeps the charcoal ember of courage from going out. Soldiers must be convinced that their commander is a person of character—someone they can trust— and that by trusting, watching, and emulating the commander, they will be able to maintain their strength and dignity, sustain the operation's momentum, and even avert disaster.

On two occasions, both as a relatively junior officer, I was faced with combat situations during which I had to draw on my own will in order to control my fear and to retain my ability to lead. The first took place early in February 1968. I was serving in an armed helicopter platoon in Vietnam. My wingman, Chief Warrant Officer 2nd Class Tommy Sandefur—the oldest, most experienced aviator in the platoon and the one who had the trust of every platoon member (officer, warrant officer, and enlisted soldier alike)—was killed on operation. This event virtually paralyzed the platoon. Before I knew it, the others were circulating a petition saying that they weren't going to fly anymore. A mass "turning in of flight wings" was about to take place! "What do you do now, Captain?" I asked myself. I had to let them know that Tommy's death had shattered me as well. I, too, was afraid of being killed, but my conscience as a man and as a soldier told me that I had to go on. I confided to them that when diving on a target or taking machine-gun fire while lining up the rocket attack run, I was nearly paralyzed with fear, but that I had to control it or perish. Even after I knew that the message had gotten through to them, I still had to keep my cheerleading outfit on—encouraging them, nurturing them, and most of all controlling my own fear and uncertainty. In the end, I succeeded, and there was no interruption of the mission flight schedule.

The second incident, which also occurred in Vietnam, took place three years later, while I commanded an Armored Cavalry troop. Our 150-man ground reconnaissance outfit worked on security operations in the northern central part of the country. My leadership dilemma began when we were occupying a night defensive perimeter. Just before midnight, we began taking small-calibre mortar fire. The mortars, which caused a great flurry of activity, were followed by the biggest explosion I'd ever heard or seen. One of our armoured vehicles had been hit. We evacuated the crew from the burning vehicle and stood guard as it burned all night. At first light, we established that the blast had killed eight regional force soldiers (allies) and one American, leaving a crater 15 feet (4.5 m) deep and 20 feet (6 m) across. Ordnance personnel determined that a bomb weighing 250 pounds (about 122 kg) had caused the explosion. Although we continued with our daily security mission, people speculated wildly about where the bomb had come from.

The next night we were again subjected to incoming artillery, but fortunately without the accompanying "big bang." However, one of my tank commanders called me over to show me a torpedolike object lying next to his tank. It was another 250-pound (122 kg) bomb that had been crudely rigged to detonate aboveground. When we asked a repatriated Viet Cong in our employ about this discovery, he described a terror tactic that the Viet Cong had developed using captured U.S. munitions. The enemy would reconnoitre locations that would provide all the desirable characteristics for a night defence position. They would then bury a captured 250-pound (122 kg) bomb in a shallow trench at that position, attaching a small charge to lift it just above ground level. The bomb could then be set off with a very crude point-detonating fuse system. The detonation would be preceded by mortar attacks to cause our troops to move from cover, thereby increasing casualties.

This was indeed a terror weapon—and there wasn't a more terrified member of the troop than Captain Stan Cherrie! I could feel fear spreading through the unit. Instances of conduct bordering on malingering increased, as did requests to return to Da Nang, thereby getting away from the front lines of combat. What was needed, I felt, was an offensive reaction, not a defensive retreat. I assembled the officers and NCOs and told them that henceforth we would conduct the following nightly procedures. Three defence perimeters would be selected each night. We would make a great deal of noise while setting up the first one, and then the next; then, two hours later, we'd move to the third. Moving armoured vehicles at night with our limited night-vision equipment was extremely dangerous and would not normally be a recommended practice, even for experienced armoured warriors. But we did it. We subsequently regained our unit composure, and we were not bothered by the "lob bomb" terror tactic again. The message that I want to convey here is not that we "won." Rather, I want to emphasize the tremendous amount of energy and will it took to control my own adrenalin-fuelled fear while I was prescribing counteractions to my troops. This kind of control cannot be taught in schools, but must be gained on playing fields and in other tough spots throughout life.

8. THE INFLUENCE OF THE ENVIRONMENT

The conditions that surround the human in command can change the way that command is exercised. The pressures caused by instantaneous media coverage, space-age communications, a "zero-defects" culture, and postaction second-guessing by the civilian and military hierarchy challenge both commanders' self-confidence and their ability to command according to their training and experience. Let me first discuss what I call the *CNN factor*—the influence of the whole panoply of media, including CNN, on military operations. There's absolutely no doubt that having reporters like Christiane Amanpour, Kate Adie, or Richard Blystone present while military units are deployed *does* make a difference; anyone who believes otherwise is simply not facing reality.

A prime example of the CNN factor occurred in 1991, nearing the end of the "Hundred-Hour War" in the Persian Gulf. Among the most enduring images of that war was what came to be called the "highway of death" footage, which showed the carnage wrought, primarily by the U.S. Air Force, on the retreating Iraqi forces as they headed north toward Iraq from Kuwait City. Senior leadership in the United States (National Command Authority and military) became worried that such pictures (showing what some termed "wanton slaughter") might result in public pressure to dissolve the coalition involved in the war. Critical decisions associated with terminating the conflict were therefore made on the basis of perceived public opinion—as influenced by the media—rather than on the basis of tactical information from field commanders.

Another example of media intrusion occurred in January 1996, when the U.S. Army was preparing to cross the Sava River, which separates Croatia from Bosnia–Herzegovina. There was tremendous pressure on us to cross that river on a certain date, since the President of the United States had been told we'd cross on that particular date. The fact that the river had swollen to two and a half times its normal size—the highest level in a century—was barely taken into account as the pressure to cross mounted. And the nightly "progress" reports provided by CNN and other news organizations to the American people—99 percent of whom couldn't have told you where the Sava River was—simply fanned the flame of public opinion about the issue. Throughout it all, though, the commander on the ground stuck to his guns, protected his force, and refused to undertake an ill-advised action simply in order to hit an arbitrary deadline.

Another external factor that can affect command is "political correctness." One of what I consider to be our nation's finest warriors was passed over for promotion to brigadier general, reportedly (according to a highly placed source) because he was "carrying too much political baggage to be a general officer." Colonel Greg Fontenot commanded the 1st Brigade in Task Force Eagle, deployed in Croatia during December 1995. Before the Sava crossing, while exhorting his troops about the well-proven nasty nature of the area's three former warring factions, he used colourful, descriptive, troop-oriented language. Unfortunately, a *Wall Street Journal* reporter who was present chose to quote his words directly. When the story broke the next day, the world fell in on Colonel Fontenot. Calls were issued from the highest levels in Europe for his relief, several mandated investigations (one of which I personally conducted) ensued, and he was virtually censured by his local command. Clearly it is no longer acceptable to speak—or at least to get caught speaking—the kind of tough, realistic language used by so many U.S. military heroes in the past. This attitude has, in my opinion, *infected* our armed forces and made us an ethical shadow of what we have been in the past.

Still another factor that inevitably affects command is the "Monday-morning quarterbacking" phenomenon. Nearly every day, television shows angry members of Congress, armed with 20/20 hindsight, demanding the ouster of some high-level military officer, either for acting or for failing to act in some situation where the officer had only a fraction of the information and time now available to Congress.

Finally, I would like to touch on the impact of digitization in the army. Some suggest that by providing improved situational awareness, digitization may render the commander's traditional position of "marching to the sound of the guns" passé. Whether this prediction proves accurate or not will depend largely on the location of the situational awareness terminals and the information flow they generate. Although commanders may eventually consider this technology an asset, its introduction has caused considerable tension. For example, how do commanders fight according to doctrine that has not yet fully incorporated digitization?

9. HOW THE RESEARCH COMMUNITY CAN HELP

I would like to bring this presentation to a close by asking the research community for some help. First, I believe that we must somehow imbed strategies into our training that will reward commanders for taking prudent risks in the face of uncertainty—and just as importantly, penalize them if they don't. General Dennis Reimer, the current U.S. chief of staff, has instructed our training community to do just that; but we haven't yet determined how to accomplish the task. Perhaps if we, as a NATO military training/research consortium, put our heads together we could decide on an approach that would address this issue.

Second, I believe that we must inculcate in military personnel the attitude that perfection is one of our arch-enemies, especially when it comes to staff work. Unfortunately, our schools, our training centres, and the overwhelming majority of our senior leaders seem to constantly demand perfection. That "Do it again!" mode achieves only diminishing returns on subordinates' time and effort. Perhaps our modern computer tools—Excel spreadsheets, PowerPoint presentations, and so on—have caused this unreasonable desire for perfection. Whatever its cause, it is now out of control in our army, where it ties our combat unit staffs in knots.

There are two final areas in which I think members of all armies could use a little help: stress reduction training and developing better methods of optimizing performance over extended periods. Before each of my last two deployments (to the Gulf and to Bosnia), we underwent up to seven weeks of intense, concentrated training, with no break and little chance to sleep. By the time we deployed and were making ready for operations, all the officers were "walking wounded." This situation could have caused more than just concern: had the Hundred-Hour War been a little longer, its tactical leaders would have become unfit for combat. Each time we find ourselves in the deploy/fight mode, we seem to throw all our research results and training out the window in an attempt to accomplish everything except to prepare for the long haul. I know that there has been considerable research in this area. Why aren't we making use of it? As commanders we must continue to learn and to ensure that research recommendations are incorporated in our armies' training and operational regimens.

This wraps up my thoughts on some of the factors that influence the human in command. I thank you for your kind attention and for allowing me to be a part of this enlightening workshop.

10. REFERENCES

Fontenot, G. (1995, July–August). Fear God and Dreadnought. *Military Review, 75*, 13–24.

Franks, F. M. (1996, May–June). Battle command: A commander's perspective. *Military Review, 76*, 4–25.

Keegan, J. (1976). *The face of battle*. London, U.K.: Penguin.

Military Review (1985, August). [Cover illustration.]

United States. (1987). *Leadership and command at senior levels* (Field Manual 22–103). Washington, DC: Department of the Army.

United States. (1992). *Leadership and command on the battlefield* (TRADOC Pamphlet 525-100-1). Fort Munroe, VA: U.S. Army Training and Doctrine Command.

CHAPTER 4

COMMAND EXPERIENCES IN RWANDA

LIEUTENANT-GENERAL R. A. DALLAIRE

EDITORS' NOTE—In October 1993, the United Nations sent a lightly armed peace-keeping force to Rwanda to assist in implementing peace accords between the Rwandan government (controlled by Hutus, the country's largest ethnic group) and the Rwandan Patriotic Front or RPF (chiefly ethnic Tutsis who had fled the country after the Hutus over-threw them in the 1960s). Commanded by Canadian General Roméo Dallaire, UNAMIR (United Nations Mission for Rwanda) comprised 2,500 troops who were forbidden to use force except in self-defence. The accords, signed after a two-year civil war, were meant to end hostilities that themselves were rooted in longstanding political and ethnic tensions. But Hutu extremists resisted the power-sharing arrangements. (For details on the conflict's history, along with events before and after UNAMIR's deployment, see HRW, 1999, and Sellström & Wohlgemuth, 1997; see also Adelman & Suhrke, 1998; Bodnarchuk, 1999; Gourevitch, 1998; Keane, 1997; Klinghoffer, 1998; Leyton & Locke, 1998; "100 Days," 1999; "Republic," 1998; and "Rwanda: A Historical Chronology," 1998.)

On April 6, 1994, the presidents of Rwanda and neighbouring Burundi were killed when their plane was shot down. The event set off a 100-day "tidal wave of violence" that saw the civil war resume while government forces massacred more than 800,000 Tutsis and moderate Hutus, including the acting prime minister ("Central Africa," 1999) and 10 of the Belgian soldiers UNAMIR assigned to protect her. Belgium—a key UNAMIR contributor—promptly withdrew its forces. Two weeks after the Belgian soldiers were killed, the U.N. Security Council cut UNAMIR back to 270 troops, making no change in its mandate (HRW, 1999). "Some U.N. camps shelter civilians, but most of the U.N. peacekeeping forces . . . [can only] stand by while the slaughter goes on. They are forbidden to intervene, as this would breach their 'monitoring' mandate" ("100 Days," 1999). Not until May 17, 1994, amid a growing international outcry, did the U.N. finally agree to send 5,500 troops (UNAMIR II) to Rwanda. But disputes over costs delayed the troops' deployment.

LIEUTENANT-GENERAL R. A. DALLAIRE • *Special Advisor to the Chief of Defence Staff (Officer Professional Development 2020), Department of National Defence, Ottawa, Ontario, Canada K1A 0K2*

The Human in Command: Exploring the Modern Military Experience, edited by McCann and Pigeau, Kluwer Academic/Plenum Publishers, New York, 2000.

On June 22, 1994, the U.N. Security Council authorized France to deploy 2,500 troops (Operation Turquoise) to Rwanda as an interim peacekeeping force, with a two-month U.N. mandate.

The war ended on July 18, 1994. "The RPF took control of a country ravaged by war and genocide [Destexhe, 1995; Prunier, 1995]. Up to 800,000 had been murdered, another 2 million or so [both Tutsi and Hutu] had fled, and another million or so were displaced internally" ("Republic," 1998)—a substantial proportion of the country's population, which was an estimated 7.9 million before the war. The return of the displaced persons and the "repatriation of these refugees [were] marred by periodic outbursts of violence" ("Rwanda," 1999) that continued well into 1995. UNAMIR II took over from the French on August 24, 1994, remaining in Rwanda until March 8, 1996.

In November 1994, the U.N. Security Council set up the International Criminal Tribunal for Rwanda (ICTR), which meets in Arusha, Tanzania, to prosecute those responsible for the genocide. Trials are ongoing (for details, see ICTR, 1999; and United Nations, 1998).

In May 1998, U.N. Secretary-General Kofi Annan apologized to Rwanda's parliament, saying that "[t]he world must deeply repent this failure. . . . Now we know that what we did was not nearly enough. . . . [I]n their hour of need, the world failed the people of Rwanda" ("100 Days," 1999).

1. INTRODUCTION

My aim in recounting my experiences as commander of the United Nations Assistance Mission for Rwanda (UNAMIR) in 1993/94 is to provide my personal perspective on the nature of future military operations. Mine is fundamentally a Canadian perspective, given by a senior officer from a middle-power Western nation that has no particularly strong stake in advancing its own political or economic interests in the context of peace support operations.

We Canadians possess a mastery of technology, a strong work ethic, and perhaps an uncommon sense of altruism. These qualities are reflected in our military commitments, which, in the last few years, have been oriented toward peace support operations rather than toward traditional warfighting. The lessons we've learned and the skills we've acquired during the past decade will prove crucial in solving the complex military problems of the future. I believe that Canada's recent experiences in military operations are likely to be the norm for the next couple of decades.

In these new operational scenarios, which I am calling *conflict resolution*,[1] troops are typically deployed in-theatre (for example, into Rwanda) as part of a coalition. They operate under a complex mandate with demanding milestones, together with multidisciplinary partners (for example, political groups, humanitarian organizations, police, and organizations dedicated to rebuilding the area's infrastructure), and under continuous media scrutiny. If coalition soldiers are not intimately familiar with the complex rules of engagement (ROEs) that

---

[1] Other chapters in this volume (see, for example, Chapter 26, "Research Challenges for the Human in Command") use the term *operations other than war (OOTW)*.

control their use of force, they are doomed to mishandle complex tactical-level actions in these operations—and possibly to jeopardize the success of the whole mission.

In conflict resolution operations, many factors can conspire to compromise a commander's ability to make correct decisions. I have already mentioned the impact of complex and confusing ROEs on the average soldier. The problem worsens if field commanders also experience confusion in interpreting these rules. Because of the levels of responsibility and accountability commanders must shoulder in the field, confusion breeds caution; hence these commanders inevitably perform at a margin of safety well below the mandated level of force. This phenomenon can spread until the whole coalition operates well below the level of force necessary to accomplish the mission. Add to this the ever-present media analysis of each military decision and the equally ever-present concern of nations and governments over casualties, and coalitions often find themselves in a frustrating position: the mission becomes a secondary priority, after "ensuring the security of our troops." The result completely undermines the commander's ability to determine the best operational method for accomplishing the job.

In this chapter, I will discuss some of the lessons gleaned from my experience of conflict resolution in UNAMIR, a U.N. Chapter VI force,[2] and identify some of the skills that I feel are important for ensuring success in these often very difficult circumstances.

2. CLASSIC WARFARE SKILLS ARE INSUFFICIENT

The conventional wisdom—widespread among most militaries—is that training for war is more difficult than training for operations other than war (OOTW) or for conflict resolution. I contend that the opposite is true. The skills required for peace support operations demand a much broader range and depth of knowledge— and a much richer set of experiences—than those acquired in conventional warfighting training programs. Militaries must ensure that their personnel also develop linguistic, cultural, and analytic skills that are unique to peace support operations—skills that are not currently taught in military education and training programs.

I will use my 1993/94 field experience in Rwanda to support my assertion that conflict resolution requires an expansion of the soldier's skills beyond those of classic warfighting. However, first I will discuss a couple of military operations that occurred before Rwanda. In 1990, Canada's armed forces were asked to provide aid to the country's own civil power when a provincial government was unable to handle an insurrection by native Canadians at the Oka reserve, near Montreal, Quebec. Two key aspects of this operation made it unique. First, it was deemed crucial that no

---

[2] Chapter VI operations require the consent of the parties and usually limit the use of force to self-defence. By contrast, Chapter VII operations authorize the full use of force necessary to accomplish the mandate, as was the case, for example, in both the Korean Conflict and the Gulf War.

martyrs be made of the individuals involved in the insurrection. Second, as a result of this decision, it was ordered that in the event of a violent confrontation, our troops would take the first casualty—before any response using weapons could be made. In other words, we were sending troops in harm's way, and we were deliberately eliminating the most fundamental component of any rule of engagement—namely, that self-defence is a sufficient reason for a lethal weapons response. Although I didn't realize it at the time, this event was a significant portent of the future.

Next came the 1991 Gulf War, an event that I contend was an anomaly in the post–Cold War era, just as future conflict scenarios involving classic warfighting will be exceptions. I maintain that although there may be similar crises in the next 10 to 20 years, conflict resolution, not warfighting, will be the main context for the employment of our forces. Of course, armed forces will always need to maintain warfighting skills in order to respond to national security problems, and such responses could include offshore allied and coalition operations. But if the majority of military operations in the next couple of decades involve conflict resolution, then I suggest that a serious disconnect exists between our current training approaches—which are based on the RMA (Revolution in Military Affairs) philosophy[3]—and the human skills necessary for successfully executing conflict resolution operations. I believe that we need to realign and broaden the education of the Canadian officer corps to more closely reflect missions of the type and complexity that, realistically, we will end up facing. Although the skill sets of classic warfighting, along with the credibility they provide, will certainly remain essential and fundamental for all militaries, they will serve only as the necessary starting point for mastery of the more complex dimensions of conflict resolution.

Martin Van Creveld's book *The Transformation of War* (1991) provides a convenient starting point for thinking about the conflict resolution situations in which many modern militaries are now becoming involved. Van Creveld argues that in certain countries, the nation–state structure—that is, the triumvirate of the nation, the people, and the armed forces—is only partly formed. Africa represents one region where many nation–states have not yet really matured—where, for example, the government is not responsible to the people.[4] As a result, either by political or economic design, or perhaps due to pressures emanating from the media or other nongovernmental organizations (NGOs), militaries will undoubtedly find themselves embroiled in the trauma of these African nations as they adjust to the democratic process—a process that usually entails whole new philosophies of life.[5] The breakdown in Rwanda is a particularly brutal example of political trauma resulting from ineffective power sharing and ethnic frictions. And similar scenarios will almost certainly recur in the future.

---

[3] The Revolution in Military Affairs refers to the overwhelming information and weapon system superiority assumed to be conferred on militaries who take advantage of recent technological advances.

[4] In such cases, advocating noninvolvement on the basis of sovereignty becomes spurious, since the nations in question are *not* in fact sovereign in the sense of having a government that is determined by and responsible to the people.

[5] The same may well prove true for large portions of Asia and South America.

In my opinion, the Rwandan crisis represents a catastrophic failure by the international community, which proved unwilling to deploy even a small component of its enormous collective military power to contain the situation. Unfortunately, self-interest—not human rights—remains the dominant criterion determining world powers' involvement in such crises. The limitation is vividly exemplified by the March 1994 U.S. Presidential Decision Directive 25.[6] As a consequence, independent middle powers and countries that are committed to human rights (such as Canada) may find themselves increasingly involved in these new types of conflict resolution situations, despite lacking both the resources needed for achieving success in such missions and the willingness to tolerate casualties.

3. SOPHISTICATED TECHNOLOGY VERSUS THE SIMPLE RADIO

Ironically, even when Western armed forces have a clear technical advantage (for example, in computer and weapon systems), operations like the one in Rwanda continue to present challenges. Historically, Western armed forces have equipped and trained themselves to fight adversaries that have technological competencies similar to their own, in classic warfare scenarios. I contend that this fascination with technology, along with the assumption that such technology provides superiority, has lulled Western militaries into a form of complacency, preventing them from arriving at simpler solutions to major operational problems.

For example, in Rwanda, the most sophisticated technology used by the general population was the ordinary public radio. Since 85 percent of the population was illiterate, the radio dominated life, particularly in the country's outlying villages. Rwanda functioned not through its road systems, televisions, or newspapers, but through its radio stations. Everyone had a radio. Even people in refugee camps found ways of getting batteries to run radios. The radio was, if not the voice of God, then certainly the voice of authority, with a status that made it a powerful tool for disseminating information, misinformation, and propaganda, as well as for overall control of the masses. For instance, military forces encountered a radio station run by extremists who were explicitly inciting people to kill, but had no way of jamming it (let alone of understanding what was being said). Such situations illustrate the military's failure to really comprehend the cultural dimensions of the problem in-theatre. And I'm not talking about collecting sophisticated intelligence data here—but simply about getting readily available information from an ordinary radio broadcast!

The U.N. mission in Rwanda did not at first realize the importance of this communication method, much less appreciate its widespread influence and impact on the population. How that factor escaped us will always remain a mystery to me. And

---

[6] Published only weeks before the commencement of the genocide and civil war in Rwanda, PDD 25 essentially formalized the decision-making process to be used by the U.S. president in authorizing the use of U.S. forces or other U.S. involvement in various humanitarian or conflict resolution crises. The overriding criterion for involvement specified in the PDD is the degree of U.S. self-interest in the conflict.

when we did finally realize the radio's importance—particularly that it was the nation's dominant instrument of hate propaganda—what happened? We were told to retreat to a safe position and that we could not stop those hateful, slaughter-inciting broadcasts because to do so would have encroached on Rwanda's sovereignty! This clumsy, outdated view of international law—that is, the idea that nations must not interfere with other sovereign nations' internal affairs—remains the Western world's single most common excuse for nonintervention. Yet the world's nations should realize that the Geneva Conventions *do* allow them to intervene for humanitarian reasons in situations where national sovereignty might previously have been an obstacle (Gee, 1999). I believe that the United Nations can gain the moral and physical force to be genuinely effective in conflict resolution only if its participant nations put advancing global humanism ahead of blindly respecting the supremacy of national sovereignty.

In the end, we couldn't deploy a radio station to counter the propaganda in Rwanda. As a result, we failed miserably in our objectives and were left to witness daily escalations in the slaughter.

What advantage, then, does technological superiority provide such situations? In Rwanda, it merely encouraged a dangerous arrogance toward the belligerents, a tendency to view them—inaccurately—as unsophisticated and insignificant. This attitude served us poorly. Moreover, our supposed technological superiority was marginalized anyway by political decisions—first, not to support the mission, and eventually, to pull out.

Whatever the Rwandans lacked in technology, they more than made up for in numbers, as well as in their confidence in their abilities when faced with uniformed white people carrying guns. Still, a single platoon of militia with machetes, grenades, and old rifles should pose little threat to a section of well-trained Western soldiers—*if* those soldiers understand the rules of engagement regarding the use of force, and if their leaders are ready to act on those ROEs. But in Rwanda, the belligerents never came in platoon size. They came by the hundreds. They came by the thousands. Their military was able to maintain such large numbers by drawing on the country's disaffected youth and capitalizing on the ethnic animosities. In a country where chaos reigns, displaced people are easily recruited. How, then, does a peace-keeping force handle hundreds and thousands of belligerents (female as well as male), many of whom are intoxicated on narcotics and alcohol, and are easily incited to violence by their leaders' emotional appeals to ethnic, tribal, and religious identity? How do you handle that kind of volume and scale of threat? How many do you need to kill before they will stop? What conventional Western warfighting methods apply in such situations? What clause in the mandate handles such dilemmas, even in a Chapter VII mission? Have our rules of engagement matured to the point of guiding the answers to such moral and ethical questions?

4. CULTURAL AWARENESS

I confess that my initial view of Rwanda was biased by history and by naive pre-conceptions. To me, much of Africa was the domain of missionaries and NGOs, and it was the victim of ruthless resource extraction. But as I discovered, the quality of the political leadership in Rwanda (as well as in many other African nations) was very high. Since the numerous revolutions against colonial rule that occurred during the late 1950s and early 1960s, many of the country's leaders had been educated in North American and European colleges. The astuteness of the political and military leaders of the belligerent groups in Rwanda was quite evident in the way they counteracted Operation Turquoise, a U.N. Chapter VII coalition of French-led forces, many of whom were also participants in my Chapter VI mission. Operation Turquoise attempted to maintain a protection zone against the Tutsi-led rebel forces of the Rwandan Patriotic Front (RPF) and to protect nearly 2 million displaced Hutus. As the Chapter VI UNAMIR force commander, I negotiated the separation line and monitored, with my small force, the line between General Paul Kagame's rebel forces (RPF) and the forces of Op Turquoise, which included Jaguar jets, helicopter gunships, heavy mortars, APCs (armoured personnel carriers), and 2,500 special forces troops. There were a number of confrontational situations during Op Turquoise's two-month stay in Rwanda, including two occasions when the rebels beat the French in the field, capturing over 20 French soldiers. These incidents demonstrate that the best Western equipment and training do not necessarily lead to success. As General Kagame so shrewdly and ruthlessly pointed out, "Kigali [the Rwandan capital] can handle more body bags than Paris can." Many factors besides raw military power can influence success in complex conflict resolution situations: cultural perceptions and societal sensitivities are among the most influential.

Our experience with peace support operations in remote nations suggests that military officers need additional cultural and linguistic skills—because, for example, the local translators usually are (or are perceived to be) biased toward one faction or another. Yet should we expect our officers to master all the common international languages (like Spanish)—let alone languages as rare as Kinyarwanda? In Canada, simply implementing national bilingualism continues to pose challenges long after the policy was originally mandated. Nevertheless, cultural awareness and linguistic proficiency *are* necessities for these new operations. I maintain that militaries cannot gain and keep the initiative essential for mission success if they are unaware of the cultural nuances, the social customs, and the subtle messages that are being passed around them with impunity by the belligerents. Regrettably, training in these areas has not yet been developed in our officer corps: we still single-mindedly advocate and pursue warfighting skills that, as I have been arguing, are no longer sufficient. The solution is to provide either a linguistically adept and broadly educated officer corps or a special group of civilian/military experts in such matters. Of the two, the former option is less risky and more flexible.

5. RISK ASSESSMENT AND DECISION MAKING

The UNAMIR conflict resolution operation regularly required dealing with issues of mandate, risk, and moral ambiguity. For example, after Juvénal Habyarimana, the Rwandan president, was killed on April 6, 1994, the only legal authority left in the country was the coalition prime minister, Agathe Uwiliyingimana. She was considered key to preventing the country from sliding into civil war. It was essential that she be protected and moved to a radio station so that she could speak to her people. But by that time our mandate was over, so what was to be UNAMIR's official role in this situation? War was imminent: both sides were ready to renew the fighting, and ceasefire violations had escalated both in Kigali and in the demilitarized zone (DMZ). Twelve hours later, the Rwandans did indeed go to war, and the killing of civilians gained momentum. Technically, we could simply have packed up and left.

Yet from the start I had decided to protect the prime minister by sending in my best troops, the Belgian contingent. This decision was fraught with moral and ethical dilemmas. What justification did I have for risking soldiers' lives to protect the prime minister in such a chaotic situation? I was hoping to prevent open war and the mass killings of an ethnic minority, but was I overstepping the limit of my mandate? Tragically, by midmorning on April 7, the extremists had captured and killed the coalition prime minister and her husband. In addition, 10 of the Belgian peacekeepers who had been guarding her were massacred after being disarmed and tortured by the extremists. By 1600 hours that day, negotiations had broken down and the civil war had begun in earnest, followed immediately by the literal beheading of all the Tutsi and moderate Hutu political and judicial leaders. In the end, was my decision to try to protect the prime minister the right decision? Though the attempt was unsuccessful, was it at least morally correct? It remains my firm conviction that my decision to protect the prime minister in the pursuit of peaceful resolution was absolutely correct. The loss of those Belgian heroes—in addition to nearly a million Rwandans—is the legacy of that mission.

I then made the further decision to extract the future prime minister, Faustin Twagiramungu (who had been designated by an August 1993 peace accord to fill this position), from his encircled home and bring him to my headquarters. The extremists heard about this intercession and began verbal and military attacks on both my headquarters and me. I therefore asked the contingents in my headquarters to defend the headquarters and the prime minister designate. Was I authorized to order the contingents to do so? At that point, UNAMIR no longer had a mandate. Would my troops have fought to defend the headquarters at the risk of being wiped out? What were their own national orders at that point in time? What arguments could I have offered to persuade them to stand their ground and fight? Ultimately, why should they have risked their lives to follow a Canadian or other foreign general[7] when their own nation was not at risk, their government did not want casualties, and our chances of success were minimal?

In the end, some contingents were withdrawn and others belatedly replaced them. After six days of sporadic mortar and artillery attacks and attempts by the belligerents to overrun the headquarters we removed the prime minister designate from the country by subterfuge, and the rebel forces overwhelmed the extremists in our area. In the face of such crimes against humanity, should commanders continue to put their troops' lives at risk from a sense of moral duty, or should they cease operations, protect themselves, and withdraw because they no longer have a

---

[7] The vast majority of troops within UNAMIR were not Canadian.

mandate? My situation was not unique: such difficult operational and moral decisions presented themselves several times a day throughout Rwanda at all levels of command.

Thirteen days later, as both the civil war and the slaughter gained momentum, I received the order to withdraw all forces. I refused outright to comply with this order. We had about 30,000 Rwandans from both sides under our protection. Our departure would have guaranteed their death—as had already happened at one site when a military contingent, without orders but under national direction, retreated and left nearly 4,000 Rwandans to their fate. We found about 2,000 bodies a few weeks later. The U.N. headquarters accepted my offer to keep a reduced complement of approximately 450 troops and withdraw the rest. The 1,300 French and Belgian forces that had been evacuating white Europeans and certain Rwandans had by then withdrawn, together with the U.N. Belgian contingent. My tattered and logistically depleted force knew that no reinforcements or supplies would be forthcoming. And throughout it all, we received no formal mandate. I called our situation the "counter crimes against humanity operation," and my soldiers believed in that mission. Although a number of them became casualties over the months to follow, they pursued the mission with tireless courage.

Surely no single nation would have deserted its troops the way we were deserted by the world community in Rwanda.

Dilemmas like these will continue to confront commanders in conflict resolution situations, particularly when risk assessment is required. How far should a commander go in negotiating with a belligerent leader (one who still has blood on his hands from the morning's slaughter) to save a couple of thousand people, when the commander knows that this same belligerent is killing others by the tens of thousands? How far should a commander risk the lives of his or her own troops in order to save a few people when the belligerents are slaughtering others left and right?

A more informed and open debate on risk assessment is essential. Like other militaries, Canada's armed forces are being committed to theatres of operation when no direct threat to Canada exists. (Indeed, I would suggest that Canadians are often unaware that their forces are deploying into such operations.) How can commanders in such situations reasonably balance the risks in an operation? Lacking a direct threat to their country's national security, should their priorities change from the time-honoured military ethos of "my mission, my personnel, myself" to "my personnel, my mission, myself"? In my opinion, we have entered a dangerous and delicate period with respect to conflict resolution.

Commanders must be aware that their decisions will be influenced by such factors as national politics and international relations, factors that could well seem quite distant from the situation at hand. International agencies and NGOs will lobby and act independently of the military plan, and without consultation—or, at best, with only a cursory acknowledgment of military help. Commanders therefore have to balance many paradoxical questions: How many casualties will the different national contingents in a multinational operation absorb before actually pulling out? What will inspire troops to commit themselves to enormous personal risks when they know that other nations will withdraw after (or even before) they take casualties? Should commanders spare the lives of their troops and possibly sacrifice the mission, but then face their nation's and possibly the world's moral acrimony? Or should they commit their troops to achieving the mission using the classic casualty assessments techniques for success? Do commanders in conflict resolution situations need a whole new set of rules, equations, and doctrine to help them make such decisions?

6. CASUALTIES

The political impact of incurring casualties in conflict resolution is guaranteed to be an overriding factor in a commander's decision making. As General Kagame understood, the Western world cannot cope with casualties. This explains why the United States pulled out of Somalia in October 1993 (six months before the events that precipitated the genocide in Rwanda) with 18 killed and 72 injured, and why the Belgians decided to pull out of Rwanda within a few days of having lost 10 soldiers. I find it ironic that in the latter part of the war in Rwanda, American NGOs were all over the countryside, but with the exception of a few hundred U.S. military police and technicians required to secure the immediate perimeter of the Kigali airfield and to assist in the unloading of NGO personnel and supplies as part of the humanitarian airlift, there was no U.S. military presence in Rwanda itself.[8] And the U.S. troops that were there were under absolute orders to take no casualties.

As a final example, I faced a situation where one contingent possessed the capability to provide UNAMIR with a supply of water—water that was urgently needed, because hundreds of the displaced persons under our protection were dying of thirst every day. But this particular contingent was officially forbidden to assist us, no matter how many people were dying, because of the grave concern about suffering casualties.

This overriding concern for the avoidance of casualties will have continuing implications for the employment of our armed forces in conflict resolution operations where contributing nations are not at risk and where they have no other self-interest. It will affect simple, routine tactical decisions, such as whether or not to escort a convoy, and it will inevitably raise difficult moral questions and operational dilemmas.

7. UNCERTAINTY AND AMBIGUITY

Commanders will not find classic warfare's familiar action verbs—such as *attack*, *defend*, or *destroy*—in conflict resolution mandates. Instead, they will encounter vague and ambiguous verbs like *monitor, assist, create,* and *investigate.* The broad spectrum of interpretation that such verbs elicit often makes it difficult for commanders to decide what and/or how much to do. After all, today's commanders have

---

[8] The U.S. deployed 2,500 troops in late July 1994, only after the civil war and most of the slaughter was over. And 2,200 of those troops were located in the neighbouring countries of Uganda and Zaire (now the Democratic Republic of the Congo), not in Rwanda.

been trained in the very specific sets of actions associated with doctrine-based warfighting. Furthermore, in conflict resolution, the nuances of an agreement and the complex wording of mandates carry enormous political implications—implications that military organizations are not trained to handle, especially when they concern the delicate balance of power between rival factions in scenarios where the agreements between the factions have not been formalized. I maintain that commanders who insist on clear mandates and unambiguous decision processes should not be involved in conflict resolution, because the challenges they will face will be too complex and subtle to be explicitly addressed through simple short-term tactical objectives and readily identifiable milestones. For example, the mandate given to the military force in Rwanda did not address all aspects of the peace agreement signed by the belligerent parties. Thus, commanders and their troops were placed in a position of having to execute a mandate that the belligerent parties themselves were not fully committed to supporting due to the perception by the belligerents of shortfalls in the mandate. This situation created uncertainty and suspicion, leading to lengthy debates and frustrating meetings that inevitably watered down the original objectives and eventually undermined the peace agreement. Ultimately, this state of affairs provided an opportunity for the more cunning of the belligerents to seize the initiative and gain a temporary upper hand. Effective command under such conditions requires a leader who is able not only to maintain the intent of the mission but also to keep in view the full breadth of the peace agreement, all while dealing with extremely uncertain and fluid circumstances.

8. MORAL AND ETHICAL DILEMMAS

As important as these specific examples are for conveying the complexity of conflict resolution, they only begin to illustrate the scope and depth of the moral and ethical dilemmas awaiting commanders in the field—at *all* levels—during such operations. When a platoon commander is restricted to the Chapter VI rules of engagement, what should that commander say to his or her troops as they work their way into a village where the inhabitants have been slaughtered, where women and children have been literally hacked to pieces, but some are still alive and screaming for help? Does the platoon commander order the soldiers to help the survivors when 30 percent of the population is known to have AIDS, and the platoon personnel lack the gloves and other safety equipment needed to protect them from infection? Moreover, what happens when soldiers see a woman carrying a child on her back, in the midst of a killing spree by extremist groups, hacking to death another woman carrying a child on *her* back? Do the soldiers open fire? On whom? What are the moral implications if they do not try to stop the killing?

In such nightmarish circumstances, what possible guidance or preparation can be given to soldiers and their leaders? Are Western beliefs and values even relevant in such extreme situations? Have Western militaries put those beliefs and values to the test in leadership training programs, and are their officers and noncommissioned members (NCMs) ready for these complex and horrific challenges? Are we *really* thinking about these issues and spending time developing doctrine, solutions, and practices that support personnel legally, morally, and ethically? Or are we simply counting on existing training and hoping for the best? In Rwanda, there was so much room for interpretation, so much pressure to stay within boundaries, so much difficulty in getting even a mandate from the U.N. Security Council, that I often based my course of action on my own assessment of what various contingent commanders could handle—with or without their nations' approval.

Such are the moral dilemmas of command in conflict resolution. None of the contingents either anticipated or were prepared for a scenario like the one we faced in Rwanda. I therefore believe that my experiences and those of other military leaders during the past decade of world disorder must be rigorously analyzed and studied to extract the lessons to be learned for future commanders in the field. These issues are far too important and too complex to be discussed, debated, and resolved only as troops are about to deploy. Education, development, and training in these demanding subjects must begin the moment a potential leader enters one of our institutions. We cannot let future leaders be commissioned without far more depth and breadth of knowledge concerning the multidisciplined arena they will face, under the nation's scrutiny, on graduation. The luxury of a four- or five-year apprenticeship phase is over. Young officers and even NCMs are thrust into these operational theatres within months of leaving our colleges and training establishments.

9. ACCOUNTABILITY

Within the first few days of the renewed violence in Rwanda (that is, the killings that began after President Habyarimana's death on April 6, 1994), it appeared painfully obvious to me that the world community was uninterested in resolving the situation there. Countries that had contributed troops began to recall their forces, fearing casualties and responding to diplomatic pressure from the Belgian government. Yet moral accountability in conflict resolution in the post–Cold War era goes well beyond the lives of the military troops involved. In Rwanda, if we too had withdrawn outright when ordered to, not only would we have been abandoning to their certain death thousands of innocent men, women, and children who had been under our protection, but we would have had to live with having morally failed to *try* to avoid a catastrophe or at least try to save some of the moderate leaders on both sides in the process. History would have been warranted in painting us as the force with no clear mandate that withdrew for fear of casualties just when hundreds of thousands of people were being slaughtered. The United Nations, the contributing nations, and I myself could justifiably have been held accountable for cowardliness and a complete lack of moral fibre.

Unfortunately, such a concept of accountability has yet to be adequately discussed, debated, and resolved within the international community, let alone within the United Nations. Indeed, the debate so far has been limited to lawyers' discussions regarding whether it is legal to intervene in the sovereignty of failing nation–states and whether anyone has the authority to capture and prosecute the perpetrators of these terrible crimes. And sadly, when scapegoats are sought in order to defuse political problems, sometimes it is those in uniform—individuals who live by the doctrine of unlimited liability—who become those scapegoats, despite the fact that it is they who have just been the target of the belligerents.

Accountability for actions taken by armed forces during conflict resolution operations is increasingly being demanded at both the national and international levels. For Rwanda, as well as for the former Yugoslavia, international tribunals have been convened to investigate violations of the laws of armed conflict and crimes against humanity (for the Rwanda tribunal, see ICTR, 1999, and United Nations, 1999; for the tribunal dealing with the former Yugoslavia, see United Nations, 1997). I have already testified once at the International Criminal Tribunal for Rwanda (ongoing in Arusha, Tanzania, since November 1995), and I expect to return there in 2000. Other senior commanders will no doubt find themselves drawn, as I have been, into these international legal investigations—investigations that question them about events, actions, and decisions that were far from clear-cut, having taken place in a context much broader and more complex than that of classic warfighting.

Military leaders are certainly accountable to their own governments for their actions, but are they also accountable to the United Nations or to international tribunals? What should a nation's policy be on allowing its military commanders to testify before a U.N. commissioner or participating in international tribunals? Many commanders would feel morally compelled to participate in such inquiries, but would their governments agree? After all, commanders who testify could well find themselves in the difficult position of giving testimony that embarrasses their own government.

From the perspective of accountability, the position of the Red Cross regarding the International Criminal Tribunal for Rwanda (ICTR) and the International Criminal Tribunal for the Former Yugoslavia (ICTY) is an interesting one. During the first three weeks of the genocide in Rwanda, the International Committee of the Red Cross (ICRC) was the only international agency in the country, except for the media and UNAMIR. The ICRC lost 56 nationals who had been negotiating for the safe passage of casualties during assaults on hospitals. Yet when asked to testify at the ICTR, the ICRC refused, arguing that to do so would jeopardize the perception of its impartiality in future world hot spots! Should military personnel similarly not testify before such bodies, since militaries must also be perceived as neutral and impartial participants for future conflict resolution operations?

I believe that accountability extends much further than politics (that is, the strategic level): it reaches down to the everyday tactical level as well. For example, what are the options for Chapter VI field commanders when belligerent units surrender to their supposedly neutral and nonbelligerent force (such as a U.N. force)? Do those who surrender become prisoners of war, even though the U.N. force is not actually at war with them? Does the commander hand them over to the other belligerents, who may mistreat or even kill them? And if the commander does turn them over, will he or she be held accountable for the rival force's subsequent actions? Finally, what should the ICRC's role be in such situations? When an entire battalion and their families (nearly 2,000 people) surrendered to a UNAMIR company in Rwanda, it took some time to clarify the status of both UNAMIR and the battalion, as well as the ICRC's role. Are the U.N. commander's forces compelled to protect those who have surrendered? How far should the U.N.

commander go in defending them, given that U.N. forces comprise various contributing nations that may have quite different views on the issue? Finally, the faction leaders in many failing states are ruthless extremists who act solely according to their personal aims and may not recognize international law. How can a U.N. commander be sure that the belligerents will feel bound by the Geneva Convention and behave accordingly? (The killing of the Belgian soldiers who were captured within the first 24 hours of the war in Rwanda proved that at least one group of belligerents did not feel constrained by international law ["Rwanda: A Historical Chronology," 1998].) Such situations raise whole new dimensions of accountability and responsibility that commanders and senior officers have not traditionally spent much time reflecting on.

10. MILITARY COHESION

In contrast to former U.N. peacekeeping missions, which tended to be static in nature, today's international crises demand that U.N. involvement be dynamic, time-sensitive, and flexible. But the nature of the United Nations rarely permits such a response. For example, the day before I landed in Kigali, Burundi (the country just south of Rwanda) experienced a coup d'état. Within days, over 300,000 Burundi refugees had arrived in the south of Rwanda, an area originally assessed as requiring limited UNAMIR attention (due to the presence of moderates and of a secure border between the nations). UNAMIR's very limited resource base and the lack of attention paid by the international community to this human crisis made it impossible for me to react quickly to this new situation, to take the initiative, or to bring about an atmosphere of security in southern Rwanda, let alone in Burundi.

Several procedural factors interfere in the speed of the organization's response. The U.N. procedure for defining mission requirements, mandates, and funding mechanisms is complex and drawn-out; lengthy procedural and administrative delays are also common. Add to that the often slow decision-making processes involving extensive negotiations between the United Nations and the countries that are potential contributors to the military effort, and the result is that by the time forces are deployed, the mission and the resources may be out of sync with the actual situation in the field.

These delays create serious difficulties for commanders who are trying to establish an effective operational plan and a cohesive military coalition. Establishing military cohesion is further complicated by the enormous variance in training among member nations' militaries, along with differences in equipment availability and quality, and in the sustainability of the entire effort. The commander may appear to have an adequate number of troops, but if more than half of them do not meet minimum standards or do not have the requisite mobility and sustainability, then the commander is seriously limited in employing them. Imagine building a headquarters using staff who don't speak the same language and don't even have the same operating procedures! Although some UNAMIR participants—for example, the Dutch and the Ghanaians—had extensive experience in peace support operations and were real assets, others were there simply to gain on-the-job training, as one contingent's chief of staff explained to me. Another complicating factor in forming a functional force for peace operations is the fact that some participating nations may have terrible human rights problems of their own and therefore represent less-than-adequate role models. Lastly, in some cases a coalition's participating nations have previously been enemies in their own region of the world—and especially when adversarial sentiments linger from a time when one nation was a colony of another. Such situations make the task of establishing unit cohesion extremely delicate. Not only is it difficult for commanders to create and maintain a cohesive force under such circumstances, but the belligerents may well try to take advantage of the resulting lack of a common standard and commitment. They may play some components of the U.N. force off against others, and they may gain more freedom to act by taking advantage of the components of the U.N. force that have not had sufficient preparation and training.

11. ONE MISSION FOR ALL PARTICIPANTS

Conflict resolution requires a unified approach, with comprehensive coordination encompassing all plans—security, humanitarian, economic, and political—in ways that prove mutually supportive. Without a single overarching mission plan, it is difficult to seize and maintain the initiative as a crisis develops. It is even more difficult if the crisis is full-blown.

Often military forces are on the ground and ready to go, but the humanitarian operation is stalled because the needs haven't been fully assessed, funding isn't yet in place, or more coordination is required. Meanwhile, the political situation may be fluctuating or even may have stagnated. If we continue to be so disjointed in articulating, implementing, and coordinating these different plans, failures will continue to occur, precious resources will be wasted, and credibility will disappear.

Achieving an integrated conflict resolution plan is not a trivial task. Simply coordinating the many NGOs that may be involved presents a significant challenge—there were 169 NGOs in Rwanda! Some of these were very small, with lots of heart but little or no capability. Often they quickly became liabilities. Others were quite large, with extensive capabilities, but their actions were frequently governed as much by their media image (and the need to get resources for the next crisis) as by their humanity—sometimes seriously jeopardizing success in the current operation.[9]

The military and the NGOs have different aims and missions, and these can often be at odds. In 1994, NGOs were working behind the lines of one Rwandan belligerent group. Not surprisingly, these belligerents started using the fuel, medical supplies, and food that the NGOs had brought in for the displaced persons. Despite the fact that during the first months of the war, UNAMIR had no official jurisdiction over the activities of these NGOs (UNAMIR provided only security), the

---

[9] The extensive aid provided to 1.5 million persons in Goma, in contrast to the much lower—and at times virtually nonexistent—levels of aid for so many of the millions of Rwandans who were displaced internally is an example.

opposing belligerents immediately accused us of aiding and abetting their enemy. They did not understand the operational ethos of these NGOs—namely, to offer unconditional assistance that was unconnected to military intervention. Instead, they perceived the situation solely as evidence of favouritism on UNAMIR's part. Incidents like these complicated the political and military dimensions of the UNAMIR mission. How can commanders in conflict resolution situations work with NGOs to achieve both the military mission and the NGOs' missions, yet still appear consistent—and, more important, impartial—to the belligerents?

Our credibility was further undermined by the often rigid and narrow interpretation of the mandate by our higher headquarters—especially considering the actual situation on the ground. We were often ordered to pull out far too soon, without enough time to implement proper support strategies or to develop sound solutions that would be agreed to by all sides. Under these conditions, commanders and political decision makers can find themselves implementing completely unachievable pull-out solutions based on impossible milestones. Belligerents—particularly the extremist elements—may easily see through these supposed solutions. They may consequently use covert tactics and underground operations to preserve their power among the local populace—chiefly by sustaining people's fear levels. Eventually, the donor countries lose patience and withdraw, leaving the belligerents as strong as ever. I am adamant that conflict resolution must not be attempted unless we are willing to address all the dimensions of a problem (that is, its political, humanitarian, security, and economic factors) and to do so over the long term—for decades if necessary. Unless we are willing to make long-term commitments, we must not deploy troops under the pressure of media-driven hype. We must not risk the lives of our personnel in poorly conceived, guilt-driven humanitarian operations that are predominantly vehicles for political posturing by corrupt leaders who, in the end, have only a superficial concern for the real situation.

If you are in the business of conflict resolution, you must expect to be in it for the long haul. If you are not prepared for this type of commitment, then stay out—and learn to live with your individual and collective consciences.

12. COMMUNICATION AND THE MEDIA

All of these moral dilemmas, operational uncertainties, political sensitivities, and coordination issues happen under the close scrutiny of the media. I would argue that a productive way of looking at this unavoidable reality is to view the media as a new and positive instrument for communication. One of the responsibilities of command is to communicate mission objectives to the troops, to their families, to a nation's population, to the international community, and to organizations such as the United Nations and NATO (the North Atlantic Treaty Organization). Communication can happen directly between commanders and their troops, but it can also happen indirectly—through the media. The media also offer excellent ways to gather intelligence, to help assess the belligerents' intentions in zones that your mission cannot get into, and to get your side of the story out to the world. Putting the drama of a conflict on the world stage can actually help resolve a crisis by spurring international participation.

Some may view using the media to influence world leaders as unethical. But I disagree, particularly when those leaders show a tendency toward indifference. When world leaders deliberately abandoned the Rwandans to their plight, relegating my force to an impotent witness to the third genocide of the twentieth century (Destexhe, 1995), only the media remained with us. In some ways, the media made much of the difference. To them go well-deserved kudos for courage, determination, and a sense of global social conscience. Force commanders should therefore regard the media as an asset, not as an impediment, to the mission. In modern military operations, the media should be embraced as an essential tool for mission success, albeit one that should be employed with caution and respect. Commanders who play "coy" with the media or try to conceal information from them risk undermining their own command. If the media in Rwanda had felt that I was being anything but honest with them, they would have turned on me with a vengeance; their reporting would have focused on U.N. ineptness rather than on the human tragedy. Minimally, such a negative media image would have affected the morale of my force. But it would also almost certainly have changed the belligerents' perception of our force, thereby putting the whole mission at risk, including the safety of the 30,000 or so Rwandans under our protection.

Communicating with the media, then, is a crucial aspect of postmodern command, an integral part of the many ways that commanders can influence their troops, their opponents, and their overall situation. Consequently, commanders should not relegate these activities to expert public affairs staff alone. Commanders must therefore become comfortable with having cameras and microphones thrust in their faces, often at the most sensitive of times, and they must be able to project confident resolve and professionalism without hesitation under those trying conditions.

Communication also involves more than words alone. In addition to words (for example, in the form of orders to the troops or statements to the media), commanders also communicate through their eyes, their face, their tears, their tone of voice, and their body language. And an effective commander uses all these channels to convey to the troops a complete willingness to risk his or her own life where necessary. Effective commanders present their orders personally, stand behind them, and are there in person to see the results. This point was reinforced for me in Rwanda. Initially, I gave my staff only the mission statement and intent for the first operations order, which the staff then wrote. But we took casualties with that first operation. After that, I would not let my staff write the orders. I wrote the next dozen or so myself, with staff input, and I personally presented those orders to the troops at as many levels as I could manage. Each time, I told them that they were going to be in harm's way, and urged them to show courage, pluck, and determination. I also made clear to them our limited ability to get them to safety should they be injured or captured. And when they returned from those dangerous missions, I was there to cry with them over the loss of comrades. This is not the job of staff officers; neither is it the job of subordinate commanders alone. It is the responsibility of the most senior commander. The troops had to realize that I was also suffering when people under my command were injured or lost—that we would cry together, then collectively wipe the tears from our eyes and go back out again and again.

13. TRUST

I believe that we in the military have developed a dysfunctional syndrome whereby too many of our leaders retreat to their offices during a crisis in order to answer phone calls from higher headquarters or write reports to "cover all the bases." Many times in UNAMIR, I observed officers from various nations who, when the shelling began, went inside and started writing plans and reports rather than gathering the information personally and controlling the situation directly by their presence. A perception exists that when trouble occurs, someone higher in the chain of command should be told immediately. This is both wrong and unnecessary. But how do you cure this insidious disease—a condition all too common among those who have experienced only garrison duty? Commanders at all levels should take it for granted that in conflict resolution situations their superiors are getting updates from CNN and the other media right in their offices! Details on the situation should be provided only after the crisis has been addressed or when support from higher command is truly required. In my opinion, the rear headquarters is the last place for leaders during a local crisis. They should be well forward, where they can quickly assess the situation and make informed decisions. I spent the bulk of my first four to five days in Rwanda in either the Hutu or the Tutsi military headquarters instead of my own. Only through his or her presence can a commander's force of will and determination steer the situation in the desired direction.

Senior officers must create an atmosphere that clearly demonstrates their confidence that their subordinates will undertake the proper and competent actions. Until officers can project this confidence—a cornerstone of effective leadership— personnel at all levels will be looking over their shoulders during conflict resolution operations and lapsing into inaction. Should this happen, the mission is doomed to fail.

14. DISCIPLINE, STRESS, AND COPING

In Rwanda, significant numbers of officers and NCOs were unable to handle the pressures of the UNAMIR operational theatre, particularly during the civil war and genocide—and most particularly when deprived of water, food, and sleep and when casualties were being taken. Certain officers, for example, retreated to the safety of relief aircraft during an attack, leaving their troops under fire on the tarmac. Some NCOs withheld food and water from their soldiers. Other officers kept medication for their personal use. The pressures of the Rwandan operation turned it, for some, into an exercise in self-preservation. Discipline in their units broke down very rapidly. One such contingent actually refused to open the gates of its compound to allow another contingent to take refuge within. Trapped in an attempt to escape militia numbering in the thousands, the cornered contingent was forced to climb over the compound wall under fire. Fortunately, the contingent suffered only limited injuries in the process.

Military units that have not had the opportunity to gain self-discipline through participating in demanding and realistic peacetime exercises cannot be expected to meet the stringent disciplinary requirements of actual operations. I believe that haughty, image-obsessed, abusive leaders who demand unquestioning, instantaneous obedience from subordinates in garrison produce self-protective, survival-oriented units that disintegrate—losing their ability to function in their military roles or even secure their own welfare—within hours of a conflict's start. Only by applying day-to-day discipline considerately and according to sage standards can commanders keep units and their individuals focused, confident, committed, altruistic, and brave in operations. It is too late to expect discipline in-theatre if the troops have not internalized it before deployment.

Not surprisingly, post-traumatic stress disorder (PTSD) casualties are becoming more prevalent in conflict resolution. Even if troops were thoroughly trained in and well prepared for these types of operations, many would have trouble coping with the outright horrors often faced in operational theatres. But as I've argued in this chapter, today's militaries are *not* "thoroughly trained in and well prepared for" conflict resolution operations that include the interpretation of ambiguous orders. Combined, these problems produce extremely high stress levels. Commanders must be able to recognize in their subordinates any potentially dangerous responses to this stress. In Rwanda, UNAMIR personnel wore helmets and flak jackets when our headquarters was being shelled. One lieutenant-colonel suddenly began coming into my twice-daily Orders Group fully dressed for battle—flashlight and all. The first time he appeared this way, he seemed to be functioning normally, so I did not react. At that evening's gathering, he again turned up with everything on: however, he still seemed rational, albeit worried and faint of voice. But by the next morning, he was obviously no longer functioning. He was the sheer embodiment of fear—bordering on terror—and he was infecting many of those surrounding him. People were getting scared just looking at him. He was sent to his room under escort and evacuated from the operational theatre on the next flight. Although this action might seem precipitous, it was necessary for the well-being of both the individual and the contingent as a whole.

When military personnel succumb so spectacularly to stress, they must be removed immediately from active duty. Some, given a short break—even just a couple of days with good food, clean sheets, a wash, plenty of sleep, and an absence of risk—will recuperate and be able to return. Others become outright PTSD casualties and cannot return. Given that possibility, commanders must instill in their subordinates the knowledge that PTSD is an *injury*—that those who succumb are casualties and are in no way inferior soldiers.

Not only do commanders have a duty to be ruthless yet fair in assessing their troops' effectiveness under stressful conditions, commanders also have the difficult task of recognizing when they themselves lose their objectivity, their patience, their ability to focus, their nerve, and most importantly, their sense of humour. After all, commanders are no more immune to stress than their subordinates are.

Recognizing that fact is all the more critical, because when a commander becomes debilitated, the risks to the mission and to subordinates are so much greater.

In my view, militaries must re-examine their whole rest-and-recuperation (R&R) policy in operational theatres. A single two-week recuperation period in a six-month operation may not be the best solution, since it can jeopardize cohesion and increase stress on the remainder of the team. Whatever new approaches are devised, they must be flexible enough to allow commanders to respond to the stresses and strains of each operation and cater to the fluctuating demands on the troops. Commanders must be able to pull soldiers out, let them vent their frustration under controlled conditions, and then bring them back, according to the mission's tempo, nature, and demands. The traditional R&R formulas (those based on the shorter tour lengths of the "good old days")—along with their mythology of boozing and having a "good time"—are destructive rather than recuperative. They reflect a very poor assessment of the nature and consequences of the stresses that soldiers experience in today's operational theatres.

As I have already intimated, revamped recuperation procedures must reflect a reconsideration of soldiers' use of alcohol. In my view, allowing soldiers to use alcohol as a means of relaxation in-theatre is a surefire way of contributing to loss of instinctive judgment, slowing the ability to react, and ultimately increasing the number of casualties. More than 50 percent of Canadian casualties in operations over the past decade have been directly attributable to in-theatre alcohol consumption. I have come to the conclusion that there is no room at all for alcohol in the new generation of operational theatres, since hostile fire can come from any direction at any time where belligerents—especially extremists—operate without regard for the neutrality of your force. A soldier who is fatigued, lonely, and stressed, and who yet must react instantaneously and with sound judgment based on experience and skill, is less likely to make the right decision after drinking. Even a single drink dulls a person's abilities under physically and mentally demanding conditions. Militaries cannot afford any slackening of reflexes in the fluid, totally unpredictable scenarios of conflict resolution. Any compromise of a soldier's professional reactions is unacceptable under circumstances where unexpectedly hazardous situations can arise anytime. During conflict resolution operations, soldiers are *always* on the "front line."

15. CONCLUSION

As military operations over the past decade have shown, the world has entered an era of complex, multidimensional missions in which forces are being committed much more frequently than during the Cold War. These deployments typically occur in cultural contexts for which militaries have not traditionally been prepared—largely because such operations have been shunned by some services and downplayed by others as being unworthy of and inappropriate for warfighting forces. This perception existed throughout the Cold War and has persisted even during this past decade of conflict resolution operations. I disagree with the adage "Peacekeeping dulls the warfighting spirit."

Officers and NCMs in conflict resolution operations need a spectrum of knowledge and skills that go well beyond merely understanding how the rules of engagement restrict the use of force. In contrast to classic warfare, conflict resolution is fraught with uncertainty and ambiguity, and further complicated by fear of casualties and by national self-interest and security agendas. The sheer number of multidisciplinary agencies that must interact in conflict resolution, even at the lowest tactical levels, requires a structured and evolving body of knowledge and skills to facilitate understanding and effective cooperation throughout the mission. Our continued inability or even outright refusal to appreciate the scope and complexity of—and the necessity for innovative doctrines to guide—conflict resolution missions has cost innocent lives, resulted in unnecessary casualties, wasted enormous resources, and ensured that no real lasting success has been achieved in many troubled areas for the last decade. We can no longer take an ad hoc approach to these operations, nor can we expect that sophisticated warfighting alliances and coalitions like NATO will be the solution. Consequently, for a middle power like Canada, it will become critical to develop adaptable, resilient, task-oriented forces that are capable of successfully undertaking the full spectrum of potential operations.

It is my firm conviction that conflict resolution operations must be studied formally by our officer corps. Militaries must find the correct balance between providing (a) the training, equipment priorities, and force structures required for classic RMA-type warfighting, and (b) the much broader multidisciplinary competencies that leaders require to be able to develop innovative solutions and methods for conflict resolution. The officer corps needs a broader-based education, with increased emphasis on the social sciences in particular. Furthermore, conflict resolution operations will demand that military doctrine be modified, upgraded, or even created outright, and that changes be made in leadership training, stress management policies, and possibly even organizational structures. Unless we achieve this new balance of competencies, we will fail to meet our nations' expectations in 90 percent of the operations that we will be called upon to perform. If this fundamental change is not made, casualty levels will increase (with psychological injuries increasing the most); resource demands will never be met; military advice to democratic governments will not be accepted as credible; and trust in military leadership will erode. The challenge is before us. We must leave behind the security of familiar doctrines and accepted classic theories of warfare. We must proactively develop our leadership and force structures to enable us to execute the full spectrum of missions and tasks anticipated now and in the future.

16. REFERENCES

Adelman, H., & Suhrke, A. (Eds.). (1998). *The path of a genocide: The Rwandan crisis from Uganda to Zaire*. New Brunswick, NJ: Transaction.

Bodnarchuk, K. (1999). *Rwanda: Country torn apart*. Minneapolis, MN: Lerner.

Central Africa: The closest of enemies. (1999). In *Worlds apart: Ethnic conflict at century's end* [On-line]. Available http://www.britannica.com/worldsapart/4_print.html

Destexhe, A. (1995). *Rwanda and genocide in the twentieth century*. New York: New York University Press.

Gourevitch, P. (1998). *We wish to inform you that tomorrow we will be killed with our families: Stories from Rwanda.* New York: Farrar, Straus and Giroux.

HRW (Human Rights Watch). (1999). The genocide. In *Leave none to tell the story: Genocide in Rwanda* [On-line]. Available http://www.hrw.org/reports/1999/rwanda/Geno1-3-02.htm

ICTR (International Criminal Tribunal for Rwanda). (1999). *International Criminal Tribunal for Rwanda* [On-line]. Available http://www.ictr.org

Keane, F. (1997). *Season of blood: A Rwandan journey.* New York: Viking Penguin.

Klinghoffer, A. J. (1998). *The international dimensions of genocide in Rwanda.* New York: New York University Press.

Leyton, E., & Locke, G. (1998). *Touched by fire: Doctors Without Borders in a Third World crisis.* Toronto: McClelland and Stewart.

Gee, M. (1999, August 12). Rules of war are getting awkward. *Globe and Mail,* p. A18.

100 days of slaughter: A chronology of U.S./U.N. actions. (1999). In *Frontline: The triumph of evil* [On-line]. Available http://www.pbs.org/wgbh/pages/frontline/shows/evil/etc/slaughter.html

Prunier, G. (1995). *The Rwanda crisis.* New York: Columbia University Press.

Republic of Rwanda. (1998, March). *Background notes on countries of the world* [On-line]. Available http://www.britannica.com/bcom/magazine/article/0,5744,212598,00.html

Rwanda. (1999). In *Encyclopedia Britannica* [On-line]. Available http://www.britannica.com/bcom/eb/article/1/0,5716,66201+5,00.html

Rwanda: A historical chronology. (1998). In *Frontline: Valentina's nightmare* [On-line]. Available http://www.pbs.org/wgbh/pages/frontline/shows/rwanda/etc/cron.html

Sellström, T., & Wohlgemuth, L. (1997). *The international response to conflict and genocide: Lessons from the Rwanda experience, Study 1. Historical perspective: Some explanatory factors* [On-line]. Available http://www.um.dk/udenrigspolitik/udviklingspolitik/evaluering/1997_rwanda/book1.html

United Nations. (1997). *ICTY home page* [On-line]. Available http://www.un.org/icty/

United Nations. (1998). *Verdicts on the crime of genocide by the International Criminal Tribunal for Rwanda* [On-line]. Available http://www.un.org/law/rwanda

Van Creveld, M. (1991). *The transformation of war.* New York: Free Press.

CHAPTER 5

THE FOG OF WAR
A Personal Experience
of Leadership

COMMANDER (RETIRED)
RICHARD A. LANE

1. INTRODUCTION

In the spring of 1982, Britain's Royal Navy (RN) went to war. The event was unscheduled, unexpected, and, for many, potentially terrifying. The analysis of potential scenarios showed that the outcome was in doubt from the start. Were there enough specialist ships? What losses could be sustained? To the ship's company of HMS *Coventry*, a Type 42 air defence destroyer, these questions were academic: the ship was coming to the end of a large-scale North Atlantic Treaty Organization (NATO) exercise, and all crew members were anticipating a few days of relaxation in Gibraltar. Events, however, were to take their turn. We had heard on the BBC World Service that a diplomatic row was developing over some Argentine scrap-metal merchants in South Georgia (a remote island outcrop 850 miles southeast of the Falklands); the admiral's staff had gone into closed session and were difficult to contact; there was talk of Soviet submarines' departing the North Cape. Something was afoot. At the beginning of April, the Argentines invaded the Falkland Islands, and a British task force was sent to the South Atlantic in response. Thus began the Falklands War.

In a military community, the combination of command and leadership takes on different guises. Command can involve a barked order to a subordinate, a quiet nod of reassurance to a team member, or, to a timid junior operator, just the knowledge

COMMANDER (RETIRED) RICHARD A. LANE • *Defence Evaluation and Research Agency, Portsdown West, Portsdown Hill Road, Fareham, Hampshire, United Kingdom, PO17 6AD*

The Human in Command: Exploring the Modern Military Experience, edited by McCann and Pigeau, Kluwer Academic/Plenum Publishers, New York, 2000.

that "the Old Man" is there and will look after him or her. This chapter discusses command in a naval operation from the personal perspective of HMS *Coventry*'s operations officer during the Falklands War. It covers the transition to the war operation, the experiences of attack, and the devastation of losing a ship. Throughout, the nature of command/leadership changed with the situation. I have concluded that no matter what definition of command one uses, it is the leader's personal instinct and style that eventually carry the day.

2. TRAINING

During the Cold War era, operational training in the Royal Navy followed the traditional approaches of all NATO navies. The Soviet Union was the recognized threat, and all training was geared accordingly. Soviet orders of battle, weapon system capabilities, and tactics were second nature to the command team. Indeed, *Coventry* had just spent the previous two weeks exercising against that very kind of threat.

My responsibility as the operations officer and on-watch anti–air warfare officer was to maintain the ship's operational state and to conduct the air battle by helping to provide an umbrella of air defence to other ships in the force. Achieving this requires the skills of leadership, communication, and quickness of thought. Traditional military training plants the seeds of these requirements, and long professional warfare courses provide the deep knowledge; thereafter, one improves through experience. However, I wonder whether the traditional leadership tests—the kind that, for example, assess an officer candidate's ability to get a team to move an oil drum across a stretch of water, armed only with some rope and a few wooden poles—have relevance to leading a command team in a modern warship. In training, "taking charge" of a squad of recruits to accomplish an unusual task hinges on the crisply barked order—the louder the better. This command style was once appropriate for gunnery officers controlling manual gun systems from windswept gun direction platforms. However, it does not transfer well to the quiet, computerized modern operations room. The order of the day involves having situation awareness and communicating that awareness to the team, rather than drill-by-numbers. Being in charge of a sizable team requires knowing the team members' personalities, strengths, and weaknesses; it requires being demanding when the situation requires; and it requires knowing when to applaud and congratulate. Team members, incidentally, also respond to their leader. The more they trust the leader, the more they give without having something explicitly demanded of them. Having operated together for almost a year, HMS *Coventry*'s operations team was well-knit and effective.

Now, however, change was imminent: the goalposts had moved; the potential enemy was unknown. The reference book *Jane's Fighting Ships* (Surrey, U.K.: Jane's Information Group, updated regularly) became required reading for the team. The Argentines had never been classed as a potential enemy. We had built one Type 42 destroyer for them and had allowed a second to be built under licence in Argentina, but we had no information concerning their military capability. Any reference material was welcome: hence the need for *Jane's*. The Argentines' capability and the expected deployment of their forces were the subjects of much debate and planning. Training of the operations and weapons crews had to be changed overnight. The crews needed to know the new enemy and its likely attack procedures. The RN was being sent against a Western-equipped and -trained force, and our crews' reactions would need to be totally different from those used against the well-known Soviet procedures.

3. PREPARATIONS

The first day of the passage south was most poignant. The ships that were detailed to go to the Falklands had spent long hours receiving ammunition, spares, and supplies from ships that were returning to the United Kingdom. This was done while at sea. We had three ships alongside in succession, hastily transferring anything that they thought we would need for our venture. Finally, there was a short period of time to write a hasty note home and transfer mail to the last ship alongside before the group split; then the southbound ships were on their own. My own feelings as I sat at my radar console and watched the group disappear to the north were intense. At that point no one knew what to expect, and speculation was rife. Leaving loved ones behind is nothing new to the military community, but the sudden diversion from Gibraltar and the ominous nature of what was happening on the diplomatic front added uncertainty, and there were endless questions about likely possibilities and outcomes. Our teams needed to prepare not only for military operations, but also for ship survival. Damage control exercises were carried out, building up in complexity; operational exercises that were thought to approximate the Argentine capability were also devised. Throughout this period, however, personal thoughts were paramount.

The modern sailor is an intelligent human being. Unlike the leaders of the past, today's leaders cannot rely on blind allegiance. Therefore, giving sailors as much information as possible generally elicits a positive response. I decided that a file of all the assessment signals that had been sent from our U.K. headquarters (including some of a sensitive nature) should be kept in the operations room for anyone to read. That file became a focus of attention, with the ship's teams devouring its contents during the quiet hours at night. The signals generally covered the diplomatic efforts of the U.S. secretary of state, General William Hague, and the responses of the governments concerned. Thus it was that the perceived rights and wrongs of the affair were shown to the ship's company, and there emerged a full consensus that the ship should be sent on this mission.

In Geneva Convention terms, neither side had yet declared war. In fact, during the early days of the transit, with Hague's shuttle missions in full flight, war was by no means certain. Nevertheless, we prepared the ship for war. Would we arrive off the Falklands to conduct blockading operations? Would the Argentines back down and leave? Or would we need to evict them? People began listening compulsively to the BBC World Service. It would have been folly, though, not to prepare for the worst eventuality, so any ship's fitting or false bulkhead that was deemed surplus was ripped out and dispatched overboard. Warships of the 1970s and 1980s were constructed with the comfort of the ship's company in mind: but such extras as mess deck decorations and wooden accessories, which had seemed appropriate in a non-threatening environment, were now seen as fire or projectile risks and were there-fore discarded.

Our sailors also needed to prepare themselves from a personal point of view. The realities of a hostile environment needed to be recognized. Trying to persuade a 19-year-old sailor that he ought to make a will and sort out his personal effects is far from easy. Someone that young does not wish to confront his own mortality: he expects his officers to do that for him. During one of my nightly sessions with the commanding officer, I remember discussing whether the men should shave off their beards so that they would be safer when wearing anti-gas respirators; and whether they should take down all their personal photographs, because these created a fire hazard. Such issues may seem trivial, but a ship company's morale could be affected by a decision either way. If our decisions showed the sailors the starkness of what they might face (not that we knew either!), they might react negatively. I felt that the risk was worth taking and that the beard issue should be a personal choice. Simi-larly, I decided that photographs should be permitted around their bed spaces, pro-viding that the photos passed the scrutiny of their mess deck officer. Although it may now seem inconsequential, I felt strongly that to force sailors to shave their heads and remove personal mementos from their sleeping spaces would have a negative effect—would deny them, in some way, their right to personal choice. They might believe that we, the command, wanted to create clones of the perfect fight-ing sailor by removing their individual human traits. By allowing personal choice, we prevented the sailors from thinking that we were dehumanizing them.

First aid and damage control exercises became daily events. The reality—that there would be real casualties should the ship get hit—began to strike home, and the exercises picked up more urgency as they progressed. The operations teams set to their tasks with increasing vigour. Our aircraft carriers had now joined the fleet, so we could now conduct air defence exercises with simulations of likely Argentine capabilities and tactics. Our own anti–ship missile defence reactions were changed to reflect the situation. We had now come full circle, from an anti-Soviet to an anti-Argentine mindset. However, we were still unsure about what was facing us. Having by now received an intelligence update regarding the Argentine military's capabili-ties and limitations, we had to consider what would be the major threat to our forces. On balance, it seemed that the Argentine navy would provide the severest test to the British task force. It was flexible, well-armed, and already buoyed by the success of the initial invasion. The odds appeared to favour a naval campaign, with missile ships against missile ships—a shooting war that could be a closely run thing, since the Argentine navy had almost as many surface-to-surface missiles as we had deployed! The Argentine air force, however, was not initially assessed as posing an overriding threat. The majority of its aircraft squadrons were still in the north of the country; only a major logistical maneuver would get them into the theatre.

Thus, we became oriented to the surface threat and how to counter it. We prac-tised and exercised, honing our standard and emergency skills of detection, acqui-sition, and engagement until they became second nature. I had every confidence in my operations and weapons crews—they were motivated and, having a continuous supply of information, they were in tune with the operation's anticipated requirements. History has shown that we were wrong in our assessment of the surface threat. But this only serves to illustrate that a good enemy is unpredictable: the more the enemy makes you second-guess, the more successful that enemy will be.

Maintenance, too, became of paramount importance. We were already into the hostile environment of the South Atlantic. Equipment had to be at peak efficiency. This, alas, was not always the case. The Type 42 is a complex modern warship. Even when it is being prepared for a routine peacetime missile firing, the ship requires extensive maintenance efforts. The two 909 fire control radars were beasts to keep operational, and it was not unusual to have only one 909 working at any time. The workload of the 909 maintenance personnel was enormous, and that workload had to be managed carefully by the weapons engineer officers. Other equipment failed from exposure to the southern ocean. Our long-range air warning radar suffered a major component failure that rendered it useless. Only with some innovative engineering (the sort not offered in any manual) did the radar maintainer get that radar working again. Against all odds, that radar would actually work throughout our campaign! There were major problems with the 4.5-inch gun that were never fully resolved, and a significant defect in one of the Olympus gas turbine engines also could not be rectified. Although some spares were coming in to us by airdrop, other spares were just too large to be sent, so we had to plan for operations knowing that certain elements of our operational capability could not be realized. Of course, this was true for the other ships as well: it gave the admiral's staff a real headache, for they needed us to be at peak performance. The demands already being placed on sailors and machinery far exceeded those typical in normal peacetime operations—and the task force had not even reached its theatre of operations.

4. OPERATIONS

Toward the end of April, the Hague peace initiative was in tatters, and the British government had established a maritime exclusion zone of 150 nautical miles around the Falklands. The Argentine troops had not left the islands and showed no intention of doing so, although their warships had returned to Argentine waters. Other issues were now weighing on our minds. The Southern Hemisphere's winter, only a month away, would make operations extremely difficult—and the task force had struggled through extreme weather already. Furthermore, in the Falklands, a standoff appeared to be in progress. With these factors in mind, Operation Paraquat—the operation aimed at recapturing the island of South Georgia—was launched: A small garrison of Royal Marines on the island had been taken by the Argentines during the main invasion of the Falklands. A group of warships, led by HMS *Antrim*, was detached to South Georgia. The remainder waited with bated breath for two days as the group made the transit in radio and radar silence. Suddenly, our high-frequency radio crackled into life as we heard the recapture of the island in progress. Some of our helicopters crashed on the Fortuna Glacier, but their crews were recovered by *Antrim*'s Wessex helicopter in whiteout conditions; an Argentine submarine was caught on the surface, attacked by helicopter-launched missiles, and disabled; then the Argentines surrendered! All these events happened quickly and fired the resolve of our ship's company. The Argentine military junta in Buenos Aires could now be under no illusion as to our purpose in the South Atlantic. This action had also denied them an eastern base from which to attack our forces. The southeastern flank was now secure—we could focus our efforts on the Falklands.

On May 1, the maritime exclusion zone was extended to 200 miles and became a total exclusion zone. The task force entered it and began operations. We needed to entice the Argentine navy out from its own waters to force some action. Initially, our electronic warfare sensors detected many aircraft radar emissions that seemed to indicate a significant launch of Argentine aircraft. However, this did not make sense: if those detections were to be believed, the enemy aircraft were within 200 miles of the task force and were about to attack. As a precaution, the task force moved back to the east, away from the supposed threat. Subsequent analysis resolved the puzzle: an unusual weather condition had increased the detection range, and the aircraft were actually in mainland Argentina. The incident, however, did provide a clue that the Argentines were deploying aircraft to the south of the country and that their air force would become a player.

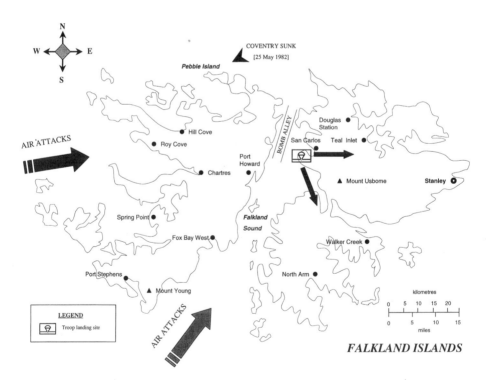

FIGURE 1. The Falkland Islands, May 1–June 14, 1982.

The Argentine navy did come out that night. Our intelligence plot showed a three-pronged formation: the aircraft carrier *25 May* and its escorts to the northwest, the two Type 42s and their escorts to the west, and the cruiser *General Belgrano* and its escorts to the southwest. One of our submarines, HMS *Conqueror*, was given the necessary rules of engagement, attacked the cruiser, and sank it. In *Coventry,* we gave no thought to whether the ship had been outside the exclusion zone or had been steaming away: we simply considered that a threat had been eliminated. The Argentines were quite clearly attempting a pronged approach against the task force's units, and one of those prongs had been dealt with. Subsequently, the Argentine T42s and aircraft carrier turned and made their way back to their own territorial waters. The Argentine navy did not repeat this action; thus, the major naval engagement that we had expected never came to fruition.

The balance appeared to have swung in our favour, but the nature of the threat remained unclear. The task force now settled into an air defence posture, with the Type 42s *Sheffield, Glasgow,* and *Coventry* stationed 40 miles up-threat and spread across the threat axis. Sea Harrier fighters from HMS *Hermes* and HMS *Invincible* were flying combat air patrol sorties. The mood of *Coventry*'s crew was dogged and resolute; no longer did I hear complaints of boredom (typical in peacetime operations!) despite the long hours of watching and waiting. There were, however, rumours that some sailors, of all ranks, were having premonitions of death. This I found to be unnerving. I had never encountered it before, and although I understood that anyone might see death as a possibility, I felt that it was unhealthy to dwell on the subject. In my view, the problem was that we had too much time for thinking; if we kept ourselves busy, perhaps those morbid thoughts would recede. Thereafter, I spent long hours talking to my teams about anything at all—from what we ourselves were doing, to the state of world politics. They had to be kept diverted.

On May 4, the enemy hit back. HMS *Sheffield* was struck by an Exocet missile that had been launched from a Super Etendarde fighter–bomber aircraft. It was the task force's first defensive action, and it turned out to be a disaster. My beliefs in my own capabilities and our own air defence protocols were brought into the sharpest of focus. Our air defence formation was classic, and the fighters were airborne. *Glasgow* reported radar contact, but *Sheffield* did not see them. Their bombers flew under our fighters without being detected, launched their missiles, and evaded without a hand having been laid on them. The air defence organization was in chaos, not only because the bombers had not been detected early enough for the fighters and the surface-to-air missiles to engage but, most importantly, because the situation had not been assessed correctly. *Sheffield* had gone off the air; *Glasgow* was reporting the contacts in vain; we in *Coventry* were supporting those reports. Yet somehow, back in the main force, our reports were not believed! Communications discipline on the anti–air warfare radio circuit, a circuit that demands clear and concise transmissions, had been lost. The assessment was that *Sheffield* had been hit by a submarine's torpedo—and no one had the real picture.

Nevertheless, we had a ship in distress that needed assistance. Our immediate reaction—especially since *Sheffield* was the same type as *Coventry*, and the Type 42 community was very close—was to leave our station and head off at full speed to assist *Sheffield*. By this time, the admiral's staff had regained the situation; they told us, quite rightly, to stay where we were. They dispatched two frigates, which succeeded in getting *Sheffield*'s survivors off and away from the area. That night we were in a most sombre mood. People we knew personally had been killed, and we had been caught with our trousers down. What had gone wrong? Not the least pertinent was the realization that *we* had been in *Sheffield*'s position only six hours previously, but after coming back into the main formation to take fuel, we had continued out to the northwest sector instead. The cold fact that it could have been *Coventry* that had been hit was not lost on the operations team. Our first taste of action had not been good; it was a hard lesson to learn and to recover from.

The following days saw the task force settle into routine operation. We had taken to bombarding Argentine troop positions ashore and using Harriers to attack strategic points, including the airfield at Stanley. We probed their defences in preparation for the beach assault that we knew lay ahead. The ship was now operating on a strict two-watch defence system; it closed up to full action stations, with everyone up and on watch, only when the ship was under direct threat of attack. Fatigue was beginning to set in—long hours spent staring into a radar screen brought on eyestrain and conjunctivitis in some. Also, there were concerns about the effects of sleep loss. A ship's motion at sea can be quite disruptive to sleep, especially when the ship does something unexpected. I clearly remember waking up once in a cold sweat to feel the engine power increase and the ship heel as it altered course. I was reminded, too, of the uniqueness of our situation when I was summoned once to the bridge for a radio conversation with a war correspondent about the shooting down of an enemy helicopter earlier that day. Given the intensity of our routine, this kind of occurrence represented an annoying distraction, especially when it interrupted a quick catnap! Coming to terms with the fact that the media were watching our every move was difficult, and it changed our way of conducting the business of warfighting. Press briefings became routine. The Falklands was the first of the "armchair" wars, and we had to make the best of it. At that time, military personnel were not trained to communicate with the media, and I, for one, found the task quite difficult.

The landing of British troops and their equipment on the island of East Falkland (via the port of San Carlos) began on May 21; from our perspective, it was a resounding success. The landing caught the Argentines unaware, and there was minimal opposition at the beachhead. But after that, the Argentine air force began to retaliate, leading the media to invoke the term Bomb Alley for that area. While the warships outside in Falkland Sound took the brunt of the air attacks, the merchant ships were able to offload their troops and equipment unscathed. Although the frigates *Antelope* and *Ardent* were sunk, the landings continued unabated. We in *Coventry* were stationed handily to the north of the Sound, where we were able to pick off enemy aircraft as they climbed out of the attack area. At last our troops were ashore, and the Argentine air force was sustaining heavy losses. We were almost in control. This perception spread among the ship's company, and from the ops room I could hear cheers each time we downed another aircraft. Although I could not deny the crew their moments of relief, I was concerned that some sailors were treating these events like a game. That night the captain reminded the ship's company of the serious nature of what we were doing.

5. ATTACK

It was becoming increasingly clear that the Argentines saw *Coventry* as the unit that was hindering their efforts: a dedicated attack on our ship was therefore looking more and more likely. Also, the fact that the date was May 25—Argentine Independence Day—should have warned us that something extraordinary would happen. The Argentines had only two air-launched Exocet missiles remaining in their arsenal; they duly attempted an attack on the main elements of the task force, which were operating out to the east of the Islands. Simultaneously, a flight of four air force A-4 Skyhawks was launched to attack the surface-to-air missile combination of *Coventry* and *Broadsword,* which was on patrol to the northwest of Pebble Island. By now our teams were truly battle-hardened; there was no possibility of our being caught unprepared or unaware. Still, things went drastically wrong.

The Exocet attack broke through the task force's air defence cordon. This time the missiles were detected, and a frigate fired chaff rockets to distract their radar-seeking heads. This defensive tactic was initially successful: the missiles veered toward the chaff bloom. However, although one of the missiles ditched in the water, the other flew through the bloom and hit the container ship *Atlantic Conveyor,* resulting in the loss of much vital equipment for the troops ashore. The most critical loss was the Chinook helicopters, which had been deemed essential for moving troops and equipment across the island to Stanley, our final objective. As a result, this operation would need to be carried out by the one remaining Chinook. But in *Coventry,* 200 miles to the west, we were oblivious to these events: we had problems of our own to contend with.

The A-4 raid had been detected 150 miles to the west of us, before it descended toward the island. The four aircraft had then vanished from our radar screens. I called to *Hermes* to provide me with some fighter support—which was sent but, regrettably, was late in arriving. Minutes later, the A-4s were redetected flying low along the coast. The aircraft were proving impossible to acquire with our 909 radars, because they were flying so low and they were masked by the coastline's land returns. Ten miles abeam of our formation, they turned out to sea and commenced their attack. Two of our Sea Harriers were approaching fast from the east to defend, but I assessed that they would not reach us in time and ordered them to break off. The leading pair of A-4s passed overhead *Broadsword,* which was just astern of us, without either of us firing a missile. *Broadsword* was hit astern by a 1,000-pound bomb that came out of the flight deck and took the nose off the Lynx helicopter. Seeing that *Broadsword* was also having difficulties with its missile system, I advised the CO that we were on our own and that he should maneuver accordingly. As the second pair of A-4s approached, I fired a missile without a fire control solution; our ship heeled to starboard and, as I later discovered, crossed the firing line of *Broadsword*'s SeaWolf missile system, thus masking *Broadsword*'s weapon arcs.

Were we fully aware of the situation? Suffice it to say that all of us were doing our jobs. The ops room was ethereally quiet, except for the constant tapping of computer keys as the operators tracked aircraft, the murmuring of voices as information was passed, and the background noise as one of our Oerlikon 20 mm guns was being fired at a target. It was exactly as I had expected it ought to be: quiet, professional, and without panic.

Until my tactical display erupted before me!

6. SURVIVAL

We had been hit by three 1,000-pound bombs, each of which had exploded. In the ensuing fireball, I was knocked out of my chair and hurled across the ops room. Several seconds later, I came to beneath a radar display that had fallen on top of me. The sights and sounds were horrific: little pockets of fire spread over the deck; cabling was sparking; emergency lights glowed; smoke was everywhere; and screams emanated from someone in the computer room below. I crawled over and tried to pull him out, but he slipped from my grasp and fell back into the inferno that had been his workstation a few moments earlier.

Even before I got to my feet, it became clear to me that the ship was in terminal decline. We were heeling at a ridiculous angle, and it was getting worse. The first bomb had entered the ship just forward of the computer room, below the ops room. The explosion created a fireball that emerged from the computer room hatch and flew through the ops room, leaving devastation in its wake. The second bomb had exploded in the forward engine room and breached the after bulkhead—thus opening the ship's two largest compartments to the sea. At that moment, all I knew was that although a minute earlier I had been defending the ship against attack, I now lay dazed and injured in the corner of the ops room. The sailors who were left with me wandered aimlessly about in shock and needed to be got out to the upper deck. I did not have time to debate, either within myself or with anyone else, whether I should take action or even whether my injuries would allow me to do so. Those sailors needed to be ordered, herded, and guided to safety through passageways now full of twisted metal and up through hatches where the ladders had been burned away—all in pitch darkness and smoke. A firmer, harsher form of leadership was now required; basic training was to be of use after all! I distinctly remember standing astride a hatch with the deputy weapons engineer officer, each of us cajoling and pulling sailors through. Ultimately we reached the highest space we could attain, adjacent to the gun direction platform. The door was jammed; sailors were squeezing in and beginning to panic. I pushed my way through and hammered the clips apart, thus freeing the door and allowing 30 men to reach fresh air and the comparative safety of the upper deck. Were all of these actions just reflexes? Did they stem from some deep sense of responsibility? Was I propelled by a determined sense of self-preservation? I suspect it was an amalgam of all three. Such is command.

The ship was going over. The life rafts were being released, and the crew were jumping into the water. Having retrieved a spare life jacket from the locker—mine had been blown off in the initial blast—I slid down the ship's side into the freezing water, swam to the nearest life raft, and was hauled on board. Half an hour earlier, I had been at my action station; now I was the only officer in a life raft that contained many more sailors than it had been designed to hold. I was thoroughly wet, as well as burned and dazed, yet those sailors still looked to me for leadership. I felt that I had failed them—that I had somehow allowed the ship to be hit. They had trusted me once, but should they trust me now? Yet there was no time for self-recrimination: the life raft was being sucked around the bow and down the sinking side of the ship. We were facing the prospect of having the ship roll over on top of us! I ordered those sailors who appeared to be fit over the side to see whether we could get some propulsion for the life raft—but to no avail. Fortunately, at the last moment, the life raft was plucked to safety by *Broadsword*'s inflatable sea boat, which towed us to its parent ship, where we gratefully clambered up the scrambling nets to safety. I was assessed as being too badly injured to remain with the rest of the ship's company and was airlifted to the hospital ship SS *Uganda*, along with a handful of others. There my burns were treated. My war was over.

7. REFLECTIONS

Lying in my hospital bed, unable to walk because of leg burns and with my face bloated to twice its normal size from flash burns, I had a great deal of time to reflect. The small group of us who had been airlifted from *Broadsword* to the hospital ship took on a depression: first we retreated into ourselves as a group, and then we retreated as individuals. I knew that I had failed to save my colleague from the computer room; I did not know how many members of my ops room team had survived (not until I returned to the United Kingdom, some four weeks later, did I discover that they had all escaped), and I felt an immense sense of guilt that I had failed them professionally. This guilt stayed with me for the remainder of my naval career and ultimately ended it. I could not—or would not—shake it off. An intense bond developed and remained among those of us who had been sent to the hospital ship. We had shared something that very few people really understood—or indeed wanted to understand—and we felt a need to protect each other. I remain unsure about whether those of the ship's company who came back uninjured experienced the same feelings. The psychological demands of operating in an intense and risky situation for almost a month (typical NATO exercises last for approximately 10 days), followed by the shock of escaping from a devastated, sinking ship and the pain of injuries, should never be underestimated. Indeed, even the hospital ship was not necessarily the sanctuary it might have been: the Argentines threatened to attack it on more than one occasion.

During operations, the ship's company had answered the call to action for 25 days. Everyone had withstood horrendous hours on duty, the pressure of attack, endlessly malfunctioning equipment, and, during off-watch periods, uncertainty about what was happening. They had responded to praise, cajoling, and, of course, during quiet periods, reassurance that everything was going to be all right—they depended on that. But during the attack's immediate aftermath, leadership methods had to be much more direct. Evacuation and survival need a much firmer, and louder, leadership style. There is no single approach to command. Command must adapt to the situation.

That day command *was* successful. No one who was left alive after the bomb blasts was killed inside the ship. Everyone escaped, even though the ship rolled over and sank within 40 minutes of being hit. But the responsibility of command doesn't end when a ship sinks. The process of reflection after such an experience also needs care. Unfortunately, the survivors' mental well-being was not well attended to. The ship's company was split up too quickly on our return to the United Kingdom, without psychological debriefing. Several of us would suffer the consequences later.

Motivating the ship's company at sea was not difficult. Our decision to keep our sailors informed about what was going on from the start meant that they were always onside and well imbued with the sentiment of returning control of the Falkland Islands to those who chose to inhabit them. Unlike the commanders of some of the ground units, we did not need to whip them into a state of frenzy. (One soldier on the hospital ship, who had broken his ankle alighting from a helicopter and had been evacuated without seeing any action, had to be physically restrained so that his personal weapons could be taken from him!)

War is horrendous, and people react differently when put in horrendous situations. Even though warfare at sea can be relatively impersonal—a weapons officer firing a missile at a radar blip probably experiences less emotional trauma than an infantry soldier fighting for ground in the enemy's sights—the result is nevertheless the same: either the opponent dies, or you do. Our militaries can train people in the team skills required by effective fighting units, whether on land or at sea; but to recreate the sinking of a ship, the need to support injured sailors, and the fight for survival is virtually impossible.

Command/leadership in war starts in basic training. I believe that certain personality characteristics need to be inherent from birth. For example, the ability to keep a clear head in stressful situations is certainly common; but the ability to sustain this clear-headedness through a lengthy period of intense high-risk operations is an unusual trait. A leader needs to set the example, motivating people by keeping them constantly aware of where they fit into the overall puzzle. In dire situations, a leader must act in a manner that makes those who are less sure want to follow that leader.

8. CONCLUSION

In this chapter, essentially a personal narrative of my experiences in war, I have attempted to highlight the many leadership and command issues that we faced in the Falklands. War is, by its very nature, unpredictable and full of surprises. Command/leadership is not just a definition: it is a real, ever-changing responsibility. The aptitude for command is assessed during interview boards at recruiting, but it must mature as service progresses. Preparation for the horrors of a sinking ship can be acquired only indirectly from the experiences of others. We must then adapt our own personalities to the requirements of the day.

When a ship is lost, its command no longer has responsibility for the mission and can relax (yet possibly go mad with self-blame). How much worse is it for soldiers, who may lose a battle and subsequently retreat, but must then regroup and fight again? It was command/leadership in the Falklands that carried the day: the British forces suffered setbacks, yet the overall goal was never lost—and the Argentine invasion force surrendered at Stanley. This success could not have been achieved with stereotyped automaton commanders who could not react to the unexpected or take reverses and come back with resolve. Command is intensely personal and must, necessarily, remain a human responsibility. Computers may provide tools that lighten the workload, aid situation awareness, and prompt decision making, but they can never emulate the humanity, resolve, courage, and sheer unpredictability of the human in command.

CHAPTER 6

COMMAND AND CONTROL IN STRESSFUL CONDITIONS

COLONEL PEER L. E. M. EVERTS

> The justice court of Heaven, after long delay,
> At last has pitied me, the tired castle, and
> Poor citizenry. Stirred by people's prayers and
> Their laments, it has relieved the frightened city.
> —J. VAN DEN VONDEL, 1637[1]

1. INTRODUCTION

The topic of how humans command under stressful conditions is an appealing one. It is especially relevant for me: as commander of Dutchbat 2 (the second of three infantry battalions provided as peacekeeping units within the United Nations Protection Force [UNPROFOR] in the former Yugoslavia), I experienced the responsibility of command first-hand while serving in Bosnia.[2] I have written this chapter based on my subjective impressions of command in the enclave of Srebrenica from July 19, 1994, to January 18, 1995.[3] My personal experiences in Srebrenica take centre stage, although I have attempted to view them against the backdrop of the general situation in the former Yugoslavia.[4]

[1] These four lines begin the elegy "Gysbrecht van Aemstel," which describes the siege of the city of Amsterdam by the city of Haarlem in 1304. Amsterdam was destroyed.

[2] Officially the Federal Republic of Bosnia and Herzegovina; often referred to simply as Bosnia.

[3] I wish to thank Carol McCann, Ross Pigeau, Ad Vogelaar, and Donna Winslow for their useful and stimulating comments on this chapter.

[4] My experiences, as described in this chapter, concern mainly the units of the battalion located inside the enclave of Srebrenica. Other units served in the areas of Sapna and Lukavac.

COLONEL PEER L. E. M. EVERTS • Royal Netherlands Army, Keislagen 37, 4823 KN Breda, Netherlands

The Human in Command: Exploring the Modern Military Experience, edited by McCann and Pigeau, Kluwer Academic/Plenum Publishers, New York, 2000.

The issue of command can be viewed in many ways. I will take a subjective perspective rather than an academic one, though this approach has its dangers. The reader is no doubt familiar with the way that the passage of time changes one's perception of the past. Events gain perspective and nuance, the sharp edges are softened, and—perhaps more important—the pleasant experiences become more pleasant, while bad experiences fade. Among the dangers of treating command subjectively, based on one's own perception and experience, are that events and situations may be taken out of context and that individuals and organizations may be viewed in the wrong light. Such an approach could also lead to a kind of lamentation—which is certainly not my intention. Nonetheless, my memories of commanding in Srebrenica[5] will always be inextricably linked with memories of unthinkable human suffering in dire conditions. Furthermore, I shall always have a deep respect for the men and women who served with the Dutch battalions during this exceptionally difficult deployment.

In the following pages, I will briefly describe the general situation in the Srebrenica area of operations. I will then discuss the nature of the conditions in Srebrenica, with the aim of describing my own perception of the stressful conditions under which operations had to be carried out. I will discuss a number of operational issues in addition to my personal experiences. Finally, I will address the issue of how command adapted procedures for operations in these conditions.

1.1. General Description of the Operational Situation

The mission given to Dutchbat 2 was (a) to support the delivery of humanitarian aid to the enclave of Srebrenica by the United Nations High Commissioner for Refugees (UNHCR),[6] as well as by other relief organizations; and (b) to create an environment that would, in general terms, favour the evacuation of wounded people, the care of the population, and the cessation of hostilities. The assumptions at the outset of the mission were that all parties would respect the safety of the enclave's inhabitants and that no weapons would be available to Bosnians inside the enclave.

The enclave itself was in a mountainous setting, with peaks as high as 1,500 m (4,900 feet). The enclave's size was approximately 225 km^2 (87 square miles). The only hardened road ran from north to south in the eastern part of the enclave. The majority of the population lived either in the city of Srebrenica or in the village of Potocari, both located well to the east within the enclave (see Figure 1).

The Bosnian Serbs controlled the area outside the enclave with about three brigades. They also had a variety of means of controlling the enclave itself. The Serbs could cover every part of the enclave with their artillery fire, and they had direct influence over the "8 Operational Group," a group of approximately 3,000 to 4,000 young men who were armed—mainly with light weapons, but they also had access to mortars and heavy machine guns.

Dutchbat consisted of a headquarters company that included two security

---

[5] In this chapter, Srebrenica and its surround are also referred to as "the enclave." An enclave is an area that is geographically separated from the country with which it is associated.

[6] The U.N.-led agency for humanitarian assistance in the former Yugoslavia.

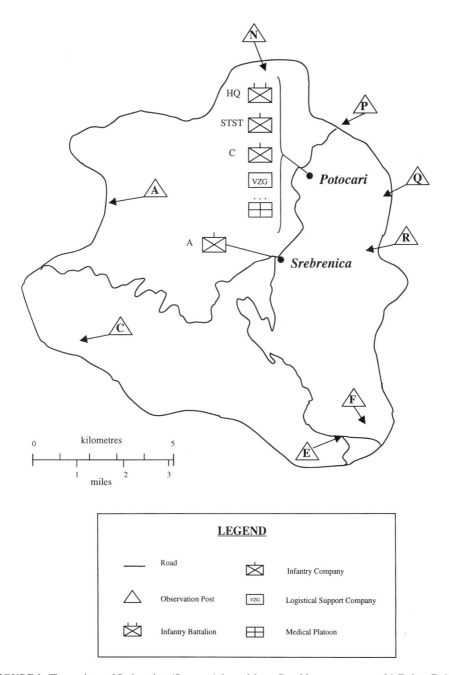

FIGURE 1. The enclave of Srebrenica. (Source: Adapted from *Dutchbat on tour*, page 26, Debut, Delft, 1995)

platoons and engineers, three rifle companies (with armoured vehicles), a direct logistical company, an engineer company, a medical company, and an indirect support unit. Of these, one rifle company was stationed outside the enclave, in the Sapna area, and an indirect support unit was stationed in Tuzla. In total, the battalion numbered approximately 1,200 women and men, of whom about 600 were stationed in the enclave itself, where they were housed mainly in two military compounds[7]—one at Srebrenica and other at Potocari. The battalion conducted its mission mainly by observing the activities of the inhabitants of the enclave and its surround from a number of posts that were situated along the enclave's border, and by patrolling along that border.

2. FACTORS AFFECTING THE OPERATION

I will first describe the factors that affected our operation in Srebrenica. Before our deployment, there was a great deal of public and media discussion in our home country concerning the mission, with a considerable range of opinion. Some asserted that the mission was not feasible; others spoke in terms of a "difficult but feasible" mission. I found it very difficult to handle the negative effects of this diversity of opinion. When soldiers are about to embark on a mission involving great uncertainty, resolve and clarity of intent are of the utmost importance. In my opinion, public discussion about the feasibility of a mission is incompatible with the need for clarity.

I will not discuss the mission's ultimate feasibility in any further detail; the events of June and July 1995 speak for themselves.[8] The equipping and arming of our battalion was also a frequent topic of discussion before our deployment, with a variety of people in the Netherlands expressing their opinions. This debate, too, was extremely annoying to me, since it was the members of my battalion who actually had to carry out the operation. Ammunition—without which, of course, weapons are useless—was a special concern. I knew that the supply of ammunition would be a problem, since I had learned from my predecessor that only 16 percent of the recommended minimum level of supply would likely be available, because of the Serb control of supplies to the enclave.

Once we were in-theatre, the ambiguity of the chain of command became an issue. Formally, the commander of HQ North-East[9] was my operational commander. However, the Serbs prevented him from ever setting foot in the enclave. Thus, the influence of his headquarters on activities in my area of operations was necessarily limited. The battalion was therefore obliged to resolve some issues with a higher level of headquarters than originally anticipated—especially issues related to convoys and leave arrangements. There was also some interaction with the Netherlands, running "officially" through a Dutch detachment in Zagreb. In

---

[7] Compounds were fenced areas that housed military personnel. They were defended by the units.

[8] On July 11, 1995, Bosnian Serb troops occupied the enclave of Srebrenica. This event led to the end of the mission of Dutchbat 3 (the third and final Dutch battalion to serve as part of UNPROFOR).

[9] HQ North-East was located in Tuzla. Responsible for operations in the northern part of central Bosnia and in the Srebrenica enclave, it was subordinate to the HQ in Sarajevo (the Bosnia–Herzegovina Command).

addition, I was often in touch with the Situation Centre of the Royal Netherlands Army in The Hague. Indeed, I was able to discuss many problems with the Centre: it was a welcome sounding board. In sum, however, the chain of command seemed ambiguous to me. In some cases it ran through one headquarters, and in some cases it ran through another.

A factor that had a profound effect on all facets of the operation in Srebrenica was the battalion's total isolation—in every respect. This isolation not only influenced the implementation of the mission, but also hampered the lines of supply; and, of course, it affected the psychological state of my personnel. For example, it quickly became quite clear to me that the battalion could not possibly be supported by troops from the higher level of command: the provision of such support would be extremely arduous, due to such factors as the poor roads and the terrain. In fact, given the geographical situation, the battalion could not count on much support at all. Thus, the enclave's isolation became an extremely significant factor in all my decision making.

Another important operational factor was that the enclave was surrounded by a number of Bosnian Serb brigades, whose strength was unknown. These units had various types of light and heavy weapons at their disposal. I knew that at the very least they had the firepower to threaten all Dutchbat positions. In addition, as already mentioned, units of the Bosnian government army—numbering between 3,000 and 4,000 personnel and equipped with light arms—were also present inside the enclave. These two parties constituted an important military factor that I had to account for in our operations.

In-theatre, the battalion's freedom of movement was extremely restricted, partly due to the terrain, but also due to deliberate actions on the part of the belligerents. The terrain's mountainous nature made the movement of vehicles relatively easy to detect by all parties; as a result, the battalion's movements could be limited using simple assets, such as mines. In fact, the enclave was surrounded by a great many minefields, whose location was not fully known. Furthermore, the belligerents sometimes refused to grant permission for certain activities to be carried out, or they simply refused to allow the use of roads, or they prohibited access to certain areas. Finally, all of the compounds and the observation posts[10] were located in such a way that they were easily observable by all parties:[11] they were therefore vulnerable to fire. These circumstances all hampered the implementation of the mission.

I must also mention that the sheer size of the population in the enclave (approximately 35,000) was a further factor in the operation. We knew from experience that large human blockades were a possibility and that such blockades can be extremely effective in restricting military operations or even making them impossible, especially in the case of "blue" missions.[12]

---

[10] An observation post is a location designed to be visible to all parties and to allow activities in the area to be observed. Normally six to ten soldiers would operate a post.

[11] The parties were the Bosnian Serbs (outside the enclave) and the Bosnians (inside the enclave).

[12] "Blue" missions are missions that are executed within the framework of the United Nations. "Green" missions are missions that take place in the context of war.

Finally, the arrangements for personnel leave—a very important consideration when operating under great pressure—meant that no more than 75 percent of the battalion was available for duty at one time.[13]

From an operational point of view, then, circumstances were complex. It was clear that the battalion was walking a tightrope, and there were plenty of opportunities for us to lose our footing. Furthermore, the risk was considerable, particularly in view of the level of political and media interest in the mission.

3. THE INTERACTION OF DUTCHBAT WITH OTHER AGENCIES

As a commander in Srebrenica—where I was totally cut off from the outside world—I became aware of many issues that, in the context of a general defence task or an operational exercise in the Netherlands, would not normally require close attention. Most of them related to interaction with the various parties involved in the conflict: in particular, our own higher command and the belligerents. Inevitably, there were conflicting interests that I had to resolve for myself, since there was little or no support from the outside.

From the time that the first Dutch battalion (Dutchbat 1) had been committed and the general situation in Srebrenica had worsened, the opportunities for passing information to the Netherlands had become more limited. One consequence was that the picture of the situation that was painted in the Netherlands was, from my perspective, not entirely aligned with the actual situation in the enclave. This distortion was exacerbated by Bosnian organizations that deliberately disseminated incorrect information concerning conditions in the enclave.[14] As a result, it was my experience that the United Nations and other agencies did not always have the correct information on which to base decisions, and this lack of information affected their assessment of the actual situation. The implication for me, as commander, was that I needed to be especially careful regarding my communications concerning the situation, in order to prevent our "home front" from becoming unduly concerned.

Because of the restricted freedom of movement and the difficulty of communications,[15] the higher levels in the chain of command could be only partly aware of the circumstances under which the battalion had to conduct its activities. Consequently, they sometimes made decisions that the battalion could not possibly implement. At times I was compelled to protest these decisions. It often seemed to require a disproportionate effort to convince others that the situation in the enclave was unique.

---

[13] During the execution of a mission, personnel have the need and the right to get rest. Depending on the duration of a mission, soldiers might get up to 21 days of leave during 6 months of duty.

[14] On one occasion, we learned through military channels that people inside the enclave were supposedly starving and that many were dead, just lying in the streets of the enclave. This was simply not true. Later it became clear that Bosnian organizations had provided this "news" to the authorities in the Netherlands.

[15] It was impossible to talk directly to higher commanders and staff officers and impossible for higher commanders to visit the enclave.

Another factor that had a strong influence on my decisions was the fact that the belligerent parties regarded Dutchbat and all its personnel as a single entity. The battalion as a whole was therefore deemed responsible for any action undertaken by its individual members. As a result, activities unacceptable to one of the conflicting parties could lead to reprisals in an entirely different location. I therefore found it necessary to ensure that the actions of individuals, groups, and platoons were as uniform as possible. Naturally, this requirement meant that individual initiative suffered, as did individual interpretation of assigned tasks. This was a very sensitive issue for my subordinate leaders—who, in peacetime situations, had been accustomed to taking initiative and exercising somewhat more freedom when carrying out their tasks.

Conducting business with the two belligerent parties was especially complicated, since negotiation with them was an extremely long and drawn-out process. In the Netherlands, we in the military are accustomed to being issued a mission and then interpreting that mission with initiative. But that was not the case for the military parties in the enclave. Our discussion partners had no authority whatsoever: all the activities of the belligerents were centrally directed.[16] So it was very time-consuming for the battalion to make arrangements with the local authorities to improve the situation within the enclave. As a result, initiatives taken by the battalion that required cooperation from the belligerents often failed to get off the ground.

Within the enclave, the battalion maintained contact with the civil administration.[17] This was an administration that dealt with the "interests" of the enclave's inhabitants, but one in which the Bosnian military leadership had absolute authority. Members of the administration were notably better off, materially, than most of the population. Also notable was the authorities' inability—or perhaps reluctance—to evenly distribute what little was available among the enclave's inhabitants. I often had the impression that the administration would approve of anything, as long as Dutchbat provided the resources and they themselves did not need to make any effort.

The battalion had ongoing interactions with several of the nongovernmental organizations (NGOs) that were working within the enclave, including Médecins Sans Frontières and the International Red Cross, as well as with U.N. military observers, UNCIVPOL (the United Nations Civil Police), and UNHCR (the United Nations High Commissioner for Refugees), who were also active within the enclave. Cooperation with these organizations was pleasant, and our efforts could often improve the assistance they were giving to the local population. Because of the enclave's geographical isolation, these organizations depended heavily on the battalion's support, particularly with regard to fuel and security. Therefore the battalion was to a significant extent responsible—at least in a moral sense—for the well-being of their members. Similarly, the battalion was responsible for the approximately 100 members of the local population who worked with us. Clearly, maintaining these relationships added to our task.

---

[16] My perception was that the Bosnian Serbs received guidance from their superiors in Pale, and the Bosnians received guidance from Sarajevo.

[17] The enclave had a president; the city of Srebrenica and some of the villages had a mayor.

The final factor that was of particular importance was the apparent powerlessness of the United Nations to improve the conditions for the enclave's population. Neither promises nor threats made by the United Nations seemed to make any difference whatsoever to the well-being of either the population or the battalion. It was my impression that Dutchbat's credibility—as a representative of the United Nations—was thus implicitly undermined, as was the confidence of all parties in the possibility that Dutchbat's mission could be successfully carried out.

4. PSYCHOLOGICAL FACTORS IN THE OPERATION

Psychological factors played an important role in the operation. I have already mentioned the battalion's total isolation—an isolation that was immediately apparent when entering the enclave, which was encircled by high mountains and dotted with Serb observation posts. Battalion personnel were very conscious of being literally surrounded by the threat posed by the Serbs, and this awareness contributed to the impression of being in the world's largest open-air prison, with all the associations and psychological implications that such an image entailed.

One aspect that left a particularly deep impression on everyone who served in the enclave was the life of the inhabitants—a life that was unimaginably harsh. There were far too many people in the small area of the enclave with inadequate shelter and food, no electricity, no sewer system, no waste disposal system worth mentioning, no shops, and no restaurants—a situation that we in the Netherlands could scarcely have imagined. Furthermore, the inhabitants were burdened by the constant threat from the Serbs, by the powerlessness of their own government to do anything for them, by the apparent powerlessness of the United Nations, and, indeed, by sheer uncertainty about whether they would live or die. Needless to say, the population's suffering did not go unnoticed by the battalion, but the battalion had neither the resources nor the permission to relieve the population's torment.

The battalion was also greatly affected by the casualties claimed by the operation. In one short period (approximately a month after taking over the area of responsibility), two excellent NCOs were injured in mine incidents. Later, three other members of the battalion were wounded. All of these personnel were lost to us because they had to be repatriated to the Netherlands. After the initial shock, everyone quickly realized that the situation was serious and that we had to be constantly alert. Personnel also soon became aware that when they were on patrol along the enclave's boundaries, they were visible to all parties, and were therefore a potential target. These factors exerted great pressure on the entire battalion, and especially on the leaders, who keenly felt the responsibility for the safety of their personnel.

The battalion's isolation and the constant impediments to the smooth implementation of leave arrangements made those arrangements a constant concern both for those tasked to implement them and for the personnel who wanted to go on leave. Nor must we forget the countless relatives and friends who worried every time a convoy of personnel on leave was delayed.

5. EXPERIENCES AND LESSONS LEARNED

Deployment is an opportunity to learn. In this deployment, the local situation and circumstances virtually dictated the way we conducted the operation and largely determined how the mission was carried out. In fact, the battalion's very survival depended on its ability to accommodate the local circumstances. The experiences described in this section became lessons that greatly influenced my decision making, and thus the battalion's actions.

5.1. Handling Risks

Approximately one month after the battalion had assumed responsibility for the enclave, minefield clearance operations were initiated in conjunction with the elimination of a number of Bosnian Serb positions. At the same time, we experienced a number of mine incidents on certain roads. As mentioned earlier, two outstanding NCOs were injured and had to be repatriated; in addition, an armoured vehicle drove over a mine and was demolished (although fortunately its crew was not injured), and a Mercedes drove over an antipersonnel mine. I am convinced that there was a direct connection between these "incidents" and the mine-clearing operations that the battalion had been carrying out elsewhere in the enclave. Furthermore, during that period the Serbs reduced their contact with the battalion,[18] resulting in the delay of several badly needed convoys.

These events had a tremendous impact on the battalion. It became quite clear to all of us that the operation was deadly serious. The situation forced a re-evaluation of the operational procedures and of what we called "skills and drills." These re-evaluations led to adaptations of the armoured vehicle, modifications in the methods of vehicle patrol, and changes in the number of soldiers who took part in a foot patrol. Furthermore, as a result of the analysis that followed these incidents, the membership of foot patrols was adjusted to include an assault engineer and a medical orderly. Because there were fewer of these personnel in the battalion, their workload became heavier than that of the other personnel. I also decided to lay the responsibility for the patrols solely on the doorstep of the company commanders, believing that this change would contribute to their control of the operations. Previously, a duty officer at the company level had been able to authorize certain patrols; in my opinion, this approach was no longer acceptable, even though the new policy would increase the burden on the commanders in the line.

Several aspects of the situation gradually became clear to me as commander. First, it was evident that both parties in the conflict could arbitrarily strike the battalion wherever they wanted. Second, the battalion was fully dependent on Serb approval for logistical and supply convoys—and therefore for the fulfillment of its mission. Finally, it became clear that promises of support from the United Nations would not improve the battalion's situation. These realizations reinforced my view that the battalion must avoid all unnecessary risks, since most risks would be

---

[18] The Bosnian Serbs had some officers who acted as liaisons to the battalion and with whom the battalion and the companies had irregular contact.

counterproductive. From that point on, the battalion precariously walked the fine line between fulfilling its mission and accommodating the interests of the conflicting parties.

Before departure, all battalion personnel had been informed of a vast number of specific and detailed rules having to do with what was and what was not acceptable regarding movement into the area of deployment. These regulations had resulted from negotiations between the United Nations and the Serbs concerning the rotations in and out of the enclave. Despite extensive discussion and stringent directives, many soldiers chose to disregard these rules. On one occasion, their actions put the entire rotation at risk: contraband items[19] caused the Bosnian Serbs to briefly hold up a convoy of more than 200 people, with no one able to come to their aid. Even I, as commander, was powerless to change the convoy's situation. I found this situation totally unacceptable; from then on, I was extremely critical of personnel who disregarded directives. In my view, the battalion's collective interests and the implementation of its mission were far more important than the freedom of individuals.

Countless stress-inducing incidents occurred during the deployment. Fortunately, most of them were resolved successfully. The battalion conducted numerous operations aimed at stopping undesirable activities by the conflicting parties and by the civilian population; in doing so, it acted with considerable restraint, partly as a result of the mine incidents mentioned earlier. However, there arose one occasion when I judged that decisive action—rather than restraint—was required. The immediate cause for my decision to act was the fact that the battalion's hospital, which was clearly recognizable, had come under direct fire on three occasions. Our action involved a deliberate deployment to seize the weapons that had been used. The decisive factors in the decision were our morale and my faith in our ability. By taking a conscious—albeit limited—risk, we were able to improve our sense of self-respect; this shift had a positive effect on the subsequent implementation of our task. An important lesson for me was that it was sometimes necessary to take risks, because doing so enabled the battalion as a whole to function better.

During the months of the deployment, there was a constant development and discussion of "What if?" scenarios, which typically assumed the worst. A great deal of time and effort was devoted to convincing battalion personnel of the gravity of the situation and to discussing how best to carry out the task using our extremely modest resources. By the end of November 1994, I was convinced that the battalion would no longer be able to fulfill its mission if supplies were not forthcoming by the middle of December. However, it seemed that in the Netherlands the situation was being judged differently. It was very difficult for me to communicate an accurate picture of the situation in the enclave.

5.2. Shortages

During the course of the deployment, the battalion experienced a growing number of shortages; increasingly, these shortages became an impediment to the

---

[19] The United Nations and the Bosnian Serbs had reached an agreement concerning what the soldiers could take on rotation. They were forbidden to take such items as cameras, video cameras, and large radios.

implementation of our task. For instance, at the end of August we were forced to begin rationing fuel and, to a more limited extent, fresh food. The imposition of rationing made it impossible for our vehicles to carry out patrols; also, the observation posts could no longer be visited on a regular basis. (My own contact with the personnel at the observation posts became restricted as well, for how could I travel in my personal vehicle while restricting travel by my troops?) Our overview of activities in the enclave thus became more limited.

With the approach of winter, the battalion was increasingly forced to undertake certain measures aimed simply at ensuring our survival. The "mini-mini-minimize" programs we instituted will be remembered by battalion personnel for years to come. As part of these programs, the battalion constructed a great number of heaters. The S4 (the person responsible for the unit's logistical support) gave detailed instructions concerning which units were tasked to chop wood for heating, the priorities for distributing it, and where and for how long it could be burned. The programs also instituted very detailed instructions concerning the use of lights and the use of water for showers (a hot shower once a week only) and laundry (cold water only). These conditions demanded that we devote even more effort to motivating and encouraging the troops and compelled me to develop a "survival strategy" under which the priority was keeping personnel fit for duty. I focused increasing attention on the personnel and logistical aspects of the deployment. In fact, the operational component of the mission became more and more subordinate to inventing the means with which to survive the winter.

5.3. Communication

I indicated earlier that only a few members of the chain of command knew the precise situation in the enclave and that, in general, the perception of the situation by the chain of command differed from what it actually was. This gap made communication about the mission extremely difficult: my ability to explain the situation was severely limited by the false conceptions that existed at other levels. I often felt a sense of being at cross-purposes in my communication with the Netherlands, particularly since the messages from my end were not always optimistic. Furthermore, I found that I had to exercise extreme restraint when describing the situation to the press and the people at home. A special lesson I have learned is that the local commander has the best knowledge of the military situation, and that it sometimes takes a great deal of personal courage on the part of that commander's superior to trust that he or she will make the right decision. When guidance for an operation is needed, shared knowledge of the local situation on the part of both superior and subordinate, coupled with good and open communication, is of the utmost importance.

In this context, it would perhaps be useful to briefly discuss the influence exerted on very high levels by decisions taken at very low levels. In general, we in the military are accustomed to having a relatively high degree of freedom within our area of responsibility. With this freedom, however, comes a caveat: the results of decisions made at a lower level can never be so extensive that the higher level must adapt its operation. In particular, it is critical that decisions made by a lower level should not draw undue attention from the local political authorities. As I have mentioned, all parties within the enclave regarded Dutchbat as a single entity. The belligerents regarded actions taken by individual battalion members as the responsibility of the battalion as a whole. With the increasing complexity of the situation in the former Yugoslavia over time, the involvement of political and senior military authorities became greater; the implications for the higher levels of decisions that were made at lower levels also grew. This shift had further consequences for the local commander's freedom to make decisions. The external factors increasingly limited the range of decisions that could be made; at the same time, communication with the lower levels was becoming more difficult. I felt obliged to issue stringent guidelines concerning the activities of the battalion's subunits, thereby restricting the freedom of the subcommanders.

5.4. Psychological Effects

Within the enclave, the battalion was fully dependent on Serb approval of logistical and leave convoys, and the Serbs dictated the routes to be taken. In November, the battalion faced two hostage situations. A supply convoy of about 20 people was "stopped" en route; at the same time, a convoy of approximately 80 personnel on leave was "stopped" in the vicinity of Zvornik. It soon became apparent that these events were linked to the bombing—by the North Atlantic Treaty Organization (NATO)—of the airfield at Ubdina. The hostage situations once again brought us face to face with the facts: the Serbs were in a position to act arbitrarily, and the United Nations was powerless to stop them. These situations were extremely humiliating: I had a sense of complete impotence. My relief was great when, after approximately 10 days, this nightmare came to an end: the soldiers and their families were reunited, and for the first time in many weeks a small quantity of diesel fuel and some food were supplied. It had now become perfectly clear to me that if push came to shove, the battalion would be on its own, and that support (apart from lip service) could be very scarce.

Duties within the enclave were often monotonous: conducting endless foot patrols, performing guard duty at the compound, and operating observation posts. The physically demanding conditions, coupled with our often poor nutrition and the constant threat of belligerent action, put the battalion's lower levels under severe pressure. There was also almost no opportunity for recreation or any other way of relieving the stress. Owing to the physical demands of the operation as well as the constant psychological pressure, there was a need for constant monitoring of personnel. The counsellors attached to the battalion played an important role in this respect. In one instance, after lengthy consultations and intensive discussions, I decided to rehabilitate a platoon. I had observed that it could no longer carry out its mission, since at least 50 percent of the unit's personnel were no longer deployable, either due to physical problems caused by patrolling in extremely heavy terrain or due to the constant psychological pressure. With the help of the counsellors, we devised a rehabilitation plan and gave the responsibility for its implementation to the company commander. It was extremely difficult to make the decision—on the basis of my subjective observations—that the unit should be required to recuperate. The unit regarded the decision as a punishment, even though everyone was aware that the situation could not continue. Only later did it become apparent that many in the platoon supported the decision. I have concluded that a commander sometimes needs the courage to make decisions that will not be met with broad support, but that, in his or her opinion, are legitimate and necessary both for the implementation of the mission and for the well-being of a large group of young people.

The more time passed, the worse the conditions for the battalion became. The ceaseless psychological pressure and work demands, combined with poor hygiene and a permanent shortage of fresh food, milk, and so on, were of constant concern. Poor communication with friends and family also complicated the situation for the soldiers: mail was dependent on the Serbs' willingness to let convoys pass, and the chances to communicate by telephone were limited. The opportunities to "let off some steam" were also very limited.

Furthermore, the battalion—especially those personnel who were working in the Potocari compound—also faced serious environmental pollution. Good living conditions are an important precondition for the satisfactory functioning of personnel. Unfortunately, we could do little to change these conditions. We took measures to seal off badly polluted areas, and many members of the battalion were given medical examinations and advice. By adapting the activities and patrol schedules, we did everything possible to accommodate the diminished resistance of the personnel. Fortunately, the personnel who were subjected to these conditions have (as far as I am aware) suffered no long-term ill effects from this exposure.

The battalion and its commanders were continually confronted with situations that they had never before seen or experienced. A number of these situations have already been discussed—for example, the inconceivable complexity of maneuvering between the conflicting interests of the belligerents, the enclave's inhabitants, and the national and international organizations. The aspect of the operation that had the most impact, however, was acting as "guard" to 35,000 people who were being forced to live in desperately poor conditions. Observing the sheer despair of men, women, and children who had absolutely nowhere to go was a unique experience for the battalion's personnel, particularly when contrasted to their personal circumstances and family situations at home in the Netherlands.

As a commander, one is given the authority and the responsibility for the use of military resources, including the use of force. One has a certain power to legitimately change the situation for the soldiers (and, in my case, for the inhabitants of the enclave as well). This power demands very careful decision making: the lives of the soldiers and potentially those of many other people are at stake. In this operation, I had to consider the needs of the inhabitants and others who were in immediate need against my battalion's situation with its shortages of essential stocks. I was walking a very thin line between the interests of my unit and those of the population, using my own moral standards and values.

Finally, I must discuss the position of the commander in situations such as this one. As much as a commander wants to be "at one" with the unit and wants to "belong," this ideal is in most cases impossible to achieve. The commander has an official position in the unit: he or she is its figurehead and representative and is personally responsible for all decisions. It was my experience that despite having an outstanding staff to support and advise me, I was always ultimately forced to consider matters personally, with the staff wanting "nothing to do with it." The commander alone must make the difficult decisions: there is no one to hide behind. If things go well and the commander is lucky, the staff and the unit reap the benefits; if things go badly, then, in my opinion, the commander alone must take responsibility. I shall never forget the special loneliness of command. In Srebrenica, this loneliness was reinforced by a sense of powerlessness and a perception of lack of support from the outside world.

6. STRATEGIES FOR COPING

In my opinion, a unit's ability to cope with the type of military and living conditions described above—total isolation, constant shortages, and the lack of understanding of the situation at higher levels—is not something that suddenly "happens." Instead, a tacit understanding of the situation forms among the unit's members, and over time they develop certain strategies for coping. In addition, the ability to deal with difficult circumstances is often an individual one: one person may be better able to cope than another.

6.1. The Battalion

Given our situation in Srebrenica, I felt that it was important to create as much stability as possible in the daily routine. We therefore held meetings at fixed times every day, with the main objective of keeping one another informed and maintaining a certain amount of social interaction. In my battalion, all subcommanders, staff officers, and NCOs gathered at 0800 hours to watch the news broadcast on RTL 4.[20] This broadcast was often our only source of information about the situation outside the enclave. After the news, we held the main staff meeting. Following the meeting, I always spoke to the company commanders separately—both to permit the discussion of confidential matters and to give them the opportunity to exchange thoughts among themselves. The daily cycle ended with a staff meeting of the section heads at 2000 hours. This meeting enabled me to prepare for the following day, as well as to get feedback concerning the events of the past day.

I stuck strictly to this schedule. The meetings not only gave everyone a chance to "let off steam" but also helped prevent the perception that we were resigned to our situation and that the staff was doing nothing. The daily routine for the units themselves also fit within this framework. Every day they followed the same routine. The exception was Sunday, when the relaxation of the routine broke up the week and gave the personnel a break. The Sunday break was also important, I felt, for marking the passage of another week and thus preventing the loss of a sense of time. The provision of personnel leave, difficult though it was to arrange, was also important for making the situation as bearable as possible.

---

[20] RTL 4 was a television station that could be received in the enclave and that gave news about the Netherlands.

In addition to the above-mentioned meetings within the battalion, I held regular meetings with all parties and relief organizations within the enclave. These meetings enabled us to explain our own situation, and proved absolutely vital once the battalion became hard pressed to carry out its assigned task. The meetings allowed us to become informed about the situation around us, especially the needs of the population, and helped in the decision-making process.

The battalion devised various ways to continue to carry out its mission. When movement by vehicle became restricted due to fuel shortages, we developed alternative strategies for allowing patrols to continue. For instance, we switched to an approach that involved setting up patrol bases, from which a platoon could carry out its orders for several days. Another approach was "enclave-hopping," whereby patrols moved from one observation post to another entirely on foot, dramatically reducing the use of vehicles and fuel. As well, battalion personnel were very inventive about such matters as energy supplies, water consumption, and methods for generating heat. At the core of all these measures was the need to provide people with a useful task that gave them a focus. If it becomes impossible to do so, a unit's morale is ultimately eroded.

Central to being able to cope in such situations is a clear understanding of the task for which one has been deployed. It is crucial that the troops continue to see the purpose of the mission and to have some tangible evidence that their efforts are having a positive effect. Our efforts were, of course, also directed toward the benefit of the enclave's inhabitants. I always insisted that support be provided for all enclave projects—whether helping to establish a water supply or to set up a rubbish dump: anything visible counted. We were certainly able to provide a great deal of medical support to the local population, attending to matters that ranged from births to deaths. This support was welcome and was gratefully accepted.

Though the battalion had limited supplies, I believed that it was better to share them with the local population. There was a practical reason for doing so: if the population thought that the battalion had a generous level of supplies, while they themselves had nothing, it was highly conceivable that the inhabitants would simply avail themselves of the battalion's supplies. I took the trouble to inform the authorities in the enclave on many occasions that we too did not have a great deal: the battalion's empty storage areas spoke volumes.

The instruction that personnel received before the deployment included training on the impact of stress as well as on how to function in stressful situations. The battalion also employed a "buddy system," under which two people were responsible for each other: each would monitor the other's behaviour, helping the other as necessary and reporting to the commander if some problem appeared likely to get out of hand. In addition, the subunit commanders and counsellors were tasked to oversee personnel care. It was my observation that this approach was successful, given the circumstances under which the battalion had to carry out its tasks.

Finally, I must observe that, in my opinion, each individual has his or her own mechanisms for dealing with stressful situations. Some individuals, however, must also be responsible for a group of other people, thereby increasing their own load and level of stress. Commanders are *always* commanders. They cannot simply say, "It's too difficult" or "I'm too tired; I think I'll just drop out for a while." A commander is responsible 24 hours a day, 7 days a week; in my own case, this responsibility lasted for almost 7 months. The full meaning and implications of this burden cannot be described in this limited space; only those with similar experience will understand what I mean.

6.2. The Commander

I shall close by providing some comments on how I dealt with the circumstances described above, both as a commander and as a person. The distinction between "person" and "commander" is deliberate. The person can take everything that he or she sees or feels to heart. The commander, on the other hand, has a special responsibility for implementing a mission and for all the personnel entrusted to him or her. As a person, one might choose a certain option on the basis of emotional considerations; as a commander, one must always try to choose on the basis of rational considerations. The greater the difference between the person and the commander, the harder it is to function properly. In an ideal situation, the two can be virtually one. I can assure you, however, that in Srebrenica the situation was not ideal; this disparity was therefore a considerable burden during my time in the enclave.

Before we deployed, I had made arrangements with two officers in the Netherlands whereby I could telephone them whenever I wanted to and discuss any concerns with them in confidence. I believed that I might need such a sounding board—an occasional chance to vent my opinions and to say what was on my mind, however negative, without consequences for the battalion or me. And, indeed, I often made use of this arrangement; it certainly contributed to my being able to hold things together. I also made an agreement with two officers from the battalion staff. I asked them to watch over me and to warn me if it looked as though I were going "off the rails." If they perceived that I was making decisions that were totally inappropriate or behaving oddly, I gave them the freedom to tell me to my face what was wrong. These people provided a very special support. I shall always remain indebted to them.

I shall now touch again on the importance of a fixed rhythm of meetings. For me, this routine contributed to order and predictability. It forced me to think about the various problems that we were encountering and to prepare solutions. I strongly preferred a regular routine: it gave me something to hold onto. Moreover, it gave me a structured opportunity to meet with people from the battalion and other organizations and to bounce my own ideas and feelings off them. The visits to the units and posts contributed, as well, to my motivation. Under the circumstances, it was an extremely pleasant experience to discuss day-to-day affairs with the soldiers: it gave me the opportunity to explain my policy—and such explanations were frequently necessary—and it was often a source of new ideas.

As for the human element of our mission—by which I mean the enclave's population—I never grew accustomed to the disgraceful conditions in which they lived. It distressed me that I could do little to alleviate their plight, even though I as a commander and we as a battalion were highly motivated to help. Such a situation is, without question, psychologically disturbing; in this sense, Srebrenica constitutes a black page in my personal history.

One final comment: it seems to me that we ask a great deal of our commanders as people and as leaders. Because a commander is entrusted with the responsibility for the people in his or her unit, he or she must be able to make careful choices and thorough preparations for difficult tasks. The military organization must therefore not hesitate to prevent unsuitable individuals from taking up command. Not only could such vigilance ultimately save lives, but it will also enhance the confidence of our personnel in the military organization.

CHAPTER 7

COMMAND AND LEADERSHIP IN OTHER PEOPLE'S WARS

COLONEL M. D. CAPSTICK

1. FROM THE COLD WAR TO OTHER PEOPLE'S WARS

> Still, it was my job. We were still a platoon with a job to do. . . . It wasn't the last time the Bosnians murdered their own people in well-staged attacks for PR reasons. At the ordinary soldier level, we had no authority to stop it, so we just had to turn away. Soldier on. (Davis, 1997, p. 168)

This quote from Sergeant (Retired) James Davis's book, *The Sharp End: A Canadian Soldier's Story*, provides a glimpse of the frustrations often encountered by the ordinary soldier during peace support operations. It summarizes his reaction to the shelling of a group of Bosnian Muslim children—allegedly by the Bosnian-Muslim Territorial Defence Force (TDF)—in front of the United Nations headquarters in Sarajevo. Frustration is not the only emotion engendered by this kind of incident: anger is another. According to Davis, "[W]e couldn't believe it. I can't speak for the others, but that morning I would have happily killed any TDF troops I saw. I was growing tired of the whole mess. These people didn't care. They were animals" (p. 168). Lightly armed, and restricted by rules of engagement that limited the use of deadly force to "self-defence," Davis and his platoon felt impotent in the face of a dangerous and degenerating situation in Sarajevo in the spring of 1992. Finally, there was an implicit message in Davis's description of powerlessness "at the ordinary soldier level"—the message that those in positions of command and authority might not be doing the job that they were entrusted with.

COLONEL M. D. CAPSTICK • *Director Land Personnel, National Defence Headquarters, Ottawa, Ontario, Canada K1A 0K2*

The Human in Command: Exploring the Modern Military Experience, edited by McCann and Pigeau, Kluwer Academic/Plenum Publishers, New York, 2000.

At about the same time as Canadian Major-General Lewis MacKenzie[1] and Lieutenant-Colonel (now Colonel) Michel Jones[2] were trying to impose some order in the chaos of Sarajevo, the 1st Regiment, Royal Canadian Horse Artillery, was preparing to deploy to Cyprus. The regiment, under my command, was to be the 58th Canadian contingent in the United Nations Force in Cyprus. Jones and his composite Battle Group, based on a battalion of Canada's francophone infantry regiment, the Royal 22ième Régiment du Canada, and augmented by members of the Royal Canadian Regiment (Davis was a member of this unit) and Combat Engineers, were the first Canadians to serve in the former Yugoslavia. They would not be the last. Both Jones's mission and my own were peacekeeping missions under Chapter VI of the U.N. Charter.[3] But that is where the similarities ended. The Cyprus mission involved peacekeeping in the classical sense of the word: uniformed belligerents, political consent, and a stable status quo, as evidenced by the famous "Green Line."[4] Jones, on the other hand, found himself embroiled in the military and political hell that was Sarajevo in 1992.

By Christmas of that year, another battalion would be deployed in Bosnia and the Canadian Airborne Regiment Battle Group would be on its way to Somalia to participate in the U.N.-sanctioned, but U.S.-led, Operation Restore Hope. In total, over 4,000 Canadian troops would spend New Year's Day of 1993 involved in other people's wars. The vast majority of the officers and NCOs appointed to lead those soldiers performed superbly. The soldiers, for the most part, did what was asked of them, and more. But some of the leaders failed, and some of the soldiers committed unconscionable acts. These failures and acts would scar the Canadian Army for the rest of the decade, precipitating an extended period of introspection and self-criticism. After all, Canada had "invented" peacekeeping, and its Army had "written the book" on involvement in other people's wars.

This was an army that was in the midst of major organizational trauma brought on by the withdrawal of the Canadian brigade group from Germany. Major cultural change was also under way: the government had just announced the unrestricted employment of women within Canada's armed forces, and there had also been policy changes with regard to homosexuals. The army's "bayonet strength" was being reduced as regiments and battalions were either struck from the order of battle, amalgamated, or designated as 10/90 (that is, 10 percent Regular force and 90 percent Reserve) Total Force units. More importantly, the Canadian Army had lost the North Atlantic Treaty Organization (NATO) mission that had been the focus of its existence for the previous 40 years. Officers and soldiers had been trained for conventional war in Europe—a war in which the survival of Western democratic principles would be at stake and the *destruction* of advancing

---

[1] MacKenzie was the Canadian general who was originally deployed to Sarajevo to establish the United Nations Protection Force (UNPROFOR) headquarters to control operations in Croatia (MacKenzie, 1993).

[2] Jones commanded the Canadian battalion that was redeployed from Croatia to open Sarajevo's airport.

[3] Chapter VI operations require the consent of both (or all) parties and usually limit the use of force to self-defence. Chapter VII operations authorize the use of force to accomplish the mandate, as was the case in both the Korean Conflict and the Gulf War.

[4] The buffer zone demarcating the portions of Cyprus under Greek control from those under Turk Cypriot control.

Warsaw Pact forces was seen as the key to victory. With the exception of General MacKenzie (one of the world's most experienced peacekeepers), everyone who was in command of troops deployed overseas in the winter of 1992/93 had "grown up" in Germany. Our mission there had been clear: we knew who the enemy was, and we knew that we would use every weapon at our disposal to kill as many as possible. The term *rules of engagement* was foreign to most of us; I myself had never heard any discussion of the legal basis for our commitment to the defence of Europe. That was a far simpler world than the one that we've been dealing with since! We have moved from the stark threat of nuclear exchanges on the highly structured Cold War battlefield to the far more complex world of peace support operations (Lewis, 1996). Doctrine, tactics, and even equipment have been adapted to meet these new conditions. But our understanding of the most vital component of operational effectiveness—command and leadership—is still rooted in the principles that worked in the last world war. This chapter will discuss some of the major issues and leadership concerns that have resulted from this situation.

2. LEADERSHIP: THE PROBLEMS

The Somalia Inquiry (a Canadian government–ordered commission with a mandate to examine the performance of the Canadian Airborne Regiment Battle Group in Somalia), the media, and the most vocal military critics all claim that the Canadian Forces (CF) are suffering a "leadership crisis" (Canada, 1997, Executive Summary). The Canadian Army's success in recent operations (including Somalia), along with my own experience, tells me that the term "leadership crisis" is extreme. However, we do have problems. Regardless of their credibility or credentials, a large number of soldiers believe the critics. The concept of trust extending through the chain of command has been seriously weakened and needs to be restored. To my mind, the problem has three main components. First, we have not reconciled our views of leadership with an army in which soldiers with an *occupational* orientation seem to outnumber those who see themselves as warriors—that is, those with a *vocational* view of their profession. Second, we have not been very successful in transforming those who have an occupational motivation into warriors; nor have we been very successful in imbuing some of those who have a vocational view of soldiering with "the warrior's honour" (Ignatieff, 1998). Finally, and most importantly, the theoretical basis for our study of leadership, developed in an era of mass armies fighting for national survival, has not been adapted to professional armies involved in other people's wars.

Almost every Western volunteer force faces the first two problems. Charles Moskos's seminal work on the vocational/occupational model (Moskos & Wood, 1988) deals with this problem in Western armies. Bercuson (1997) describes the same dynamic in a more anecdotal fashion. The hearings held by the Standing Committee on National Defence and Veterans' Affairs[5] have provided poignant evidence that a large number of our soldiers, sailors, and aviators view military service as "just

---

[5] A committee of the Canadian Parliament that recently concluded an in-depth review of the conditions of service in the Canadian Forces.

another job." This view has been magnified by worsening economic conditions, housing problems, and quality-of-life issues that have made service members even more prone to demanding that they be treated like employees in any other Canadian enterprise (O'Hara, 1998). My personal discussions with combat arms soldiers who were deployed to Bosnia in 1997 and 1998 indicate that there is also—at least among that group—a strong sense that a large number of CF members, especially those in support roles, go to great lengths to avoid operational deployment. On the other hand, there is still a "hard core" who view military service as a vocation (Sergeant Duke, a Canadian infantry NCO, quoted in O'Hara, 1998, p. 18). The challenges of leading and motivating both groups in other people's wars present particular problems.

3. THE OCCUPATIONAL SOLDIER

In the case of the occupational soldier, ensuring a clear understanding of the importance of mission accomplishment is essential. In stark terms, many of these soldiers have deployed either because they simply could not avoid it without risking their livelihood or because they needed the extra allowances. As commander in Bosnia, I actually received a letter from a tradesman's wife complaining that he was being "forced" to perform camp security tasks and that nowhere in his *contract* did it state that he was a "soldier first and tradesman second"! I wish I could say that this kind of sentiment is rare: unfortunately, it is not. In practical terms, such attitudes have led to a culture of entitlement that, once developed, is tough to reverse. Despite the fact that we were the best-supported contingent in the NATO Stabilization Force, the vast majority of complaints that came to my attention concerned things like telephone calls home and the allocation of amenities. The reality of peace support operations is that logistics, in the pure sense of the word, must be one of the primary concerns of commanders and leaders at all levels.

It is easy to dismiss most of these concerns as trivial and of little operational impact. In my view, this is a serious mistake. Today's soldiers expect far more in the way of material support than their fathers and grandfathers did in wartime, and a system's failure to provide that support erodes the essential trust in the chain of command. This is a difficult concept for senior leaders to accept. After all, we learned our profession in an era where our job was to maximize killing power by ensuring the best possible "tooth-to-tail" ratio. In his study of peacekeeping, Christopher Bellamy (1996) asserts that "soldiers in intervention operations are not, by and large, fighting for their lives or, indeed, their countries' vital interests. They are there as volunteers . . . to help others. They expect and, indeed, deserve, a bit of comfort" (p. 169). My experience as a commander supports this contention. Failure to provide an appropriate level of support will not only weaken confidence in the chain of command; it will eventually affect cohesion and unity of effort. This is especially true if soldiers perceive that the system is not interested in their welfare, or that fiscal constraints have resulted in a reduced standard of support. The challenge is to find the appropriate ways of looking after the soldiers' welfare while at the same time maintaining the operational effectiveness of the force. In my experience, many soldiers with a more occupational motivation have unreasonable and unrealistic expectations of military service. Those in support roles are often accustomed to working regular hours in jobs that have readily identifiable civilian equivalents; some units, even on operations, adopt a "garrison mentality" with respect to their daily routines and duties. This attitude only widens the gulf between support units and the more vocationally oriented combat units that they are designed to support. That gulf between the "guys in the rear with the gear" and the combat units "at the sharp end" has existed since Napoleon's day; it will never be completely eliminated. But my experiences in both Cyprus and Bosnia suggest that commanders must do everything possible to close the gap by ensuring an equitable distribution of both supplies and amenities. In the longer term, the Army must learn how to clearly explain the true nature of the military profession to the young Canadians who walk into the recruiting centre looking for a job.

4. THE ROGUE WARRIOR

Soldiers on the other end of the occupational/vocational spectrum present another set of challenges. Motivated by a desire to *soldier*, taught to fight, and steeped in the image of the rough, tough warrior, these soldiers are often frustrated by the constraints of peace support operations. I have had soldiers tell me that they did not join the Army to be social workers or babysitters. Davis's (1997) description of his experiences vividly conveys that sense of frustration. In my view, countering it, maintaining operational discipline, and ensuring that the soldiers understand the limited nature of peace support operations are among the most important challenges facing tactical-level leaders in the field. It has long been a cliché that peace support operations are a section commander's war, where the aim is to settle problems at the lowest possible level. Based on personal observation, however, I am not confident that we have given our junior leaders (officers and NCOs) the intellectual and theoretical tools to do the job. Too often, leaders adopt the exaggerated macho style made popular in American movies and thus convey a rogue image that is incompatible with the principles of peace support operations—and, in fact, would be dangerous in war. This problem is, in fact, the main thesis of Winslow's (1997) work on socio-cultural factors in the Canadian Forces, commissioned in support of the Somalia Inquiry. Some of Winslow's specific conclusions are arguable: for example, was the in-theatre presence *per se* of alcohol in Somalia the problem, or was the failure really due to the leaders' inability to control the overconsumption and abuse of alcohol? In addition, I am uncomfortable with the implication that peacekeeping and the "combat paradigm" are incompatible and that the attitudes that Winslow encountered might, somehow, be applicable to warfighting. To my mind, the rogue behaviours described by Winslow (see also this volume, Chapter 20) would probably be even more dangerous in war than they were in the peace support operations in Somalia. That being said, Winslow's main themes (especially those concerning the friction between the occupational and vocational models and the importance of both formal and informal leadership) are supported by my own observations.

5. THE WARRIOR'S HONOUR

Michael Ignatieff (1998) addresses many of the same concerns in the context of ethnic conflict within failed states. He describes the concept of "warrior's honour" as "both a code of belonging and an ethic of responsibility" (p. 117). It is this code that permits warriors to distinguish "between combatants and non-combatants, legitimate and illegitimate targets, moral and immoral weaponry and civilized and barbarous usage in the treatment of prisoners and of the wounded" (p. 117). He goes on to state that without these codes, "war is not war—it is no more than slaughter" (p. 117). In essence, it is this sense of a warrior's honour that differentiates the soldier from the thug and the warlord; and it must also differentiate between the mechanic at Canadian Tire[6] and the mechanic in the Canadian (or any other) Army. The challenge for today's military leader is to develop that code of belonging in those whose motivation is occupational. At the same time, those with a vocational motivation, corrupted by the "Rambo mentality," need to be taught the ethic of responsibility. The values and ethos described in the newly published manual *Canada's Army* (Canada, 1998) are those described as necessary by Ignatieff and found to be wanting in the Canadian Forces by Winslow (1997). The importance of these fundamentals in peace support operations cannot be overstated. The consequences of poor discipline, excessive use of force, mistreatment of the local population, or a lack of professionalism are, most often, mission failure.

6. LIMITED WAR, UNLIMITED LIABILITY

Woven through the problems of trying to reconcile the occupational/vocational friction within the Army is the entire question of understanding combat motivation and leadership in the context of peace support operations conducted by a professional volunteer army. This question has become more profound as operations have become more complex and dangerous since the end of the Cold War. Unfortunately, our leadership theory, and our understanding of the regimental system and combat motivation, is based on history. But today's Canadian soldier has no more in common with the Cameronians (Scottish Rifles) featured in Baynes's classic *Morale* (1967) than with a Roman Legionnaire! The Canadian soldiers who attacked Vimy Ridge and went ashore at Normandy came from an entirely different society; they held different values, and they were motivated by the simple fact that they had to kill or be killed. (See Blackburn, 1997, for a description of Canadian society and the motivation of soldiers in 1939.) Of course there are immutable principles, or basics, of command and leadership that transcend history and are common across a variety of cultures. Still, a review of the literature reveals that virtually every one of the classic works on military leadership is rooted in the experience of global war in the first half of the twentieth century. Given the massive cultural change of the past few decades, it is essential that the military and academic communities combine to redress this situation.

---

[6] A retail chain specializing in auto repair and hardware in Canada.

The challenge for commanders and leaders in peace support operations is to adapt the classic leadership theories and principles to the realities of today's soldiers and operational context. The essential first step is for commanders at all levels to appreciate the qualitative difference between fighting in our own nation's wars and being involved in someone else's. That difference is not subtle: it goes to the heart of the principle of unlimited liability and raises the basic question "Is this hell-hole worth one Canadian (or American, or Dutch, or British) life?" Davis (1997) is eloquent in this regard, as is Stewart (1994) in his description of his time commanding the first British battalion in Bosnia. In short, this aspect of peace support operations will always be ambiguous, because there can be no prescriptive answer to the basic question. At best, commanders can hope to achieve an appropriate balance between two imperatives: mission accomplishment and force protection. At the strategic level, leaders (political and military) are often forced to decide this balance in full view of the media and world opinion. The two-year debate concerning the use of air power to deter Bosnian Serb aggression against the designated U.N. "safe areas" in Bosnia (including Sarajevo, Srebrenica, Bihać, and three other towns), given the risk to UNPROFOR troops on the ground, is a classic example of this dichotomy at the strategic level. The challenge is no less critical at the tactical level, where officers and NCOs are faced with daily ethical dilemmas of this nature. (Everts—this volume, Chapter 6—offers numerous examples in describing his experience commanding a battalion at Srebrenica.)

In practical terms, these considerations present a number of challenges for leaders and commanders on peace support operations. The importance of logistics and personnel support have been discussed earlier in this chapter, and commanders must be very careful not to jeopardize either the quality or quantity of their support structure. Food, medical support, leave, and amenities all have a direct impact on mission success and should be a major focus for all leaders.

7. THE NEED TO EVOLVE LEADERSHIP STYLES

In my view, many of the patriarchal practices that have developed along with our regimental system are no longer appropriate for our professional Canadian soldiers employed in a peacekeeping or peace support role. Today's soldiers are older and better educated than their World War II counterparts. Most are married, have children, and are more than capable of making their own decisions; they therefore expect and demand that their experience, expertise, and professionalism be respected. In addition, the operational tempo during a peace support operation is usually slower than that expected in war, and relatively junior NCOs and officers have far more freedom of action and responsibility. Leaders at all levels need to accept these facts and learn how to take advantage of the soldiers' experience by adopting consultation as a regular part of their planning process and battle procedure.

Leaders also need to be very careful to avoid any perception that officers and NCOs can take advantage of their positions to make their lives more comfortable than those of their subordinates or to avoid compliance with unpopular policies.

The testimony of soldiers before the Somalia Inquiry indicates that the issue of double standards was an important one in the Canadian Airborne Regiment. Winslow (this volume, Chapter 20), in describing the events at the Bacovici Hospital in Bosnia (another incident of leadership failure), demonstrates that the officers' flouting of the alcohol consumption policy gave the soldiers licence to do the same. In the past, soldiers expected officers to come from a different social class and to affect idiosyncratic dress and social habits. During World War II, it was common practice in the Canadian Army to permit the soldiers' field canteens to sell nothing stronger than beer, while officers' messes were also stocked with spirits (Blackburn, 1997). Today's Canada is an egalitarian society, and today's soldier has no respect for the artificial class differences that used to be common in the Army and were essential to the operation of the regimental system.

8. MISSION SUCCESS AND TEDIUM

Another fact of life on peace support operations is the tedium that comes with mission success. In other words, when the unit is doing its job, the situation is under control. An inevitable byproduct is boredom and inattention—a situation that carries a high degree of risk with respect to both force protection and mission accomplishment. Vehicle accidents are a leading cause of death among the world's peacekeepers; commanders must therefore be ruthless in enforcing speed limits and traffic regulations. Negligent handling of weapons and blasé attitudes toward the mine threat are other symptoms of boredom that can result in death or serious injury. I saw all of these occur in both Cyprus and Bosnia: the only antidote is to maintain a high standard of operational discipline at the unit and subunit levels. The key to maintaining operational discipline is to maintain trust throughout the chain of command. Junior officers and NCOs are faced with having to make tough decisions with respect to disciplinary questions, and they need to have absolute confidence that they will be backed up by the chain of command when they have done the "right thing." It is too easy for junior leaders to keep the peace within their small units either by ignoring minor disciplinary lapses or by resorting to informal corrective action. Winslow's (1997) study of the Canadian Airborne Regiment in Somalia points out numerous examples of both methods and the possible tragic results.

Prior to leaving for Cyprus, I had established some simple disciplinary guidelines for the unit leadership. Given the static nature of the operation, and the risks presented by boredom, I "laid down the law" concerning negligent weapons discharges and sleeping on duty. Early in the tour, a young Reserve force soldier was caught sleeping in his observation post by a junior NCO. It would have been a simple matter for the NCO involved to take informal action to correct the situation. But the commanding officer had set the policy, and the NCO involved had the duty to enforce it as stated. Even though the soldier involved was not a criminal or a disciplinary problem, I had little choice but to sentence him to detention once he was found guilty. Despite the fact that both the junior NCO and I had options, and neither of us wanted to see the soldier in a cell, our duty was clear. The NCO had to enforce the unit policy to the best of his ability, and I had to back him up. The signal to the soldiers was clear and simple: we meant it! The signal to the unit's officers and NCOs was also clear: if you did the right thing, the chain of command would back you up.

9. NOT THE SAME AS WAR

The dominant fact that commanders and leaders need to bear in mind is that a peace support operation is not the same as war. The nation's survival is not at stake, nor is the kill-or-be-killed imperative a major factor for maintaining combat motivation. The mandate may well be vague, the rules of engagement unwieldy, and the definition of victory elusive. Soldiers must be motivated by their sense of professionalism and their personal pride in their skills. Commanders, in turn, are responsible for ensuring that the troops are given the tools to do the job, that the rules are clearly explained, and that every effort is made to provide an appropriate level of force protection. Soldiers deployed on peace support operations commonly express feelings of frustration with the mission; the natural fear of injury or death; uncertainty as to the reaction of the politicians and the media to the use of force; deployment stress caused by family or financial problems; and a strong sense that their efforts are not really appreciated by the Canadian public and political leadership. Except for the stress that results from the violence of the environment and the natural fear of death, commanders and leaders in Canada's earlier wars did not have to deal with most of these stressors in real time. For example, in World War II, communication with families at home was maintained by mail—mail that was censored in-theatre and moved across the Atlantic by ship. In Cyprus, we paid for our own phone calls home; most of us spoke to our families once a week. In Bosnia five years later, large numbers of soldiers could call home daily, and many had access to Internet e-mail. At the same time, modern communications means that the soldiers know exactly what the media are or are not saying about their performance and the value of the mission. The end result is that soldiers remain connected to their families; the downside is that, in some cases, problems back home can cause real stress that affects individual performance. I remember being taught, as a young officer cadet, that providing one hot meal a day, ensuring that the troops had clean, dry socks, and getting the mail up with the rations were the important aspects of maintaining morale. It's a little more complicated than that today!

10. CONCLUSION

It is clear to me that certain aspects of the Army's leadership theory and training need to be modernized to reflect the realities of Canadian society. Although there is no doubt concerning the essentiality of the values and military ethos described in *Canada's Army* (Canada, 1998, Chapter 2), the real test is how they are applied to leadership in today's context. It is, in my view, essential that the Army better define the elements of combat motivation, cohesion, and leadership in peace support operations. This is a necessary precursor to a review of army leadership doctrine as well as educational and training methods. A multidisciplinary partnership between the Canadian Army and the research community needs to be established to accomplish this.

It is also clear that both theory and practice need to consider the cultural and demographic "facts of life" within Canadian society and Canada's army. In the first instance, it is evident that Canadian society is no longer willing to accept an army made up of soldiers who "[swear] continuously, [drink] regularly and [do] not give a damn about social norms from the civilian world" (Davis, 1997, p. 16). This is not to say that soldiers should become "civilians in uniform" or that the leadership should try to impose unrealistic standards of moral behaviour on the troops. Just the opposite: leaders must strive to ensure that our core values and military ethos contribute to an army that can be successful in peace *and* in war. The personnel and discipline policies that result must be appropriate to an army of experienced soldiers who are ready to take on a greater share of responsibility. There can be only one goal: the development of a Canadian Army that lives according to the "warrior's honour" code and reflects the values of Canadian society.

11. REFERENCES

Baynes, J. (1967). *Morale—A study of men and courage: The Second Scottish Rifles at the Battle of Neuve Chapelle, 1915*. London, U.K.: Cassell.

Bellamy, C. (1996). *Knights in white armour: The new art of war and peace*. London, U.K.: Hutchinson.

Bercuson, D. (1996). *Significant incident: Canada's Army, the Airborne and the murder in Somalia*. Toronto: McClelland and Stewart.

Blackburn, G. G. (1997). *Where the hell are the guns?* Toronto: McClelland and Stewart.

Canada. (1997). *Dishonoured legacy: The lessons of the Somalia affair—Report of the Commission of Inquiry into the Deployment of Canadian Forces to Somalia*. Ottawa: Commission of Inquiry into the Deployment of Canadian Forces to Somalia [Somalia Inquiry].

Canada. (1998). *Canada's Army* (CFP 300/B-GL-300-000/FP-000). Ottawa: Department of National Defence.

Davis, J. R. (1997). *The sharp end: A Canadian soldier's story*. Vancouver: Douglas and McIntyre.

Ignatieff, M. (1998). *The warrior's honour*. Toronto: Viking Press.

Lewis, P. (1996). A short history of United Nations peacekeeping. In B. Benton (Ed.), *Soldiers for peace: Fifty years of United Nations peacekeeping* (pp. 24–41). New York: Facts on File.

MacKenzie, L. (1993). *Peacekeeper: The road to Sarajevo*. Vancouver: Douglas and McIntyre.

Moskos, C., & Woods, F. (1988). *The military: More than just a job?* Washington, DC: Pergamon-Brassey's.

O'Hara, J. (1998, April 13). Fighting mad: Canada's troops are suffering—and angry. *Maclean's, 111*(15), 14–18.

Stewart, R. (1994). *Broken lives*. London, U.K.: HarperCollins.

Winslow, D. (1997). *The Canadian Airborne Regiment in Somalia: A socio-cultural inquiry*. Ottawa: Commission of Inquiry into the Deployment of Canadian Forces to Somalia.

ESTABLISHING COMMAND INTENT—A CASE STUDY
The Encirclement of the Ruhr, March 1945

LIEUTENANT COLONEL (RETIRED) WILLIAM M. CONNOR[1]

1. INTRODUCTION

In March 1945, during the campaign against Germany, the United States Army conducted an operation that showed its proficiency: the encirclement of the Ruhr.[2] The establishment of command intent was central to the success of this operation. While U.S. Army doctrine at the time did not explicitly describe the meaning and composition of the term *command intent* (sometimes also called *commander's intent*), the conduct of this operation demonstrated an understanding of these concepts that had been acquired through practice at all tactical levels. The encirclement of the Ruhr, conducted both to deny resources to the German army and to draw the remainder of the Germany army's forces to battle in the region's defence, had always been one

---

[1] The views expressed in this chapter are those of the author and do not necessarily represent the official policy or position of the U.S. Department of the Army, the U.S. Department of Defense, or the U.S. Government.

[2] An industrial region of roughly 16,000 km² (approximately 6,200 square miles) in northwest Germany (between the Lippe and Ruhr Rivers) that was strategically important for the German war material production system and for its steel, synthetic oil, and chemical industries.

LIEUTENANT COLONEL (RETIRED) WILLIAM M. CONNOR • *Combined Arms Doctrine Directorate, United States Army Command and General Staff College, Fort Leavenworth, Kansas, USA 66027*

The Human in Command: Exploring the Modern Military Experience,
edited by McCann and Pigeau, Kluwer Academic/Plenum Publishers, New York, 2000.

of the campaign's strategic objectives. However, the encirclement and its exact direction and force requirements were decided only as operations progressed (SHAEF, 1946).[3] Implicit command intent guided the tactical decisions made as the operation progressed and linked subordinates' exercise of initiative and coordination by tactical formations in the decentralized execution of operations. This decentralized execution of operations is the desired outcome of the mission command approach.

2. DOCTRINE

Mission command as an explicit philosophy of command and control was first enunciated as doctrine in a publication of the British Army (United Kingdom, 1995). Its clear antecedent was a German concept of command commonly called *Auftragstaktik*, explained by von Spohn (1907) and analyzed by Fitzgibbon (1990). The concept is widely known, although different organizations have interpreted it differently: the U.S. Navy and the U.S. Marine Corps have also adopted mission command into their command and control doctrine, albeit as *mission control* and *mission command and control*, respectively (United States, 1995, 1996).

> Mission Command is designed to achieve unity of effort at all levels; it depends on decentralization. It requires the development of trust and mutual understanding between commanders and subordinates throughout the chain of command, and timely and effective decision-making together with initiative (a quality of a commander) at all levels, the keys to "getting inside" the enemy's decision–action cycle. (United Kingdom, 1995, p. GL-8)

Mission command aims to accomplish missions through the decentralized execution of operations. The mechanism through which doctrine prescribes achieving these decentralized operations is subordinates' initiative.[4] To empower subordinates to use their initiative and to achieve unity of effort during the decentralized execution of operations, mission command further outlines major elements. The most salient of these are the commander's intent (United Kingdom, 1995) and orders structured as "mission-type orders" (United States, 1994). Trust and mutual understanding create the environment for subordinates' exercise of their initiative.

---

[3] For general histories of the encirclement of the Ruhr, see MacDonald (1973), Pogue (1954), Toland (1965), and Weigley (1981). The Combat Studies Institute prepared a study of the same operation (Connor, 1987) for HQ, TRADOC (Headquarters, U.S. Army Training and Doctrine Command), to support developing U.S. Army doctrine at the operational level of war.

[4] In this context, initiative is the subordinate's assumption of responsibility to decide on and initiate independent actions either (a) when his or her commander's concept of operations or order no longer applies or (b) when presented with an unanticipated opportunity that could lead to the accomplishment of the commander's intent. It is distinguished from tactical or operational initiative, which involves seizing and dictating the terms of action throughout the operation, forcing the enemy to react to the actions of the friendly forces. The former type of initiative is a function of the individual; the latter occurs through forces.

Common to both mission command and U.S. mission-type orders is the idea that orders should direct the subordinate unit to perform a mission without specifying how to accomplish that mission. Mission command emphasizes that such orders should contain the minimum of control measures so as not to unnecessarily limit the freedom of action of subordinates (United Kingdom, 1995). This stricture is also implicit in the concept of mission-type orders (United States, 1997a). Subordinates then decide how best to achieve the assigned mission within their delegated freedom of action.

Commander's intent is central to this doctrine. Specifically, the doctrine emphasizes the requirement for the subordinate to understand (a) the higher commander's intent and (b) the subordinate's responsibility to fulfill that intent. It also emphasizes the role of the commander's intent in achieving unity of effort within the operation and in focusing or disciplining subordinates' exercise of initiative (United Kingdom, 1995; United States, 1997b; see also Leser, 1997). U.S. doctrine also asserts the role of the commander's intent in guiding subordinates' decisions (unity of effort) in the absence of explicit orders (initiative). Thus, the commander's intent in mission command is the starting point for the subordinates' disciplined exercise of initiative in achieving decentralized execution of operations to accomplish missions.

> The Commander's Intent is a clear, concise statement of what the force must do to succeed with respect to the enemy and the terrain and to the desired end state. It provides the link between the mission and the concept by stating the key tasks that, along with the mission, are the basis for subordinates to exercise initiative when unexpected opportunities arise or when the original concept of operations no longer applies. (United States, 1997b, p. 5-9)

U.S. Army doctrine during World War II accorded well with mission command. The doctrine for operations stressed offensive action, although it also acknowledged that defensive actions would be necessary. For offensive operations during a war of movement, doctrine emphasized immediate orders and rapid action. Even in defensive missions, operations doctrine required maximum offensive actions for success. For both, it also specified superior mobility and surprise (United States, 1941).

> By the prompt exercise of initiative, endeavors must be made to deprive the enemy of his freedom of action and prevent the coordinated employment of his forces. . . . Opportunities for decisive action must be exploited immediately. . . . Open warfare requires the widest possible exercise of *initiative* by commanders of all echelons in the execution of the general mission assigned to the command. (United States, 1941, p. 113)

Pre-war doctrine on command also reflected characteristics and principles found in mission command.

> The criterion by which a commander judges the soundness of his own decision is whether it will further the intentions of the higher commander. Willingness to accept responsibility must not manifest itself in a disregard of orders on the basis of a mere probability of having a better knowledge of the situation than the higher commander. . . . [A]ny independence on the part of a subordinate commander must conform to the general plan for the unit as a whole. (United States, 1941, p. 24)

It emphasized the commander's responsibility for taking action in the absence of orders or in the event of situations no longer covered by orders. In both cases, however, the commander had to be guided by the "general plan of the operations or the mission of the whole command" (United States, 1941, p. 24). To ensure that subordinates understood the "general plan," doctrine noted the importance of personal conferences between higher commanders and their subordinates to keep the subordinates informed of the "plans and intentions of their superiors" (United States, 1941, pp. 24–25). This doctrine also urged commanders to use "simple and direct plans and methods" and to "communicate to subordinates clear and concise orders, which gives them freedom of action appropriate to their professional knowledge, to the situation, to their dependability, and to the team play desired" (United States, 1941, pp. 22, 29).

Doctrine cautioned staff officers to "prescribe only such details or methods of execution [in orders] as are necessary to insure that the actions of the subordinate unit concerned will conform to the plan of operations for the force as a whole" (United States, 1940, p. 49). There was, however, no specific requirement to write the commander's intent in the orders, nor was there anything specific in the pre-war doctrine about its content.

3. BACKGROUND

As early as May 1944, General Dwight D. Eisenhower's staff—Supreme Headquarters Allied Expeditionary Force (SHAEF)—had considered operations subsequent to the Allied landing on the continent of Europe. The final phase of these operations was crossing the Rhine River, with the primary attack north of the Ruhr and a secondary attack from the Frankfurt area joining the main effort in the vicinity of Kassel. The operation would then continue northeast to take Berlin, the capital of Germany (Eisenhower, 1970, vol. 4, p. 1933; SHAEF, 1946).

The failure of the German Ardennes counteroffensive in December 1944 provided an opportunity to defeat the German army west of the Rhine. Looking beyond that phase to the next, SHAEF planners identified main crossing sites between north of the Ruhr and around Frankfurt. Eisenhower approved the main attack in the north across the Rhine River against the Ruhr, but added a second major crossing in the south by forces in excess of the main effort. The potential missions included advancing against Berlin, north to cut communications with the Ruhr, or east toward Leipzig (Eisenhower, 1970, vol. 4, pp. 2232–2234, 2238; MacDonald, 1973, pp. 2–5; Pogue, 1954, p. 405; SHAEF, 1946).

Operations aimed at closing to the Rhine River and defeating the German army commenced February 8 in the north and continued in succession to the south. First (U.S.) Army made a crossing of opportunity over the Rhine River at Remagen on March 7. General Eisenhower ordered General Omar Bradley, 12th Army Group commander, to build up the bridgehead and to be prepared to exploit that success without detracting from the main crossing in the north. Third (U.S.) Army then executed hasty crossings of the Rhine on March 22 at Oppenheim and near Boppard. Thus, by the night of March 23–24, there were two major crossings in the south

(MacDonald, 1973, pp. 135–293; HQ, First U.S. Army, After-Action Report, 1–31 March 1945).[5]

One of the two encircling forces, VII Corps in First (U.S.) Army, had been activated on November 26, 1940, at Fort McClellan, Alabama; on January 3, 1941, Colonel J. Lawton Collins, an impatient infantryman eager to escape staff work in Washington, had arrived as the corps chief of staff. He and the corps had initially trained and participated in all the General Headquarters maneuvers from June through September 1941, and defended the west coast of the United States against invasion. Collins commanded 25th Infantry Division in Hawaii, Guadalcanal, and New Georgia during 1942 and 1943, while VII Corps deployed to England in 1943, arriving on October 6, 1943, and was assigned to First Army. Now a major general, Collins returned to command VII Corps on February 12, 1944, training and preparing the corps and its divisions for the invasion of Europe, code-named Operation Overlord.

VII Corps had covered nearly 1,000 km (621 miles) from Utah Beach in Normandy and had taken 140,000 German prisoners by the time it moved its divisions into the Remagen bridgehead on March 14, 1945 (MacDonald, 1973, pp. 323–324). By August 25, it had led the breakout at St. Lo, stopped the German counterattack at Mortain, and crossed the Seine River. VII Corps then exploited its success, working its way toward the German border during early September; the corps took nearly 25,000 German prisoners in the Mons pocket alone. Three months of fighting at the German West Wall included actions in the Huertgen Forest, the seizure of Aachen, and finally penetrating the West Wall by December 16. The German Ardennes offensive next involved Major General Collins and VII Corps when Britain's Field Marshal Sir Bernard L. Montgomery specifically requested them. VII Corps concluded this operation successfully by January 17 (Collins, 1979, pp. 198–297: Weigley, 1981, pp. 538–566).

Collins's staff served with him almost without interruption through the campaign—on average, there were two incumbents for each of the primary staff positions (that is, chief of staff, and G-1 through G-4). Among his principal staff officers was the corps chief of staff, Colonel Richard C. Partridge, who had served first as the corps G-3 during the invasion. Collins replaced the incumbent corps G-3 with Partridge; later, in Normandy, he sent Partridge, an artillery officer, to command an infantry regiment. Partridge was wounded shortly after that, but he returned to duty, and Collins brought him back to VII Corps as its chief of staff, in which position he served until the end of the war. Collins also replaced the original corps artillery commanding general (CG) with Brigadier General (later General and vice chief of staff of the U.S. Army) Williston D. Palmer, who commanded for the duration of the campaign. Among the divisions of VII Corps, 3d Armored Division (3AD), along with its commander, Major General Maurice Rose, had served the longest in VII Corps. Of the others, 104th Infantry Division (104ID) had arrived in-theatre only the preceding fall, but Major General Terry de la Mesa Allen, one of the U.S. Army's most

---

[5] The U.S. Army documents, such as After-Action Reports, cited throughout this chapter do not appear individually in the References list following the chapter. All such documents are archived at the Combined Arms Research Library, U.S. Army Command and General Staff College, Fort Leavenworth, Kansas, USA.

dynamic trainers and division commanders, commanded it. Also, 1st Infantry Division had seen lengthy service with VII Corps, dating back to the breakout from Normandy (Collins, 1979, pp. 198–297). During the European campaign, VII Corps issued only twenty field orders, or an average of two per month, to control operations; many of these simply "confirm[ed] oral orders CG VII Corps."[6]

4. PLANNING

SHAEF directed the encirclement of the Ruhr; 12th Army Group and Ninth and First (U.S.) Armies planned it; and XIX and VII Corps of those armies, respectively, and 2d Armored Division (2AD) and 3AD from within those corps, executed it. (Although 21st Army Group commanded Ninth Army, they did not really embrace the encirclement, as the following text points out.) The seizure of the Ludendorff bridge at Remagen by First Army forces nearly two weeks before a deliberate crossing of the Rhine in the north created the opportunity for the double envelopment. But it was not certain when another crossing, especially at Eisenhower's preferred location for the secondary crossing in the south, would occur. With the crossing of Third (U.S.) Army forces (also under 12th Army Group) in the south, however, the shape of the plan formed. Complicating matters was the fact that 12th Army Group did not control both Ninth and First Armies. It controlled only First Army, while 21st Army Group controlled Ninth Army (Pogue, 1954, pp. 417–426).

21st Army Group directed crossings in the north by Second (British) Army north of the key communications centre of Wesel and by Ninth (U.S.) Army south of it, securing a firm bridgehead, and developing operations aimed at isolating the Ruhr and at penetrating deeper into Germany. Ninth Army was instructed to cross the Rhine River south of Wesel, protect 21st Army Group's right flank, and develop a bridgehead south of the Lippe River. In the second phase of operations, Ninth Army was to continue protecting the bridgehead's southern portion and to pass a corps through Second Army's right flank to advance and secure the Hamm–Muenster line. Ninth Army decided to use XVI Corps to cross and establish the beachhead and to use XIX Corps to expand the bridgehead to the east. XIII Corps was to hold the west bank of the Rhine until relieved (HQ, Ninth U.S. Army, After-Action Report, 1–31 March 1945).

South of the Ruhr, First (U.S.) Army's participation was limited until Third (U.S.) Army's crossings of opportunity (from March 22–24, 1945) effected the secondary crossing in the area that Eisenhower had desired from the start. SHAEF then directed a major thrust to meet 21st Army Group in the vicinity of Kassel–Paderborn. 12th Army Group directed First and Third Armies first to link up in the Hanau–Giessen area and then to drive north or northeast to join with 21st Army Group. First Army would then link up with 21st Army Group forces (HQ, 12th Army Group, G-3 Reports, 25 March–5 April 1945). Thus, the balance between the encirclement's northern and southern arms was changing.

---

[6] One of the orders prepared by VII Corps for this operation, Field Order 18, was included as a historical vignette in the 1997 edition of FM 101-5, *Staff organization and operations* (United States, 1997b).

SHAEF's location at Reims precluded close control and coordination of the two army groups. Moreover, 12th Army Group was also badly located, with no headquarters farther forward than nearly 100 miles (approximately 160 km) from the Rhine (MacDonald, 1973, pp. 339–340). When rapid movement started, therefore, it would not be able to respond to changing events with sufficient alacrity. The position of 21st Army Group between SHAEF and Ninth (U.S.) Army also added to the command and control problems. The initial directive from Montgomery to Ninth Army, for example, did not mention any linkup with First (U.S.) Army or any such contingency; nevertheless, Lieutenant General William Simpson, commanding Ninth Army, deployed his forces to execute just such a mission (Pogue, 1954, p. 430; HQ, Ninth U.S. Army, After-Action Report, 1–31 March 1945).

General Eisenhower commanded ninety divisions organized into three army groups and nine armies.[7] Sixty of these divisions were infantry, twenty-five were armoured, and five were airborne (MacDonald, 1973, p. 322; Weigley, 1981, p. 668). The supply problems that had halted the Allied offensive drive the previous fall would not recur. The ports of Antwerp and Marseilles now received adequate supplies for all three army groups. Railways had been repaired or constructed up to the Rhine, and pipelines had been laid to supplement them. Highway transport assets now existed to provide support to forward units east of the Rhine. In addition, aerial resupply aircraft airlifted supplies forward and evacuated casualties on return flights (MacDonald, 1973, pp. 324–328; Ruppenthal, 1959, pp. 367–389, 405–458; SHAEF, 1945).

The German army that opposed this overall force consisted nominally of 60 divisions, but its effective strength was equivalent to only about 26 divisions, all short of equipment, ammunition, and supplies. Nor would these shortages be made good, for German industrial production had finally peaked and was now declining. Just as surely, the quality of personnel replacements was declining. Moreover, the Ruhr could not sustain the German forces defending it, because it merely produced basic goods and materials for final assembly or manufacture into battle matériel elsewhere in Germany. The shortages rendered German tactical doctrine irrelevant or ineffective (MacDonald, 1973, pp. 301–302, 335–339; Pogue, 1954, pp. 427–429).

5. OPERATIONS

The encirclement of the Ruhr occurred in phases, initiated by 21st Army Group's crossing of the Rhine in the north. The first phase, which took place March 24–29, 1945, in the north and March 25–28 in the south, established army group

---

[7] The army groups' composition was as follows: 21st Army Group comprised First (Canadian) Army, Second (British) Army, and Ninth (U.S.) Army; 12th Army Group comprised First (U.S.) Army, Third (U.S.) Army, and Fifteenth (U.S.) Army (the latter army formed especially for occupation duties in Germany behind First and Third Armies); and 6th Army Group comprised First (French) Army and Seventh (U.S.) Army. Ninth (U.S.) Army was eventually placed under 12th Army Group as well. In addition, Eisenhower commanded First Allied Airborne Army, consisting of five airborne divisions; this army was never assigned to an Army Group, although one of the divisions—XVIII Airborne Corps' 17th (U.S.) Airborne Division—ultimately became part of 21st Army Group's Second (British) Army.

bridgeheads and penetrated German defences. The second, March 30–April 1 in the north and March 29–April 1 in the south, consisted of exploitation and linkup. The third, April 1–4 in both sectors, involved consolidation and continuation of operations.

Collins's command techniques emphasized and supported the exercise of initiative by his subordinates. When he received a mission, he first conducted a mission analysis to determine whether he needed further information or clarification. He emphasized maintaining a continuous mental estimate of the situation, which he brought into focus with a new mission. His decisions about an operation included the immediate objectives and the more distant objectives, the basic scheme of maneuver, and the zones of action. Before issuing a written order, he first made an oral presentation to and held a discussion with his major subordinate commanders, preferably in a group but individually if necessary. He personally outlined his principal decisions, important enemy dispositions, and principal terrain features. Only after this oral presentation and discussion did he issue a written order; however, his oral orders and decisions initiated action. He emphasized the importance of such discussions, stating that orders should not be issued without prior warning or consultation with major subordinate commanders. He cautioned against allowing this process to become a "council of war," and he expected subordinates to participate in order to obtain clarification and coordination among their actions before they commenced their own planning. If he could not assemble his major subordinate commanders, he visited them individually as time permitted, with priority given to the commander who would be making his main effort (Collins, 1966, pp. 3–8). It was not unusual for these visits to take place on a strip of straight road where Collins could land in a Piper Cub aircraft (Collins, 1979, p. 313).

During operations, Collins personally visited major subordinate units to obtain information on enemy reactions and on major difficulties encountered by those subordinates. He gave priority to the subordinate units that were conducting the main effort, and he sent general and special staff officers to visit the other subordinate units; these officers reported matters of a critical nature within their areas of authority to the corps chief of staff. Collins usually received an early update at his headquarters and then spent most of the day in the field. He first visited the units that were conducting the operations of the greatest importance, checking with their commanders face to face on the battle's progress. If necessary, he made on-the-spot changes to details or concepts. He did not restrict himself to the major subordinate units' headquarters: he also visited units two or three echelons down. An aide always accompanied Collins, noting any changes he made in instructions. When Collins returned to VII Corps headquarters, the notes were typed up, and Collins assembled with the staff after supper to review the day's events and the changes that he had directed. Following coordination within the staff of the changes Collins had directed and of any other changes needed to support those directions, the G-3 prepared and distributed a daily operations memorandum (OPNS MEMO) confirming Collins's oral instructions and adding any other information or instructions developed in the evening staff meeting. Collins disdained the approach of conducting operations solely from the command post (Collins, 1966, pp. 13–18).

5.1. Operations: First Phase

In the first phase in the north (see Figure 1), Ninth (U.S.) Army's XVI Corps established the bridgehead through which Ninth Army's XIX Corps moved in the second phase. At 1800 hours on March 23, artillery fire and diversionary attacks commenced in support of the crossing of the Rhine. By nightfall on March 24, XVI Corps divisions had crossed and pushed inland 3 miles (4.8 km), joined their bridgeheads, and nearly achieved a breakthrough—one that the Germans viewed as the most serious threat to their defence (HQ, Ninth U.S. Army, After-Action Report, 1–31 March 1945). The German command reacted to the Allied moves. They committed 2d Parachute Division, which had been positioned just south of the American crossing. The terrain and road net east of the American landing sites favoured the defence, and by nightfall on March 25, elements of 116th Panzer Division and another division had entered the fight south of the Lippe River. By the morning of March 26, these German actions had prevented an American breakout (HQ, Ninth U.S. Army, G-2 After-Action Report, 16–31 March 1945). On March 28, however, just to the north, paratroopers from 17th (U.S.) Airborne Division[8] mounted tanks that belonged to the British 6th Guards Armoured Brigade and advanced 17 miles (27 km), outflanking the forces opposing Ninth Army. Now XIX Corps could cross the Rhine River, start progressing north of the Lippe River, and outflank the defences facing XVI Corps to the south. But XIX Corps could not complete its concentration and move until March 30 (HQ, Ninth U.S. Army, After-Action Report, 1–31 March 1945; MacDonald, 1973, pp. 302–320).

The attack in the south commenced on March 25, initiated by First (U.S.) Army forces that were in contact with the enemy; the Allied forces achieved solid initial successes that day. First Army's VII Corps passed the enemy's main defensive positions, with 3AD leading the VII Corps attack and 104ID following it (HQ, VII Corps, 23 March 1945, Field Order 18; HQ, VII Corps, June 1945, OPNS MEMO 181). In the centre of First Army, III Corps gained only 7 to 8 km (4 to 5 miles), but its 7th Armored Division (7AD) was ordered for commitment the next day. On the right of First Army, the V Corps attack gained a road junction leading to the linkup point with Third (U.S.) Army (HQ, 12th Army Group, Letter of Instructions Number Eighteen, 25 March 1945; HQ, First U.S. Army, After-Action Report, 1–31 March 1945; HQ, VII Corps, After-Action Report, 1–31 March 1945). By March 25, 1945, General Eisenhower had decided to isolate the Ruhr from the north and south by encirclement, with the junction point being the Kassel–Paderborn area; to reduce the encircled forces; and to prepare for further advance into Germany (Eisenhower, 1970, vol. 4, pp. 2349, 2354; Pogue, 1954, pp. 434–436; SHAEF, 1946).

The next day, in VII Corps, 3AD advanced nearly half the distance to the Dill River, taking Altenkirchen, its initial objective. III Corps advanced nearly 50 km (31 miles) in the centre, and V Corps reached the town of Limburg and the Lahn River. On March 27, the pace of the attack accelerated: 3AD drove nearly 35 km (22 miles)

---

[8] From XVIII Airborne Corps, one of five airborne divisions that constituted First Allied Airborne Army, the ninth of the armies under Eisenhower's command and the only one not attached to an army group; after the linkup, 17th Airborne Division became part of Second (British) Army.

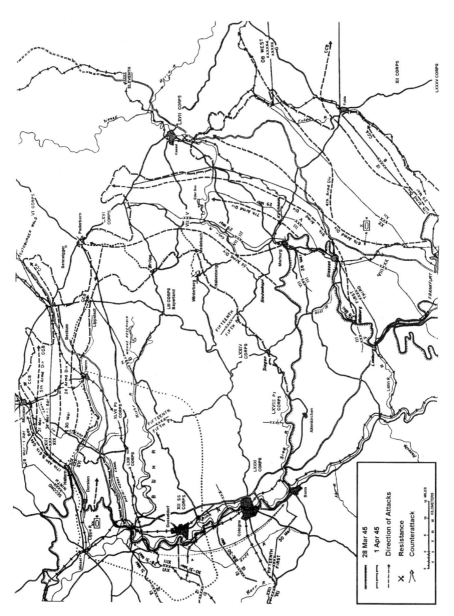

FIGURE 1. Encircling the Ruhr.

in the north, crossing the Dill River in two places, while 7AD of III Corps crossed the Dill River in four places. Most important, 9th Armored Division of V Corps linked up with Third (U.S.) Army on March 28, just as Ninth (U.S.) Army's attack stalled in the north. Nor was this the only good news of the day in the southern breakout, for 3AD had exploited its crossing of the Dill River another 35 km (22 miles) to Marburg (HQ, VII Corps, After-Action Report, 1–31 March 1945; HQ, First U.S. Army, After-Action Report, 1–31 March 1945). The initial phase of the southern part of the encirclement was now ended also (HQ, First U.S. Army, After-Action Report, 1–31 March 1945; HQ, VII Corps, After-Action Report, 1–31 March 1945; HQ, 12th Army Group, G-3 Reports, 25 March–5 April 1945).

5.2. Operations: Second Phase

By March 28, 1945, 21st Army Group had made advances of 25 km (15.5 miles) by Ninth (U.S.) Army and nearly 50 km (31 miles) by the British 6th Guards Armoured Brigade and 17th (U.S.) Airborne Division, immediately north of Ninth Army. But XIX Corps could not attack until March 30, so the only possibility for exploitation on March 29 came in the south. In 12th Army Group, First (U.S.) Army had advanced 100 km (62 miles) and formed, with Third (U.S.) Army, a bridgehead that was 150 km (93 miles) wide in terrain that was not favourable to the offence (HQ, 12th Army Group, G-3 Reports, 25 March–5 April 1945; Eisenhower, 1970, vol. 4, p. 2364; SHAEF, 1946). 12th Army Group directed First Army to link up with 21st Army Group forces at Paderborn (HQ, 12th Army Group, Letter of Instructions Number Nineteen, 28 March 1945). First Army then directed VII Corps (already the inner corps) to make the main effort, supported by V Corps on its right, or outer, flank. III Corps was to support VII Corps directly on its right, but it was pinched out and held in reserve (HQ, First U.S. Army, After-Action Report, 1–31 March 1945).

VII Corps had only 3AD and 104ID available to make the effort, and the assigned objective was more than 100 km (62 miles) away. Nevertheless, VII Corps directed 3AD to reach Paderborn in one day's time (HQ, VII Corps, 29 March 1945, Field Order 19). These orders were received at about 2200 hours on March 28, and the attack began at 0600 hours on March 29, 1945. However, the personal reconnaissance of the lead force, starting at 0400 hours, got 3AD off to a good start for what would be First (U.S.) Army's longest single-day advance in the European campaign: 110 to 150 km (68 to 93 miles) by road. Indeed, the only significant problem occurred in the vicinity of Brilon, some 40 km (25 miles) from the advance, when soldiers discovered a warehouse full of champagne. They finally halted 25 km (15.5 miles) short of the division's objective, Paderborn, at 2200 hours that evening, amid reports of possible resistance ahead (HQ, VII Corps, G-3 Periodic Reports, 25 March–5 April 1945; HQ, VII Corps, After-Action Report, 1–31 March 1945; HQ, First U.S. Army, After-Action Report, 1–31 March 1945; Barnwell, 1947; United States, 1946).

The next day, the German army defended Paderborn using the elements of three major formations. These forces held 3AD's lead elements 10 km (6 miles) from Paderborn that day, and the division commander, Major General Maurice Rose, was killed in action late that afternoon (United States, 1946). VII Corps also received intelligence indicating that German counterattack forces were building around Winterberg, southeast of Paderborn. 104ID took the road junctions of Hallenberg, Medebach, and Brilon, while 1st Infantry Division began moving north to hold the area between 9th Infantry Division, attached from III Corps, and 104ID (HQ, VII Corps, After-Action Report, 1–31 March 1945; HQ, VII Corps, G-3 Periodic Reports, 25 March–5 April 1945; HQ, VII Corps, June 1945, OPNS MEMO 183).

German attacks began on March 31 against 104ID. These attacks, the increasing resistance around Paderborn, the 3AD reorganization necessitated by Major General Rose's death, and the need to prepare a coordinated attack caused the VII Corps commander to contact Ninth (U.S.) Army's commander directly to suggest a change in the linkup point. Based on the progress of XIX Corps and its 2d Armored Division (2AD) since the night of March 29, the two commanders agreed to link up at the village of Lippstadt, halfway between Paderborn and 2AD's lead elements (HQ, VII Corps, After-Action Report, 1–31 March 1945; HQ, VII Corps, G-3 Periodic Reports, 25 March–5 April 1945).

The second phase of the encirclement in the north really began with the dash of the British 6th Guards Armoured Brigade and the U.S. 17th Airborne Division on March 28, 1945 (see Figure 1). Montgomery ordered exploitation from the 21st Army Group bridgehead and advance to the Elbe with Ninth (U.S.) Army and Second (British) Army abreast. He expanded Ninth Army's sector to north of the Lippe River in the area of the latest advance, modified the use of the Rhine bridges and road net in the vicinity of Wesel to help Ninth Army, and assigned Ninth Army the tasks of linking up with First (U.S.) Army and reducing the Ruhr (MacDonald, 1973, pp. 319–320, 357–359).

Lieutenant General Simpson assigned the breakout and linkup with First (U.S.) Army to XIX Corps, which already had one combat command (CCA) of 2AD east of the Rhine in response to oral orders from him. XIII Corps was to regroup and follow XIX Corps over the Rhine on March 31, 1945. XVI Corps was to defend against German forces in the Ruhr from the Rhine to Paderborn, protect the Ninth (U.S.) Army's right flank, and cooperate in reducing the Ruhr pocket (HQ, Ninth U.S. Army, After-Action Report, 1–31 March 1945; HQ, 2d Armored Division, After-Action Report, March 1945).

XIX Corps lost no time in executing these orders, but the density of forces in the bridgehead slowed down its introduction into operations. On March 27, CCA, 2AD, had moved east of the Rhine; on March 28, it had moved north of the Lippe. The rest of the division followed CCA on March 28, and XIX Corps' 83d Infantry Division moved up preparatory to crossing the Rhine. By 2100 hours on March 29, 2AD had attacked in the vicinity of Haltern. During March 30, the division's elements crossed the Dortmund–Ems Canal approximately 25 km (15.5 miles) from Haltern and advanced another 25 km (15.5 miles) to the east, enveloping the division's objective, Hamm, from the north. There was some resistance in the southern sector, but the advance was not held up significantly; indeed, finding crossings over the Dortmund–Ems Canal created the most significant delay (HQ, Ninth U.S. Army, After-Action Report, 1–31 March 1945; HQ, 2d Armored Division, After-Action Report, March 1945).

By nightfall the next day, the division had cut the Ruhr–Berlin autobahn east of Hamm. With this success, approximately 65 km (40 miles) from its starting point, the division commander sent one force to seize and block the pass through the Teutoburger Wald, some 40 km (25 miles) further east; it had achieved its mission by the following morning. At the same time, Ninth (U.S.) Army received a telephone call from VII Corps to the south outlining the problems at Paderborn and suggesting linkup at Lippstadt, midway between Beckum, where 2AD had cut the autobahn, and Paderborn. CCB moved out at 0150 hours on April 1, 1945, in response to Lieutenant General Simpson's orders to conduct the linkup, while the forces of CCA advanced east to the pass through the Teutoburger Wald. CCB's right column initially had the mission of effecting the linkup, but enemy resistance held it up, so CCB's left column, which had completed the capture of Beckum, received the task (HQ, Ninth U.S. Army, After-Action Reports, 1–31 March and 1–30 April 1945; HQ, Ninth U.S. Army, G-3 After-Action Report, 012400–152400 April 1945; HQ, XIX Corps, After-Action Report, 012400–302400 April 1945; HQ, 2d Armored Division, After-Action Reports, March and April 1945).

On April 1, 1945, the commanding general of VII Corps sent a force from 3AD to Lippstadt (HQ, VII Corps, June 1945, OPNS MEMO 184). Because this force was also part of the planned coordinated attack on Paderborn, the attacks started half an hour late. This attack on Paderborn nevertheless succeeded; among the prizes taken were 136 German artillery pieces. Late in the day, that force, meeting weak resistance in its push west, made radio contact with elements of CCB, 2AD; by 1530 hours, the two had made physical contact at Lippstadt, closing the Ruhr pocket (HQ, VII Corps, After-Action Reports 1–31 March and 1–30 April 1945; HQ, VII Corps, G-3 Periodic Reports, 25 March–5 April 1945; HQ, 3d Armored Division, After-Action Report, 1–30 April 1945).

6. OUTCOME AND ANALYSIS

Although relieved the next day by 8th Armored Division of XVI Corps, CCA and 2AD would take nearly two days to fight their way through the pass at the Teutoburger Wald, by which time Ninth (U.S.) Army was under the command of 12th Army Group (HQ, Ninth U.S. Army, After-Action Report, 1–30 April 1945; HQ, 2d Armored Division, After-Action Report, April 1945). In the south, 3AD would also take nearly two days to reorganize to continue operations to the east (HQ, 3d Armored Division, After-Action Report, 1–30 April 1945). The encirclement's southern arm had covered nearly 300 km (186 miles) in the seven days since the breakout from the Remagen bridgehead, while its northern arm had covered about 100 km (62 miles), albeit in just three days (HQ, 12th Army Group, Report of Operations [Final After-Action Report], 31 July 1945).

Trapped in the Ruhr pocket were Germany's Army Group B, including Field Marshal Walther Model, Fifth Panzer and Fifteenth Armies and parts of First Parachute Army, seven corps, and nineteen divisions, as well as various antiaircraft and local defence troops, a total of nearly 350,000 troops. The reduction of the Ruhr pocket would take another two weeks to accomplish, consuming nearly eighteen divisions and leaving only eight divisions in Ninth and First (U.S.) Armies to advance to the east toward Berlin under the direction of 12th Army Group. The casualties were comparatively light for the encircling forces. They reported over 20,000 POWs processed through the cages, as well as 66 German tanks and assault guns and nearly 100 German artillery and antiaircraft artillery pieces destroyed. First Army took 197,374 POWs and killed or wounded another 50,000 Germans before entering the Ruhr pocket (HQ, 12th Army Group, Report of Operations [Final After-Action Report], 31 July 1945; HQ, First U.S. Army, Combat Operations Data, 1945; HQ, First U.S. Army, After-Action Report, 1–30 April 1945).

The Ruhr had been selected as an objective even before the Allies landed in Europe, and all major commanders appear to have understood this. Thus, the command intent was well established and understood for a long time by those who would have to act on it. The original concept in the campaign plan was modified to take advantage of two unexpectedly easy crossings of the Rhine in the south before the main effort began in the north. The encirclement was not spelled out at first, however. Instead, the orders simply called for the creation of a bridgehead in the north by Second (British) and Ninth (U.S.) Armies and in the south by First and Third (U.S.) Armies before attempting the linkup. The next modification came on March 28, when the success of First Army's breakout had become clear. Only then were the executing echelons finally given orders that would lead directly to the encirclement. Symptomatic of the understanding of the command intent was the inclusion of orders to 2AD in the north to link up with 12th Army Group forces, even though 21st Army Group's orders had not assigned that task.

The echelon that should have controlled the linkup forces during execution, 12th Army Group, could not do so for two reasons. First, part of the encircling force (2AD) came from another army group. Second, the tactical command post (CP) was located too far from the front to control the linkup. Although the planning echelons—Ninth and First (U.S.) Armies—were close enough to exercise control, neither army's headquarters crossed the Rhine. Only the corps headquarters did. The linkup was eventually effected between VII Corps and Ninth Army, principally on the initiative of Major General Collins, aided by artillery spotter planes at the end. This part of the operation was not very well carried out by higher echelons; rather, initiative at the executing level rescued the linkup.

Techniques that commanders developed during the campaign in fulfillment of the doctrine contributed to the exercise of initiative within subordinates' understanding of the command intent. Collins's practice of giving only one or two immediate objectives to each major subordinate command, along with a distant objective toward which to proceed without orders, allowed his subordinates freedom of action and exercise of initiative. The information from which Collins's subordinates could glean an understanding of command intent was probably communicated personally—for example, both during his initial briefing of his subordinates and during his daily visits to them.

The establishment of the command intent—encircling the Ruhr—enabled the forces on both sides of the encirclement to direct their efforts toward fulfilling that intent. Thus, on April 1, when 2AD found the task force that it had intended to use for the linkup engaged, it could direct another, less-engaged force to effect the linkup. Likewise, when the original concept of operations—meeting at Paderborn— no longer obtained, Collins proposed an alternative spot for the linkup. He further exercised personal initiative in communicating directly across an army group boundary to establish that linkup point. Finally, with elements of his corps defending at Winterberg, attacking at Paderborn, and moving to Lippstadt, Collins positioned himself with the task force from 3AD that was making the linkup—the main effort that day for his corps, First (U.S.) Army, and 12th Army Group. Subordinates' initiative in defending Winterberg and attacking Paderborn ensured success there, but those were now supporting efforts.

Using orders that fit the modern definition of "mission-type orders" further allowed subordinates' exercise of initiative. Collins's use of an immediate objective and a deeper objective in his orders to subordinates may constitute a form of implicit intent. Likewise, restricting his orders to one or two critical missions for each subordinate unit contributed to communicating an implicit intent. Finally, using face-to-face meetings with major subordinate commanders (or individual commanders) to issue orders allowed for the possibility that some form of intent would be communicated in those meetings. Collins's daily meetings with his subordinates would also have kept them abreast of any revisions of his intent, as well as of detailed, explicit instructions.

However, that exercise of initiative required coordination that would not stifle subordinates' exercise of initiative. The implicit command intent provided that essential element of coordination in the encirclement of the Ruhr. With the command intent as its guide, 3AD's operations could emphasize speed and distance in its advance from Marburg to Paderborn. When the lack of lateral communications hindered coordination between its subordinates, those subordinates had to take initiative to accomplish the mission and fulfill the command intent as they understood it. The establishment and understanding of command intent allowed 3AD to resume operations the day after Major General Rose was killed. It likewise guided other subordinate elements in VII Corps and other forces in their decisions and actions during the encirclement of the Ruhr.

The establishment of the commander's intent in this case study rested on a foundation of trust and mutual understanding within the chain of command. This trust was born of the experience and maturity of the teams created by the commanders involved during the campaign in Europe. At the higher levels, this trust and mutual understanding extended back before World War II. The generals had in many cases begun their acquaintance while training at the United States Military Academy in West Point, New York, and the U.S. Army's manageable size after World War I had allowed each of them to know nearly every officer in his own branch, as well as the outstanding ones in the other branches. They had also undergone similar schooling aimed at building a common doctrinal foundation among the Regular officers. Closer to home, the VII Corps staff and major subordinate commands also showed a long familiarity with each other. Thus, for example, Major General Collins trusted Colonel Partridge to run his CP smoothly while Collins was away from it; in addition, Collins delegated authority to his corps artillery commander and engineer officer to give orders in their areas to subordinate units without his prior approval.

Nor was this trust and mutual understanding merely a product of pre-war personal relationships and education. The U.S. Army in the European campaign became a learning organization, and both lessons learned and proven combat techniques were disseminated in a variety of forms. Army Ground Forces Observers analyzed combat operations that the War Department used for training in the continental United States and distributed the results of those analyses to forces in the field. In-theatre, since the ground forces were rarely pulled off-line for training, forces from the division level up prepared and distributed their own lessons learned and promulgated revised procedures for combat operations. This learning process appeared to create a common understanding, at least within the units of the field armies (Doubler, 1994).

7. CONCLUSIONS

The encirclement of the Ruhr accomplished the reduction of a major defensive position with far fewer casualties than either a frontal assault or a penetration would have produced. The forces on the other side of the Ruhr on April 1 were well placed to continue the advance; indeed, after consolidation that lasted until April 4, they gained 400 km (248 miles) or more (from the crossing of the Rhine to the final stopping point on the Elbe or the Mulde). This encirclement effectively destroyed the continuity of the German defence, by leaving only patchwork formations to stop the Allied forces and by leaving the German forces to the north and south with assailable flanks (MacDonald, 1973, pp. 373–406; Pogue, 1954, pp. 439–440).

While U.S. Army doctrine at the time did not explicitly define command intent or specify how and where it was to be communicated, it did place responsibility on subordinate commanders to determine an "intention" and to adjust their decisions and actions accordingly. Moreover, it emphasized the importance of subordinates' initiative during operations, and it specified that explicit and excessive tasks should be limited in orders to subordinates. Without explicit doctrine, subordinates' understanding and the establishment of command intent had to be implicit. The decisions and operations in the encirclement of the Ruhr exhibited that implicit understanding of and acting on intent. This case study corroborates Pigeau and McCann's (this volume, Chapter 12) paradigm of implicit intent, with a base of shared experience by the commanders before and during the war and within VII Corps during the campaign. Collins's command methods provided frequent opportunities for verbal and nonverbal interactions, supporting another Pigeau and McCann (this volume, Chapter 12) proposition. Thus, an implicit command intent contributed effectively to mission success.

The establishment of command intent provided both freedom of action for subordinates' initiative in the decentralized execution of operations and essential but minimum coordination of decisions and actions among the forces executing the encirclement of the Ruhr. While the commander's intent provides guidance for subordinates' initiative, it can and should also provide a framework for coordination of action leading to unity of effort. In fact, it constitutes a key coordinating role in the exercise of initiative. Again, Pigeau and McCann (this volume, Chapter 12) note that the conduct of decentralized operations relies very heavily on implicit intent.

The commander's intent by itself cannot achieve the decentralized execution of operations based on subordinates' exercise of disciplined initiative sought by the philosophy of mission command. It must be communicated through mission-type orders and founded on an environment of trust and mutual understanding. The commander also creates and maintains this climate before and during operations. Even if a commander assumes command during the conduct of operations, he or she still can and must create an environment of trust and mutual understanding. Also, as noted by Vogelaar and Kramer (this volume, Chapter 15), mission command requires a certain level of resources, a fact that may explain the lack of *Auftragstaktik* in German actions in this case.

The U.S. Army ended its European campaign with a superb example of successful decentralized execution of operations conducted using initiative combined with an understanding of the commander's intent. It would not rediscover the operation level of war until 1982 (United States, 1982).

8. REFERENCES

Barnwell, W. G. (1947). *Operations of the Third Armored Division in closing the Ruhr pocket.* Fort Leavenworth, KS: U.S. Army Command and General Staff College.

Collins, J. L. (1966). *Generalship study: Questionnaire prepared for a study of requirements of senior commanders for command–control support.* Washington, DC: Headquarters, Department of the Army.

Collins, J. L. (1979). *Lightning Joe: An autobiography.* Baton Rouge: Louisiana State University Press.

Connor, W. C. (1987). *Analysis of deep attack operations: The encirclement of the Ruhr, 24 March–1 April 1945.* Fort Leavenworth, KS: Combat Studies Institute, U.S. Army Command and General Staff College.

Doubler, M. D. (1994). *Closing with the enemy: How GI's fought the war in Europe, 1944–1945.* Lawrence, KS: University of Kansas Press.

Eisenhower, D. D. (1970). *The papers of Dwight David Eisenhower: Vols. 1–5. The war years* (Alfred D. Chandler, Jr., Ed.). Baltimore: Johns Hopkins University Press.

Fitzgibbon, S. S. (1990, April). Colonel von Spohn's "Art of Command." *British Army Review 91,* 7–11.

Leser, J. W. S. (1997, September–October). Initiative: The power behind intent. *Military Review 77*(5), 59–64.

MacDonald, C. B. (1973). *The last offensive.* Washington, DC: Office of the Chief of Military History.

Pogue, F. C. (1954). *The supreme command.* Washington, DC: Office of the Chief of Military History.

Ruppenthal, R. G. (1959). *Logistical support of the armies: Vol. 2. September 1944–May 1945.* Washington, DC: Office of the Chief of Military History.

SHAEF (Supreme Headquarters Allied Expeditionary Force). (1946). *A Report by the Supreme Commander to the Combined Chiefs of Staff on Operations in Europe of the Allied Expeditionary Force 6 June 1944–8 May 1945.* Washington, DC: SHAEF.

Toland, John. (1965). *The last 100 days.* New York: Random House.

United Kingdom. (1995). *Command* (Army Doctrine Publication, Vol. 2). London, U.K.: Ministry of Defence, Chief of the General Staff.

United States. (1940). *Staff officers' field manual: The staff and combat orders* (Field Manual 101-5). Washington, DC: War Department.

United States. (1941). *Field service regulations: Operations* (Field Manual 100-5). Washington, DC: War Department.

United States. (1946, May). *Operations of the First U.S. Army in encircling the Ruhr area, 25 Mar–1 Apr 45.* Fort Leavenworth, KS: U.S. Army Command and General Staff College.

United States. (1982). *Operations* (FM 100-5). Washington, DC: Department of the Army.

United States. (1994). *Department of Defense dictionary of military and associated terms* (Joint Publication 1-02). Washington, DC: Office of the Chairman of the Joint Chiefs of Staff.

United States. (1995). *Naval command and control* (Naval Doctrine Publication 6). Washington, DC: Department of the Navy.

United States. (1996). *Command and control* (Marine Corps Doctrine Publication 6). Washington, DC: U.S. Marine Corps.

United States. (1997a). *Operational terms and graphics* (Field Manual 101-5-1). Washington, DC: Department of the Army.

United States. (1997b). *Staff organization and operations* (Field Manual 101-5). Washington, DC: Department of the Army.

von Spohn, K. (1907). *The art of command* (British General Staff, Trans.). London, U.K.: Her Majesty's Stationery Office.

Weigley, R. F. (1981). *Eisenhower's lieutenants*. Bloomington: Indiana University Press.

CHAPTER 9

TIME, TEMPO, AND COMMAND

COLONEL J. SERGE LABBÉ

1. INTRODUCTION

Despite having recently adopted maneuver warfare and mission command as warfighting and command philosophies, many armies, including the Canadian Army, continue to support their commanders with decision-making processes that presume that time is a controllable commodity—that it can somehow be manipulated for one's use. However, this assumption runs counter to the reality of operations, where success is largely determined by a commander's ability to make decisions faster than the opponent and to take action as soon as possible.

Just as important, time is the essence of *tempo*—the rhythm or pace of activities in operations, relative to that of the enemy. Together, tempo, firepower, simultaneity, and surprise constitute the essential ingredients for attacking an opponent's cohesion and thus that opponent's will to fight. Tempo is a state of mind, and is a function of (a) the speed both of decision making and of plan execution, and (b) the speed of transition from the one activity to the other.

Applying tempo with a view to causing paralysis or inaction in an enemy (or belligerents) requires that commanders have both sufficient professional knowledge of the conduct of operations and sufficient field experience to exercise effective and timely military judgment based on an informed understanding of the situation—in short, a recognitive quality referred to as *intuition*.[1] The intuitive commander who

---

[1] Current British Army doctrine classifies "intuition" as "a *recognitive* quality, based on military judgement, which in turn rests on an informed understanding of the situation based on professional knowledge and experience" (United Kingdom, 1994b, p. 2-17). Rogers (1994) argues that "intuition is about sifting rapidly through your memory bank of past experiences in order to make decisions" (p. 41). This

COLONEL J. SERGE LABBÉ • *Plans and Policy Division, International Military Staff, North Atlantic Treaty Organization (NATO) Headquarters, Boulevard Léopold III, B-1110 Brussels, Belgium*

The Human in Command: Exploring the Modern Military Experience,
edited by McCann and Pigeau, Kluwer Academic/Plenum Publishers, New York, 2000.

uses mission command must be complemented by a staff with a similar mindset. Therein lies the challenge for our training philosophies and professional development institutions for the next century.

I will argue in this chapter that the manner in which decision-making aids are currently used by staffs to support their commanders mistakenly assumes an "ownership" of time and cannot therefore cope with the current and anticipated tempo of operations against asymmetrical[2] or even conventional threats. I will examine deficiencies in current practices and suggest that command in the information age will be supported effectively only by a command-driven training and professional development system—one that promotes both initiative and intuition, and that optimizes the human in command through the appropriate use of decision-making processes, together with a digitization strategy that addresses all the components of command.[3]

2. TIME

2.1. The Time-Competitiveness of Operations

Warfighting is and will continue to be "time-competitive." This reality is particularly exacerbated by developments in technology, which armies attempt to harness to "accelerate the pace of movement with unequalled velocity, and to maintain an unrelenting operational tempo" (Scales, 1997, p. 41). While the desire to enhance the tempo of operations against potential adversaries is a worthwhile goal, it is questionable whether commanders can maintain complete situational awareness through the fog and friction of conflict and whether their staffs are similarly capable of providing timely options for consideration.

This is not a new problem. In his article "Intuition: An Imperative of Command," Rogers (1994) compares the results of two reports assessing the speed of decision making:

> In a research opinion paper, "Decision Making Theory Applied to the Conditions of Ground Combat," produced for the Army in 1990, it was found that the time it took US division commanders to issue orders after mission receipt was on average 2-1/2 hours, with the maximum time being 5 hours. In 1980, BDM Corporation in the United States hosted a conference on tactical warfare. As part of the conference, two retired German generals from World War II, Hermann Balck and Friedrich Wilhelm von Mellenthin, were invited to develop a plan for the use of a US division in defence in the NATO context against a Soviet enemy. The report from the conference states

is consistent with research conducted by Fallesen (this volume, Chapter 13), which concludes that "[a] recognitional approach is desirable whenever decisions need to be made rapidly" (p. 191).

[2] Asymmetrical warfare (Matthews, 1998) is a term in common usage within the U.S. defence community. It is akin to maneuver warfare in that it seeks to exploit the weaknesses of potential adversaries while avoiding their strengths. Hence, it is not a new concept, but one attributed to the use of non-conventional means to pre-empt, disrupt, and/or dislocate opponents' strengths.

[3] The Canadian Army has two such components—the human and the doctrinal; the British Army has three (see footnote 4).

that the two generals accepted the challenge and goes on to say: "General von Mellenthin at one point turned to the American participants to announce that they would not take long. He observed that in Russia they normally had about five minutes to make such decisions." He went on to say that it took another ten minutes to issue the orders. (Rogers, 1994, p. 45)

Notwithstanding certain extenuating circumstances associated with this comparison, the German generals attributed the significant difference in the speed of decision making to *fingerspitzengefühl* ("fingertip feeling"). They were describing the process of intuitive decision making. However, just as revealing was the fact that in arriving at their decisions, neither general considered the element of time. This is contrary to the battle procedure espoused by the Canadian Army, wherein consideration and apportionment of time to the various levels of command is paramount (Canada, 1997). British Army doctrine is even more prescriptive:

> Thus a running check on the situation and the time in hand to make decisions, to complete planning and to issue orders must be maintained at every level of command. The *one third:two thirds rule*, whereby one level of command takes only one third of the *time remaining* before committal for decision-making and the issue of orders, is a good rule of thumb. In most circumstances it is advisable to conduct a preliminary analysis on the time in hand before the estimate process (including mission analysis) is initiated. Following this initial time analysis, time deadlines should be issued to the staff. (United Kingdom, 1994b, p. 8-5)

Such an approach to operations presupposes either an element of "ownership" of time—some form of control—or that time is infinite. In reality, a commander who wishes to get inside and stay inside the adversary's decision cycle must seek to accomplish all actions as quickly as possible. Staff systems that either ignore the time factor or assume that time is available in indefinite quantities cannot provide commanders with the products necessary to optimize the decision–action cycle; nor can they inculcate the requirement for intuitive, command-driven decision making.

When the Boyd decision–action cycle (Allard, 1996) is applied to history (Figure 1), the time-competitive nature of warfighting is readily obvious. Furthermore, if we accept the prognosis that in future operations, observations will be in real time, orientations will be continuous, and decisions will be taken immediately, it follows that commanders will need to act quickly (often in less than an hour), and to do so on a continual basis for the duration of a campaign or operation.

2.2. Risks and Potential Threats in the Information Age

Literature addressing future conflict confirms that the pace of the decision–action cycle will continue to accelerate. Furthermore, operational decision making will have to address the full spectrum of new forms of conflict, including asymmetrical threats. In this regard, Arquilla and Ronfeldt (1997), in their compendium of articles *In Athena's Camp: Preparing for Conflict in the Information Age*, provide a troubling insight into the risks and potential threats challenging commanders and staffs

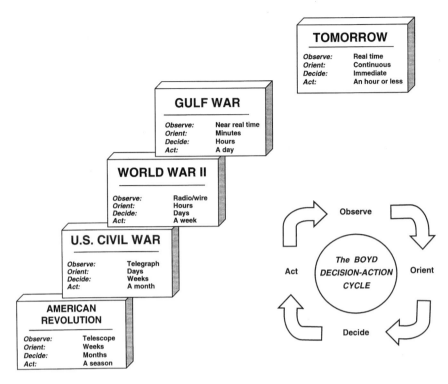

FIGURE 1. Time and command.

who employ traditional decision-making tools. Some of their recurring themes, listed below, involve matters that are certain to have an impact on the nature of future conflict:

- First, we live in an interwar period—between the Cold War and the cyber war, or "information age *blitzkrieg*"—where large-scale conventional conflicts are an aberration. Conflicts are localized and nonlinear in nature, and they are prosecuted by smaller, more lethal combat units, at intensified tempos. "Information, in all its dimensions, will enhance both the destructive and the disruptive capabilities of small units for all the services. . . . In the new epoch, decisive duels for the control of information flows will take the place of drawn-out battles of attrition or annihilation; the requirement to destroy will recede as the ability to disrupt is enhanced" (Arquilla & Ronfeldt, 1997, p. 2).

- Second, we have entered an age of global disorder, an age in which networked transnational criminal organizations, warlords, and other nonstate actors will exploit the information revolution to the detriment of nation–states and alliances. "Information-age threats are likely to be more diffuse, dispersed, nonlinear, and multidimensional than were industrial-age threats. This will place ... military (and police) forces under growing pressures to formulate new concepts for organization, doctrine, strategy, and tactics" (Arquilla & Ronfeldt, 1997, pp. 5–6).

- Finally, what is known as the Revolution in Military Affairs (RMA) is but an evolutionary first step toward Alvin and Heidi Toffler's "Third Wave" (Arquilla & Ronfeldt, 1997, p. xix) of conflict, which proffers that "conflicts will increasingly depend on, and revolve around, information and communications—[or] 'cyber' matters—broadly defined to include the related technological [and] organizational ... structures of a society" and "that the information revolution is not solely or mainly about technology; it is an organizational as well as a technological revolution" (Arquilla & Ronfeldt, 1997, pp. 4–5).

Although these insights may appear futuristic to more conventional policy makers and planners, they do corroborate the necessity of having to deal with sophisticated, networked, information-age adversaries—adversaries with organizations that are better structured than are traditional military hierarchies to respond to the rapid pace of information-based conflict. Not only will these adversaries challenge our own decision–action cycles, but their decision–action cycles will become increasingly difficult to penetrate. Hence the requirement to control both operational-level and tactical-level tempo.

3. TEMPO

The importance of tempo—the rhythm or pace of activities on operations, relative to that of the enemy—is grounded in the maneuverist approach to warfare, which several armies have recently adopted as the doctrinal basis for operations at all levels of conflict. One of the basic tenets of maneuver warfare is that it is often more desirable and less costly to attack an enemy's will (or its belief in its ability to win) through pre-emption, dislocation, and disruption than it is to physically destroy that enemy.

Furthermore, the combined effects of physical destruction *and* pre-emption, dislocation, and disruption will be more intense in the absence of cohesion. "At its simplest, cohesion is unity. It is a quality that binds together constituent parts, thereby providing resilience against dislocation and disruption. It minimises vulnerability to defeat in detail and the adverse effects of preemption" (United Kingdom, 1994a, p. 2-5). Given that "the qualities that promote cohesion are also those that if attacked destroy it" (United Kingdom, 1994a, p. 2-8), an adversary's cohesion is best attacked through tempo, firepower, simultaneity, and surprise.

Tempo has three elements: the speed of decision, the speed of execution, and the speed of the transition from one activity to the other. Although the last two elements imply the ability to physically maneuver more rapidly than an enemy, all three are heavily time-dependent, and all three imply an intellectual dimension—a state of mind that is implicit in the U.S. and British Army definitions of maneuver warfare. Rogers (1994) concludes that

> [i]n essence, manoeuvre warfare can be broken down into two components. First, the physical ability to move and apply force faster than the enemy, which in simple terms relates to equipment and technology, and second, . . . the speed of decision-making. If all things are equal, then decision-making relative to the enemy becomes all important. (p. 41)

Thus tempo is a vital component of maneuver warfare and is directly affected by the attitude that both commanders and staffs have toward decision-making processes.

4. COMMAND

4.1. Current Practices

Despite significant technological advances aimed both at enhancing commanders' situational awareness and at accelerating the decision–action cycle, the continued staff use of time-consuming strategies for aiding decision making runs contrary to the precepts of maneuver warfare and mission command. There are four main reasons for this situation: corporate views on initiative, the manner in which decision-making aids are used, digitization strategies, and training and professional development philosophies.

Professional armies in peacetime tend to develop a corporate consciousness that suppresses initiative in training and therefore in operations. An officer who touts the status quo and solves problems in accordance with established procedures is a desirable commodity. Yet a military culture that rewards success only through promotion, while at the same time discouraging innovative risk-taking—or even the questioning of a superior's decision—may not encourage the type of behaviour necessary for the successful prosecution of operations.

Colonel Douglas Macgregor (1997) quotes a former senior observer/controller at the National Training Center at Fort Irwin, California, who states that "commanders are not taking risks. We continue to see cookie-cutter approaches with regard to tactics, like keeping two up and one back, . . . that generally result in frontal attacks instead of any really innovative or risk-taking effort on the part of unit commanders" (p. 63). He goes on to quote Lieutenant General Theodore Stroup, who, in 1996, as the U.S. Army's assistant chief of staff for personnel, referred to "stifled initiative, lack of trust of subordinates and a culture that overemphasizes perfection" (Macgregor, 1997, p. 63) in field training. The Canadian Army is no different. In our training establishments and professional development institutions, significant deviations from the norm, unless rewarded by overwhelming success, are used by instructors and directing staff as examples of what happens when principles and procedures are not followed.

It is human nature to avoid risk and error. But the desire to attain certainty in a profession fraught with friction and chaos often produces commanders who suffer from "paralysis by analysis" or risk aversion. In attempting to find the one conclusive piece of information that will solve the problem, commanders will delay making decisions—or, worse still, avoid making them altogether. Yet calculated risk-taking, together with the appropriate state of mind, is the foundation of maneuver warfare. Nonetheless, in an attempt to reduce the risk associated with taking decisions, most armies have introduced decision-making procedures that require commanders to commit themselves (in a timely manner) to particular courses of action.

These procedures are meant to standardize, streamline, and expedite the decision-making and planning process, thereby maximizing the likelihood that commanders will make the most informed decisions possible. But by their very nature, these procedures are time-dependent. Moreover, in an attempt to minimize risk in decision making, well-intentioned staffs have propagated the use of procedures for generating multiple options. Fallesen (this volume, Chapter 13) argues that

> [p]rocedures that are advocated for reasons like these can take on a life of their own and can end up being followed as if the procedures themselves—and not the problem needing to be solved—were the objects of thinking. In the past, requiring decision makers to follow those processes often resulted in false adherence to the procedures, producing only "look-alike" and "throw-away" courses of action. But the real downside to this behaviour is the false impression that it gives—that is, that a rational, objective process has been followed. Furthermore, planning time is wasted on options that are not particularly useful for building the plan. A related but more general problem is that too much emphasis is typically placed on the decision step, and not enough time is left for detailed planning. (p. 187)

As a result, these procedures—although originally intended to assist commanders in making timely decisions—have in fact slowed down the decision–action cycle. The Canadian Army has gone so far as to adapt the Boyd decision–action cycle as the four stages of its battle procedure and recommends the use of the following aids to decision-making: the estimate process, the operation planning process (staff estimate), intelligence preparation of the battlefield, wargaming, decision support templates, targeting, and synchronization matrices (Canada, 1997).

Despite the availability of modern technology and of efficient, well-trained staffs, the stated "requirement" for simultaneous or "concurrent option comparison" (Fallesen, this volume, Chapter 13, p. 187) often yields solutions that are based on flawed or outdated information and/or solutions that are implemented too late to allow the commander to enter and stay inside the opponent's decision–action cycle. Consequently, these aids for decision-making, as currently instantiated, can be used only in "battle preparation"; they are not helpful for "battlefighting" (Rogers, 1994, p. 46). Worse yet, such procedures tend to promote "cookie-cutter" approaches, resulting in predictable solutions that lack the bold and imaginative flair so essential for success in operations and that smack of an "attritionalist" mindset— the antithesis of the maneuverist approach.

A further attempt to "guarantee certainty" in war is reflected in the concept of the Revolution in Military Affairs (RMA). The digitization of the battlefield, which promises near–real-time situational awareness for commanders at all levels, is a laudable goal. But here too the solution may contribute to the problem. In an effort to satisfy the information requirements of commanders, digitization has produced a flow of data that often causes information overload. The net effect is to draw commanders back to their headquarters, where the bulk of the data flow terminates, and away from the point of main effort on the battlefield, where they would be able to gain a feel (*fingerspitzengefühl*) for what is really occurring and would thereby be able to influence the battle effectively.

Finally, professional development and training institutions have promoted neither the mindset nor the background necessary for effectively applying maneuver warfare and mission command. Although it would be unfair to expect our entire corps of officers and noncommissioned officers to be current in the practices of two recently introduced warfighting and command philosophies, there are two issues that have not, in the past, been satisfactorily addressed. Both have a serious impact on our ability to generate intuitive officers and noncommissioned officers who are capable of exercising mission command.

The first problem is the absence of a climate that fosters productive thinking. In the Canadian Army, for instance, the pace of daily activity is such that, whether at the unit level or in senior-level headquarters, little time is set aside for visionary thinking or brainstorming: in short, there is too little time to think. There are few formal or informal venues for conceptualizing, for discussing new ideas, or for articulating and debating views on the *raison d'être* of our profession—that is, warfighting. Over time, there has been such a demand on the curricula of our staff colleges for nonwarfighting issues that most "thinking time" has been eradicated with a view to preserving the core subjects. Indeed, there are those who view time set aside for thinking during staff college courses as a luxury. Such an approach cannot produce officers capable of independent thought and action.

The second problem is that the Canadian Army, like most others, has seen its operations and maintenance budgets repeatedly and drastically diminished, to the point where field training is the exception rather than the rule. Battalion commanders can actually command for two years without being subjected to a brigade-controlled exercise. The amount of time that officers (and, increasingly, noncommissioned officers) are spending with troops in field units has been reduced to dangerously low levels. Field sense and intuitive judgment, based on experience and knowledge derived from years of field soldiering together with training and professional development, are in danger of falling short of the requirements for grooming the senior officer corps—grooming that is critical for exercising mission command in an army that has adopted maneuver warfare as its warfighting philosophy. Peacekeeping commitments and other priority taskings, however essential, continue to exacerbate this situation by pre-empting the conduct of scheduled training events at all levels.

Although the Canadian Army, like the armies of many other nations, has adopted maneuver warfare and mission command, neither the corporate mindset nor the tools required to accelerate decision making have kept pace with the introduction of these warfighting and command philosophies. Given that the "human component of a command system has primacy" (Canada, 1997, p. i), we must address these concerns with the aim of optimizing the human in command.

4.2. Supporting Command in the Information Age

Before directly addressing the issue of optimizing the human in command, it is first necessary to situate maneuver warfare and mission command in the information age. Mission command, according to the British Army Directorate of Land Warfare paper "Command in the Digitised Era," is "fundamental to the manoeuverist approach and the tempo required for the future operational environment" (United Kingdom, 1998, p. A-1). That same document further emphasizes that "the views and intent of commanders, . . . which [are] fundamental to cohesion and will in CJ [combined joint] forces, [are] linked directly to the advantages of mission command and a chain of commanders with the responsibility, freedom of action, decisiveness and drive to exploit all circumstances through initiative and surprise" (United Kingdom, 1998, p. A-1).

Additionally, mission command

> applies not only to operations but also to much of the regulation of the Army's affairs in peacetime. It is to be used at all levels of command. . . . It requires the development of trust and mutual understanding between commanders and subordinates throughout the chain of command, and timely and effective decision-making, together with initiative (a quality of a commander) at all levels, the keys to "getting inside" the enemy's decision–action cycle. (United Kingdom, 1994b, p. 2-4)

This recognition that mission command applies in peacetime as much as on operations is a necessary precondition if mission command is to endure as a command philosophy. After all, it is a natural extension of the fundamental belief that armies must train as they are going to fight. It therefore presupposes that we would want to develop an officer and noncommissioned officer corps of "prudent risk-takers" by providing an environment that proactively encourages the use of initiative at all levels. It is therefore fortuitous that the Canadian Forces has adopted a peacetime managerial philosophy—Defence 2000—that, in its purest form, is wholly consistent with the precepts of mission command. With its overarching principles of devolution and empowerment, innovative decision making and risk management, as well as accountability, this philosophy should complement other efforts to develop a corporate mindset that promotes the qualities sought in our leaders if they are to exercise effective mission command.

The following sections recommend alternative strategies in the four areas that are critical for ensuring support for command in the information age: initiative, the manner in which aids to decision-making are used, digitization strategies, and training and professional development.

4.2.1. Initiative

Before addressing the problem of how to promote initiative in the information age, it is important to be aware of what "initiative" is and what it is not. Macgregor (1997) provides a good perspective:

> [I]nitiative is not the result of an untutored individual response based on a sudden, creative impulse. Rather the successful exercise of initiative in battle involves recognizing the relationship of an individual's personality attributes—physical and moral courage,

intelligence and character—to developed professional expertise and making decisions under the adverse conditions of combat that will contribute to mission success. In this sense, the exercise of initiative presupposes a concrete knowledge of the higher commander's intent, tactics and weaponry, extraordinary self-confidence and a willingness to accept responsibility for taking actions that were neither planned in advance nor ordered by higher headquarters. (p. 63)

So how do we develop initiative? In today's resource environment, simulation technology is the key. Tactical and command and control trainers should be employed to encourage the use of different approaches to problem solving. Officers should be challenged to defeat the enemy through pre-emption, dislocation, and disruption rather than by physical destruction; they should be told to, as Macgregor puts it, "break the rules" (1997, p. 66) and to practise, practise, practise. One of the great advantages of simulation systems is their ability to drive home lessons learned in a convincing yet harmless manner.

4.2.2. Aids to Decision Making

It is also necessary to reassess how aids to decision making can be used in helping commanders make timely decisions. There is no suggestion here that these tools are superfluous in supporting commanders. On the contrary: on the many occasions when sufficient time is available (such as during battle preparation), decision aids can be of great importance in helping a commander appreciate the full extent of the factors affecting a particular situation. Tools such as the operation planning process, wargaming, decision support templates, and synchronization matrices must be taught in our staff colleges and employed in operational units as instruments both for "training the mind" and for fulfilling the "managerial expectations" of peacetime soldiering.

But the issue of when and how decision-making aids should be used must be carefully studied. While their importance in battle preparation is unquestioned, they must be employed in battlefighting as staff *tools*, the focus being not on the time-consuming process of producing multiple, largely similar options, but rather on supporting the commander's intuitive decision by indicating "difficulties and ways of overcoming those difficulties" (Rogers, 1994, p. 47)—in other words, as a "safety check." It is important that decision-making aids not engender a checklist mentality. They cannot be employed as a substitute for initiative or innovation in plan development. Decision aids must not become an end unto themselves; otherwise, we risk developing a mindset where these tools are used as a crutch by cautious commanders who are paralyzed by analysis and who have unimaginative staffs producing predictable options for situations already overtaken by events.

We should consider Fallesen's (this volume, Chapter 13) suggestion that there needs "to be an emphasis on activities other than optimal decision procedures" (that is, option comparison) to include other important activities such as "situation assessment, forecasting, wargaming, synchronization, and contingency planning" and that "these activities should be formed around how humans actually think" (pp. 186–187). Indeed, recent research by Fallesen (this volume, Chapter 13) indicates that when problem solving, officers in command positions use "a concurrent option comparison strategy . . . in less than 5 percent of the cases" (p. 195), while "*informal* approaches were used more than half of the time," with the "recognition approach [intuition] . . . used most often when the thinker was familiar with the situation" (p. 194).

4.2.3. Digitization

> Digitization of the Battlespace, especially within the Land Component, offers substantial opportunity for enhancing the way in which command is exercised in the Future Army era, primarily through the ability to achieve superior tempo. (United Kingdom, 1998, p. 1)

Both maneuver warfare and mission command have the potential for being enhanced by digitization. However, it is necessary to thoroughly analyze "how the conceptual, moral and physical components[4] of C2 [command and control] should be developed in line with the technical aspect of digitization. . . . The relationship between the human and technical components of command will therefore be of paramount importance if the Army is to operate effectively, as part of a CJTF [Combined Joint Task Force] or within a National force structure" (United Kingdom, 1998, p. 3-4). Furthermore,

> Digitized Situational Awareness should be optimised to support Mission Command at each level of command . . . and should . . . provide greater freedom of movement for commanders. . . . Cognitive skill and decisiveness must not be impaired by the quest for digital perfection—information overload and the fog of war should be assumed, as should the effects of C2W [command and control warfare] and deception. (United Kingdom, 1998, pp. A-2 to A-3)

Digitization of the battlefield must provide commanders with the requisite information, at the right time, and in an understandable format or presentation. This is not an insignificant issue to address. Despite all the cautionary warnings about information overload, Bran Ferren, Disney Engineering's executive vice president, claims that "the problem at this stage of our evolution as a species isn't too much information, it's too little and/or bad and incomplete information" (1998, p. 5-4). He goes on to state that "when we design the BV [battlefield visualization] systems of the future, we need to remember what computers do well and what *we* humans do well—and let each do its own 'thing' best" (Ferren, 1998, p. 5-6), and he concludes emphatically that

---

[4] The current British Army command model is based on a system that comprises three aspects of command (leadership, decision making, and control), three basic components of command (the conceptual, the moral, and the physical), and a command support organization. "The *conceptual* component of command requires a sound philosophy of command, based on the establishment of a common doctrine. The second, the *moral* or human component, centres on the ability to get soldiers to fight, hence the requirement for leadership and other qualities of command. . . . The third, the *physical* component, relates to the technical means of command and the ability to exercise command" (United Kingdom, 1994b, p. 1-5).

Information Overload within the context of Battlefield Visualization is a Myth. By gaining a better grasp of how human beings acquire and understand complex dynamically changing environments in the Real World, we can build Interactive Presentation Environments (as contrasted to visual displays) that enhance human performance. In the near term the consequences of this requires technology that gives decision makers *radically more information* (ideally at the full capacity of human sensory systems) so their brains can better perform the information fusion and correlation tasks. The motivation should be to get the information into the one processor known to be capable of accomplishing this task brilliantly—the human brain. In order to accomplish this we have to understand how WE work and get the BV [battlefield visualization] systems to adapt to us, rather than the other way around. (Ferren, 1998, p. 5-14)

Contrary to the statements made by McCann and Pigeau (1996), this quote by Ferren suggests that the scientific theories and approaches used to support control must in fact directly complement those used to support command.[5] As a result, digitization must focus on providing "effective information transfer into and out of human beings" (Ferren, 1998, p. 5-8) through the use of ergonomically designed "interactive presentation environments" designed to enhance human command performance, rather than through single-modality graphical displays.

Also, digitization work must take a "comprehensive approach to the conceptual, moral and physical components of command" (United Kingdom, 1998, p. 6). In Ferren's words, "[t]here is an inseparable relationship between Art, Science, Doctrine and Technology in BV [battlefield visualization]. You can't work the solutions independently, or the final product will suffer. This is a highly iterative and synergistic challenge that will be continuously evolving for the foreseeable future" (1998, p. 5-8).

Finally, mission command must drive digitization requirements, not the other way around. Furthermore, the unique demands of armies on operations are such that off-the-shelf systems designed for commercial applications are unlikely to provide the requisite capabilities needed by armies in the information age. Requirements must be identified and developed by the users, and research and development must be either conducted internally by defence scientific establishments or contracted out to the private sector with very prescriptive requirements. The economies of scale associated with collaborative research and development, as well as the potential benefits that would accrue from interoperability, argue strongly for multinational efforts in battlefield digitization.

Thus there is every reason to believe that "digitization will deliver more relevant and timely information, potentially enabling a much more rapid decision–action cycle" (United Kingdom, 1998, p. 2), provided that it is appropriately developed and focused. Digitization must be used to enhance decentralized execution, initiative, and independent action; it must not be allowed to fuel the desires of senior commanders to see and control everything. Digitization will not eliminate chaos and uncertainty on the battlefield: indeed, nothing can. To the contrary, it must be used to promote the initiative and decentralization necessary for creating confusion and disorder in the mind of the enemy.

---

[5] In their article "Taking Command of C²," McCann and Pigeau (1996) "conclude that Command is qualitatively different from Control and argue that, for this reason, scientific theories providing knowledge and support for Command must differ from those of Control" (p. 2).

4.2.4. Training and Professional Development

Command in the information age presupposes an understanding of maneuver warfare and mission command and their application in peace, crisis, and conflict. The conduct of mission analyses and the articulation of the commander's intent— the purpose, the method, and the desired end state—together with a coherent and innovative strategy for conducting operations, are essential for the well-being of all armies as we approach the twenty-first century. This requires a visionary approach to training and professional development, one that embraces the imperatives of continuing fiscal constraints.

Success is predicated on an intelligent officer and noncommissioned officer corps in which each member is capable of independent thought. Officers and noncommissioned officers must be encouraged to think outside the mold, and more time must be set aside during the daily military routine as well as during courses for the development of vision based on innovative, productive thought. The use of professional journals as a means of promoting debate on the full spectrum of issues related to the profession of arms is essential. Doctrinal sessions and simulation technology should be used to hone the tactical and operational skills of appropriate commanders at all levels of command.

Rogers points out that "[t]here is an increasing tendency in peacetime to focus on procedures that are quantifiable and easily measured" (1994, p. 50). To avoid this detrimental tendency, we must structure and harmonize our peacetime decision-making processes and managerial methods to more closely resemble how we will conduct operations. We must re-establish "command pull" based on intuitive decision making rather than relying almost exclusively on "staff push," which so often provides overly detailed solutions that are too late and that reflect the "staff intent" rather than the "commander's intent."

Finally, it is vital that we develop leaders who are capable of making intuitive decisions while at the same time exercising judgment. Only well-developed, well-honed intuition will allow commanders to make correct and timely decisions during the conduct of future operations.

> Once a commander has received his orders and mission, he will use intuition to decide on his plan. This will be a rapid process that will be based on his experience and knowledge, emphasising the effect he wants to have on the enemy and his design for battle to achieve that effect—in other words, his "intent."
>
> In reality, most commanders formulate a plan based on one or two options very soon after receiving orders. In a battle command situation, commanders will make decisions without recourse to their superiors but within the framework provided by their superiors' "mission command/commander's intent." If time allows, the commander will then use his staff or subordinates as a "safety" check. (Rogers, 1994, p. 47)

Our approach to the development of future leaders must therefore address the three components that help promote intuition—training, experience, and technical ability.

- We must develop training philosophies that promote initiative and the willingness to take decisions without necessarily having all the requisite information. This approach should not be misconstrued as endorsing the development of a careless mindset with respect to decision making; rather, it should be viewed as a means of countering "paralysis by analysis." Careful consideration of the proper balance between training and testing is required—on the basis that "learning from mistakes is more effective than learning from success, and so experimentation with ideas should be encouraged, and officers should not be penalized for making honest mistakes" (Rogers, 1994, p. 49).

• Officers and noncommissioned officers who demonstrate early potential for rapid advancement relative to their peers should be given increased opportunities for command, field, and operational experience. Both time with troops and instructional experience in training establishments and professional development institutions, where our "best and brightest" can promote leadership qualities in future generations of officers and noncommissioned officers, are fundamental for fostering sound military judgment and intuition. Notwithstanding the benefits of simulation, there is ultimately no substitute for field training, so any training philosophy must reflect an appropriate balance between the two.

• Staff officers and commanders alike must be masters of both the "art" and the "science" of command. Not only must they be able to optimize the capabilities of digitization, they must be intimately involved in clearly articulating the command and control imperatives that "battlefield visualization" should provide. Increased emphasis on the development of high-technology skills and an understanding of digitization is required.

The already extensive U.S. Army experience would suggest that the harmonization of maneuver warfare and mission command with the supporting training and digitization strategies can best be accomplished through the use of battlefield laboratories. A similar approach, with a focus on command and control that includes attention to organizational structures and information flow, would work for other modern armies, including the Canadian Army.

5. CONCLUSIONS

If we are to give credence to Alvin and Heidi Toffler's "Third Wave" of conflict (Arquilla & Ronfeldt, 1997, p. xix), asymmetrical threats will bring with them adversaries who will challenge our decision–action cycles while making their own cycles increasingly difficult for us to penetrate. We must develop commanders who are capable of making timely decisions based on intuition, thereby accelerating tempo in an effort to get inside and stay inside the decision–action cycles of adversaries. Maneuver warfare and mission command will provide the warfighting and command philosophies. Aids to decision making must support commanders, not slow down their decision making. Appropriate training, experience, and technical competence can contribute significantly to the development of leaders capable of making intuitive decisions, keeping the human in command not only relevant but also dominant into the next century.

6. REFERENCES

Allard, Kenneth. (1996). *Command, control, and the common defense* (Rev. ed.). Washington, DC: National Defense University.

Arquilla, J., & Ronfeldt, D. (Eds.). (1997). *In Athena's camp: Preparing for conflict in the information age.* Santa Monica, CA: RAND.

Canada. (1997). *Command* (CFP 300(3)/B-GL-300-003/FP-000). Ottawa: Department of National Defence.

Ferren, B. (1998, February). Modern fictions: How two big wrong ideas are blurring the vision of battlefield visualization. In Army Science Board 1997 Summer Study Final Report, *Battlefield visualization* (pp. 5-1 to 5-16). Arlington, VA: Army Science Board.

Macgregor, D. A. (1997, August). Initiative in battle: Past and future. *Marine Corps Gazette*, 62–67.

Matthews, L. J. (Ed). (1998). *Challenging the United States symmetrically and asymmetrically: Can America be defeated?* Carlisle Barracks, PA: U.S. Army War College Strategic Studies Institute.

McCann, C., & Pigeau, R. (1996). Taking command of C². In *Proceedings of the Second International Command and Control Research and Technology Symposium* (pp. 531–546). Washington, DC: National Defense University.

Rogers, C. T. (1994, March). Intuition: An imperative of command. *Military Review*, 38–50.

Scales, R. H. (1997, July). Cycles of war. *Armed Forces Journal International*, 38–42.

United Kingdom. (1994a). *Operations* (Army Doctrine Publication, Vol. 1). London, U.K.: Ministry of Defence, Chief of the General Staff.

United Kingdom. (1994b). *Command*. (Army Doctrine Publication, Vol. 2). London, U.K.: Ministry of Defence, Chief of the General Staff.

United Kingdom. (1998). *Command in the digitized era* (Army Doctrine Committee (ADC)/P(97)11). Upavon, U.K.: Ministry of Defence, Directorate General Development and Doctrine.

CHAPTER 10

UNITED STATES ARMY LEADERSHIP DOCTRINE FOR THE TWENTY-FIRST CENTURY

COLONEL JOHN P. LEWIS, LIEUTENANT COLONEL CRANSON A. BUTLER, LIEUTENANT COLONEL TIMOTHY CHALLANS, LIEUTENANT COLONEL DONALD M. CRAIG, and LIEUTENANT COLONEL JONATHAN J. SMIDT

1. INTRODUCTION

What does it take to foster and develop Army leaders of character, competence, and high standards who can achieve excellence every day? These leaders must influence their soldiers in a positive manner, operate to successfully accomplish the mission, and improve both their subordinates and the organization. In this chapter, leadership is defined as influencing people—by providing purpose, direction, and

COLONEL JOHN P. LEWIS • *508 South Broadway, Leavenworth, Kansas, USA 66048*   *LIEUTENANT COLONEL CRANSON A. BUTLER* • *P.O. Box 1781, Forest Park, Georgia, USA 30297-1781*   *LIEUTENANT COLONEL TIMOTHY CHALLANS* • *United States Military Academy, West Point, New York, USA 10996*   *LIEUTENANT COLONEL DONALD M. CRAIG* • *Center for Army Leadership, United States Army Command and General Staff College, Fort Leavenworth, Kansas, USA 66027*   *LIEUTENANT COLONEL JONATHAN J. SMIDT* • *Center for Army Leadership, United States Army Command and General Staff College, Fort Leavenworth, Kansas, USA 66027*

The Human in Command: Exploring the Modern Military Experience,
edited by McCann and Pigeau, Kluwer Academic/Plenum Publishers, New York, 2000.

motivation—while operating to accomplish the mission and improving the organization. Leaders operate to achieve the short-term goals of accomplishing missions: from personnel administration and vehicle maintenance to combat victory. In addition, leaders are responsible for focusing beyond the immediate to ensure that they leave the people and the unit better than they found them.

The U.S. Army describes effective leaders using a new doctrinal framework consisting of values, attributes, skills, and actions that are valid whether the leaders are sergeants, civilian directors, or four-star generals. Written as an inspirational narrative, the doctrine—FM 22-100, *Army Leadership* (United States, 1999)—is intended to serve the force in the new millennium and to bring the leadership framework to life with historical vignettes and examples. The examples distinguish between the skills that remain constant and those that change as a leader moves through three levels of leadership: direct leadership, organizational leadership, and finally strategic leadership.

This chapter describes the U.S. Army's new leadership doctrine: the framework, its components, and its interrelationships. Figure 1 illustrates this doctrine and

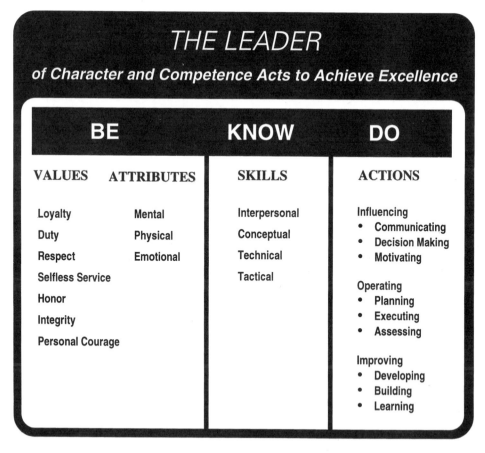

FIGURE 1. The U.S. Army leadership framework.

provides a graphical synopsis of the Army's leadership philosophy—one that focuses on character and on leadership excellence and that highlights Army leaders' tremendous moral responsibility to the people they lead and to the country they serve.

2. CORE CONCEPTS OF THE LEADERSHIP FRAMEWORK: BE, KNOW, DO

We begin by highlighting one of the U.S. Army's time-honoured leadership maxims: "Be, Know, Do." This exhortation forms the centrepiece of our new doctrinal framework and describes our expectations of leaders in any situation. First, *Be* the person of character to whom our nation and Army can entrust sons, daughters, and missions. Second, *Know* your profession and your people, so that your decisions are informed and accurate. Finally, set the example by behaving honourably at all times, and *Do* the right things to guide the organization and its people to success.

2.1. "Be"

The "Be" aspect of the framework comprises the personal *values* that an individual brings to the job of leadership and the mental, physical, and emotional *attributes* that are either inherent or developed during the leader's career.

Because the U.S. Army is a values-based organization, its comprehensive framework of core leadership principles grows out of the seven Army values: *loyalty*, *duty*, *respect*, *selfless service*, *honor*, *integrity*, and *personal courage* (LDRSHIP).[1] The U.S. Army espouses an "ideal" character for its soldiers, derived from these values.[2] The Army's focus on common values and strong character is crucial. Because the Army draws soldiers and Department of the Army civilians (DACs) from an increasingly diverse society, the organization must now more than ever work to instill and

---

[1] U.S. Army commanders present their soldiers with small cards that briefly define each of these values, as follows:

- Loyalty—Bear true faith and allegiance to the U.S. Constitution, the Army, your unit, and other soldiers.
- Duty—Fulfil your obligations.
- Respect—Treat people as they should be treated.
- Selfless Service—Put the welfare of the nation, the Army, and subordinates before your own.
- Honor— Live up to all the Army values.
- Integrity—Do what's right, legally and morally.
- Personal Courage—Face fear, danger, or adversity (physical or moral).

The soldiers sign and carry these cards as part of their commitment to the fundamental principles of their military profession.

[2] The ideal character traits of soldiers and Army civilian employees are discussed extensively in the new leadership manual (United States, 1999) and contribute to a larger initiative throughout the U.S. Army, beginning in basic training and continuing through operational assignments using videos, presentations, and discussion groups.

develop leadership dimensions that transcend different backgrounds so that all members can achieve common purposes in the future.

Army values help define the U.S. Army's corporate culture, but it takes more to define an individual's character. Attributes combine with values to make up a leader's character. Doctrinally, the key attributes that constitute a leader's character are divided into three sets: mental, physical, and emotional. These attributes deserve elaboration.

A leader's *mental attributes*, which are honed over time, include will, self-discipline, initiative, judgment, self-confidence, intelligence, and cultural awareness. Will is the inner drive that compels soldiers and leaders to keep going when they are exhausted, hungry, afraid, cold, and wet—when quitting would be easier. A self-disciplined leader is in control of his or her impulses, having developed the habit of doing the right thing regardless of the consequences. But such a leader can also take initiative when the "right thing" is not obvious, when the situation changes, or when the plan falls apart. The specific course of action depends on the leader's good judgment and on his or her ability to size up situations quickly. Leaders have the self-confidence needed to complete a mission, because they have mastered the required skills through hard work and dedication. Throughout any decision cycle—in training or in combat—intelligent leaders think, learn, reflect, and apply what they have learned. Finally, because the Army encompasses diversity in its units and operates in foreign countries, modern leaders must be culturally aware.

Physical attributes required by leaders—including health fitness, physical fitness, and military and professional bearing—must also be developed. Health fitness includes all the activities involved in maintaining good health—from having routine physical and dental exams to avoiding substance abuse, obesity, and smoking. Physically fit soldiers and Department of the Army civilians (DACs) can handle stress better, work longer and harder, and recover faster than those who are not fit. Military and professional bearing means looking, behaving, and performing in a way that conveys pride in oneself, one's unit, and the institution.

Emotional attributes influence how leaders feel inside and how they interact with those around them. A leader's self-control, balance, and stability are powerful attributes for motivating subordinates. For example, self-controlled leaders keep a handle on their own emotions but tap into their subordinates' emotional resources by displaying the appropriate amount of passion. Balanced leaders display the right emotion for the situation and can also read the emotional states of others. Stable leaders remain steady and level-headed under pressure. By behaving calmly in the face of danger—even if they are not actually feeling calm—leaders provide an invaluable example of how to act most effectively.

2.2. "Know"

Army values and attributes form the foundation of character. Character, in turn, serves as the basis for knowing and doing. Leaders' knowledge falls into four categories: interpersonal skills, conceptual skills, technical skills, and tactical skills. *Interpersonal skills*, which involve competence in dealing with people, include coaching, teaching, counselling, motivating, and empowering. *Conceptual skills*, which reflect competence with ideas, include sound judgment, the ability to think creatively, and the capacity to reason analytically, critically, and morally. Leaders with appropriate *technical skills* possess the necessary expertise to successfully perform all of their assigned tasks and functions. *Tactical skills* enable a leader to make the correct decisions about how to employ and maneuver forces on the battlefield. The first three of these skill domains combine to enhance the last in accomplishing a mission.

2.3. "Do"

The values and attributes that leaders embody (that is, those listed under the heading "Be"), along with the skill sets that they develop (that is, what they "Know"), are all merely prerequisites to "Do"-ing—the fundamental purpose of any army—or, indeed, of any organization. Leadership truly begins when leaders act, when they put character and competence to use in (a) influencing people, (b) operating to accomplish a mission, and (c) improving their organizations (see Figure 1).

Leaders *influence* subordinates at lower levels in the organization mainly through direct face-to-face encounters—such as when a team leader gives instructions, recognizes achievement, and encourages hard work. At higher echelons, leaders also use indirect influence to guide their organizations. Squad leaders, for example, know what the division commander wants, not because the general has briefed each one personally, but because the commander's intent has been passed through the chain of command.

"Do"-ing's *operating* component refers to short-term mission accomplishment—getting the job done on time and to standard—and includes planning and preparation, executing, and assessing. Planning and preparation involves developing detailed, executable plans, arranging unit support, and conducting rehearsals. Executing involves meeting mission standards, taking care of people, and efficiently managing resources. Assessing actions involve validating the efficiency and effectiveness of any system or plan—both before and after executing it.

Through the *improving* component, leaders set priorities and establish a balance among competing demands. (Doing so can often require making a sacrifice now in order to achieve future gains in unit proficiency.) Leaders facilitate their subordinates in training that brings them to a level of mastery that holds up under the stress of combat. While higher headquarters do support training, the leader must be directly involved in three ways. First, leaders must invest time and effort in helping their subordinates develop. Second, leaders are responsible for building—spending time and resources on improving teams, groups, and units. As part of the third action, learning, leaders seek self-improvement and organizational growth, taking responsibility for leading change.

2.4. Levels of Leadership

"Be, Know, Do" forms the centrepiece of the U.S. Army's leadership doctrine. It succinctly encapsulates the values, attributes, competencies, and practices that good leaders must embody and display. But in many instances, the precise ways in which leadership manifests in a given situation depend on the size of the unit or organization, the number of people involved, and the planning horizon. These variations suggest that there are different *levels of leadership*, depending on span of influence, and that these different levels demand different attributes, competencies, and practices. The U.S. Army categorizes leadership among its units and organizations in three levels: the *direct* level, the *organizational* level, and the *strategic* level. The context that each level provides is critical in determining the skills required by that level's leaders and the actions that those leaders will undertake. As a result, one set of skills and actions is not adequate for all situations. Some are appropriate only for the strategic leader; some are also required at the organizational level. The rest of this chapter explores the various aspects of the leadership framework's *skills* and *actions* components (Figure 1) at the direct, organizational, and strategic levels.

3. DIRECT LEADERSHIP

Direct leadership is face-to-face, first-line leadership. It occurs in teams, squads, sections, platoons, and batteries—and even in squadrons and battalions—when subordinates see their leader on a continual basis. Thus the direct leader's span of influence may range from a handful of people to several hundred. This level involves more certainty and less complexity than the organizational and strategic levels involve. Direct leaders are close enough to see—very quickly—whether things are working or not, and how to address any problems that are revealed.

3.1. Direct Leadership Skills

U.S. Army soldiers and civilians serve around the world—training, supporting, fixing, guarding. Whatever the conditions or the mission, direct leaders adopt a common set of principles and skills for performing their actions, as described in this section.

The interpersonal skills described in U.S. Army doctrine emphasize the attributes required for improving relationships within an organization. When considering communication, for example, the doctrine asserts the importance of active listening, two-way communication, and nonverbal communication. Team building is one of the direct leader's most important responsibilities. The direct leader must also develop supervisory skills so as to minimize the chance that a subordinate's oversight or mistake, or some other circumstance, will derail a mission, although it takes time to hone one's sense of how much latitude different soldiers and teams can handle. Pervading everything is the requirement for counselling skills—the ability to challenge, encourage, and critique subordinates for the purpose of developing them.

Direct leaders are responsible for developing their mental or conceptual skills so that they can handle the full range of possible missions, from the simple and routine to the complex and unusual. The ability to reason critically is crucial for understanding a military situation, finding causes, arriving at justifiable conclusions, making good judgments, solving the problem, and learning from the experience. Whether facing a new problem or an old one, direct leaders must be able to think creatively to find the best approach. Leaders must also be able to reason morally, to do the right things for the right reasons. For areas that require judgment, U.S. Army values (see Section 2.1, "'Be'") provide the guide. Finally, the conceptual skill of reflective thinking keeps leaders open to feedback from multiple perspectives—those of superiors, peers, and subordinates—feedback that they can assess and apply for continual personal improvement.

Direct leaders must also be skilled with the technical tools of their trade—from the towing winch on the front of a vehicle to the computer that tracks soldiers' assignments. The closer leaders are to equipment, the greater their technical competence must be, including knowledge of what equipment works best in what situations. In fact, part of direct leaders' technical ability is being expert enough to teach their people how to operate equipment.

Tactical skills at this leadership level involve solving battlefield problems—which arise rapidly and are dynamic—regardless of whether or not the unit is in contact with the enemy. Developing the necessary tactical skills can be a challenge, since units frequently cannot train together due to lack of resources or time. But such constraints do not relieve direct leaders of their responsibility for training their units in basic warfighting skills: adaptive leaders find ways to prepare and motivate people under any conditions. To achieve success, the direct leader must combine basic tactical skills (like doctrine and fieldcraft) with technical knowledge and interpersonal skills (like communication).

3.2. Direct Leadership Actions

Leadership skills serve as the raw material for leadership actions. The new U.S. Army doctrine clearly distinguishes between knowing something and doing something. Knowledge (in the form of skills) is certainly necessary—indeed, critical—for military leaders, but skills alone are not sufficient: leadership begins only when people undertake action, thereby applying what they know.

3.2.1. Influencing Actions

Among the direct leader's influencing actions—communicating, decision making, and motivating—the latter is the most important. While the direct leader must indeed ensure smooth and complete two-way communication and well-considered decisions, his or her ability to motivate subordinates is paramount. A common misperception, even within the force, is that U.S. Army leadership is authoritarian in style. But the U.S. Army schools, units, and culture have all identified the leader's ability to delegate as crucial for building teams and cementing loyalty. People want to be recognized for their work. Good direct leaders empower their subordinates by training them for the work they expect, giving them the resources they need, and then getting out of their way and letting them work. This tremendous expression of trust is one of the best ways to develop subordinates into future leaders.

3.2.2. Operating Actions

Leaders at all levels are responsible for planning, preparing for, and successfully executing missions and for continually assessing their units, their soldiers, and themselves. Planning aids coordination, builds subordinates' confidence in themselves and the organization, and helps ensure success with a minimum of wasted effort— or, in combat, the minimum number of casualties. While leaders are planning, their soldiers can be preparing. A leader can simultaneously develop a plan and prepare his or her unit to execute that plan by issuing a warning order, which provides advance notice of a task or mission and initial guidance on preparing for it. Based on this guidance, subordinates can, for example, draw ammunition, rehearse key actions, inspect equipment, conduct security patrols, or begin movement while the leader completes the plan. Successful execution means accomplishing the mission on time and to standard, while caring for soldiers. In both training and combat, the leader sets realistic, challenging, attainable goals and then communicates and enforces standards of excellence. Finally, assessment occurs throughout a unit's operations, as leaders observe and refine their activities both within a given execution cycle and in preparation for the next such cycle.

3.2.3. Improving Actions

Finally, leaders strive to leave a unit better than they found it. Like anyone who sets aside money to save for the future, leaders know that planning and sacrifices made now are investments that pay huge dividends later. They labour constantly to develop subordinates, build teams, and learn as individuals and units. Of course, the Army as an institution has a responsibility for developing soldiers, but at the heart of this endeavour are individual leaders who are dedicated to mentoring their subordinates—whether soldiers or civilians—by observing, coaching, teaching, counselling, and assessing them. For the U.S. Army, mentoring is an inclusive process that involves everyone under a leader's charge. Beyond improving an organization's individuals, leaders build cohesion with purposeful attention to forming, enriching, and sustaining teams. The leader's aim is to foster the development of a group that is viewed by its members as having meaning and value that run deeper than their own self-interest. Finally, leaders are responsible for instilling lessons from the past and for capturing those that they learn on the job. This requires a climate that supports initiative and underwrites honest mistakes. A "zero-defects" atmosphere stifles learning and reduces performance proficiency to a level that merely maintains the status quo.

   The direct leader's skills, knowledge, and actions are required at all leadership levels, because all leaders function in a direct leadership role at least part of the time. But the demands of the organizational and strategic levels' increasing complexity and responsibility require additional skills and actions from leaders at those levels.

4. ORGANIZATIONAL LEADERSHIP

An organizational leader's span of influence encompasses between several hundred and several thousand people. This type of leadership is undertaken by military leaders at the brigade level through the corps level, by military and civilian leaders from the directorate level through the installation level, and by Department of the Army civilians from the Assistant Secretary level through the Undersecretary of the Army level. Organizational leaders focus on planning and mission accomplishment across timespans of two to ten years. Their role is to establish policies and an organizational climate that support their subordinate leaders. Organizational leaders generally operate through more levels of subordinates—and thus more indirectly—than do direct leaders. In addition, they have staffs to help them lead their people and manage their organization's resources.

4.1. Organizational Leadership Skills

Organizational leadership skills differ from direct leadership skills in degree but not in kind. That is, while the skill sets for both leadership levels are the same, organizational leaders must deal with more complexity, more people, greater uncertainty, and a greater number of unintended consequences. They influence people through policy making and systems integration more than through face-to-face contact.

At the organizational level, leaders can no longer know all their subordinates. They substitute a general but more refined understanding of the human dimension for the individualized perceptions of subordinates that are provided by the direct leader's close interpersonal relationships. Because organizational leaders may be remote from their subordinates in time and distance (and because subordinates' ability to check back with them is typically diminished), organizational leaders must often change the way they communicate. Additionally, they supervise differently.

The organizational leader's complex environment—with its multiple abstract problems—demands patience and careful analysis on the leader's part. The additional conceptual skills that U.S. Army doctrine identifies at the organizational level include (a) establishing intent, (b) filtering information, and (c) systems understanding.

Intent is a leader's personal expression of an operation's desired end state, along with guidance on how to achieve that state. An organizational leader must establish clear and concise intent, including the mission's overall purpose, the acceptable risk, and the expected results. Since organizational leaders are typically further away than direct leaders are, in both time and space, from the point of execution, they must describe the collective goal and empower subordinates rather than simply list tasks for individuals. Then, because organizational leaders are on the receiving end of tremendous amounts of information, they must be able to filter that information effectively in order to achieve a broad perspective on and understanding of the entire situation. They must communicate clearly to their staff which information they need, and then hold the staff accountable for providing it. Finally, organizational leaders must view their units as being made up of systems, considering how those systems work together, how the use of one affects the use of others, and how to get the best performance from the whole. While direct leaders think about tasks, organizational leaders integrate, synchronize, and fine-tune systems.

Despite mounting pressures, organizational leaders must maintain the technical skills they mastered as direct leaders. Although the Army is so complex that organizational leaders cannot be as proficient at all skills as a trained subordinate, they must at least be proficient in the critical direct leadership skills that they need in order to evaluate tactical training and set an example for their subordinates. But because they head larger, more complex organizations, organizational leaders must also master technical skills that lie outside their original area of expertise. In particular, they must develop resourcing and predictive skills. For example, when priorities shift unexpectedly—as, for example, is the case when an emergency deployment occurs—organizational leaders must be able to evaluate the new objectives, anticipate requirements, and efficiently allocate any available resources. Because their decisions have wider-ranging effects than those of direct leaders, organizational leaders must be sensitive to the "ripple" effects of their actions on both the mission and the climate.

Lastly, organizational leaders must master the tactical skills of synchronization (at the tactical level of war) and orchestration (at the operational level). Synchronization involves arranging actions in time, space, and priority to focus maximum military power at a decisive point in time and space. Orchestration, the more complex skill, includes synchronization. Organizational leaders at and above the corps level orchestrate by applying the complementary and reinforcing effects of all military and nonmilitary assets to overwhelm opponents at one or more decisive points. Both synchronization and orchestration require leaders to bring together their interpersonal, conceptual, and technical skills and apply them to warfighting tasks.

4.2. Organizational Leadership Actions

Organizational leaders' actions have far greater consequences for more people over a longer time than direct leaders' actions do. Because the connections between actions and their effects are sometimes more remote and therefore more difficult to see, organizational leaders spend more time thinking about what they are doing and how they are doing it than direct leaders do.

When organizational leaders act, they must translate their intent into action through the larger number of people that work for them.

4.2.1. Influencing Actions

At the organizational level, influencing actions go beyond simply getting the order out. Influencing entails marshalling the activities of staff and subordinate leaders to move toward the organization's objective. Influencing involves constant communication and reinforcement of the commander's intent and concept, continual assessment and adjustment of decisions based on available feedback, and motivation of subordinates through the leader's presence.

Decision making for organizational leaders is more complex than it is for direct leaders, because more people are involved, more factors must be considered, and each decision has more wide-ranging effects. Organizational leaders are far more likely than direct leaders to be required to make decisions with incomplete information. They must determine which decisions to make themselves, and which ones to delegate to lower levels. In determining the right course of action, they consider possible ripple effects and think far into the future—at least months, and sometimes even years in the case of certain directorates.

Organizational leaders are responsible for establishing and maintaining a climate that motivates each member of their entire organization—a climate that promotes Army values, fosters the warrior ethos, encourages learning, and cultivates creative performance. The foundation for a positive organizational climate is a healthy ethical environment, but such an environment alone is insufficient. There is no substitute for the leader's presence at the key points of the battle or at the toughest times in the organization's life. The simple acts of seeing the soldiers and listening to their views go a long way toward building an effective unit. At the same time, visits to the troops afford organizational leaders an opportunity to share the view from the top.

Leaders owe it to their organization and their people to share as much information as possible. Effective communication is fostered by encouraging open dialogue, by practising active listening, and by permitting subordinate leaders and staff to have a forthright, open, and honest voice in the organization without fear of negative consequences. Leaders who communicate openly and who genuinely reinforce team values send a message of trust to subordinates, and benefit from subordinates' good ideas.

Paradoxically, organizational leaders' face-to-face communication must be more powerful, more focused, and more unequivocal than direct leaders'. Because leaders at this higher level move quickly from one project to another and from one part of the organization to another, they must be careful that the right message goes out. Organizational leaders must, for example, be very conscious of the nonverbal messages they transmit, ensuring that their personal mannerisms, behavioural quirks, and demeanour do not contradict a spoken message.

Finally, in order to disseminate information broadly and rapidly, organizational leaders must also develop effective communications networks. The more adept they become at recognizing, establishing, and using such networks, the more successful they will be. Memoranda, notes, and e-mail, as well as formal and informal meetings, interactions, and publications, are among the tools of an effective communicator. Organizational leaders must know the audiences that each communication method reaches and use the methods accordingly.

4.2.2. Operating Actions

The scope and complexity of organizational leaders' responsibilities dictate that these leaders be supported by a well-trained, competent staff. Selecting and training such a staff are among the organizational leader's most important responsibilities. Wise leaders constantly share their thoughts and guidance with their staff, so that the latter can provide support according to the leader's guidelines. Furthermore, the leader provides the staff with opportunities to tackle challenging problems (together with clear guidance on how to do so)—an approach that builds proficiency and fosters an attitude that the staff can overcome any obstacle. But leaders also make sure that staff members have opportunities to celebrate their successes and to recharge their batteries.

When organizational leaders—whether NCO, officer, or civilian—commit to executing an action, they must mass the effects of available forces on the battlefield, including supporting assets from other services. The process actually starts in the planning stage as leaders align forces, resources, training, and other supporting systems. The organizational leader provides the intent, but the intent is potentiated through encouraging initiative among—and delegating authority to—subordinates. At the brigade or directorate level, leaders can no longer personally supervise the unit's operations. Effective organizational leaders therefore delegate authority and accountability and support their subordinates' decisions. Successful delegation involves convincing subordinates that they are empowered, that they do indeed have the freedom to act independently. Empowered subordinates have, and know that they have, more than the responsibility to get the job done. They have the authority to operate in the way that they see fit, limited only by the leader's intent.

Ongoing assessment at the organizational level is critical for determining unit weaknesses and for pre-empting mistakes. Thorough assessment and identification of the causes of problems are essential both for developing subordinate leadership and for improving processes. The ability to assess a situation accurately and reliably requires instinct and intuition based on experience and learning. It also requires a feel for the reliability and validity of information and its sources. Organizational leaders can gather assessment information in several different ways, including asking questions of subordinates to determine their level of knowledge and understanding, and checking for synchronized plans. Assessment may also require delving into the electronic databases on which situational understanding depends. But it involves more than just measurement: in fact, the way that a leader assesses something can influence that very thing. (For example, suppose a commander wants to track fuel usage. By the time that idea gets down to the motor sergeant, it has been reinterpreted as a desire to *limit* fuel usage; before long, the word gets around that only high-priority missions are authorized. The commander never actually wanted anyone to change anything, just to measure what was going on. Consider also that the mere presence of a senior commander changes everyone's behaviour, so that the senior commander will probably never get a personal view of how things actually work.) Assessment can produce useful, high-quality feedback; but in a dysfunctional command climate, it can backfire and send the wrong message about priorities.

4.2.3. Improving Actions

Improving actions are those actions that leaders take today in order to improve their organization and their subordinates for tomorrow. These actions—developing, building, and learning—are harder to undertake at the organizational level, because leaders at this level must rely more on indirect leadership methods. Furthermore, the payoff for actions aimed at developing subordinates and improving the organization may not be evident for years. In fact, organizational leaders may never directly experience the benefit of having helped a subordinate develop, since most subordinates typically go on to work for someone else. The organization's greater size makes the challenge greater, but the rewards also increase: organizational leaders can influence large numbers of people and improve large segments of the Army.

Just as leadership begins at the top, so does developing. Organizational leaders keep a focus on where the organization needs to go and on what all its leaders must be capable of accomplishing. They continually develop themselves, and, as they did when they were direct leaders, they search for and seize opportunities to mentor their subordinate leaders. Effective organizational leaders grow leaders at all levels of their organization by designing a development program and integrating it into everyday training. Such programs aim to capture learning during the course of everyday duties, ensure timely feedback, and allow for reflection and analysis. Leaders develop best when they can practise what they have learned and receive straightforward feedback in rigorously honest reviews.

By building the right teams and systems, and by formulating appropriate contingency plans, the organizational leader ensures that the organization is prepared for a variety of conditions and uncertainties. In wartime, the building of combat power derives from task organization, resourcing, and preparation while at the same time meeting the organization's human needs. Commanders must preserve and recycle organizational energy throughout the campaign. In peacetime, the main component of potential combat power is the embedded collective skill and unit readiness that result from hard, continuous, and challenging training to standard. Organizational leaders build solid, effective teams by developing and training them, and then sustain those teams by creating healthy organizational climates.

Organizational leaders create a learning environment that allows people within their organizations to profit from their own experiences and from the experiences of others. How leaders react to failure and encourage success now is critical for excellence in the future. Subordinates who feel they need to hide mistakes deprive others of valuable lessons. Organizational leaders set the tone for an honest sharing of experiences by acknowledging that not all experiences (even their own) are successful. They encourage subordinates to examine their experiences, and make it easy for them to share what they learn. Continuous learning occurs throughout the organization, and organizational leaders ensure constant teaching at all levels: the organization as a whole shares knowledge and applies relevant lessons. They put systems in place to collect and disseminate those lessons so that individual mistakes become organizational tools. This approach improves unit programs, processes, and performances.

5. STRATEGIC LEADERSHIP

Strategic leaders are the U.S. Army's highest-level thinkers, warfighters, and political–military experts. Some strategic leaders work in institutional settings within the United States; others work in a variety of regions around the world. Strategic leaders concern themselves with the total environment in which the Army functions. They simultaneously sustain the Army culture, envision the future, convey the vision to a wide audience, and personally lead change. Their decisions take into account Congressional hearings, Army budgetary constraints, new systems acquisition, civilian programs, research, development, and interservice cooperation, among other factors. Strategic leaders actually have a dual focus. On the one hand, they must look at the environment outside the Army today in order to understand the context for the institution's future role. On the other hand, they must know and have a feel for the current force so that they can anchor their vision in reality.

Strategic leadership requires techniques that differ significantly in both scope and skill from those exercised by organizational and direct leaders. The strategic environment is characterized by high levels of uncertainty, complexity, and ambiguity. It is also tremendously volatile. Strategic leaders must therefore be able to work amid chaos, think in multiple time domains, and operate flexibly in order to manage change. Moreover, strategic leaders must interact with other leaders over whom they have minimal authority. While direct and organizational leaders focus mainly on the short term, strategic leaders must maintain a long "future focus." They spend much of their time looking toward the mid-term and positioning the organization for long-term success, even as they contend with immediate issues.

5.1. Strategic Leadership Skills

Like direct and organizational leaders, strategic leaders must live by Army values and set an example for their subordinates. But strategic leaders also face some substantially different challenges. Strategic leaders affect the culture of the entire U.S. Army, and they may find themselves involved in political decision making at the highest national or even global levels. Therefore, nearly any task that a strategic leader sets out to accomplish requires more coordination, takes longer, has a wider impact, and produces longer-term effects than a similar organizational-level task.

Strategic leaders must continue to use the interpersonal skills they developed as direct and organizational leaders, but their position's scope, responsibilities, and authority require that these skills—especially those involving communication and negotiation—be more sophisticated. Communication is complicated because this leadership level spans a wide array of staff, functional, and operational components that interact with each other and also with external agencies. In addition, strategic leaders communicate not only with the organization but also with a large external audience that includes the nation's political leaders, the media, and the American people. It is essential that these leaders both exemplify integrity and trustworthiness and be able to convincingly project those qualities. One of the most prominent differences between strategic leaders' communications and those of other types of leaders is the greater importance of symbolic actions—for example, the message conveyed by the leader's explicit support of U.S. Army traditions.

Many of the relationships between organizations at the strategic level are lateral, entailing no clear subordination. Therefore, strategic leaders must often rely heavily on negotiating skills in order to obtain the cooperation and support necessary for accomplishing a mission or for meeting the command's needs—as is the case, for example, in NATO (North Atlantic Treaty Organization) operations. Strategic leaders persuade others of their viewpoint's validity through engaging in dialogue; exchanging perspectives, assumptions, and concepts; gathering information; clarifying issues; and enlisting support from subordinates and peers.

Strategic leaders are skilled at reaching consensus and at building and sustaining coalitions. Whether designing unified commands, joint task forces, and policy working groups, or determining the direction either of a major command or of the U.S. Army as an institution, strategic leaders weld people together for missions lasting months or years. Using peer leadership rather than strict positional authority, strategic leaders oversee progress toward their envisioned end state and monitor the health of the relationships necessary to achieve that state. Interpersonal contact sets the tone for professional relations: strategic leaders must be tactful and discreet. They should stay aware of, and respond astutely to, a diversity of styles, needs, desires, and perceptions.

The conceptual skills required of a strategic leader are exponentially greater than those needed by organizational and direct leaders. Strategic leaders must be able to comprehend national security and theatre strategies, operate at the strategic and theatre levels, and improve their vast and complex organizations. Strategic leaders must have more than just knowledge: they must have wisdom. They must deal effectively with diversity, complexity, ambiguity, change, uncertainty, and conflicting policies; develop well-reasoned positions; and then communicate their views and advice to the nation's highest leaders.

Strategic leaders must create a comprehensive personal frame of reference—based on schooling, experience, self-study, and reflection on current events and history—that encompasses their organization and where it fits into the strategic environment. They do so by being (a) open to new experiences and input from others, including subordinates; (b) reflective, thoughtful, and unafraid to rethink and learn from past experiences; and (c) comfortable with the abstractions and concepts common in the strategic environment.

Strategic leaders design compelling visions for their organizations, either alone or in concert with others. They handle complexity by encompassing it, expanding their frame of reference to fit the situation rather than reducing the situation to fit their preconceptions—but always without losing sight of U.S. Army values. Because of their maturity and wisdom, they can tolerate ambiguity, knowing that they will never have all the information they want. Instead, they carefully analyze events and decide when to make a decision, realizing that they must innovate and accept risk. Once they make a decision, strategic leaders must be able to clarify the situation, however uncertain and ambiguous, for both the Army and the nation; translate their vision and concepts for others; and use that vision and those concepts to create a plan, gain support, and focus subordinates' work.

Strategic leaders operate on a broad canvas; not surprisingly, this level requires broader technical skills as well. Since the Cold War ended, the international stage has become more confusing. Threats to U.S. national security can come from a number of quarters, including regional instability, insurgencies, civil wars, terrorism, the proliferation of weapons of mass destruction, and drug trafficking. To counter such diverse threats, the strategic leader needs a broad enough perspective and sufficient flexibility to plan and execute a wide array of missions, from warfighting to peacekeeping to humanitarian assistance. Strategic leaders identify the military conditions necessary for achieving the political ends desired by their nation's civilian leaders. They synchronize the effects of operations within various domains of conflict to attain these goals. And in order to operate effectively on the world stage (often in cooperation with one or more allies), strategic leaders must call on their international perspective and on their relationships with policy makers in other countries.

Technology has given strategic leaders advantages in force projection, in command and control, and in combat power. It has also increased the tempo of operations, the speed of maneuvers, the precision of firepower, and the pace at which information is processed. But along with all its advantages, technology also increases complexity: large organizations that are moving quickly are harder to control. Strategic leaders who understand and leverage emerging military technologies will be better able to resource, allocate, and exploit the many systems under their control.

5.2. Strategic Leadership Actions

Military and civilian strategic leaders who operate at the highest levels of the U.S. Army, Department of Defense, and national security establishment face highly complex demands from both inside and outside the Army. Strategic leaders must tell the Army story, make long-range decisions, and shape the Army culture in ways that effectively influence the force and its partners inside and outside the United States. They plan for contingencies across the range of military operations and allocate resources to prepare for those contingencies, while assessing the threat and the nation's readiness. Conscious of their responsibility to improve the Army, strategic leaders develop their successors, lead changes in the force, and optimize systems and operations. This section addresses the influencing, operating, and improving actions they use.

5.2.1. Influencing Actions

Strategic leaders act to influence not only their own organization but also its outside environment. Like direct and organizational leaders, strategic leaders influence through personal example as well as by communicating, making decisions, and motivating. The external environment's diversity and complexity sometimes create difficulties in identifying the sources of factors that affect the organization, especially in fast-paced situations like theatre campaigns. Strategic leaders meet this challenge by becoming masters of information gathering. They also seek to control the information environment in ways that remain consistent with U.S. law and U.S. Army values. Such actions can range from conducting psychological operations campaigns that systematically deceive the enemy and degrade its morale to managing everyday media relationships. Strategic leaders identify trends, opportunities, and threats that could affect the Army's future and address them proactively.

One of the strategic leader's most important activities is communicating his or her vision within the Army. If that vision is to provide purpose, direction, and motivation, the strategic leader must gain commitment from the organization as a whole and must relentlessly spread the vision throughout the organization in order to make it a reality. Whether by nuance or overt presentation, strategic leaders vigorously and constantly communicate what kind of organization the U.S. Army is, what it is doing, and where it is going—to the Army itself, as well as to the American people, who support their Army with money and lives. Whether working with other branches of government, federal agencies, the media, other militaries, the other services (that is, the U.S. Navy and the U.S. Air Force), or their own people, strategic leaders rely to a great extent on writing and public speaking (at conferences and press briefings) to help them reinforce the central messages that the Army wants to convey. Because they direct so much of their communication at agencies outside the Army, strategic leaders must avoid using parochial language while also remaining sensitive to the Army's image.

Strategic leaders' decisions—whether made by operational leaders who are deploying forces or by service chiefs who are initiating budget programs—often result in a major commitment of resources. Such decisions are not only expensive but also difficult to reverse. Strategic leaders therefore rely on timely feedback throughout the decision-making process in order to avoid making a decision that is based on inadequate or faulty information. Because decisions at this level are so complex and depend on so many variables, leaders may be tempted to analyze things endlessly: the next batch of reports or the next dispatch will always provide new information. Effective strategic leaders, however, have the perspective, wisdom, and courage to know *when* to decide. In peacetime, strategic leaders' decisions may not see completion for 10 or 20 years, and may need constant adjusting along the way. By contrast, a strategic leader's decision at a critical moment in combat can alter the course of a war.

A healthy culture—the shared set of values and assumptions members hold about their organization—is a powerful tool that can guide an institution. A cohesive culture molds the force's morale, reinforcing an ethical climate built on Army values, especially that of mutual understanding and respect. One task of the strategic leader is to shape this culture to support his or her vision, accomplish the mission, and improve the force, by cultivating a challenging, supportive, and respectful working environment for soldiers and DACs.

Large, complex organizations like the U.S. Army are diverse, containing many subcultures—for example, civilian and reserve components, heavy and light forces, and special operations forces. Gender and ethnic differences also distinguish different groups within the force. The challenge for strategic leaders is to ensure that all these subcultures remain part of the larger Army culture and that they share Army values. Strategic leaders do this by working with the best that each subculture has to offer and by preventing subcultures from fostering unhealthy competition with each other, with outside agencies, or with the rest of the Army. Strategic leaders appreciate the differences that characterize each subculture and treat all members of the Army with dignity and respect.

5.2.2. Operating Actions

Actions taken by strategic leaders that involve planning, executing, and assessing can relate to either the short term or the long term. Ideally, the organization will have standing procedures and policies in place for many routine actions, thereby allowing leaders to concentrate their imagination and energy on the most difficult tasks facing the organization.

While strategic-level planners must balance competing demands from across the vast structure of the U.S. Department of Defense, the fundamental aims of these planners are the same as those of direct- and organizational-level planners: establish priorities and communicate decisions. The challenge is to stay on top of the many different demands being made by the large number of players who can influence the organization. Strategic planners must adopt multiple vantage points, looking at the mission from other players' viewpoints in order to achieve coordination.

Allocating resources—whether in peacetime or during a war—is another major responsibility of strategic leaders. In peacetime, strategic leaders decide which programs get funded and are accountable for the implications of those choices. For example, strategic leaders determine how much equipment can be pre-positioned for contingencies without degrading current operational capabilities.

Although the nature of the next war has not been defined for today's strategic leaders, they must be able to prepare the appropriate force based on hints in the international environment. Questions they must consider include the following: Where is the next threat? Will we have allies? What are our national and military goals? What is the exit strategy? Strategic leaders address the technological, leadership, and moral considerations associated with fighting on an asymmetrical battlefield. These leaders are at the centre of the tension between traditional warfare and the newer kinds of multiparty conflicts that are emerging in stability operations, and they consider and account for the ramifications of switching repeatedly among offensive, defensive, stability, and support actions.

Strategic leaders manage joint, interagency, and multinational relationships and oversee the relationship between their organization, as part of the nation's total defence force, and the national policy apparatus. They use their knowledge of how things work at the national and international levels to influence opinion and build consensus for the organization's missions, gathering support from diverse players in order to achieve their vision. Strategic leaders clarify national policy for their subordinates, explaining the perspectives that contribute to a given policy. Leaders at this level develop policies that reflect national security objectives, and they prepare the organization to respond to missions that span the spectrum of military actions.

To optimize operations, strategic leaders align various initiatives so that different factions are not working at cross-purposes. For example, they focus research and development efforts on achieving combined arms success. Strategic leaders must coordinate timelines and budgets so that compatible systems are fielded together. But they must also plan for the force to have optimal capability across time. This requirement means making plans to integrate new equipment and concepts into the force as they are developed, rather than waiting until all the pieces are ready before fielding an entire system.

Finally, strategic leaders must assess many elements of the strategic environment. Like leaders at other levels, they must first assess themselves: their leadership style and their strengths and weaknesses. They must also understand the present operational environment—including the will of the nation's people, expressed in part through law, policy, and decisions. Strategic leaders must survey the political landscape and the international environment, because both these factors affect the organization and shape the future strategic requirements that are the overarching concern at this level.

5.2.3. Improving Actions

A fundamental goal of strategic leaders is to leave the Army better than they found it. Improving institutions and organizations involves an ongoing tradeoff between today and tomorrow. Wisdom and a refined frame of reference are tools that allow strategic leaders to understand what improvement is and what change is needed. Knowing what to change—and when—is a constant challenge: which traditions should remain stable, and which long-standing methods need to be modified? Improving actions at the strategic level call for experimentation and innovation; but because these organizations are so complex, quantifying the results of changes can prove difficult.

The U.S. Army is decentralizing the learning process in order to become more flexible and efficient. Several questions have emerged as this shift has progressed, including how to share good ideas across the entire institution, and how to incorporate the best ideas into doctrine (thus establishing an Army-wide standard) without discouraging the decentralized learning process that generated the ideas in the first place. These and other challenges face the strategic leaders of the learning organization the Army seeks to become.

Strategic leaders develop the intellectual capital of the Army as a whole by choosing the best people and ideas to invest in for the future. They judge which ideas best bridge the gap between today's organization and that needed tomorrow and determine how best to resource those ideas and the people responsible for them. In other words, strategic leaders must maintain an environment that elicits important ideas from others, nurtures those productive thinkers, and implements necessary changes. The concepts that shape the thinking of strategic leaders will become the intellectual currency of the coming era: the soldiers and DACs who develop those ideas become trusted assets themselves. Strategic leaders also develop individual subordinates through deliberate mentoring—sharing the benefit of their perspective and experience. Mentoring at the strategic level involves introducing a protégé to the institutional Army's important procedures and players. Mentoring also has a more subtle and conceptual connotation—the notion of investing in a rising leader's ideas, efforts, projects, and learning. The potential moral and ethical implications associated with mentoring at this level make the strategic leader's responsibility especially weighty.

Strategic leaders, with their vision and audacity, spearhead the process of change in the U.S. Army. But strategic leaders do more than just recognize trends and opportunities: they actually drive innovation. Strategic leaders build their organizations by being proactive rather than reactive, and by anticipating change while simultaneously shielding their organizations from unimportant and bothersome influences. They use "change drivers"—technology, education, doctrine, equipment, and organization—to control the direction and pace of change. Strategic leaders and their advisory teams are the Army's "futures people."

As an institution, the U.S. Army must remain committed to learning from the experience of others and to applying what it has learned to understand the present and prepare for the future. Strategic leaders therefore conduct technical research, monitor emerging threats, study projected future trends, and develop leaders for the next generation. Furthermore, through their personal example and through their resourcing decisions, they sustain the culture and policies that encourage leader development in all three categories: self-study, operational experience, and institutional learning.

6. CONCLUSIONS

To the U.S. Army, leadership means influencing members of the Total Army (that is, Active members, Reserve members, and DACs), members of other government agencies, and the nation by providing purpose, direction, and motivation. It means operating to accomplish today's missions, both foreign and domestic. And it means improving the institution—making sure its people are trained and its equipment and organizations are ready for tomorrow's missions, any time, anywhere. Leaders must operate to achieve the short-term goals of accomplishing missions, from personnel administration and vehicle maintenance to combat victory. In addition, leaders are responsible for focusing beyond the immediate future, in order to leave the people and the unit better than they found them. U.S. Army leadership doctrine asserts that leadership actions are the same no matter what the level, but that emphasis and specifics differ. At the direct level, the doctrine emphasizes influencing and operating, whereas at the organizational level, it focuses on operating and improving. The strategic-level leader is almost completely occupied with improving the organization and with charting the course for years ahead.

7. REFERENCE

United States. (1999). *Army Leadership* (Field Manual 22–100). Washington, DC: Department of the Army.

HUMAN PROBLEMS IN ORGANIZATIONAL DEVOLUTION

COMMANDER JEFF PENROSE

1. INTRODUCTION

In 1994, the Australian Federal Police (AFP) embarked on a program of corporate reform whose purpose was to change the organization from a rigid paramilitary structure to one that employed self-empowered teams. The thrust for the reform came from the recognition by the AFP executive that opportunities for crime now exist on a global scale and that the sheer scale of this enlarged criminal environment poses unique challenges for law enforcement. The idea was to develop a law enforcement organization whose structure, work practices, and processes are sufficiently flexible to meet these challenges.

Most law enforcement agencies, including the AFP, have favoured a traditional hierarchical organizational structure based on the military concept of *command and control*—an all-encompassing term used to describe structure, systems, and processes as well as the accompanying leadership traits. Traditionally, command and control in organizations like the AFP was quite rigid, but had the advantage that the roles of managers and employees were simple, clear, and relatively stable (Hirschhorn & Gilmore, 1992). But this structure was also inefficient, especially since there were many levels and ranks in the hierarchy. Decision-making processes were generally isolated from the working level, producing such problems as ineffective decisions (because the decision makers had incomplete information) or lack of commitment by those on the working level to decisions that were made by their superiors without their input.

COMMANDER JEFF PENROSE • *Australian Federal Police, P.O. Box 401, Canberra, Australian Capital Territory, Australia 2601*

The Human in Command: Exploring the Modern Military Experience,
edited by McCann and Pigeau, Kluwer Academic/Plenum Publishers, New York, 2000.

The AFP executive had determined that in the face of the emerging criminal environment, the AFP's future relevance required that the organization make the following changes:

- Move away from an organizational structure based on a paramilitary model.

- Recognize that segmenting the organization into divisions had the effect of dividing the AFP's resources.

- Remove many of the centrally imposed autocratic control mechanisms.

- Develop and motivate its personnel through genuine trust and empowerment.

The result was the implementation of the National Teams Model (NTM), an organizational structure that was felt to be operations-focused and based on flexible, multiskilled, empowered teams.

But within 12 months of introducing the NTM, the AFP experienced a significant drop in work quality and productivity. The decline was caused partly by insufficient monitoring and poor quality control by the organization—problems that themselves resulted from delays in defining the new roles of supervisors and in conducting management training. More importantly, though, the program's limited success stemmed from the failure to explain the overall NTM concept to employees. For example, the AFP commissioner had to dispel the widespread but inaccurate perception that empowerment through the NTM meant that one could do what one liked. On the other hand, middle managers in the AFP complained that they had been disempowered—that their traditional authority to manage had been devolved to operating teams. A significant number of senior officers and traditional front-line managers consequently left the organization. Other concerns included uncertainty about the kind of leadership that would be required to manage complex or crisis situations. The prevailing opinion, especially among those who had worked in the traditional environment for many years, was that there had been little wrong with the traditional command and control approach. Many felt that it had been clear and effective, and they regarded the new organizational structure as confusing and wasteful.

As a consequence of these and other concerns, KPMG Consulting was engaged to independently evaluate the reform program's progress. Their study found a serious lack of understanding regarding the purpose and implications of the new NTM structure, particularly with respect to the important roles that empowerment, responsibility, and accountability play in the model (KPMG, 1997).

This chapter attempts to analyze and put into perspective the pitfalls of devolution in the AFP, thereby aiding other organizations that may consider taking this approach. The analysis will focus on three concepts: empowerment, responsibility, and accountability. I will discuss how these principles were applied in the context of the AFP's self-empowered work teams, and I will outline the remedies that the AFP undertook to address the ensuing problems.

2. THE NATIONAL TEAMS MODEL

The AFP's original hierarchical structure contained the divisions, branches, and sub-units typical of most traditional organizations. The new NTM has a semihierarchical network structure. Both are illustrated in Figure 1. The move from a rigid, linear paramilitary structure (the hallmark of the old AFP organization) to a structure based on *organic circles* resulted in much confusion over how the new NTM would actually function. Although it has been argued (Cannon, 1996) that structures based on networks or interrelationships are flexible and decentralized, and that they represent a shift from a command economy to a more democratic and federal economy, the full implications of the move to NTM were not appreciated by the AFP before implementing that move.

Mintzberg's (1989) theory of organizational design can clarify how the NTM's nested circles work together. Mintzberg proposes that every organization comprises six basic parts, which can be applied to the NTM as follows:

- an *operating core*, where self-empowered operational teams carry out basic work focused on the AFP's core business;

- a *strategic apex*, or top executive management, characterized in corporate governance (that is, executive decision-making) arrangements;

- a *middle line*, or middle management, that creates a hierarchy of authority between the strategic apex and the operating core;

- a *technostructure*, which plans and formally controls the work of others through policy and standards;

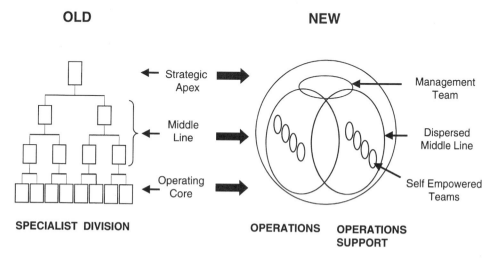

FIGURE 1. The AFP structure: Old and new.

- a *support staff*, which provides a multitude of internal services in traditional support roles; and

- an *ideology*, which is most often referred to as the culture found within the formal and informal organization.

Mintzberg (1989) further posits that human activity in organizations relies on two fundamental and opposing requirements: (a) the division of labour into tasks and (b) the coordination of those tasks. Indeed, according to KPMG (1997), poor coordination of work contributed significantly to the AFP's suboptimal performance when the NTM was implemented. The consultants concluded that the coordination problems stemmed from a lack of understanding of how responsibilities should be devolved in the organization. Key to Mintzberg's theory is the notion of *deriving configurations*. Previous research in organizational design has focused on arranging personnel resources along linear dimensions rather than on exploring how an organization's attributes could be arranged into interconnected types. Mintzberg defines a *configuration* as a system of networks or interrelationships that shape any organization. A plethora of literature supports his view on network organizations (Cannon, 1996; Peters, 1992; and Shapiro, 1995).

The next section will explore several factors—empowerment, accountability, authority, hierarchy, and responsibility—that were brought into sharp focus when the AFP devolved into a self-directed work team structure.

3. ISSUES IN DEVOLUTION

Organizations can become more flexible and more responsive to the marketplace by flattening their management hierarchies (Higgs & Rowland, 1992). Devolution entails distributing decision making and accountability to those who work closest to the point where goods and/or services are produced and delivered to the customer—that is, those who work at the operating core. The Australian Commonwealth Government recognizes the value of devolution and has sought to create performance-based structures, systems, and cultures that emphasize innovation (Reith, 1996). As a reflection of this policy, governments at both the federal and state levels have implemented public-sector reform programs and legislation to devolve greater authority to chief executive officers. The introduction of new public-sector management practices in the early 1990s encouraged the devolution of management responsibility to lower levels within the public service (Harman, 1994), albeit with an increased obligation on managers, senior executives, and politicians to check on and account for the performance of subordinates.

In Australia's law enforcement community, recent revelations of police corruption, mismanagement, poor supervision, and questionable work practices have caused adjustments to, and in some cases the rewriting of, law enforcement accountability frameworks. But these changes have resulted in a misalignment between the high levels of parliamentary accountability demanded by the public and the risk-managed approach that characterizes devolved responsibilities under managerial reform programs. Understanding the different requirements of parliamentary and managerial accountability is the first step in identifying why confusion arises about how devolution will operate in these new flattened structures. What is the difference? Parliament has high accountability to the public, while public-sector CEOs have been asked to adopt contemporary private-sector business management practices and to risk-manage their business processes. Who needs to understand it? People employed in the public sector and those who deal with the public sector. How does understanding the difference help identify the source of the confusion? Properly informed public-sector employees will, it is hoped, develop the human skills needed to work in this new environment. And how does identifying the source of the confusion help? If you know where the confusion lies, you can implement strategies to prevent or resolve the resulting problems.

The NTM structure has certainly reduced the AFP's management hierarchies. But with devolution and delegation to the operating-core level comes the need to establish new kinds of control systems (Byham & Cox, 1988). Lack of control and lack of check on the devolution of responsibility reflect an abdication of management responsibilities. Front-line and middle managers in the AFP continue to grapple with this paradox in leading and managing self-empowered teams.

It was the opinion of KPMG (1997) that devolution would continue to have an adverse affect on AFP's overall effectiveness, particularly because those managers who were accustomed to using traditional command and control approaches perceived a loss of power, authority, and purpose. KPMG (1997) recommended that the AFP develop training programs for all levels aimed at explaining (a) the purpose of devolution and empowerment and (b) their implications for the responsibility and accountability of various AFP personnel.

3.1. Empowerment

KPMG (1997) also recommended that devolution include sufficient empowerment to ensure that workers have sufficient authority over the resources necessary for carrying out their functions effectively. Empowerment, and its effect on the new roles in the workforce, proved somewhat difficult for the AFP to understand, articulate, and implement during reform. (Some had trouble understanding what was required. Others understood, but had a hard time implementing—sometimes because they failed to articulate their understanding to all affected managers and workers. In some cases, those who did understand took the general confusion as a licence to do as they liked.) A useful definition of empowerment is "the degree to which a group is able to make and influence decisions" (MAB/MIAC, 1996, p. 108). Employees feel empowered when they have a sense of influence, competence, meaningfulness, and choice (Thomas & Venthouse, cited in Coleman, 1996). In organizations structured like the AFP, therefore, teams must be empowered at the operating core, where direct contact with customers and suppliers occurs. In the AFP's experience, such empowerment improves the morale of teams that work at this level. But people are sometimes told that they have been empowered when in fact they have not been (Mills, 1992). Instances of this demoralizing incongruity have occurred in the AFP's transition to its new, devolved organizational structure.

Blanchard, Carlos, and Randolph (1996) contend that the three keys to empowerment are as follows:

- replacing hierarchy with self-directed teams,
- sharing information with everyone, and
- creating autonomy by setting boundaries.

In implementing the NTM, the AFP has indeed abandoned its traditional steeply hierarchical structure; but a degree of hierarchical organization remains, since teams working at the operating core are still subordinate to those working at the strategic apex. These levels have different degrees of authority and empowerment. A common challenge in empowering an organization's lower levels involves the difficulty of balancing the need to delegate authority with the continuing need for a degree of hierarchical relationship (Coleman, 1996). In these new flattened structures, executives at the strategic apex and middle-line managers are clearly responsible for performing this delicate balancing act between delegating authority and maintaining control. But team leaders who work at the operating core must recognize that they, too, are part of management, and that therefore they also need to be involved in this process. Kriegel and Brandt (1996) believe that the best way to achieve such a balance is to encourage *ownership*, by giving employees as much control as possible over their destiny. Employees must be given information, responsibility, and the authority to make decisions, and then be held accountable for the results.

According to Blanchard, Carlos, and Randolph (1996), the sharing of information is another crucial element in successful empowerment. But within the AFP, there is still confusion about how to share information at all levels in the organization and about the value of sharing information to empower people. Some consider removing information barriers as potentially threatening precisely because information can equal power. The AFP has invested considerable time and effort in developing and implementing information management practices and systems that will permit a more effective sharing and use of corporate information.

Empowerment does not happen overnight simply because information is transferred; nor does the mere transfer of responsibility from a boss to a subordinate automatically produce the desired effect. Rather, true empowerment results from gradual delegation requiring substantial top-management involvement (Bartlett & Goshal, 1995). In the AFP, it has also required the establishment of a new hierarchy of corporate policy and a significant investment in drafting new policies, guidelines, and operating procedures that complement a flattened structure and an empowered workforce.

3.2. Accountability

The empowerment of employees requires that they be accountable for their actions. Ostroff (cited in Stoner, Yetton, Craig, & Johnston, 1994) suggests that managers who work in organizational structures that involve self-directed teams need to be able to say "empowerment" and "accountability" in the same sentence. He also points out that employees require a systematic program aimed at developing their empowerment skills so that they can gain the necessary confidence to assume mutual accountability for allocated projects.

In the Australian public sector, accountability is defined as "the obligation on public officials to report on, justify, and be judged for actions taken in an official capacity when called upon to do so by those with the necessary authority" (Harman, 1994, p. 54). Just as there are different levels of empowerment throughout the AFP (KPMG, 1997), there are also corresponding levels of accountability at the strategic apex, the middle line, and the operating core.

Since traditional hierarchical structures become flattened in organizations that adopt a self-directed team approach, such organizations need very clear rules regarding accountability; otherwise, the lines of accountability can become unclear and ultimately dissipate (Shapiro, 1995). Katzenbach (cited in Proehl, 1996) argues that teams within these new structures must be committed to a common purpose, common performance goals, and a common approach to their task, for which they are mutually accountable. But accountability in these structures will vary for each individual or team (MAB/MIAC, 1996).

Even in the absence of a flattened organizational structure, executives who work at an organization's strategic apex often find that maintaining accountability is a complex activity, especially when they must explain their actions to many different bodies. The AFP, for example, has multiple reporting lines both for the organization and for its members, resulting in a horizontal and vertical reporting matrix. Vertical accountability characterizes the relationship between the AFP and government ministers, auditors, and the ombudsman. Horizontal accountability occurs in dealings with external bodies, such as the judicial system and educational or technical accreditation bodies.

The AFP has found that ensuring accountability requires more than simply providing information or answering questions. It can be reliably achieved only by having employees set goals, report on results, and be openly responsible for the consequences of getting things right or wrong. The human side of managing accountability in new organization structures like the AFP's demands careful leadership, especially since some employees will seek to avoid decisions when they realize that they will be held accountable for the results of those decisions (Coleman, 1996). In time, the traditional boundaries that inhibit the AFP's performance will disappear, and people will recognize that their responsibilities extend beyond a literal, narrow interpretation of their job description or role. Katzenbach and Smith (cited in Coleman, 1996) conclude that a sense of mutual accountability derives from commitment and trust and from allowing employees to share in the rewards of mutual achievement. The leaders or managers who are most likely to achieve good performance will be those who successfully balance empowerment, responsibility, and accountability, while at the same time treating people as partners and willingly sharing information, authority, and resources (Coleman, 1996).

3.3. Authority

KPMG (1997) concluded that if the AFP is to operate effectively, team members in the new NTM structure will need sufficient levels of authority and command over resources to carry out their functions effectively, a conclusion also supported by Proehl (1996). Handy (1996) makes an interesting extension of this point, suggesting that employee attitudes have changed in revitalized organizations that, like the AFP, have actively recruited and hired new professionals. The new professionals will accept authority only when it is based on something they agree with and is being exercised by someone they deem worthy of respect. For them, authority must be earned. Therefore, the hardest part of managing authority in these new structures is negotiating consent. Coleman (1996) explains that in negotiating consent, it is necessary to obtain commitment from employees at the operating core. Obtaining commitment requires that employees align themselves with the organization's core ideology (recall Mintzberg's model in Section 2, "The National Teams Model")—which in turn allows them to be granted sufficient authority to perform their functions effectively.

Stephens and Becker (1994) summarize three different types of authority found in these new organizations:

- *Personal authority:* one party obeys another either due to the existence of an interpersonal bond or due to the personal qualities of the latter.

- *Competent authority:* one party defers to the judgment of another in recognition of the latter party's expertise.

- *Institutional authority:* one party perceives his or her relationship with another party (a putative authority holder) to fall within a socially established, or institutionalized, category in which the appropriate model of exchange is one of *obedience*.

Although the exercise of institutional authority—that is, authority associated with position—works well for organizations where work consists largely of routine tasks (Savage, 1995), procedures that involve the simple issuing and following of orders are not appropriate in the new flexible organizations (Hirschhorn & Gilmore, 1992). Competent authority—that is, authority based on knowledge or information—is fast becoming a more important determinant of success in such organizations, since in many situations, the individual with institutional authority may not be the one with the most up-to-date information needed to perform a given task. Effective performance also demands that subordinates challenge their superiors (Hirschhorn & Gilmore, 1992) and that superiors listen to and seriously consider alternative views.

The AFP has undertaken a continuing program of reprofiling its workforce to ensure that employees have the skills to meet these emerging challenges. Any reprofiling program means an investment in either funding early retirement packages or upskilling the organization to meet the demands of the new structure, or both. The AFP has found that people operating in this new structure are indeed devolving responsibility and sharing authority. The process by which authoritarian control yields to participation may occasionally prove volatile, as the informal organization rises to challenge the new formal system (Halal, 1996). The AFP's new structure is not immune to such volatility, especially since discussions suggesting authoritarian control can sometimes be perceived as reverting to the nasty habits of command and control. Employees report feeling particularly demotivated after being told that they have the authority to make choices and decisions, and then having that power undermined by an anxious or distrustful boss (Kriegel & Brandt, 1996). It is critical that managers and leaders in the new structures understand the human component of command and leadership. The art of command and leadership will be exhibited by those who can situationally balance the organization's needs with those of the individual.

3.4. Hierarchical Structures

There has been a good deal of confusion concerning the degree of hierarchy that is or should be used to structure organizations that are evolving toward self-empowered teams. Some commentators assert that hierarchies are dead (Peters, 1992). Others argue that hierarchies are inherent in all organizations (Shapiro, 1995); indeed, Mills (1992) claims that there is no such thing as a nonhierarchical organization, except in a two-person partnership. Hilmer and Donaldson (1996) note that large companies such as Nike and McDonald's manage the delivery of consistent services across huge networks through hierarchies, where members in different areas—for example, sales, management, and marketing—add value in different ways and at different levels. They contend that it is absurd to think that every member of an organization can be simply guided by a vision, and report to the CEO.

Organizations based on self-empowered teams are emerging with flattened hierarchical structures, but in some cases, the lines of authority have become blurred (Wilson, 1996): such organizations are often characterized by structures in which employees report to more than one person, have many job responsibilities, and work in several different areas. The issue of hierarchical structure is related to those of accountability and authority—which, according to Jacques (cited in Shapiro, 1995), are the principal factors by which an organization manages the production of its products and services. The distribution of accountability and authority determines the hierarchy's health.

Handy (1996) proposes that professional organizations have two kinds of hierarchies: one based on *status* and the other on *task*. A status hierarchy dictates, for example, that some people in an organization are paid more than others because of their knowledge, experience, and proven ability. But people of higher status will not necessarily lead a group; that task should fall to the person with the most appropriate skills. In a task hierarchy, the role dictates who's who. In 1997, the AFP embarked on the laborious task of comparing people's roles or jobs to the skills that they bring to those roles or jobs, using competencies as one of the methods for evaluating the skills gap. It has recently introduced a remuneration strategy based on the skills a person brings to his or her role.

Research undertaken by Hilmer and Donaldson (1996) suggests that many organizations that consider themselves to be leading examples of the teams approach to organizational structure nevertheless have plant managers and different grades of technicians. The hierarchical relationships that have been maintained in these organizations are not inconsistent with flexibility, empowerment, and self-directed teams. Reporting on their investigation of these new organic organizations, Ashkenas, Ulrich, Jick, and Kerr (1995) conclude that most have some form of up/down structure, since some members of an organization inevitably have more authority and responsibility for making decisions, setting direction, and giving direction. Remuneration is therefore based both on the person's contribution and on his or her position in the hierarchy. On the basis of their findings, Ashkenas and his colleagues propose a model of four ideal "healthy" hierarchies—based, respectively, on information, competence, authority, and reward—for such organizations.

The principal question for the AFP is "How much hierarchy should be retained during the transition to a self-directed teams structure?" It seems clear that some degree of hierarchical structure must be maintained, since the critical factors of accountability, responsibility, authority, and reward are manifest to some extent through hierarchy. In fact, the AFP's flattened structure, with self-empowered work teams at the operating core, can provide a good foundation for participative management. But the currently blurred relationships in the hierarchy must be clarified through training, communication, and consultation.

3.5. Trust and Responsibility

Trust is an organizational value that is intimately linked to responsibility. Employees tend to take on more responsibility when trusted—although the organization's reward system must reinforce this tendency by recognizing any additional responsibility undertaken by its employees (Coleman, 1996). According to Handy (1996), trust is one of the principal means of control in team-based organizations. He further suggests that organizations based on trust should be more effective, more creative, more fun, and cheaper to operate. Trust and the sharing of responsibility do not entail an abandoning of management responsibility. Management remains responsible for setting the organization's direction, making decisions that the team cannot make, ensuring that people stay "on course" toward goals, offering guidance, and assessing performance (Byham & Cox, 1988).

According to Handy (1996), self-empowered teams like those in the AFP exist within two concentric circles of responsibility. The inner circle encompasses those tasks for which the team is explicitly accountable—a baseline. The outer circle delimits the extent of the team's authority. In matters that fall into the area between the two circles, teams have both the freedom and the responsibility to initiate action, at their discretion. This area, called the white space, is where the hard work of management and leadership comes into play. Effective management of the white space of responsibility in organizations like the AFP means trusting people and allowing them the freedom to take risks, to make mistakes, and not to be second-guessed. Communication, especially listening to employees, is critical for building trust (Coleman, 1996). Communication includes providing information, letting employees know about changes that will affect them before such changes are implemented, and sharing items of interest. In organizations that are structured like the AFP, it is imperative that the communication process be two-way to ensure that employees at the operating core, the middle line, and the strategic apex are advised of both potential problems and significant successes.

4. THE CHALLENGES OF DEVOLUTION

The new organizations that are based on a team approach are not the visible, tangible institutions that they used to be. Handy (1996) points out that as these organizations devolve responsibility and accountability, they will become increasingly "virtual," a shift that will make the task of coordinating their work quite complicated. This observation applies equally to the AFP as it becomes decentralized, both within Australia and globally. A challenge for the AFP, therefore, is to effectively coordinate the organization's work without losing control. Successfully meeting this challenge will require new and different means of control (Coleman, 1996). A useful view of what might be required is offered by Simons (1995), who reasons that managers must reconcile the difference between creativity and control in order to give control to all humans in these new structures, particularly those who have not had much control before. He posits that these new organizations need to establish new kinds of control systems. In fact, Handy (1996) contends that new organizations like the AFP will always tend to be slightly out of control, with their structures flexing and their people innovating. Because the AFP must respond quickly to its operating environment and undertake different kinds of work, it must encourage flexibility as an organizational value. And to achieve that flexibility, it must give its employees the latitude to operate independently, as long as they remain within the mainstream guidelines set by the strategic apex and the technostructure.

Mintzberg (1989) offers six ways to describe how organizations like the AFP can coordinate their work. He maintains that these coordination mechanisms constitute the most basic elements of structure—the "glue" that holds an organization together. They are particularly useful for understanding how to tackle devolution.

- *Mutual adjustment:* the process of informal communication between self-empowered teams at the operating core.

- *Direct supervision:* the issuing of orders or instructions, usually from the strategic apex.

- *Standardization of work processes:* the process, in the technostructure, of developing and issuing work processes, instructions, policies, or guidelines to be carried out in the operating core.

- *Standardization of outputs:* the process, in the technostructure, of developing and issuing plans that specify subunit performance targets or outline the dimensions of products to be produced.

- *Standardization of skills:* training that is established by standards, policy, and planning initiatives in the technostructure.

- *Standardization of norms:* the result of alignment of functions based on a
  shared set of beliefs and values.

Coordination of work in the AFP will rely primarily on the standardization of skills,
through formal training and through giving the professional staff control over their
work (Mintzberg, 1989). The technostructure must assume primary responsibility
for generating the skill standards for the operating core, although some of these
standards will originate from external sources. But considerable discretion will be
given to the professional who works at the operating core.

The AFP is rewriting its policies so that the new professionals have the flexibility to apply their skills in ways that suit the variable nature of their work. A substantial investment has been made in building operational computing systems that
have enough flexibility to successfully coordinate these emerging work demands.
The gap in leadership and management skills needed to operate in this new environment, as identified by KPMG (1997), will be addressed through a significant
investment in reskilling the workforce. A team leader development program aimed
at the strategic apex, middle line, and operating core will provide people with the
opportunity to gain the skills they need in order to effectively coordinate work in
this new environment.

The term *command and control* remains very much part of the Australian policing community's lexicon, although using it has recently become unfashionable
because of the move to participative organizational structures. There continues to
be a tension between the need to devolve and the need to be able to build rigid
structures for complex or crisis situations. Some researchers (McCann & Pigeau,
1996; Pigeau & McCann, 1995) argue that the military interpretation of command
and control has placed undue emphasis on control—especially through attempts to
solve command problems solely by the progressive application of technology. The
AFP has also found that technology alone does not resolve the problems associated
with devolution and with controlling or coordinating work. Evidence now indicates
that such issues must be addressed by concentrating on the critical role that humans
play in command.

One component of control that has been neglected is the capability, within a
flattened structure, to construct highly accountable, hierarchically based teams for
dealing with complex or crisis situations. Research shows that law enforcement and
military teams spend very little of their operational time working in crisis situations.
Sherriton and Stern (1996) conclude that organizations may not realize that they
have the capacity, in these new structures, to construct collateral or temporary organizational structures within the existing structure. For example, a collateral organizational structure could be the very rigid, steep hierarchy needed to provide high
levels of accountability in complex or crisis situations. Mink (1992) supports this
conclusion, contending that successful organizations will be those whose structure,
processes, policies, and technology create the fewest constraints. Organizations like
the AFP must recognize that either the strategic apex or the middle line will be
responsible for deciding to establish a collateral structure. In addition, either the
strategic apex or the middle line must articulate an accountability framework for
the collateral structure and determine the devolved boundaries within which it will
operate.

5. CONCLUSIONS

This chapter has aimed to identify and review the many effects of flattening an organization's structure and devolving responsibility to its operating core. The review has been set in the context of the AFP's recent experience with building self-directed teams, systems, and cultures that emphasize innovation and devolution. I conclude that resolving the problems with devolution in flattened structures will require the following actions:

- adopting an integrated approach to changing the culture and the key components—an approach that develops the organization incrementally;

- understanding that succeeding in this aim requires a long-term commitment to redeveloping the structures, systems, and processes that affect everyday organizational life; and

- developing the organization's human side, so that its people are equipped to cope with these emerging trends.

This position is reinforced by the following observation from the KPMG (1997) review of the AFP reform program's progress:

> [C]onquering the problems associated with devolution in these new structures means changing the entrenched culture of independence and separateness to one of corporate unity, consultation and cohesion. (p. 5)

There are many similarities between both the command and control systems and the cultures of law enforcement agencies and the military. My observations may therefore assist military organizations that are undergoing devolution. In addition, this review provides a background for identifying training topics and initiatives that should be undertaken to develop the human skills needed in order to operate effectively in these new organizations. The research community should consider developing a mechanism for identifying projects and exchanging material that will assist in overcoming the difficulties associated with flattened organizational structures and devolved responsibilities.

6. REFERENCES

Ashkenas, R., Ulrich, D., Jick, T., & Kerr, S. (1995). *The boundaryless organization: Breaking the chains of organizational culture*. San Francisco: Jossey-Bass.

Bartlett, C. A., & Goshal, S. (1995, May–June). Changing the role of top management: Beyond systems to people. *Harvard Business Review, (73)*3, 132–142.

Blanchard, K., Carlos, J. P., & Randolph, A. (1996). *Empowerment takes more than a minute*. San Francisco: Berrett-Koehler.

Byham, W., & Cox, J. (1988). *Zapp!—the lightning of empowerment: How to improve productivity, quality, and employee satisfaction*. New York: Ballantine.

Cannon, T. (1996). *Welcome to the revolution: Managing paradox in the twenty-first century*. London, U.K.: Pitman.

Coleman, H. J. (1996). Why employee empowerment is not a fad. *Leadership and Organizational Development Journal, (17)*4, 29–36.

Halal, W. E. (1996). *The new management: Democracy and enterprise are transforming organizations.* San Francisco: Berrett-Koehler.

Handy, C. (1996). *Beyond certainty: The changing world of organisations.* Sydney, Australia: Random House.

Harman, E. (1994). Accountability and the challenges for Australian governments. *Australian Journal of Political Science, 29,* 1–17.

Higgs, M., & Rowland, D. (1992). All pigs are equal. *Management and Education and Development, 23*(4), 349–362.

Hilmer, F. G., & Donaldson, L. (1996). *Management redeemed: Debunking the fads that undermine corporate performance.* New York: Free Press.

Hirschhorn, L., & Gilmore, T. (1992, May–June). The new boundaries of the boundaryless company. *Harvard Business Review, 70*(3), 104–115.

KPMG. (1997). *The journey—organisational change: Evaluation of Program One and beyond.* Canberra: Australian Federal Police.

Kriegel, R., & Brandt, D. (1996). *Sacred cows make the best hamburgers.* Sydney, Australia: HarperCollins.

MAB/MIAC (Management Advisory Board / Management Improvement Advisory Committee). (1996). *2 + 2 = 5: Innovative ways of organising people in the Australian public service.* Canberra: Australian Government Publishing Service.

McCann, C., & Pigeau, R. (1996). Taking command of C². In *Proceedings of the Second International Command and Control Research and Technology Symposium* (pp. 531–546). Washington, DC: National Defense University.

Mills, D. Q. (1992, August). The truth about empowerment. *Training and Development, 46*(8), 31–32.

Mink, O. G. (1992). Creating the new organisational paradigms for change. *International Journal of Quality and Management, 9*(3), 21–35.

Mintzberg, H. (1989). *Mintzberg on management: Inside our strange world of organizations.* New York: Free Press.

Peters, T. (1992). *Liberation management: Necessary disorganisation for the nanosecond nineties.* London, U.K.: Macmillan.

Pigeau, R., & McCann, C. (1995). Putting the "command" back into command and control: The human perspective. In *Proceedings of the Command and Control Conference, September 26, 1995.* Ottawa: Canadian Defence Preparedness Association.

Proehl, R. A. (1996). Enhancing the effectiveness of cross-functional teams. *Leadership and Organizational Development Journal, 17,* 3–10.

Reith, P. (1996). *Towards a best practice Australian public service: Discussion paper.* Canberra: Australian Government Publishing Service.

Savage, C. M. (1995). *Fifth generation management: Co-creating through virtual enterprising, dynamic teaming and knowledge networking.* Boston: Butterworth-Heinemann.

Shapiro, E. (1995). *Fad surfing in the boardroom: Reclaiming the courage to manage in the age of instant answers.* Sydney, Australia: HarperCollins.

Sherriton, J., & Stern, J. (1996). *Corporate culture, team culture: Removing the hidden barriers to team success.* New York: American Management Association.

Simons, R. (1995, March–April). Control in an age of empowerment. *Harvard Business Review, (73)*2, 80–88.

Stephens, M., & Becker, S. (1994). *Police force, police service: Care and control in Britain.* London, U.K.: Macmillan.

Stoner, J., Yetton, P., Craig, J., & Johnston, K. (1994). *Management.* Australia: Prentice Hall.

Wilson, P. (1996). *Empowering the self directed team.* Shawnee Mission, KS: National Press.

Part II

The Science of Command

CHAPTER 12

REDEFINING COMMAND AND CONTROL

ROSS PIGEAU and CAROL McCANN

1. INTRODUCTION

> Our soldiers ... weren't about to let impassable roads stand in the way of getting food to the elderly. When the vehicles had gone as far as they could go, these same soldiers threw rucksacks on their backs, filled them with food and then ran up the snow-covered roads to greet the eternally grateful "snowed-in."
>
> —McNally (1997, p. 5), about a peacekeeping operation in Bosnia

> I held to the old-fashioned idea that it helped the spirits of the men to see the Old Man up there, in the snow and sleet and the mud, sharing the same cold, miserable existence they had to endure.
>
> —General Matthew Ridgway, quoted in Schnabel (1964, p. 9)

> [Private] Haggard now took charge of the situation, in the absence of leadership from any NCO. . . . With the help of [Private] Berthelot, a Bren gunner, [Private] Haggard now organized an attack on [a] position . . . which was subsequently found to have been held by about 50 [enemy soldiers] with four machine-guns.
>
> —Memorandum, Historical officer at Canadian Military HQ at Dieppe, 1942

> In the execution of my orders I allowed divisional commanders as much liberty of action as possible. While I sometimes felt their methods could have been bettered, I considered that they would execute a plan they had made

ROSS PIGEAU and CAROL McCANN • *Defence and Civil Institute of Environmental Medicine, 1133 Sheppard Avenue West, Toronto, Ontario, Canada M3M 3B9*

The Human in Command: Exploring the Modern Military Experience,
edited by McCann and Pigeau, Kluwer Academic/Plenum Publishers, New York, 2000.

themselves and believed in with more vigour than a potentially better plan, imposed from above.

> —Quote in McAndrew (1996) from the memoirs of General
> E. L. M. Burns, who commanded 1st Canadian Corps
> during the Italy campaign in World War II

Lawrence had irrevocably broken with traditional methods of fighting a war. He had "thrown away the books." He started this new kind of war, his mind uncluttered, unbiased, free, and ready to create from original materials, battle-winning combinations.

> —Mrazek (1968, p. 131), describing Lawrence of Arabia

Human creativity, initiative, resolve, problem solving, leadership, and trust play crucial roles in military operations. For command and control (C^2) to be effective in the full range of missions that modern militaries encounter, it is essential that it be human-centred. We have previously argued that C^2's human component has been chronically under-emphasized and under-researched (Pigeau & McCann, 1995). The military has gotten swept away all too easily by the allure of technology (for example, battlefield digitization): as a result, C^2 has become obscured in conceptualizations of rigid structure and process. We have also argued that existing definitions of command and control have provided little guidance either to the military or to industry for allocating the scarce resources necessary for supporting command (Pigeau & McCann, 1995). To redress this problem, McCann and Pigeau (1996) offered a new definition of C^2, one that "emphasizes the critical role of Command [that is, human will] while acknowledging the necessary contribution of Control [that is, technology]" (p. 533). In this chapter, we will explore this new definition's implications, and we will demonstrate its explanatory power for elucidating C^2 organizational structures and leadership.

2. WHY IS A NEW C^2 DEFINITION NECESSARY?

Definitions are not merely rhetorical devices used by ivory-tower intellectuals for arguing the finer points of semantics. A definition, when properly constructed, should concisely embody a concept's essence, giving that concept significance and precise meaning, and encapsulating its nature and key qualities. A definition provides an authoritative anchor for deriving new ideas and interpretations. It should be neither ambiguous nor redundant; nor should it be simply descriptive.

Consider the definitions of command, control, and C^2 shown in Figure 1. Notice that fully half the definition of command is dedicated to the notion of control; similarly, a large portion of the definition of control relates to command. By defining command in terms of control and defining control in terms of command, such circular cross-references induce confusion.

Notice also that the definition of C^2 shown in Figure 1 does little more than restate the previous two definitions. Furthermore, it devotes more words to how C^2 should be *attained* than to what C^2 actually *is*. "[P]ersonnel, equipment, communications, facilities and procedures" are certainly important for conducting C^2, just as "planning, directing, co-ordinating and controlling" are necessary for ensuring its

---

Command: The authority vested in an individual of the armed forces for the direction, co-ordination, and control of military forces. (NATO, 1988)

Control: That authority exercised by a commander over part of the activities of subordinate organizations, or other organizations not normally under his command, which encompasses the responsibility for implementing orders or directives. (NATO, 1988)

Command and Control: The exercise of authority and direction by a designated commander over assigned forces in the accomplishment of the force's mission. The functions of command and control are performed through an arrangement of personnel, equipment, communications, facilities and procedures which are employed by a commander in planning, directing, co-ordinating and controlling forces in the accomplishment of his mission. (NATO, 1988)

FIGURE 1. Typical definitions of command and control.

success. But to what end are these capabilities and activities directed? What is C^2's *purpose*?

We have already discussed the essential differences between the independent concepts *command* and *control* (see Pigeau & McCann, 1995). Briefly, we view *command* as the authoritative and responsible expression of creative human will for the attainment of a mission, whereas we view *control* as the application of structure and process for the purpose of bounding the mission's problem space. C^2 should do more than simply restate these two concepts. It should be *consistent* with command and with control (as separate concepts), but it should also make a unique contribution on its own. We believe that the following definition makes such a contribution, and we devote the remainder of this chapter to expanding and exploring its implications, particularly in the areas of organizational structure and leadership.

Command and control: *The establishment of common intent to achieve coordinated action.*

3. TYPES OF INTENT

Key to our definition of C^2 is the concept of *intent*, which we currently define as *an aim or purpose along with all of its associated connotations*. A close look at this definition reveals that intent itself comprises two elements: explicit (or public) intent, and implicit (or personal) intent. To clarify the difference between the two components, consider the following abbreviated military orders:

- Take hill X by 1300 hours.
- Escort merchant ship Y across the Atlantic.
- Airlift medical supplies Z to Country Q.

Each order can be taken as an explicit directive to accomplish a specific aim or purpose. As such, each must be physically communicated using some modality (for example, spoken, shown with a gesture, written, grunted, and so on) and physically transmitted using some medium (for example, electronically, by courier, or through simple proximity). Orders are examples of explicit intent. They may be short and terse, or they may contain detailed instructions, guidelines, and constraints. Either way, they are a commander's primary mechanism for initiating and maintaining goal-directed action among subordinates.

But explicit intent is only the tip of the iceberg (see Figure 2). Recall that by our definition, intent includes the *associated connotations* of an aim (for example, an order) as well as the specific aim itself. Any overt order from a commander, no matter how meticulously stated, contains a vast network of additional (implicit) intents that inevitably qualify it. The order to "Take hill X by 1300 hours" may seem simple and straightforward, but more is intended by this statement than is immediately obvious—including, but not limited to, expectations that the order's recipient will achieve the objective in the following ways:

- with the fewest civilian casualties,

- without wasting scarce artillery resources,

- while conducting the operation in the best tradition of one's regiment, and

- without embarrassing the nation in front of CNN.

In our complex multicultural world, implicit expectations, beliefs, and values influence the interpretation of explicit intent in pervasive and subtle ways.

INTENT

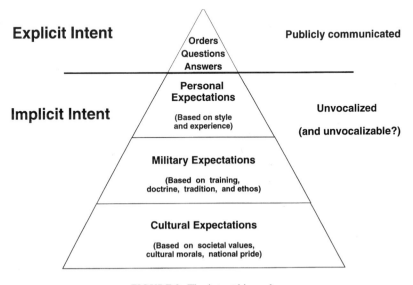

FIGURE 2. The intent hierarchy.

Implicit intent refers to all of the connotations latent within a specific (that is, explicit) aim. An individual's implicit intent is a combination of habits, experiences, beliefs, and values that reflect personal, military, cultural, and national expectations. Implicit intent is also consistent with the concept of tacit knowledge. Polanyi (1967), for instance, has argued persuasively that we know more than we can say, and a growing body of evidence supports that position (Berry & Dienes, 1991; Davids & Myers, 1990; Dienes & Berry, 1997; Horvath et al., 1994; Reber, 1989; Shirley & Langan-Fox, 1996). Studies have shown that patterns and associations[1] are learned unconsciously in many complex tasks and that this knowledge can be used in problem solving. But this research has rarely gone beyond identifying the knowledge necessary for performing simple tasks. Our notion of implicit intent is much broader than (though still consistent with) the current concept of tacit knowledge, and includes deep beliefs based on religion, morals, and values that are to a large extent unconscious and pervasive.[2]

Figure 2 is more than just a metaphorical depiction of intent. The layers' arrangement and size convey their relative importance and influence in an overall intent hierarchy. Explicit intent is just the smallest, most visible aspect of overall intent; it is built on a whole set of implicit and largely uncommunicated (partly for reasons of expediency) personal expectations—for example, expectations regarding how explicit military orders should be executed. These personal expectations are in turn influenced and supported by a deeper, larger set of military expectations regarding how such orders should be carried out in general. Finally, military expectations are themselves built on a still larger foundation of national interests and cultural expectations that justify the need for a military in the first place.[3]

In an ideal world, all levels in the intent hierarchy would coexist harmoniously—that is, there would be no conflicting expectations, beliefs, or values. But such harmony virtually never occurs. For example, personal accounts of the U.S. Army's My Lai incident in Vietnam (Kelman & Hamilton, 1989) or the Canadian Army's Somalia incident (Canada, 1997b) reflect the stress and confusion induced by perceived inconsistencies between explicit orders and implicit cultural beliefs and values. Another example is the internal conflict that may be produced when a soldier, despite observing grossly inhuman actions on the part of belligerents, must obey a standing military directive of noninterference (as might be the case, for example, in peacekeeping operations). Both situations create inconsistencies between the explicit and implicit layers of intent.

Inconsistencies may also exist within the layers of implicit intent itself. Simply being a member of the armed forces, for instance, may be incompatible with an

[1] We hesitate to use the word *rules* here, since we agree with Pleasants (1996) that the idea of an unconscious rule is nonsensical.

[2] Many aspects of beliefs can, of course, be consciously communicated; but it is a common psychoanalytic observation (Freud, 1926/1963) that we cannot articulate all of our beliefs in all of their nuances. Our actions often speak louder than our words.

[3] The intent hierarchy includes more levels than these, of course. For the reader's convenience, however, this chapter concentrates only on these four.

> **Proposition 1:** *Conflicts between layers in the intent hierarchy can be reconciled by either (a) modifying one or both conflicting values, or (b) tolerating the inconsistency.*
>
> **Proposition 2:** *Modifying lower-level expectations (that is, more fundamental values) will be more arduous and stressful than modifying higher-level expectations.*
>
> **Proposition 3:** *Tolerating inconsistent expectations (or values) is stressful, and the amount of stress is directly proportional to the severity of the inconsistency.*

FIGURE 3. Propositions about the intent hierarchy.

individual's belief in pacifism or nonaggression.[4] Or a drill sergeant may need to reconcile his or her role as a tough authoritarian with that of being a caring, loving parent and spouse. Conflicts between layers in the intent hierarchy can be reconciled by either (a) modifying one or both conflicting values, or (b) tolerating the inconsistency. (See Figure 3 for our propositions about the intent hierarchy.)

The intent hierarchy's pyramidal shape reflects Proposition 2's suggestion that beliefs, values, and morals that have had more time to instill themselves—those that were acquired during childhood, for instance—will be more enduring and resistant to change.

4. SHARING INTENT

Thus, an intent hierarchy is the set of expectations and beliefs residing within a single individual. For coordinated C^2, however, intent must be shared among multiple members of a team or organization. Sharing explicit intent (for example, military orders) requires a markedly different strategy than sharing implicit intent (that is, values).

Sharing explicit intent begins with initiating explicit communication, usually in the form of written instructions or verbal directives.[5] This requirement may seem trivial, but communication between two or more individuals is a remarkably complicated and error-prone activity, one to which a considerable amount of theoretical research is being addressed—see, for example, the work that has been done in conversation theory (Pask, 1976; Pask, 1980; Pask & Gregory, 1987) and layered protocol theory (Taylor, 1988a). Sharing explicit intent efficiently requires that at least three conditions be met: (a) a common language must exist; (b) the parties who are attempting to communicate must have a baseline level of literacy in that language; and (c) a communication medium must be available. Deficiencies in one or more of these conditions will hamper the sharing of explicit intent. Hence commanders must

---

[4] Although it is unlikely that such an individual would voluntarily join the military in the first place, countries that practise conscription or mandatory service will undoubtedly have military members who experience such conflicts.

[5] Communication is not restricted to verbal language; much information is passed using verbal prosody (that is, all of the elements that accompany verbalization but aren't verbal themselves: for example, pacing, tone of voice, inflection, and rhythm), gestures, facial expression, eye contact, and body position (Argyle & Cook, 1976; Ekman & Friesen, 1969; Siegman & Feldstein, 1987).

be articulate in the language of their subordinates, and must have a reliable communication channel—which may be as simple as sharing the same physical space or as complicated as communicating via digital satellite.

Although these conditions are necessary for efficient communication, they are not sufficient. The opportunity for conducting constructive *dialogue* is also crucial. Sharing explicit intent is as much about backbriefs,[6] questions, and arguments as about articulation and literacy. For example, one implication of conversation theory (Pask, 1976) is that a subordinate must be able to reiterate an order *using different words*—otherwise, the commander has little assurance that the order was actually *understood*, not simply *heard*. The intricacies and requirements for effective dialogue are too complex to discuss here: see Taylor's (1988a, 1988b) discussion of layered protocol theory for an in-depth discussion of the topic.

As we have said, explicit intent—even if shared—is only the tip of the iceberg. Explicit intent alone is rarely sufficient for ensuring operational success. Operations evolve and develop unique tempos and problems that can quickly supersede even the most meticulous plans. In C^2, it may be neither desirable nor possible to devote sizable amounts of time to sharing explicit intent.

Given the pervasive "fog" and "friction" (Clausewitz, 1833/1976) of operations, only overlapping implicit intent can maximize success. Establishing shared implicit intent is a critical *preparatory* activity (that is, it must be done before operations begin), one to which commanders must devote considerable time and effort. Furthermore, it is a long-term activity that must be supported by the military organization as a whole. Commanders must support the development of shared implicit intent by augmenting education and training with leadership, team building, and continual personal interaction with subordinates. In these ways, commanders establish a command climate that fosters trust, confidence, motivation, creativity, initiative, pride, discipline, and esprit de corps. In every stage of its members' careers, from basic training to retirement, the military organization must continually reinforce and enlarge shared implicit intent among its members.

Understanding and optimizing a phenomenon as elusive as the sharing of expectations and beliefs is a significant psychological and social-psychological problem. For example, team decision-making literature has placed much emphasis on shared mental models (Cannon-Bowers, Salas, & Converse, 1993; Kraiger & Wenzel, 1997; Rouse, Cannon-Bowers, & Salas, 1992). Moreover, social psychologists who study attitudes emphasize the effect of beliefs and intentions on subsequent behaviour (Ajzen & Fishbein, 1980), as well as the role of expectations concerning others in establishing subjective norms:

> [I]n forming a subjective norm, an individual takes into account the normative expectations of various others in her environment. That is, she considers whether specific individuals and groups think she should or should not engage in the behavior and she uses this information to arrive at her subjective norm. (Ajzen & Fishbein, 1980, p. 73)

But a person's subjective norm is not influenced by just anyone. It is affected only by *salient others*—that is, individuals or groups who have subjective value and

---

[6] In a backbrief, people who have received a briefing are asked to reiterate the content of that briefing in their own words, to ensure that they have understood the briefing.

importance to that person. Salient others may include peer group members, authority figures, and respected members of society (or of an institution). In the military, salient individuals include supervisors, peer group members, commanders, and sometimes even opponents.

The theory of implicit learning argues that much is learned unconsciously (Reber, 1989). We maintain that sharing implicit intent is at least as much about unconsciously learning subjective norms and developing normative beliefs as about consciously seeking opinions and achieving consensus. Furthermore, research on implicit learning has shown that a consistent set of stimuli is more easily learned (unconsciously) than inconsistent stimuli.[7] Therefore, the first key to developing shared implicit intent is to expose military members to a consistent set of organizational values. The second key is to provide the time, opportunity, and institutional encouragement that permit personnel to be exposed to one another's expectations and beliefs. Mess dinners, unit functions, religious gatherings, operational exercises, informal briefings, casual conversations—all are venues for sharing (that is, implicitly learning) the subtle expectations and beliefs that will become the foundation for operationally relevant shared implicit intent.

Thus far we have been rather informally discussing the notion of shared intent between individuals. Dividing intent into two components—explicit and implicit intent—allows for a more formal treatment of the topic. Figure 4 illustrates four possible ways that individuals can share their intent hierarchies. Two of these mechanisms (dialogue and socialization) are bidirectional; the other two (internalization and externalization) are unidirectional. Our nomenclature for describing these four ways of sharing intent closely follows that proposed by Nonaka (1994). Although his work concentrates on how knowledge is created and transferred between and among individuals within organizations, we believe that his scheme can be extended to the creation and sharing of expectations, beliefs, and intent hierarchies.

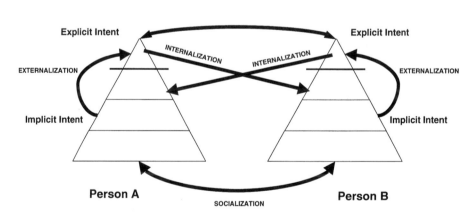

FIGURE 4. Mechanisms for sharing intent.

---

[7] Apparently individuals focus on and learn the pattern of invariances in the stimuli, to use Gibson's term (1969).

- *Dialogue (explicit to explicit):* We have already mentioned the importance of dialogue for sharing explicit intent. Dialogue in C² involves the reciprocal communication of specific information between participants in order to elucidate objectives—and possibly the processes by which those objectives may be attained. Except in the special case of an autocratic leader (see Section 7, "Common Intent and Leadership"), dialogue by definition involves bidirectional communication.

- *Socialization (implicit to implicit):* Sharing implicit intent involves displaying and learning tacit behaviour through nonverbal social interaction, usually within a common context or environment. For example, new recruits learn how to behave in the presence of senior officers partly by observing how other military personnel behave. Unlike dialogue, which communicates concentrated information on a specific topic relatively quickly, socialization imparts diffuse but very rich information over extended periods. But because this information is remarkably subtle, people require numerous exposures in many different contexts in order to "figure someone out" or "understand where someone is coming from." The gradual accumulation of experience provides an increasingly large base from which to make more refined inferences during subsequent socialization. Like dialogue, socialization is a bidirectional activity.

- *Internalization (explicit to implicit):* Each of us unconsciously *internalizes* the explicit messages of others, no matter how those messages are communicated. Recall that implicit learning (Reber, 1989) is the unconscious learning of environmental consistencies; in this sense, internalization is an aspect of tacit learning. The skeptical raising of an eyebrow, the faint murmur of an apology, even the expressive lilt of enthusiasm—all add context and meaning to a verbal message, particularly if the meaning inferred is consistent with the verbal message itself. But inconsistencies can exist between what individuals say and what they do. In such cases, the information that is internalized by the recipient may actually contradict the message intended by the sender. What is being internalized (that is, unconsciously learned) is the inconsistency, and as we will see in Section 5, "Common Intent," the accumulation of such inconsistencies can pose serious barriers to establishing common intent. Internalization is a unidirectional process involving the transfer of the sender's explicit intent to the receiver's implicit intent.

- *Externalization (implicit to explicit):* Art, music, problem solving—in fact, most expressive acts—are externalizations of sentiments and realizations that, before they are expressed, exist only as vague ideas or desires within the mind. Nonaka (1994) believes that metaphor "plays an important role in the externalization process" (p. 19). Metaphor is a powerful tool for resolving the paradox of explicating emotions and thoughts that are in principle not explicable. Metaphor allows inexpressible (but nonetheless deeply felt or intuited) knowledge to be associated with expressible knowledge, permitting new links to be established between concepts. These new concepts can then be further explored and refined. A parable, for example, is a form of metaphor that communicates not only knowledge but also expectations (whether religious or cultural). Externalization is a unidirectional process through which an individual makes available his or her personal implicit intents—often for the purpose of transmitting them to others through dialogue.

Nonaka's (1994) real insight lay in realizing that although "each of the four modes of knowledge conversion can create new knowledge independently, the central theme of the model . . . hinges on a dynamic interaction between the different modes of knowledge conversion" (p. 20). Rarely do dialogue, socialization, internalization, or externalization take place in isolation. More often, they interact in complex ways, and this complex set of interactions yields the rich fabric of our society and culture. Yet despite this dynamic interplay among the four ways of sharing intent, we maintain that two of them (socialization and internalization) are ubiquitous and occur almost continuously, whereas the other two (dialogue and externalization) occur episodically, coming into play specifically and only when thoughts or ideas need to be communicated. As a result, we posit that in general, sharing explicit intent involves dialogue and externalization, while sharing implicit intent involves socialization and internalization. (See Figure 5.)

Before proceeding to Section 5, "Common Intent," we want to note that just as conflicts arise within an individual's intent hierarchy, conflicts between people's intent hierarchies are also quite common. Army, navy, and air force personnel may harbour unspoken prejudices against one another, gender differences may contribute to tension in the ranks, and cultural differences among the various components of an international force may hamper operational effectiveness. Resolving such differences is a major command problem. As is true for conflicts within an individual, there are only two general strategies for dealing with such conflicts: (a) modifying one or both intent hierarchies, or (b) tolerating the inconsistencies.

5. COMMON INTENT

Having sketched the components of intent and described how these components may be shared, we now return to our definition of C^2 and its central concept of common intent. We posit the following definition for the latter phrase:

Common intent: the sum of shared explicit intent plus operationally relevant shared implicit intent.

The establishment of common intent is the precursor for coordinated action. Against this referent, mission states are compared; in the case of a mismatch, corrective action can be taken. But common intent is not simply the shared understanding that results from explicit communication: it is also the web of shared connotations implicit in that understanding. Both the implicit and the explicit elements must be present in order for common intent to be established.

Proposition 4: *Sharing explicit intent (via dialogue and externalization) is facilitated by wide-bandwidth communications using a stable language and protocol.*

Proposition 5: *Sharing implicit intent (via socialization and internalization) is facilitated (a) by frequent and extended opportunities for verbal and nonverbal interaction, and (b) by having a rich base of experiences from which to draw.*

FIGURE 5. Propositions about sharing intent.

Proposition 6: *To compensate for the relative lack of shared implicit intent, joint and combined operations will require greater amounts of shared explicit intent (for operations of comparable size) to achieve a given level of common intent.*

FIGURE 6. Proposition about common intent.

One important factor in establishing common intent is time. Sharing implicit intent is a time-consuming activity that must occur well before operations begin. Typically there is insufficient time during operations for sharing expectations, values, and beliefs.[8] Therefore, to achieve the necessary level of common intent, commanders must adjust the amount of detail in orders, gauge the correct level of discussion, or allow time for feedback—that is, they must increase explicit intent.

But during operations, time is such a critical commodity that in most militaries, the activity of planning and disseminating orders must itself be proceduralized—and personnel must be trained to carry out the resultant procedures. If there is insufficient time to draft and disseminate explicit detailed orders, commanders must either compromise common intent—thereby possibly jeopardizing the operation—or adopt a strategy that may appear suboptimal. For example, the commander of a coalition force may elect to use only a subset of that force (say, only individuals from countries that share the greatest implicit intent) for a key coalition task, in an attempt to maximize the probability that the task will be successfully carried out. (See Figure 6.)

To a lesser degree, joint commanders face a similar quandary. Personnel from different military services within the same nation will share national beliefs, but they will differ in service-specific values—indeed, the various services often pride themselves on having unique traditions and standards. Establishing common intent in these circumstances can also require significant effort.

Given that common intent for an operation is the sum of shared explicit and implicit intent, what is the appropriate balance between the two types of intent? We propose that the organizational structure that supports command, along with the commander's leadership style, affects this balance.

---

[8] Operations and exercises, however, are themselves excellent opportunities for building shared implicit intent for future operations.

6. COMMON INTENT AND ORGANIZATIONAL STRUCTURE

We believe that the common intent component in our definition of C^2 can provide new and useful insights into such issues as the structure of military organizations. Figure 7 illustrates how various levels of shared explicit and implicit intent are linked to either centralized or decentralized C^2 structures.

A preponderance of explicit intent paired with a low level of implicit intent characterizes highly centralized organizations. (See Figure 8.) Long chains of command, copious rules and regulations, rigid standard operating procedures, extensive contingency planning, large and detailed operations orders—all are indicative of centralized C^2. In highly centralized organizations, creative decision making occurs mainly at higher levels in the chain of command, and it is expected that subordinates will be told not only what to do but also how to do it. In stable, well-bounded operational environments, centralized C^2 promotes efficiency and speed of response. It explicitly apportions resources to suit the operation's known needs, and coordinates the effort to obtain known objectives.

But centralized organizations still require some amount of shared implicit intent in order to work effectively. Even in stable, well-defined real-world situations, no set of operating procedures is exhaustive and no plan is complete. Inevitably, operational personnel will need to make informed intentional interventions in the procedures of centralized organizations. (It is well known by unions, for example, that the opposite approach—that is, "working to rule," or making no interventions beyond those prescribed in job descriptions and formal procedures—is an effective strategy for slowing service delivery and product manufacturing.) Shared implicit intent facilitates spontaneous intervention even in centralized organizations, because subordinates share knowledge of how the system is intended to work.

On the other hand, achieving common intent with a preponderance of shared implicit intent at the expense of shared explicit intent is often associated with a

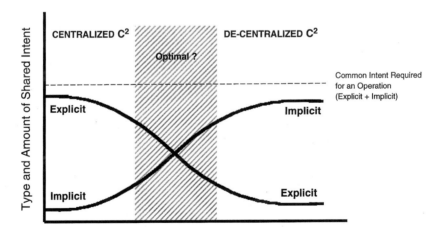

FIGURE 7. Levels of shared explicit and implicit intent in organizations.

Proposition 7: *Centralized C² organizations promote explicit intent instead of implicit intent to achieve a given level of common intent. Conversely, decentralized organizations promote implicit intent instead of explicit intent.*

FIGURE 8. Proposition about intent and organizations.

decentralized C^2 structure. Decentralized organizations characteristically spread decision-making authority downward to subordinates, empowering them with command initiative and independence. Sometimes called maneuver warfare (Hooker, 1993) or mission command (Canada, 1997a), decentralized C^2 attempts to capitalize on the intelligence, motivation, and situation awareness of those personnel most closely associated with the current operational situation. Commanders in decentralized organizations give directives for what must be accomplished without mandating the precise mechanisms for a mission's attainment. The central tenet of such organizations is individual initiative, and what stops such an organization from degenerating into chaos is, we posit, the high levels of shared implicit intent among its members. Each individual must understand and share (perhaps unconsciously) the organization's overarching intent as well as its commanders' specific intents.

Of course shared implicit intent, by itself, is insufficient to ensure organizational effectiveness. Some structure is needed in order to bound the problem space and guide effort. But what form should this decentralized organizational structure take? Does such a structure involve more than simply the flattening of steep and rigid hierarchies?

> How do we create structures that move with change, that are flexible and adaptive, even boundaryless, that enable rather than constrain? How do we simplify things without losing both control and differentiation? How do we resolve personal needs for freedom and autonomy with organizational needs for prediction and control? (Wheatley, 1992, quoted in Mathews, 1996, p. 28)

Wheatley (1992) uses the metaphors of chaos theory and fractal structures to answer these questions. Instead of looking for control, she advocates seeking order. Problems complex enough to require human volition usually will, given sufficient energy (that is, motivation and initiative), generate spontaneous organizational order, possibly in the form of autonomous teams and specific communication protocols.[9] Since the universe seems to produce order spontaneously given sufficient energy flow (for example, see Kaufmann, 1995), Wheatley proposes that complex problems addressed by humans (who themselves are complex) will also spontaneously generate order, if freedom for innovation is allowed. But we must caution that although Wheatley's use of fractal and quantum metaphors is novel and insightful—she devotes her entire 1992 book to this approach—in the end, she offers merely metaphors, which lack explanatory and predictive force. In contrast, Mathews (1996) attempts to describe what he calls "holonic organizational architectures"—that is,

---

[9] Katzenbach and Smith (1993) offer examples of the characteristics of excellent teams and describe how they form in business and industry.

architectures that, following a biological metaphor, resemble cellular structures. A holon (a term that Mathews borrows from Koestler, 1967) is an autonomous unit or entity that is made up of smaller autonomous units while at the same time itself being a member of a larger autonomous unit. From this foundation, Mathews deduces three properties that holonic systems may be expected to have—properties that are universal and potentially measurable: (a) autonomy (holons must display self-sufficiency—that is, have their own energy sources and system integrity); (b) system dependency (a holon's autonomy is in the service of the larger autonomous unit of which it forms a part); and (c) recursivity, or self-similarity (each holon resembles in structure those holons greater and lesser than itself).

The message underlying our introduction of all these new terms is that our thinking about decentralized organizational structures demands new concepts. The problem of how best to harness the creative will that results from successfully sharing implicit intent is a provocative and challenging area for research. Although attempts at modelling and empirically evaluating alternative organizational structures are becoming more common in the scientific literature (for example, see Curry, Kleinman, & Pattipati, 1997; Entin, Kerrigan, & Serfaty, 1997; Kemple, Drake, Kleinman, Entin, & Serfaty, 1997; Levchuk, Pattipati, & Curry, 1997), these studies necessarily limit themselves to known parameters of the task and the environment. They offer important insights into adaptive organizational structures that are based on shared *explicit* intent, but they do not address organizations that are built on shared *implicit* intent. The processes of socialization, internalization, and, to some extent, externalization are admittedly difficult to study empirically, but if we are correct in hypothesizing that the success of a decentralized C^2 organization depends on shared implicit intent, new scientific approaches will have to be developed. An intriguing possibility is Carley and Lee's (1997) work on C^2 adaptation using Monte Carlo techniques and simulated annealing.[10] Although their approach is very algorithmic, they do stress and investigate the nonlinear and adaptive nature of evolving organizational structures.

We wish to stress that our definition of C^2 and its implications are meant to be value-free. We do not favour one organizational structure over another. Rather, we hope that the discussion so far shows that our framework is consistent with a range of organizational structures. There may be good a priori reasons for choosing one structure under certain circumstances and the other under different circumstances. If the problem domain is well known and stable, centralized C^2 will likely yield faster and more efficient responses. When the problem domain is ill defined and open, decentralized C^2 may be more effective. Of course in the real world, it may not be clear which C^2 structure is more appropriate. Indeed, finding the correct balance is a difficult challenge that probably occupies the minds of many senior commanders.

Senior commanders should also be aware that human and environmental factors may influence the adoption of a centralized or decentralized C^2 structure. For example, university-educated people form a greater and greater proportion of

---

[10] Simulated annealing is a heuristic process that attempts to find the optimal solution to a computational problem in a manner analogous to the physical process of annealing a solid.

the military population, and a university education typically fosters independent thought and action; these individuals may therefore expect more autonomy and command responsibility, forcing military organizations to become more decentralized. On the other hand, advances in information technology will permit the transmission of finer-grained military information to senior commanders. As a result, those commanders may develop a tendency toward micromanagement (a form of centralization). Optimally, a flexible organizational structure that is capable of adapting to various operational exigencies—that is, the type of organizational structure depicted in Figure 7's central portion—may be the best strategy. But how such flexibility might be achieved remains unknown at present.

7. COMMON INTENT AND LEADERSHIP

We have defined common intent as the sum of shared explicit intent plus operationally relevant shared implicit intent. We have also shown that "sharing" can be viewed as a form of explicit and implicit learning comprising four submechanisms (dialogue, socialization, internalization, and externalization). But understanding the motivation for sharing, as well as the means by which it is facilitated, represents an ongoing challenge for leadership.

It is often said that leadership is the art of influencing others (Hays & Thomas, 1967). Although we agree that there is much of art in leadership, this definition already presumes a particular approach to leadership—that is, that the only way to lead is through influence. Influencing others is certainly one effective method for attaining objectives, but it may not be the best technique for every situation. Under certain circumstances, leadership by simple direction (that is, giving orders) can be more effective. For this reason, we prefer to consider leadership as acting with others to accomplish the leader's (or the organization's) objectives. Viewing leadership in this way allows us to discuss it from the perspective of sharing explicit and implicit intent. Also, this view reaffirms Hollander's (1993) observation that any discussion of leadership is incomplete without a parallel discussion of followership.

Leadership has been studied from a number of perspectives: charismatic or transformational; situational or transactional; and managerial (Chemers & Ayman, 1993; Conger & Kanungo, 1988; Yukl, 1989). A dimension suggested by Katz and Kahn (1978) allows all leadership styles to be situated along a common continuum based on social-psychological distance. Although Katz and Kahn's original formulation centred on charismatic leadership, we believe that the idea of a social-psychological distance between leader and follower allows us to consider a wide range of leadership styles.

Figure 9 depicts this continuum. On the figure's left side is autocratic leadership, a leadership style commonly associated with more centralized forms of authority. In extreme cases, autocratic leaders stand aloof from their followers. They take explicit advantage of their authority to effect goal-oriented action, regardless of their followers' views or emotional needs (the word *subordinate* rather than *follower* is probably more apt in such instances). Autocratic leaders view subordinates solely as the means to organizational ends and feel that subordinates should be told

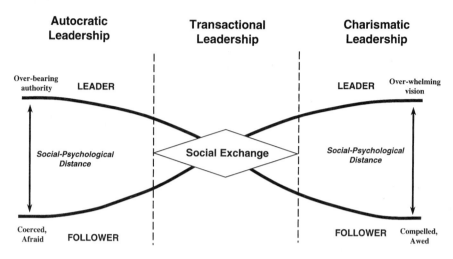

FIGURE 9. Leadership styles.

exactly what to do and how to do it. For their part, subordinates do not follow autocratic leaders so much as they accede to or comply with the leader's wishes—often
due to fear of experiencing reprisals if their performance is deemed inadequate. The
social-psychological distance between autocratic leaders and their subordinates,
therefore, reflects a highly goal-oriented, authoritarian behaviour on the part of the
leader paired with rule-governed, submissive, and often fear-induced compliance on
the part of the subordinate. This leadership style is reminiscent of Korten's (1968)
authoritarian model.

We posit that in order to establish common intent in C^2, extremely autocratic
leaders must rely almost exclusively on the unilateral propagation of orders (that
is, the use of explicit intent), with dialogue between the leader and subordinates
limited to confirmations that the leader's orders have been heard and understood.
(See Figure 10.) Autocratic leaders are not concerned with their subordinates'
implicit intents—if they even recognize that those intents exist. They limit their
interactions with subordinates to goal-related issues. Autocratic leaders impose their
authoritative will on subordinates with the expectation that subordinates will
comply unquestioningly with their directives. The possibility that a conflict could

---

Proposition 8: *An autocratic leader imposes his or her explicit intent on the follower, without
acknowledging the follower's implicit intent.*

Proposition 9: *A charismatic leader indoctrinates the follower into the leader's intent
hierarchy.*

Proposition 10: *A transactional leader encourages the sharing of leader and follower intent
hierarchies.*

FIGURE 10. Propositions about intent and leadership.

exist between their own expectations and those of their subordinates, if they consider it at all, is dismissed as incidental and inconsequential.

At the opposite end of the continuum in Figure 9 lies the charismatic (also called transformational by Bass, 1988) leadership style. In 1924, Max Weber laid much of the theoretical foundation for the current work in charismatic leadership: see Conger (1988) for a review of the topic. Originally Weber's work was adapted from theology, a field in which charisma means "endowment with the gift of divine grace" (Bass, 1988, p. 43); his thinking remains very consistent with more contemporary theories, which describe charismatic leaders as people skilled in

> articulating and focusing a vision and mission; creating and maintaining a positive image in the minds of followers, peers, and superiors; exhibiting a high degree of confidence in themselves and their beliefs; setting challenging goals for followers; providing a personal example for followers to emulate; showing confidence in and respect for followers; behaving in a manner that reinforces the vision and mission of the leader; and possessing a high degree of linguistic ability and nonverbal expressiveness. (House, Woycke, & Fodor, 1988, pp. 100–101)

The above quote reinforces the importance of discussing leadership from the perspective of both leader and follower. It is the interaction between the two that defines the style of leadership.

Bass (1988) describes eight distinguishing characteristics of strong charismatic leaders: (a) expressive behaviour, (b) self-confidence, (c) self-determination, (d) insight, (e) freedom from internal conflict, (f) eloquence, (g) a high activity and energy level, and (h) followers who identify with them. Space limitations prevent us from discussing each of these factors, but one of them—freedom from internal conflict—is particularly important for our concept of common intent. Recall that there are only two general methods for dealing with internal conflicts in the intent hierarchy: changing one's expectations until they are internally consistent (an approach that often produces acute stress) or tolerating the inconsistencies and coping with the resultant chronic stress. To the follower, a charismatic leader appears to be one of those rare individuals who have accomplished the former undertaking. Through vision, insight, and will, the charismatic leader has constructed a personally consistent view of the world and has successfully applied that view to attaining particular ends. The leader's apparent freedom from internal conflict—particularly when paired with self-confidence, insight, eloquence, and the other traits outlined by Bass (1988)—is powerfully attractive to followers who, until encountering the charismatic leader, have coped with their own internal conflicts by tolerating them (perhaps unconsciously). The chronic stress that such followers are experiencing motivates them to adopt the charismatic leader's vision (that is, Item (h) above) and intent hierarchy.[11] Thus the leader is "idealized and becomes the model of behavior to be emulated" (Bass, 1988, p. 51). Although indoctrination has the effect of reducing the ideological distance between leader and follower, in extreme cases the leader is "sufficiently distant from membership to make a simplified and magical image

---

[11] "Those in psychological distress are prone to join a charismatic leader's coterie," notes Bass (1988, p. 50) in summarizing Galanter's (1982) work on religious sects.

possible" (Katz & Kahn, 1978, p. 546), thereby reinforcing the social-psychological distance between the two.

We have concentrated on the extreme ends of the continuum shown in Figure 9 because we want to elucidate the consequences of those extremes of leadership style for the sharing of intent. The autocratic leader imposes his or her intent hierarchy on followers, and the charismatic leader indoctrinates followers into his or her intent hierarchy. Most leadership styles, of course, lie somewhere between these two extremes. Figure 9 suggests that convergence from either end toward the centre is associated with an increase in social interaction. From the follower's perspective, the emphasis becomes less on tolerating an autocratic leader's rule or on adopting a charismatic leader's vision, and more on engaging in transactions (Chemers, 1993) or goal-oriented partnerships (for example, teams or work groups). Although less extreme styles of autocratic and charismatic leadership (for example, managers and mentors, respectively) are still possible within this transactional leadership style, the dominant emphasis is social exchange.

> Leaders and followers approach their relationship with needs that require *mutual fulfillment*. Needs are oriented both toward the rational goals of the group and [toward] each individual's interest in group success, as well as toward the more personal emotional needs of each person (Schein, 1985). These needs, while *not always rational* [or] *completely conscious*, are the critical moderators of the relationship. (Chemers, 1993, p. 299; italics added)

A key element in the concept of transactional leadership is mutual fulfillment, which can range from a concrete exchange of commodities (for example, remuneration for services rendered) to an abstract exchange of social-psychological influences (for example, motivation, direction, or satisfaction). The leader ensures that followers receive the requisite skills, incentives, and resources to do the task. Followers complete the implicit bargain with the leader (House, Woycke, & Fodor, 1988) by accomplishing the mission competently and with initiative. As Chemers states in the above quote, the needs exchanged between leaders and followers are "not always rational [or] completely conscious." This view is consistent with our positions that (a) much of the intent hierarchy is unconscious, and (b) sharing implicit intent is largely an unconscious process of socialization and internalization. It may even be the case that leaders and followers harbour their own unconscious (implicit) theories of what constitutes an "ideal" leader, further complicating the social exchange process (for example, see Ayman, 1993). Indeed, the complexities of social interaction may explain the proliferation of transactional theories—for example, path–goal theory (House, 1971; House & Shamir, 1993), rolemaking theory (Graen & Scandura, 1987), situational leadership theory (Hershey & Blanchard, 1977), attribution theory (Lord & Maher, 1990), and, to some extent, contingency theory (Fiedler, 1993).[12]

Our intention in this section is only to show that common intent is consistent with a wide range of leadership styles, not to discuss the entire topic of leadership. We have described leadership styles involving the leader's imposition of his or her

---

[12] Contingency theory is perhaps more about a leader's relationship with the situation and with the organization as a whole than about his or her way of relating to a specific follower.

detailed explicit intent (that is, autocratic leadership), the leader's indoctrination of followers into his or her implicit intent hierarchy (that is, charismatic or transformational leadership), and extended socialization resulting from leader–follower interactions (that is, transactional leadership). Earlier in this chapter, we expressed dissatisfaction with the common definition of leadership, noting its bias toward a particular leadership style (that is, one that involves influencing others, rather than simply directing them). We suggested instead that leadership should be considered as the act of getting others to achieve particular objectives, regardless of the strategy used to do so. We are now in a position to provide a precise definition of leadership that is consistent with our general definition of C^2:

Leadership in C^2: the act of resolving intrapersonal and interpersonal conflicts for the purpose of achieving common intent.

8. CONCLUSION

> The current state of command and control theory is . . . characterised by an inchoate level of conceptual development, a diffuse focus, and a set of highly conjectural, largely undeveloped hypotheses concerning seemingly random aspects of the command and control process. (Foster, 1988, p. 213)

> The mystery that seems to cloak the world of command and control systems has confounded a good many military people and defense specialists for years. (U.S. General Robert T. Herres, 1992, p. xv)

Both the scientific and the military communities continue to be frustrated about the state of command and control theory and C^2 systems development. Major advances in information technology and in weapons delivery have certainly changed C^2's face and pace, but these changes have occurred within a philosophical and conceptual vacuum. Those responsible for "doing" command and control are increasingly burdened by a dizzying array of operational commitments, with only confusing concepts and poorly designed systems to help them. It is a tribute to human fortitude and determination that our militaries are as successful as they are.

We do not pretend to have resolved this large, complex conundrum—no one book chapter could possibly do so. Nevertheless, we are adamant that a fresh perspective on C^2 must be advanced, if only to spark controversy and force a reassessment of the field's fundamental assumptions. To this end, we reassert what may seem obvious: only humans command. All other concepts, technologies, doctrines, standard operating procedures, training, systems development, and so on, must support this pivotal axiom. We believe that C^2 must be defined and discussed from a uniquely human perspective—one that is consistent with prevailing operational experience, yet provides novel and productive avenues for improving overall effectiveness and efficiency. Defining command and control in terms of common intent represents a first step in that direction.

We offer only a new framework, not a theory, for discussing C^2. Our purpose in discussing organizational structure and leadership is to situate our definition within the context of relevant scientific work, not to make a substantive contribution to these well-established fields. That having been said, we nonetheless believe that our perspective on command and control both offers a provocative new way of viewing the problem and establishes a new language for discussing it.

Finally, the reader may have noticed that we have limited our discussion to the first half of the definition—that is, what common intent is and how it is established. We have not yet investigated how well the mechanisms or implications of "achieving coordinated action" apply in actual C^2 situations. But we have found the idea of common intent to be remarkably rich and fruitful. We invite the scientific community to expand this effort and extend our knowledge of C^2 from the human perspective.

9. REFERENCES

Ajzen, I., & Fishbein, M. (1980). *Understanding attitudes and predicting social behavior.* Englewood Cliffs, NJ: Prentice-Hall.

Argyle, M., & Cook, M. (1976). *Gaze and mutual gaze.* Cambridge, U.K.: Cambridge University Press.

Ayman, R. (1993). Leadership perception: The role of gender and culture. In M. M. Chemers & R. Ayman (Eds.), *Leadership theory and research: Perspectives and directions* (pp. 137–166). New York: Academic Press.

Bass, B. M. (1988). Evolving perspectives on charismatic leadership. In J. A. Conger & R. N. Kanungo (Eds.), *Charismatic leadership: The elusive factor in organizational effectiveness* (pp. 40–77). San Francisco: Jossey-Bass.

Berry, D. C., & Dienes, Z. (1991). The relationship between implicit memory and implicit learning. *British Journal of Psychology, 82,* 359–373.

Canada. (1997a). *Command* (CFP 300(3)/B-GL-300–003/FP-000). Ottawa: Department of National Defence.

Canada. (1997b). *Dishonoured legacy: The lessons of the Somalia affair—Report of the Commission of Inquiry into the Deployment of Canadian Forces to Somalia.* Ottawa: Commission of Inquiry into the Deployment of Canadian Forces to Somalia [Somalia Inquiry].

Cannon-Bowers, J. A., Salas, E., & Converse, S. (1993). Shared mental models in expert team decision making. In N. J. Castellan, Jr. (Ed.), *Individual and group decision making* (pp. 221–246). Hillsdale, NJ: Erlbaum.

Carley, K., & Lee, J. (1997, June). *C² adaptation in a changing environment.* Paper presented at the Third International Command and Control Research and Technology Symposium, National Defense University, Washington, DC.

Chemers, M. M. (1993). An integrative theory of leadership. In M. M. Chemers & R. Ayman (Eds.), *Leadership theory and research: Perspectives and directions* (pp. 293–319). New York: Academic Press.

Chemers, M. M., & Ayman, R. (Eds.). (1993). *Leadership theory and research: Perspectives and directions.* New York: Academic Press.

Clausewitz, K. von. (1976). *On war* (P. Paret and M. Howard, Trans.). Princeton, NJ: Princeton University Press. (Original work published 1833)

Conger, J. (1988). Theoretical foundations of charismatic leadership. In J. A. Conger & R. N. Kanungo (Eds.), *Charismatic leadership: The elusive factor in organizational effectiveness* (pp. 12–39). San Francisco: Jossey-Bass.

Conger, J. A., & Kanungo, R. N. (Eds.). (1988). *Charismatic leadership: The elusive factor in organizational effectiveness.* San Francisco: Jossey-Bass.

Curry, M. L., Kleinman, D. L., & Pattipati, K. R. (1997, June). *Mission modelling as a driver for the design and analysis of organisations.* Paper presented at the Third International Command and Control Research and Technology Symposium, National Defense University, Washington, DC.

Davids, K., & Myers, C. (1990). The role of tacit knowledge in human skill performance. *Journal of Human Movement Studies, 19,* 273–288.

Dienes, Z., & Berry, D. (1997). Implicit learning: Below the subjective threshold. *Psychometric Bulletin and Review, 4*(1), 3–23.

Ekman, P., & Friesen, W. V. (1969). The repertoire of nonverbal behavior: Categories, origins, usages, and coding. *Semiotica, 1*, 49–98.

Entin, E. E., Kerrigan, C., & Serfaty, D. (1997, June). *Performance under traditional and non-traditional architectures.* Paper presented at the Third International Command and Control Research and Technology Symposium, National Defense University, Washington, DC.

Fiedler, F. E. (1993). The leadership situation and the black box in contingency theories. In M. M. Chemers & R. Ayman (Eds.), *Leadership theory and research: Perspectives and directions* (pp. 1–28). New York: Academic Press.

Foster, G. D. (1988). Contemporary C^2 theory and research: The failed quest for a philosophy of command. *Defense Analysis, 4*(3), 201–228.

Freud, S. (1963). *A general introduction to psychoanalysis.* (J. Riviere, Trans.). New York: Pocket Books. (Original work published 1924)

Galanter, M. (1982). Charismatic religious sects and psychiatry: An overview. *American Journal of Psychiatry, 139*(2), 1539–1548.

Gibson, E. H. (1969). *Principles of perceptual learning and development.* New York: Appleton-Century-Crofts.

Graen, G. B., & Scandura, T. A. (1987). Toward a psychology of dyadic organizing. In L. L. Cummings & B. Staw (Eds.), *Research in organizational behavior: Vol. 9* (pp. 175–208). Stamford, CT: JAI Press.

Hays, S. H., & Thomas, W. T. (1967). *Taking command.* Harrisburg, PA: Stackpole Books.

Herres, R. T. (1992). Introduction. In T. P. Coakley, *Command and control for war and peace* (pp. xv–xvii). Washington, DC: National Defense University Press.

Hershey, P., and K. Blanchard. (1977). *Management of organizational behavior: Utilizing human resources.* Englewood Cliffs: NJ: Prentice-Hall.

Hollander, E. P. (1993). Legitimacy, power and influence: A perspective on relational features of leadership. In M. M. Chemers & R. Ayman (Eds.), *Leadership theory and research: Perspectives and directions* (pp. 29–48). New York: Academic Press.

Hooker, R. D. (Ed.). (1993). *Maneuver warfare: An anthology.* Novato, CA: Presidio Press.

Horvath, J. A., Forsythe, G. B., Sweeney, P. J., McNally, J. A., Wattendorf, J., Williams, W. M., & Sternberg, R. J. (1994). *Tacit knowledge in military leadership: Evidence from officer interviews* (Technical Report 1018). Alexandria, VA: U.S. Army Research Institute for the Behavioral and Social Sciences.

House, R. J. (1971). A path–goal theory of leader effectiveness. *Administrative Science Quarterly, 16*(3), 321–338.

House, R. J., & Shamir, B. (1993). Toward the integration of transformational, charismatic and visionary theories. In M. M. Chemers & R. Ayman (Eds.), *Leadership theory and research: Perspectives and directions* (pp. 81–108). New York: Academic Press.

House, R. J., Woycke, J., & Fodor, E. M. (1988). Charismatic and noncharismatic leaders: Differences in behavior and effectiveness. In J. A. Conger & R. N. Kanungo (Eds.), *Charismatic leadership: The elusive factor in organizational effectiveness* (pp. 98–121). San Francisco: Jossey-Bass.

Katz, D., & Kahn, R. L. (1978). *The social psychology of organizations.* New York: Wiley.

Katzenbach, J. R., & Smith, D. K. (1993). *The wisdom of teams: Creating the high-performance organization.* Boston: Harvard Business School Press.

Kaufmann, S. (1995). *At home in the universe.* Oxford, U.K.: Oxford University Press.

Kelman, H. C., & Hamilton, V. L. (1989). *Crime of obedience: Toward a social psychology of authority and obedience.* New Haven, CT: Yale University Press.

Kemple, W. G., Drake, J., Kleinman, D. L., Entin, E. E., & Serfaty, D. (1997, June). *Experimental evaluation of alternative adaptive architectures and command and control.* Paper presented at the Third International Command and Control Research and Technology Symposium, National Defense University, Washington, DC.

Koestler, A. (1967). *The ghost in the machine.* London, U.K.: Hutchinson.

Korten, D. C. (1968). Situational determinants of leadership structure. In D. Cartwright & A. Zander (Eds.), *Group dynamics* (pp. 351–361). New York: Harper and Row.

Kraiger, K., & Wenzel, L. H. (1997). Conceptual development and empirical evaluation of measures of shared mental models as indicators of team effectiveness. In M. T. Brannick, E. Salas, & C. Prince (Eds.), *Team performance assessment and measurement: Theory, methods, and applications* (pp. 63–84). Mahwah, NJ: Erlbaum.

Levchuk, Y. N., Pattipati, K. R., & Curry, M. L. (1997, June). *Normative design of organizations to solve a complex mission: Theory and algorithms.* Paper presented at the Third International Command and Control Research and Technology Symposium, National Defense University, Washington, DC.

Lord, R. G., & Maher, K. J. (1990). Leadership perceptions and leadership performance: Two distinct but interdependent processes. In J. Carroll (Ed.), *Advances in applied social psychology: Business settings, Vol. 4* (pp. 129–154). Mahwah, NJ: Erlbaum.

Mathews, J. (1996). Holonic organizational architectures. *Human Systems Management, 1,* 27–54.

McAndrew, W. (1996). *Canadians and the Italian campaign.* Montreal: Art Global.

McCann, C., & Pigeau, R. (1996). Taking command of C^2. In *Proceedings of the Second International Command and Control Research and Technology Symposium* (pp. 531–546). Washington, DC: National Defense University.

McNally, G. (1997). Making a difference, and making Canada proud: A report from Bosnia. *Defence Matters, 2*(4), 4–7.

Mrazek, C. (1968). *The art of winning wars.* New York: Walker.

NATO (North Atlantic Treaty Organization). 1988. *Glossary of Terms and Definitions* (STANAG. AAP-6(R)). Brussels, Belgium: NATO.

Nonaka, I. (1994). A dynamic theory of organizational knowledge creation. *Organizational Science, 5*(1), 14–37.

Pask, G. (1976). *Conversation theory: Applications in education and epistemology.* Amsterdam: Elsevier.

Pask, G. (1980). Developments in conversation theory, Part I. *International Journal of Man–Machine Studies, 13,* 357–411.

Pask, G., & Gregory, D. (1987). Conversational systems. In J. Zeidner (Ed.), *Human productivity enhancement, Vol. 2* (pp. 204–235). New York: Praeger.

Pigeau, R., & McCann, C. (1995). *Putting "command" back into command and control.* In *Proceedings of the Command and Control Conference, September 26, 1995.* Ottawa: Canadian Defence Preparedness Association.

Pleasants, N. (1996). Nothing is concealed: De-centring tacit knowledge and rules from social theory. *Journal for the Theory of Social Behaviour, 26*(3), 233–255.

Polanyi, M. (1967). *The tacit dimension.* London, U.K.: Routledge and Kegan Paul.

Reber, A. (1989). Implicit learning and tacit knowledge. *Journal of Experimental Psychology: General, 118*(3), 219–235.

Rouse, W. B., Cannon-Bowers, J. A., & Salas, E. (1992). The role of mental models in team performance in complex systems. *IEEE Transactions on Systems, Man and Cybernetics, 22*(6), 1296–1308.

Schein, E. H. (1985). *Organizational culture and leadership.* San Francisco: Jossey-Bass.

Schnabel, J. F. (1964, March). Ridgway in Korea. *Military Review,* 3–13.

Shirley, D. A., & Langan-Fox, J. (1996). Intuition: A review of the literature. *Psychological Reports, 79,* 563–584.

Siegman, A. W., & Feldstein, S. (Eds.). (1987). *Nonverbal behavior and communication* (2nd ed.). Hillsdale, NJ: Erlbaum.

Taylor, M. M. (1988a). Layered protocols for computer–human dialogue. I: Principles. *International Journal of Man–Machine Studies, 28,* 175–218.

Taylor, M. M. (1988b). Layered protocols for computer–human dialogue. II: Some practical issues. *International Journal of Man–Machine Studies, 28,* 219–257.

Wheatley, M. J. (1992). *Leadership and the new science.* San Francisco: Berrett-Koehler.

Yukl, G. (1989). Introduction: The nature of leadership. In G. Yukl (Ed.), *Leadership in organizations* (pp. 1–11). Englewood Cliffs, NJ: Prentice-Hall.

CHAPTER 13

DEVELOPING PRACTICAL THINKING FOR BATTLE COMMAND

JON J. FALLESEN

1. INTRODUCTION

Battle command as conceived of by the United States Army consists of leadership and decision making. This chapter deals with the thinking that contributes to the decision-making function. The chapter's aim is to indicate how the U.S. Army Research Institute for the Behavioral and Social Sciences (ARI) has investigated battle command thinking and what ARI has found out about thinking that can improve an officer's command performance. The research depicts the complexities of instrumental processes and emphasizes the importance of situational factors, individual experience, beliefs, and attitudes. In the past, instructional materials for commanders have been based on formal models of thinking; however, the research described here conforms to less formal assumptions. The informal approach comes from areas referred to as *everyday thinking* and *naturalistic decision making*. This area of study has started to delineate important understandings about cognitive processes in battle command. Efforts that have been taken to improve thinking for battle command are summarized here, and broad research issues are identified.

In 1995, we developed an exploratory program of instruction (Fallesen, Michel, Lussier, & Pounds, 1996) to provide alternative approaches to thinking. This instruction, referred to as *practical thinking*, grew from our research on command and control and general cognition. The traditional approach bases instruction for

JON J. FALLESEN • *United States Army Research Institute for the Behavioral and Social Sciences, Fort Leavenworth Field Unit, P.O. Box 3407, Fort Leavenworth, Kansas, USA 66047-0347*

The Human in Command: Exploring the Modern Military Experience,
edited by McCann and Pigeau, Kluwer Academic/Plenum Publishers, New York, 2000.

thinking on optimal decision theories or classical logic; however, few people follow optimal models or use classic logic. Practical thinking, on the other hand, takes a descriptive approach, basing instruction on how battle commanders think as they are developing the desired results. Practical thinking is related to the emerging field of naturalistic decision making and includes both critical thinking and creativity.

The essence of command has to do with conceptual thought—understanding, visualizing, deciding, planning, monitoring, and communicating. Pigeau and McCann (this volume, Chapter 12) discuss the meaning of command and control, reinforcing the importance of establishing (understanding, visualizing, deciding) and implementing (planning, monitoring, communicating) intent. Advancements in command and control systems and in technology for weapons and sensors are aimed at providing better information to a commander to support these processes. But the richer sources of information, combined with complex geopolitical situations (some of which are illustrated in this volume by Capstick, Chapter 7; Winslow, Chapter 20; and Everts, Chapter 6) and the unknowable means and intent of potential adversaries, may in the future strain a commander's cognitive capacity. Even if uncertainty does not increase, the commanders of the future will still face significant challenges. One reason is the trend for units to be responsible for more missions and more different threats, in more theatres of operations, with smaller force structures. At the same time, the civilian sector is less willing to accept casualties, which in turn creates a higher demand for reducing the uncertainty in the risks taken. The situational influences and their interactions create high levels of ambiguity, dynamism, and complexity—all pointing to a greater need for (a) versatile ways to think in the face of uncertainty and (b) ways to overcome uncertainty.

2. BACKGROUND

In 1990, I led a small ARI team that worked on a chapter of a draft manual to replace FM 101-5 (United States, 1984); the new manual was to be called *Field Manual on Command and Control for Commanders and Staff*.[1] We offered ideas for describing the command and control process that were based on our findings from more than 10 research projects on commander and staff performance (Fallesen, 1993). The main assumption that we questioned was whether command and control doctrine should be based on optimal decision theory. We had observed that the command and control processes espoused by doctrine and training did not match what we and others had observed commanders and staffs doing in field, laboratory, or classroom settings. There was considerable debate at that time about the "right model" for command and control as an optimal decision-making process. We felt that there needed to be an emphasis on activities other than optimal decision procedures. Activities that we felt were important—for example, situation assessment,

---

[1] The draft was substantially changed and retitled before eventual publication in 1997.

forecasting, wargaming, synchronization, and contingency planning—had not been described very thoroughly in doctrine. Our position was that these activities should be formed around how humans actually think—not based on what economic theory suggests is an optimal way. Our draft chapter for the *Field Manual* tried to capture these points, as indicated in the following excerpt.

> The commander and staff need to share an understanding of command and control activities, why they are important, and what results from each. The activities should not be *prescribed* as a fixed sequence of procedures. Nor do the products have clear and definite end states. There are an endless number of ways in which the activities may be linked. Specific sequences will be determined by situational factors, including the strategies of the commander, whether hostilities are pending or in progress, the level of command, the capabilities of the threat, results from one activity determining what activity needs to be done next, and so on. The amount of effort required to perform various command and control activities and the thoroughness of resulting products are highly dependent on situational factors. Mission goals, time available, uncertainty, and experience determine what needs to be done and how it can be done. . . . Command and control is a dynamic enterprise with high stakes. To gain the proper leverage on the battlefield, command and control activities must be understood thoroughly and performed with ingenuity and insight. (Fallesen, Lussier, & Michel, 1992, pp. 30–31)

We also tried to infuse more practicality into the formal expression of doctrine. For example, a major change that we proposed concerned the number of options to consider in planning. We suggested that doctrine should require that no more than one course of action should be considered unless there are explicit reasons for having more. Our point was that the requirement for multiple options to be generated concurrently seemed to be recommended solely so that formal procedures for concurrent option comparison could be used. Procedures that are advocated for reasons like these can take on a life of their own and can end up being followed as if the procedures themselves—and not the problem needing to be solved—were the objects of thinking. In the past, requiring decision makers to follow those processes often resulted in false adherence to the procedures, producing only "look-alike" and "throw-away" courses of action. But the real downside to this behaviour is the false impression that it gives—that is, that a rational, objective process has been followed. Furthermore, planning time is wasted on options that are not particularly useful for building the plan. A related but more general problem is that too much emphasis is typically placed on the decision step, and not enough time is left for detailed planning (Lussier, 1992).

The coordinating author approved our draft chapter and included it in the draft for review. Shortly thereafter, the coordinating author's boss called me to his office. He thanked us for our effort, but dismissed our work as too revolutionary. He told me that the Army was not ready for anything so new. Yet from a research perspective, our recommendations did not seem new at all; we were just balancing the suitability of optimal decision theory with procedures that we saw already in use. We felt that optimal decision theory did not merit the amount of print and influence it had received in doctrine, especially when contrasted with the activities that we chose to emphasize and describe instead. Prior to our proposed description, doctrine had indeed conceded that there would be occasions when time would be too short for the complete optimal-decision-theory–based approach, but doctrine had not provided much detail about an abbreviated process. In our view, doctrine should be written for the typical case—not for an ideal one that might occur only during institutional education. Since this polite rejection of our recommendations, subsequent doctrine documents have picked up more of the quality of situational decision making and have emphasized more practical and natural guidance.

Then, as now, there are two prevailing ways of considering procedures for battle command thinking and tactical decision making. One way is a formal mode, where *process* is paramount. Individuals adopt this mode according to the extent to which they are inclined to value formality and explicitness of process. This valuing stems from an epistemic belief about what constitutes truth and acceptable thinking. Doctrinal authors and instructors who need to convey descriptions of a desired process favour straightforward and explicit descriptions. The most explicit descriptions come from the implications of optimal decision theory, even though real-world conditions may not conform to the constraints of the theory. Proponents of this view believe that the structure imposed by optimal decision theory can optimize decision making, and that failure to follow the tenets of the theory exists because of problems with training, learning, or willingness to expend effort.

The opposing way of viewing military decision procedures involves assuming that the commander's and staff's *knowledge* guide the process. This mode is characterized by informal procedures that are not generalizable, but rather depend on how an individual thinks and what an individual knows. Commanders and staff (and researchers who are trying to capture actual behaviours) tend not to rely on explicit, formal decision prescriptions. Proponents of this informal view maintain that there is no widespread lack of knowledge or diligence among commanders and their staffs. Instead, they suggest that when doctrine and practice don't match, the explanation lies in the fact that a tactical leader's thinking has evolved through roughly three decades of repetition into the application of prudent, expedient, and natural reasoning processes. Mismatches between doctrine and observed processes are not a result of failure to learn *the* process; rather, they are a result of ill-fitting formal models of thought. The natural reasoning processes involved are admittedly complex and are dependent on individual knowledge and intentions in a specific situation. Proponents of this view believe that tactical decision makers should invest most of their mental effort in constructing and executing a plan that accomplishes a unit's mission and not be focused on optimizing a decision. Optimization may not be an appropriate goal in the time-pressured, complex realm of battle command.

Actual procedures for determining what to do depend on a whole range of factors, such as experience, the stakes involved, the time available, attitudes, decision-making style, and style of knowledge use. These factors combine and manifest themselves as different ways and styles of thinking. In our team's early interactions with doctrinal authors, we were trying to define an alternative doctrinal description of the process, drawing on an informal, practical model that incorporated situational characteristics. We realized that there was considerably more groundwork to do.

3. COMPARISON OF FORMAL AND INFORMAL THINKING

Our research observations, as well as those of others, showed a mismatch between how military thinking is actually done and the focus of doctrinal procedures and training materials. The difference is usually attributed, especially for the formal camp, either to poor training or to having a lack of time to complete the recommended procedures. But we prefer to explain the difference in terms of the different amounts of *explicitness* in the formal and informal models of thinking. Table 1 contrasts the formal and informal models. This contrast is an extension of Galotti's (1989) review. A particular emphasis of informal thinking is to be well versed in thinking skills that can be tailored to specific problems with different demands for mental accuracy, speed, and effort. Thinking skills like problem finding, situation understanding, and self-assessment of thinking quality are more important in informal thinking. Equally important is to consider one's limitations in understanding, especially those that stem from habitual ways of looking at problems. Informal thinking implies giving more attention during training and personal development to experience, intentions, holistic thinking, and adapting to situational differences. On the other hand, formal approaches emphasize the procedures that should be followed to produce thoughts, plans, and conclusions. While there may not be actual differences in the underlying cognitive mechanisms between formal and informal thinking (Walton, 1990), the two views do suggest that different approaches ought to be taken when one wants to *improve* thinking.

The differences between the two styles of thinking can be clarified by considering specific types of problem solving within each category. Two types of problem solving can be described for each mode. Formal approaches can be broken down into *analytic* and *procedural* types (see Table 2). Informal approaches can be separated into *recognitional* and *dominance* approaches. Analytic and recognitional approaches operate best when knowledge already exists and the situation is familiar. The processes common to both involve the application of rules to the existing and apparent knowledge one has about a problem. Procedural and dominance approaches, by contrast, provide ways to think when there is not a great deal of knowledge and the situation is relatively unfamiliar.

Formal approaches tend to be prescriptive, guiding how one thinks about what one knows. For example, the analytic approach recommends using formal means of analysis to quantify or objectify aspects of a problem. These aspects are broken down and recombined using analysis. Analytic approaches tend to focus on structured ways of comparing courses of action in symmetric formats (for example, a decision matrix or a linear additive model). Analytic guidance is contained in the comparison and selection steps of the U.S. military decision-making process. Procedural approaches enumerate a sequence of steps that are believed to lead to a single optimal solution. Procedural guidance involves laying out the processes for making military decisions. Procedural steps are taught in U.S. Army institutional courses, such as the Officer Basic and Advanced Courses, the courses offered at the Combined Arms Services Staff School, and the Command and General Staff Officer Course (CGSOC).

Table 1.   Comparison of Formal and Informal Approaches to Thinking

Comparison factor	Formal thinking	Informal thinking
Views about knowledge	Knowledge exists or can be determined with certainty; it is structured hierarchically; it is explicit and unambiguous.	Some uncertainty always exists; *knowing* is relative to one's view of the world; it is structured in nonhierarchical "weblike" patterns; it is affected by values, attitudes, feelings.
Views about goals	Goals are accepted as given or as what is typical; little attention is paid to what goals should be or how they could differ.	Goals are checked, determined iteratively by the thinker; aim is to solve the right problem or a solvable one; give and take between goals and solution.
Views about outcomes	An optimal outcome is possible and desired, even if it's theoretical; solutions are justifiable to outside authority.	A satisfactory outcome is good enough (satisficing), but good solutions don't necessarily exist; solutions stand on common sense or a result they achieve.
Order of process	Process is sequential, usually linear, and aligned to some so-called ideal model; following the process is believed to result in the answer.	Process is opportunistic and fluid; process depends on what is figured out (one conclusion leads to another); process is streamlined to expedite solution.
Control of process	Systematic; rule-bound; regulated by algorithmic or probabilistic procedures; oriented on belief that "process is paramount."	Heuristic; makes exceptions to rules; flows according to interim results of thinking; oriented on end goals, problem substance, and what is expedient.
Nature of process	Formal logic; analytical; closed system; self-contained rules of thought; converges to answer; all premises are known or knowable.	Everyday logic; tends toward holistic; openness of thought; creative and divergent; some premises are implied or unknowable; irreducibly dynamic.
Aim of process	Find truth or falsity of conclusions; form and structure of arguments makes statements right or wrong; persuade others that a position is correct.	Common sense, everyday experience, and existing beliefs make statements believable or less believable; thinking is imperative to action.
Preciseness in process	Thoughts should be exact, error-free; precise, absolute measurements; quantitative amounts.	Thoughts have varying degrees of uncertainty; thoughts have different degrees of association; "fuzzy" comparative amounts; qualitative amounts.
Types of problems	Limited to well-bounded, well-understood problems.	Suited to everyday problems that are irreducibly dynamic and complex.

Table 2. Four Problem-Solving Approaches Organized by Two Types of Process and Formality

Predominant cognitive process	Formal	Informal
Rules, knowledge	Analytic—deliberate rule-following or transformation of knowledge	Recognition—nonconscious use of rules or knowledge
Search	Procedural—deliberate search process	Dominance—desire to find dominance guides search

Informal approaches are more descriptive than prescriptive. Informal approaches try to explain thinking and recognize that it is not always a linear, deliberate, and conscious process. (The military community might think of these natural procedures as "intuition," but intuition is an ill-defined and inexact term that we will forgo in this chapter.) The informal approaches do presume that the ways of thinking are natural. Improvements should adapt to the natural behaviours, not try to replace them. Improvement is a bit problematical in informal approaches, because these approaches make no claim that optimal outcomes exist. The conditions that illustrate the potential advantage of informal approaches come from several assumptions:

- People are not ideal rationalizers. Their bounded rationality comes from the way that cognition functions. Cognition has evolved over time to allow efficient and life-sustaining processing.

- Thinking is a uniquely personal matter. Processes are idiosyncratic to an individual and to his or her perception of what the problem is.

- Thinking starts from what is already known or believed to be true. It is more complex than is captured by an input–process–output model.

There are many ways of solving problems using informal approaches. We focused on two in our research (see Table 2). One informal approach is based on recognitional processes. In this approach, noticeable cues trigger the recognition of a pattern from memory. A match of a situation, in turn, triggers a habitual way of acting or responding in that type of situation. A recognitional approach is desirable whenever decisions need to be made rapidly. Klein (1993) refers to this approach as recognition-primed decision making. The usual guidance given for producing improvement is to ensure lots of experience from on-the-job-training, practice, surrogate experiences, or case study. The improvement in behaviour results from repetition and from the pairing of recognitional processes with action. Repeated exposure, action, and feedback allow the person to notice intricate situational cues and to refine the assessments and actions that prove to be best.

A second informal approach is based on dominance structuring (Montgomery, 1993). In dominance structuring, a set of processes is activated in order to test whether a particular solution is better than any others. The starting assumption in this decision process is that some course of action ought to dominate the others. The search processes test various problem frames to come up with a solution where dominance is likely to be found, and considers various problem parameters by which it might be judged as dominant. Dominance might provide elaboration for a hunch, an intuition, or a feeling about a particular option. Although specific techniques have not been developed for improving dominance processing, being aware of how it works should enhance performance. Another way of viewing the recognition approach is that the processes rely on and use stored knowledge that has passed dominance testing in previous experiences.

We felt that by examining these informal approaches, which depart from normal doctrinal and educational description, we could provide guidance for improving these important—but less generally familiar—processes. We turned our attention to cognitive skills rather than to doctrinal descriptions of processes because we knew that the skilled use of knowledge was important, regardless of the linkages and sequences contained in a group process. Our idea was that focusing on cognition might provide a better way of improving performance, by replacing a task-oriented focus that is primarily concerned with formal procedures and observable behaviours. Combining the idea of skills with cognition meant that we were sensitive to the fact that quality of performance varies and should be able to be improved with practice. The face validity of the assertion that performance is variable is illustrated by the noticeable differences in ways of thinking among commanders, across different conditions, and across time. Psychological factors that influence these different cognitive skills include an individual's beliefs about knowledge, his or her standards of thinking quality (Paul, 1993), how much the individual capitalizes on continuing opportunities to learn, and his or her attitudes.

We felt that attitudes were especially important in informal modes of thought. Most human emotions and attitudes are out of conscious focus, but they have a strong influence on judgment. Since our attitudes so strongly affect our thinking in informal, natural models, it is worthwhile to consider what kinds of attitudes and emotions are desirable. Some of the desired attitudes about thinking that commanders and staff could profit from include the following (adapted from Walton, 1990):

- *Persistence*—realizing that if one line of thought or action is not working, another may work.

- *Plasticity of process*—realizing that prescribed processes are not sacrosanct for solving novel, ill-defined problems, and understanding that eventual success may depend on adapting or discovering a new process of thinking that will help reach a solution.

- *Consistency*—reasoning with the same standards regardless of the issue, the position, or who supports it; maintaining consistent standards and procedures of thinking that are independent of the desired outcome.

- *Active fair-mindedness*—making a special effort to find out whether one's ideas will work by imagining what is wrong with them; often involves simply looking at the other side or trying to imagine what it would take to persuade someone who holds an opposing view to believe differently.

- *Openness*—being open to different and multiple possibilities; being ready to put aside negative thoughts and allow ideas to emerge concerning something that is contrary to one's initial or long-held beliefs.

- *Detachment of ego*—separating the things that influence one's self-esteem from one's reasoning (for example, by not getting caught up in being on the right side of an argument, or by rationalizing why failure was out of one's control).

- *Retraction of commitment*—being open to changing one's mind about a preferred solution or even about how the problem itself is defined. Once mental effort is expended or some sense of closure is reached, there is a natural preference for sticking with an initial commitment; to be truly open, one needs to be willing to change an earlier commitment to thoughts or planned actions.

- *Willingness to expend effort*—a willingness to engage in deeper, more thorough thinking (for example, the consideration of side effects), even when the effort may not seem prudent. This attitude is related to that of active fair-mindedness, and is perhaps most necessary when confidence in a certain solution is high from the beginning.

- *Tolerance of uncertainty*—knowing that it is all right not to know something. There is often an advantage to having to think through problems to figure them out, instead of using minimal cues to interpret a situation and making hasty and incorrect recognitions.

- *Willingness to learn*—realizing, even when one is in a position where one is expected to already have the knowledge and experience to perform acceptably, that learning anew is desirable too. When something that has already been learned is reviewed, a fuller, deeper understanding may be achieved; one is reminded of finer points that may have been forgotten, and the information may be combined with what has been learned since.

These 10 attitudes were identified as desirable qualities of thinking. They also indicate important attributes of ways of thinking. This is especially useful because our recommendations put increased emphasis on informal thinking, with its inherent lack of prescription regarding ways to think. We propose attitudes in addition to specific ways of thinking partly because a person's qualities and standards of thinking are hard to distinguish from that person's ways of thinking. (For example, does creativity happen because someone is skilful or because he or she has an attitude that values creativity?) With "healthy" attitudes like these and the values and attributes described by Lewis, Butler, Challans, Craig, and Smidt (this volume, Chapter 10), it may be that the conceptual thinking skills will form largely by themselves. Better understanding of the relationship between attitudes, beliefs, and skills is a current area of ARI research that we hope will reveal acceptable ways to improve conceptual abilities.

4. FINDINGS ABOUT BATTLE COMMAND THINKING AND IMPROVING THINKING

In view of the position described above on informal thinking, we proceeded to try to discover what kinds of processes tactical leaders actually use in their situated problem solving. This research took two tracks. One track was designed to develop a better empirical understanding of the thinking processes used by tactical leaders. This work surveyed officers on their approaches to problem solving and on their detailed strategies and solutions. A second track examined various ways of improving the practical thinking of leaders.

4.1. Officers' Problem-Solving Approaches and Strategies

The first track surveyed the approaches and strategies used by U.S. Army officers when faced with tactical problems (Pounds & Fallesen, 1997). Approaches were operationalized to be a categorization of decision-making behaviour as described in Table 2. Strategies were listed in terms of short statements describing the problem-solving processes defined for this study: 19 choice strategies and 29 information-processing ones, all derived from a review of the problem-solving literature. Each strategy was expressed as a short description (for example, *identify problems in accomplishing the goals, deconflict information, consider the relevancy of information*, and *choose the option that had occurred most often in the past*). After each of 82 participants in the study had worked through three problems individually, they indicated the approach they had used and rated the importance of each strategy. The problems consisted of one case reported from a participant's own military experience and two scenarios (called "enemy over the river" and "rescue the ambassador" [adapted from Schmitt, 1994]) in which the participant was assigned the role of commander. For both scenarios, the participant reported what he or she had been thinking while solving the problems; these presentations were recorded.

The striking finding with regard to doctrine was that *informal* approaches were used more than half of the time. The recognition approach was used most often when the thinker was familiar with the situation, and the dominance approach was used the most when the situation was relatively unfamiliar (see Figure 1). As expected, the analytic approach required the most mental effort, and recognition required the least. The five most important strategies (dealing with goals, facts, criteria, problems with goals, and visualization) were common components of all four approaches (Fallesen, 1996), while the seven least important strategies were unique to the informal approaches. This finding, together with the prediction of approaches by strategy importance, indicates that most strategies are associated with more than one approach. It seems that the higher-level approaches consist of complex combinations of both formal and informal strategies.

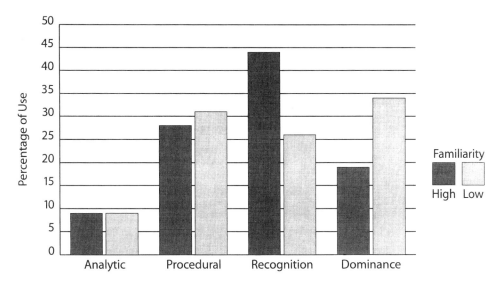

FIGURE 1. Use of problem-solving approaches for two levels of familiarity.

One of the most important findings was that a concurrent option comparison strategy was used in less than 5 percent of the cases. In the majority of cases, individuals did not follow what was the prevailing guidance at the time—that is, to generate multiple options before evaluating them in order to compare all options at the same time. On the other hand, thinking was rarely limited to single, narrow options. Multiple options were almost always considered sequentially (rather than concurrently) after a potential problem, concern, or opportunity was identified following investigation of an initial option. When only a single option was considered, it was likely to be considered in greater depth than when two or more options were considered. This result confirmed that doctrinal guidance about generating at least three options concurrently was not followed most of the time.

More specifically defined strategies emerged from qualitative analysis of the audio recordings. We identified 22 new strategies, including *organizing understandings, monitoring one's own knowledge, negotiating among goals, prioritizing goals*, and *compensating for missing information*. Several high-order classes of knowledge, called themes, were also identified from the transcripts. The themes seemed to provide an organizing function and in some cases were the predominant basis for a decision on a course of action. Examples of themes included *acting to limit the enemy's available options, acting to promote broad flexibility in future options*, and *exercising caution to protect against unknown risks* (Pounds & Fallesen, in press).

4.2. Improving the Practical Thinking of Leaders

In the second research track, we studied ways to improve thinking through cognitive instruction techniques. We were sensitive to the fact that most cognitive instruction is of a general nature and is geared toward children. We recognized that instruction for adults should place more emphasis on the motivation that helps a person to consider how he or she thinks. In addition, instructional approaches that provide examples of thinking may be more effective with adults than they would be with children. Instruction that provides examples of deep, concentrated thinking can help show why it is important to build up versatility in thinking skills.

We developed instruction in what we called practical thinking (Fallesen et al., 1996). We used this approach along with U.S. Army instructors to teach a CGSOC class. The practical thinking lessons consisted of 12 hours of instruction; the schedule and level of detail were influenced by the amount of time available from the larger battle command course in which these were embedded. The lessons were separated into six sessions. Table 3 describes each lesson's title, basic concepts, and purpose, and summarizes the lesson's content. Students reported significant gains in expertise because of the lessons (see Figure 2). The development of lesson materials provided a model for defining battle command topics that were later incorporated into the CGSOC's core curriculum.

In two other studies using a cognitive skill approach, we also found significant improvements. The first study (Cohen, Freeman, & Thompson, 1997) attacked the problem of premature or overly simplified situation understanding. To counter this problem, training in three strategies was provided: looking for hidden assumptions that could lead to an incorrect situation assessment, handling unexpected information that would require changing one's situation understanding, and having the leader explicitly consider how to decide. Officers who received the training had accuracy scores that were 25 percent higher than those in the group that did not receive the training. The second study tested ways to check for relevancy of information (Fallesen & Pounds, 1998). The cognitive requirement for training was based on an analysis of problem-solving strategies that showed that a more thorough

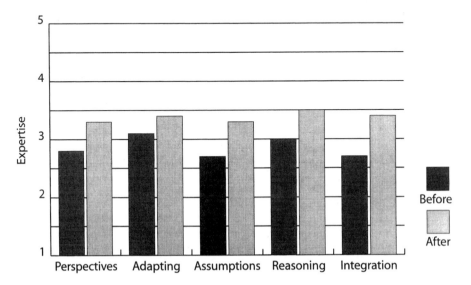

FIGURE 2. Changes in expertise of critical thinking attributed to practical thinking lessons.

Table 3. Summary of Practical Thinking Lessons

Lesson topic	Basic concepts	Purpose	Content summary
Introduction	What are different ways of thinking? What are some of the key components of thinking?	Provide a course overview. Describe rationale and philosophy. Stimulate students to consider how they think. Set expectations through an overview of topics and introductory exercises.	Practical thinking aims to capture the strengths of how we think about everyday problems, calling on experience more than on formal models. Practical thinking includes creative and critical elements. Thinking is a rich interchange among problems, possibilities, evidence, goals, and values.
Multiple perspectives	Think outside the box. Thinking is often bound with unnecessary limits.	Demonstrate ways to (a) broaden perspectives, (b) take different perspectives, or (c) find a better perspective when assessing situations and solving problems.	Whenever we reason, we do so with some perspective. Any defect or restriction in that perspective is a possible source of problems. Taking multiple perspectives helps us understand situations, be creative, and reason about solutions. Techniques, guidelines, and attitudes for altering perspective are described.
Strategies for adapting to the situation	There is no single right way to think. Need to learn to be aware of how thinking works and how to guide thinking.	Demonstrate the reasons why procedures need to be adapted, what factors are involved, and ways to think about adaptation. Provide a bridge between formally taught tactical decision making and the skills in these lessons.	Effective performance depends on adapting to tasks and situations. For unfamiliar problems, one must think about how to think and decide. It is like *triage* for decisions. Questions can help guide thinking: What are the goals of and obstacles to thinking? How familiar is the situation? How important is the problem to be solved? How much time is available? How much effort is required? What's important now?
Finding hidden assumptions	Some assumptions are hidden as "beliefs" when there is no true basis for them. Explore other possibilities.	Increase awareness of the assumptions that we make unknowingly. Provide techniques for identifying hidden assumptions and handling unexpected events.	Cases like Pearl Harbor, the Battle of the Bulge, and the Shuttle disaster indicate assumptions that were ignored or treated as facts. Check assumptions by asking what else could this be; what else could explain this? Once assumptions are identified, judge their plausibility. Keep track of unexpected events; explain them in accordance with other understandings.
Practical reasoning	Limit the extent that attitudes unjustly influence reasoning, and recognize when there is a failure to reason critically.	Make explicit what reasoning techniques are commonly used. This serves to demonstrate fallacies of arguments and different ways to reason. Describe and assess standards of reasoning, attitudinal pitfalls, and reasoning fallacies.	Knowledge is key in reasoning. There are different ways to prepare for uncertainty, but uncertainty is inevitable. We can fill in our gaps in knowledge by creative and critical exploration. Five standards of reasoning, four pitfalls, and eight biases are discussed. Quick-start questions: What if? What else? So what? What specifics? Is there a weak link? What is unexpected?
Integrative thinking	Learn from experience. Understand cause and effect relations. Put the big picture together.	Demonstrate differences in integrative thinking. Address how it is acquired and how it relates to expertise and intuition. Provide guidance for developing integrative thinking.	Integrative thinking involves understanding the relationships among events and concepts. Levels of integrative thinking are reliance on authority, awareness of complexity, reflection, emerging synthesis, and mastery. To improve it, resolve uncertainties, spend more time understanding problems, apply practical thinking techniques, and practise patience and persistence.

consideration of tactical objectives resulted when officers used a relevancy-checking strategy. Based on this result, instruction was developed to improve discrimination of relevant information, goals, actions, and conclusions. Usually relevancy checking occurs as an automatic and nonconscious check of the applicability of one's knowledge to the current situation. The instruction brought explicit attention to the importance of deliberate relevancy checking, ways of doing it using "What else?" and "What if?" questioning, and practice exercises. Subjects who received the training showed positive benefits compared to a control group who did not receive the training. All of these studies on cognitive instruction showed that gains can be achieved through techniques that remind thinkers of explicit ways to safeguard their natural ways of thinking with reflective and thought-provoking questions.

5. CONCLUSIONS

Our failed attempt at writing doctrine led us away from explicit descriptions of battle command procedures and toward a focus on practical thinking and on the cognitive skills that extend to any chosen or designed procedures for battle command. U.S. Army doctrine has been repeatedly updated since our original attempts to change it, and it now contains more of the flavour that we were aiming for. Even so, we are not content that an adequate understanding of practical thinking has been achieved. A major goal of the NATO (North Atlantic Treaty Organization) Human in Command Workshop at which the paper on which this chapter is based was first presented was to identify contemporary research issues of interest to the NATO military community. In response to this, and based on our experience, we believe that the two tracks of research described in this chapter should continue to identify the conceptual thinking patterns of commanders and staff and to explore ways of improving them. Improvement in conceptual thinking can lead to more knowledge, as well as to knowledge that is more differentiated and that can be applied more flexibly. Instruction in conceptual thinking promotes more ways of thinking, and will also, it is hoped, promote more versatility of the kind that will be needed to meet the demands made by future situations. With practice over time and elaborated in depth, instruction in conceptual-thinking skills should allow thinking to occur more quickly and more efficiently and not occur as a ponderous mental struggle. An indirect benefit of instruction should be to build commanders' confidence in their cognitive skills so that they will be more likely to see a way to think through a problem, rather than ignore it, frame it more simply than is justified, or look to someone else to offload the task to.

   All of the behavioural research community for military applications should consider helping develop better understandings of basic battle command skills, as well as advanced skills at expert levels. More specifically, research will need to expand the military's understanding of cognitive behaviours in command and its understanding of interactions between those behaviours and the commander's experience, attitudes, and beliefs about knowledge. Research addressing skill improvement will need to consider how to impart or demonstrate the deep, concentrated ways of thinking required by commanders under high levels of battlefield uncertainty. Research should consider how to encourage tactical leaders to understand their own thinking without interfering with it. Self-awareness about one's cognitive skill, standards, and attitudes may be an important component of ways to improve informal, natural approaches like dominance structuring. Improved self-awareness affords an individual commander the opportunity to understand his or her thinking processes better and to discover improved ways of practical thinking. Diligence in scientific approach and in testing development initiatives will continue to be necessary as well.

6. REFERENCES

Cohen, M. S., Freeman, J. T., & Thompson, B. B. (1997). Training the naturalistic decision maker. In C. E. Zsambok & G. Klein (Eds.), *Naturalistic decision making*. Mahwah, NJ: Erlbaum.

Fallesen, J. J. (1993). *Overview of Army tactical planning performance research* (Technical Report 984). Alexandria, VA: U.S. Army Research Institute for the Behavioral and Social Sciences.

Fallesen, J. J. (1996). Understanding and improving tactical problem solving. In *U.S. Army Research Institute Principal Scientist Colloquium Special Report 26*. Alexandria, VA: U.S. Army Research Institute for the Behavioral and Social Sciences.

Fallesen, J. J., Lussier, J. W., & Michel, R. R. (1992). *Tactical command and control process* (Research Product 92-06). Alexandria, VA: U.S. Army Research Institute for the Behavioral and Social Sciences.

Fallesen, J. J., Michel, R. R., Lussier, J. W., & Pounds, J. (1996). *Practical thinking: Innovation in battle command instruction* (Technical Report 1037). Alexandria, VA: U.S. Army Research Institute for the Behavioral and Social Sciences.

Fallesen, J. J., & Pounds, J. (1998, May). *Identifying and testing a naturalistic approach for cognitive skill training*. Paper presented at the Fourth Conference on Naturalistic Decision Making, Warrenton, VA.

Galotti, K. M. (1989). Approaches to studying formal and everyday reasoning. *Psychological Bulletin, 105*, 331–351.

Klein, G. A. (1993). A recognition-primed decision (RPD) model of rapid decision making. In G. A. Klein, J. Orasanu, R. Calderwood, & C. E. Zsambok (Eds.), *Decision making in action: Models and methods* (pp. 138–147). Norwood, NJ: Ablex.

Lussier, J. W. (1992). *Early decisions and concurrent option comparison in problem solving groups* (Research Report 1618). Alexandria, VA: U.S. Army Research Institute for the Behavioral and Social Sciences.

Montgomery, H. (1993). The search for a dominance structure in decision making: Examining the evidence. In G. A. Klein, J. Orasanu, R. Calderwood, and C. E. Zsambok (Eds.), *Decision making in action: Models and methods* (pp. 182–187). Norwood, NJ: Ablex.

Paul, R. (1993). *Critical thinking: How to prepare students for a rapidly changing world*. Santa Rosa, CA: Foundation for Critical Thinking.

Pounds, J., & Fallesen, J. J. (1994). *Understanding problem solving strategies* (Technical Report 1020). Alexandria, VA: U.S. Army Research Institute for the Behavioral and Social Sciences.

Pounds, J., & Fallesen, J. J. (1997). *Problem solving of mid-career Army officers: Identification of general and specific strategies* (Research Note 97-21). Alexandria, VA: U.S. Army Research Institute for the Behavioral and Social Sciences.

Pounds, J., & Fallesen, J. J. (in press). *Problem solving of mid-career Army officers: Identifying natural reasoning* (Technical Report). Alexandria, VA: U.S. Army Research Institute for the Behavioral and Social Sciences.

Schmitt, J. F. (1994). *Mastering tactics: A tactical decision game workbook*. Quantico, VA: Marine Corps Association.

United States. (1984). *Staff organization and operations* (Field Manual 101-5). Washington, DC: Department of the Army.

Walton, D. N. (1990). *Practical reasoning: Goal-driven, knowledge-based action-guiding argumentation*. Savage, MD: Rowman and Littlefield.

CHAPTER 14

COMMAND AND CONTROL
A Biased Combination?

LIEUTENANT COLONEL PER-ARNE PERSSON, JAMES M. NYCE, and HENRIK ERIKSSON

1. INTRODUCTION

When seeking a theoretical basis for research in command and control (C^2), researchers tend to favour control-related concepts, which are amenable to rational scientific inquiry. For example, the topic of control has strong ties to systems theory, to information management, and to control technologies. Command, on the other hand, as a human-centred term that has emerged from the military vernacular, seems to be less tied to scientific theory. Compared to control, command has attracted relatively little theoretical effort. As a result, control—strongly related to mechanistic and systems theory, along with their more accessible research methods—has been used inappropriately, albeit perhaps inevitably, to guide social control and organizational design. This approach has yielded designs that are perhaps more appropriate for meeting the criteria of scientific management than for accommodating human needs such as autonomy and creativity.

As a result, we humans have become alienated from our own social control mechanisms. Military social meaning—that is, the situational and institutional aspects of command and control—has become neglected, and the human actors less

LIEUTENANT COLONEL PER-ARNE PERSSON • Swedish National Defence College, P.O. Box 27805, S-115 93 Stockholm, Sweden   JAMES M. NYCE • School of Library and Information Management, Emporia State University, 1200 Commercial Street, Emporia, Kansas, USA 66801-5087 and Swedish National Defence College, P.O. Box 27805, S-115 93 Stockholm, Sweden   HENRIK ERIKSSON • Department of Computer and Information Science, Linköping University, S-581 83 Linköping, Sweden and Swedish National Defence College, P.O. Box 27805, S-115 93 Stockholm, Sweden

The Human in Command: Exploring the Modern Military Experience, edited by McCann and Pigeau, Kluwer Academic/Plenum Publishers, New York, 2000.

visible. We have failed to build a robust, analytically informed scientific foundation for what is called "command and control." This chapter analyzes the agenda that informs the present state of C^2 research, discusses why various difficulties have evolved, and outlines some of their consequences.

In addition, we describe a qualitative research approach based on grounded theory[1] that can serve as a generic model both to advance research into command and to resolve the pragmatic issues that face commanders. This approach grew out of a study of the 1993/94 United Nations operations in Bosnia (Persson, 1996, 1997)—a study that led to an alternative way of thinking about command and control.[2] First, however, we will re-examine the common concepts of command and control, trace their origins and meanings, and raise some questions about certain fundamental assumptions that the C^2 research community has taken to be self-evident. Unless these issues are addressed—that is, as long as researchers accept the traditional cognitive and individual models without questioning their underlying assumptions—C^2's theoretical foundation will remain weak.

2. SCIENCE VERSUS ART IN COMMAND AND CONTROL

Is command and control a scientific or an artistic endeavour? Over the centuries, theoreticians have taken both perspectives. When C^2 was viewed as a scientific enterprise, the goal was to design military organizations as clockwork mechanisms (Morgan, 1986) using mathematical principles (Gat, 1989), and then manage them accordingly. This attitude, which was directed toward opponents as well, prevailed well into the twentieth century. The result was an ongoing struggle to achieve social control through rationalistic means that reflected the political and institutional contexts of their times. In this pragmatic approach, which became increasingly scientific, such inventions as discipline, training, doctrine, legal systems, and various technologies were common mechanisms for achieving control. Today, the legacy of mechanized control is one of servitude to an engineering mission, with scientific management being the dominating philosophy.

The other historical perspective on C^2 puts creative genius first. Here command and control is considered to be more art than science. Inspired by intuition, creative leaders are allowed to move beyond formal frameworks (Gat, 1989) and adapt

---

[1] A grounded theory is inductively derived from a study of a phenomenon—that is, discovered, developed, and provisionally verified through systematic data production/collection and analysis. These analytic and interpretive procedures are *nonmathematical* and applicable to various kinds of data—usually observations, interviews, photos, videos, and texts, but occasionally also quantified data (Strauss & Corbin, 1990).

[2] We visited Macedonia early in 1994 to better understand the context of an international operation. We later interviewed 16 returning Swedish officers from the first two Nordic Bosnia battalions. The interviews and conversations covered command practices and difficulties, communication issues, coalition-related events, standard operating procedures, and related competence issues. The interviews varied between one and two hours in length, and 11 of them were audiotaped. Official after-mission reports and documents completed the data. The qualitative analysis led to a theory for C^2 that provides a foundation for further studies (see Section 4.1, "The Grounded Constraint Theory").

quickly to war's inherently nonorderly character. Adapting dynamically to shifting circumstances requires guidance from principles other than those of purely mathematical computation (Howard, 1983).

The unpredictable and unavoidable "frictions of war" discussed by Karl von Clausewitz (Howard, 1983) may thus be managed either through formal control mechanisms (for example, planning and engineering) or by focusing on human will, with its inherent ability to improvise. We will look more closely at both positions.

3. BACKGROUND: THE DEVELOPMENT OF COMMAND AND CONTROL

It is often difficult to understand the social actions, meanings, and mechanisms commonly associated with the concept of "command and control."[3] The control behaviours now exhibited in society are ingredients of what Beniger (1986) calls the *control revolution.* The success of certain theories and control mechanisms has contributed to defining what science is, and has even influenced what is perceived as being rational and logical (Goody, 1996). But as long as the social concepts behind those theories and mechanisms remain unanalyzed (and often even unrecognized), future research efforts, even if sound—that is, based on a solid theoretical foundation, while also taking account of the real (empirical) world, and conducted according to prevailing research standards—may fail to illuminate what is really going on. The military community will be left with few means of understanding the terms and agents that constitute the social and pragmatic business of C^2. To give one example, although Van Creveld (1985) states that military personnel require motivation as well as coordination, the latter concept (which is more easily reducible to law and science) receives *much* more attention in the literature.

3.1. Thought and Science: A Scientific Foundation for C^2?

Historically, there have been a number of attempts to establish a science of war. For example, siege warfare was long regarded as the ideal form of warfare because of its mathematical and thus scientific nature. During the Enlightenment, thinkers believed that warfare could be "reduced to rules and principles of universal validity and possibly even mathematical certainty" (Gat, 1989, p. 139). Why have military thinkers and scientists attempted to quantify and derive rules for war? First, many have believed that such an approach would help make war more intelligible and thus more controllable—a goal justified by the horrors of war throughout the ages. Second, some of these efforts may have been aimed at making the profession of war more socially respectable—that is, at legitimizing the craft and institutions

---

[3] Van Creveld (1985) maintains that a problem exists with the term itself, pointing out that it tends to conceal people's will and actions, and suggesting instead that the single word *command* be used to describe the manifold activities now grouped under command and control, just as the word *management* is used elsewhere.

of command. We interpret this "domestication" of war and its institutions as an answer to the loss of influence that aristocracies experienced under the control mechanisms of the modern nation–states, and the strategies those aristocracies applied in order to be socially recognized.

When one attempts to summarize previous thinking about war—that is, the art and the acts of command—certain features stand out. Because the practice of command and control in the military is complex and pragmatic, its theory base is weak. The theories that do exist are very old: they can be traced back to ancient Greek and Roman practices (Parker, 1995).[4] These theories form the foundations for today's doctrines (Leonhard, 1994). Their typical view of battle management— as an orderly, controllable process (Samuels, 1995)—leads to an interpretation of command that includes (a) an institutional legal framework, (b) socially recognized and formally empowered individuals who act as leaders using a cluster of formalized mechanisms, (c) and a socially constructed supporting ethos or culture. The ongoing search for ways to reduce complexity and to gain control has made scientific management an important concern for the military.

In modern times, the international C^2 research community has similarly attempted to establish a scientific foundation for military command. In the United States, research based on a concept of a science of command and control began to take form in the late 1970s (Levis & Levis, 1994). But as Levis and Levis point out, despite much effort and thought, little success has been achieved in designing and integrating military systems. Also, the appeal of authors (such as von Clausewitz) who make order versus chaos the primary issue in command and control may have set the community up for failure. What troubles us is neither the choice between order and chaos nor the remedies proposed for dealing with that choice—either more planning, more control, or the acceptance of chaos. Rather, it is the notion that only hard science—a science that tends to de-emphasize the critical role of the human in command and control—can succeed in improving military systems. This bias, along with its lack of success, requires us to rethink the entire command and control domain.

3.2. Concepts and Technologies

The term *command* is usually used to describe both the act of commanding and the position held by those who command (that is, those who are "in command"). Although its theoretical basis is weak, this approach does tie command acts and events to the social world. *Control*, on the other hand, means both "regulate" or "supervise" *and* the tool with which one does so. In order to be meaningful, control presupposes a goal.[5] This requirement easily leads to a focus on closed systems, or at least to a simplified treatment of the control object as if it were

---

[4] See Hoskin, Macve, and Stone (1997) for an insightful discussion of historical conditions and thinking.

[5] The word *control* apparently has origins in old commercial or social practices. It derives from the medieval French word *contre-rolle*, which meant the duplicate register that was used as a standard for comparison by someone who was consequently named *controlleur*.

a closed system. Indeed, a stable (closed) system is a prerequisite for training and assessment, where standards must be established beforehand and where predictability is an asset. During this century, the concept of control has been incorporated into systems theory and cybernetics, thereby acquiring some theoretical prestige. But such associations have obscured its original meaning—with its connotation of a fixed standard—although that meaning still carries significant semantic weight, particularly with its connotations of real-world practicality.

In fact, successive developments in control and information technology have probably been driven by issues of practicality. Such modern information techniques as written forms, contracts, formal procedures, and even the use of money are means of establishing reliable and stable relations between people. Compared to the spoken word, these techniques allow communication over long distances and over long time periods, and when a number of people are involved, they allow complex patterns of cooperation (Beniger, 1986; Goody, 1996; Hoskin & Zan, 1997). Practical control methods such as writing made complex chains of reasoning (formal logic, mathematics, and so on) possible and facilitated the tracking and recording of transactions (Goody, 1996). Because it allowed the calculation of costs, profits, and losses, this capability proved crucial to early and medieval commerce (Hoskin & Zan, 1997).

When used in the "command and control" context, control also has practical meanings. To command is itself an act of control, in which a person who is socially recognized as being in authority directs another person or persons toward a goal. But practical meaning does not yield analytical precision. Though the concept of control turns up in everyday usage, its common meaning when used in that way lacks a scientific foundation (unlike the concept of control in the context of systems theory). This limitation, we believe, has restricted the study of one of the most dynamic social institutions known—namely, war.

3.3. Research Rationales

Thus far we have briefly described some of the factors contributing to control's conceptual and scientific dominance in military thought—a dominance that has come at the expense of the more human and social concept of command. Command implies a human who is wielding a power that is socially sanctioned by an organization in the pursuit of a mission. It embodies the fields of psychology, sociology, and history. But control has been driven by developments in information technology (Beniger, 1986), where coordination and goals have been emphasized. Consequently, information systems developers have had trouble grasping the importance of human and social factors in their designs. This gap in understanding has contributed to many of the difficulties encountered in modern information systems, which are designed mainly to handle control functions rather than to support the social practice of command. Kammerer (1997) warns against accepting a military machine culture that focuses on technology and neglects the deeper analysis of such a culture's impact on war and leadership.

4. QUALITATIVE CONTRIBUTIONS: THE BOSNIA STUDY

4.1. The Grounded Constraint Theory

In order to better understand command and control—and subsequently to create a theory that would promote its development—we used the U.N. operations in Bosnia during 1993 and 1994 as a field site. Our research was oriented toward devising methods for studying command and control during this period of great change. We hoped to generate an empirically grounded theory—that is, a theory that takes into account the situated, social, and often nonorderly components of command and control.[6] To that end, we made an early strategic decision to use qualitative research methods. Interviews of Swedish officers who were returning from Bosnia served as our main source of empirical data; we also analyzed evaluations that were conducted by the units themselves and by the military authorities.

The U.N. coalition forces in Bosnia were confronted with extreme physical and social adversity (Breakwell, this volume, Chapter 23; Everts, this volume, Chapter 6). Our data revealed that formal structures and procedures, along with more informal practices, were used to overcome the problems. In addition, the operation required intense communication and personal interaction; improvisation, compromise, and negotiation skills proved vital. Old rules sometimes had to be violated or replaced with new ones. Because the purpose of this phase of the research was to develop a grounded theory for control (and command), a uniting concept that framed all these actions had to be developed (Strauss & Corbin, 1990). We therefore used the concept of *constraint management* in the final step of the analysis, in order to make sense of the multitude of approaches used by the coalition forces (Persson, 1997). The theory was then named *constraint theory*, because of the command teams' seemingly continuous need to manage one form of constraint or another.

In Bosnia, command activities concentrated on reducing the existing constraints to mission success without creating unmanageable new constraints. Although the term *constraint theory* is also used in computer science, we use it here to highlight what we see as a central element of command and control—that is, the situated management of sets of constraints. The term emphasizes important issues that the C^2 literature has so far either neglected or failed to take very seriously: in effect, we wish to focus analytic attention on what others have tended to dismiss as the "frictions" of war. In Bosnia, for example, unavoidable conflicts resulted from actions and events that could not be evaded. Indeed, such phenomena seem to have been encountered so frequently that their critical importance in command needs to be considered.

The importance of constraints in war is well known. But the Bosnia material suggests that researchers may need to rethink both what is meant by "constraint" (that is, the objects and actions that fall into this category) and how these objects

---

[6] Something is "situated" when it is given meaning by a specific institution, society, or culture and when it is defined in history and space—that is, when it pertains only to a specific time, place, and social context.

and actions are negotiated (managed). Moving in this direction will encourage and allow questioning of the traditional approaches to command and control. For the most part, traditional models and solutions in the literature have favoured rules and "rational" approaches. The underlying assumption has been that individuals and institutions work "best" if they are rule-bound and rational. The proof offered by advocates of this viewpoint is a pragmatic one: such approaches, they argue, not only reduce the complexity of war, but also can result in "right thought" and "proper action." But studies of command have yielded little evidence that what is "right" or "proper" can be adequately specified either for individuals or for institutions. Keegan (1976) for example, has clearly documented the confusions and the difficulties of battle. Redefining "constraint"—and in the process, elucidating why the traditional research community has defined the term the way it has—will provide opportunities to expand and strengthen the command paradigm.

4.2. Preliminary Conclusions

We believe that constraint theory's qualitative base and empirical origins give it analytic strength. It provides a means for understanding how and why pragmatic operations in war are executed and what they mean for those who carry them out. In particular, the theory can help illuminate what is done, by whom, and why (that is, the relationships between goals and actions) in more depth. In other words, qualitative methods, and what these methods presuppose about the social order, will expose the practices traditionally masked by the term "command and control." For example, as C^2 is currently construed, only control is considered necessary for achieving a given goal or organizing a social action. What is often overlooked (and rarely even acknowledged) is the close relationship between goals and social actions. In many ways, the social context gives rise to and even defines the goal. Standard C^2 technologies and models not only obscure social institutions and practices, they treat them only in (or reduce them to) individual and cognitive terms. This narrow approach privileges rationality and establishes strong links to control theory. The role of complexity in any given situation is in turn underplayed. The result disguises cause and effect in the social world. But it is only a short step analytically from useful reduction to misunderstanding and rationalizing what constraint is and means in social terms, and consequently what kind of action is necessary to confront or circumvent (a set of) constraints within a certain context. The Bosnia study (Persson 1996, 1997) shows that command and control may be more usefully recast into such terms as resources (material and personnel, as well as human competence—for instance, expertise), opportunity, and autonomy.

5. EXPANDING CONSTRAINT THEORY

5.1. Bosnia Revisited: Logistics and Autonomy

As we worked through the interview transcripts, we were struck by how military personnel in Bosnia perceived organizational structures as constraints to be managed. The structures often needed to be adapted, and sometimes even ignored. Officers and soldiers constantly worked to overcome frictions and constraints, especially in the area of logistics. Logisticians must juggle the situated, the social, and the institutional aspects of military life (Pagonis & Cruikshank, 1992), and their accounts brought to the surface a number of previously neglected issues. For example, it became clear that competent logisticians must be masters of both formal and informal (often innovative) methods for accomplishing their tasks, as well as of formal and informal communication channels. Unfortunately, logistics is an aspect of command that has been neglected as a topic of study, compared to tactics and operations (Van Creveld, 1977; Lynn, 1993). Logistics stands out as the area where command must be practised primarily by humans rather than by automated routines and predetermined actions.

The reality of applied logistics in the military contrasts strikingly with the term's meaning in industry, where production and transportation are designed to proceed automatically, thus being (at least ideally) easy to control.[7] Battlefield logistics and supply flows are affected by unpredictable events, making the resulting nonlinearities and discontinuities difficult to control and automate. Some researchers are now discovering that the military's well-established control mechanisms (that is, its rules and procedures) are bolstered by a rich collection of innovative strategies for ensuring the successful completion of a mission—often by personnel who wish to preserve their autonomy for precisely this purpose. Pagonis and Cruikshank (1992), for instance, describe how radio equipment is sometimes reported as having been broken in battle in order to prevent interference from higher echelons.

The insight that grew out of our analysis is that command and commanding, including various kinds of control, are actually instruments for achieving and preserving both social control and autonomy. This means that behind the efforts to overcome operational constraints is a constant search for autonomy, a central concern of all social interaction. The military phrase *freedom of action* calls for the practical implementation of the abstract concept autonomy and implies a certain dialectics. In one example of its centrality, Nandan (1997) refers to and exploits Giddens's term *dialectic of control*. This term, says Nandan, is largely unexplored in management studies and implies the analysis of power relations, meaning that subordinates have some resources at their disposal, and hence can influence the activities of their superiors. Further, Nandan continues, if studies on management control neglect issues of power and the possibility of resistance, they are deficient from a theoretical point of view, a deficiency that is likely to lead to incomplete prescriptions for designing or modifying management control systems. Thus, when it comes to C², our "grounded" term *constraint management* also points to the need for balance. Furthermore, we interpret the common military concept *mission tactics* as the operationalized *balancing between autonomy and control* considered necessary by Walsham (1993). One of the ideas behind this concept, we believe, is to legitimize the ongoing situated adjustment of the autonomy–control balance.

---

[7] The military meaning of logistics appeared around 1840, whereas the modern industrial meaning did not crystallize until 1960.

Autonomy presupposes efficient feedback mechanisms among those who control. Feedback—a prerequisite for choosing correctly among command actions—is a mutual and social affair in which both delays and misunderstandings should be avoided. Looking more closely at the roles played by autonomy, opportunity, and constraint should help us understand command, as well as how to teach and practise it.

5.2. Related Work on Constraints in Computer Science

Researchers in computer science have developed various programming techniques based on the notion of constraints (Kumar, 1992). These techniques provide an alternative to the more procedural, functional, and object-oriented programming methods. In constraint modelling, programmers attempt to formally define the constraints of a given problem. Constraint approaches therefore work best when applied to problems with constraints that *can* be formally defined. As previously noted, many command problems fall outside that category. Still, the principle of constraint satisfaction can prove useful in illuminating command issues.

In the two-dimensional example illustrated in Figure 1, constraints A and B delimit an area of possible solutions (called the *solution space*). Solutions within this area can be compared according to a defined goal function, which assigns a score to each solution based on how closely it fits a set of preferred objectives. The goal function might, for example, call for minimizing losses, maximizing speed, and neutralizing enemy forces. It is possible to generalize the example in Figure 1 to allow for more than two dimensions (variables) and constraints. Because many aspects of

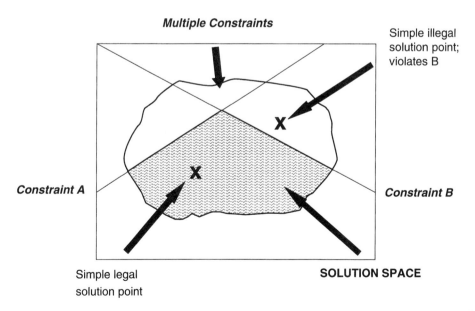

FIGURE 1. Example of constraints and solution space.

command are fuzzy and therefore difficult to describe as sets of well-defined constraints and goal functions, the formal application of constraint theory within computer science is limited to subareas that can be defined using such terms (for example, certain problems in logistics).

But constraint theory's importance for command extends beyond the theory's usefulness in solving a small category of problems. By requiring constraints to be defined in formal terms, this approach provides an opportunity to think about the consequences of reducing human artifacts to formal statements, laws, and standard procedures. Those who write and think about command issues in strictly rational terms do so from a seldom-questioned epistemological stance toward the world. Failing to recognize this stance prevents an important question from being asked: what is won and lost analytically and pragmatically by restricting thought and analysis in this way?

Working with constraint theory can strengthen our understanding of the role played by constraints in complex work and complex organizations. More importantly, because sufficient parallels seem to exist between the management of constraints (a) in a situation like that faced in Bosnia and (b) in certain problems in the domain of computer science, constraint theory could be the basis for an *analogy set*—a common language[8] that could encourage collaborative design and development of C^2 systems. Using this analogy set could lead to innovative work in knowledge development and operations support. Further, adding a qualitative component to this effort would help researchers elicit what is significant and important to the organizations and individuals concerned. In short, this approach would allow us to understand what informants (and often C^2 researchers themselves) take for granted, thereby improving the ways in which information technology is incorporated into command and control.

5.3. Command and Control: The Situated, the Social, and the Institutional

Thus far, this chapter's argument can be summarized as follows. Little attention has been paid to the premises that underlie the command and control research and literature. Events, actions, and objects that fall under the command and control rubric have been treated as though they were natural objects—and thus best understood in terms of general rules, laws, and principles. In short, it is commonly believed that command and control events and actions can be reduced to universal rules and principles that may even have mathematical validity and certainty. This epistemological position, like any other, necessarily demands tradeoffs. For example, those who take this position typically end up ignoring any role that might be played by culture and society (for which, after all, rules and laws are difficult to build) in the command and control community.

Van Creveld (1977) reminds us that war is a cultural event, not a natural one. The C^2 community—whose agenda is to integrate individuals, institutions, and technology for war (see, for instance, Van Creveld, 1977, p. 180)—disregards this fact at

---

[8] Constraint logic programming (CLP) is an example of a recent approach to constraint satisfaction (Pountain, 1995), used for scheduling and transportation planning.

its own peril. Do we wish to construct a science of command that captures only the rational and rule-bound components of human interaction and neglects everything else? Opting for nature and rule may validate certain prejudices toward knowledge and epistemology, but this position (a kind of naive positivism[9]), if not challenged, will continue to inhibit research. Further, if we want to interpret the objects and events of command as human artifacts, it may be best to avoid the kinds of analytic reductions that occur when we resort to terms like "rule" and "law." Demands for rigour and precision will not yield the scientific clarity that the C^2 community hopes for. In short, C^2 research has been weakened because it confuses nature and culture: where war is concerned, the research denies any distinction between natural and social fact. Constraint theory, on the other hand, does not rely on rules or laws. It supports description and interpretation rather than explanation and prediction.

6. DISCUSSION

6.1. Implications for Command, Control, and Logistics

Constraint theory approaches promise to unite the different concepts of command and of control. Consequently, constraint theory can help explain how command is exercised in the military—that is, how military commanders try to find pragmatic ways to solve the recurring control crises that characterize war (Beniger, 1986). As this chapter has argued, some of these techniques and methods have a very long tradition and reflect a strong need to find high-level abstract methods, applicable in a multitude of situations, for leveraging social control.

In logistics, the contradictions between the very old (social control practices and the struggle for autonomy) and the newer (scientific and rational) approaches are extremely visible. Supply management—that is, the set of situated actions that ensures everyday survival (Van Creveld, 1977; Lynn, 1993)—became known as *logistics* at the beginning of the nineteenth century. The new term signified the more systematic action that had by then become necessary; advances in transportation technologies made the shift seemingly inevitable. Modern industrial logistics reduced the art and craft of survival (that is, constraint management) to a set of objects, actions, and operations that can be counted, transforming these in turn into a set of continuous processes that are easily controlled and (ultimately) automated (Beniger, 1986).

A paradox appeared. Being a successful logistician appears to demand pragmatism, the recognition that the situated, the social, the institutional, and the innovative count for more than anything else. Yet logistics is also a domain in which

---

[9] Few people today believe that positivism, which holds that only observation and experiment can yield valid results about the (social) world, can be taken seriously, particularly as grand theory. In the C^2 research community, however, positivism has become synonymous with common sense, particularly when it comes to how this community understands human behaviour and social life. In brief, this kind of naive positivism strongly informs this community's approach to making sense of society and the social world. The influence of positivism and its consequences are discussed at some length in Miser and Quade (1985).

rules, measures, and quantities are deemed paramount. Rules and measures are originally designed to help achieve certain goals; they are human instruments that enable particular kinds of social interaction and negotiation. Military campaigns are indeed subject to logistical constraints, but commanders in the field must be prepared to compensate creatively for sudden shortfalls.

Equating logistics with things like production flows, processes, transportation, and just-in-time delivery causes a tendency to give priority to quantitative, not qualitative, aspects of logistics. Quantities are useful for planning and predicting, whereas quality evolves through the inevitable need to use supplies creatively and dynamically. Qualitative logistics uses imaginative thinking to solve pragmatic problems. Hence, logistics primarily involves human processes (processes that are not easily understood) and constraint management. Focusing on using logistics to create quality makes possible a new model of command—a domain that, like logistics, requires bringing together and managing the situated, the social, and the institutional. Such a foundation will in turn foster the design of systems that support the key command elements (particularly autonomy) necessary for successful military operations.

6.2. Research for Informed Redesign of Command Practices

New operational and control technologies have changed the conditions for social actions. Holley (1988) argues that new technologies, however brilliantly they solve problems, have little or no impact unless they become institutionalized—that is, fully incorporated into an organization. Holley also points out that von Clausewitz paid little attention to advances in weapons technology: he regarded numbers (manpower) as the decisive element in war. Nor did he question the notion of geniuses and their roles: for him, geniuses and manpower, in the absence of more adequate concepts, defined war. For von Clausewitz and his contemporaries, the humans *were* visible and in command.

We believe that modern command technologies are largely taken for granted. Because they deal mostly with control and with quantities, these technologies reinforce a certain kind of rationality and institutionalization that inhibit change. Only when a technology's underlying assumptions are exposed can a sufficiently informed theory[10] emerge. Without such work, pragmatic, incremental change in military practice cannot occur. To move beyond this limitation, it will be necessary to encourage research efforts that challenge what the C^2 community has taken for granted. As the Bosnia study reveals, qualitative methods can make a strong contribution to such research efforts, revealing new aspects of a seemingly well-known domain.

Looking carefully at what logisticians do may help the C^2 community advance beyond its current emphasis on rule and law. In addition, it may resolve the old dispute over whether war has more to do with art than with science. Pagonis and Cruikshank (1992) demonstrate the social character of command and logistics in

---

[10] By *informed theory* we mean a theory that is underpinned by science, systematically arrived at, and either traceable to data or supported by recognized scientific method.

the field. Implicit in our argument is the difficulty, if not the impossibility, of describing in formal terms the set of social and situated interactions that constitute war. This is not to say that science completely fails in helping researchers understand war. But it does means that the C^2 community must rethink the kinds of projects it undertakes with regard to command and must foster exploration into and making sense of war as a social process. However brutal war is, it is a form of social interaction. It is a human artifact. Therefore, more than anything else, war is a social artifact. It is a form of social exchange, governed by tradition, convention, and even law. It is a product of history and a negotiation over power. As such, it has more to do with the social world than with the natural world.

6.3. Further Studies

We have argued that the C^2 community needs a research agenda based on the acknowledgment that war is a social institution. Research that employs qualitative methods and theory can encourage the investigation of important command (and control) practices that the literature has largely ignored, and may produce knowledge and tools that will help command practitioners succeed in an uncertain world. Although commanders' attempts to achieve their goals are often impeded by the enemy, they are more often frustrated by internal constraints—especially in logistics, where very precise economic control mechanisms and the attendant reduction in personal autonomy (that is, innovation) threaten the social aspects of command.

We believe that constraint theory, as outlined in this chapter, can help reorient the command research agenda. If leadership is interpreted within a social context as those actions necessary for achieving personal autonomy in the pursuit of mission objectives, and if command is considered as one strategy for doing so, both concepts stand to gain theoretical weight. From this perspective, autonomy is not a one-way affair: leader and led alike need autonomy, often from each other. The social interaction must allow for sufficient real-time communication (feedback) to create this mutual perception. Feedback mechanisms within the entire control process must be designed accordingly.

Constraint theory's focus on social factors, as well as its emphasis on resources (material and human, including human competence and expertise), opportunity, and autonomy, can contribute to the design of information systems, to modelling efforts, and ultimately to doctrine and strategy. It can also encourage cooperation between military practitioners, systems designers, and computer scientists. Current work at the Swedish National Defence College aims at gaining a better understanding of the mechanisms related to command and at introducing a scholarly treatment of logistics into the college's curriculum. Accomplishing these goals would enable us to address the problems of how to preserve and negotiate mission and command autonomy when confronted by constraints that undercut the freedom to act, as can be the case both when dealing with enemies and when dealing with allies who want their share of victories. Further, this new understanding would in turn help staff stay in command and no longer be overshadowed by their own control mechanisms.

7. WORKSHOP POSTSCRIPT

We are convinced that there are good reasons for trying to distinguish between theory and practice when speaking of command and control. Otherwise, much remains hidden with respect to the social and situated actions underlying these concepts, including their communicational role and content.

The presentations given at the NATO (North Atlantic Treaty Organization) Human in Command Workshop illustrated the growing difficulties that many militaries are experiencing in establishing effective command practices, doctrines, and training that are relevant, for example, in operations other than war (OOTW) or in working with new defence concepts. Our discovery of the importance of making *autonomy* a central concern in command was supported by the presenters' repeated calls for "autonomy of action" and their vivid descriptions of how military personnel achieve such autonomy through social interaction—for example, when passing a roadblock in Bosnia (see Vogelaar & Kramer, this volume, Chapter 15; Everts, this volume, Chapter 6), when negotiating with militia in Rwanda (Dallaire, this volume, Chapter 4), or when detecting and neutralizing hostile missiles at sea (Lane, this volume, Chapter 5). Pigeau and McCann (this volume, Chapter 12) also allude to autonomy in their discussion of decentralized organizations.

The discussion by Winslow (this volume, Chapter 20) about military culture and the Canadian regimental system is, in our opinion, an account of how autonomy has been managed and the consequences of misdirected efforts and tolerance. The Canadian Airborne Regiment comprised three commandos, which represented different parent regiments and reflected the geographic, linguistic, and cultural divisions in the Canadian Army. Regimental traditions, group bonding, and unit cohesion are assumed to be valuable for efficiency. The system consequently allowed a considerable autonomy: units did not mix, lived separated from each other, did not mingle socially, and even displayed open antagonism toward each other. In this way, francophones and anglophones could remain separate and develop their own subcultures and ways of doing things, along with an associated identity, seeing other combat troops and noncombat personnel as inferior. Winslow describes how "walls of silence" (this volume, Chapter 20, p. 305) rose when investigators tried to determine what had happened in various cases of misconduct. Winslow's chapter title, "Misplaced Loyalties," captures the situation effectively; such loyalties grew out of the accepted, even sanctioned, autonomy, which eventually fed on itself.

New force structures also suggest changes for command and control. Armed forces around the world are being transformed from organizations consisting chiefly of young conscripts into groups of professional soldiers who are often experts in their field (Capstick, this volume, Chapter 7). Such personnel expect and must be accorded some level of autonomy: otherwise, both recruitment and retention can be jeopardized. Command practices, attitudes, and values must be consistent with such structural changes and what they imply. Traditional disciplinary practices must be questioned, and the proper combination of formal and informal control mechanisms must be reassessed. All these requirements suggest that the role of autonomy merits considerable theoretical and practical attention. Whenever military personnel must deviate from their original goals, interpret the implications of such deviations, or even change the goal according to actual events, they will need autonomy and hence a capacity for constraint management.

Finally, *leadership* is another theme that was frequently raised during the workshop presentations. We would object, however, to labelling leadership as simply a technical skill acquired through formal training. "Textbook" leadership skills are neither appropriate nor efficient in circumstances such as those found in Bosnia or Rwanda, where the need for situated autonomy was great, but where on the whole such autonomy was denied. Leadership theories should both recognize command situations like these and make them intelligible. To that end, the C^2 community needs a more informed understanding of constraint management and command autonomy. The leadership models that would emerge as a result would be stronger both analytically and pragmatically.

8. ACKNOWLEDGMENTS

The study described in this chapter is supported by the Swedish National Defence College and is part of a larger effort aimed at establishing a scientific foundation for studying and teaching command and logistics. By providing a valuable occasion for further discussions and feedback, the June 1998 NATO Human in Command Workshop advanced this chapter considerably.

9. REFERENCES

Beniger, J. R. (1986). *The control revolution: Technological and economic origins of the information society*. Cambridge, MA: Harvard University Press.

Gat, A. (1989). *The origins of military thought from the Enlightenment to Clausewitz*. Oxford, U.K.: Clarendon Press.

Goody, J. (1996). *The East in the West*. Cambridge, U.K.: Cambridge University Press.

Holley, I. B., Jr. (1988). Doctrine and technology as viewed by some seminal theorists of the art of warfare from Clausewitz to the mid-twentieth century. In R. L. Pfaltzgraff, Jr., U. Ra'anan, R. Shultz, & I. Lukes (Eds.), *Emerging doctrines and technologies: Implications for global and regional political–military balances* (pp. 13–34). Lexington, MA: Lexington Books/D. C. Heath.

Hoskin, K., Macve, R., & Stone, S. (1997, July). *The historical genesis of modern business and military strategy*. Paper presented at the Fifth Interdisciplinary Perspectives on Accounting Conference, Manchester, U.K. Available http://les.man.ac.uk/IPA/papers/73.html

Hoskin, K., & Zan, L. (1997, July). A first "discorso del maneggio": *Accounting and the production of "management discourse" at the Venice Arsenal, 1580–1650*. Paper presented at the Fifth Interdisciplinary Perspectives on Accounting Conference, Manchester, U.K. Available http://les.man.ac.uk/IPA/papers/94.html

Howard, M. (1983). *Clausewitz*. Oxford, U.K.: Oxford University Press.

Kammerer, J. (1997, September–October). Preserving mission-focused command and control. *Military Review (77)*5, 65–70.

Keegan, J. (1976). *The face of battle*. London, U.K.: Cape.

Kumar, V. (1992). Algorithms for constraint-satisfaction problems: A survey. *AI Magazine, 13*(1), 32–44.

Leonhard, R. R. (1994). *Fighting by minutes: Time and the art of war*. Westport, CT: Praeger.

Levis, A. H., & Levis, I. S. (Eds.). (1994). *Science of command and control: Part 3. Coping with change.* Fairfax, VA: AFCEA International Press.

Lynn, J. A. (Ed.). (1993). *Feeding Mars: Logistics in Western warfare from the Middle Ages to the present.* Boulder, CO: Westview Press.

Miser, H. J., & Quade, E. S. (Eds.) (1985). *Handbook of systems analysis: Vol. 1, Overview of uses, procedures, applications, and practice.* Chichester, U.K.: Wiley.

Morgan, G. (1986). *Images of organization.* London, U.K.: Sage.

Nandan, R. K. (1997, July). *The dialectic of management control: The case of the Fiji Development Bank.* Paper presented at the Fifth Interdisciplinary Perspectives on Accounting Conference, Manchester, U.K. Available http://les.man.ac.uk/IPA/papers/5.html

Pagonis, W. G., & Cruikshank, J. (1992). *Moving mountains: Lessons in leadership and logistics from the Gulf War.* Boston, MA: Harvard Business School Press.

Parker, G. (Ed.). (1995). *The Cambridge illustrated history of warfare: The triumph of the West.* Cambridge, U.K.: Cambridge University Press.

Persson, P.-A. (1996). *From theoretical pragmatism to pragmatic theory: A qualitative analysis of coalition command and control* (No. 3). Stockholm: Swedish National Defence College, Department of Military Technology. Also appears in *Proceedings of the Second International Command and Control Research and Technology Symposium* (pp. 416–435). Washington, DC: National Defense University.

Persson, P.-A. (1997). *Toward a grounded theory for support of command and control in military coalitions* (Licentiate thesis 607). Linköping, Sweden: Linköping Studies in Science and Technology.

Pountain, D. (1995). Constraint logic programming. *BYTE Magazine, 20*(2), 159–160.

Samuels, M. (1995). *Command or control?: Command, training, and tactics in the British and German armies, 1888–1918.* London, U.K.: Frank Cass.

Strauss, A., & Corbin, J. (1990). *Basics of qualitative research: Grounded theory procedures and techniques.* Newbury Park, CA: Sage.

Van Creveld, M. (1977). *Supplying war: Logistics from Wallenstein to Patton.* Cambridge, U.K.: Cambridge University Press.

Van Creveld, M. (1985). *Command in war.* Cambridge, MA: Harvard University Press.

Walsham, G. (1993). *Interpreting information systems in organizations.* Chichester, U.K.: Wiley.

CHAPTER 15

MISSION COMMAND IN AMBIGUOUS SITUATIONS

A. L. W. VOGELAAR and E.-H. KRAMER

> Never tell people *how* to do things. Tell them *what* to do and
> they will surprise you with their ingenuity.
> —GENERAL GEORGE S. PATTON

1. MISSION COMMAND

The military performance of the German army during the first years of World War II fascinates many military analysts. For example, Wilson (1989) asserts that "[i]t was, in the opinion of many, the greatest military victory of modern times" (p. 3). Within a period of only six weeks, the German army defeated the combined forces of Britain, France, Belgium, and the Netherlands. It has been argued that this success was attributable to a superior German military doctrine called *Auftragstaktik*. *Auftragstaktik*—translated as "mission command"—is a system of decentralized command under which a subcommander is assigned a mission without being told how it should be accomplished. *Auftragstaktik* assumes that subcommanders think and act relatively autonomously.

There has been a recent trend within the Dutch Army toward acceptance of the mission command (MC) philosophy (called *Opdracht Gerichte Commandovoering* in Dutch). The MC philosophy seems particularly suited to army operations in the post–Cold War era, an era in which it is very difficult to plan every operation in great detail in advance and detailed planning must be left to local commanders on the ground (Egter van Wissekerke, 1996). Dutch military doctrine (Netherlands, 1996) suggests that MC should be applicable in all operations and in both

A. L. W. VOGELAAR and E.-H. KRAMER • Royal Netherlands Military Academy, P.O. Box 90154, 4800 RG Breda, Netherlands

The Human in Command: Exploring the Modern Military Experience,
edited by McCann and Pigeau, Kluwer Academic/Plenum Publishers, New York, 2000.

operational and peacetime situations. It is, however, doubtful whether MC can be implemented fully in operations with significant political implications, such as U.N. operations (Egter van Wissekerke, 1996). In these instances, higher commanders may feel compelled to intervene in the decisions of their subcommanders, thus short-circuiting MC. In this chapter we will explore whether, and under what conditions, MC is applicable in peace support operations such as those undertaken by the United Nations Protection Force (UNPROFOR). The focus of our study is on the application of MC at the battalion level and its implications at the platoon or group level. The study is based on interviews with Dutch soldiers—privates, noncommissioned officers (NCOs), and officers—who served with UNPROFOR.

This chapter consists of five sections. In the next section, we describe the Dutch doctrine of mission command. In Section 3, "Dutch Troops in UNPROFOR," we provide background information about Dutch involvement in UNPROFOR and briefly describe the design of our study. In Section 4, "Mission Command in Dutchbat and Logtbat: Results of Interviews," we assess whether MC could have been successfully implemented during that UNPROFOR operation.[1] Finally, in Section 5, "Conclusions," we offer some lessons about MC's applicability in the context of peace support operations.

2. MISSION COMMAND IN THE DUTCH ARMY

The Dutch Army's leadership policy has been oriented toward a mission command philosophy since the early 1990s. In a 1991 document, the commander-in-chief prescribed that military leadership at every level should be based on two central themes: (a) freedom of action (a phrase that was later replaced by "autonomy of action") and (b) mutual trust (Wilmink, 1991). The central idea behind these themes was that the inherent capabilities of commanders at every level in the organization should be used as much as possible.

In the most recent Dutch military doctrine (Netherlands, 1996, pp. 107–113), the first of these two themes, autonomy of action, has been explicitly covered by MC, the rationale being the same as that used to explain the successes of *Auftragstaktik* (Egter van Wissekerke, 1996; Nelsen, 1989)—namely, that

- in the chaos of war, decisions are best made by the subcommanders who are directly involved in the operation;

- decentralization creates commitment and stimulates courage at every hierarchical level;

- decentralization prevents information overload up and down the hierarchy; and

---

[1] It should be mentioned that only certain parts of the MC doctrine had been enacted as a formal policy of the Dutch Army at the time of the UNPROFOR operation we studied.

- local commanders are thereby encouraged to act on the most directly available and the most recent information.

The Dutch Army conceives MC as consisting of five elements, as described in the following passage:

> A superior commander guarantees that his subcommander understands what is expected of him (**clear objectives**) through his presentation of the broader context and his intentions (Element 1) and the objectives to be met by the subordinate commander (Element 2). The provision of **adequate means** (Element 3) makes it possible for the subcommander to be successful. By giving **autonomy** over the way the mission is accomplished (Element 4), and by refraining from giving too many instructions (Element 5), a superior commander encourages a subcommander to take effective and timely initiatives without the hindrance of inefficient and inappropriate procedures.

The boldfaced terms in this passage, along with the supporting concept of mutual trust, will be elaborated on in Section 4, "Mission Command in Dutchbat and Logtbat: Results of Interviews."

In order for the five elements of MC to be achieved, at least three further factors must be in place:

- *Initiative.* MC presumes that commanders at every level in the chain of command are able and willing to take full initiative. Commanders should be trained and encouraged to take initiatives and risks instead of simply following orders. In both the Israeli and the German systems, for example, officers are taught that they have not only the *opportunity* but also the *duty* to make decisions (Gal, 1986; Nelsen, 1989). Furthermore, they are taught that making no decision at all is worse than making a wrong decision. This kind of attitude is possible only in the absence of a "zero-defects mentality" (Reimer, 1996)—that is, in an environment that allows mistakes to be treated as learning experiences.

- *Common intent.* MC requires a high level of shared intent (Pigeau & McCann, this volume, Chapter 12) between superior and subordinate commanders to permit coordinated action to be achieved during an operation. Pigeau and McCann assert that in decentralized command and control structures, considerable effort will need to be invested in creating shared implicit intent between commanders.

- *Mutual trust.* In a system of decentralized command, commanders at higher hierarchical levels rely on their subordinates' initiatives. Thus, trust between commanders is an important precondition for MC; it is also central to the Dutch decentralized leadership policy. Mishra (1996) distinguishes four dimensions of trust: competence, openness and honesty, concern, and reliability. In the decentralized command context, mutual trust must take several forms. First, superior commanders must be able to trust their subordinate commanders to act in accordance with the superior's intentions. Second, commanders at the same level in the hierarchy who are dependent on each other must each be aware of how the other(s) will react in certain situations.

Third, when accepting a dangerous mission, a subordinate commander must be able to trust his or her superior commander's decision-making capability and integrity. In addition, subordinate commanders must be able to trust that their higher commanders will support them to the extent possible. Mutual trust is therefore essential to the success of decentralized command; when it is absent, decentralized command will fail.

In short, MC is a system of decentralized command that requires competent and enterprising commanders at every level in the chain of command. Furthermore, it requires an organizational environment in which commanders trust each other's competency and share each other's intent.

3. DUTCH TROOPS IN UNPROFOR

When the nation of Yugoslavia disintegrated in the early 1990s, Bosnia–Herzegovina[2] was declared an independent state. As a consequence of independence, disputes began to erupt between the Bosnian Serbs, on the one hand, and the Bosnian Croats and Bosnian Muslims, on the other. When the fighting escalated to the level of "ethnic cleansing," resulting in streams of refugees, the United Nations developed an international military force—the United Nations Protection Force (UNPROFOR)—intended to neutralize the fighting and provide humanitarian assistance. From 1992 onward, the Dutch Army contributed to the transport of humanitarian supplies in UNPROFOR. In cooperation with the Belgian armed forces, the Dutch Army provided a transport battalion that was deployed in central Bosnia. In 1994, an infantry battalion (Dutchbat) and a support unit (Support Command) were provided to the United Nations. Dutchbat was deployed as a peacekeeping unit. Support Command and the transport battalion merged in 1995, becoming a logistic and transport battalion that we refer to as Logtbat, a general term referring to the Dutch transport units in UNPROFOR from 1992 on.

Logtbat had two main tasks: (a) transporting food and goods for humanitarian purposes under the authority of the United Nations High Commissioner for Refugees (UNHCR),[3] and (b) supplying the UNPROFOR units. The transports were carried out by convoys consisting of white trucks with clear U.N. signage. These convoys were led by platoon commanders.

Part of Dutchbat (that is, one infantry company and some staff and support units) was deployed in Simin Han, near Tuzla, with the remainder (two companies and the battalion staff) assigned to the enclave of Srebrenica from the beginning of 1994 to the middle of 1995. Dutchbat's mission was (a) to provide military assistance to the UNHCR and other recognized relief organizations; and (b) to create conditions that would allow the wounded to be evacuated, the inhabitants to be protected and taken care of, the living conditions of the population to be improved, and the hostilities to be stopped. The main tasks of Dutchbat's infantry units were

---

[2] Officially the Federal Republic of Bosnia and Herzegovina; hereafter referred to as Bosnia.

[3] The U.N.-led agency for humanitarian assistance in the former Yugoslavia.

to operate observation posts (OPs) on the confrontation lines and to send out patrols to gather information about the belligerents' activities. The OPs and patrols were led mainly by group commanders (sergeants). Srebrenica was one of the five Bosnian towns that, along with the city of Sarajevo, had been declared safe areas by the United Nations; therefore, Dutchbat's task was also to demilitarize the enclave (see Everts, this volume, Chapter 6).

In the next section, we assess to what extent and under what conditions MC could have been implemented in Dutchbat and Logtbat. For this analysis, we draw on material from interviews conducted in a larger study of the issues confronting Dutch lieutenants and sergeants during the UNPROFOR operations (see Vogelaar et al., 1997). The study was based on 18 in-depth interviews with Dutchbat soldiers and 28 in-depth interviews with Logtbat soldiers ranging in rank from private to lieutenant colonel.

4. MISSION COMMAND IN DUTCHBAT AND LOGTBAT: RESULTS OF INTERVIEWS

In this section, we first consider whether the platoon and group commanders of Logtbat and Dutchbat were permitted autonomy of action (elements 4 and 5 of the Dutch mission command doctrine outlined in Section 2, "Mission Command in the Dutch Army"). After concluding that autonomy was realized to only a small degree, we assess whether this lack of autonomy can be explained by lack of adequate means (element 3), by lack of clear objectives (elements 1 and 2), or by lack of mutual trust.[4]

4.1. Autonomy of Action?

The last two elements of the MC doctrine assert that subcommanders should be free to make their own decisions and to take initiative. The issue in UNPRO-FOR, therefore, was whether subcommanders were autonomous or restricted. From our interviews, we conclude that the platoon commanders and group commanders of both Logtbat and Dutchbat were both restricted and autonomous in their actions.

From one perspective, Logtbat platoon commanders and Dutchbat platoon and group commanders operated quite autonomously. Logtbat platoon commanders led their convoys of trucks through Bosnia far from the military compound. They were forced to solve many problems by themselves en route. The group commanders (and sometimes the platoon commanders) of Dutchbat operated OPs for several weeks at a stretch, where they stayed for long periods with their soldiers. They also led the patrols. They, too, were required to perform these tasks far from the compound.

From another perspective, however, there were many restrictions on these commanders. First, there were strict rules for conducting patrols and driving convoys.

---

[4] As previously noted, mutual trust is not explicitly mentioned in the Dutch MC doctrine, but it is nevertheless considered a *sine qua non* of MC.

Patrols followed only fixed routes and had to be executed as ordered by higher commanders in the operations room (ops room), even when the subordinate commander thought that another patrol or route would provide more information. There were rules for the order of the cars in convoys, for the routes to be taken, for maximum speed, and so on. Second, there were explicit rules concerning interaction with combatants and with the local population. For example, platoon and group commanders were not allowed to let their soldiers associate with the local population. Thus, the soldiers were not allowed to provide aid (food, medical help, and so on) directly to the inhabitants. Third, they were constrained by UNPROFOR's rules of engagement, which were intended to prevent partiality and escalation of the conflict—and which instructed armed UNPROFOR personnel to use force "to the minimum extent necessary" and "in self-defence" only. Finally, there were rules concerning safety measures, such as the wearing of helmets and bullet-proof vests, and the position and loading of weapons. These and other rules restricted the autonomy of the platoon commanders and the group commanders in the operations.

The progress of patrols and convoys was often closely monitored by their superior commanders on radio from the ops room. In a number of cases, higher commanders intervened in the decisions of subordinate commanders, to the latter's frustration. In one instance, a group commander's decision to disarm a belligerent was overruled by his superior, who told the group commander to leave the scene immediately. In another case, a convoy commander who had just decided to stop over for the night (because driving further in the dark would be too dangerous) was ordered to drive on to the compound that same night. Although these examples could be countered by many instances in which subordinate commanders were left to make their own decisions without interference, the fact remains that subcommanders' initiatives could always be overruled by higher commanders on the radio. Whether such interventions took place depended on the superior commander, the subordinate commander, and the situation.

We conclude, then, that platoon commanders and group commanders were somewhat restricted in their autonomy. Whereas they were autonomous with respect to the internal functioning of their subunits (for example, in determining the division of tasks among their soldiers, in handling their soldiers' problems, and so on), they were also restricted by rules and by the ever-present possibility that higher commanders could overrule their decisions.

In the following subsections, we will assess whether higher commanders felt that these restrictions were necessary, and under what conditions autonomy of sub-commander action could have been implemented in the operation. An overview of the results is presented in Table 1.

4.2. Adequate Means?

The MC philosophy requires that a commander provide his or her subordinate commanders with the means to perform their assignments. This element of MC (element 3 in the description in Section 2, "Mission Command in the Dutch Army") implies that conditions must be established in which subunits can be successful. At least two

Table 1. Reasons for Limited Autonomy of Action for Platoon and Group Commanders

	Logtbat	Dutchbat
Adequate means?	Adequate for task fulfillment, but not for safety.	Inadequate for task fulfillment and for safety.
Clear objectives?	Continual need to resolve dilemma between safety and assignments. Tension between providing assistance and keeping a distance from people in need.	Continual need to resolve dilemma between safety and assignments. No control over situation. Ambiguity of how to deal with provocations from local belligerents. No clear criteria for success.
Mutual trust?	Individual rotation system prevents trust. Little experience with this type of operation. Group and platoon commanders often young. Changes in policy after rotation. Changes in the chain of command.	Preparation time too short for such an operation. Little experience with this type of operation. Group and platoon commanders often young. High levels of frustration following provocations. Changes in the chain of command.

aspects of this element must be considered: (a) task fulfillment and (b) the soldiers' safety.

For Logtbat, the sufficiency and the adequacy of the means for task fulfillment were not an issue. The convoy commanders' task was to drive convoys of trucks from one place to another through Bosnia. Although in theory this was a relatively simple task, there were nevertheless many associated problems to be dealt with, requiring initiative and firmness on the part of the convoy commanders. The roads were often narrow, mountainous, and slippery. Often there were accidents, including some in which soldiers were wounded. Commanders were required to undertake negotiations at roadblocks, where the convoy could be held up for hours if the local belligerents so desired. Convoys could also be stopped along the way by oncoming traffic or by would-be plunderers. Despite the range and uniqueness of the problems, we conclude from our interviews that each convoy commander found his or her own way to handle them. There were virtually no cases of convoy commanders who consistently failed in their assignments.

More problematic were those situations involving the soldiers' safety. During periods when there was no ceasefire in effect, certain routes became very dangerous, since the warring parties were shelling one another's positions. In some cases, the belligerents also targeted UNPROFOR trucks. Because the trucks were "soft-skinned" (that is, not bulletproof), the drivers and passengers risked being hit.[5] To reduce the chances of incurring casualties, soldiers were required to wear helmets and bulletproof vests. Furthermore, the convoys were accompanied on the most

---

[5] Nine soldiers were wounded in this kind of incident on October 25, 1993.

dangerous routes by Warrior tanks from the United Kingdom, and often by tow trucks or ambulances.

The adequacy of the means proved to be a far bigger issue for Dutchbat. As noted earlier, part of Dutchbat's mission was to create conditions in which wounded people could be evacuated, the population could be protected and cared for, the living conditions of the population could be improved, and the hostilities could be stopped. For the two infantry companies of Dutchbat that were deployed in the Srebrenica enclave, the mission implied that they should protect the people in the enclave from any Bosnian Serb aggression and that they should disarm the Muslim belligerents (because Srebrenica was to be demilitarized). For the infantry company in Simin Han, the mission implied that they should patrol part of the confrontation line between the Bosnian Serb area and the Bosnian Muslim area in order to prevent aggressive acts between the two parties. However, Dutchbat did not have the means to perform those tasks that called for the actual use of force (see also Everts, this volume, Chapter 6), such as the protection of Bosnian Muslims from Bosnian Serb forces. Dutchbat was therefore limited to patrol and observation tasks that resulted, at best, in notes and descriptions of enclave activities.

Not only were some tasks impossible to carry out, the safety of the Dutch soldiers was also not assured. The battalion was typically dispersed in small units at OPs and on patrols. If the belligerent parties had wanted to harm these units (for example, by shelling them or by taking hostages), the units could not easily have defended themselves. Dutchbat was therefore very vulnerable. Both the Muslims and the Bosnian Serbs used that vulnerability to their own advantage. Bosnian Serb belligerents fired close to the Dutch positions to prove that they could indeed hit them. Muslim belligerents fired on Dutchbat soldiers and blamed the Bosnian Serbs, in order to incite Dutchbat against the Serbs. Dutchbat's only recourse was to protect itself as best it could, and to protest to the United Nations. Again, there was no possibility of using force, since Dutchbat was, in the end, dependent on the goodwill of the warring parties.

In summary, Logtbat convoy commanders possessed adequate means to complete the tasks they were given. The only issue—albeit a crucial one—was the safety of the soldiers driving the convoys. Even with the means available, the drivers' safety could not be assured. Dutchbat was not capable of accomplishing many portions of its mission and also could not assure the safety of its soldiers. The only tasks that it could undertake were those involving observation. The battalion had far too few personnel and inadequate weapons to be able either to protect the population or to stop hostilities.

4.3. Clear Objectives?

The first two elements of MC require that orders be given to subordinates in a way that ensures understanding of the commander's view, the objectives to be met, and the way the subcommander's task fits into the broader context of the assignment given to the entire unit. The effectiveness of MC is based on the possibility of commanders at lower levels taking initiative. The tasking requires, therefore, that a clear objective exist, as well as that it be communicated.

In the UNPROFOR operation, both the nature of the conflict and the objectives to be met were unclear. UNPROFOR had a high political profile. The international community in general, and Europe in particular, wanted something to be done to stop the conflict in the former Yugoslavia, but at the same time, no one wanted to be drawn into a war. Therefore, the U.N. forces were mandated to provide humanitarian help and to suppress the fighting between the different parties, but with restrictions.[6] The first and most important task for the peacekeeping units was to "show the flag." The assumption was that the mere presence of the United Nations and their observation of the activities in the former Yugoslavia should help to de-escalate the fighting: the warring parties would see that the world was not keeping itself aloof from developments in Bosnia and that aggressors would ultimately be punished. Second, UNPROFOR was ordered to be strictly neutral, so that none of the warring parties could accuse it of favouritism. Finally, because of concern about possible escalation of the war through unintended aggression, UNPROFOR troops were quite restricted in their use of force. They were limited by the rules of engagement described earlier, by the number of military personnel on the ground, and by the extent of permissible military buildup. These were some of the conditions under which Dutch UNPROFOR troops had to operate. Mockaitis (1997) concludes that UNPROFOR was hopelessly outgunned from the outset, trying to fulfill an impossible task with inadequate resources. Added to this problem was the fact that the belligerents were not at all influenced by UNPROFOR: the U.N. presence had no effect on the hostilities. Yet the continued fighting caused many dangerous situations for UNPROFOR soldiers, who were forbidden to take the kind of action for which soldiers are trained—namely, cover yourself and fire back. Furthermore, the ongoing hostilities hampered humanitarian transport. For the battalion commanders of Logtbat and Dutchbat, this was a very complex situation.

Uncertainties in the broader context of UNPROFOR meant that Logtbat faced a number of dilemmas and ambiguities. One dilemma was the continual need to weigh the importance of any particular humanitarian assignment against the safety of the soldiers driving the trucks. It was not acceptable to seriously endanger the lives of soldiers who had insufficient means of protection. Yet the reason that the military—rather than a civilian organization—had been tasked to provide the humanitarian support was precisely because the situation was dangerous. Therefore, a commander could not cancel an assignment simply because of some anticipated threat. It was necessary to determine, in each case, whether the threat was serious enough to warrant such a decision. The pressure to ensure the full safety of the troops was very great, but the credibility of the military unit required that certain risks be accepted.

Part of Logtbat's mission was to bring humanitarian aid to the population. For some soldiers, there was an ambiguity in ostensibly providing aid to people they could not directly see, while at the same time not being permitted to take any initiatives to aid the people they *could* see, many of whom were obviously in need. Many soldiers had come to Bosnia with the idea of providing help to the

---

[6] The parties had not, however, as in some cases of U.N. involvement, come to a prior agreement that had to be implemented.

population, and they assumed that they would be welcome. In many cases, reality proved different. Soldiers were fired on while driving aid convoys from warehouse to warehouse. Sometimes they passed angry and dangerous local inhabitants who threw bricks at their convoy and who were obviously not pleased with UNPRO-FOR's presence. Yet elsewhere, they encountered people living in miserable circumstances who asked for food or who wanted to exchange goods or services. The emotional impact of these situations made the requests of these people very hard for the soldiers to resist. But higher commanders discouraged contact between soldiers and locals because of the risk of endangering the passage of convoys or the safety of the encampments by the unpredictable consequences of raising the inhabitants' expectations.

The ambiguities and dilemmas inherent in the UNPROFOR mission itself also affected Dutchbat in the performance of its tasks. One of the biggest problems for the Dutchbat commanders was a sense of lack of control. As noted earlier, Dutchbat was not adequately armed for tasks requiring the use of force. Its commanders therefore decided to give priority to the safety of their soldiers, rather than to being assertive in the mission. They chose to fulfill the routine tasks of observing and patrolling, but to avoid disarming Muslims or driving Bosnian Serbs out of the enclave. It was, however, very difficult to transmit this intention to the lower ranks, because this was not formal U.N. policy. The incident previously described, in which a group commander was suddenly ordered to stop disarming a belligerent, was one example of the consequences of this lack of communication.

Another issue for Dutchbat was the desire to see some degree of improvement as a consequence of its presence in the enclave. But there were no criteria for measuring the operation's success, and in fact, the situation could hardly be regarded as optimistic. Would the fighting have been heavier if Dutchbat had not been there? Or was Dutchbat's presence in Srebrenica merely a welcome interlude that was allowing both parties to prepare for battle? Dutchbat soldiers at OPs or on patrol observed that, despite their presence, both parties were busily improving their military positions. While there were, indeed, fewer victims in the region, was this shift due to UNPROFOR's presence? Finally, had Srebrenica really become a safe area, and if so, had Dutchbat actually made a contribution in that regard? The ambiguity of the situation, coupled with the frustration, caused Dutchbat morale to suffer, making it very difficult for Dutchbat commanders to keep their soldiers motivated for the mission.

In summary, the higher commanders of both Dutchbat and Logtbat were confronted with a number of dilemmas and ambiguities that made it very difficult to communicate clear objectives to their subordinates. The balance between the success of the mission and the safety of their soldiers was at times very precarious. In what situations could the safety of the soldiers be put at risk? Various factors had to be weighed: the fact that the soldiers were trained to cope with danger but lightly armed, the importance of the mission, and public opinion about the usefulness of the Army and the acceptability of casualties. A second precarious balance concerned the requirement to maintain a certain distance between the soldiers and the local population. On the one hand, UNPROFOR's success depended on its neutrality. Furthermore, close relations between the local people and the soldiers were a concern from the standpoint of safety. On the other hand, respondents from both Logtbat and Dutchbat said that their motivation improved dramatically whenever they had the chance to help people who, in return, were grateful. As one sergeant said, "At one point I took the initiative to go into the houses of the poor and give them cartons of juice. We felt like Santa Claus. We lived on that action for months."

For MC to be effective in an organization, commanders at each level should decide how assignments can best be completed and ensure that the safety of their subordinates is not unnecessarily put at risk. When it is unclear whether the assignment or the safety of personnel should get priority, a decentralized command and control organization requires a high level of shared implicit intent between different levels of command, as well as open communication channels. Goals and objectives must be adjusted to the realities of the situation. Both battalions experienced many instances in which the ambiguities described above resulted in friction between higher and lower command levels.

4.4. Mutual Trust?

In order for a superior commander to permit a subordinate commander to exercise independence of action, a basic precondition must be in place: the superior must believe that the subordinate can be trusted to fulfill the mission as completely as possible without further prescriptions. There were some specific conditions that prevented mutual trust in these operations.

Logtbat used a system of personnel rotation whereby every two months, a third of the Logtbat soldiers in Bosnia were replaced by newcomers drawn from several different units in the Netherlands. These new military personnel then worked alongside the experienced soldiers—one third of whom had been in Bosnia for two months, while the other third had been there for four months. An advantage of such a rotational system is that experienced soldiers' knowledge of the local situation (for example, information about roads) can easily be passed along to the newcomers. A disadvantage is that group cohesion—essential for helping group members to pull each other through hard times or through dangerous situations—is reduced. Furthermore, it is more difficult to establish high levels of mutual trust between different hierarchical levels, since this factor takes time to develop. For example, a superior commander at the compound will not necessarily know how a new subcommander who is leading a convoy will react in a dangerous situation. The subordinate, in turn, will not know what the superior commander expects the subordinate to do in unforeseen circumstances, and may therefore make a decision that is very different from the superior's intention. Their mutual trust must develop gradually over time.

A number of other factors compounded the negative effect of the lack of familiarity between members of Logtbat. First, for most of the commanders at the platoon and group levels, UNPROFOR was the first operation inside a war zone. It was hard for anyone (including the commanders themselves) to predict how these commanders would react under stress. Second, some of the platoon and group commanders were very young and inexperienced. Many had been posted to Bosnia within a year after graduating from basic training, and they lacked, for example, the experience necessary to handle personnel problems. Third, a new superior commander sometimes changed the previous commander's policy completely. In such a situation, the platoon commander, who was accustomed to the intentions of the superior commander's predecessor, had to adjust to the expectations of the new commander. Fourth, the chain of command in Bosnia was different from that in the Netherlands. When a platoon was at the compound, the company commander was in charge. However, convoys were controlled from the ops room, which was grouped at the battalion level. Therefore, during operations (for example, the driving of convoys), the platoon commander received orders directly from the battalion. The company commander was outside this chain of command. In a number of cases, this dual command led to conflicts between the personnel in the ops room, who were responsible for the operations, and the company commander, who was responsible for the well-being of the platoons. These conflicts also served to inhibit the trust that platoon commanders placed in their superior commanders.

In contrast to Logtbat, Dutchbat was rotated as a whole. Even so, there was the general impression that the battalion was not sufficiently trained to establish the requisite level of mutual trust. Although the infantry battalion had been assembled between nine and seven months before leaving for Bosnia, some platoons were not filled until the last few months before departure, and the subsidiary units were assigned to the battalion only in the last six weeks before departure. This was considered too late to allow the personnel in question to become familiar with the basic routines of working together, and it prevented mutual trust from being established between several of the units.

Another issue related to mutual trust was that commanders did not always know how their subordinates would react to the unexpected and ambiguous situations that occurred in Bosnia. Subunit frustration grew due to the continued fighting, the many provocations by the belligerents, and the wounding of Dutch soldiers (see also Everts, this volume, Chapter 6). It was assumed that subordinate commanders and soldiers would handle these frustrations in a professional way. But commanders could never be absolutely certain whether a member of one of their subunits might not, under stress, react in an unexpected or irrational way (for example, shooting back when provoked). In a peace support operation like the one in Bosnia, where it was impossible to prevent a massive attack from one of the warring parties, a commander could not afford any risks. Therefore, superior commanders strictly controlled their subordinates' behaviour.

As was the case for Logtbat, the Dutchbat chain of command was different from that in the Netherlands. In Dutchbat's case, however, it was the company commanders in Srebrenica who gave direct orders during operations to the group commanders at the OPs or on patrols, thus bypassing the platoon commanders. (Platoon commanders were still responsible for personnel matters in their platoons and for contacts with the local population in their areas.) Platoon commanders did not adjust well to these changes in their command authority and responsibilities. As far as they were concerned, this situation completely contradicted MC. Moreover, the fact that the role of the platoon commanders was not clear at the group level also contributed to a lack of mutual trust between platoon commanders, on the one hand, and group commanders and soldiers, on the other.

In summary, mutual trust between commanders at different hierarchical levels was negatively affected by a number of factors. The system of personnel rotation in Logtbat inhibited the commanders from establishing a cohesive team. For Dutchbat, despite the benefits of its unit rotation system, it was nevertheless felt that preparation time for the battalion's deployment had been too short. And this impression may have been intensified by the extremely difficult and frustrating operational situation with which Dutchbat had to cope. Other factors that negatively affected mutual trust in both battalions were the fact that many officers and NCOs had never previously been deployed to a war zone and the fact that the command structure in Bosnia was different from what they were accustomed to in the Netherlands.

5. CONCLUSIONS

In most army operations, companies, platoons, and even groups of soldiers must operate relatively autonomously, and this requires decentralization of command (Murray, 1992). Recent Dutch Army doctrine advocates that leadership should be based on mission command (MC). The essence of MC is that a subcommander is assigned a mission without being given an exact specification of how that mission should be accomplished. There is, however, some doubt concerning the feasibility of using MC in missions with a high political profile. The central question in this chapter was whether and under what conditions MC can be applied in peace support operations like those undertaken by UNPROFOR. This question was addressed by focusing at the platoon and group command levels. We found that commanders at these levels were given only partial autonomy of action and that there were a number of reasons for this lack of autonomy.

For MC to be successful, certain requirements must be met. The first requirement is that the units tasked to carry out a mission should be supplied with adequate means to do so. This requirement was not met in UNPROFOR, especially in the case of Dutchbat. The soldiers were too lightly armed to operate in the hostile environment of Bosnia. Actual peacekeeping proved to be impossible, because the warring parties were unwilling to attend to the official terms of UNPROFOR and they heavily outnumbered Dutchbat in both personnel and equipment. Thus it was impossible to accomplish the parts of the mission where the use of force might be necessary. Under such conditions, it proved very difficult for superior commanders to give autonomy to their subordinates (the platoon and group commanders). While there were sufficient means (personnel, trucks, and so on) to perform the tasks in Logtbat's humanitarian mission, the safety of the convoys was a problem. Almost all of Logtbat's soldiers were involved in dangerous incidents at one time or another during the deployment. Many times they realized they had been very lucky indeed to escape without injury.

A second requirement of MC is that orders should be given so that subcommanders fully comprehend the view of the commander, the objectives to be met, and the broader context of their assignments with respect to the performance of the entire unit. This proved to be a problem for both Logtbat and Dutchbat. Both the nature of the conflict and the objectives to be met were unclear; thus the units in

Bosnia were presented with a very ambiguous situation that permitted them only to react. One of the biggest problems for both battalions was keeping the right balance between the satisfactory performance of their assigned tasks and the safety of their soldiers. Logtbat and Dutchbat were required to perform their tasks under "acceptable" levels of risk, but this criterion was so unclear that different commanders interpreted it differently. Furthermore, the perception of risk sometimes changed rapidly as a consequence of certain events or new information; as a result, friction could easily arise between commanders at different levels. Establishing the appropriate standard for risk was difficult: some subordinate commanders were considered by their superiors to be "thrill seekers" who took too many risks, while others were perceived as not willing to take enough risks. Finally, there was a strong sense of frustration because of the lack of success in the mission. In these complex circumstances, it was very difficult to meet this second requirement of MC.

A third requirement of MC is that subcommanders should be given autonomy in how they satisfy their assignments, without being given detailed instructions. In this way, initiative at lower levels is encouraged. However, this approach introduces a certain amount of uncertainty into the behaviour of the system, and that uncertainty can be of concern to higher commanders (Kipnis, 1996). Therefore, a crucial precondition for autonomy is a high level of mutual trust between commanders at different hierarchical levels. They must be confident of each other's competence. In this operation, however, mutual trust was impeded by several factors. For example, Logtbat used a personnel rotation system that reduced the opportunity for commanders and subcommanders to become familiar with each other, and thereby prevented the establishment of shared implicit intent (Pigeau & McCann, this volume, Chapter 12). Furthermore, junior commanders had no experience in the role of neutral third party to a conflict. In both Logtbat and Dutchbat, the usual chain of command was also altered, which led to conflicts between commanders who should have been able to rely on each other. The lack of mutual trust caused higher commanders to give very precise orders, their justification being that very small mistakes could have drastic consequences. The requirement for mutual trust was therefore not met in this operation.

Our study shows that few of the requirements for MC were met in UNPRO-FOR. The next question is whether this gap was a consequence of the nature of the operation or a lack of preparation for MC on the part of the organization. It is our view that both factors were pertinent. The nature of the operation meant that it was almost impossible to implement MC in some respects. Dutchbat, in particular, lacked sufficient means to carry out the operation, partly because the international community initially thought that a merely symbolic presence of the United Nations in Bosnia would be sufficient for success. Also, it was virtually impossible to establish clear objectives for this operation. Does this mean that MC is not suitable for operations like UNPROFOR—that is, for operations with a high political profile? Generalizing from the results of this operation is difficult, because UNPROFOR itself caused specific problems that we believe would have arisen with any system of command. What we can conclude is that a clear mandate and sufficient means to accomplish the mission are desirable preconditions for a successful implementation of MC. If these conditions are not satisfied, MC is possible only when mutual trust and shared implicit intent are very high. Subcommanders will need to know exactly how their superiors think about certain situations, and superior commanders should be sure that their subordinates are sufficiently qualified to cope with the range of anticipated problems. For successful implementation of MC in missions with a high political profile, it is essential that the organization prepare itself to meet the requirement of high mutual trust. Because the establishment of trust takes time, commanders who will need to work with each other in deployments must train together intensively and at length.

6. ACKNOWLEDGMENTS

Both authors are lecturers at the Royal Netherlands Military Academy in Breda. We are grateful to our colleagues Jolanda Bosch, Annemarie Witteveen, Max Metselaar, Herman Kuipers, Frans Nederhof, and Coen van den Berg, who participated in this study.

7. REFERENCES

Egter van Wissekerke, F. J. D. C. (1996). Opdrachtgerichte commandovoering als leidend doctrinebeginsel van de Koninklijke Landmacht [Mission-oriented command as a leading doctrine principle in the Dutch Army]. *Militaire Spectator, 165*, 481–497.

Gal, R. (1986). *A portrait of the Israeli soldier.* New York: Greenwood Press.

Kipnis, D. (1996). Trust and technology. In R. M. Kramer & T. R. Tyler (Eds.), *Trust in organizations: Frontiers of theory and research* (pp. 39–50). Thousand Oaks, CA: Sage.

Mishra, A. K. (1996). Organizational responses to crisis: The centrality of trust. In R. M. Kramer & T. R. Tyler (Eds.), *Trust in organizations. Frontiers of theory and research* (pp. 261–287). Thousand Oaks, CA: Sage.

Mockaitis, T. (1997). Civil conflict intervention: Peacekeeping or enforcement? In A. Morrison, D. A. Fraser, & J. D. Kiras (Eds.), *Peacekeeping with muscle: The use of force in international conflict resolution* (pp. 31–50). Clementsport, NS: Canadian Peacekeeping Press.

Murray, W. (1992). *German military effectiveness.* Baltimore: Nautical and Aviation Publishing.

Nelsen, J. (1989). *Auftragstaktik*: A case for decentralized combat leadership. In L. J. Matthews & D. E. Brown (Eds.), *The challenge of military leadership* (pp. 26–39). Washington, DC: Pergamon-Brassey's.

Netherlands. (1996). *Landmacht Doctrine Publicatie I* [Royal Netherlands Army Doctrine Publication I]. The Hague, Netherlands: Royal Netherlands Army, Doctrine Committee/Sdu.

Reimer, D. J. (1996, January–February). Leadership for the 21st century: Empowerment, environment and the golden rule. *Military Review, 76*(1), 5–9.

Vogelaar, A., Kramer, F., Metselaar, M., Witteveen, A., Bosch, J., Kuipers, H., & Nederhof, F. (1997). *Leiderschap in crisisomstandigheden: Het functioneren van pelotons-en groepscommandanten in UNPROFOR* [Leadership in crisis circumstances: The functioning of platoon and group commanders in UNPROFOR]. The Hague, Netherlands: Sdu.

Wilmink, M. J. (1991). *Leidinggeven in de Koninklijke Landmacht* [Leadership in the Dutch Army]. The Hague, Netherlands: Beleidsdocument.

Wilson, J. (1989). *Bureaucracy: What government agencies do and why they do it.* New York: Basic Books.

CHAPTER 16

DYNAMIC DECISION MAKING IN COMMAND AND CONTROL

BERNDT BREHMER

1. INTRODUCTION

Decision making is a central aspect of command and control, yet it has received very little systematic study. One reason for this neglect may be the lack of a conceptual framework with which to guide research. This chapter presents an initial attempt to develop such a framework, one that has been inspired by a frequently cited quotation from the elder Moltke, a well-known 19th-century military commander (Hughes, 1993). Simpkin (1985) provides what I believe is the best interpretation of Moltke's viewpoint:

> Moltke maintained that the operational plan should seek to insure that the first contact between the main bodies occurred under the most favourable circumstances possible, and that "no plan survive[s] contact." After this, it was a matter of responsiveness and opportunism. (p. 14)

The quote suggests two different kinds of military decision making. The first one, planning, is clear enough. But what happens once the plan is put in place, and contact is initiated with the enemy? I propose that at this point, the form of *control* changes. Specifically, it changes from feedforward control (by means of the plan) to feedback control—where the military must respond to the enemy's response to its actions. The decision task now becomes *dynamic*. Viewing command and control from this new perspective—that is, as dynamic decision making—might give us some insights.

BERNDT BREHMER • *Department of Operational Studies, Swedish National Defence College, P.O. Box 27805, S-115 93 Stockholm, Sweden*

The Human in Command: Exploring the Modern Military Experience,
edited by McCann and Pigeau, Kluwer Academic/Plenum Publishers, New York, 2000.

It is the purpose of this chapter to discuss command and control from this perspective.

Section 2, "Fundamental Properties of Dynamic Decision Making," describes the fundamental characteristics of dynamic decision tasks and the demands that these characteristics make on decision makers. Military decision problems are, however, not only dynamic, but also complex and opaque: these aspects are discussed in Section 3, "Additional Properties of Military Decision Situations." Section 4, "The Nature of Decision Making in Dynamic Tasks," concerns itself with the nature of decision making in dynamic, complex, and opaque tasks, proposing that such decision making be seen as a matter of achieving control. The requirements for achieving control are then discussed. Section 5, "Approaches to Research on Decision Making in Dynamic Tasks," describes the research strategy of using microworlds—that is, computer simulations—to study dynamic decision making. The results obtained with this strategy are then reviewed in Section 6, "Results of Research." Finally, Section 7, "Conclusions," discusses some implications for understanding and improving command and control decision making.

2. FUNDAMENTAL PROPERTIES OF DYNAMIC DECISION MAKING

A dynamic decision problem has four properties (Brehmer & Allard, 1991):

- It requires a series of decisions.

- The decisions implemented are not independent.

- The state of the environment changes, both autonomously (for example, as a consequence of enemy actions) and as a consequence of the decision maker's own actions.

- Time is an important factor.

Let me amplify these properties of dynamic decision making with reference to a nonmilitary example, so as to avoid getting bogged down in tactical and operational details. Consider the decision problems facing a fire chief, who is charged with the task of extinguishing forest fires. From his or her command post, the fire chief receives information about fires from a spotter plane. On the basis of this information, the fire chief deploys firefighting units to the fire(s). These units report back about the situation and their actions. Using this new information, together with additional information from the spotter plane, the fire chief issues new commands to the firefighting units. This sequence continues until the fire has been extinguished.

The forest fire problem has all four characteristics of dynamic decision making. First, it obviously requires a series of decisions. Second, these decisions are not independent. Current decisions will constrain those that can be made in the future (for example, if the fire chief sends all available assets to one location, none of those assets can be used in some other location except after some period of time). It is also possible to remedy past errors with subsequent decisions (for example, having noted that he or she has sent too few firefighting units to a given location, the fire chief can compensate for this error by sending more units, provided they are available). Third, the state of the fire inevitably changes. It can change autonomously—as a consequence of, for example, the strength and direction of the prevailing wind—and it can change as a consequence of the firefighting units' own activities as ordered by the fire chief. Finally, the decision-making problem has temporal constraints—which, in the case of firefighting, are of three types:

- Decisions must be made as the need arises.
- The fire, a temporal process, must be managed through other temporal processes.
- Differences in time scale must be recognized and accommodated.

These temporal constraints, which also apply in military command and control situations, are amplified in the following sections.

2.1. Lack of Control over the Timing of Decisions

When facing a dynamic decision problem, decision makers have little control over exactly when decisions must be made. For example, the fire chief cannot wait until he or she is completely satisfied with a decision before it is enacted. Decisions must be made quickly, as and when required, depending on how the fire develops. This constraint introduces an element of stress into the decision-making process.

Decision makers in such situations confront two separate kinds of problems: (a) handling the "core" decision task—that is, making the decisions that are required to control the aspects of the environment that are of concern—and (b) controlling the overall decision situation, so as to avoid overload and remain capable of making the core decisions. In the firefighting example, the core decision task is to fight the fire. In order to do so efficiently, the fire chief must have time to gather information pertaining to decisions, to think about options, and so on. Such a considered approach is possible only if the fire chief can find a strategy that does not force him or her to make decisions at a pace so rapid that it leaves no time to think. The fire chief must, for example, refrain from micromanaging the firefighting units' activities, since doing so would leave insufficient time for considering strategic issues. Expert dynamic decision makers in other domains such as process control (Bainbridge, 1981) and air traffic control (Sperandio, 1978) are able to handle both these aspects of their decision task. In command and control warfare, an important additional aim is to deny the enemy the possibility of controlling the decision situation; losing this aspect of decision control would undermine the commander's ability to exercise command.

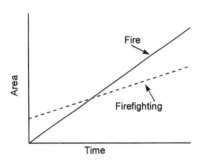

FIGURE 1. Basic characteristics of the firefighting scenario for a simple case involving constant wind and a homogeneous forest.

2.2. Control of One Temporal Process by Another Such Process

In the firefighting scenario, the fire is a process with temporal characteristics. The mechanisms available to the fire chief for exercising control also constitute a process. The tactical opportunities are determined by the relationship between these two processes: the *controlling* process and the *controlled* process. Figure 1 illustrates this relationship, showing the basic characteristics of the firefighting scenario for a simple case involving constant wind and a homogeneous forest.

The slopes of the two lines express the "efficiency" of the fire and of the firefighting processes, respectively—that is, the rate at which the fire will spread and the rate at which firefighting resources can be applied. The intersection of the two lines (that is, the point after which the fire will spread faster than the firefighters can control it) changes position in direct relation to the number of firefighting units. The figure shows the relationship between the two lines, and suggests that certain strategies may work better under certain circumstances. To the left of the intersection between the two lines, the fire chief is stronger than the fire—that is, the available firefighting units can cover more area than the fire can, per unit of time. Under these circumstances, a strategy involving a direct attack on the fire is likely to succeed. But to the right of the crossover point, such an approach ceases to be effective: the fire is spreading faster than the firefighting units can cover the ground. The fire will therefore grow, despite the firefighting units' best efforts to attack it directly. Two strategies are possible in this case. The first involves encircling the fire, containing it, and waiting until it burns down to a size that makes direct attack possible again. The other involves dividing it into smaller fires and directly attacking each small fire. These three strategies are the only possible strategies in any spatio-temporal problem, whether the problem involves fighting fires or fighting battles.[1]

Implicit in Figure 1 is the fact that events in the real world (in contrast to activities that take place in a person's mind or within a computer) require a finite amount

---

[1] I am not, of course, attempting to reduce war to Heinrich von Bülow's geometric principles, which Clausewitz (1976) so harshly—and justly—criticizes. Figure 1 simplistically implies that the only factor governing military success would be the number of soldiers. If that were true, Alexander the Great's defeat of 200,000 Persians at Issus in 333 B.C. with an army of just 30,000 ought to have been impossible. Obviously, the number of soldiers is not by itself an adequate measure of military strength. Figure 1 is merely intended to illustrate a principle, not to reduce a complex situation to a single factor.

of time. For example, decision makers cannot get immediate information about the results of actions: feedback delays are inevitable. Thus, a significant aspect of handling dynamic decision-making processes involves coping with delays.

Control engineers distinguish among three kinds of delays. The first is *dead time*: the time interval between the moment that a command is given and moment that it starts to take effect. The second kind of delay is the interval between the moment that a command takes effect and the moment that some specified percentage of the full goal has been reached. This is called the system's *time constant*. The third type of delay is the time taken for a report to be received after an action has been taken: the *report delay*. In the firefighting example, the dead time is the time required for the firefighting units to mobilize and get ready to go. The time constant is the time required for the units to reach the fire and to extinguish it. The report delay is the interval between an action—for example, moving from one location to another, or extinguishing a fire within one's area of responsibility—and the point at which the information about this action reaches the fire chief.

A commander cannot control a military system that incorporates delays solely on the basis of the information provided at any single moment in time: this information is always out of date. The dead time and time constants inherent in a military system mean that information about enemy actions arrives too late to permit the commander to effectively counter those actions. Hence, it is important for the commander to know the enemy's intentions so as to gain the time required for an appropriate response; similarly, it is important to use surprise to deny this time to the enemy. Delays in reporting can involve both information about the enemy and information about the actions and location of the commander's own forces. In the former case, a delay means that the commander will make a decision that pertains to the state of the system at some earlier point in time, not to the current state. In the latter case, it means that the commander does not know exactly what forces are available for the task. Out-of-date reports indicating that the commander's units are occupied with some earlier task may lead him or her to believe that fewer units are available for a new task than are actually available.

Modern information technology aims at diminishing—and perhaps eliminating—delays of the third kind.[2] Other forms of technology, such as air transport, have successfully reduced dead time and time constants. But neither kind of delay has been completely eliminated, although the pace of battle has increased. The ability to understand and handle the delays in the military system will probably therefore remain an important aspect of a commander's competence for the foreseeable future.

---

[2] Keegan (1987) notes, however, that modern information technology can create a false impression of timely and accurate information. He describes how Hitler, whose headquarters was equipped with the most modern information technology available at that time, overestimated the accuracy of the information that the technology provided to him. On the basis of this information, he issued inappropriate orders to his subordinates; he was surprised and enraged when the effect was not what he had anticipated.

2.3. Different Time Scales

A third temporal aspect of dynamic decision making is that of relative *time scales*. In the firefighting problem, there are two important time scales: a fast time scale characterizes the work of the individual firefighting units, while a slower time scale characterizes the fire chief's work. The fire chief's job is not to extinguish fires but to coordinate the efforts of the individual firefighting units to ensure that they operate in concert. Without this coordination, the collective efforts of the firefighting units might prove futile, despite their efficiency as individual units. Obviously, the interpretation of the firefighting task should not be made solely in terms of either of these time scales.

Differences in time scale also characterize the fighting of battles. The time scale relevant to fighting at the platoon level is clearly different from that at the division level. A concept related to time scale is *feedback delay*. All three kinds of delays discussed above are relevant here. Activities characterized by faster time scales, such as fighting at the platoon level, are also characterized by shorter feedback delays than are activities characterized by slower time scales, such as fighting at the division level. Thus, there is less dead time at the platoon level: getting something started takes less time here than it does at the division level. Time constants are also shorter: the tasks set out for the platoon can usually be achieved faster than the tasks set out for a division. Finally, information about the results usually reaches platoon commanders faster than it reaches division commanders.

Despite the close connection between the concepts of time scale and feedback delay, it is nevertheless useful to differentiate between the two. The time scale concept denotes the totality of activity of a given level—for example, the division level in contrast to the platoon level. The feedback delay concept, on the other hand, usually denotes relations at the level of specific behaviours.

3. ADDITIONAL PROPERTIES OF MILITARY DECISION SITUATIONS

The dynamics of a battle, of course, differ fundamentally from those of firefighting. One critical difference is that the adversary in a battle has intentions: the adversary will not necessarily respond predictably to the commander's actions. Physical processes like fires, on the other hand, are not malicious: they do not intentionally make things difficult for those dealing with them. This difference is important for modelling the control of battles. I will return to this point after briefly discussing two additional characteristics of "real-world" decision tasks in general, and of battles in particular: *complexity* and *opaqueness*.

As a concept, complexity resembles the concept of time in that, as Saint Augustine commented in his *Confessiones* (Augustine, 397/1983), we know what it is until we are asked to define it.[3] For this discussion, however, I restrict the meaning of

---

[3] The best general conceptualization of complexity is in terms of Ashby's Law of Requisite Variety (Ashby, 1956), which suggests that a system is complex to the extent that its controller cannot generate the requisite variety of responses needed for its control. Consequently, complexity cannot be defined in absolute terms; rather, it must be defined in relation to some controlling system.

complexity to *the interrelationships among processes in a task*. These interrelation-ships require the decision maker to formulate his or her goals clearly and to strike a balance among them, taking into account the various side effects that every action will have.[4] The interrelationships may, of course, also be treated as a matter of feed-back. Feedback is not limited only to that information provided to the decision maker. There is also feedback from the decision maker to the decision task, by which the decision maker changes the state of the system that he or she is trying to control. The third characteristic of dynamic decision tasks listed in Section 2, "Fundamen-tal Properties of Dynamic Decision Making"—that is, that the state of the decision task changes both autonomously *and* as a consequence of the decision maker's actions—alludes to this aspect. Distinguishing between the two kinds of feedback is important. Otherwise, a commander may fall prey to a situation similar to the one that occurred in the 1905 Russo-Japanese war: while the Russians advanced, the Japanese retreated in an orderly and pre-planned fashion, giving the Russians the impression that the Japanese were fleeing. As a result, the Russians were defeated in battle at Mukden (now Shenyang, China).

Opaqueness refers to a lack of transparency about the decision situation. There are two kinds of opaqueness: the first is due to a lack of information about the system's current state, and the second results from lack of information about the system's inner structure and the relationships among its various subprocesses. In military situations, lack of transparency often stems from the enemy's active attempts to hide its assets and their locations. But opaqueness may also result when the enemy makes no attempt to deceive. As Watts (1996) points out, the spatial and temporal distribution of battlefield information means that a commander can never have access to more than just part of it, even with the resources provided by modern information technology.[5] Thus an important aspect of decision making in these kinds of tasks involves making inferences about the system's state (that is, about the enemy, and perhaps about one's own forces as well). Section 2.2, "Control of One Temporal Process by Another Such Process," describes an important cause of opaqueness: feedback delays, which make it difficult or impossible for the com-mander to have relevant information about the state of the battle.

4. THE NATURE OF DECISION MAKING IN DYNAMIC TASKS

The traditional view of decision making, as reinforced by normative decision theory,[6] considers it the resolution of the dilemma of choice. Normative decision theory

---

[4] For a discussion of the need to balance goals in command and control, see Coakley (1991).

[5] Those who expect modern information technology to solve this problem should remember that an important part of the information needed by the commander—including, especially, the enemy's inten-tions—is hidden under the enemy's skin, and therefore beyond the reach of any known information technology.

[6] Normative decision theory was developed to help decision makers cope with uncertainty. It requires the decision maker to specify all possible courses of action, and to describe each course of action in terms of the possible outcomes, their values, and the probability for each outcome. The theory then requires the decision maker to compute the expected value for each course of action, and to choose the course of action with the highest expected value. When the consequences unfold over time, this

asserts that the decision maker generates alternatives and evaluates these alternatives according to some criterion, usually *expected value*. But this conception is difficult to apply to dynamic decision making, mainly because of the importance of time. Decision trees for dynamic tasks can become very large very rapidly, especially if the task is broken into chunks that occupy short timespans. Moreover, the notion that decision making involves simply the resolution of choice dilemmas rarely captures why the decision is being made in the first place.

An alternative view takes the *objective* of dynamic decision making as the point of departure. The objective of dynamic decision making can be regarded as achieving control over some aspect of the environment (Brehmer, 1992). Control theory might therefore serve as a useful alternative to traditional decision theory for dynamic tasks.[7] Control theory, part of engineering science, mathematically models how one process controls another process (see also the discussion of the strategy problem in dynamic decision making in Section 2.2, "Control of One Temporal Process by Another Such Process"). In the case of firefighting, control theory should suggest ways of using the firefighting process to fight the fire (which, as noted above, is also a process). But as Bainbridge (1981) notes in discussing the modelling of process operators, control theory's actual equations are of little use for modelling human decision making, since the equations require measured signals as input. Modelling human perception as if it involved single signals for input to an internal control model is not reasonable: perception is based on patterns and gestalts rather than on single signals. A recent attempt to use control theory to model firefighting (Svensson, 1998) illustrates this problem quite clearly: the only aspect of firefighting tactics that could be modelled was regulating the water pressure in the firehose to match the fire's temperature. The strategic issues illustrated in Figure 1 could not be modelled in this way.

But even if the control theory equations themselves are not useful, the theory can nevertheless provide us with a useful metaphor. Specifically, it identifies the four general conditions required for control:

- There must be a goal (the *goal condition*).

- It must be possible to ascertain the state of the system to be controlled (the *observability condition*).

- It must be possible to change the state of the system (the *change condition*).

- There must be a model of the system that describes what will happen if we do something to the system (the *model condition*).

---

step is handled by constructing a decision tree. Decision trees rapidly become unwieldy when the decision problem is considered in real time, and it becomes impossible to make decisions because constructing the decision tree takes too long. Moreover, it is often not possible to construct the whole decision tree because it is impossible to collect the information that is needed to do so. Hence, as pointed out by Simon (for example, 1956), "bounded rationality" is the best a decision maker can hope for.

[7] See Toates (1975) for an introduction to control theory in contexts other than the automatic control of machines.

The goal condition is required for defining the reference signal for control. The control system attempts to reduce the difference between this reference signal and the feedback signal, which describes the system's state. Observability ensures that the control system uses the actual state of the system—for example, how far its output is from the reference signal—in computing how the system should be changed. The change condition ensures that the control system can indeed change the system's state so that the differences between the reference signal and the system's state (as indicated through feedback) can be reduced. The model tells the control system how to accomplish this reduction. In decision-making terms, the decision maker has a goal that he or she seeks to attain. After observing the system's state, the decision maker notes whether a difference exists between the actual state and the goal state. The decision maker then consults his or her model of the task in order to find a way to reduce the difference between what is and what ought to be, while staying within the limits of what can be changed in the system.

Two of these conditions (the observability condition and the change condition) pertain to the system, while the other two (the goal condition and the model condition) pertain to the decision maker. It would be tempting to conclude that the research problem in dynamic decision making is simply to understand how observability and change affect the goals and models people develop. But that approach would be too simplistic. Neither observability nor the possibility for change are objective conditions that can be defined independently of the system doing the observing and the one being changed. For example, observability for a process engineer is not the same as observability for a process operator, and the changes in a computer's state differ significantly from those that pertain to its operator's state. As a result, interface design becomes vital: considerable effort must be spent on creating interfaces that allow the system's operator to acquire adequate information about the system's state and that provide the operator with the means for changing it.

Furthermore, the four conditions are not independent. For example, the extent to which the observability condition can be met determines the quality of the models that can be developed. The models that are developed to control systems with low levels of observability (such as many industrial processes) are necessarily imperfect, and the level of control made possible by those models will therefore also be less than perfect. If the decision maker's model of the system is imperfect, he or she will not be able to formulate adequate goals; this situation will lead to even lower levels of control. One can posit, therefore, that the decision maker's mental model is the most important factor in successful control, since it suggests both reasonable goals and the level of system performance. The control theory metaphor thus suggests that the primary focus when studying command and control should be on the quality of the mental model developed by the commander.

The mental model concept has found many uses in cognitive psychology (see, for example, Rogers, Rutherford, & Bibby, 1992). Here, the term is defined in the control theory sense, as the representation of the task that allows the decision maker to compute inputs to the system that change the system's state in the direction of the goal state. As such, it is an intervening variable. Whether it is a structure in long-term memory or a construction in short-term memory—or perhaps both—is currently impossible to say; detailed evidence on this point is lacking.[8] To understand this aspect, more detailed studies of how commanders make their decisions are needed.

The conditions under which military command and control is exercised typically involve limited observability. The enemy, of course, does its utmost to deny the commander full observability. Moreover, as noted earlier, the temporal and spatial distribution of battlefield information on the battlefield generally prevents the commander from obtaining a complete picture of the situation (Watts, 1996). Finally, the enemy's intentions are hard to ascertain. Hence, the models that a commander can develop are less than perfect. The commander's control over the battle's outcome will consequently also be less than perfect (and that would be true even if the commander had an infinite capacity to process the information that can be obtained). No wonder Clausewitz (1976) and others have stressed the role of chance in battle. This limitation also makes clear why commanders themselves represent a major source of Clausewitzian friction (Watts, 1996).

With this in mind, I now turn to the results of studies of dynamic decision making to gain some insights into what can be expected from commanders and other decision makers who must cope with complex dynamic decision problems. But first I will describe the approaches that are used for this type of research.

5. APPROACHES TO RESEARCH ON DECISION MAKING IN DYNAMIC TASKS

Knowledge about human performance in complex dynamic tasks can be gained from many sources. One source is case studies, such as those provided by military history.[9] But knowledge from case studies is not well-suited to the development of general theories regarding human decision making. Case studies have too many degrees of freedom relative to their number of observations, so they can only provide support for—not rejection of—a large number of interpretations. Systematic observation and field studies (for example, from the process industry) provide another source of knowledge about human performance in dynamic tasks. But decisions in these situations usually involve considerable specific knowledge about the process and the plant. Without the guidance of some kind of theory, as well as a deep understanding of the system with which the operators work, it is difficult to untangle results that are specific to the process being studied from results that pertain to the control of dynamic systems in general. A third source of knowledge is psychological research. Results from such research may also be somewhat limited, in that they are typically derived from laboratory studies with college students as subjects. The resultant findings must eventually be tested against other data, such as those obtained from case studies. In addition, laboratory studies can increase the utility of case studies by providing guidance for data collection. In this chapter, I

---

[8] Brehmer (1998) reviews and discusses mental models for control.
[9] A well-known book by Dixon (1976) provides many examples of commanders' failures to cope with complexity and dynamics.

limit my consideration of research results to those derived from psychological research. The testing of these results through case studies must follow.[10]

5.1. Microworlds

Psychological research on dynamic decision making in the laboratory became possible only after computers enabled researchers to create the necessary interactive environments, which paper-and-pencil experimental paradigms cannot provide. The computer environments developed for this kind of research have come to be called *microworlds*. Research on dynamic decision making using microworlds began independently in Australia, in Germany, in the United States, and in Sweden during the 1970s.

In microworld experiments, subjects interact with and control computer-simulated systems such as forest fires, companies, or developing countries over some period of time. (Frensch & Funke, 1995, describe a variety of microworlds.) Microworlds are not intended to be high-fidelity simulations. Instead, they represent systems in the same manner that woodcuts represent scenes—it is possible to recognize what is being represented, but there is little detail. Nevertheless, microworlds can simulate the fundamental characteristics of decision problems—namely, complexity, dynamic behaviour, and opaqueness.

5.2. Strategies in Microworld Research

Research using microworlds has followed two different strategies. The first I will call the *individual differences strategy*. In such research, all subjects interact with the same microworld under the same conditions. The subjects are then divided into two or more groups according to their performance. The analysis then attempts to explain differences in subjects' performance in terms of their scores on psychometric tests, such as intelligence tests or personality tests, or in terms of their behaviour while performing the task. While the practical aim of this research may be to find a way of predicting performance with complex tasks, from a theoretical viewpoint, studies like these also contribute to a better understanding of the demands that the microworld places on decision makers. If, for example, subjects who have high scores on tests of spatial ability perform better than those who have low scores, it is reasonable to infer that accomplishing the task presented by the microworld in question requires spatial ability.

The other strategy is the *experimental strategy*: here, the microworld's properties are varied, and the effects of these variations are assessed using between-subjects or within-subjects designs. For example, one experimental group may control microworld events that feature feedback delays, while another group controls events that present no such delays; the subsequent analysis compares the performance of the two groups. The experimental strategy yields information about what people can and cannot do under different circumstances. If performance is lower in situations that incorporate feedback delays compared with those

---

[10] Dörner (1996) describes results from both experiments and case studies.

that do not contain delays, researchers can conclude that people find such delays problematic.

The individual differences and experimental strategies can be combined in order to ascertain how different microworld characteristics affect the performance of subjects with different characteristics—for example, how subjects with different levels of intelligence perform when presented with delays.

6. RESULTS OF RESEARCH

Research with microworlds has produced a remarkably stable picture of human performance in complex dynamic tasks. In cases where comparisons can be made, the results from studies using microworlds agree with those from process control—for example, with respect to the effects of feedback delays (Brehmer, 1992).

6.1. Results from Studies of Individual Differences

Studies that focus on individual differences indicate that there are large individual variations in behaviour and performance in microworlds. It has generally proved difficult to find any consistent relationship between microworld performance and performance on psychometric tests, but there are clear differences in behaviour between subjects who perform well and subjects who perform less well. The former behave in a more systematic way, collect more information before making decisions, evaluate their decisions more carefully, test causal hypotheses about the system with which they are working, and exhibit more self-reflection—that is, they think about the reasons for their successes and failures to a greater extent—than do subjects who perform less well. Schaub and Strohschneider (1989) found that when managers of large German and Swiss companies participated as subjects in a microworld experiment, they showed the same kinds of behaviours as college students in a control group, but with a greater frequency of the beneficial behaviours. Since it seems hard to believe that the managers were born with these abilities (for example, more systematic approaches to information gathering), these results suggest that people can be trained to cope with complex dynamic tasks. Extending these results to military command and control might suggest that the commander's staff can and should contribute to the systematic handling of a decision-making task—for example, by ensuring that they collect adequate information and evaluate alternative courses of action before the commander makes a decision.

But the particular factors that lead to improved performance are not yet known in any detail. Practice alone does not seem to be enough. Rigas (1998) found that repeated exposures to the same microworld did not lead to better performance. Nor did instruction in systems thinking and in the behaviours that are needed to control a dynamic system lead to better performance in a complex microworld (Dörner, Kreuzig, Reither, & Stäudel, 1983). However, systematic self-reflection, where the subjects were induced to actually think about their successes and failures, *did* result in performance improvement (Tisdale, 1992), as did teaching subjects specific rules for handling complexity in the context of the microworld that they were to control

(Jansson, 1995). Senge and Sterman (1992) advocate combining the analysis of single business cases with microworlds training, so that the case material gives direction to the learners' experimentation with the microworld. Specifically, they recommend that managers first help create a microworld simulation of their business, and then run the simulation and examine the results as a way of understanding their business better. These findings suggest that the main problem faced by subjects trying to control complex dynamic tasks is that of developing hypotheses concerning the relevant variables in the system. In the absence of such hypotheses, providing general methods for handling complexity seems to be of little help.

6.2. Results from Experimental Studies

Studies using the experimental strategy elucidate the general problems that people experience when making complex dynamic decisions. Although no general theory of dynamic decision making currently exists, the results to date can be summarized in terms of two main principles (Brehmer, 1995b). And when combined with the conclusions from the studies on individual differences, these results may be seen as steps toward developing a general theory.

The first principle, *overemphasis on the here and now*, refers to the tendency for decision makers to attend only to the information currently at hand—that is, their tendency to believe that this information alone provides a representative picture of the system's current state and, as a result, to experience difficulties in accommodating feedback delays. This interpretation is consistent with results from studies of decision making under conditions of uncertainty, which often find that decision makers tend to ignore the limitations of sample information (which is usually all they can get) and to consider such information to be representative of the population at large. Tversky and Kahneman (1974) posit that decision makers rely on this "representativeness heuristic" because they lack the statistical techniques for handling sampled data. When considered in conjunction with the results from dynamic decision making, these results may indicate a fundamental characteristic of decision makers: that they rely on perceptual information ("the world as it seems to be" according to the input of the decision maker's senses) and that they do not process this information any further. This hypothesis is supported by recent conclusions from research on naturalistic decision making—for example, that decision makers often rely solely on their recognition of a situation and seem to perform little or no analysis before selecting a course of action (Klein, Orasanu, Calderwood, & Zsambok, 1993). But the hypothesis needs further investigation. Note that these results cannot be interpreted as support for the hypothesis that people have difficulty developing adequate mental models for complex systems. In fact, managing the implications of delays proves difficult for people even when they are informed in advance of the delays' existence and nature (Brehmer, 1995a). Providing the information required to form an adequate mental model does not by itself seem sufficient to ensure accurate dynamic decision making.

The second principle, *lack of systems thinking*, alludes to the tendency for decision makers who are handling dynamic problems to think linearly—that is, to believe that actions and results are directly related and to ignore the side effects of actions. This tendency can also be viewed as an overreliance on information that is readily available, along with a tendency to ignore what must be inferred—such as side effects. This behaviour of the decision maker is obviously similar to that described above, but in the preceding instance, the decision maker ignores the task's temporal characteristics. Here, the decision maker ignores the task's systems characteristics. It is not yet clear, though, whether the two instances actually represent (a) separate cases of a single form of behaviour (that is, taking into account only what can be seen directly when making a decision) that has two different consequences (ignoring feedback delays and ignoring side effects); or (b) two completely different forms of cognitive deficit (ignoring temporal relations and ignoring side effects). Another interpretation of this experimental result holds that subjects simply have not developed the mental models needed to go beyond the information given and to make the required inferences. Whatever the explanation, subjects working with complex dynamic systems clearly have problems with feedback delays and side effects in complex dynamic decision tasks. In this respect, their performance resembles that of people who work with such systems in the "real world" (Senge & Sterman, 1992; see also the quotations from Axelrod, 1976, and Forrester, 1971, below).

Although individuals do differ in their approaches, the results of studies on dynamic decision making nevertheless indicate that almost everyone exhibits these tendencies to some extent. Nor are the results limited to this domain. Similar observations have been made in studies of process operators (Brehmer, 1998) and in studies of business managers—where, for example, failure to account for the effect of feedback delays is a common cause of bankruptcy (Senge & Sterman, 1992).

7. CONCLUSIONS

Following the lead of the elder Moltke—as quoted in this chapter's introduction— I have distinguished two aspects of command and control decision making: planning and dynamic decision making. Although Moltke does not use the specific term dynamic decision making, his description of what happens "after contact" seems to be matched quite well by the modern conception of dynamic decision making. Viewing military command and control as a dynamic decision-making problem illuminates the general demands made on the commander and assists in the development of hypotheses about commanders' decision-making behaviour and about how to help commanders make effective decisions. Any hypotheses that are developed in this way—that is, on the basis of results from experimental studies in the process industry and in management—will of course need to be validated and augmented in the context of military command and control.

The results of the studies reviewed in this chapter provide concrete directions for future work. Specifically, these results indicate that delays and complexity can be expected to cause difficulties for commanders due to inadequate mental models. The lack of appropriate mental models for dealing with dynamic decision problems has been observed not only in the laboratory and in studies of process operators, but also in the decision making of high-level managers. Axelrod (1976) characterizes the models of the elite decision makers in his study as revealing

> [a] picture of the decision maker . . . [as] one who has more beliefs that he can handle, who employs a simplified image of the policy environment that is structurally easy to operate with and who acts rationally within the context of his simplified image. (p. 244)

His conclusions are based on in-depth studies of the "causal maps" ("mental models," in my terminology) of decision makers who had the experience necessary to develop adequate models. One reason that the models are not corrected is that they are not explicit. Forrester (1971) argues that

> [t]he mental model is fuzzy. It is incomplete. It is imprecisely stated. Furthermore, within one individual, a mental model changes with time and even during the flow of a single conversation. The human mind assembles a few relationships to fit the context of a discussion. As the subject shifts, so does the model. . . . Each participant employs a different mental model to interpret the subject. Fundamental assumptions differ but are never brought into the open. (p. 53)

When a model is not explicit, decision makers have trouble pinpointing the exact reasons why decisions based on the model fail to have the intended consequences. Consequently, the decision maker will also have difficulty making the necessary changes in the model. The remedy being suggested, therefore, is to develop some way of making a mental model concrete and explicit, so that it can be confronted and inspected. Simulations may well be the answer, as they have been in the process industry and in management. A simulation forces a mental model to become explicit, especially when the decision maker helps construct the simulation (Senge & Sterman, 1992). When decision makers have provided input to the model builder in the form of beliefs about the system's causal relations and loops, they can later examine the consequences of these beliefs when the model is run under different conditions and after different modifications. Because the beliefs are externalized in the computer model, they are made explicit in a way that they are not in a purely mental model. New beliefs can be substituted for the old beliefs and their consequences examined until the decision maker finds a model that does what he or she wants it to do. While in principle, it may be possible do this kind of modelling "in one's head," the results of studies of real decision makers (described above) suggest that mental modelling is very difficult or even impossible without access to some form of cognitive aid, such as a simulation. The conditions under which simulations will be effective is, of course, a matter for further research.

8. REFERENCES

Ashby, W. R. (1956). *An introduction to cybernetics.* New York: Wiley.

Augustine, Saint. (1983). Från *Bekännelser* (Bok XI) [From *Confessiones* (Book XI)]. (H. Lyttkens, Trans.). In K. Marc-Wogau, (Ed.), *Filosofin genom tiderna* [The development of philosophy] (pp. 322–338). Stockholm: Bonniers. (Original work published 397)

Axelrod, R. (1976). Results. In R. Axelrod (Ed.), *The structure of decision: The cognitive maps of political elites* (pp. 221–248). Princeton, NJ: Princeton University Press.

Bainbridge, L. (1981). Mathematical equations or processing routines? In J. Rasmussen & W. B. Rouse (Eds.), *Human detection and diagnosis of systems failures* (pp. 259–286). New York: Plenum Press.

Brehmer, B. (1992). Dynamic decision making: Human control of complex systems. *Acta Psychologica, 81,* 211–241.

Brehmer, B. (1995a). Feedback delays in complex dynamic tasks. In P. A. Frensch & J. Funke (Eds.), *Complex problem solving: The European perspective* (pp. 103–130). Hillsdale, NJ: Erlbaum.

Brehmer, B. (1995b). *Mänsklig styrning av komplexa system* [Human control of complex systems] (MDA Report). Stockholm: Arbetsmiljöfonden.

Brehmer, B. (1998). *Mentala modeller: Operatörers kunskap om dynamiska, komplexa och ogenomskinliga system* [Mental models: Operators' knowledge about dynamic, complex and in-transparent systems]. Unpublished manuscript, Swedish National Defence College, Stockholm.

Brehmer, B., & Allard, R. (1991). Real time, dynamic decision making: The effects of complexity and feedback delays. In J. Rasmussen, B. Brehmer, & J. Leplat (Eds.), *Distributed decision making: Cognitive models of cooperative work* (pp. 319–334). New York: Wiley.

Clausewitz, K. von. (1976). *On war* (P. Paret and M. Howard, Trans.). Princeton, NJ: Princeton University Press. (Original work published 1833)

Coakley, T. P. (1991). *Command and control for war and peace.* Washington, DC: National Defense University Press.

Dixon, N. F. (1976). *On the psychology of military incompetence.* London, U.K.: Futura.

Dörner, D. (1996). *The logic of failure.* New York: Metropolitan Books.

Dörner, D., Kreuzig, H. W., Reither, F., & Stäudel, T. (Eds.). (1983). *Lohhausen: Vom Umgang mit Unbestimmtheit und Komplexität* [Lohhausen: On dealing with uncertainty and complexity]. Bern, Switzerland: Huber.

Forrester, J. W. (1971). Counterintuitive behavior of social systems. *Technology Review, 73,* 52–68.

Frensch, P. A., & Funke, J. (Eds.). (1995). *Complex problem solving: The European perspective.* Hillsdale, NJ: Erlbaum.

Hughes, D. J. (Ed.). (1993). *Moltke on the art of war.* Novato, CA: Presidio Press.

Jansson, A. (1995). Strategies in dynamic decision making: Does teaching heuristic strategies by instruction affect performance? In J.-P. Caverni, M. Bar-Hillel, F. H. Barron, & H. Jungermann (Eds.), *Contributions to decision making I* (pp. 213–232). Amsterdam: Elsevier.

Keegan, J. (1987). *The mask of command.* New York: Viking.

Klein, G. A., Orasanu, J., Calderwood, R., & Zsambok, C. E. (Eds.). (1993). *Decision making in action: Models and methods.* Norwood, NJ: Ablex.

Rigas, G. (1998). *Decision making processes in a simulated ecological system.* Manuscript submitted for publication, Uppsala University, Uppsala, Sweden.

Rogers, Y., Rutherford, A., & Bibby, P. A. (Eds.). (1992). *Models in the mind: Theory, perspective, and application.* London, U.K.: Academic Press.

Schaub, H., & Strohschneider, S. (1989). *Die Rolle heuristischen Wissens beim Umgang mit einem komplexen Problem oder: Können Manager wirklich besser managen?* [The role of heuristic knowledge when interacting with a complex problem—or: Are managers really able to manage?] (Memorandum 71). Bamberg, Germany: Lehstuhl Psychologie II.

Senge, P., & Sterman, J. D. (1992). Systems thinking and organizational learning: Acting locally and thinking globally in the organization of the future. *European Journal of Operational Research, 59,* 137–150.

Simon, H. A. (1956). Rational choice and the structure of the environment. *Psychological Review, 63,* 129–138.

Simpkin, R. E. (1985). *Race to the swift: Thoughts on twenty-first century warfare.* London: Brassey's Defence Publishers.

Sperandio, J. (1978). The regulation of working methods as a function of work-load among air traffic controllers. *Ergonomics, 21,* 195–202.

Svensson, S. (1998). *Solving tactical problems using control engineering: Systems identification and modeling* (Report 10:17). Lund, Sweden: Lund University, Department of Fire Safety Engineering.

Tisdale, T. (1992). Self-reflection and its part in action regulation. In B. Brehmer & J. Leplat (Eds.), *Simulations, evaluation and models: Proceedings of the Fourth MOHAWC [Modeling of Human Action in Work Contexts] Workshop* (pp. 78–89). Roskilde, Denmark: Risø National Laboratory.

Toates, F. (1975). *Control theory in biology and experimental psychology.* London, U.K.: Hutchinson.

Tversky, A., & Kahneman, D. (1974). Judgment under uncertainty: Heuristics and biases. *Science, 185,* 1124–1131.

Watts, B. D. (1996). *Clausewitzian friction and future war* (McNair Paper 52). Washington, DC: National Defense University, Institute for National Strategic Studies.

CHAPTER 17

SELF-ASSESSMENT OF COMMAND PERFORMANCE AND FEEDBACK IN MULTIFORCE TRAINING

ANGELO MIRABELLA, GUY L. SIEBOLD, and LIEUTENANT COLONEL (RETIRED) JAMES F. LOVE

1. INTRODUCTION

The increasing prevalence of multiforce (multiservice, joint service, and multinational) operations highlights the need to better understand how to *train* and *evaluate* multiforce command staffs, especially for the *planning* phases of combat and peacekeeping operations at high echelons. Here the "dynamics of human interaction that constitute the essence of command" (Foster, 1988, p. 204) pose the most severe challenge to training. *Assessment* of how well these dynamics are being shaped in training exercises poses an especially difficult and complex problem. In assessing combat planning, we have neither the structure (for example, standard operating procedures, software, and equipment) nor the hard data (for example, casualties and objectives reached) that are available in the execution phases of combat. Yet to effectively train people in combat planning skills, we need to link

ANGELO MIRABELLA • United States Army Research Institute for the Behavioral and Social Sciences, 5001 Eisenhower Avenue, Alexandria, Virginia, USA 22333-5600   GUY L. SIEBOLD • United States Army Research Institute for the Behavioral and Social Sciences, 5001 Eisenhower Avenue, Alexandria, Virginia, USA 22333-5600   LIEUTENANT COLONEL (RETIRED) JAMES F. LOVE • 317 James Street, Falls Church, Virginia, USA 22046

The Human in Command: Exploring the Modern Military Experience,
edited by McCann and Pigeau, Kluwer Academic/Plenum Publishers, New York, 2000.

those skills to explicit training objectives, measure how well the skills are performed, and use the measurement results to provide training feedback. Even more challenging is training for peacekeeping operations and assessing the human dynamics involved. Peacekeeping tasks and outcomes are less structured, more uncertain, and less well defined—and therefore more difficult to observe and measure—than combat tasks. Peacekeepers must plan operations involving a complex mixture of social, economic, and political tasks as well as supporting police or combat tasks. We need to find innovative ways to assess the skills and performance of these difficult-to-observe tasks. But from a scientific as well as a military perspective, we also need to find ways to validate the effectiveness of the assessments to support training feedback.

2. CURRENT APPROACHES TO COMMAND MEASUREMENT

Current measurement approaches fall into two broad categories. The first is the use of observer/controllers (O/Cs) to observe training exercises, make judgments about various aspects of collective performance, and then record those judgments on checklists, on rating forms, or in critical incident notes. The primary purpose for doing this—at least in the U.S. military establishment—is to provide data and documentation for diagnostic training feedback. The U.S. Army refers to such feedback as the *after-action review* or AAR. It is based on the Socratic method, by which a mentor with the requisite experience to recognize problems and recommend solutions highlights that information by drawing it out of the trainees themselves. The mentor functions as a facilitator, a guide.

The quintessential application of the AAR methodology is to be found at the National Training Center (NTC), Fort Irwin, California. At NTC, battalion task force training exercises for brigades that fight offensive and defensive missions against a cadre enemy force are conducted over many square miles of desert terrain (Dryer, 1989; Stafford, 1990). A dozen or so O/Cs, in utility vehicles, follow key personnel within each battalion to observe and document performance problems during the planning and execution phases of defensive or offensive missions. Some O/Cs focus on specific subordinate units. Others assess major battlefield functions, such as Intelligence or Command and Control, across the battalion (Mirabella, 1997; Sulzen, 1997). The senior O/C and a staff of analysts compile the O/C observations, along with extensive electronic data on maneuvers and casualties. Results are used to conduct a task force after-action review with the battalion's commander, staff, and company officers. Though carefully structured according to a customary NTC format, the AAR is intended to encourage the commander and his or her subordinates to identify performance problems and solutions that occurred during training—from their own perspectives.

The second category of measurement approach is the use of electronic data streams or other hard data. In the O/C judgment approach, the O/C is the "ruler" for measuring performance: thus, this approach is subjective. Hard data approaches, in contrast, are designed to increase objectivity through the use of mechanical or electronic devices for assigning scale values to performance. This is sometimes referred to as the *statistical* approach. The scales of measurement here are at the interval or ratio level. Some examples are found in the Universal Joint Task List (UJTL) (United States, 1996b), the Army Command and Control Evaluation System (ACCES) (Halpin, 1996), and the Army Training Analysis and Feedback System (ATAFS) (Brown et al., 1997). For example, the UJTL task measures include percentages, minutes, hours, days, and frequencies. The task "Analyze Courses of Action (COAs)" is measured in part by the percentage of COAs wargamed against potential enemy COAs. The ACCES uses similar measures applied to generic tasks such as "Planning Process," "Course of Action Analysis," and "Information Exchange." For example, one measure of planning is the time from implementation of the plan until the time the plan is changed. The ATAFS measures various aspects of tactical performance, including weapon movements, firings, and kills. It also provides routines for quickly compiling tabular and graphical materials for use in after-action reviews.

2.1. Limitations of Observer/Controller (O/C) Judgments

There are a number of problems with using O/Cs for measuring mission planning performance and generally for assessing the complex human dynamics in command.

2.1.1. Logistics

First, using dedicated O/Cs imposes a heavy overhead burden. The world-class O/Cs at the National Training Center (NTC) do a splendid job of observing, documenting, and analyzing training performance, but at an enormous cost—a cost that is not routinely affordable. Also, in some circumstances outside of NTC, there may be no personnel available to serve as O/Cs other than personnel from the unit or staff being trained.

Second, an O/C cadre may have a restricted view of mission planning activities. In joint training environments, particularly, such activities may take place in dozens of staff elements and subgroups of those elements, distributed over large areas within a training facility or location, or even distributed geographically at multiple training sites. In any event, the O/C may be hard pressed to assess the trainee's view of training events—for example, the trainee's situational awareness (Zazanis, 1998).

2.1.2. Measurement Issues

Current and evolving measurement approaches have limited utility for supporting AARs at higher echelons—that is, those that stress planning and mission management rather than tactical control. The use by O/Cs of sequential event-based checklists was reported to be only marginally helpful in supporting AARs in a simulation-based training event involving a multiservice Battalion Task Force (Mirabella, Sticha, & Morrison, 1997). The checklists were designed to allow the O/C to compare expected with actual performance and to note discrepancies between the two (Bell et al., 1997). They *were* useful for generating indices and for documenting overall performance trends from day to day. However, scales intended for rating generic team processes during the same event were reported by O/Cs to be of no use for preparing or conducting AARs. Generic measures included "communication," "team coordination," "situational awareness," and "team adaptability."

The events-based approach is consistent with a view of battle as a predictable linear sequence of combat events. But as Pigeau and McCann (1995) note, "[t]he world of C^2 is in principle non-linear and uncertain. . . . [H]uman users are notoriously imperfect followers of procedures" (p. 4). The approach is therefore unlikely to capture the "dynamics of human interaction that are the essence of command" (Foster, 1988, p. 204). In contrast, the generic-measures approach described above is derived from the language and methods of psychology; it may thus be too *abstract*, too far removed from specific combat events, to be usefully applied to the multiforce training environment. Research on its use in such an environment suggests as much (Mirabella et al., 1997). Both the events-based and the generic-measures approaches *have* been used successfully by the U.S. Navy, but only in the relatively constrained, structured, tactical environment of a Navy Combat Information Center (Paris, Johnston, & Reeves, this volume, Chapter 18).

2.2. Limitations of Electronic Data Streams or Other Hard Data

A key problem with hard data approaches is that their utility in providing remedial feedback is not clear-cut. ACCES and UJTL employ "statistical" dimensions—for example, percentage, duration, quantity, and distance—to measure the outputs of a process. But these measures don't indicate what combat behaviours need to be modified. Moreover, their "statistical" approaches toward feedback have received some negative comment (for example, at the 1997 Universal Joint Task List Conference, Joint Warfighting Center, Fort Monroe, Virginia) as being too rigid, restrictive, and fine-grained for the fuzzy character of training at high echelons. These comments may be particularly valid for mission planning and management at the joint operational level. The ATAFS approach does provide methods for converting hard numbers into feedback procedures. It is a very imaginative, inventive system for doing so. But it is designed for measuring and remediating tactical skills, not the softer operational skills implied by the expression "command."

An additional problem with hard data approaches is that data collection and analysis are time- and labour-intensive. ACCES data compilation may require several days at the end of an exercise. Accordingly, this approach cannot support feedback in a timely fashion. The ATAFS *is* designed to provide timely feedback. Although the system is not currently designed to support command training, its underlying concepts may be generalizable to evolving digital command environments. In fact, as command staff functions move increasingly from grease-pencil–and–acetate-map environments to digital environments, the use of hard data to support after-action reviews may require some innovative new thinking and research. The U.S. Army's evolving Battle Command System is being developed to support operations up to joint and combined joint operations. Its rich electronic data stream should provide new opportunities to measure and remediate soft skills.

2.3. Impact of Limitations

An extreme example of the difficulty in using current measurement approaches is found in the training of Joint Air Operations, managed by a Joint Forces Air Component Commander (JFACC). The JFACC's Air Operations Center (AOC) contains more than 1,000 people organized into dozens of planning cells and engaged in complex group activities. The challenge of assessing command skill levels to support training feedback under these circumstances is intimidating. Although this training is bounded by standard operating procedures (SOPs), the detailed command activities involve very fluid, complex, interactive, and cyclical group dynamics.

2.4. Need for Innovation in Measurement/Feedback Methodology

The limitations described and illustrated above partly explain the need for innovation in measurement methods. But equally important is the current insufficient effort at providing *command* performance feedback, particularly in interservice training. Even the Army, which has invested substantial resources in AARs and AAR methodology, uses this approach mainly for assessing tactical performance and the "control" aspects of command and control (Brown et al., 1997; Dyer, 1994; Meliza & Tan, 1996; Sulzen, 1997).

The performance measurement/feedback deficit is far more pronounced in the joint arena, even though AAR principles and practices are explicitly and thoroughly detailed in a formal joint training manual (United States, 1996a). "Hot washes" (that is, short summary briefings about exercise pluses and minuses in key areas) and after-action reports do provide good training feedback in training events at the Commander in Chief (CINC) and Joint Task Force (JTF) levels. However, these events occur at the end of two- or three-week rotations, are aimed primarily at senior leadership, and deal as much with training system and training management problems as with staff performance problems. Some O/Cs— called observer/trainers (O/Ts) in the joint arena—may hold specific subject-matter AARs following an exercise. These are called *facilitated after-action reviews (FAARs)*.

According to psychological principles, effective training requires that feedback be provided (a) frequently and (b) soon after the targeted performance (Fedor & Buckley, 1987; Weinstein, Goetz, & Alexander, 1988). Feedback effectiveness has been shown to decrease over time in an inverse exponential manner: that is, effectiveness drops sharply at first, and then levels off (Klein, 1991).

Theory also recognizes that trainees have valid and valuable insights into training progress and effectiveness (Dominick, Reilly, & McGourty, 1997; Keesling, Ford, & Harrison, 1994; Mirabella et al., 1997; Zazanis, 1998). For example, evidence from NTC exercises supports the validity of self-assessment for battalion task force training. In these exercises, effectiveness ratings by battalion staff personnel agreed with ratings by O/Cs (Keesling et al., 1994). A wealth of knowledge may therefore remain untapped in the experiences of trainees—knowledge that could be extracted through enhanced self-assessment tools and methods.

The foregoing limitations prompted the U.S. Army Research Institute for the Behavioral and Social Sciences to initiate research aimed at developing an innovative approach to command performance measurement and related training feedback. The approach is described below.

3. A SELF-ASSESSMENT APPROACH TO COMMAND PERFORMANCE MEASUREMENT

The thrust of our research has been to develop methods of accomplishing the following goals:

- Convert abstract joint training doctrine into analyzed battle functions.

- Convert analyzed battle functions into training objectives (TOs), detailed tasks, and self-assessment questions.

- Derive checklists and rating forms (that is, measurement tools) that can be used by trainees to self-assess the performance of their command cell in a simulation-based training exercise.

- Conduct a mini–after-action review (mini-AAR), drawing on the preliminary self-assessments of all the participants. A mini-AAR is an AAR conducted after each exercise shift by separate command staff cells in order to improve individual cell performance and to augment later staff-wide AARs.

The notion, in effect, is to use the trainee as a surrogate O/C to assess team performance. That performance would mainly reflect command activities, yet it should be anchored to clearly defined TOs. The data from the trainees are intended to supplement, not replace, other available sources of assessment data for use in AARs. The trainees' data are also intended to measure TO-derived processes and products of command planning cells, including such abstract concepts as "adherence to commander's intent." The trainees complete these assessments before convening, staff cell by staff cell, in mini-AARs. These latter two procedures are essentially steps in the Delphi technique (Linstone & Turoff, 1975).

In its original applications, Delphi was used to facilitate experts' efforts to solve fuzzy, complex national policy problems involving the management and use of nuclear weapons. The experts were asked to generate and document solutions individually and then convene for group discussion to reconcile differences and achieve a consensus. Differences might have resulted from different premises or experiences. The various solutions were factored into the consensus solution. Thus Delphi is a mechanism for increasing the reliability of subjective measurement. We are proposing that this technique be adapted and used as a method of training assessment and diagnostic feedback for command and staff training.

An adaptation of Delphi appears well suited to assessing staff training performance, especially the softer skills inherent in mission planning and executive management. These softer skills are important at higher-echelon levels, especially in joint environments. A key step in applying Delphi to command measurement is to develop self-assessment instruments as tools that trainees can use to express their opinions about training progress and deficiencies. This step is described below. But first we need to ask whether trainees would have sufficient knowledge and experience to judge the adequacy of their collective performance. This question is part of the broader issue of the validity of the self-assessment approach for the multiforce environment. A conclusive answer lies in research yet to be done. But available research suggests that the preliminary answer is yes. From her extensive review of the literature on peer assessment, Zazanis (1998) concludes that "[r]esearch suggests that [peer evaluations] are extremely reliable and highly valid" (p. 1). Her follow-up research compared trainee and instructor ratings of special forces team training performance. She concluded that trainees were more effective than instructors at assessing interpersonal performance: "These results strongly suggest . . . that peer evaluations may offer a method of measuring motivation and interpersonal skills, attributes that are difficult to measure in other ways" (Zazanis, 1998, p. 4). Further support for the use of trainees as sources of assessment data was cited earlier in this chapter (Dominick et al., 1997; Keesling et al., 1994; Mirabella et al., 1997). In any case, trainees can and should be provided with performance anchors and standards before a training exercise starts. This is simply good instructional design practice. Finally, Delphi can bring together people with a range of past experiences and present perspectives on training progress to help fill experience and knowledge gaps.

3.1. Development of Measurement Instruments

A four-step model for developing and using self-assessment instruments is summarized in Figures 1 through 4. In Step 1 (Figure 1), a subject matter expert (SME) compiles and reviews doctrine and combat theory for a selected battle function—for example, "coordinate, synchronize, and integrate joint fires." The SME then analyzes the function to define a set of tasks, key players, and linkages to other combat elements or echelons. These tasks are those involving the unit staff as a whole entity, not those involving each staff section or the interactions among the sections (Fields, Taylor, Moore, Mullen, & Moses, 1997).

In Step 2 (Figure 2) the SME, working with an instructional design specialist, produces a training guidebook. This document details inputs, processes, and outputs for each staff cell, as well as interactions among cells. The guidebook also includes sets of self-assessment questions (Love, 1998a). These questions, in turn, are the foundation for Step 3, in which self-assessment checklists and rating forms are designed for specific training exercises.

In Step 3, an SME and an instructional specialist produce self-assessment tools, such as performance checklists and task flowcharts. An example of a self-assessment checklist for a division artillery staff exercise, S-3 section, is shown in Figure 3 (Mirabella & Love, 1998). In this exercise, each staff member was asked to rate the section's products and processes/outputs for a just-completed mission shift.

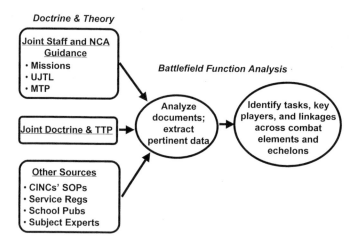

FIGURE 1. Convert doctrine from source documents into analyzed battlefield functions.

3.2. Use of Instruments in Mini-AARs

Figure 4 shows how self-assessment tools might be used in an expanded research or test application of the Delphi method. In Procedure 1, each staff cell (team) member independently assesses the cell's performance at the tasks it carried out over the preceding daily shift. (Shifts in joint training exercises are typically 12 hours long.) For the sake of illustration, assume that the test bed is a Joint Task Force training exercise and that the research focus is on joint fires training. Cells would be teams of four or five people contributed by Intelligence (J2), Operations (J3), and the Fire

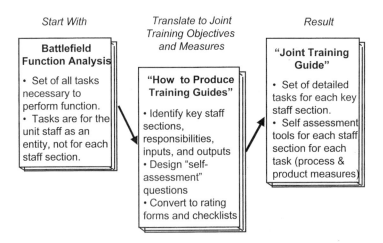

FIGURE 2. Convert analyzed battlefield functions into training objectives.

Partial Self-Assessment Checklist

DivArty S-3 Section

Date, Time, Prepared by:	Not applicable	Opportunity for improvement	Satisfactory	Commendable
Assessment of Products/Outputs				
Field Artillery Support Plan				
DivArty commander's guidance				
Movement orders				
Mission changes				
Assessment of Processes				
How well were FA assets allocated and prioritized?				
Were changes in allocation projected over time IAW div OPORD?				
Were instructions for timely detection/attack of HPTs given?				
Were requirements for positioning of all FA assets determined?				
Were make-up of basic loads & the RSR determined?				

FIGURE 3. Derive instruments applicable to processes, products, and outputs.

Control Element (FCE) for the day and night shifts. In Procedure 2, a mini-AAR, the cell (team) leader brings the cell members together to review their ratings, discuss their differences, and generate a group rating for the cell on its tasks. Members also talk about how to improve cell performance. Any available standards or performance anchors could be consulted, including such items as planning documents and statements of commander's intent. In Procedure 3, the cell's products would be rated for quality and timeliness by other staff cells. These staff cells would be those that received those products as mission inputs during their own exercise shift. Examples of rating forms for this intercell measurement approach are given in Love (1998c). These intercell measures can be used experimentally to "validate" judgments made by the producing cell. Operationally, they can either contribute to

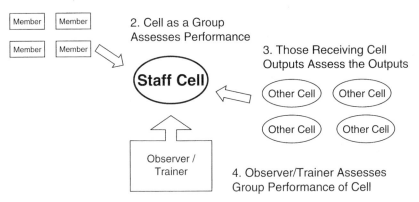

FIGURE 4. Research application of self-assessment.

the mini-AARs as part of the Delphi process or provide inputs to a final staff-wide AAR. Procedure 4 would be used only in an experimental application, unless resources permit operational use. Here an observer/trainer would complete the same checklist as the cell members. The two sets of data could then be compared in studies of consistency and convergent validity. The entire cycle described above would be repeated daily.

3.3. Preliminary Test Applications

3.3.1. Blue Flag

We've developmentally tested this approach at Blue Flag, a recurring event used for training Joint Air Operations commanded by a JFACC (Commander, 9th U.S. Air Force, in this particular case) and involving U.S. Army, U.S. Navy, U.S. Marine Corps, and Allied (including Canadian) forces. A set of joint force TOs for targeting and their derivative self-assessment instruments were produced and tested. The methodology was well received by the command staff of the host unit. A model guidebook on how to develop joint TOs and related self-assessment instruments was produced (Love, 1998c). This guidebook outlines the phases of a joint air campaign planning mission. It then converts each phase into a TO by detailing information or decisions flowing to the phase, processes carried out during the phase, and information or decisions flowing from that phase to subsequent phases of operation. Further efforts to develop and test the method in a corps-level Joint Task Force environment, with a focus on joint fires training, are needed. To support such an effort, a guidebook for developing training objectives and self-assessment instruments to assist training feedback for corps-level application of joint fires training was produced (Love, 1998b).

3.3.2. Division Artillery Staff Training

A further effort to pilot test the self-assessment approach was made in a division artillery staff training exercise at Fort Hood, Texas, in January 1998 (Mirabella & Love, 1998). Though not conducted in a joint environment, this exercise provided a suitable opportunity to pilot test portions of the assessment method. At the end of each of two days of exercises, self-assessment instruments were administered to four staff teams (cells), each of which had been responsible for a major command and staff function: Operations, Fire Control Element, Fire Support Element, and Targeting. For a number of administrative reasons, the anticipated mini-AARs were not held. At the end of the exercises, a survey was administered to measure the participants' perceptions about the value and effectiveness of the self-assessment approach. The approach was judged to be a useful and timely way to bring to the surface training problems that might otherwise have been overlooked. Further development and implementation of the method were viewed as having value to Army staff training.

In practice, self-assessment rating sheets would be administered to all trainees at the end of each day's exercise. The trainees would take 10 or 15 minutes to fill out the sheets and would then assemble with their respective team (cell) leaders for mini-AARs. Here they would compare and discuss their ratings to determine how to improve performance in subsequent exercises.

4. CONTINUING RESEARCH ISSUES

Theory indicates that frequent, thorough, and immediate training feedback is the most effective, but in joint and multinational environments the reality is that feedback to staff cells is minimal. It occurs, if at all, at the end of days or weeks of training. Is the self-assessment approach a viable solution to the feedback problem? To answer this question, a number of research steps need to be taken. First, the entire method needs to be administered, to establish whether both trainers and trainees perceive that it is feasible and that it adds significant value to their training. Until now, only portions of the method have been tested. The results of those tests have been encouraging, but far from conclusive.

Second, empirical evidence is needed showing that self-assessment enhances training effectiveness sufficiently to justify its use. Would a Joint Task Force be better prepared to go to war if self-assessment were added to its arsenal of training tools? Experimental answers to this question are not feasible outside a laboratory setting, but quasi-experimental approaches may provide useful approximations—for example, identifying two comparable staff exercises in succession, and then applying daily self-assessment in one case, but only at the beginning and at the end of all the exercises in the second case. Percentages of "satisfactory" performance ratings for the first and last days of the training rotations would provide a basis for comparison.

Third, the reliability and validity of the self-assessment measurement tools would need to be addressed if summaries of the measures were to be considered for use in training management applications (such as trend analysis) or for characterizing training status by cell within an exercise shift or across exercise days. Reliability and validity issues would also need to be resolved if the tools were considered for uses other than training—for example, to compare operational or training systems. Such issues would be less critical if the self-assessment tools were used primarily as job aids to support training feedback. In this latter case, the self-assessment checklists would serve primarily to facilitate discussion during the mini-AAR. Again, surrogates to experimental research would be required—for example, convergent measurements, such as correlations of assessments by trainees and by O/Cs using identical measurement scales. Such measurements were used, with encouraging results, in the Army Research Institute's program on the "Determinants of Effective Unit Performance at the National Training Center" (Keesling et al., 1994).

A final issue is the design and use of self-assessment tools and methods. This issue has many researchable dimensions. For example, how much time should be allocated to the mini-AAR? How can self-assessment be applied across distributed sites? What types of staff cells would benefit most from the approach? Can other sources of data, such as O/C checklist and rating data or electronic data streams, be incorporated into the self-assessment approach? Can assessment data be summarized to yield indices of training progress or even of combat readiness? What impact would self-assessment have on leadership, morale, or cohesion?

5. CONCLUSION

Current or currently evolving measurement approaches have limited utility for assessing command performance and supporting after-action reviews in multiforce training exercises. A complementary measurement approach is needed. Self-assessment, combined with the Delphi technique, has promise for supporting AARs at higher echelons, which stress human-in-command planning and mission executive management. But research is needed to validate the effectiveness of this approach for enhancing command training and for designing a prototype self-assessment system.

6. AUTHORS' NOTE

The views and findings in this chapter are those of the authors and should not be construed as an official position or policy of the U.S. Army Research Institute for the Behavioral and Social Sciences, the U.S. Department of the Army, or the U.S. Department of Defense.

7. REFERENCES

Bell, H. H., Dwyer, D. J., Love, J. F., Meliza, L. L., Mirabella, A., & Moses, F. L. (1997). *Recommendations for planning and conducting multi-service tactical training with distributed interactive simulation technology: A four-service project* (Research Product; AD-A32 8480). Alexandria, VA: U.S. Army Research Institute for the Behavioral and Social Sciences.

Brown, B., Wilkinson, S., Nordyke, J., Riede, D., Huyssoon, S., Aguilar, D., Wonsewitz, R., & Meliza, L. L. (1997). *Developing an automated training analysis and feedback system for tank platoons* (Research Report 1708; AD-A32 8445). Alexandria, VA: U.S. Army Research Institute for the Behavioral and Social Sciences.

Dominick, P. G., Reilly, R. R., & McGourty, J. W. (1997). The effects of peer feedback on team member behavior. *Organization Management, 22*(4), 508–520.

Dryer, D. A. (1989). *An analysis of ground maneuver concentration during NTC deliberate attack missions and its influence on mission effectiveness* (AD-A219 884). Thesis, Naval Postgraduate School, Monterey, CA.

Dyer, J. L. (1994). *A comparison of information in the Joint Readiness Training Center archival records* (Research Report 1659; AD-A27 7676). Alexandria, VA: U.S. Army Research Institute for the Behavioral and Social Sciences.

Fedor, D. B., & Buckley, M. R. (1987). Providing feedback to organizational members: A reconsideration. *Journal of Business Psychology, 2*(2), 171–180.

Fields, H. T., Taylor, H. G., Moore, B. R., Mullen, W. J., & Moses, F. L. (1997). *Analysis of the function to coordinate, synchronize, and integrate fire support as accomplished by an army corps acting as a joint task force* (Research Product 97-10; AD-A32 8260). Alexandria, VA: U.S. Army Research Institute for the Behavioral and Social Sciences.

Foster, G. D. (1988). Contemporary C^2 theory and research: The failed quest for a philosophy of command. *Defense Analysis, 4*(3), 201–228.

Halpin, S. M. (1996). *The army command and control evaluation system (ACCES)* (Research Product 96-04; AD-A31 7213). Alexandria, VA: U.S. Army Research Institute for the Behavioral and Social Sciences.

Keesling, W., Ford, P., & Harrison, K. (1994). Application of the principles of training in armor and mechanized infantry unit. In R. F. Holz, J. H. Hiller, & H. H. McFann (Eds.), *Determinants of effective unit performance: Research on measuring and managing unit training readiness* (pp. 137–178). Alexandria, VA: U.S. Army Research Institute for the Behavioral and Social Sciences.

Klein, S. B. (1991). *Learning principles and applications*. New York: McGraw-Hill.

Linstone, H. A., & Turoff, M. (1975). *Introduction*. In H. A. Linstone, & M. Turoff (Eds.), *The Delphi method: Techniques and applications* (pp. 3–12). Reading, MA: Addison-Wesley.

Love, J. F. (1998a). *How to produce training guides from battlefield functions* (Research Product 99-03). Alexandria, VA: U.S. Army Research Institute for the Behavioral and Social Sciences.

Love, J. F. (1998b). *Joint fires training guide for a corps JTF* (Research Product 99-02). Alexandria, VA: U.S. Army Research Institute for the Behavioral and Social Sciences.

Love, J. F. (1998c). *Joint targeting planning training guide* (Research Product 99-04). Alexandria, VA: U.S. Army Research Institute for the Behavioral and Social Sciences.

Meliza, L. L., & Tan, S. C. (1996). *SIMNET Unit Performance Assessment System (UPAS) version 2.5 user's guide* (Research Product 96-05; AD-A28 5805). Alexandria, VA: U.S. Army Research Institute for the Behavioral and Social Sciences.

Mirabella, A. (1997). *Analysis of battlefield operating system (BOS) statements for developing performance measurement* (Technical Report 1062). Alexandria, VA: U.S. Army Research Institute for the Behavioral and Social Sciences.

Mirabella, A., & Love, J. F. (1998). *Self-assessment based mini-after action review (SAMAAR) methodology: Developmental application to division artillery staff training* (Technical Report 1086). Alexandria, VA: U.S. Army Research Institute for the Behavioral and Social Sciences.

Mirabella, A., Sticha, P., & Morrison, J. (1997). *Assessment of user reactions to the multi-service distributed training testbed (MDT2) system* (Technical Report 1061). Alexandria, VA: U.S. Army Research Institute for the Behavioral and Social Sciences.

Pigeau, R., & McCann, C. (1995). Putting "command" back into command and control: The human perspective. In *Proceedings of the Command and Control Conference, September 26, 1995*. Ottawa: Canadian Defence Preparedness Association.

Stafford, C. A. (1990). *The relationship between operational graphics and battlefield success* (AD-A238-338). Thesis, Naval Postgraduate School, Monterey, CA.

Sulzen, R. H. (1997). *National Training Center research element Fort Irwin, California, 1986–1996* (Research Special Report 30; AD-A32 6056). Alexandria, VA: U.S. Army Research Institute for the Behavioral and Social Sciences.

United States. (1996a). *Joint training manual for the armed forces of the United States* (CJCSM 3500.03). Washington, DC: Joint Chiefs of Staff.

United States. (1996b). *Universal joint task list* (CJCSM 3500.04A). Washington, DC: Joint Chiefs of Staff.

Weinstein, C. E., Goetz, E. T., & Alexander, P. A. (1988). *Learning and study strategies*. San Diego, CA: Academic Press.

Zazanis, M. M. (1998). Peer evaluations: What do they buy you? In *1997 in-house researcher colloquium* (Special Report 35) (pp. 1–5). Alexandria, VA: U.S. Army Research Institute for the Behavioral and Social Sciences.

CHAPTER 18

A SCHEMA-BASED APPROACH TO MEASURING TEAM DECISION MAKING IN A NAVY COMBAT INFORMATION CENTER

CAROL PARIS, JOAN HALL JOHNSTON, and DARIAN REEVES

1. INTRODUCTION

Certain military events that have taken place in the last decade—such as those involving the U.S. Navy's ships USS *Stark*, USS *Vincennes*, and USS *Saratoga*—collectively illustrate the great potential for human error in highly complex, stressful environments like that in the Navy Combat Information Center (CIC). The Tactical Decision Making Under Stress (TADMUS) program, sponsored by the Office of Naval Research, was implemented to improve training methods in order to maintain and enhance individual and team performance processes and outcomes in complex environments (Cannon-Bowers, Salas, & Grossman, 1991; Salas, Cannon-Bowers, & Johnston, 1997). Empirical evidence from TADMUS research has highlighted the need to refine current measurement and diagnostic strategies for assessing the accuracy and timeliness of tactical decision-making outcomes. The

CAROL PARIS • *Naval Air Warfare Center Training Systems Division, Code 4961 12350 Research Parkway, Orlando, Florida, USA 32826-3224*   JOAN HALL JOHNSTON • *Naval Air Warfare Center Training Systems Division, Code 4961 12350 Research Parkway, Orlando, Florida, USA 32826-3224* DARIAN REEVES • *Sonalysts, Inc., 3051 Technology Parkway, Suite 290, Orlando, Florida, USA 32826*

The Human in Command: Exploring the Modern Military Experience,
edited by McCann and Pigeau, Kluwer Academic/Plenum Publishers, New York, 2000.

main purpose of this chapter is to develop a conceptual framework for deriving a measurement strategy for reliably assessing, evaluating, and diagnosing team tactical decision-making outcomes. We also generate a number of research propositions and describe research plans intended as an initial test of this framework.

2. BACKGROUND

A primary requirement for establishing training effectiveness is to have reliable and valid performance measurement tools with which to compare the performance of individuals and teams across various training strategies. In order to be most informative, performance measurement tools should provide a description of behaviours, criteria for distinguishing between effective and ineffective behaviours, and an explanation of why the behaviours occurred so that their causes can be remediated or reinforced (Cannon-Bowers & Salas, 1997; Johnston, Smith-Jentsch, & Cannon-Bowers, 1997). Additionally, the complexity of military environments requires that assessment, evaluation, and diagnosis address both individual and team-level performance processes and outcomes (Cannon-Bowers & Salas, 1997; Johnston et al., 1997). Therefore, the development of performance measurement tools has been a primary focus of the TADMUS program (Cannon-Bowers & Salas, 1997; Johnston et al., 1997).

To date, much of the effort in the TADMUS program has been applied to developing effective measures of team processes, individual processes, and individual outcomes. For example, the Anti–Air Warfare Team Observation Measure (ATOM) has been demonstrated as a reliable tool for assessing team processes and for supporting debriefing after team training exercises (Smith-Jentsch, Ricci, Campbell, & Zeisig, 1997). In addition, the Behavior Observation Booklet (BOB) and Sequenced Actions and Latencies Index (SALI) collectively combine accuracy and latency ratings to permit examination of a series of actions and their respective outcomes at an individual level (Johnston et al., 1997). However, a reliable and usable measure of training for the last important category—team outcomes—has proven to be more elusive.

To develop a team outcome measurement tool, we reviewed U.S. Navy publications and conducted task analyses with subject matter experts to identify the major tasks that the Air Warfare (AW) team performs in the "detect-to-engage" sequence. Within a Navy CIC, responsibility for threat management is delegated according to the nature of the threat—air, surface, or subsurface. The focus of our research included the five watchstations responsible for air threat management: Tactical Action Officer, Air Warfare Coordinator, Tactical Information Coordinator, Identification Supervisor, and Electronic Warfare Supervisor. The primary AW team tasks include reporting the detection of a track, performing correlation and formal identification, identifying and prioritizing threats, taking actions in accordance with the rules of engagement, and monitoring an engagement with threat reassessment and prioritization (Dwyer, 1992; Johnston et al., 1997). Next, subject matter experts identified the response time requirements for each of the AW tasks at the level of the significant scenario events in the TADMUS research scenarios. The result was the Air Warfare Team Performance Index (ATPI) (Johnston et al., 1997), with which we hoped to measure both accuracy and latency for significant team performance outcomes.

However, for several reasons, the ATPI was not fully successful as a measurement tool. First, the complex nature of teams conducting tactical decision making in stressful (fast-paced and ambiguous) scenario exercises makes evaluating performance difficult and labour-intensive for the observers (Johnston et al., 1997). Consequently, a comparison of observer assessments resulted in low reliability (Johnston et al., 1997). Second, as TADMUS research findings from various experiments accumulated, it became apparent that the ATPI needed further development in order to establish linkages between team-level knowledge and outcomes so that feedback on team performance could be more effective (Johnston et al., 1997; Marshall, Christensen, & McAllister, 1996). The original ATPI was designed only to provide diagnostic information at the task level; it provided no linkages for diagnosing specific deficiencies in the knowledge required to perform the team AW task.

3. CONCEPTUAL FRAMEWORK

The first step in designing an effective team outcome tool for addressing knowledge deficiencies was to develop a theoretical framework from which team performance outcomes and diagnoses could be operationalized. Understanding and modelling problem-solving and decision-making processes have been the focus of research efforts for many years. However, most models are portrayed as sequential information-processing tasks, beginning with information gathering or situation assessment, followed by environmental interpretation, uncertainty reduction, and finally action selection, implementation, and feedback (see Nickerson and Feehrer's [1975] descriptive model; the process models of Clancey [1985] and Rasmussen [1988]; the timeline model of Brecke and Garcia [1995]; and finally, the recognition-primed models described by Klein [1989, 1993], Klein and Calderwood [1990], Noble, Grosz, and Boehm-Davis [1987], and Zsambok and Klein [1997]). Moreover, the majority of such models have focused on the individual, not on the team, as the information processor.

More recently, Hinsz, Tindale, and Vollrath (1997) conducted a synthesis of the group and team literature in order to advance the concept that a team organizes itself to process information in much the same way as an individual does. These authors stress that "at the group level, information processing involves the degree to which information, ideas, or cognitive processes are shared, and are being shared among the group members, and how this sharing of information affects both individual- and group-level outcomes" (p. 43). We have adopted the Hinsz et al. approach—an approach based on the amount and type of information shared among team members—to operationalizing team effectiveness. Our ATOM measurement tool addresses the amount of information shared (that is, team communication processes), and the ATPI focuses on the type of information shared (that is, detect-to-engage information).

In addition, we needed to find a more specific information-processing model that would enable diagnosis of team performance. As part of their research efforts in support of the TADMUS program, Marshall and her colleagues have been developing and validating a problem-solving framework whereby they have proposed and tested a *hybrid schema* model of cognitive processing (Marshall, Christensen, & McAllister, 1996). A *schema* (meaning "form," "shape," or "figure") is an acquired framework or highly organized body of knowledge about a topic. Marshall (1995) describes how schemas are created and modified, how they are selected for use, and how memory stores change as a result of learning (that is, through the strengthening of connectivity among schema elements). Schemas are portrayed as efficient, goal-oriented cognitive mechanisms: they are developed for the purpose of solving problems. Marshall identifies the same information-processing tasks found in other problem-solving theories, but she goes further, also specifying how behaviours—at the individual or team level—can be tied to the tasks, thus enabling specification of training interventions for remediation. This model allows us to take what we know about how individuals learn about their role as part of a team problem-solving task (for example, AW), use that knowledge to structure what we want individuals to learn with regard to performing team tasks and how we want them to learn it, and then use that same knowledge to build the test instruments that we need to measure changes in team performance.

Marshall has advanced the development of her model based on empirical evaluation of tactical teams, and her approach confirms what has been discovered regarding the role of shared team mental models, or common perceptions of the environment and task that support team performance (see Cannon-Bowers, Salas, & Converse, 1993; Duncan et al., 1996; Stout, Cannon-Bowers, & Salas, 1996). For these reasons, Marshall's schema approach seems best suited to guide team performance measurement development. More detail on the approach is provided in the next section.

3.1. Schema Model of Tactical Decision Making

Marshall's schema model comprises four knowledge components that support a decision maker's perception of and attention to a task's situational cues, as well as retrieval of and access to information stored in long-term memory:

- *Identification* involves the knowledge required to recognize a potentially hostile situation. Effective identification involves recognizing a situation by focusing on the particular configuration of features. In a Navy CIC, such configurations tap an individual's knowledge of platforms and weapons, thereby allowing operators to identify specific tracks, project the future actions of those tracks, and ultimately assign threat potential to them. Effective identification further requires the timely and accurate reporting of the ongoing state of those features to fellow team members, within and beyond ownship.

- *Elaboration* involves the knowledge needed to determine what tasks have high priority. Elaboration taps the background store of information that summarizes what has been learned previously about similar situations; it enables operators to create mental models of particular situations. Effective elaboration includes the application of previous knowledge (for example, of mission profiles) to the current situation, so that the most reliable and acceptable hypothesis can be formulated regarding the intent of a specific track. In effect, the individual maps the current experience onto a template that he or she develops from previous experience, and then either consciously or unconsciously attempts to match each part of this template with some aspect of the current situation (Marshall, 1995).

- *Planning* involves the knowledge that guides how and when an individual or team reacts to different parts of the situation. It entails the application of rules and strategies to the current situation, and enables connection of a goal state to a set of possible actions that will realize that state. Effective planning arises from (a) a solid body of experience/knowledge that addresses the appropriateness and optimal timing of specific responses to potential threats, and (b) rules of engagement that define the current situational constraints and provide the specific framework within which the knowledge must be implemented.

- *Execution* involves the knowledge that guides implementation of plans and determines who should perform the required actions. Effective execution requires sufficient follow-through by all team members to accomplish the stated objectives.

These four categories cover both declarative and procedural knowledge. Declarative knowledge is conceptual knowledge that tends to be static and hierarchical in nature. By contrast, procedural knowledge refers to "rule" knowledge, and is related to skill acquisition and performance. It operates according to "If . . . , then . . ." rules: for example, "If A is true, then do B." One might envisage a continuum of knowledge components for tactical decision making, anchored at one end by declarative knowledge (identification) and at the other end by procedural knowledge (planning and execution). Elaboration has elements of both declarative and procedural knowledge.

Declarative and procedural knowledge types are closely tied to schema instantiation and usage—that is, how and when schema components are utilized. Developing and operationalizing a performance measurement tool for the AW team task (specifically for the detect-to-engage sequence) requires, in addition, that we understand the processes by which schema components are instantiated.

To understand schema instantiation, it is necessary to understand that for years, cognitive psychologists have tried to ascertain whether humans process information in a simultaneous/parallel fashion or in a sequential manner. The parallel mode of processing, which operates on declarative, conceptual types of knowledge, is explained by models of pattern recognition, commonly called connectionist models or neural nets (for example, McClelland, Rumelhart, and the PDP Research Group, 1986). The sequential mode of processing, which operates on procedural knowledge, is explained by models of skill acquisition, frequently represented by production or rule-based systems (for example, Anderson, 1983).

Both models have been faulted for shortcomings. One criticism levelled at production models is that they do not easily recognize patterns (identification); they deal primarily with procedural knowledge (planning and execution). And production models are unlike humans in another important way: the models do not make mistakes; they always perform systematically and logically. Connectionist models, on the other hand, are capable of modelling both performance and learning (for example, through the adjustment of weights associated with the connections within a neural net), but they do not excel in logical sequences of actions such as those required for planning and execution. Marshall's (1995) model of complex cognitive processes, by contrast, capitalizes on the strengths of both approaches—the strength of the production system for modelling sequences of actions and the strength of the connectionist approach for modelling pattern recognition. The model is, therefore, *hybrid* in nature, embracing both the parallel and sequential modes of processing. Thus, it can explain how a team of tactical decision makers can engage in parallel pattern recognition processes (for example, the identification of radar contacts) early in a tactical response, as well as sequential decision making processes later, in the planning and execution phases of that response.

Given that the schema knowledge components may be characterized as either declarative in nature with parallel functioning, or procedural in nature with sequential functioning, how do they operate once the "detect-to-engage" schema is instantiated? Marshall suggests that the schema and all of its knowledge components are activated simultaneously. The retrieval of declarative knowledge probably facilitates the retrieval of procedural knowledge, and vice versa. The entire schema is available to working memory, which Marshall characterizes as a blackboard on which any schema component may write. Therefore, the various components can share inputs and outputs and can send queries to each other. In that sense, the schema components control the mode of processing, depending on which component is sending information to the blackboard (Marshall, 1995).

There tends to be some ordering of schema contributions, given that identification and elaboration knowledge are used to plan a solution. Thus, the input to the planning component of the model is the output from the elaboration production system coupled with the output from identification knowledge. Together, they provide necessary and sufficient information for the planning production system to set a series of goals and to call on the appropriate execution knowledge for achieving them. Thus, Marshall's schema theory affords us the ability to understand which knowledge components may be utilized at various points in the task and how the output of one component might affect another.

We emphasize that Marshall's model was developed to explain decision making at the individual level. However, we draw an analogy between her work and TADMUS team research regarding group-level performance. We could say, for instance, that when a group is formed, the knowledge store of all team members is immediately instantiated and is *potentially* available, simultaneously and continuously throughout the task. Each team member serves as a unique knowledge component, *capable* of providing relevant inputs to the team information-processing task. However, Hinsz et al. (1997) propose that this capability does not automatically translate into effective team performance. Team members must have an understanding of how to contribute their knowledge in ways that help them to function effectively. As events unfold during a team task and team members make their inputs known, the team begins to share a common mental model of the existing state of affairs (that is, a situation assessment). This common knowledge, or "team mental model" (see Cannon-Bowers et al., 1993; Duncan et al., 1996; Stout et al., 1996), ultimately affects what information is shared and the degree to which that information is shared (Hinsz et al., 1997).

Here, then, we see the hybrid nature of the information-processing task at the team level. The connectionist aspects reside in the networked knowledge or experience base possessed by, or available to, the team members. It is this experience base that allows team members to collectively recognize situations and respond appropriately. The serial nature is captured by the flow of information (the *team process*) as events unfold. Note that the measurement tool we describe here does not attempt to capture this team process. These behaviours (for example, information exchange, communication, error correction, and initiative) are assessed by the ATOM tool. The ATPI tool is designed to be used in conjunction with the ATOM to capture key incremental outcomes (or mini-snapshots) of those processes—outcomes that are tied to critical phases of the decision-making task. Team timeliness and accuracy at each step in the task should lead to a positive overall outcome. Assessing the outputs depicted in the ATPI is a first step in understanding and describing both the connectionist and the serial aspects of the team's information-processing task.

It should be noted that this measurement tool cannot track all of the communications passed among team members. Nor does it yet include such behavioural indicators as keystroke input and eyescan patterns of the operator display interface. A fuller understanding of schema development could be obtained if all of these pieces of information could be aggregated into one picture. Cannon-Bowers, Burns, Salas, and Pruitt (1998) and Zachary, Bilazarian, Burns, and Cannon-Bowers (1997) describe such a system that is currently being developed, the Advanced Embedded Training (AET) System. This system includes the capability of integrating and assessing all three types of behaviours. Currently, the accuracy and latency behaviours evaluated by the ATPI cannot encapsulate the state of any schema component, but they can provide valuable indicators of how well those schema are functioning, indicators that could facilitate a debriefing and feedback session and promote team expertise. With validation, this tool could be expanded to include the finer-grained behaviours that constitute the higher-level actions currently represented. Furthermore, with the successful mapping of behaviours to schema, the tool could be adapted to other team task domains.

In sum, Marshall's approach seems best suited to provide the theoretical grounding for operationalizing the team AW task. The hybrid nature of her model is essential and perhaps unique; few hybrid models currently exist. Her approach aptly specifies the nature of the processing that occurs as the "detect-to-engage" schema is instantiated. It explains what knowledge prerequisites facilitate performance at various stages of task execution. Marshall's model, then, effectively supports our effort to assess and diagnose team performance deficiencies.

4. APPLICATION OF THE COGNITIVE SCHEMA MODEL TO OPERATIONALIZING TEAM PERFORMANCE OUTCOMES

The first step in developing a modified ATPI was to map the AW detect-to-engage tasks to the knowledge requirements proposed by Marshall. The consensus among subject matter experts (SMEs) was that the first two tasks in the AW sequence—detection and entity type identification—required a significant amount of identification knowledge. Marshall et al. (1996) provided substantial empirical support for this determination. The next two tasks—threat identification and threat prioritization—were found by SMEs to require extensive elaboration knowledge. Cohen, Freeman, and Wolf (1996) and Halpern (1998) have conducted a considerable amount of research on an aspect of elaboration knowledge called critical thinking, and their findings support this proposition. Extensive planning knowledge is required for acting in accordance with the rules of engagement, which include giving warnings to a known hostile track, illuminating a hostile track with radar, covering the track with surface-to-air missiles, and providing conditional engagement orders. Last, SMEs proposed that extensive execution knowledge was required to conduct a shooting of a known hostile track.

Next, SMEs assisted in the development of performance accuracy and latency requirements for priority tracks in each of four 30-minute TADMUS scenarios. They identified specific actions that an expert team would need to perform with respect to individual air and surface craft or tracks (corresponding to performance accuracy). They also identified the normative times by which the actions should take place (performance latency). Thereby, an ATPI was developed for each TADMUS scenario. In sum, each team task was tied to its specific knowledge requirements for the purpose of linking patterns of performance deficiencies with their respective knowledge requirements. For example, if a team is consistently not performing warning calls to hostile aircraft, then we presume that it is deficient in its use of planning knowledge.

4.1. Using the ATPI Schema-Based Tool

Figure 1 illustrates coding aspects of the modified ATPI. The first column indicates the acquisition time for each radar contact, the time at which detection is lost, and the contact's bearing and range. The second column specifies the track number assigned to the contact, as well as the platform type (for example, for an air contact: commercial, helo, tactical). The remaining columns map the important "detect-to-engage" tasks to appropriate knowledge categories. Note that the blocks below contain accuracy and latency codes for each key track (aircraft) in each team task, recorded by observers. The observer circles "0" for no action, "X" for incorrect action, ">" for correct but delayed action, or "⇐" for correct and timely action. Timely actions include those occurring prior to and at the "normative time," indicated in brackets. Delayed actions include those occurring subsequent to the normative time. If an action is not necessary, then assessment is not applicable (shown by shaded portions). If an action is optional, then it appears in the

SCENARIO ONE MINUS (Rev. 980810)		IDENTIFICATION (I)		ELABORATION (E)	PLANNING (STAGE 1) (P-1)		PLANNING (STAGE 2) (P-2)			EXECUTION (E)
Acq. Time Detec. Lost Brg/Rge	Track No. Craft Type	Detect	Entity Type ID	Threat ID /Threat Prioritization	Query	Final Warning	Illuminate	Cover w/ Weapons	Conditional Orders (If...Then)	Decision to Engage
0:00 -- 279/97	7022 Comm Air	0 <= (3:00) >	0 X <= (4:00) >	0 X <= (5:00) >	0 <= (9:30) >	0 X	0 X	0 X	0 X +	0 X
0:00 -- 071/41	7026 Hostile Helo	0 <= (3:00) >	0 X <= (6:00) >	0 X <= (7:00) >	0 <= (7:00) >	0 X	0 X	0 X	0 X +	0 X
0:00 -- 319/35	7027 Comm Helo	0 <= (3:00) >	0 X <= (5:00) >	0 X <= (6:00) >	0 <= (6:00) >	0 X	0 X	0 X	0 X +	0 X
0:00 In & Out 054/32	7030 Host. Air-1	0 <= (3:00) >	0 X <= (7:00) >	0 X <= (7:30) >	0 X	0 X	0 X	0 X	0 X +	0 X
10:30 15:42 Intermittent 106/122	7037 Host. Air-2	0 <= (13:00) >	0 X <= (14:30) >	0 X <= (15:00) >	(see second appearance below)					
10:48 15:42 Intermittent 107/122	7040 Host. Air-3	0 <= (13:00) >	0 X <= (14:30) >	0 X <= (15:00) >	(see second appearance below)					
11:18 -- 108/121	7041 Host. Air-4	0 <= (14:00) >	0 X <= (20:00) >	0 X <= (22:00) >	0 X	0 X	0 X	0 X	0 X +	0 X
11:42 -- 108/119	7042 Host. Air-5	0 <= (14:00) >	0 X <= (20:00) >	0 X <= (22:00) >	0 X	0 X	0 X	0 X	0 X +	0 X
27:18 -- 123/47	7037 Host. Air-2	0 <= (27:45) >	0 X <= (28:30) >	0 X <= (29:00) >	0 <= (29:30) >	0 <= (30:00) >	0 <= (30:30) >	0 <= (29:00) >	0 X · +	0 X

FIGURE 1. Data collection sheet (excerpt).

worksheet with double borders. We do not penalize a team for not taking an optional action, but we can assess whether taking those actions resulted in better performance overall.

As an example of the instrument's application, consider Track 7022, the first track that appears in Figure 1. Team members must apply identification knowledge to detect the aircraft by the third minute into the scenario; track platform type identification (that is, aircraft) must be performed by the fourth minute. By the fifth minute, team members must apply elaboration knowledge to identify threat potential and then prioritize the track for monitoring potential actions with respect to the rules of engagement. By nine minutes and thirty seconds into the scenario, planning knowledge should emerge in the form of a query (that is, a first warning). Again, each task is tied to its specific knowledge requirements for the purpose of linking patterns of performance deficiencies with respective knowledge requirements.

5. RESEARCH PROPOSITIONS

Teamwork (and selected taskwork) performance assessments exist for five-person AW teams as a result of their participation in the TADMUS Decision Making Evaluation Facility for Tactical Teams (DEFTT) experiments, which included AW scenarios designed to study tactical decision making in demanding operational situations (Johnston, Koster, Black, & Seals, 1998). This information will be used to make a known-groups comparison in order to assess the validity and reliability of the modified ATPI (Johnston et al., 1997). For comparison purposes, we identified the 10 best-performing teams and the 10 worst-performing teams from these experiments; we also identified teams in those categories that reported high and low levels of previous CIC experience. We will evaluate each team's performance using communications that were recorded during their interactions on the four TADMUS scenarios. Where possible, recorded keystroke actions will be added to the ATPI assessments to develop a more accurate determination of the timeliness of team tactical decision making.

The following are three major propositions we plan to test once raters have been trained to use the new format:

- The modified ATPI format was redesigned to enable raters to reliably assess team performance. Therefore, the first proposition is that the redesign will result in high levels of interrater agreement.

- Team performance scores on the ATPI will be significantly higher for those teams known to have high teamwork performance (as measured by the ATOM) than for those teams with low teamwork performance. In other words, we anticipate a high correlation between team outcome measures and team process measures.

- Teams with high levels of CIC experience will have significantly higher ATPI scores than teams with little CIC experience.

In addition, consistent with Marshall's schema theory and Klein's (1993) Recognition Primed Decision (RPD) theory, we predict the following:

- Inexperienced CIC teams will show strong patterns of deficiencies for both latencies and accuracy in the four schema knowledge components: that is, they will show weaker relationships, or correlations, among the four knowledge components than teams with high levels of CIC experience. According to RPD theory, experts simultaneously recognize both the problem and prototypical solutions. Expert knowledge is considered highly compiled, while that of novices is more fragmented and loosely connected. In other words, experts and novices may both have the same number of pieces of information stored in memory, but the expert's knowledge is more efficiently organized. Consequently, the relationship between the pattern-recognizing schemas proposed by Klein (1993) (or Marshall's identification and elaboration schema) and Klein's problem-solving schemas (or Marshall's planning and execution schema) is likely to be greater for experts than for novices.

- Expert and trained teams, in comparison to novice teams, will perform identification, elaboration, planning, and execution activities more rapidly and efficiently (with fewer errors), and will do so on a greater number of significant tracks.

By distinguishing novice from expert performance, and knowing how each group is likely to perform, we are better able to tailor training to suit each group. This tool promises to provide a useful strategy for assessing and diagnosing these differences.

Although it is too early to report statistics, preliminary analyses of the data with this tool show trends that support the first two propositions (that is, ATPI outcome scores are correlating with the ATOM process measures, and interrater agreement is high).

6. IMPLICATIONS OF THE COGNITIVE SCHEMA MODEL AND THE ATPI FOR TRAINING TACTICAL SKILLS AND IMPROVING TEAM PERFORMANCE

Marshall (1995) advances the notion that adopting schema theory to diagnose decision-making performance has many positive implications for training, and is in accordance with the educational literature that promotes using case-based reasoning (CBR) to train problem-solving skills (Kolodner, 1997). She (Marshall, 1995) suggests that training to develop decision-making schemas focuses on engaging the learner to play an active role in developing the schema, similar to the way that CBR does. Instructors act as facilitators whose responsibilities include making the new information pertinent, pointing out explicit links to other, known information, and providing understandable examples to help the individual make the appropriate connections; thus, the trainee learns how to take new incoming information and relate it to previously stored knowledge. By drawing on the learners' interests and prior experiences, instructors can promote schema development. Using the four schemas as a basis for diagnosis enables the instructor to shape the nature of the information presented to trainees, as well as the order in which it is introduced. Access to performance diagnosis on the basis of the four schemas can enable explanation of both the encoding of knowledge in, and the retrieval of knowledge from, memory (Marshall, 1995). Like CBR, schema-based instruction differs from other instructional approaches in the following ways (Kolodner, 1997; Marshall, 1995):

- It de-emphasizes the quantity of factual details, and redirects emphasis to the integration of those details. Although bits of factual information accrue steadily as part of identification and elaboration knowledge, they should never become the central focus of learning. Instead, it is important for the learner to strive to integrate the facts that are essential, rather than striving to acquire more and more facts.

- It emphasizes active use of the domain knowledge. Successful learning is measured in terms of one's ability to integrate and apply knowledge, not merely one's ability to recall. Schema-based tests should include novel situations that require individuals to apply their schema-based knowledge.

- It suggests that domain knowledge should be introduced in a top-down, rather than a bottom-up, fashion. Because schema construction occurs when new, incoming information is linked to old, previously stored knowledge, an appropriate background store of knowledge is necessary (although not sufficient) as a foundation for new schemas. It is therefore imperative that an instructor begin by introducing the *fundamental* situations, ideas, and events and their distinguishing characteristics (that is, the core units of the discipline) as a foundation for schema construction. These fundamentals should be introduced not one at a time, but more or less simultaneously. In this way learners are given a "big picture" of the domain, so that they can begin to organize their knowledge about it in meaningful chunks. This segment of instruction allows individuals to acquire the necessary identification knowledge for schema development.

- Schema-based instruction explicitly targets the development of links that are central to the schema. It repeatedly stresses how and why different elements of the domain are related. Situations or examples can be explored, one at a time, to provide necessary insights that provide the foundation for elaboration knowledge. Visual representations are also useful for enhancing connectivity and template formation.

- Planning and execution knowledge should be specifically taught and demonstrated. Individuals don't always understand the importance of planning, and instructors often fail to provide them with models of how to construct and execute their plans. Optimal instruction would include a small number of heuristic problem-solving strategies, a full and detailed explication of each, and rigorous training and extended practice in applying them. A hierarchical structure of assessment (identify individual elements and combine them logically as needed) is most appropriate for evaluating planning and execution knowledge, given that several skills are required.

Schema assessment does present certain challenges. Schemas are highly individualized, and no single test item can possibly assess schema knowledge in the same way that it can assess a solitary fact. A test of a specific piece of information will not be a fair test of schema development. Therefore, it is important that we develop a means of examining the common schema knowledge possessed by a team of individuals, without rewarding or penalizing individuals for their unique schema components (drawn from individualized experience) (Marshall, 1995). It is toward this end that we have developed the modified ATPI.

In creating the ATPI measurement tool, we hope to be able to utilize the diagnostic information it provides to develop training for the four tactical decision-making competencies. To be most effective, that training should be tailored to respond to the specific knowledge deficiencies unique to each team. Marshall's schema model allows us to accomplish this goal. Useful training strategies may include (but are not limited to) the following:

- More problem practice to develop recognition and identification skills. Information must be presented until the learner perceives and deals with it in a consistent manner (that is, develops consistent mapping processes).

- Critical thinking training to sharpen elaboration skills for alternative hypothesis generation and testing (Cohen et al., 1996; Halpern, 1998).

- Heuristics training to teach ways to avoid the pitfalls commonly associated with the shortcut strategies (for example, representativeness, confirmation bias) often used by decision makers.

- Cross-training to develop shared mental models of team member roles and information requirements so that proper team coordination may occur; also, more problem practice to develop procedural skills to enhance planning and execution.

- Feedback that follows immediately when actions are performed during training scenarios, rather than at the debriefing session that customarily occurs at the end. Anderson (1993), in a later version of his production rule system, asserts that the delay between a production's application and the moment of feedback affects the rate of learning. Therefore, intrateam feedback provided during task execution may increase the opportunities to strengthen schema connections and improve team performance. That feedback is likely to be more specific and better linked to the situation than feedback given subsequent to task execution (Rasker, Schraagen, Post, & Koster, 1998). Intrateam feedback or team self-correction strategies can be trained, and have been demonstrated to be very effective in improving team performance (Smith-Jentsch et al., 1997).

- Metacognitive training to provide the "big picture" of the decision-making task, the steps involved, the skills required, and the contributions of each watchstation to the overall task and its outcome. Metacognition, or the ability to monitor and evaluate one's cognitive processes and learning, has been found to be highly predictive of learning in all instructional contexts (Cohen et al., 1996). (Critical thinking and heuristics training, mentioned earlier, exemplify the use of metacognition.) Through metacognitive training, team members can learn to monitor and correct their own performance, as well as that of fellow team members.

- Probing techniques, or instructor-facilitated guided practice, to assist teams in recognizing their own deficiencies and correcting them. Team self-correction is important because it can enable teams to access the knowledge needed to perform the task. Both team self-correction and probing techniques can be trained (Smith-Jentsch et al., 1997). Both are effective in speeding and shaping schema development in the proper directions. Specifically, instructors can help their teams to develop a common understanding of the task, balance task demands, and utilize all task resources.

7. SUMMARY AND CONCLUSIONS

In this chapter, we have presented a cognitive schema theory on which to base a tool for measuring team tactical decision-making performance (ATPI) that would serve to support tailored training applications for novices and experts. An experimental approach and propositions were described that would permit the development of a reliable and valid measure. Once validity is established, we expect to transition this measure from a paper-and-pencil–based tool to a computerized tool. For example, ATOM has been implemented on a hand-held computer for training purposes with reasonable success. Computerization of the tool has allowed for more rapid data processing and some automatic data capture (Pruitt, Burns, Wetteland, & Dumestre, 1997). In addition, it is hoped that, with its validity established, this instrument will be integrated into the training regimen on U.S. Navy ships to contribute to a thorough diagnosis and debriefing of team training. By demonstrating the efficacy of the ATPI approach, we can provide a foundation for guiding future tactical training strategies. Success of this strategy would provide (a) an expanded ability to train tactical decision-making skills for novices and experts, (b) reduced costs and greater efficiency of training; and (c) a potential to integrate products and findings with future embedded shipboard training.

8. REFERENCES

Anderson, J. R. (1983). *The architecture of cognition*. Cambridge, MA: Harvard University Press.

Anderson, J. R. (1993). *Rules of the mind*. Hillsdale, NJ: Erlbaum.

Brecke, F. H., & Garcia, S. K. (1995). *Training methodology for logistic decision making* (AL/HR-TR-1995-0098). Brooks AFB, TX: U.S. Air Force, Human Resources Directorate, Technical Training Research Division.

Cannon-Bowers, J. A., Burns, J. J., Salas, E., & Pruitt, J. S. (1998). Advanced technology in scenario-based training. In J. A. Cannon-Bowers & E. Salas (Eds.), *Making decisions under stress: Implications for individual and team training* (pp. 365–374). Washington, DC: American Psychological Association.

Cannon-Bowers, J. A., & Salas, E. (1997). A framework for developing team performance measures in training. In M. T. Brannick, E. Salas, & C. Prince (Eds.), *Team performance assessment and measurement: Theory, research and applications* (pp. 45–62). Hillsdale, NJ: Erlbaum.

Cannon-Bowers, J. A., Salas, E., & Converse, S. A. (1993). Shared mental models in expert team decision making. In N. J. Castellan, Jr. (Ed.), *Individual and group decision making* (pp. 221–246). Hillsdale, NJ: Erlbaum.

Cannon-Bowers, J. A., Salas, E., & Grossman, J. D. (1991, June). *Improving tactical decision making under stress: Research directions and applied implications.* Paper presented at the International Applied Military Psychology Symposium, Stockholm, Sweden.

Clancey, W. J. (1985). *Heuristic classification* (STAN-CS-85-1066). Stanford, CA: Stanford University.

Cohen, M. S., Freeman, J. T., & Wolf, S. (1996). Metarecognition in time-stressed decision making: Recognizing, critiquing, and correcting. *Human Factors, 38*, 206–219.

Duncan, P. C., Rouse, W. B., Johnston, J. H., Cannon-Bowers, J. A., Salas, E., & Burns, J. J. (1996). Training teams working in complex systems: A mental model–based approach. In W. B. Rouse (Ed.), *Human/technology interaction in complex systems, Vol. 8* (pp. 173–231). Stamford, CT: JAI Press.

Dwyer, D. J. (1992). An index for measuring naval team performance. In *Proceedings of the Human Factors Society Thirty-Sixth Annual Meeting* (pp. 1356–1360). Santa Monica, CA: Human Factors and Ergonomics Society.

Halpern, D. F. (1998). Teaching critical thinking for transfer across domains: Dispositions, skills, structure training, and metacognitive monitoring. *American Psychologist, 53*(4), 449–455.

Hinsz, V. B., Tindale, R. S., & Vollrath, D. A. (1997). The emerging conceptualization of groups as information processors. *Psychological Bulletin, 121*(1), 43–64.

Johnston, J. H., Koster, A., Black, E., & Seals, M. (1998). A learning-methods approach to designing team training simulations: Lessons learned from the Tactical Advanced Simulated Warfare Integrated Trainer (TASWIT-Device S14A13). In *Proceedings of the 1998 Command and Control Research and Technology Symposium* (pp. 721–730). Monterey, CA: Naval Postgraduate School.

Johnston, J. H., Smith-Jentsch, K. A., & Cannon-Bowers, J. A. (1997). Performance measurement tools for enhancing team decision making. In M. T. Brannick, E. Salas, & C. Prince (Eds.), *Team performance assessment and measurement: Theory, method, and application* (pp. 311–327). Hillsdale, NJ: Erlbaum.

Klein, G. A. (1989). Recognition-primed decisions. In W. Rouse (Ed.), *Advances in man–machine systems research, Vol. 5* (pp. 47–92). Stamford, CT: JAI Press.

Klein, G. A. (1993). A recognition primed decision (RPD) model of rapid decision making. In G. A. Klein, J. Orasanu, R. Calderwood, & C. E. Zsambok (Eds.), *Decision making in action: Models and methods* (pp. 138–147). Norwood, NJ: Ablex.

Klein, G. A., & Calderwood, R. (1990). *Investigations of naturalistic decision making and the recognition-primed decision model* (Research Note 90-59). Alexandria, VA: U.S. Army Research Institute for the Behavioral and Social Sciences.

Kolodner, J. L. (1997). Educational implications of analogy: A view from case-based reasoning. *American Psychologist, 52*(1), 57–66.

Marshall, S. P. (1995). *Schemas in problem-solving.* New York: Cambridge University Press.

Marshall, S. P., Christensen, S. E., & McAllister, J. A. (1996). Cognitive differences in tactical decision making. In *Proceedings of the 1996 Command and Control Research and Technology Symposium* (pp. 122–132). Monterey, CA: Naval Postgraduate School.

McClelland, J. L., Rumelhart, D. E., & the PDP Research Group. (1986). *Parallel distributed processing: Explorations in the microstructures of cognition, Vol. 2.* Cambridge, MA: MIT Press.

Nickerson, R. S., & Feehrer, C. E. (1975). *Decision making and training: A review of theoretical and empirical studies of decision making and their implications for the training of decision makers* (NAVTRAEQUIPCEN 73-C-012801). Cambridge, MA: Bolt, Beranek, and Newman.

Noble, D., Grosz, C., & Boehm-Davis, D. (1987). *Rules, schema and decision making* (Office of Naval Research R-125-87). Vienna, VA: Engineering Research Associates.

Pruitt, J. S., Burns, J. J., Wetteland, C. R., & Dumestre, T. L. (1997). ShipMATE: Shipboard Mobile Aid for Training and Evaluation. In *Proceedings of the Human Factors and Ergonomics Society Forty-First Annual Meeting* (pp. 1113–1117). Santa Monica, CA: Human Factors and Ergonomics Society.

Rasker, P. C., Schraagen, J. M. C., Post, W. M., & Koster, E. R. (1998). The effects of two types of information exchange on team self-correction. In *Proceedings of the First Symposium of the Human Factors and Medicine Panel on Collaborative Crew Performance in Complex Operational Systems.* Edinburgh, U.K.

Rasmussen, J. (1988). A cognitive engineering approach to the modeling of decision making and its organization in process control, emergency management, CAD/CAM, office systems and library systems. In W. B. Rouse (Ed.), *Advances in man–machine systems research, Vol. 4* (165–243). Stamford, CT: JAI Press.

Salas, E., Cannon-Bowers, J. A., & Johnston, J. H. (1997). How can you turn a team of experts into an expert team?: Emerging training strategies. In C. Zsambok & G. Klein (Eds.), *Naturalistic decision making* (pp. 359–370). Hillsdale, NJ: Erlbaum.

Smith-Jentsch, K. A., Ricci, K. E., Campbell, G. E., & Zeisig, R. L. (1997). Shaping mental models of the scenario-based training process: A preliminary validation of shipboard instructor training [CD-ROM]. In *Proceedings of the Nineteenth Annual Meeting of the Interservice/Industry Training, Simulation, and Education Conference* (pp. 164–173). Washington, DC: National Security Industrial Association.

Stout, R. J., Cannon-Bowers, J. A., & Salas, E. (1996). The role of shared mental models in developing team situation awareness: Implications for training. *Training Research Journal, 2*, 85–116.

Zachary, W., Bilazarian, P., Burns, J., & Cannon-Bowers, J. A. (1997). Advanced embedded training concepts for shipboard systems. In *Proceedings of the Nineteenth Annual Meeting of the Interservice/Industry Training, Simulation, and Education Conference* (pp. 670–679). Washington, DC: National Security Industrial Association.

Zsambok, C. E., & Klein, G. (Eds.). (1997). *Naturalistic decision making.* Mahwah, NJ: Erlbaum.

CHAPTER 19

COMMUNICATION OF INTENT IN MILITARY COMMAND AND CONTROL SYSTEMS

LIEUTENANT COLONEL LAWRENCE G. SHATTUCK and DAVID D. WOODS

1. INTRODUCTION

Military command and control (C^2), air traffic control, and nuclear power plant control rooms are examples of distributed supervisory control systems. Distributed supervisory control systems are hierarchical and cooperative. They involve remote supervisors who work through intelligent local actors to control some process. A remote supervisor typically provides plans and procedures to multiple local actors. However, these plans and procedures are often inadequate to cope with the unanticipated variability of local situations (Woods & Roth, 1988). As a result, local actors must adapt the plans and procedures to the situation based on their understanding of the remote supervisor's intent. The research reported here investigated how remote supervisors (senior commanders) who are separated by both time and space from local actors (subordinate commanders) impart their presence by

LIEUTENANT COLONEL LAWRENCE G. SHATTUCK • Department of Behavioral Sciences and Leadership, United States Military Academy, West Point, New York, USA 10996   DAVID D. WOODS • Cognitive Systems Engineering Laboratory, Ohio State University, 1971 Neil Avenue, Columbus, Ohio, USA 43210

The Human in Command: Exploring the Modern Military Experience, edited by McCann and Pigeau, Kluwer Academic/Plenum Publishers, New York, 2000.

communicating intent to permit coordination and adaptation of underspecified plans and procedures.

Normally, plans and procedures are developed by designers before a system is implemented or by remote supervisors who have an incomplete (or inaccurate) view of the local situation. These plans and procedures often do not aid local actors in their process control tasks if followed in a rote manner. In a field study of a human–intelligent machine system, Roth, Bennett, and Woods (1987) observed that correct problem-solving paths deviated from predetermined plans and procedures in 78 percent of cases. Deviations were found to be the norm because domain experts and designers are unable to anticipate all possible local conditions. Plans and procedures are therefore underspecified, requiring technicians to "supply knowledge and act outside of the scope and direction" of the expert system (Roth et al., 1987, p. 496).

Woods, O'Brien, and Hanes (1987) also found in their studies of nuclear power plants that "good operations require more than rote rule following" (p. 1745). They identified two types of errors that occurred when "events demanded a relatively variable sequence of component actions and extensive feedback from the environment in order to adapt to unpredictable constraints or disturbances" (p. 1743).

- In "Type A" problems, "rote rule following persisted in the face of changing circumstances that demanded adaptable responses" (p. 1743).

- In "Type B" problems, "adaptation to unanticipated conditions was attempted without the complete knowledge or guidance needed to manage resources successfully to meet recovery goals" (p. 1743).

Local actors either failed to adapt plans and procedures to local conditions or adapted them without considering the intent of the remote supervisor.

Suchman (1987) supports the concept of local actors' adapting plans and procedures. She asserts that "plans are inherently vague" and that "actions must be contingent upon the circumstantial and interactional particulars of actual situations" (p. 185). Local actors cannot blindly follow predetermined plans and procedures issued by remote supervisors or by system designers without regard for local conditions.

Local actors need a framework or context for adapting their plans and procedures when responding to novel situations. They must understand the supervisor's underlying intent with regard to the plans and procedures. *Webster's New World Dictionary* defines intent as "a purpose; object; aim." *Webster's II New Riverside University Dictionary* defines intention as "an aim that guides an action." In communicating intent, the remote supervisor explains the goals of the system (the object or aim) and the reason for pursuing the goals (the purpose). This description provides a framework for adapting the existing plans and procedures to respond to novel situations. Intent is the means by which the remote supervisor imparts his or her *presence* to local actors. This sense of presence helps local actors to respond in the same way that the supervisor would if the supervisor were able to view the situation through the eyes of the local actors.

The concept of imparting presence is context-free. However, communication of intent is context-specific and relies on the capacity of the remote supervisor to have established his or her presence with the local actor prior to the situation at hand. Presence, as used in this chapter, is analogous to the concept of intent discussed by Pigeau and McCann (this volume, Chapter 12).

There is an inherent tradeoff for the remote supervisor in establishing the framework for adaptation. Supervisors must determine the latitude or flexibility they will give actors to adapt plans and procedures to local situations. Supervisors who establish centralized control inhibit local actors. These supervisors show little regard for the impact of local situational factors. At the other extreme are supervisors who give local actors complete autonomy. In such cases, remote supervisors are then "out of the loop," and the response across multiple local actors is coordinated and synchronized only by coincidence. In fact, the system may actually move away from its goals or end state. Somewhere between these extremes are systems in which local actors are able to modify and implement procedures to achieve the supervisor's intent based on an analysis of local conditions and a sense of the supervisor's presence.

This chapter uses the distributed supervisory control system as a theoretical framework for examining the communication of intent in military command and control systems. We discuss the conceptual components of distributed supervisory control and relate this model to military command and control. Next, we report the results of a study that used a mixed-fidelity simulation to investigate the communication of intent in army combat units. Finally, we discuss the implications of the findings with respect to communicating intent, imparting presence, and individual differences.

2. A MODEL OF DISTRIBUTED SUPERVISORY CONTROL SYSTEMS

Military C^2 systems, nuclear power plants, air traffic control networks, and many industries exhibit some form of distributed supervisory control. Although these domains are very different in their specific objectives, they have distinct similarities in the underlying structures and functions used to achieve their objectives or end states. Despite their ubiquitous nature, little has been written about the characteristics of such systems. Any model of distributed supervisory control that could be applied across diverse domains must conform to the following scheme:

> A **remote supervisor** uses a **communications process** to provide **local actors** with **plans and procedures** and to impart his or her **presence**. The **degree of control** established by the remote supervisor influences the ability of the local actors to adapt to unanticipated conditions based on the actors' assessments of their local environments.

The boldfaced terms in this description are purposely generic so that they can be applied to distributed supervisory control systems in any domain. Each of these terms will now be discussed in greater detail. Later, we will explain how these terms apply to military command and control systems.

2.1. Remote Supervisor

Advances in communication and automation have made it unnecessary for supervisors and actors to be at the same location. Supervisors now can be separated by both space and time from their subordinates. Technology affords a greater span of control, but has its pitfalls. For example, supervisors who attempt to function as local actors will quickly lose sight of high-level organizational goals. They cannot continuously monitor all processes, filter information, and determine the appropriate course of action for each local actor. They must remain detached from the details of the local actors' environments so that they can evaluate the system's progress relative to the high-level goals.

Before controlling a process, the remote supervisors and local actors may engage in cooperative activities, including planning, training, and rehearsals. During periods of low activity in controlling a process, the need for the supervisor and actors to exchange information is minimal. When an unanticipated time-sensitive event occurs, however, a remote supervisor must rely on local actors to provide him or her with the information needed to assess the situation and formulate a plan at the very time that the actors are busiest. Woods (1994) describes this ebb and flow of activity as characteristic of systems in which cognitive activity is distributed across multiple agents. If the supervisor's intent is effectively communicated before an unanticipated event, actors are more likely to make proper decisions with respect to overall system goals. Supervisors will not become mired in one local situation and lose sight of the system's goals. Thus, during peak periods, actors are able to devote more cognitive resources to controlling the local situation and less to the task of updating the supervisor.

2.2. Local Actors

We use the term "local actors" to describe those autonomous human or machine agents that interact with subsystems. A remote supervisor and local actors have different perspectives on the environment. Local actors operate at the sharp end (Reason, 1990), where they interact directly with the process being controlled. They have privileged access to a narrow portion of the system. Remote supervisors operate at the blunt end: they can influence the control process only indirectly, through policies, plans and procedures, and the allocation of resources.

Local actors have specific goals and are able to continuously monitor local changes in system status. These local conditions, in turn, affect how the actors respond to the plans and procedures of their remote supervisors. For example, if the local actors cannot communicate with the remote supervisor, the local actors must rely on the plans and procedures that have previously been provided to them. If local situations are such that the plans are no longer valid, the local actors must modify the plans and then implement the modified plans on their own. Even then, however, the local actors cannot act independently. They must reconcile their actions with their supervisor's intent and coordinate their activities with those of other local actors. Failure to coordinate their activities with other agents could result in system failure.

2.3. Communications Process

The methods used for communicating between the remote supervisor and the local actors include voice, text, and graphics. Exchanges can occur face to face, electronically, or through written correspondence. The functions of the communications process include

- distributing plans and procedures;

- specifying the degree of control;

- imparting presence; and

- updating agents on the status of the system.

A remote supervisor will communicate plans and procedures to local actors, but the actors are not expected to implement them until some future point in time—when the system may be in a different state, one that might not have been anticipated by the supervisor. (For example, at Time T_1, when the system is in State S_1, the plan is to implement Procedure P_1. However, at a later Time, T_2, the system is in State S_2, and Procedure P_1 may not apply.) The content of the communication may consist of nothing more than the procedure itself, or it may contain additional information, including system goals, rationale, constraints, and other considerations (Klein, 1993). It is vital that the local actors understand the intent, so that when local conditions are different from those envisioned by the remote supervisor, the actors (if given the latitude) can take the action(s) that will move the system closer to its goal state.

2.4. Plans and Procedures

Distributed supervisory control system functions are based on plans and procedures (or guidelines). Plans and procedures are often developed by designers in conjunction with domain experts long before a system is operational. By their very nature, such plans and procedures are brittle. The plans and procedures specify what actors should do and how they should do it for each state of the system. But designers and experts are not able to predict every situation, system state, or set of interactions for which plans and procedures should be developed.

Plans and procedures are also developed just before beginning (or even during) the control process. These situation-specific plans and procedures require supervisors to have an accurate view of the control process. Since remote supervisors cannot directly observe the process, local actors must devote both time and cognitive resources to updating the supervisor's knowledge of the local situation when time is critical and cognitive resources may be committed to near-capacity.

2.5. Degree of Control

There is an inherent tradeoff for the remote supervisor in establishing the framework for adaptation. Supervisors must determine how much latitude or flexibility they will give local actors to adapt plans and procedures to local situations. According to Ashby (1956), "only variety can destroy variety" (p. 207). If in some game, D can make ten moves, but R can make only one move, then the variety in the outcomes will be as large as the variety in D's possible moves. If, however, R can make two moves rather than one, then the variety of outcomes is reduced by as much as 50 percent. The remote supervisor determines the number of "moves" available to the local actors vis-à-vis the environment by the degree of flexibility afforded to the actors.

Remote supervisors establish the degree of control they exert on local actors through plans and procedures. Specific, detailed plans and procedures establish centralized control and reduce the actors' flexibility to adapt to unanticipated variety in the local environment. Generalized plans and procedures increase the flexibility of local actors but decrease the likelihood that there will be a coordinated response across the system.

3. MILITARY C² AS A TYPE OF DISTRIBUTED SUPERVISORY CONTROL

The characteristics of the distributed supervisory control system described above are easily applied to the domain of military command and control. Senior commanders are remote supervisors. Before the onset of hostilities, they (and their staffs) engage in a deliberate, self-paced decision-making process to formulate a plan. The plan is then communicated to subordinate commanders for implementation. These subordinate commanders are the local actors in the military C² system. Senior commanders differ in the degree of control they exert on subordinate commanders. Through written plans, standard operating procedures, or experience, senior commanders make known the amount of flexibility that subordinate commanders have in carrying out their assigned missions.

Unique to the military C² system is that this domain includes an intelligent, uncooperative, unpredictable enemy that attempts to exploit weaknesses in the plans of the friendly forces. Detailed battle plans do not remain viable much past the onset of hostilities. When confronted with unanticipated events, subordinate commanders must initiate an event-driven decision-making process. Their task is to identify and achieve the senior commander's higher-order objective, even if the specified mission can no longer be accomplished. Subordinate commanders must rely on the senior commander's statement of intent to bound the space of acceptable solutions.

In most distributed supervisory control systems, intent is communicated passively. It is implied in the procedures and is difficult to discern. However, in the domain of military command and control, senior commanders work diligently to develop a statement of intent that is communicated to subordinate commanders before starting a tactical operation. Such explicit statements of intent ought to increase the likelihood that local actors will make decisions in accordance with the goals of the remote supervisor. We propose that research results concerning the communication of intent in a military C^2 system could be extended to improve local actor compliance with remote supervisors in other domains.

The present study used active-duty infantry and armour battalions to investigate how intent guides the event-driven decision-making process so that the senior commander's higher-order objectives are achieved. In a mixed-fidelity simulation (see Figure 1), four army battalion commanders and their staffs developed tactical operation orders based on a brigade (next higher echelon) operation order that they were provided. The battalion commanders and their staffs disseminated the orders, which included statements of intent, to subordinate company commanders. These company commanders (four per battalion) developed their own operation orders and briefed them back to the battalion commanders.

An investigator then reviewed copies of the battalion and company operation orders. Two types of anomalies were created for each battalion. In the first anomaly, the unit was blocked from completing its specific mission but could still achieve the battalion commander's higher-order objectives. In the second anomaly, the unit had unexpected success relative to the specific mission and had to decide what to do next. In both cases, the battalion commander's statement of intent provided sufficient information to aid the company commanders in responding to the anomalies.

The battalion commanders were presented with both anomalies. They were asked how they expected the subordinate company commanders to respond to the anomalies. Their answers became the basis for evaluating the responses of their subordinate company commanders. The anomalies were then presented to the company commanders. While being videotaped, the company commanders used a think-aloud protocol as they considered how to respond to the anomalies. The battalion commanders watched the videotapes and judged the responses of their subordinates relative to their own responses. Finally, former battalion commanders, serving as neutral observers, watched the videotapes. The neutral observers provided valuable commentary on the intent process within each of the battalions.

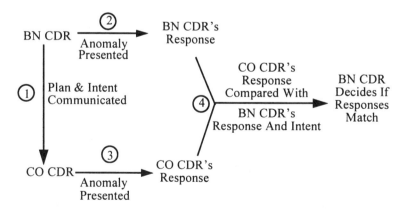

FIGURE 1. Sequence of events for tactical simulation.

4. RESULTS OF THE SIMULATION

Four battalions, each with four company commanders, were each given two anomalies, generating thirty-two problem-solving episodes. General information extracted from the verbal protocols included the following:

- a summary of the company commander's response;

- the judgment of the battalion commander regarding whether or not the company commander's response matched the battalion commander's intent;

- the basis for the company commander's response;

- references by the company commander involving coordinating his or her actions with those of other actors engaged in actions that will be affected by the company commander's actions—for example, adjacent/lateral commanders and higher commanders;

- references by the company commander to any element of the plan; and

- length of the protocol.

Battalion commanders judged that the company commanders' responses matched their intent in only seventeen of the thirty-two episodes (53 percent). In three episodes, however, the responses matched only by coincidence. In these cases, the company commanders chose to remain in place not because they understood the battalion commander's intent but because they misinterpreted the information available to them. In three other episodes, although the battalion commanders judged the decision of the company commanders to match their own, the decisions were in fact substantially different. Battalion commanders considered them a match because the company commanders were "thinking along the right lines." If these six episodes are considered mismatches, then the responses matched in only eleven of thirty-two episodes (34 percent).

The amount of time the company commanders had worked for the battalion commanders varied from as little as one week to as long as twenty-one months. Table 1 summarizes the responses of the company commanders to the anomalies based on the length of time they had worked for their battalion commanders. These data do not suggest that the ability of the company commanders to match their battalion commander's intent is linked to the length of time they have worked for their battalion commanders.

A detailed analysis of the think-aloud protocols identified six distinct categories of utterances. These categories were used to parse the protocols and to identify the type of information used by the company commanders to respond to the anomalies. The six categories are as follows:

- need for more information;

- system status;

Table 1. Summary of Company Commanders' Responses Based on Their Time in Command

Time in command	Number of company commanders	Possible correct responses	Responses judged correct by battalion commanders	Actual number of correct responses
1 week	1	2	0	0
3 months	2	4	3	2
8 months	3	6	3	3
9 months	4	8	2	0
13 months	2	4	4	2
20 months	2	4	3	3
21 months	2	4	2	1
Total	16	32	17	11

- reference to procedures;
- reference to intent;
- course of action; and
- coordination activities.

Company commanders who were successful in matching their battalion commander's intent first determined the system status (that is, the disposition of friendly and enemy forces). They made specific references to procedures and to the statement of intent in the battalion operation order. They also acknowledged that they had to coordinate their activities with the commanders of adjacent units before taking any action.

Company commanders who were unsuccessful in matching their battalion commander's intent generally did not refer to the battalion commander's statement of intent. In addition, these commanders exhibited several other behaviours. Some commanders exhibited flawed domain knowledge. For example, one commander's incorrect knowledge of tactics and time/distance factors caused him to initiate a system response that could not have been completed in the time available. A few commanders had a low tolerance for situational uncertainty. They decided not to act until they were given more information to reduce their uncertainty. In some instances, commanders misassessed the information available to them. Even though they were given information on the status of the environment (that is, enemy units), they did not incorporate it into their mental model of the system. Some commanders also exhibited a rigid adherence to procedures despite situational information that indicated they were facing a novel, unanticipated situation. When a major unanticipated event occurred on an adjacent part of the battlefield, these commanders would not deviate from their assigned mission, even though the event jeopardized the higher-order goals of the system.

5. IMPLICATIONS OF RESULTS FOR DISTRIBUTED SUPERVISORY CONTROL SYSTEMS

The results of this study suggest several areas that can be explored to improve communication of intent, and, therefore, the performance of distributed supervisory control systems confronted with unanticipated variability.

5.1. Path versus State Solutions

Rich and Knight (1991) believe that solutions to problems can be either paths or states. Military doctrine suggests that intent should focus on state solutions; yet in practice, solutions are often paths. The doctrine states that intent is designed to "focus subordinates on what has to be accomplished in order to achieve success, even when the plan and concept of the operation no longer apply" (United States, 1993, p. 6-6). In implementing the doctrine, commanders are taught that their intent statements ought to include the following components: purpose, method, and end state. In this study, the method sections provided by commanders were often very specific. In a sense, they established a canonical path through a Problem Space (see Figure 2). The method tells the local actor to proceed from Start State to State 2, State 3, and, finally, to the End State: this constitutes a path solution. An actor may progress unimpeded through the Problem Space. Or, as is the case for Local

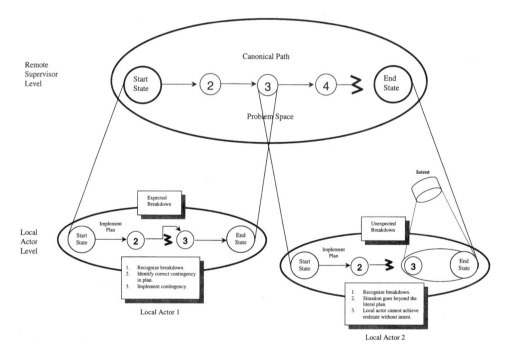

FIGURE 2. Path solutions (Remote Supervisor and Local Actor 1) versus a state solution (Local Actor 2).

Actor 1, there may be an obstacle that prevents the system from reaching the End State as planned. However, in this case the event (or breakdown) that blocked mission accomplishment is not unexpected, so there is a contingency plan that can be implemented. Even though a breakdown occurs, Local Actor 1 still follows a preplanned path through the Problem Space.

For Local Actor 2, on the other hand, the event that occurs between State 2 and State 3 is unanticipated. There is no preplanned alternative path through the Problem Space to the End State. To permit movement through the Problem Space to the End State, the intent statement—rather than being very specific—should illuminate and bound a Solution Space, giving the local actor the opportunity to find a state solution. Actors should be free to move through the Solution Space based on their analysis of the local situation. The intent, then, should *guide* the local actor's adaptation process.

5.2. Ambiguity of Natural Language

The ambiguity of natural language presents an obstacle to distributed supervisory control systems that are confronted with unanticipated variability. Misunderstandings arise when remote supervisors and local actors do not share a common understanding because they are separated by both space and time. Suchman (1987) states that many expressions "rely upon their situation for significance" (p. 58). In describing distributed decision-making systems, Fischoff and Johnson (1990) state that "people need to translate their thoughts into some language before those [thoughts] can be shared with others. Their ability to use the language sets an upper limit on the system's coordination of decision making, as does the system's procedures for information sharing" (p. 38). They also state "that terms will unwittingly be used differently" (p. 41) by agents in the system.

These difficulties are compounded in distributed supervisory control systems because intent is communicated from the remote supervisor to the local actor at Time 1 and in Context A, but is often not interpreted and implemented until Time 2 and in Context B. Remote supervisors should therefore make every attempt to ensure that local actors clearly understand the supervisor's intent. Embedding the intent in hypothetical contexts is one method that can be used to check the local actors' understanding.

5.3. Flexibility versus Synchronization

Highly coupled, technologically laden systems call for flexible yet synchronized responses to anomalous, unanticipated situations. In distributed supervisory control systems, a remote supervisor oversees multiple actors, each controlling a local process. It is not enough for local actors to implement the correct procedure. The procedure must be initiated at the correct time and place relative to the actions of the other agents in the system. Decisions made and implemented in isolation can interact in unexpected ways and actually prevent the system from reaching its goals. Military history is replete with examples of commanders who erred either on the side of providing tremendous latitude to subordinate commanders with no requirement to coordinate their activities, or, in contrast, on the side of retaining centralized control so that all actions would be synchronized. The former approach leads to autonomous military organizations that lose the synergism that emerges from coordinated activities. The latter approach prevents subordinate units from exploiting transient windows of opportunity on the battlefield.

5.4. Imparting Presence

Remote supervisors have no means of controlling a process except through the actions of local actors. However, plans and procedures are too brittle to completely guide the decision-making processes of these actors: decisions must be tailored to the local situation. A remote supervisor with high-level system knowledge and a clear understanding of system goals, if placed in the local situation, would effectively adapt the plans and procedures based on local conditions. Remote supervisors, however, must remain in a position that allows them to retain a comprehensive view of the entire system. Since they cannot be physically present with the local actor, they need to impart their presence to guide the adaptation of plans and procedures.

When remote supervisors impart their presence, they are equipping local actors with the strategic-level goals, constraints, and tradeoffs of the system. Presence empowers a local actor to make decisions similar to those that the supervisor would make if the supervisor were at the actor's location. Communicating intent is the primary means by which remote supervisors impart their presence.

6. CONCLUSION

Van Creveld (1985) states that when "[c]onfronted with a task and having less information available than is needed to perform that task, an organization may react in either of two ways. One is to increase the information-processing capacity, the other to design the organization, and indeed the task itself, in such a way as to enable it to operate on the basis of less information. These approaches are exhaustive; no others are conceivable" (p. 269).

Those who design distributed supervisory control systems must choose one of the two alternatives proposed by Van Creveld (1985). Advocates of technology-based solutions will undoubtedly seek to increase the organization's information-processing capacity. The logic behind this approach rests on the idea that increasing the ability to process information will reduce the amount of uncertainty. Less uncertainty will result in better (and probably more centralized) control of the system.

Uncertainty, however, is not a function of information-processing capacity so much as it is a function of the designer's inability to predict and identify all conceivable states of the system. As stated earlier, complex, highly coupled distributed systems often confront remote supervisors and local actors with unanticipated states. Designing distributed supervisory control systems that have the ability to function with less information requires that local actors have a variety of responses at their disposal and the authority to implement them at their discretion. The process of imparting supervisor presence through the communication of intent is thus essential and worthy of further investigation.

7. REFERENCES

Ashby, W. R. (1956). *An introduction to cybernetics*. New York: Wiley.

Fischoff, B., & Johnson, S. (1990). The possibility of distributed decision making. In Committee on Human Factors, Commission on Behavioral and Social Sciences and Education, & National Research Council (Eds.), *Distributed decision making: Report of a workshop* (pp. 25–58). Washington, DC: National Academy Press.

Klein, G. A. (1993). Characteristics of commander's intent statements. In *Proceedings of the 1993 Symposium on Command and Control Research* (pp. 62–69). McLean, VA: Science Applications International.

Reason, J. (1990). *Human error*. New York: Cambridge University Press.

Rich, E., & Knight, K. (1991). *Artificial intelligence*. New York: McGraw-Hill.

Roth, E. M., Bennett, K. B., & Woods, D. D. (1987). Human interaction with an "intelligent" machine. *International Journal of Man–Machine Studies, 27*, 479–525.

Suchman, L. (1987). *Plans and situated actions: The problem of human–machine communication*. Cambridge, U.K.: Cambridge University Press.

United States. (1993). *Operations* (Field Manual 100-5). Washington, DC: Department of the Army.

Van Creveld, M. (1985). *Command in war*. Cambridge, MA: Harvard University Press.

Woods, D. D. (1994). Observations from studying cognitive systems in context. In A. Ram & K. Eiselt (Eds.), *Proceedings of the Sixteenth Annual Conference of the Cognitive Science Society* (Part II, Section A: Keynote Address). Mahwah, NJ: Erlbaum.

Woods, D. D., O'Brien, J. F., Hanes, L. F. (1987). Human factors challenges in process control: The case of nuclear power plants. In G. Salvendy (Ed.), *Handbook of Human Factors* (pp. 1724–1770). New York: Wiley.

Woods, D. D., & Roth, E. M. (1988). Cognitive systems engineering. In M. Helander (Ed.), *Handbook of human–computer interaction* (pp. 3–43). Amsterdam: Elsevier.

CHAPTER 20

MISPLACED LOYALTIES
Military Culture and the Breakdown of Discipline in Two Peace Operations

DONNA WINSLOW

> In the infantry, they take care of their own. That's the way it's done.
> —Canadian Soldier

1. INTRODUCTION

In December 1992, Canadian Forces personnel, as part of a coalition of forces led by the United States, were deployed for service to Somalia. Many of the Canadian personnel involved in the deployment belonged to the Canadian Airborne Regiment Battle Group, itself made up largely of soldiers from the Canadian Airborne Regiment (a paratroop battalion). On the night of March 16–17, 1993, near the city of Belet Huen, Somalia, soldiers from Two Commando of the Canadian Airborne Regiment beat and tortured a bound 16-year-old Somali youth, Shidane Arone, resulting in his death.[1] The consequences of this incident have been far-reaching, not only for the Battle Group that was deployed to Somalia, but also for the Canadian Forces as a whole. The investigations that followed, the media coverage,

---

[1] It is important to note that Canadians were not the only ones involved in serious human rights abuses in Somalia. Belgian and Italian paratroopers were also scrutinized by inquiries in their own lands (see Omaar & de Waal, 1993).

DONNA WINSLOW • Program for Research on Peace Security and Society, Centre on Governance, Vanier Hall, Room 284, University of Ottawa, Ottawa, Ontario, Canada K1N 6N5

The Human in Command: Exploring the Modern Military Experience,
edited by McCann and Pigeau, Kluwer Academic/Plenum Publishers, New York, 2000.

and the ensuing public inquiry shook the Canadian military establishment to its core.

Representatives of the Canadian military maintained that the events that occurred in Somalia were "isolated incidents" and the result of the actions of a few "bad apples." Yet subsequently, on another peace operation thousands of miles from Somalia, in Bacovici in the former Yugoslavia, Canadian soldiers were once again involved in serious incidents indicating a severe breakdown of discipline. From October 1993 to May 1994, a Battle Group based on the 12e Régiment blindé du Canada (12 RBC) served in Bosnia–Herzegovina.[2,3] At the end of the tour, members of the incoming unit received information on and reported various incidents of misconduct by the outgoing unit, including misuse of alcohol, sexual misconduct, insubordination, violence, and black market activities. During the ensuing military police investigations, various other concerns came to light regarding the state of discipline and overall effectiveness of the unit. The Military Board of Inquiry into the events in Bacovici concluded that the operational environment could not be blamed for the shortcomings, but that flaws existed in the units prior to deployment. Some of these flaws, according to the Inquiry, found their roots in military culture.[4]

The explanations for the incidents in Somalia and Bacovici are many and varied. In this chapter, I will focus on a group analysis and on the culture of the units, a culture that emphasized regimental loyalty. British military journals have, over the years, debated the pros and cons of the regimental system, addressing such issues as morale versus conservatism, autonomism versus centralization, resistance to change, exclusiveness undermining cooperation, and so on. Though loyalty is perceived as a positive state in the military, it is my intention to show that highly intense unit cohesion can, at times, be divisive. Exaggerated loyalty to the group can lead members to work at counterpurposes to the overall goals of a mission—or even to the goals of the Army and to those of the Canadian Forces as a whole.

I will begin by explaining how cohesion and loyalty are considered important components of combat effectiveness. The emphasis on primary groups[5] in military sociology began during World War II, when studies emerged emphasizing mechanical forms of social solidarity (for example, bonding and cohesion). Sociologists felt that morale rooted in a feeling of unity gave soldiers the courage to fight. After

---

[2] Officially the Federal Republic of Bosnia and Herzegovina; hereafter generally referred to as Bosnia.

[3] In Bacovici, there were members from one Army regiment, the R22eR (the Royal 22e Régiment du Canada, popularly known as the "Van Doos"), and from one armoured unit, the 12 RBC, in addition to reservists and support staff. The Canadian Airborne Regiment Battle Group that was deployed to Somalia also had reservists and support staff; however, the bulk of its members came from the Canadian Airborne Regiment, which has since been disbanded.

[4] For the purposes of this chapter, *culture* will be defined as a social force that controls patterns of organizational behaviour. It shapes members' cognitions and perceptions of meanings and realities. It provides affective energy for mobilization and identifies who belongs to the group and who does not (Ott, 1989).

[5] The term *primary groups* refers to small groups in which social behaviour is governed by face-to-face relationships. This concept is reminiscent of Tönnies's (1887/1957) notion of *Gemeinschaft*, which refers to a social state in which belonging is pervasive and in which primary group relations predominate. Individuals exhibit strong allegiance to their group, and the group exerts social control over the individual members.

briefly examining the literature concerning mechanical solidarity (bonding and cohesion), I will describe how cohesion and loyalty are reinforced in Canadian military culture.

Like other military organizations around the world, the Canadian Forces (CF) have developed a culture characterized by an emphasis on hierarchy and tradition, represented symbolically in rituals, customs, distinctive dress, and insignias. Members of the CF share this culture, which is transmitted through the generations. Canada's overall military culture also comprises specialized subcultures based on land, sea, and air capabilities. In this chapter, I will focus on the Canadian Army's organization, an organization based on the regimental system. I will describe this system, which places special emphasis on "belonging" and "loyalty," and note that these are valuable aspects of the regimental system. However, in the two cases described below, strong group bonding also had negative effects: regimental loyalty became misplaced and contributed to a breakdown in command and control.

2. METHOD

From 1995 to 1997, I conducted research that focused on the socio-cultural causes for the events that took place in Somalia in 1993. The study was done for the Canadian government's Commission of Inquiry into the Deployment of Canadian Forces to Somalia, more popularly known as the Somalia Inquiry. This work was published as one of the Commission's Research Studies (Winslow, 1997). Also, from May 1997 to April 1998, I carried out archival research at the Department of National Defence in Ottawa on the Canadian deployment to the former Yugoslavia.

The analyses and interpretations concerning Army culture are based on over 50 in-depth interviews held with military personnel from a variety of ranks, in addition to several focus groups held with military families. Thirty interviewees were selected randomly from a list of personnel deployed to Somalia. The remaining interviews were added when the soldiers and officers from the original sample suggested other possible interviewees. Interviews were conducted on military bases across Canada and in Ottawa.

Quotes from these interviews appear in this chapter; however, the text has been altered to conceal the identity of the interviewees. For example, French was translated into English, and the vocabulary was "levelled" so that officers could not be distinguished from noncommissioned members (NCMs), nor men from women. To ensure fidelity in the changes, a copy of the altered quotation was sent back to the interviewee, so that he or she could check that I had in fact captured the sense of the original statements. From this point on, I refer to every interviewee as "Canadian soldier."

Documentary research concerning the Canadian deployments to Somalia and to the former Yugoslavia is based on library research and on lengthy archival research carried out at the Somalia Inquiry and the Department of National Defence. In addition to viewing numerous videos on the deployments, I read thousands of pages of testimony to the Military Boards of Inquiry that were convened to investigate the events in Somalia and Bacovici, as well as the testimony and background documents from the Somalia Inquiry. Information concerning regimental traditions and customs was gathered from the documents described above and from the work of such authors as Kellett (1986), Parker (1995), and Strachan (1997).

3. COHESION

Military organizations are structures for the coordination of activities meant to ensure victory on the battlefield. Though this structure has taken, in modern times, the form of a permanent force maintained in peacetime for the eventuality of armed conflict, it can still be characterized as a culture organized around its primary purpose—war. This factor organizes the way that military forces do business and orients all the basic assumptions, spirit, and beliefs, along with the characteristic ways of doing things, that are shared by members of the organization. In particular, members of military organizations view strong interpersonal relationships and unit cohesion as necessary aspects of land warfare. Loyalty is encouraged at all levels, because military values and structures grant primacy to collective goals.

In this section, I will begin by reviewing the literature concerning the importance of cohesion and unity of effort in the military. I will also describe the importance of primary relationships in the Canadian Army and explain how policy and the regimental culture work to reinforce group cohesion. In the military, group allegiance is considered essential for combat effectiveness. Military culture emphasizes "belonging," while military training rewards group performance. Strong affective ties bind soldiers into a fighting unit, one for which they are willing to sacrifice their lives.

3.1. Mechanical Solidarity

Studies emphasizing mechanical solidarity in military organizations became popular during World War II. In the United States, Marshall (1947) studied the effect of morale on the willingness to fight and noted the importance of unity among soldiers. In an extensive study of the U.S. military, Stouffer and a team of researchers at the U.S. War Department (Stouffer et al., 1949) confirmed Marshall's findings. They concluded that the primary group "served two principal functions in combat motivation": it "set and enforced group standards" of behaviour, and it "supported and sustained . . . individual[s]" in stresses that they would not otherwise have been able to withstand (pp. 130–131). Thus a primary group can generate norms of its own or use its informal sanctions to enforce (or not enforce) organizational standards.

Shils and Janowitz (1948), who debriefed *Wehrmacht* prisoners of war, also conducted an important study of affective relationships. They found that affective relationships (the primary group bonding), were responsible both for cohesion in the German *Wehrmacht* and for the soldiers' willingness to continue fighting in spite of incredible odds: "In the army, when isolated from civilian primary groups, the individual soldier comes to depend more and more on his military primary group. His spontaneous loyalties are to its immediate members, whom he sees daily and with whom he develops a high degree of intimacy" (p. 285).

Although some authors in the period since World War II have continued to emphasize the importance of primary groups in combat motivation (see Savage & Gabriel, 1976), others began to observe a decline in primary groups. For example, Moskos (1970) saw ideology (tacit patriotism) as being more important than group cohesion for combat motivation. Moskos (1976) went on to assert that the importance of the primary group for combat soldiers had been overstated. This view has been challenged by Segal and Segal (1983), who maintain that the importance of primary relationships has not declined. They support their argument with empirical evidence of strong affective ties in combat units and the implementation of military policies designed to foster group cohesion.

3.2. Cohesion and Loyalty in the Canadian Military

Mechanical solidarity is also reinforced by the larger organization. Officers and soldiers are expected to respect values and norms that transcend individual self-interest in favour of a goal that is presumed to be higher. According to the official statement on Canadian military ethos, "it is essential for all members to clearly display loyalty, first to the country, then to the group, and finally to each member of the chain of command, both senior and junior to them before taking thought for themselves." The ethos statement goes on to say that "teamwork is essential to the survival and success of the military unit" (Canada, 1994, pp. ii–iii). In his critique of this document, Parker (1995) points out that "the subordinating of the self to the team, the concepts of service and sacrifice, the moral justification for the existence of the military institution, and the need for loyalty to the country, one's comrades and the command structure are all examples of the values needed by the benevolent military patriarchy" (p. 60).

In the Oath of Service taken by each recruit, whether an officer or a noncommissioned member, the soldier swears allegiance to something larger than him- or herself. According to Neill (n.d.), this is "the first step in ethical socialization to the in-group—bringing the new recruit into a body of individuals drawn together by a common purpose and thus, a common bond, subordinating individualism to group identity" (p. 14). Because of the nature of ground warfare, the Army places special emphasis on reinforcing unit bonding, team playing, and supporting one's comrades (particularly under fire). One key component of unit bonding is the regimental culture, which emphasizes group solidarity and cohesion.

In the Army, combat skills and values are learned through a socialization process that begins when a soldier enters basic training. The aim is to instill new attitudes, responses, and loyalties in the recruit as he or she learns new skills. Trainees begin as almost complete strangers to one another, and within just a few hours most begin to develop friendships with a bunkmate or two. Because the group is newly formed, it offers little defence to the assault of initial socialization. Then, as recruits begin to rely on each other, strong bonds build—strong enough, the military hopes, that they will go into battle for each other. "A little private out in the trenches doesn't know beans all about why he is there, except he is there with his buddies and they will die for one another. It's as simple as that" (Canadian soldier, quoted in Harrison & Laliberté, 1994). Recruits are reconstructed into soldiers through an enculturation process that encourages group solidarity through various methods that promote teamwork and group responsibility.

Having come from a civilian society that elevates the individual, recruits are now immersed in a world where the institutional value of the group reigns supreme. One has to be a team player or risk ostracism. "To the ordinary civilian—ostracism may not seem such a horrible fate. So, if you get kicked out of one group, you can just join another, may be the reaction. But remember that a member of the military is not free to just join another group" (Peck, 1983, p. 219). In its emphasis on teamwork, the military deliberately intensifies the power of group pressure within its ranks. Teamwork (cohesion) is seen as the only way a leader can marshal the capabilities of each individual member for the pursuit of a common goal.

> You have a bond. You have a bond that's so thick that it is unbelievable!—It's the pull, it's the team, the work as a team, the team spirit! I don't think that ever leaves a guy. That is exactly what basic training is supposed to do. It's supposed to weed out those who aren't willing to work that way.—And that's the whole motivation, that when somebody says we want you to do something, then you'll do it. You'll do it because of the team, for the team, with the team and because the team has the same focus. (Canadian soldier, quoted in Harrison & Laliberté, 1994, p. 28)

The group is made responsible for each member (Rampton, 1970), even though it may seem manifestly unfair to make the group suffer for the individual. In this way, the soldier learns to depend on his or her peers and on the adequacy of their performance. The extreme to which this can go is demonstrated by a 1995 event that took place at Canadian Forces Base (CFB) Gagetown, where Reserve officer candidates beat, harassed, and abused another candidate because the individual was messy and disorganized: "His bed was always poorly made and he got the others in his room into trouble. So they beat him up and harassed him" (Cotton, cited in Winslow, 1997, p. 63).

Researchers noticed the potential negative impact of strong bonding as early as the 1940s. Brotz and Wilson (1946) noted that, in the U.S. Army, bonding was so strong that "[c]overing up for, defense of and devotion to one's buddy was expected" (p. 374). This form of loyalty can lead to stonewalling and the refusal to give up one's buddies to investigators. My interviewees also noted that group bonding prevents individuals from speaking out against inappropriate behaviour:

> We're so connected, physically and mentally, that if there's one person that we admire, who does good work, who gains the respect of others, of his superiors and colleagues, the others will group around him. If he incites his group to racist behaviour, they'll follow, even if they don't agree, because they won't distinguish themselves from the group. Because the group's all you've got. If you're in battle, no one else is looking out for you. You can't count on your family; they're in another world. (Canadian soldier)

Thus, group bonding is a double-edged sword. According to Janowitz (1974), primary groups that are highly cohesive can impede the goals of a military organization, because they are informal networks. They work only when they are well articulated with formal authority. This is an important point to remember, since, on peace operations, small units are often sent to isolated spots far from formal authority.

There is also some debate in the literature as to whether army socialization actually changes people. For example, Bercuson (1996) posits that "the attitudes and values that a candidate brings to officer training are far more important in determining the degree to which he or she will embrace the military ethos than any socialization he or she will be subject to at [CFB] Gagetown or elsewhere" (p. 109). At the very least, socialization reinforces certain values and promotes group cohesion. I agree with Chatman (1991) that while there may be value congruence at entry, socialization experiences contribute significantly to changes in the person/organization fit during the recruit's first year. In the Canadian Army, group bonding in the form of regimental allegiance plays an important role in the period after basic training in setting the new military identity.

4. THE REGIMENTAL SYSTEM

> [Regimental culture] has at its core all of the values, mores, and beliefs which allow the Army to maintain itself in times of peace and war. This ancient system is shared by both [the] Regular and [the] Reserve components of the Army. It is a common bond which is designed to unite men and women in times of duress and whatever its current failings, the Regimental system can surely be credited with much of the success achieved by the Army during its history. (Canada, 1996, p. 7-1/12)

According to Cotton (1990), a regiment's essence is tribal and corporate, rather than instrumental and bureaucratic. A common set of values, such as pride in the regiment, are presumed to enhance the potential for effective collective action; at the same time, the regimental system orients primary group bonds into organizationally approved channels (Kellett, 1980). Thus the regimental system is supposed to be one of the major networks by which primary groups are articulated with formal authority.

4.1. Regimental Traditions

The Canadian Army possesses a strong regimental tradition—a tradition that is based in many respects on the British system, but with some uniquely Canadian twists. At the heart of the Canadian Army lie three infantry regiments that reflect the geographic and linguistic divisions in Canada—western anglophone (the PPCLI, or Princess Patricia's Canadian Light Infantry), central and eastern anglophone (the RCR, or Royal Canadian Regiment), and central francophone (the R22eR, or Royal 22e Régiment [the "Van Doos"]).[6] These territorial divisions define areas of recruitment, training, and residence for regimental members and give each regiment a certain flavour or character.

---

[6] Each regiment is in turn divided into three infantry battalions. There are also armoured units (such as the Lord Strathcona's Horse [Royal Canadians], the Royal Canadian Dragoons, and the 12e Régiment blindé du Canada) and three artillery regiments (the 1st and 2nd Regiments of the Royal Canadian Horse Artillery and the 5e Régiment d'artillerie légère du Canada). These elements, along with combat engineers and other units, are organized into the 1st and 2nd Canadian Mechanized Brigade groups and the 5e Brigade mécanisé du Canada (Bercuson, 1996).

Regiments transmit their traditions from generation to generation.[7] Regimental lore is compiled in a regimental book, which is the "bible" of regimental tradition. Regiments maintain museums honouring their glorious past. These museums contain historical artifacts and displays relating the regiment's history, in addition to rolls containing the names of members fallen in battle. Regiments also have their own archives containing war diaries, photographs, and documents concerning regimental history. Each regiment publishes its own history, which junior members are expected to learn (Bercuson, 1996). Messes, which are dining and social clubs, are repositories of regimental tradition; they create an informal atmosphere in which the transmission of military culture can continue after hours.

The distinctiveness of each regiment is also marked by unique regimental insignia, such as shoulder badges, buttons, buckles, colours of kit, and distinctive tailoring of uniform, headgear, and mess dress. Regiments also have their own unique music, rituals, and taboos. As Trice and Beyer (1984) have shown, rites serve to socialize, integrate, and assign social identity. Entry into a regiment is marked by both formal and informal rites of passage. While the formal ceremonies welcome individuals into the larger group, it is the informal rites that bond members to the primary group.

In January 1995, the Canadian public was shocked by videotaped scenes of humiliating and at times disgusting initiation rites in One Commando of the Canadian Airborne Regiment. It may seem incomprehensible to an outsider that the initiates actually participated voluntarily in these rites. Yet the importance of the ritual was, in part, a reflection of the nature of the unit's requirements at this stage. Initiates were strangers to each other and to the Airborne. The bonding of the initiation pulled them together in a very short period of time. The impact of this extreme form of initiation was noted as early as the 1950s, when Aronson and Mills (1959) showed that an initiate who endures severe hazing is likely to find membership in a group all the more appealing. In these rituals, soldiers are proving their readiness to participate in the group regardless of the personal cost, and thus gaining peer group acceptance. As one soldier put it, "I am proud to have done it, it proves to myself and others that as a member of the Canadian Airborne Regiment, I will face and overpass any challenge or tasking given to me" (Commission of Inquiry into the Deployment of Canadian Forces to Somalia [Somalia Inquiry], Document Book 5, Tab 1, One Commando Canadian Airborne Regiment, Miscellaneous—Other—Negligent Performance of Duty, CFB Petawawa, Ontario, p. 10).[8] Thus, both formal and informal experience promote the dependence of the individual on the group.

---

[7] Studies of regimental ethos show that the combat arms are the greatest supporters of regimental symbols and traditions. Flemming (1989) concluded that 98 percent of combat officers supported regimental symbols and traditions (compared with 75 percent of support officers); 87 percent of combat senior NCOs and 71 percent of combat junior ranks showed similar support (compared with 63 percent and 58 percent, respectively, for support trades). Overall, 83 percent of respondents in combat classifications and trades supported regimental symbols and traditions, compared with 65 percent in support classifications and trades (cited in Kellett, 1980).

[8] Copies of the Somalia Inquiry's exhibits and transcripts are located in the government publications section of the Morissette Library at the University of Ottawa, Ontario, Canada.

An example of how the bonding of a group can lead soldiers to defy authority can be found in the testimony given by members of One Commando to the Somalia Inquiry. They had difficulty "remembering" details concerning the initiation rite. Another example surfaced when Corporal Christophe Robin, the only black initiate in the One Commando video, reviewed the video at the Somalia Inquiry. Even though he was shown in humiliating circumstances—on his knees, with "I love KKK" written on his back—he still did not want to hurt the good name of the Airborne Regiment and was reluctant to criticize his former unit.[9]

4.2. The Regimental Family

According to Loomis (1996), the regiment is a pseudo-kinship organization.[10] One is considered a member of a regiment for life. This link continues throughout a member's career in the military and after retirement. "The Regimental Family permeates all facets of one's life from pseudo-birth as a new member to death" (Loomis, 1996, p. 60). The concept of family is strong, and it is reinforced daily. The following quote is taken from *The Army* (Canada, 1984), which was the first manual to provide land force doctrine for the period 1986–1995.[11] In a letter to the reader found at the beginning of the manual, Major-General G. H. J. Lessard, Chief of Land Doctrine and Operations for the Chief of Defence Staff, notes that it was at that time "the army's keystone manual and thus the basis of all land force doctrine" (Canada, 1984, p. ii):

> Briefly, the soldier must want his Regiment, his comrades and those around him to survive. The Regiment is his family, where he is not alone. It provides a situation in which his human needs can be met and thus, it is very important to him. As a consequence, the peril to the Regiment's survival from an attacking enemy becomes so threatening that the soldier's natural fear of loneliness and death, as well as his disinclination to take life, is less than his fear of losing those who provide him [with] safety, security, a firm sense of belonging, affection, status and prestige, order, system and structure. The Regiment provides the opportunity for him to become the best soldier in the world; he fights for something more than himself; he fights for his comrades and the Regiment; and indirectly, for his home and his family. (Canada, 1984, pp. 3/7–3/8)

Regiments are powerful entities in the Canadian Army. A regiment influences the career advancement of its members by administering career assessment and promotion boards and by providing recommendations to promotion boards at National Defence Headquarters (Bercuson, 1996). There are also strong associations that act to defend the interests of the regiment—sometimes to the detriment of the interests of the Army or those of the CF as a whole. As Granatstein (1997) notes, "[t]he Regimental system has become a problem, a closed shop that too often pits one

[9] Testimony of Corporal Robin to the Commission of Inquiry into the Deployment of Canadian Forces to Somalia [Somalia Inquiry] (Transcripts, Vol. 6, pp. 1033–1038).

[10] A regiment is often referred to as a "family," and the family nature of the system is underscored by nicknames such as "old man" for the commanding officer (CO) and "auntie" for the second in command (2 I/C). When a battalion is out in the field on exercises, the bivouac (the semipermanent tented camp) is commonly referred to as "home" (Irwin, 1993).

[11] It is important to note that *Canada's Army*, the new manual published in 1998 (Canada, 1998), specifically warns against placing primary group loyalty above organizational and national loyalty.

Regiment against another, that rallies the generals from the Regiment to secure key postings for favoured officers, and that can divide the army with the argument that it is 'our turn' for some position" (p. 11).

Each regiment has a semiofficial oversight and advisory entity known as "the Senate," "the Regimental Guard," "La Régie," or, in slang terms, "the Godfathers." These groups comprise serving general officers from the regiment and honorary appointees, such as retired generals from that regiment. The role of these advisors is to oversee the regiment's long-term well-being. An important part of the advisors' mandate is to provide advice and input on key promotions and appointments within the regiment. In addition to the regimental senate, there is a regimental executive that is responsible for managing regimental business; the executive consists of the various commanding officers (and often the regimental sergeant-majors as well). The colonel of the regiment, who is chosen from among the regiment's most distinguished members, is usually a former high-ranking officer who has been retired for several years (Loomis, 1996).

> The colonel of the regiment is, in theory, just a figurehead; in practice, he is likely to be a whole lot more. It is very rare that any major plans for the regiment would be instituted by army headquarters without consulting the colonel of the regiment. His opinion is often sought by the battalion COs on personnel problems, morale issues, and ceremonial matters. Like the senior serving member, he can be an important lobbyist for his regiment in the higher echelons of the army. (Bercuson, 1996, p. 125)

The senior serving member is the regiment's highest-ranking currently serving officer. According to Bercuson, "senior serving members have no formal authority in the regiment. They are not part of the regimental decision-making structure, and they are certainly not part of the battalion chain of command" (Bercuson, 1996, p. 124). They are, nonetheless, very important to the regiment, since they look out for its interests. No matter how far up he or she is in the chain of command, the senior serving member is expected to put in a good word for the regiment and to influence decisions bearing on its welfare (Bercuson, 1996). Kellett (1986) notes that reverence for regimental customs and traditions can undermine discipline, citing instances in which regiments have managed to "elude" orders that challenged or modified a cherished custom: "Tradition turns into traditionalism and risks becoming dysfunctional" (p. 75).

Clearly, regiments have structures of formal and informal authority that affect the Army's functioning. This observation is interesting, given that one of the original intents of the British regimental system was to direct the loyalty of the officer corps toward the *lesser* institution (the regiment), not the greater one (the Army)—in other words, to divide and conquer the Army itself: "Rivalry and competition between the regiments then internalizes any inclination in the army's officer corps as a whole to act more cohesively" (Strachan, 1997, pp. 196–197). The focus on regimental customs in Britain was a mechanism that diverted militarism into "safe" channels, thus protecting civilian society from a unified military: "In the army's case, part of the problem is not that it cannot lobby, but that the regimental system has meant that it is lobbying against itself, and that suits its political masters only too well" (Strachan, 1997, p. 233).

5. EXAGGERATED LOYALTIES

The regimental system can be "a pervasive and often unforgiving milieu within which all combat arms and most other Army personnel live their daily lives" (Canada, 1996, p. 7-1/12). The corporate nature of regiments has many advantages, but there can also be disadvantages, such as the development of an "us-versus-them" attitude. Unit pride can become so exaggerated that one respects only the members and/or officers of one's unit, ignoring and possibly resenting those outside the group. What is clearly an effective and necessary attitude for the battlefield can then become an exaggerated force that undermines good order and discipline. In Bacovici, A Company, which was from the R22e Regiment, was attached to the 12e Régiment blindé du Canada (12 RBC) for the mission in Bosnia. Because of the strong sense of regimental identity, the members of R22eR were reluctant to take any problems to the commanding officer (CO), who was not from the R22eR. On the other side, the CO (a member of 12 RBC) allowed A Company to behave autonomously. As a result, members of the unit messed, lived, and performed their duties apart from the rest of the regiment. Headquarters (formal authority) thus exercised little control over the company, and there was a breakdown in command and communication. What is more surprising is that this situation was not seen as abnormal: "They were, after all, Van Doos and therefore not part of the 12 [RBC] tribe per se" (Canada, 1996, p. 7-9/12).

The members of the Canadian Airborne Regiment (CAR) believed themselves to be part of an elite unit, a cut above the ordinary infantry soldier. CAR members saw other combat troops and noncombat personnel as inferior. They called them "legs," which apparently means "*l*ack *e*nough *g*uts." As one interviewee said, "the Airborne doesn't interact with the legs." Unit pride also affected their relationship with officers:

> They didn't seem to respect the higher ranks that weren't Airborne as much as ordinary soldiers might. An officer walking by might not be saluted by an Airborne soldier, whereas most every other private on the base would salute him. To get them to do something, it was better to get their warrant officer to order, rather than a warrant officer from outside the Airborne. (Canadian soldier)

Unlike the parent regiments, the CAR was a constituted unit without permanent membership. However, it too reflected the linguistic and geographic divisions in the Canadian Army. It was divided into three commandos, each representing one of the parent regiments: Two Commando (western anglophone/PPCLI), Three Commando (central and eastern anglophone/RCR), and One Commando (central francophone/R22eR). Some of my interviewees felt that the purpose of having the three commandos was so that the regiments could track their own people and thus control promotion and performance evaluations. The result was that commando units in the CAR did not mix with one another on a regular basis. They lived on base in separate barracks. They did not mingle with each other socially; in fact, they openly displayed antagonism toward one another. In particular, the francophones and anglophones remained separate. Like the parent regiments, each commando began to develop its own subculture—that is, its own way of doing things and an associated identity.[12] The Airborne Regiment's three commando units had difficulties working together as team, a situation that undermined overall unit cohesion, command, and control.

In addition, officers from the Airborne's other commando units were reluctant to report the problems in Two Commando to the chain of command. In Somalia, they were left on their own. A number of incidents that occurred in October 1992, before deployment, indicated a significant breakdown of discipline in Two Commando during the critical period of training and preparation for operations in Somalia. Military pyrotechnics were discharged illegally at a party in the junior ranks' mess; a car belonging to the duty NCO was set on fire; and various Two Commando members expended illegally held pyrotechnics and ammunition during a party in Ontario's Algonquin Park, near their base in Petawawa. The illegal possession of these pyrotechnics was the result of theft from the Department of National Defence (DND) and the making of false statements. A search conducted on the soldiers' premises uncovered ammunition stolen from DND, as well as 34 Confederate flags. When I interviewed officers from the other commandos, they told me that they were aware of the problems in Two Commando but that it was "none of [their] business." Not reporting on other units can lead to the nonreporting of discipline problems.

In the former Yugoslavia, there was a similarly widespread tendency for all personnel in the chain of command to concern themselves almost exclusively with their own subordinate commands: "The command structure of 'A' squadron was reticent to concern itself with anything which occurred in the Engineer Sq[uadro]n and vice versa. Although army culture has inculcated officers and [senior] NCOs not to overlook a fault, there has been a growing tendency not to meddle in the affairs of others" (Canada, 1996, p. 4-4/23).

5.1. Primary Group Loyalties

The regimental system is designed to permit the flow of information up the chain of command, but when primary group bonds are strong, information is retained at the lower levels; thus, bad news does not travel up. Officers, as a result, may simply be unaware of trouble in their unit.

> [When you are] in a leadership position, the guys won't tell you bad news. 'Cause the chain of command is such that your major is not going to tell you things are really bad down here. What he'll say is we're doing a bunch of investigations and checking things out here. As a CO that's what you hear, unless the troops know that you're going to find out some other way. So it's always been there, those kind of problems within the chain of command. Only good news goes up. (Canadian soldier)

At the Somalia Inquiry, evidence was presented that suggested that the chain of command, during both the predeployment period and the in-theatre period, failed

---

[12] One Commando, with its R22eR background, was French and sported the fleur-de-lys flag (the flag of the Province of Quebec) in its barracks. Two Commando, drawn from the PPCLI, began to flout authority by adopting the rebel flag of the American Confederacy; Three Commando, from the RCR, became known as quiet professionals with the motto "Never pass a fault."

as a mechanism for passing and seeking information. As mentioned above, several serious disciplinary problems had occurred throughout the period from early 1992 until the CAR's deployment to Somalia in December 1992. Yet few officers in the chain of command were aware of these problems. Many senior officers in the chain of command, from Major-General Lewis MacKenzie to General John de Chastelain, testified to the Somalia Inquiry that they were ignorant of the CAR's state of fitness and discipline.

In Bacovici, soldiers accused of black marketeering were not charged; instead, they were disciplined by having to put their illegal profits into the regimental fund. The CO and the regimental sergeant-major, who were with the 12 RBC, were never made aware of the matter; thus, the incident was kept within the R22eR (Canada, 1996). Similarly, soldiers testified that frequent incidents involving drinking beyond the limits set by established policy were not reported up the chain of command, so as not to humiliate the regiment (Canada, 1996).

Information that may tarnish the regiment's reputation may be hidden. "Whistleblowing" is perceived as going against the corporate nature of the military, which encourages its members to "not wash their dirty laundry in public." The act of denouncing wrongdoing to outsiders, particularly civilians, is not well accepted.

> There are some things you just don't talk about. I knew some guys who were taking drugs, but I didn't say anything. Being a stool pigeon is worse than being a homosexual. There's a climate of fear. It's better not to talk about certain things, for your own security. It's not as if they're going to kill you, but it's just something you don't do. It's like a code of behaviour. (Canadian soldier)

> Every unit likes to take care of its own dirty laundry. There's no regimental commander that wants to get up in front of the general. That's why we try to handle our own. It is understandable that a soldier would want to keep any news of wrongdoing within his regiment. (Canadian soldier)

> Guys'll stick together. They won't rat on anybody. But the other commandos are like that too. What goes on inside, stays inside. You have to belong. If you don't—well, it's just too bad. It's your family. You have to live with them. These are the guys you're going to war with. . . . They're the ones who'll be covering you. You have to be able to trust them all. (Canadian soldier)

It is also important to note that residence in foreign lands while on peace missions can intensify the sense of bonding and the view that the primary group is an extended family. Bonds of loyalty can then lead a regiment's members to protect one another, sometimes by covering up for one another or by setting up walls of silence.

> The pressure is so strong that beyond the group, right and wrong lose their meaning. Only the group matters—until it's just too much, and things start to come out on the outside. Like with Somalia. If it hadn't come out from the outside, it probably never would have come out. I tried to talk with some guys at that time. They wouldn't talk. Silence. If they talk, they're screwed. Somebody'll find out about it sooner or later. In the infantry, it's different. The group is smaller. You're trained for war, much more brutally, and you're isolated. No connections to the outside. (Canadian soldier)

Because of fierce loyalty, there was a tradition of protecting each other in Two Commando of the Canadian Airborne Regiment. At CFB Petawawa, just before the regiment was deployed to Somalia, in-group loyalty was so strong that authorities were unable to find out who had participated in the burning of an officer's car. Investigations encountered only a wall of silence concerning this serious breach of discipline. Walls of silence are erected when the soldiers refuse to give up one of their comrades. "Not only might a schismatic group of this kind foster and maintain inappropriate norms, but by assuring anonymity through norms of group loyalty and by imposing severe sanctions for violations of the solidarity norm, it can facilitate acts of subversion and defiance" (Wenek, 1993, p. 17).

This pattern was repeated in-theatre. The Somalia Inquiry's report contains excerpts from a soldier's diary showing that, shortly before the torture and death of Shidane Arone, other Somalis had been severely beaten by soldiers from the Canadian Airborne Regiment (Canada, 1997, Vol. 5, p. 1418). At the time, these acts went unreported. The perpetrators of Arone's torture and death might therefore have felt that they were operating in a permissive atmosphere—an atmosphere in which such acts were somehow "unofficially" approved of. Even if these acts were not "unofficially" approved of, the tradition of group loyalty suggested that individual perpetrators would not be held accountable.

6. CONCLUSIONS

The CF has an ethos of cohesion, teamwork, and loyalty, all sustained by cultural phenomena (physical artifacts, collective mental frameworks and manifestations, and collective action patterns). This culture has a long historical tradition that is rooted in the definition of the CF as a combat force. Thus, military ethos is shaped by Canadian policy decisions to maintain a combat force. Combat readiness, in turn, shapes the organization's values and goals, reinforcing primary group bonding, which is seen as a necessary component of combat effectiveness.

Primary group bonding is reinforced through formal and informal socialization; however, the intense bonding deemed necessary for combat is a double-edged sword. This chapter has shown how misplaced loyalty can lead to stonewalling, preventing the proper investigation of criminal activities. Group bonding also prevents individuals from speaking out against inappropriate behaviour, which can therefore continue unchecked. The chain of command thus becomes short-circuited by the strong affective ties that it has itself encouraged. The strong affective ties that are encouraged by combat norms create highly cohesive units; however, these ties can also impede the good functioning of the overall organization. Research indicates that one way to control this tendency is to ensure that the unit is well articulated with formal authority (Kellett, 1980). Thus, primary group loyalty must be encouraged only in an environment of strong leadership and discipline.

Of particular importance is leadership and discipline at the level of the small unit—particularly in the role of junior NCOs. It is through these officers that the formal demands of the organization are linked with the norms and sanctions of the small group itself (George, 1976). On a 1998 field trip to the Canadian area of operations in the former Yugoslavia, I had an opportunity to observe successful units in operation. Older, more experienced NCOs were paired with young, inexperienced troops. The commanding officer and the officer commanding, accompanied by senior NCOs, visited every unit in the area of operation on a regular (almost weekly) basis, thus ensuring close supervision of even the most isolated units. And in these isolated posts, mature NCOs with extraordinary leadership capabilities were chosen to supervise the group. In this way, hierarchical cohesion can be maintained along with peer cohesion at the lowest working level.

Discipline and leadership offset strong group identification. A unit with a strong sense of professionalism and discipline would therefore be less likely to commit infractions, because its individuals are invested in an identity that has components of self-discipline and ethics embedded in it. In the best of all worlds, Canadian military ethos prescribes this self-discipline and ethical code for all soldiers and officers. Nevertheless, personal discipline, self-control, and commitment to high standards of personal conduct need to be continually reinforced by leadership at all levels, from junior to senior. The cultivation of in-group identity needs to be balanced with respect for military authority and the rule of law. Priorities need to be clearly established within the regimental collective and within individual units so that a healthy balance of loyalties is firmly established. The role of leadership in this is clear—leaders are the primary agents by which an organization's culture and role norms are modelled, transmitted, and maintained. "Culture is created in the first instance by actions of leaders; culture also is embedded and strengthened by leaders" (Schein, 1985, pp. 316–317).

7. ACKNOWLEDGMENTS

An earlier version of this chapter was published in August 1998 as "The Role of Culture in the Breakdown of Discipline during Peace Operations" (*Canadian Review of Sociology and Anthropology, Special Issue: Organizational Crisis, 35*, 345–368).

I wish to thank Chairman Gilles Letourneau and Commissioners Robert Rutherford and Peter Debarats from the Commission of Inquiry into the Deployment of Canadian Forces to Somalia, in addition to the Commission staff, for their assistance and technical support during my time at the Somalia Inquiry. I also wish to thank the commanders and staff of the Canadian military bases I visited, the members of the Somalia Inquiry Liaison Team, and the CF Personnel Applied Research Unit. On the academic side, I am grateful to the Faculty of Social Sciences at the University of Ottawa and to my research assistants Jason Dunn, Irving Gold, and Richard Veenstra. Financing for the research into military culture was received from the Somalia Inquiry; a research grant from the University of Ottawa was used to study the Bacovici records at the Department of National Defence.

I also wish to thank the Department of National Defence and the members of the Canadian Forces deployed in the former Yugoslavia for arranging a field trip to the Canadian area of operations. I am well aware that such a trip requires time and energy to organize. I am extremely appreciative of the support given to me during this visit, which took place in October 1998.

8. REFERENCES

Aronson, E., & Mills, J. (1959). The effect of severity of initiation on liking for a group. *Journal of Abnormal and Social Psychology, 59*, 177–181.

Bercuson, D. (1996). *Significant incident: Canada's Army, the Airborne, and the murder in Somalia.* Toronto: McClelland and Stewart.

Brotz, H., & Wilson, E. K. (1946). Characteristics of military society. *American Journal of Sociology, 51*, 371–375.

Canada. (1984). *The Army* (CFP 300/B-GL-300-000/FP-000, Interim 1). Ottawa: Department of National Defence.

Canada. (1994, October). *Canadian Forces Officers General Specification, Revision 2* (A-PD-150–001/AG-001). Ottawa: Department of National Defence.

Canada. (1996). *Command Control and Leadership in Canbat 2: Part 1, The Board Report.* Ottawa: Department of National Defence, Board of Inquiry.

Canada. (1997). *Dishonoured legacy: The lessons of the Somalia affair—Report of the Commission of Inquiry into the Deployment of Canadian Forces to Somalia.* Ottawa: Commission of Inquiry into the Deployment of Canadian Forces to Somalia [Somalia Inquiry].

Canada. (1998). *Canada's Army* (CFP 300/B-GL-300-000/FP-000). Ottawa: Department of National Defence.

Chatman, J. A. (1991). Matching people and organizations: Selection and socialization in public accounting firms. *Administrative Science Quarterly, 36*, 459–484.

Cotton, C. A. (1990). Commitment in military systems. In T. C. Wyatt & R. Gal (Eds.), *Legitimacy and commitment in the military.* New York: Greenwood Press.

Flemming, S. B. (1989). *The hearts and minds of soldiers in Canada: The Military Ethos Scale (MES) in retrospect.* Ottawa: Department of National Defence, Operational Research and Analysis Establishment, Directorate of Social and Economic Analysis.

George, A. L. (1976). Primary groups, organization and military performance. In Office of Military Leadership, United States Military Academy (Ed.), *A study of organizational leadership.* Harrisburg, PA: Stackpole Books.

Granatstein, J. L. (1997). *For efficient and effective military forces: A paper prepared for the Minister of National Defence.* Ottawa: Department of National Defence.

Harrison, D., & Laliberté, L. (1994). *No life like it: Military wives in Canada.* Toronto: James Lorimer.

Irwin, A. (1993). *Canadian infantry platoon commanders and the emergence of leadership.* Unpublished master's thesis, University of Calgary, Calgary, Alberta.

Janowitz, M. (1974). *Sociology and the military establishment.* Beverly Hills, CA: Sage.

Kellett, N. A. (1980). *Combat motivation* (Report No. R77). Ottawa: Department of National Defence, Operational Research and Analysis Establishment.

Kellett, N. A. (1986). *Regimental customs and tradition* (DSEA Staff Note 12/86). Ottawa: Department of National Defence, Operational Research and Analysis Establishment, Directorate of Social and Economic Analysis.

Loomis, D. G. (1996). *The Somalia affair: Reflections on peacemaking and peacekeeping.* Ottawa: DGL Publications.

Marshall, S. (1947). *Men against fire.* New York: Morrow.

Moskos, C. (1970). *The American enlisted man.* New York: Russell Sage.

Moskos, C. (1976). The military. *Annual Review of Sociology, 2*, 55–77.

Neill, D. A. (n.d.). *Canadian military ethics.* Unpublished manuscript.

Omaar, R., & de Waal, A. (1993). *Somalia: Human rights abuses by the United Nations forces.* London, U.K.: Africa Rights Report.

Ott, J. (1989). *The organizational culture perspective.* Chicago: Dorsey Press.

Parker, R. O. (1995). *The influences of organizational culture on the personnel selection process.* Unpublished doctoral dissertation, York University, North York, Ontario.

Peck, M. S. (1983). *People of the lie: The hope for healing human evil.* New York: Simon and Schuster.

Rampton, G. M. (1970). *Effects of basic military training on quantitative dimensions of personality* (Research Report 70/1). Ottawa: Canadian Forces Personnel Applied Research Unit [available in microform at the National Library of Canada, Ottawa].

Savage, P., & Gabriel, R. (1976). Cohesion and disintegration in the American Army. *Armed Forces and Society, 2,* 340–376.

Schein, E. H. (1985). *Organizational culture and leadership.* San Francisco: Jossey-Bass.

Segal, D., & Segal, M. (1983). Change in military organization. *Annual Review of Sociology, 9,* 151–170.

Shils, E., & Janowitz, M. (1948). Cohesion and disintegration in the *Wehrmacht* in World War II. *Public Opinion Quarterly, 12,* 280–315.

Stouffer, S., Suchman, E. A., DeVinney, L. C., Star, S. A., & Williams, R. M. J. (1949). *The American Soldier: Vol. 1. Adjustment during army life.* Princeton, NJ: Princeton University Press.

Strachan, H. (1997). *The politics of the British Army.* Oxford, U.K.: Clarendon Press.

Tönnies, F. (1957). *Community and society* (C. P. Loomis, Trans.). East Lansing: Michigan State University Press. (Original work published 1887)

Trice, H., & Beyer, J. (1984). Studying organizational cultures through rites and rituals. *Academic Management Review, 9,* 653–669.

Wenek, K. W. J. (1993). Behavioural and psychological dimensions of recent peacekeeping missions. *Forum: Journal of the Conference of Defence Associations Institute, 8*(5), 13–19.

Winslow, D. (1997). *The Canadian Airborne Regiment in Somalia: A socio-cultural inquiry.* Ottawa: Public Works and Government Services Canada.

CHAPTER 21

MORALE, COHESION, AND CONFIDENCE IN LEADERSHIP
Unit Climate Dimensions for Canadian Soldiers on Operations

MAJOR PETER J. MURPHY and
MAJOR KELLY M. J. FARLEY

1. INTRODUCTION

Any book of military quotations amply illustrates the importance that renowned military leaders across history have ascribed to high morale and capable command. Xenophon (circa 394 BC/1960) was sure that the army "stronger in soul" would be victorious in battle; Napoleon felt that "moral considerations" accounted for three-quarters of the outcome in war (Wintle, 1989); and Montgomery (1958) stated that "the morale of the soldier is the greatest single factor in war." But how did these leaders gauge the level of morale in their own forces and in those of their opponents? How did they assess the impact of leadership? Commanders' perceptions of subordinates' attitudes and morale may be crucial ingredients for command decision making with regard to readiness and the commitment of forces to combat operations. If command assessments of subordinate attitudes and mood and of subunit

MAJOR PETER J. MURPHY • Directorate of Human Resource Research and Evaluation, National Defence Headquarters, Ottawa, Ontario, Canada K1A 0K2   MAJOR KELLY M. J. FARLEY • Director Land Personnel 2-2, National Defence Headquarters, Ottawa, Ontario, Canada K1A 0K2

The Human in Command: Exploring the Modern Military Experience, edited by McCann and Pigeau, Kluwer Academic/Plenum Publishers, New York, 2000.

cohesion and morale are inaccurate, organizational effectiveness and performance may suffer.

What evidence exists regarding the accuracy of military commanders in their assessments of human factors? United States Army officers in World War II were found to have had consistently inflated views of their subordinates' attitudes toward a range of military issues (Stouffer, Suchman, DeVinney, Star, & Williams, 1949b). Korpi (1965) demonstrated that modern-day commanders in the Swedish army had "very unreliable notions of the opinions in their units" (p. 302), and that officers were generally unaware that their perception of subordinate morale might be inaccurate. Indeed, the greater the commander's subjective confidence in such assessments, the greater the absolute error and positive bias (that is, the more certain the commanders were that their assessments of morale were accurate, the more incorrect they were likely to be, and the more likely they were to have erred in the direction of believing that morale was better than it actually was). Higher-ranking officers tended to express greater confidence in their assessments, but they also exhibited increased error in those assessments. More recently, there have been suggestions (for example, see Winslow, 1997) that the disturbing events in the Canadian contingent in Somalia can be partly attributed to a failure by some commanders to accurately perceive the prevailing attitudes, norms, and values in some unit subcultures, leading to erroneous judgments regarding the units' readiness for peace support operations.

Military leaders have recourse to a range of behavioural science research and expertise that may contribute both to command effectiveness and to individual and group performance. A review of the literature and of recent conferences (such as Psychological Readiness for Multinational Operations: Directions for the Twenty-First Century, a July 1997 NATO [North Atlantic Treaty Organization]/Partnership for Peace Workshop held in Heidelberg, Germany) demonstrates that behavioural science research within the military is extensive and expanding. Staples of research into the human or psychological dimension of military performance include morale (Gal & Manning, 1987; Manning, 1991); cohesion (Henderson, 1985); combat motivation (Stewart, 1988); combat stress (Solomon, 1993); fatigue (Krueger, 1991; Murphy & Mombourquette, 1998); decision making (Hartle, 1989); and issues relating to survival, evasion, resistance, and escape (Murphy & Farley, 1997). Unfortunately, this source of expertise is at times neglected—occasionally with tragic consequences. Inquiries into the July 1988 incident in which USS *Vincennes* shot down a civilian passenger jet have suggested that implementation of well-established behavioural science findings might have prevented the tragedy (Bales, 1988).

This chapter examines three of the more traditional components of the psychological dimension of military effectiveness: morale, cohesion, and confidence in leadership. These factors are often presumed to correlate highly with each other (Gal, 1986). For example, it is plausible that morale should be boosted by high confidence in leadership, and that high levels of morale should be fostered by cohesion. But laboratory studies of cohesion and performance (for example, Bowers, Urban, & Morgan, 1992) have failed to support such relationships, possibly because such studies fail either to capture the complexity of authentic group interaction or to consider other mediating factors that are crucial components of unit climate. Recent field research by Farley (1995) with deployed military personnel has confirmed a strong relationship, as found by Stouffer and his colleagues (Stouffer, Lumsdaine, et al., 1949a; Stouffer, Suchman, et al., 1949b) in the U.S. Army during World War II, between the human climate factors of morale and strain. Soldiers with poor morale are more likely to show signs of illness than are personnel with strong morale. This relationship, often intuitively recognized, has obvious ramifications for commanders who are trying to maximize operational effectiveness. This chapter extends Farley's research by exploring the dynamic interplay of three unit climate factors: morale, cohesion, and confidence in leadership. The data are drawn from the Human Dimension of Operations (HDO) project, an ongoing research study involving deployed Canadian Forces (CF) personnel.

2. THE HUMAN DIMENSION OF OPERATIONS (HDO) PROJECT

Optimal operational effectiveness is a primary goal of every military organization. Conventional efforts to enhance operational performance generally focus on training and on materiel aspects, such as equipment acquisition and streamlined support. In recent years, many military forces have become increasingly aware of the importance of undertaking research into the human dimension of operational performance. This awareness has been fostered by both an acceptance of responsibility for the psychological welfare of military personnel and their families (Hobfoll et al., 1991) and a recognition that the psychological components of military performance are crucial to effectiveness (Marshall, 1997).

The CF recognizes that research should underpin the development of policy and procedure. This awareness is reflected in the amount of personnel research conducted throughout the CF organization into such issues such as quality of life (Eyres, 1997; Thivierge, 1998); selection procedures for specific occupations—for example, military police (O'Brien, 1997) and flight crew (Adams-Roy, 1996; Pelchat, 1997); occupational stress (MacLennan, 1996; Murphy, Dobreva-Martinova, & Farley, 1998a, 1998b); performance appraisals (Mombourquette, Noonan, & Uchiyama, 1997); harassment (Davis, 1998); diversity (Ewins, 1997); and monitoring and assessing the impact of attrition (Bender & Tseng, 1996), downsizing (Murphy & Mombourquette, 1997), and gender integration (Davis, 1997; Tanner, 1996). At the vanguard of behavioural science research into operational effectiveness within the CF is the HDO project.

2.1. Background

In November 1995, the Canadian Army expressed interest in developing a psychometric instrument that could be used by commanding officers (COs) to measure human dimensions of combat readiness within units before and during deployment. The instrument was to be developed with the ultimate goal of allowing COs to administer, score, and interpret it with or without specialist advice. Dimensions such as morale, cohesion, and confidence in leadership were to be included.

There were several catalysts behind the resulting HDO project (Farley & Murphy, 1996). One major impetus stemmed from recognizing that the stress of operations can adversely affect both individual and group performance, as well as the short- and long-term well-being of personnel—and, consequently, their families. Another incentive for commencing the project was the acknowledgment that empirical measurement of particular aspects of unit climate such as morale and leadership could assist commanders to command more effectively. Such information would provide commanders with an additional tool in their command and decision-making toolbox. Furthermore, while previous research has clarified many of the psychological aspects of wartime service, peace support operations—a new phenomenon since the end of the Cold War—have not been studied as extensively. The diverse factors associated with contemporary peacekeeping deserve research attention, since for many military organizations (including the CF), peace support operations have become the most common operational activity over the last decade. The HDO project was a CF response to the clear need to study the diverse factors associated with contemporary peacekeeping.

The HDO project is conducted on behalf of the Canadian Army by the Operational Effectiveness Section at the Directorate of Human Resource Research and Evaluation (DHRRE) (formerly the Personnel Research Team [PRT]). DHRRE is a corporate resource within the Personnel Group whose mandate involves responding to research requests from within Canada's Department of National Defence and the CF. The multidisciplinary DHRRE comprises members with backgrounds in psychology, sociology, operations research, mathematical modelling, and computer science. DHRRE's mandate is to enhance the Defence team's operational effectiveness, human resource management, strategic planning, and well-being through sponsor-driven research.

2.2. A Model of Stress and Performance in Operations

The HDO project is based on a particular model of stress and performance in operations[1] (Murphy, Farley, & Dobreva-Martinova, 1997). As shown in Figure 1, the model incorporates four components: stressors, moderators, coping, and outcomes. Each of these components can be considered at individual, group, and organizational levels. The model encourages a multidisciplinary approach to research. The theoretical framework is designed to aid understanding of the human dynamics of the deployment cycle[2] and to indicate appropriate training and interventions that will enhance individual and organizational well-being and performance. The model

---

[1] In this chapter, the terms "operations," "operational deployment," and "deployment," unless otherwise specified, refer to overseas deployments on peace support missions, such as U.N. peacekeeping. Military training exercises within Canada are not included in this definition.

[2] The deployment cycle comprises three stages: predeployment, deployment, and postdeployment. Predeployment usually entails intensive training, typically for one to three months, depending on warning time. Peace support operations usually involve a six-month deployment overseas. Postdeployment refers to the process of returning to one's country and the subsequent period of readjustment to life at home, as well as activities associated with returning the unit to its routine nonoperational activities. Postdeployment periods normally last two to three months.

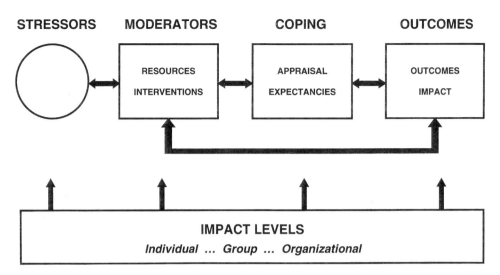

FIGURE 1. Operational effectiveness: stress research model.

is constantly being refined through the interplay of theoretical and applied research considerations.

2.2.1. Stressors

The model begins with a stressor component. Stressors are events or conditions that can cause stress in individuals (see also Breakwell, this volume, Chapter 23). Reactivity to stressors, of course, varies considerably between individuals, just as situations vary greatly both within and across peace support operations. While this study builds on previous research that sought to identify the stressors experienced by CF personnel on peacekeeping tours, the stressors for each deployment appear to be fundamentally different. Stressors may be acute or chronic; they may be specific to the operational theatre or more occupational in nature, or they may be general life events or daily hassles that are not specific to the military. We emphasize the chronic and cumulative stressors of deployment, because such stressors are more generic across peace operations and therefore presumably more amenable to study and intervention. In a sense, the deployment cycle—including the predeployment and postdeployment phases—is considered to be one large composite stressor comprising numerous potential component stressors. For various reasons, not the least of which is to develop comparative data, HDO project researchers are also studying occupational stressors experienced by personnel who are not operationally deployed.

2.2.2. Moderators

Moderators are factors that can impinge on the appraisal process (part of the coping component), thus influencing a stressor's impact. Moderators can include perceptions of organizational support, task satisfaction, and effective leadership. Certain interventions, such as psychological debriefing, are specifically tailored to act as moderators of stress; but many moderators—such as physical fitness, strong group cohesion, and ample recreational assets—are essentially resources. Our model adopts many of the tenets in Hobfoll's (1995, 1997) Conservation of Resources theory. This approach postulates that those with the greatest resource pool are the most resilient when under stress, while those with the fewest resources are likely both to be more vulnerable to stress and to act defensively—and hence maladaptively—when faced with the loss of scarce resources. Groups that are under stress and have minimal resources may use existing resources inappropriately, unwisely, or destructively. Many support programs and interventions aim to either provide or replenish individual and group resources in the form of personal, social, informational, financial, materiel, or other assets.

2.2.3. Coping

Psychological coping has attracted a great deal of conceptual and research activity (Zeidner & Endler, 1996.) In this model, coping is regarded as the appraisal process whereby an individual evaluates a stressor, possibly classifies it as a threat or a challenge, and (if it is so classified) determines how to adapt and which coping resources to marshal. Much of this appraisal process may occur subconsciously and can be governed by habitual response patterns, including expectancies about specific stressors and about one's own ability to cope. The model views coping as a process with both trait (or personality) and situational components. We therefore accept that both the dispositional and the contextual approaches to determining coping responses have value. It is assumed that individuals have a range of coping behaviours available and that they will selectively use those behaviours depending on stressor characteristics, situational factors (such as prevailing group norms and organizational culture), and individual preferences and tendencies. At this stage of the project, greater emphasis is placed on the intraindividual approach to coping and appraisal—that is, attempting to identify basic behaviours and strategies used by military personnel on deployment. The study of group coping processes is a potentially valuable field for further research.

2.2.4. Outcomes

Ample research has documented the potentially deleterious effects of stress on well-being. Adverse outcomes in the physical, affective, cognitive, and social/behavioural arenas are widely recognized. A particular interest of the HDO project is the constellation of serious postdeployment reactions that constitutes post-traumatic stress disorder. In an effort to transcend the usual emphasis on health outcomes in studies of occupational stress, this model addresses several additional consequences, such as changes in commitment and morale. We envision that the project will eventually measure and predict key *performance* outcomes. But because peacekeeping missions can present extremely complex and demanding task environments, the process of identifying and operationalizing pragmatic, universal, and meaningful performance measures is inherently difficult. Many commanders are interested in morale and leadership outcomes, and as this chapter attests, considerable progress is being made in measuring such outcomes. Of course, many of the postulated outcomes may function dually—that is, they may also link back into the deployment cycle as moderators.

2.3. Research Design

The HDO project surveys are intended to be administered before deployment, during deployment (up to three times), and after deployment to all CF contingents that are deployed on peace support operations. Operational and resource constraints have sometimes required us to modify this plan, but in the two years since the project's inception, about 7,000 surveys have been completed. In addition, several component surveys from the project have been included in CF-wide personnel surveys in order to provide normative information on personnel who are not operationally deployed.

Surveys are administered by military psychologists. Pre- and postdeployment surveys are usually completed in barracks, while the three deployment surveys are usually administered on bases or in the field. Surveys are completed anonymously. To date, one or more stages of the surveys have been administered to five different contingents: four in Bosnia-Herzegovina and one in Haiti. Various measures are taken; some—such as critical incidents during the tour—are taken only once, while some are repeated at different stages. Other component instruments include measures of strain, stressors, coping techniques, serious stress reactions, perceived organizational support, unit climate, family issues, postdeployment adjustment issues, the deployment in perspective, and positive aspects of the deployment. A complete repeated-measures design is not feasible given the number of concepts addressed by the HDO model. But some of the measures are repeated, and one of these—unit climate—provides the data presented in this chapter.

3. THE UNIT CLIMATE PROFILE

Unit climate is a multidimensional construct that comprises individual- and group-level psychological characteristics that are presumed to exist in military units and to affect their performance. Many of the climate dimensions (for example, cohesion, morale, and style of supervision) are probably common to almost all work groups. Others (for example, combat readiness) may be suggested by the traditional military role, structure, and culture, and therefore may be unique to military organizations. To measure the climate dimensions of military units and subunits, the Canadian Forces has developed an instrument called the Unit Climate Profile (UCP). The Unit Climate Profile (UCP) is the cornerstone of the HDO project, in the sense that it is the major deliverable of interest to the project sponsor. Nevertheless, the value of the more comprehensive HDO project has now been recognized, and the UCP has become a subproject of the wider HDO study.

3.1. Development

The UCP was developed within a conceptual framework proposed by Wild (1988), who postulated that the human dimension of operational readiness rests on several psychological components, including (a) confidence, (b) proficiency (achieved through training and experience), and (c) understanding of and motivation toward combat missions. Each of these components may be mediated by aspects of leadership, such as leadership behaviours, perceptions of leadership competence, and perceptions of leaders' genuine concern for personnel under their command. Reeves and Hansen (1989) adopted this conceptual model to develop a psychometric instrument called the Human Dimension Combat Readiness Index—Experimental (HDCRI-X). Items for this instrument were drawn from focus group research and from other similar instruments used by U.S. and Israeli forces. Farley (1995) subsequently refined the HDCRI-X to create the initial version of the UCP. This study used the UCP-56, a version of the UCP that includes 56 Likert-type items (see Section 3.2, "Scales," for further details). The response scale has five categories, ranging from *strongly agree* through a neutral response to *strongly disagree*. Scores can range from –2 (very negative) through 0 (neutral) to +2 (very positive).

The UCP was pilot tested on an infantry company. Figure 2 shows the results of the two administrations: predeployment (48 hours before the company departed for a theatre of operations) and deployment (after five months in-theatre). Respondents reported feeling less positive about all climate dimensions on the second administration. In four of the eight dimensions, the difference was statistically significant. The final four subscales relate to confidence in leadership at different levels of command in the company.[3] The pilot study further demonstrated that morale is variable over time and indicated that the UCP is sensitive to these changes.

3.2. Scales

The UCP-56 incorporates eight dimensions: *Morale/Cohesion* (17 items), *Professionalism* (6 items), *Ideology* (6 items), *Leadership Skills* (12 items), and *Confidence in Leadership* at four levels (*section commander*—3 items; *platoon warrant officer*—6 items; *platoon commander*—3 items; and *company commander*—3 items).

Here are some examples of the kinds of items covered in each dimension:

- "My platoon is ready for combat." (Morale/Cohesion)
- "It feels good to be part of my platoon." (Morale/Cohesion)

---

[3] Subsequent research within the HDO project used variations of the Confidence in Leadership factor, including a single combined subscale comprising new items.

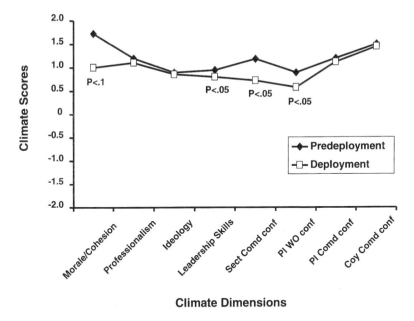

Climate Dimensions

FIGURE 2. Unit Climate Profile: Sample pilot study results.

- "I think I would perform better in battle than other members of my platoon." (Professionalism)

- "Differences in rank should not be important after hours." (Ideology)

- "My immediate supervisor lets other supervisors interfere with my work group." (Leadership Skills)

- "My Section Commander is respected by section members." (Confidence in Section Commander)

- "My Platoon Warrant Officer stands up for the troops." (Confidence in Platoon Warrant Officer)

- "In the event of combat, I have confidence in my Platoon Commander." (Confidence in Platoon Commander)

- "My Company Commander is respected by those in the company." (Confidence in Company Commander)

3.3. Utility of the UCP

The results of the UCP and other components of the HDO project are discussed with relevant commanders, allowing interpretation of the findings and the identification of opportunities to incorporate the information in the exercise of command. Trend analyses are conducted by comparing UCP profile dimensions and such other factors as stress levels over the stages of deployment. Figure 3 presents an actual UCP. Again, scores can range from –2 (very negative) through 0 (neutral) to +2 (very positive). For this infantry company, confidence in leadership (indicated by the four right-hand scales in Figure 3) tended to increase over the duration of the deployment. Compared to other companies in the same contingent, this group reported fewer disciplinary problems, repatriations, visits to sick parade, and other negative personnel outcomes. In one contingent, commanders requested that the instrument be expanded to include additional leadership dimensions (the UCP-62). A non–combat arms version of the UCP was developed and tested for support troops.

Clearly there are reasons to exercise discretion when reporting on certain components of the HDO project—in particular, with the UCP. In recognition of the sensitive nature of this information, no attributable results are provided outside the contingent. That is, information on individual units is offered only to those units' commanders, who may then use that information as they see fit. The CF's military psychologist in the Bosnia theatre of operations has conducted briefings on research findings, and DHRRE research officers have provided feedback to commanders in Haiti. But the sponsor receives no attributable data. In short, there is no intention to use the HDO project as a means of performance appraisal. DHRRE reports research findings to the sponsor and to appropriate agencies within the CF, but does so with an awareness of the sensitivities that even nonattributable data can entail.

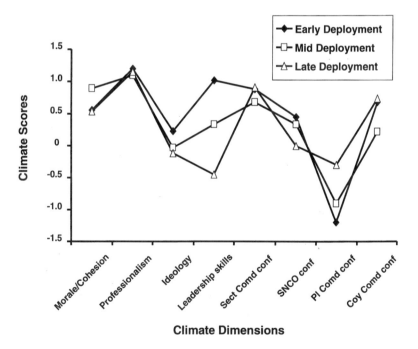

FIGURE 3. Unit Climate Profile for a deployed infantry company.

4. CURRENT STUDY

The analysis presented here uses UCP data from three CF contingents that were deployed on peace support operations in the middle to late 1990s. In response to a theoretical reformulation of unit climate dimensions and statistical analysis of the UCP-56, three new subscales—*Morale, Cohesion*, and *Confidence in Leadership*—were derived.

4.1. Subscales

The new subscales differ from the UCP's previous subscales in that Morale and Cohesion are now separate factors, while Confidence in Leadership has become a vertical factor (that is, it is drawn from different levels of leadership, as opposed to being drawn from a particular rank level). The Morale subscale comprises items that tap individual and platoon-level morale. The Cohesion subscale derives from items that tap mutual support and social interaction at the platoon level. The subscale rating Confidence in Leadership contains items that relate to the platoon commander, the platoon's senior noncommissioned officer (SNCO),[4] and the company commander.

4.2. Contingents

Each of the three contingents[5] was deployed for six months on a peace support operation sometime during the 1996–1998 period. One contingent served in Haiti; the other two were deployed to Bosnia. The Haiti contingent was made up of subunits comprising mainly francophone members. The Bosnia contingents consisted largely of anglophone members. The operational situations varied between and across contingents, as well as across time within contingents. None of the surveyed contingents were subjected to major armed conflict. Survey sample sizes ranged from a minimum of 200 to a maximum of 600. The Bosnia contingents comprised about 1,200 personnel; the Haiti contingent, 800. All contingents contained both combat arms subunits and support subunits, at a ratio of about 1:2. Most of the subunits were deployed from standing forces, although some subunits (notably military police and engineering) were made up of augmentees drawn from across the CF.

4.3. Results and Discussion

Figure 4 shows the three subscales for Contingent 1. Unfortunately, no predeployment scores were obtained for this contingent. The postdeployment measures were taken between six and seven months after the contingent returned to Canada. For this and all subsequent figures, the number 6 on the vertical axis represents a neutral score. Scores higher than 6 represent positive attitudes (for example,

---

[4] This new term—platoon SNCO—is more inclusive than the previously used "platoon warrant officer," as it allows the consideration of other senior NCO ranks such as sergeant.
[5] Ethical considerations preclude our providing more detailed information on the contingents surveyed.

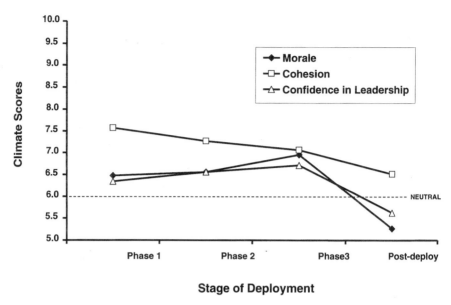

FIGURE 4. Climate subscale scores for Contingent 1.

positive morale), whereas scores lower than 6 represent negative attitudes. In Figure 4, all subscales show positive scores (higher than 6) during the three deployment phases—a welcome sign.

Figure 4 depicts some interesting trends. For example, the Morale subscale and the Confidence in Leadership subscale appear to covary quite closely, while the Cohesion subscale follows a more independent course. As morale and confidence in leadership increase from Phase 1 through to Phase 3, cohesion declines significantly, and as morale and confidence in leadership start to decline during the postdeployment phase, cohesion continues to decline as well. The significant drop in all scores in the postdeployment phase appears worthy of further analysis.[6] Note that although cohesion is in constant decline, it remains in the positive band during all phases.

Contingent 2's subscale scores appear in Figure 5. The most striking trend here is the significant drop in scores across all three subscales between predeployment and Phase 1. Once again, morale and confidence in leadership appear to covary in a similar pattern across most phases, except between Phases 2 and 3, where morale declines as confidence in leadership increases—a counterintuitive result. While confidence shows continual improvement during the deployment phases, it does not return to its predeployment level. Morale shows a slight upturn and a subsequent decline during deployment. Cohesion appears again to be an autonomous factor: it declines throughout the deployment cycle, and to a different degree than the other

[6] For this contingent's postdeployment survey results, see Murphy and Farley (1998).

subscales do. Interestingly, the scores for all three subscales reflect more positive attitudes toward these climate factors than were exhibited by Contingent 1.

Figure 6 presents Contingent 3's subscale scores. These results again show a marked covariance between morale and confidence in leadership, with an overall pattern of decline, followed by (slight) increase, followed by decline. Cohesion scores are much higher than those for the other two subscales, but this factor again declines constantly across the phases.

Figure 7 clearly shows the characteristic pattern for the Cohesion score across the three contingents. Although the contingents display different levels of cohesion, all share a remarkably similar consistent decline in this factor throughout the deployment cycle. The continued decline in cohesion during postdeployment, a surprising and disturbing finding, warrants further study. Perhaps soldiers get too much of one another during the close-quarters living that is typical of deployed operations. Or perhaps the characteristic influx of "new blood" into subunits following operational deployment creates additional tension among returned peacekeepers.

The three contingents' Confidence in Leadership subscale scores appear in Figure 8. Again, several distinct trends emerge. The scores decline significantly from predeployment to Phase 1 of the deployment in both contingents for which predeployment data are available. Confidence then consistently increases from Phase 1 to Phase 2. In the contingent for which we have postdeployment measures, this factor again displays a worrisome decline. The postdeployment declines for each subscale may indicate a general malaise or burnout syndrome among veterans of peace support operations—at least in this contingent.

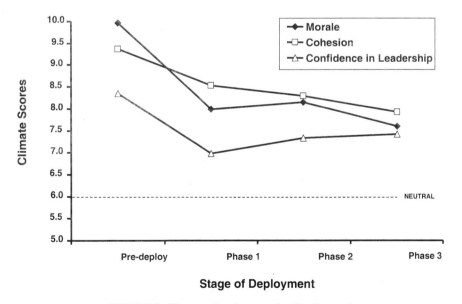

FIGURE 5. Climate subscale scores for Contingent 2.

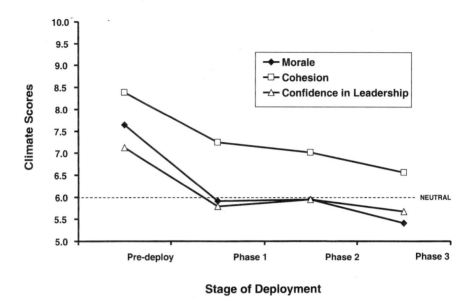

FIGURE 6. Climate subscale scores for Contingent 3.

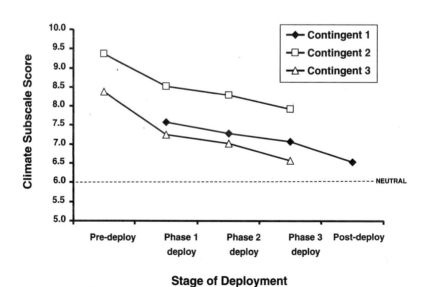

FIGURE 7. Cohesion subscale scores for all contingents.

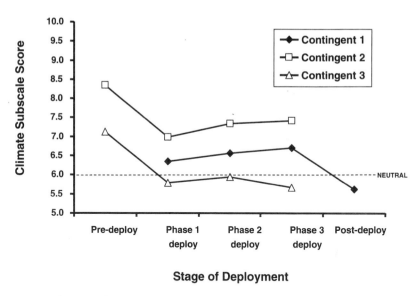

FIGURE 8. Confidence in Leadership subscale scores for all contingents.

The Morale subscale (see Figure 9) shows trends similar to those for Confidence in Leadership. Morale declines significantly between predeployment and Phase 1 in both contingents for which predeployment data are available. The scores consistently exhibit a small increase Phase 1 and Phase 2, but the changes between Phases 2 and 3 are more diverse. Discussions with commanders about these findings suggest that situation-specific characteristics of each deployment may account for the inconsistency. Discussions with deployed soldiers further suggest that a deployment's closing phase can be especially stressful, particularly if end-of-mission dates remain uncertain.

The preceding discussion highlights some interesting and consistent relationships. Of course, it may be misleading to talk about morale or cohesion or any unit climate factor for an entire contingent. Furthermore, we are not suggesting that every deployment will necessarily follow a fixed pattern. Figure 10 shows the UCP's sensitivity and the considerable complexity in human factors among individual subunits of the same contingent—in this case, Contingent 2 at mid-tour.

A few points should be emphasized about the results illustrated in Figure 10. The two infantry subunits have the highest Morale scores among the subunits shown. These two subunits consisted largely of regular service personnel, whereas the subunits with relatively low Morale scores comprised augmentees gathered from throughout the military. Augmentee units presumably had less time to develop cohesion and morale, and the scores tend to confirm that supposition. Interestingly, though, the Confidence in Leadership scores do not follow this pattern. The subunits display widely different scores on this subscale, with one augmentee unit

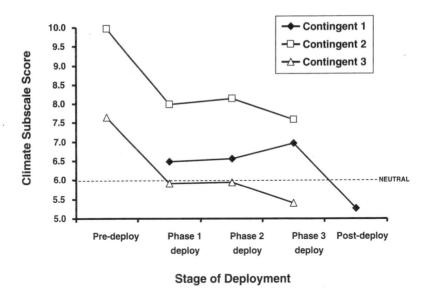

FIGURE 9. Morale subscale scores for all contingents.

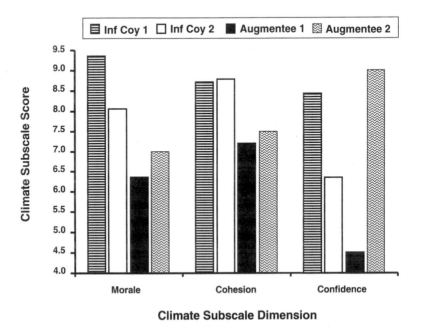

FIGURE 10. Comparison of subunit subscale scores for Contingent 2 at mid-tour.

(which might be, say, a military police detachment) exhibiting the highest level of confidence in leadership and the other showing a dramatically low score. These results suggest that morale and confidence in leadership are not necessarily strongly linked. Cohesion, which shows the least variation in score levels across units, once again displays considerable autonomy as a factor. Also interesting is the statistically significant difference between the two infantry companies on the Morale factor and the Confidence in Leadership factor. These companies were drawn from the same regiment, were billeted at the same location during deployment, and had similar operational duties. Yet discreet discussions confirmed that there were indeed tangible differences between the two infantry companies in morale and other factors.

5. CONCLUSIONS

There is great potential for the data being collected from the Human Dimension of Operations project. This chapter presents only a small sample of analyzed data from a single component of the project. Such findings as the lack of a consistent link between morale and confidence in leadership, the disconcerting malaise that seems to set in during the postdeployment phase, and the need to distinguish between morale and cohesion could all have an impact on training, policy, and support activities.

But the UCP is not without deficiencies. For example, its design limits its use to junior personnel, certain subscales tap more than one factor, and some critics maintain that the instrument focuses too narrowly on individual commanders. In an attempt to rectify these and other problems, we have developed and are currently testing a new version of the UCP. Designed for use by all ranks, the new UCP includes subscales that measure individual morale, satisfaction, and commitment; leadership effectiveness; and group morale, readiness, and performance. These measures were developed through concurrent theoretical reformulation and psychometric analysis during the 12 months in which the UCP-56 was being administered.

5.1. The Deployed Military Psychologist

The establishment of the *force military psychologist* position with the Canadian Contingent Stabilization Force (CCSFOR) has also played a part in helping the HDO project begin to fulfill its potential. This individual provides an effective conduit for channelling survey results back to commanders and can also integrate such data with information from other sources—sources that are available only to bona fide members of a contingent.

The military psychologist's role is to enhance the operational effectiveness of deployed units by applying behavioural science methods and practices. To date, the military psychologist's duties have included giving advice and instruction on managing and preventing fatigue, surviving in a hostage situation, and handling dead bodies; coordinating and conducting critical-incident debriefs and end-of-tour debriefs; counselling; conducting reactive research (for example, studying the impact of an alcohol policy on effectiveness); and administering HDO surveys. In June 1998, the military psychologist established a program designed to identify soldiers who are at high risk of developing serious postdeployment stress reactions after returning to Canada. In response to strong endorsement by commanders in the field, the chief of the land staff directed in October 1997 that a military psychologist be included in all future missions of battalion-size and larger groups mounted by the Canadian Army. The presence of military psychologists in operational theatres, though common in many military forces, is a relatively recent development in the Canadian Army.

5.2. The Future

As a dynamic long-term study, the HDO project is continually being improved. For example, the surveys for the current rotation to Bosnia have been redesigned into a digitally scannable format, and portable scanning technology is being acquired to allow more timely feedback of the results to commanders. It may well become possible to develop, administer, scan, and analyze small surveys within a day. When used in conjunction with other unit indicators, the UCP can enhance commanders' decision making and spearhead the monitoring of critical human dimensions of combat readiness within units both before and during operations. As the UCP is further refined, we intend to publish formal guidelines to help commanders interpret the new version of the instrument. Because the HDO project database now allows for complex analysis, we can examine relationships between the various components of the research model.

The HDO project clearly has significant future potential, and it is already paying dividends. It represents a rare research opportunity: the attempt to measure the impact of stress on military performance in authentic military environments. Each time we administer the survey, we are rewarded with useful information about the human dimension of operations. Component projects (such as measuring dimensions of unit climate) are helping commanders understand subunit dynamics and make command decisions. Component instruments (such as the Unit Climate Profile) are being employed in applied and other research projects. The growing database has been used in comparative research involving operations other than peacekeeping. Personnel who are not operationally deployed, along with those who have previous peacekeeping experience, are also being surveyed so that we can develop comparative norms and monitor the long-term impact of peacekeeping duties. Furthermore, the HDO model is suitable for causal modelling, which can reveal interrelationships among the numerous relevant constructs and hence provide information that aids in prediction. With such information, the CF can assess whether to develop and implement interventions and other programs (such as selecting personnel specifically for peacekeeping duties). The information could also help us design and target stress prevention programs for personnel who are at risk of serious postdeployment maladjustment. Programs could also be developed to address the more common stressors and subclinical stress reactions of generic peacekeeping duties—which, though milder, may nevertheless significantly reduce operational efficiency and interfere with the effective management and leadership of deployed personnel.

The HDO project will provide information that will help us design interventions at the individual, group, or organizational level to improve operational effectiveness and enhance the well-being of service personnel and their families. One of the project's major emphases involves developing valid ways to measure various aspects of unit climate. Commanding officers have already reported that they find the UCP to be a valuable aid. Current criticisms relate to the length of time between the survey's administration in a contingent and the provision of feedback to commanders. Technology is being acquired with a view to narrowing this time gap. It is hoped that commanders will soon be able to receive preliminary results within a few days after a survey has been administered.

Many commanders, especially those who have actively—and in some cases creatively—used information and advice drawn from the HDO project, have encouraged this chapter's authors to continue their efforts in applied operational research. But there remains considerable skepticism about the project, summed up by the comments of one recent survey respondent: "If a CO needs a questionnaire to gauge the morale of his men, he should not be a CO." The same soldier, however, commented adversely regarding several human factors in his unit, including leadership. In our opinion, the complexity of the findings provided by the Human Dimensions of Operations project to date only reinforces the need for regular, impartial empirical monitoring of various human factors. To extend Sun Tzu's (circa 490 BC/1988) famous dictum: *Know your enemy, know yourself, and know the human factors in your unit, so that in a hundred operations—be they battles or peace support—you will never fail.*

6. ACKNOWLEDGMENTS

The opinions expressed in this chapter are those of its authors and do not represent the official policy of the organizations with which the authors are affiliated.

We are indebted to the following people for assistance in various aspects of the research project from which this chapter was drawn: Steve Eyres, Claude Gingras, Tzvetanka Dobreva-Martinova, Colin Mombourquette, Alan Okros, Sue-Anne Robertson, Sharon Stairs, and André Thivierge.

7. REFERENCES

Adams-Roy, J. E. (1996). *CAPSS—Predicting success at Basic Flying Training: Cross-validation results* (Research Report 96-3). Willowdale, ON: Department of National Defence, Canadian Forces Personnel Applied Research Unit.

Bender, P., & Tseng, S. (1996). *Results of the 1996 Officer Force Reduction Program: Vol. 1. Overall results* (Research Note 96/02). Ottawa: Department of National Defence, Personnel Operational Research Team.

Bowers, C. A., Urban, J. M., & Morgan, B. B. (1992). *The study of crew coordination and performance in hierarchical team decision making* (Report TR-92-01). Orlando, FL: University of Central Florida, Team Performance Laboratory.

Davis, K. D. (1997). *Chief of Land Staff gender integration study: The regular force training and employment environment* (Sponsor Research Report 97-2). Ottawa: Department of National Defence, Personnel Research Team.

Davis, K. D. (1998). *Chief of Land Staff gender integration study: The experience of women who have served in the combat arms* (Sponsor Research Report 98-1). Ottawa: Department of National Defence, Personnel Research Team.

Ewins, J. E. (1997). *Canadian Forces Diversity Survey: A population analysis* (Technical Note 1/97). Ottawa: Department of National Defence, Personnel Research Team.

Eyres, S. A. T. (1997). *A plan to assess perceptions of improvements to quality of life in the Army* (Research Report 97-1). Ottawa: Department of National Defence, Personnel Research Team.

Farley, K. M. J. (1995). *Stress in military operations* (Working Paper 95-2). Willowdale, ON: Department of National Defence, Canadian Forces Personnel Applied Research Unit.

Farley, K. M. J., & Murphy, P. J. (1996). *Refinement and implementation of the Unit Climate Profile* (Briefing Note). Ottawa: Department of National Defence, Personnel Research Team.

Gal, R. (1986). Unit morale: From a theoretical puzzle to an empirical illustration—an Israeli example. *Journal of Applied Social Psychology, 16*(6), 549–564.

Gal, R., & Manning, F. J. (1987). Morale and its components: A cross-national comparison. *Journal of Applied Social Psychology, 17*(4), 369–391.

Hartle, A. E. (1989). *Moral issues in military decision making.* Lawrence, KS: University of Kansas Press.

Henderson, W. D. (1985). *Cohesion: The human element in combat.* Washington, DC: National Defense University Press.

Hobfoll, S. E. (1995). Conservation of resources and traumatic stress. In J. R. Freedy & S. E. Hobfoll (Eds.), *Traumatic stress: From theory to practice* (pp. 29–47). New York: Plenum Press.

Hobfoll, S. E. (1997, March). *Communal contexts of disaster and traumatic stress.* Paper presented at the Stress: Vulnerability and Resiliency Conference, Banff International Conference on Behavioural Science, Banff, AB.

Hobfoll, S. E., Spielberger, C. D., Breznitz, S., Figley, C., Folkman, S., Lepper-Green, B., Meichenbaum, D., Milgram, N. A., Sandler, I., Sarason, I., & van der Kolk, B. (1991). War-related stress: Addressing the stress of war and other traumatic events. *American Psychologist, 46*(8), 848–855.

Korpi, W. (1965). A note on the ability of military leaders to assess opinions in their units. *Acta Sociologica, 8,* 293–302.

Krueger, G. P. (1991). Sustained military performance in continuous operations: Combat fatigue, rest and sleep needs. In R. Gal & D. Mangelsdorff (Eds.), *Handbook of military psychology.* Chichester, U.K.: Wiley.

MacLennan, R. N. (1996). *Factor structure and validation of the CFOSQ* (Research Report 96-1). Willowdale, ON: Department of National Defence, Canadian Forces Personnel Applied Research Unit.

Manning, F. J. (1991). Morale, cohesion and esprit de corps. In R. Gal & D. Mangelsdorff (Eds.), *Handbook of military psychology* (pp. 453–470). Chichester, U.K.: Wiley.

Marshall, R. P. (1997). *A preliminary framework for managing stress in deployed operations* (Working Paper 12/97). Canberra, Australia: 1st Psychological Research Unit.

Mombourquette, C. J., Noonan, L. E., & Uchiyama, J. M. (1997). *Development of the Canadian Forces personnel appraisal system.* Ottawa: Department of National Defence, Personnel Research Team.

Montgomery, B. L. (1958). *The Memoirs of Field-Marshal the Viscount Montgomery of Alamein, K.G.* London: Collins.

Murphy, P. J., Dobreva-Martinova, T., & Farley, K. M. J. (1998a). *Factor structure of the Canadian Forces Occupational Stress Questionnaire: 1996 Omnibus Survey data.* Ottawa: Department of National Defence, Personnel Research Team.

Murphy, P. J., Dobreva-Martinova, T., & Farley, K. M. J. (1998b). *Selective item analysis of the Canadian Forces Occupational Stress Questionnaire: 1996 Omnibus Survey data—Work environment issues.* Ottawa: Department of National Defence, Personnel Research Team.

Murphy, P. J., & Farley, K. M. J. (1997). *Hostage survival skills for Canadian Forces personnel* (Operational Effectiveness Guide 97-1). Ottawa: Department of National Defence, Personnel Research Team.

Murphy, P. J., & Farley, K. M. J. (1998). *The postdeployment status of CF personnel: Preliminary findings* (Research Note 98-1). Ottawa: Department of National Defence, Personnel Research Team.

Murphy, P. J., Farley, K. M. J., & Dobreva-Martinova, T. (1997, October). *A conceptual approach to the study of stress in peacekeeping personnel.* Paper presented at the NATO Research and Technology Organization Aerospace Medical Panel Symposium on Aeromedical Support Issues in Contingency Operations, Rotterdam, Netherlands.

Murphy, P. J., & Mombourquette, C. J. (1997). *An analysis of personnel issues relating to service at CFS Alert* (Research Report 97-3). Ottawa: Department of National Defence, Personnel Research Team.

Murphy, P. J., & Mombourquette, C. J. (1998). *Fatigue, sleep loss and operational performance: A guide for commanders* (PRT Operational Effectiveness Guide 98-1). Ottawa: Department of National Defence, Personnel Research Team.

O'Brien, S. G. (1997). *PSO processing of applicants for occupation transfer to military police (MP 811): Interim selection procedure* (unpublished Technical Note). Ottawa: Department of National Defence, Personnel Research Team.

Pelchat, D. W. (1997). *Introduction of CAPSS and revised aircrew selection centre test procedures* (unpublished Technical Note). Ottawa: Department of National Defence, Personnel Research Team.

Reeves, D. T., & Hansen, R. J. (1989). *Development of the Human Dimension Combat Readiness Index— Experimental (HDCRI-X)* (Technical Note 10/89). Willowdale, ON: Department of National Defence, Canadian Forces Personnel Applied Research Unit.

Solomon, Z. (1993). *Combat stress reaction: The enduring toll of war.* New York: Plenum Press.

Stewart, N. K. (1988). *South Atlantic conflict of 1982: A case study in military cohesion* (Research Report 1469). Alexandria, VA: U.S. Army Research Institute for the Behavioral and Social Sciences.

Stouffer, S. A., Lumsdaine, A. A., Lumsdaine, M. H., Williams, R. N., Smith, J. L. K., Star, S. A., & Cottrel, L. S. (1949a). *The American soldier: Vol. 2. Combat and its aftermath.* Princeton, NJ: Princeton University Press.

Stouffer, S. A., Suchman, E. A., DeVinney, L. C., Star, S. A., & Williams, R. M. J. (1949b). *The American soldier: Vol. 1. Adjustment during army life.* Princeton, NJ: Princeton University Press.

Sun Tzu. (1988). *The art of war* (T. Cleary, Trans.). Boston: Shambhala. (Original work published circa 490 BC)

Tanner, L. (1996). *A synopsis of female participation in the Regular Force of the Canadian Forces* (Research Note 96-08). Ottawa: Department of National Defence, Personnel Operational Research Team.

Thivierge, J. A. A. (1998). *Development and administration of a questionnaire on conditions of service and quality of life in the Reserve* (Technical Note 98-2). Ottawa: Department of National Defence, Personnel Research Team.

Wild, W. (1988). *Proposal for studying the human dimension of combat readiness* (Technical Note 5/88). Willowdale, ON: Department of National Defence, Canadian Forces Personnel Applied Research Unit.

Winslow, D. (1997). *The Canadian Airborne Regiment in Somalia: A socio-cultural inquiry.* Ottawa: Public Works and Government Services Canada.

Wintle, J. (Ed.). (1989). *The dictionary of war quotations.* London: Hodder and Stoughton.

Xenophon. (1960). *Anabasis, Books 1–7* (C. L. Brownson, Trans.). London: Heinemann. (Original work published circa 394 BC; translation originally published 1918)

Zeidner, M., & Endler, N. S. (Eds.). (1996). *Handbook of coping: Theory, research, applications.* New York: Wiley.

CHAPTER 22

COPING WITH INTERROGATIONS

JON CHRISTIAN LABERG, JARLE EID, BJØRN HELGE JOHNSEN, LIEUTENANT BÅRD S. ERIKSEN, and LIEUTENANT KENNETH K. ZACHARIASSEN

1. INTRODUCTION

Sun Tzu (circa 490 BC/1988), among others, has emphasized the importance of obtaining information about the enemy from those who know the enemy best. Throughout the history of warfare, the capturing and interrogation of enemy soldiers has thus provided a vital source of information (Keegan, 1993). A prisoner of war (POW) can potentially provide invaluable facts about the status of the adversary, and a number of methods for tapping this information can be used: formal interrogations, informal chats, or unobtrusive surveillance (Watson, 1978). The flow of information and its value during this process will depend on a number of factors, including the knowledge and skill of the interrogator, the resistance and fighting spirit of the prisoner, and the nature of the interactions between the two (Gal & Mangelsdorff, 1991; Richardson, 1978).

A substantial proportion (from 8 to 10 percent) of soldiers who take part in current international operations are taken as hostages (Flach & Ziljmans, 1997); generally, soldiers have problems coping with this situation. One reason for this difficulty is the sense of lack of control (Hillman, 1981) that results when a soldier is

JON CHRISTIAN LABERG, JARLE EID, and BJØRN HELGE JOHNSEN • *Royal Norwegian Naval Academy, P. O. Box 25, N-5034 Ytre Laksevåg, Norway and University of Bergen, Christiesgt. 12, N-5015 Bergen, Norway* LIEUTENANT BÅRD S. ERIKSEN *and* LIEUTENANT KENNETH K. ZACHARIASSEN • *Royal Norwegian Naval Academy, P. O. Box 25, N-5034 Ytre Laksevåg, Norway*

The Human in Command: Exploring the Modern Military Experience,
edited by McCann and Pigeau, Kluwer Academic/Plenum Publishers, New York, 2000.

taken out of a predictable environment and is faced with uncertainty, fear, and fatigue, as well as possible sensory deprivation and physical harm, with little possibility of influencing the future (Strentz, 1984, 1987). In addition, reduced self-efficacy expectations (Bandura, 1997) and inadvertent "slips" may also contribute to defeat.

Despite the international agreements and formal conventions regarding the interrogation of POWs—NATO (1989, 1994a, 1994b), The Hague Conventions (Hague Conference, 1999), the Geneva Conventions (ICRC, 1983), and the U.N. *Universal Declaration of Human Rights* (United Nations, 1948)—reality is at times different (Mangell, 1992). POWs know that they must protect information about their own troops, yet they fear both the pressure from the enemy if they resist interrogation and the consequences for their own troops if they do not. Interestingly, although many will yield to the pressure, it is known that many prisoners won't (McGrath, 1975). Thus, an important challenge for both operational and human purposes is to understand the psychological mechanisms at work in this situation.

Considerable resources have been devoted to refining the various methods for manipulating POWs into compromising their own forces—methods based on psychological principles developed and elaborated during World War II (Watson, 1978). For example, Watson (1978) refers to statements made by a German interrogator, who indicates that he had used techniques that were aimed at creating a relaxed atmosphere in which imprisoned fighter pilots did not realize that they were being interrogated. Most of the available knowledge about interrogations stems from anecdotal material, primarily from the Korean War. Watson (1978) concludes that a majority of the POWs in the Korean War did provide information they were supposed to withhold. Referring to Biederman's interviews with 220 pilots who were interrogated by Chinese Communists, Watson (1978) notes that more than half of the interrogations lasted for more than 24 hours, while 10 percent lasted for more than a month. Forceful methods (torture) were considered less effective than nonforceful methods, unless pain was self-inflicted—as, for example, when prisoners were forced to assume a stressful position over time. Almost all prisoners were involved in conversations with the interrogators, even if such interactions were not part of the code of conduct. Biederman concluded that total silence was probably far more stressful than talking—even if the latter approach meant saying only a few words. Interrogators may thus manipulate a prisoner by taking advantage of the prisoner's need to speak and to please the interrogator to some extent.

Interrogators may thus use *direct* strategies, *indirect* strategies, or a combination of both, in order to make prisoners talk. Direct methods usually include straightforward questions about troops, weapons, names of commanding officers, and operational information, using various degrees of brutality (Peters & Nichol, 1992). Indirect methods may include inducing frustration or the use of deception—for example, pretending to help or support the prisoner by acting as, say, a nurse, a fellow prisoner, or a journalist, thereby reducing the prisoner's awareness of the purpose of the contact (Watson, 1978). It must be noted that trained interrogators would not regard direct and indirect strategies as separate approaches; an interrogator's strategy for interrogating each POW will be based on a synergy between the two strategies—taking account of the POW's personality.

In essence, therefore, an interrogator's goal is to reduce prisoners' resistance by manipulating their sense of reality and identity. The prisoner's strategy, correspondingly, is to resist these manipulations, maintain a sense of reality, and protect his or her identity as a soldier. The underlying assumption is that a prisoner who is aware that the enemy will use any available means to gather information will have a better chance of resisting even indirect methods of interrogation. On a practical level, a prisoner can achieve success chiefly by two methods: first, by restricting his or her communication to only that information specified in the Geneva Convention (that is, name, rank, military number, and birth date); and second, by remaining as "invisible" as possible in order to reduce his or her attractiveness as a source of information to the enemy. The interrogators may be expected to focus on those prisoners who seem most likely to provide relevant information as quickly as possible (Flach & Vullinghs, 1996).

Most military units provide their soldiers with a lecture on the theory of interrogation; fewer units also provide practical training for such incidents (Ramsay, 1996). Although practical training in resisting interrogation is generally regarded as important for operational skills, unfortunately, there is a lack of empirical data supporting this assumption. Such data could provide a basis for developing better education programs for coping with POW situations—for example, training in techniques for concealing vital information. Training could also be expected to improve performance in a number of other ways: by providing an opportunity to rehearse and automate desirable behaviour; by increasing knowledge about the tactics of the interrogators and thereby increasing perceived coping; by reducing the stressful effects of the situation (for example, fear); and by reducing the negative effects on the soldier if information is compromised (Strentz, 1984, 1987). The object of the present study, therefore, was to test the hypothesis that practical training in a realistic situation, including feedback from experienced officers of the Norwegian special forces, would help soldiers to cope better during interrogations than would simply receiving instruction provided in lectures.

The study was designed as a part of the annual ranger maneuver at the Royal Norwegian Naval Academy (RNoNA) in Norway. An element in this maneuver is the experience of being captured by special forces and kept in a simulated POW camp for about 24 hours. Cadets are exposed to a number of physical and psychological stressors, including, among other things, interrogation. The cadets are prepared for this part of the maneuver, although they do not know in detail what incidents they will face. In addition to their general education in warfare, leadership, ethics, and military psychology at the RNoNA, cadets receive lectures about interrogation methods and POW camps. However, they do not receive any specific training in coping with interrogation before participating in the ranger maneuver. To our knowledge, there were no data previously available on cadets' performance during interrogation, but anecdotal information indicated that a large proportion of the cadets generally did compromise their information. Therefore, the maneuver provided an opportunity to measure the effects of a practical training intervention, as well as the baseline effects of the theoretical training. We were also interested in the effects of *indirect* versus *direct* interrogations, with a view to determining whether there would be any modification of the POWs' behaviour as a result of these different interrogation methods. By indirect methods, we mean the use of deception to gather information from the prisoner. We are unaware of any other experimental study of this kind having been undertaken.

2. METHOD

2.1. Subjects

Fifty-eight cadets at the Royal Norwegian Naval Academy took part in an eight-day ranger maneuver in which a simulated prisoner-of-war training exercise was included. All cadets had had a minimum of two years of previous service and training before entering the RNoNA, and they had been stringently selected for admission.

The cadets had been divided into seven teams of about eight members each at the start of the academic year, with each team's composition balanced with regard to occupational branch, and these teams were well established by the time of the ranger maneuver. It was therefore decided to keep the established teams as units for the study, allocating three teams to the experimental condition and four to the control condition. The experimental group numbered 23 cadets, and the control group 35.

2.2. Procedure

To determine whether practical training would improve performance during the interrogation sessions that were included in the ranger maneuver, three teams of cadets (the experimental group) were randomly selected to participate in a pre-training interrogation session, while the remaining four teams (the control group) participated in the regular academy briefing only. The cadets were not aware of this manipulation, and the control group received no information about the pretraining session. Both groups received lectures and a brief demonstration of various forms of interrogation (that is, the regular academy briefing) before the ranger maneuver started.

2.2.1. Pretraining Interrogation Session

The pretraining interrogation session was held at a fortress in the Bergen area about three weeks before the ranger maneuver. Unaware of the actual purpose of the trip, the experimental group was assigned to a bus trip to the fortress. En route, the bus drove into an ambush; all the cadets were taken as prisoners by special forces. This attack was performed with speed and professionalism, using blank ammunition, grenades, and other effects. Prisoners were treated roughly; after being handcuffed and blindfolded, they were driven to a barracks within the fortress. There the prisoners were stripped, dressed in special prisoner clothes, and finally placed in stress positions in small groups in several bunkers. Loud noise (clips of various radio programs in foreign languages, distorted music, and so on) was played in the background, and the prisoners were not allowed to communicate with one another. During the next eight hours, each prisoner was subjected to interrogation sessions, with "rough" and "soft" interrogations being run in an unpredictable pattern. Most prisoners were also exposed to deceptive plots. The pretraining session lasted for a total of ten hours, including eight hours of interrogations and a two-hour debrief session with the head of the special forces who were performing the interrogations. Each POW was subjected to at least two interrogations, one "rough" and one "soft." Time constraints prevented interrogators from conducting purely indirect interrogations, but the "soft" interrogations involved deceptive elements common to an indirect approach. Each interrogation lasted between five and fifteen minutes.

2.2.2. The Ranger Maneuver

The ranger maneuver was an eight-day continuous exercise during which each team participated in a series of infantry disciplines and other tasks. Cadets were permitted only a minimum of food and sleep, and team members took turns as team leader every 24 hours. The physical and mental demands on the cadets were high, and the cadets were required to solve a number of problems and to prepare and perform a number of military missions during the maneuver. Senior officers tracked each team, observing and correcting the team's performance.

2.2.3. The Interrogation Session

During the ranger maneuver, an interrogation session was performed on each of three consecutive days, with a third of the cadets (one troop, comprising either two or three teams) participating each day. Since the level of sleep deprivation was not the same for teams who participated on different days, one of the experimental teams was allocated to each day. Each troop was captured in the morning, while riding on a truck. The procedure for the capturing and imprisonment of the POWs was as described above for the pretraining session, except that the POW camp was located outdoors in the maneuver area. The interrogators were specially trained at the Norwegian Defense Intelligence and Security School (NoDISS). Each prisoner underwent four interrogations during the night, and the troop was debriefed and released in the morning. The interrogators were not aware of the experimental design, or that any cadets had had pretraining.

The interrogations were videotaped, and neutral observers scored prisoner communications as one of four types: *Compromising Statements*; *Big 4* (name, rank, military number, and birth date); *Irrelevant Material*; or *Total Silence*. The observers also coded interrogations as *Direct* or *Indirect*. The main dependent variable was the percentage of Compromising Statements made by the prisoner. In addition to the actual communication, we also measured prisoners' ability to cope with the interrogations (using a 10-point scale), as scored by both the interrogator and the observers. Finally, the observers measured time in interrogation.

2.3. Questionnaires

Before starting on the ranger maneuver, each cadet completed a questionnaire that included several standard instruments that were required for other studies (for example, a 30-item Coping Style Questionnaire, and questions pertaining to self-efficacy expectations for the maneuver). At the end of the maneuver, a second questionnaire was used to evaluate their experiences and to measure potential after-effects of participating in the exercise. In particular, cadets evaluated their own performance during the interrogation sessions, using a 10-point scale. Interrogators evaluated each cadet after each interrogation session.

3. RESULTS

The statistical analyses included Yates's chi-square, and two-way analysis of variance (ANOVA). Significant main effects and interactions were followed up by LSD tests.

Mean scores are based on an unequal number of subjects per session. This attrition is due to the fact that the interrogators focused only on those POWs from whom they believed they would be able to obtain further information. The number of subjects in each session is presented in Table 1.

Figure 1 shows the percentages of the four types of communication broken down by condition. Whereas 54 percent of the communications were categorized as Compromising in the control group, only 12 percent were Compromising in the experimental group; this difference was statistically significant. There was no difference in the amount of Irrelevant Material, which made up 26 percent of the communications in the control group and 22 percent in the experimental group. The Big 4 represented only 9 percent of the communications in the control group, but 61 percent in the experimental group—another statistically significant difference. Finally, 11 percent of the communications in the control group and 4 percent of those in the experimental group were Total Silence.

Figure 2 shows the communications broken down by type of interrogation: direct and indirect. Generally, the experimental (pretrained) group performed better than the control group during direct interrogations, having, for example, no

Table 1.   Number of Subjects per Session

	1	2	3	4
Experimental group	23	21	19	3
Control group	34	33	19	7

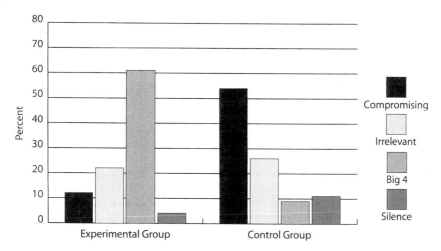

FIGURE 1. Types of communications by condition.

instances of Compromising statements and a larger proportion of Big 4 statements. Indirect interrogation had the effect of significantly reducing Big 4 communications in both groups (compared to direct interrogation): from 24 percent to 0 percent in the control group, and from 61 percent to 5 percent in the experimental group. Moreover, the percentage of Compromising statements increased under indirect interrogation from 22 percent to 37 percent in the control group, and from 0 percent to 15 percent in the experimental group. All these differences were statistically significant.

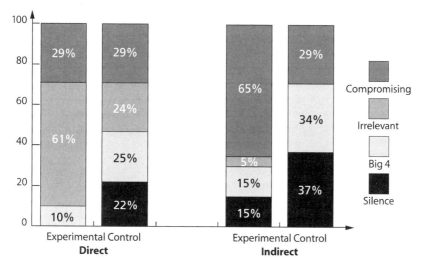

FIGURE 2. Types of communications during direct and indirect interrogation.

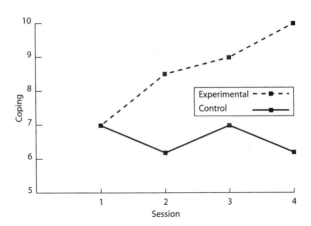

FIGURE 3. Ability to cope with interrogation (interrogators' assessments).

The interrogators' assessments of prisoners' coping ability are shown in Figure 3. Both groups scored equally well during the first interrogation (Session 1), but interestingly, prisoners in the experimental group (that is, those with pretraining) were assessed as coping increasingly better in successive sessions, while the coping ability of the control group was relatively unchanged. A two-way ANOVA on coping was performed with Session (1 to 3) as the repeated measure factor[1] and Group (experimental versus control) as the between-subjects factor. A significant main effect of Group was found, attributable to higher coping scores in the experimental group (7.75) compared with the control group (6.04). There was no significant main effect of Session. However, there was a significant interaction between Group and Session, due to the different patterns of change in coping over sessions. Follow-up tests revealed that the groups were significantly different in both Sessions 2 and 3.

The interrogators' and cadets' evaluations of coping were analyzed using a two-way MANOVA with a 2 (interrogators versus cadets) by 2 (experimental group versus control group) design. The interrogator's score was taken as the average score given to each cadet across four sessions, and the cadet's score was the cadet's post hoc evaluation of his or her own coping. The analysis revealed an effect of pretraining, with significantly higher coping scores in the experimental group compared to the control group. This effect was evident for both the interrogators' and the cadets' evaluations of coping, although the cadets' self-assessments were higher than the assessments they received from the interrogators (see Figure 4).

The mean duration of the interrogation sessions for the two groups is shown in Figure 5. On average, all cadets spent approximately 5 minutes in the first session. Subsequently, time in interrogation was higher for the control group. A two-way ANOVA confirmed this impression; there was a significant main effect of Group due to the longer durations for control group interrogations compared with those

[1] Due to the small number of subjects in Session 4, that session was excluded from the analysis of variance.

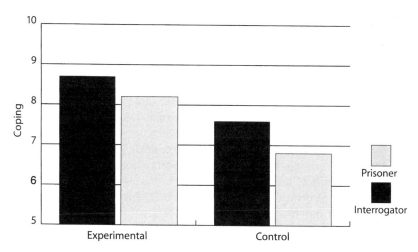

FIGURE 4. Coping (cadets' and interrogators' assessments).

undergone by the experimental group. During Session 3, the control group spent more than twice the time (32 minutes versus 15 minutes, respectively) in interrogation compared with the experimental group. A significant main effect of Session was attributed to changes in duration of interrogations across sessions. There was no significant interaction effect.

4. DISCUSSION

The objective of this study was to test the hypothesis that practical training would assist prisoners in coping with interrogation. The results showed that the experimental group (that is, the group that had been pretrained) made significantly fewer

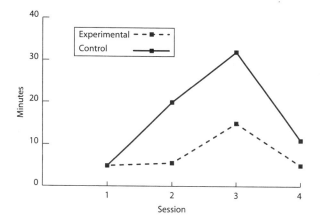

FIGURE 5. Duration of interrogation (observers' monitoring).

Compromising statements than the control group (12 percent versus 54 percent). Pretraining had a stronger beneficial effect when direct methods rather than indirect methods of interrogation were used, although the pretrained group still did significantly better in all cases.

Since these results are silent on the time perspective of coping with interrogations, it should be added that of the three POWs in the pretrained group who compromised, two did so during an indirect interrogation that was conducted only a few minutes before the end of the exercise.

In addition, the pretrained group scored significantly higher on the interrogators' assessments of coping, and spent significantly shorter time in interrogation. This latter difference may have occurred because the interrogators eventually discounted the pretrained group as being unavailable or uninteresting for further interrogation. This result may have important implications for POWs.

One mechanism that might explain the positive effect of pretraining is the development of an effective *schema* for this kind of situation. Schemas are mental representations of categories of objects, events, and people. For example, in a person who has developed a schema for "baseball game," hearing those two words might activate whole clusters of information, including the rules of the game, images of players, and so on. There are several types of schemas (Searleman & Herrmann, 1994); some take the form of a *script*, which contains knowledge about how common events unfold. It is possible that the cadets who participated in the pretraining session had developed a better script for the interrogations, and therefore were more able to resist the pressure to reveal information. Although the effectiveness of the script developed after pretraining might have been somewhat reduced by the slightly different setting, the pretrained group was better able to detect an interrogation in a different context (that is, an indirect interrogation) than the control group, who had not received extra training (15 percent of Compromising statements versus 37 percent; see Figure 2).

According to Bandura (1997), the expectations that are acquired about the probability of success in a given situation will largely determine the outcome in that situation. Bandura calls these expectations *self-efficacy expectations*; a person's expectations of success in a given situation may be enough to create that success and even to blunt the impact of minor failures. Self-efficacy beliefs may play an important role in the actual coping ability of prisoners in extreme situations, such as wartime interrogations under harsh conditions.

One of the major stressors in the ranger maneuver setting used in this experiment was sensory deprivation. There are an abundance of data showing that low stimulus levels create a need for stimulation (Zubeck, 1969), a need that in this setting might have been satisfied to some extent by social contact through talking. However, the social contact was channelled entirely through the interrogator, and the interrogator also controlled what was discussed: this arrangement might have resulted in the making of some compromising statements. This conclusion is strengthened by the fact that the three prisoners in the pretrained group who compromised did so during indirect interrogations. It should be noted that the totally silent group probably demonstrated the most irrational behaviour. By remaining silent, they increased their own sensory deprivation; in addition, their silence ensured that they would not be given POW status.

Practical training thus seems to reduce compromise in an interrogation situation. This result both suggests the need for further understanding of POWs' behaviour and communication, and also gives us valuable data to contribute to future education in this special field. However, it should be noted that this study evaluated coping during a brief interrogation session only (less than 24 hours); longer periods of interrogations are likely to produce different results (McGrath, 1975). Nonetheless, it could be argued that the ability to withstand compromise for 24 hours may be of great operational value, especially during war. Further studies are needed to clarify the effects of long-term interrogations and imprisonment, as well as the mechanisms at work in these kinds of situations.

5. CONCLUSION

We conclude that practical training had a significant impact on cadets' ability to cope with interrogation in this simulated POW situation. A possible explanation for this effect is that cadets with pretraining had developed a script for this situation, and that higher self-efficacy expectations assisted them in coping.

6. REFERENCES

Bandura, A. (1997). *Self-efficacy: The exercise of control*. New York: W. H. Freeman.

Flach, A., & Vullinghs, H. F. M. (1996). *Prisoners of war and soldiers taken hostage: Occurrence and prevention of negative psychological after-effects*. The Hague, Netherlands: Royal Netherlands Army (RNLA), Behavioural Sciences Department.

Flach, A., & Ziljmans, A. (1997). Psychological consequences of being taken hostage during peace operations. In J. L. Soeters & J. H. Rovers (Eds.), *NL ARMS (Netherlands Annual Review of Military Studies) 1997: The Bosnian experience* (pp. 141–151). Breda, Netherlands: Royal Netherlands Military Academy.

Gal, R., & Mangelsdorff, A. D. (Eds.). (1991). *Handbook of military psychology*. Chichester, U.K.: Wiley.

Hague Conference on Private International Law. (1999). *The Hague Conventions on Private International Law* [On-line]. Available: http://www.hcch.net/e/conventions/

Hillman, R. (1981). The psychopathology of being held hostage. *American Journal of Psychiatry 138*, 1193–1197.

ICRC (International Committee of the Red Cross). (1983). *Basic rules of humanitarian law in armed conflicts (Geneva Conventions and their additional Protocols)* [On-line]. Available: http://www.icrc.org/eng/party_gc

Keegan, J. (1993). *A history of warfare*. New York: Random House/Vintage.

Mangell, L. (1992). *Irakgislan och deres anhöriga ett år efteråt* [The Iraqi hostages and their affiliates one year later].

McGrath, J. (1975). *Prisoner of war: Six years in Hanoi*. Annapolis, MD: Naval Institute Press.

NATO (North Atlantic Treaty Organization). (1989, May 16). *Treatment of exercise prisoners of war during NATO exercises, with Annex A and B* (STANAG 2074). Brussels, Belgium: NATO.

NATO (North Atlantic Treaty Organization). (1994a, June 28). *Procedures for dealing with prisoners of war* (STANAG 2044). Brussels, Belgium: NATO.

NATO (North Atlantic Treaty Organization). (1994b, December 6). *Interrogation of prisoners of war* (STANAG 2033). Brussels, Belgium: NATO.

Peters, J., & Nichol, J. (1992). *Tornado down*. London, U.K.: Penguin.

Ramsay, J. (1996). *SAS: The soldiers' story*. London, U.K.: Macmillan.

Richardson, F. (1978). *Fighting spirit: Psychological factors in war*. London, U.K.: Leo Cooper.

Searleman, A., & Herrmann, D. (1994). *Memory from a broader perspective*. New York: McGraw-Hill.

Strentz, T. (1984). *Preparing the person with high potential for victimization as a hostage. FBI Law Enforcement Bulletin*, 183–208.

Strentz, T. (1987, November). A hostage psychological survival guide. *FBI Law Enforcement Bulletin*.

Sun Tzu. (1988). *The art of war* (T. Cleary, Trans.). Boston: Shambhala. (Original work published circa 490 BC)

United Nations. (1948). *Universal Declaration of Human Rights* [On-line]. Available: http://www.un.org/Overview/rights.html

Watson, P. (1978). *War on the mind: The military use and abuse of psychology*. New York: Basic Books.

Zubeck, J. P. (1969). *Sensory deprivation: Fifteen years of research*. New York: Appleton.

CHAPTER 23

STRESSORS FACED BY COMMANDERS IN THREE OPERATIONAL ENVIRONMENTS
The Gulf, Bosnia, and Northern Ireland

GLYNIS M. BREAKWELL

1. BACKGROUND

The findings reported in this chapter are extracted from a series of studies conducted since 1993 by the author and Major General Keith Spacie. These studies have focused on the stressors experienced by senior British Army commanders in three operational environments: the Gulf War, Bosnia–Herzegovina[1] (during humanitarian and peace support operations), and Northern Ireland (in preceasefire and non-ceasefire periods). Of interest are the stressors' effects on decision-making processes and on command effectiveness. By recording the commanders' experiences in these environments, the problems they encounter, and the methods they use to overcome those problems, we hope to discover ways to improve the practice of command. This research aims to increase understanding of the challenges faced by commanders in

---

[1] Officially the Federal Republic of Bosnia and Herzegovina; hereafter generally referred to as Bosnia.

GLYNIS M. BREAKWELL • *Centre for Defence Psychology, School of Human Sciences, University of Surrey, Guildford, United Kingdom, GU2 5XH*

The Human in Command: Exploring the Modern Military Experience,
edited by McCann and Pigeau, Kluwer Academic/Plenum Publishers, New York, 2000.

different operational contexts, including the characteristics that commanders need in order to be effective.

Our studies make a distinction between *stress* and *stressors*. The word stress has been misused so often in common parlance that its precise meaning has become vague and distorted. In our studies and in this chapter, we define stress as a subjective state that occurs in an individual who is faced with demands that he or she finds impossible to satisfy (Cooper, 1986). The demands can call for physical action, mental agility, or emotional strength. The defining characteristic of stress, however, is that the individual *feels* incapable of satisfying the demands. Stress is therefore a subjective phenomenon. The demands that induce stress in one individual will not necessarily cause another to react the same way. Stress reactions are idiosyncratic, but can include physiological, psychological, and behavioural changes (Brown & Campbell, 1994). The precise pattern of symptoms will be determined by the sources of the stress (that is, the demands that cannot be met), by the individual's history (that is, past experiences), and by the context in which the stress must be faced. The first of these factors, the sources of stress, are termed the *stressors*—that is, those features of an individual's experience that have the capacity to induce stress reactions. They are deemed to be stressors if the individual involved reports that they have actually resulted in stress symptoms. This chapter focuses on the type and magnitude of the stressors reported by commanders in the three operational contexts investigated.

2. METHOD

This research was designed to tap the full complexity of a commander's experiences in operational tours—particularly experiences that involved intense conflict where lives were at risk. Respondents were interviewed individually, sometimes in the context of the theatre of operation during the tour, but more often at the end of the tour. Interviews were usually tape-recorded (with the respondent's agreement) to allow for subsequent in-depth analysis. Interviews typically lasted between 1.5 and 2 hours, although some were much longer, and each interview was divided into two stages. In Stage 1, both the author and Major General Spacie interviewed the respondents. In Stage 2, Major General Spacie withdrew, in order to allow respondents to discuss more sensitive issues concerning stressor experiences and reactions. Anonymity was assured for all respondents. To reinforce this promise, material collected in Stage 2 of the interviews was not disclosed to Major General Spacie.

In the Bosnia and Northern Ireland studies, all respondents completed a short questionnaire just before the interview session ended. The questionnaire required that they rate their experiences during the target tour (the tour that was the topic of the interview), and then compare that tour on a number of dimensions with other operational tours that they had previously completed. The questionnaire items were developed from the interviews conducted in the Gulf War study (see Section 3, "Interview Samples"). Each item referred to one of the stressors reported by interviewees as having been significant during the Gulf War's Operation Desert Storm.

The results presented in this chapter are drawn primarily from analyses of questionnaire data from the Bosnia and Northern Ireland studies. Breakwell and Spacie (1997) present some of the conclusions from the qualitative analyses of interview material from the Gulf War and Bosnia studies.

3. INTERVIEW SAMPLES

Three sets of interviews were conducted and analyzed:

Gulf War: During the 1993–95 period, we interviewed 51 officers about their experiences in the Gulf War. Our interviewees represented 83 percent of the senior operational commanders and principal staff officers and 76 percent of their administrative and logistics counterparts deployed in Operation Granby by the British Army. Senior officers from all ranks above major were represented in this sample, and their experience of stressors formed the basis for items in the questionnaires that we subsequently administered to officers who served in Bosnia and Northern Ireland.

Bosnia: A total of 47 officers who served in Bosnia as part of Operation Grapple (deployments 1, 2, 4, 5, and 6) were interviewed during 1995 and 1996. The sample included virtually all commanders and key staff officers from the operation's unit, one-star, and three-star levels, as well as a representative cross-section of subunit commanders and one warrant officer.

Northern Ireland: In 1997 and 1998, we interviewed 51 officers who had served in Northern Ireland. The sample comprised the then-current brigade commanders and their chiefs of staff, together with their immediate predecessors; the chief of staff for the British Army's headquarters in Northern Ireland; a majority of the unit commanding officers who were then serving or had recently served in-theatre; and one company commander.

Although the sample sizes may appear small, they constitute a substantial percentage of the senior British Army officers involved in these three operations since 1993. Table 1 shows the breakdown of the samples by rank.

4. OPERATIONAL CONTEXT IN BOSNIA AND NORTHERN IRELAND

The British Army deployment to Bosnia, code-named Operation Grapple, followed a June 1992 decision by the U.N. Security Council to send a humanitarian force led by NATO (the North Atlantic Treaty Organization) comprising French, Canadian, British, and Spanish troops to Bosnia–Herzegovina. The U.K. element of this force

Table 1. Breakdown of Interview Samples by Rank

	Gulf War	Bosnia	Northern Ireland
Lieutenant General	1	1	—
Major General	1	—	—
Brigadier	5	10	7
Colonel	7	—	—
Lieutenant Colonel	27	18	38
Major	10	17	6
Warrant Officer 1	—	1	—

consisted of an armoured infantry battalion, a medium reconnaissance squadron, a reduced engineer regiment, a composite logistics regiment, and a one-star command group provided by brigade headquarters in Germany. The British force initially deployed in November 1992 for a six-month tour, a tour that has been renewed every six months since then. In 1994, the U.K. infantry element was increased by a further battalion (mechanized); at the same time, the reconnaissance component and the engineers were each increased to a full regiment. A number of other countries also contributed contingents at that point. Command of the multinational force rotated among the participating countries, and the command structure changed repeatedly between 1992 and 1995 (the period when our interviewees were in-theatre).

At first, the military forces operated with a peacekeeping mandate in support of the United Nations High Commissioner for Refugees (UNHCR),[2] their primary task being to ensure delivery of supplies to those who needed aid. With the 1993 establishment of U.N.-designated "safe areas" (around five Bosnian towns, as well as the city of Sarajevo), the military forces assumed a more positive protection role, although they were still forbidden to intervene actively, other than through negotiation. In February 1994, a general ceasefire between the Bosnian Croat and the Bosnian Muslim forces changed the pattern of operations (at Op Grapple's deployment 4); but the Cessation of Hostilities Agreement signed in mid-1994 was short-lived. After its breakdown, the Bosnian Serbs took military hostages from U.N. forces, NATO initiated air strikes, British troops withdrew from Goražde (one of the U.N. safe areas), and the United Nations deployed a heavily armed Rapid Reaction Force together with other units to reinforce in-theatre assets. By September 1995, the British force in Bosnia comprised 8,800 personnel (up from 3,500 in April that year). Early in Op Grapple, British troops were deployed to Bosnia with little theatre-specific training. By the close of the period studied, the British Army had developed training packages that dealt comprehensively with the military issues salient in Bosnia.

Operations in Northern Ireland differ from those in Bosnia in a number of ways. For example, only U.K. forces have been involved, and they have worked

---

[2] The U.N.-led agency for humanitarian assistance in the former Yugoslavia.

closely with the Royal Ulster Constabulary, which has operational primacy. Because operations in the Province have been ongoing for nearly 30 years, individuals have accumulated considerable experience; the operational base has become sophisticated; and procedures are well honed. For members of the British Army, General Service tours in Northern Ireland typically last either 6 months (roulement) or 24 months (resident). Resident troops may be accompanied by their families. Home Service (Royal Irish) troops also operate in Northern Ireland. Members of these troops may have either full-time or part-time appointments, but cannot be deployed anywhere outside the Province. Our interviews included both General Service and Home Service troops.

The operational background in Northern Ireland during 1994 through 1998, when our interviewees served in that theatre, can be summarized as follows. Overall, it was a period of relatively low military activity. Ceasefires were agreed to in August 1994 (lasting until February 1996) and in mid-1997. On both occasions, ceasefire led to a less overt military presence and a greater focus on improving relations between the security forces and the community. Before the first ceasefire, there was a period that saw numerous Provisional IRA attacks against security forces and commercial targets, as well as an increase in sectarian attacks. During the summer of 1995, in the so-called "marching season," there were some periods of severe unrest and confrontation between the Protestant community and the security forces, and similar problems have recurred annually, although to a lesser degree, since then. After the February 1996 end of the first ceasefire, unrest and violence increased both in the Province and on the mainland, troops returned to the streets, and the in-theatre contingent had to be reinforced. For the deployed troops as well as for the belligerents and civilians, a threat to life and limb existed throughout the period studied. The political sensitivity of even very small incidents involving the security forces increased as the peace talks accelerated.

5. COMPARISON OF STRESSORS

The Gulf War interviews revealed that certain aspects of operational experience constitute significant potential stressors. We therefore asked senior commanders in the Bosnia and Northern Ireland studies to rate the presence of these aspects during their target tours (see Table 2). Given the very different contexts of the latter two operational settings, we hypothesized that the patterns of stressors experienced by respondents in the two environments would be different.

Table 2 presents the mean ratings for each of 21 different potential stressors. Respondents rated each stressor on a five-point scale: 1 represents a rating of minimal; 2, limited; 3, moderate; 4, considerable; and 5, very great. In the questionnaire, each potential stressor was addressed by a single item.[3]

---

[3] The use of multi-item indicators (that is, several questions aimed at measuring each potential stressor, with varied wording—a method that is desirable because it provides stronger confirmation of any trends) was deemed impractical given the interviews' time constraints.

Table 2. Potential Stressors Identified in Gulf War Study, with Comparison of Mean Ratings for Northern Ireland Tour against Bosnia Tour

Potential stressor[a]	Northern Ireland tour (n = 51)	Bosnia tour (n = 47)
Difficulties in defining objectives of the mission	1.76	2.80*
Unpredictability of the factions	2.98	4.09*
Problems gaining accurate information	2.90	3.62*
Exposure to physical danger	2.29	2.94*
Casualties among your soldiers	1.45	2.07*
Equipment deficiencies	1.78	2.47*
Language problems	1.13	2.87*
Problems dealing with noncombatant civilians	2.47	3.02*
Media interference	1.82	2.47*
Workload	3.71	4.00*
Lack of support from high command	1.49	2.04*
Problems with chain of command	2.06	3.04*
Problems with the efficiency of the force	1.98	3.70*
Problems with suitability of prior training	2.10	3.00*
Fatigue	2.96	3.28
Difficulty in interpreting rules of engagement	1.72	2.02
Difficulty of keeping within rules of engagement	1.79	2.02
Problems maintaining neutrality	1.86	2.26
Interference from U.K. politicians	1.86	2.13
Interference from non-U.K. politicians	1.63	1.98
Problems arising from separation from family	1.84	1.89

[a] All items were rated on a 5-point scale (where 1 = "minimal" and 5 = "very great").
*$p < .05$.

The differences between the ratings for Northern Ireland tours and Bosnia tours were assessed using *t* tests from independent samples, as shown in Table 2. The pattern of differences is largely as we predicted. Interviewees perceived operations in Bosnia as having been characterized by more difficulties in defining the mission objectives, greater unpredictability in the factions' behaviour, and greater problems in obtaining accurate information. The exposure to physical danger was also greater in Bosnia, where there were more casualties among the soldiers than in Northern Ireland. Equipment deficiencies, language differences, and difficulties in handling noncombatants were also more problematic in Bosnia. Media interference was perceived as having been greater, and so was workload. In contrast to operations in Bosnia, Northern Ireland operations were perceived to have had more support from high command, and fewer problems related to the chain of command, to a lack of efficiency within the force, or to the unsuitability of prior training.

Some of the commanders in the Northern Ireland sample were interviewed in-tour, and others post-tour. Being asked about these issues during a tour could conceivably predispose interviewees to emphasize the stressors' significance. But analyses of the in-tour and post-tour subsets' responses showed no differences in the ratings.

6. RELATIONSHIPS BETWEEN STRESSORS

In the analysis outlined above, fatigue is treated as a separate stressor. But fatigue may also be treated as an indicator of the effect of other stressors—that is, as an indirect measure of subjective stress. Statements made by our interviewees support the hypothesis that reported levels of fatigue correlate with reported levels of subjective stress: in other words, stressed troops are tired troops. We therefore conducted further analyses to explore which potential stressors explain the variation in fatigue (as an index of stress). Stepwise linear regression analyses showed that in the Bosnia sample, 45 percent of the variance in fatigue is explained by variation in three stressors: lack of support from high command, media interference, and workload. In the Northern Ireland sample, 39 percent of the variance in fatigue is explained by just two stressors: difficulty in keeping within the rules of engagement, and workload.

Workload is clearly a major predictor of fatigue. But when we run analyses that excluded workload as a predictor, the picture becomes more interesting. For the Bosnia sample, fatigue is then predicted by lack of support from high command (20 percent of the variance) and by media interference (8.8 percent of the variance). For the Northern Ireland sample, when workload is excluded, fatigue is predicted by exposure to physical danger (18.5 percent of the variance), interference from non-U.K. politicians (9 percent of the variance), and problems related to being separated from family (9 percent of the variance). These results indicate that stress may originate in quite different types of stressors in different operational contexts. Identifying the salient stressors within a specific operational context is an important step in helping forces know what to expect and how to cope with stress reactions in that environment.

7. NORTHERN IRELAND AND BOSNIA TOUR EXPERIENCES COMPARED WITH OTHER OPERATIONAL TOURS

Respondents were also asked to compare their experiences on the target tour (that is, in Northern Ireland or in Bosnia) with some other operational tour in which they had participated. The other tours chosen by our interviewees included earlier tours in Northern Ireland (in a more junior appointment), the Falklands War, the Gulf War, and Cyprus. Interviewees were asked to estimate whether the target tour involved more or less—using a 5-point scale, where 1 represented "much less" and 5 represented "much more"—of nine potential stressors (compiled, in the interests of brevity, from the original set of twenty-one, with the addition of one item—calling for an explicit assessment of the level of stress experienced—that had not been included in the earlier list). Table 3 summarizes the mean ratings on each of the nine characteristics.

A series of *t* tests were conducted to determine whether Northern Ireland tours differed significantly from Bosnia tours when each were compared to other tours. Table 3 shows that for all factors except level of public interest/concern, respondents rated the Northern Ireland and Bosnia tours differently relative to

Table 3.   Mean Ratings for Northern Ireland Tour and Bosnia Tour Compared to Other
Operational Tours

Factor[a]	Northern Ireland tour compared with all others ($n = 49$)	Bosnia tour compared with all others ($n = 46$)
Specificity of mission objective	3.59	2.43**
Clarity of rules of engagement	3.49	3.26*
Clarity of chain of command	3.67	2.23**
Equipment deficiencies	2.65	3.81**
Media management problems	2.88	3.57**
Political interference with execution of mission	3.02	3.66**
Level of personal danger	2.76	3.77**
Level of stress you experienced	3.59	4.02*
Level of public interest/concern	3.47	3.83

Note. Each sample n reflects the fact that some respondents had no experience of other operational tours.
[a] All items were rated on a 5-point scale (where 1 = "much less" and 5 = "much more").
* $p < .05$. ** $p < .002$.

comparator operational tours. The Bosnia tour was perceived as having involved
less mission specificity, less clarity in the rules of engagement, and less clarity in the
chain of command than other tours, when compared to the Northern Ireland tour.
Moreover, the Bosnia tour was rated as having suffered from greater equipment
deficiencies, more media management problems, and more political interference
with the execution of the mission. Finally, both the level of personal danger and the
level of stress were rated as higher. Figure 1 illustrates this pattern by showing the
variation around zero—that is, the point where the target and comparator tours
would be regarded as the same. For ease of interpretation, the nine characteristics
are coded so that a positive difference indicates that the stressor is greater in the
target tour, whereas a negative difference indicates that the stressor is lower in
the target tour.

Table 4 helps illuminate this pattern by further breaking down the comparison
into those between two Northern Ireland tours, between a Bosnia tour and an
earlier Northern Ireland tour, between a Northern Ireland tour and an earlier
Bosnia tour, between a Northern Ireland tour and an earlier Gulf tour, and between
the Bosnia tour and an earlier Gulf tour. Comparisons with other theatres of operation are not included, because too few respondents made them. No one interviewed
had done two tours in Bosnia, so it was impossible to compare the target tour with
an earlier Bosnia tour.

These comparisons reveal what appear to be relatively small changes between
one Northern Ireland tour and a later one in the same theatre of operations. But
virtually all the changes seem to be positive: the later tour is reported as having had
greater mission specificity, greater clarity in the chain of command; fewer equipment
deficiencies, fewer media management problems, and less personal danger. Notably,
however, the later tour's level of stress is somewhat higher. These trends might

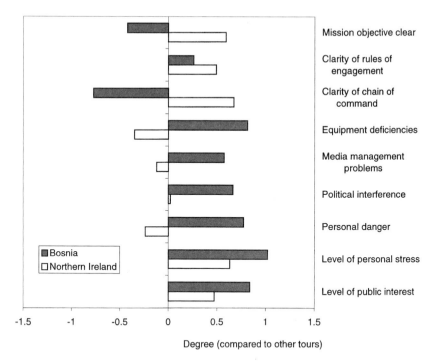

FIGURE 1. Comparison of stress factors between Bosnia tour and Northern Ireland tour.

reflect the changing operational context in Northern Ireland, but they might also be a product of the fact that each interviewee would have been at a more junior rank in the earlier tour and therefore would have been called on to undertake quite a different set of activities. Unfortunately, these data do not allow an analysis that separates effects due to changes in an interviewee's position and those due to changes in the overall operational context.

The comparisons between a tour in Bosnia and a tour in Northern Ireland echo those revealed in the direct comparisons between the two independent samples from the two studies. Respondents made the comparisons shown in Table 4 based on their experiences in the two operational environments at different times. The mirror-image assessments reflected in columns 2 and 3 of Table 4 tend to corroborate each other. Whether the Bosnia tour took place earlier or later than the Northern Ireland tour, the former was perceived to have involved more stress, more danger, and so on, than the latter.

The Gulf results must be interpreted carefully. Only a small subset of the sample used a Gulf tour as the comparator, and not all of these respondents were there during the actual war. Nevertheless, the profile that emerges is striking in some respects: Gulf tours were perceived as having been characterized by more equipment deficiencies, higher levels of public interest, and clearer mission objectives when compared with later tours in Northern Ireland and Bosnia (particularly the latter). With regard to clarity in the chain of command, Gulf tours were

Table 4. Mean Ratings of Comparisons between Tours in Northern Ireland, the Gulf, and Bosnia

Factor[a]	Northern Ireland tour compared with earlier Northern Ireland tour (n = 31)	Bosnia tour compared with earlier Northern Ireland tour (n = 32)	Northern Ireland tour compared with earlier Bosnia tour (n = 8)	Northern Ireland tour compared with earlier Gulf tour (n = 7)	Bosnia tour compared with earlier Gulf tour (n = 8)
Specificity of mission objective	3.45	2.34	3.63	2.71	1.88
Clarity of rules of engagement	3.00	3.00	3.38	4.29	3.13
Clarity of chain of command	3.29	2.00	4.00	3.57	2.00
Equipment deficiencies	2.48	4.19	2.12	2.57	2.13
Media management problems	2.74	3.63	2.00	2.43	3.38
Political interference with execution of mission	3.00	3.75	1.88	2.71	3.00
Level of personal danger	2.29	3.81	2.75	3.00	3.38
Level of stress you experienced	3.48	4.25	2.86	3.00	3.25
Level of public interest/concern	2.58	4.13	3.00	2.43	2.50

[a] All items were rated on a 5-point scale (where 1 = "much less" and 5 = "much more").

perceived as having had more than later Bosnia tours, but less than later Northern Ireland tours.

8. CONCLUSIONS

These studies constitute the first large-scale systematic analysis of British Army officers' assessments of potential stressors in different operational theatres. The data reveal clear differences between tours in the Gulf, Bosnia, and Northern Ireland with regard to officers' estimates of particular stressors' intensity. When we asked General Sir Rupert Smith, who has held senior command positions in all three theatres, to comment on our studies' findings, he emphasized the very different natures of the three operational environments. He noted, for example, that the environments differed fundamentally in the nature of the adversarial relationships involved. In the Gulf, the situation was explicitly war, and the adversaries were clearly defined and fairly stable. In Bosnia, the situation was not war—not for the United Nations, at least—but rather a peacekeeping/humanitarian intervention. For the U.N. forces there, who found themselves vilified and sometimes attacked, both the nature of the adversaries and the forces' own objectives were opaque. In Northern Ireland, the situation is again not war—in fact, currently, it is peace. But the situation can become adversarial at the wish and under the control of any of the factions. Moreover, in Northern Ireland, operational primacy is vested not in the Army but in the police and in the procedural relationships between the two forces that have grown up over decades. Whereas tours in the Gulf and Bosnia represented one-off experiences for virtually all interviewees (at least at the time the interviews were conducted), tours in Northern Ireland have long been a commonplace part of the typical British Army career. In these varying contexts, the command stressors might well be expected to vary.

This chapter has focused on how specific stressors varied in intensity across the three operational environments. Identifying the nature of these variations is only the first step in the process of making recommendations on how to deal with them. Other aspects of these studies have linked the experience of potential stressors to changes in decision-making processes and to changes in command effectiveness. Furthermore, the studies illuminate some of the ways commanders attempt to neutralize potential stressors. Detailed analysis of the interview data indicates specific elements of procedure and training that can be improved to help officers deal successfully with these types of stressors.

Understanding the patterns of stressors that characterize different theatres of operation will help militaries equip their officers to handle those stressors more effectively. It is also important to recognize that these constellations of stressors may well change over the course of a prolonged operation. Generating a corporate memory for stressors and the reactions that they engender is a crucial task for operational analysis in any theatre. It is therefore vital to introduce an appreciation of the individual and organizational impacts of these stressors into the general training of commanders.

9. ACKNOWLEDGMENTS

The author is grateful to the interviewees who provided the data on which these studies are based, and to the U.K. Ministry of Defence (Army) for its support in investigating the issues discussed.

10. REFERENCES

Breakwell, G. M., & Spacie, K. (1997). *Pressures facing commanders* (Occasional Paper No. 29). Camberley, U.K.: Strategic and Combat Studies Institute.
Brown, J. M., & Campbell, E. A. (1994). *Stress and policing.* Chichester, U.K.: Wiley.
Cooper, C. L. (1986). Job distress. *Bulletin British Psychological Society, 39,* 325–331.

CHAPTER 24

TRAINING OF HIGHER-LEVEL JOINT COMMANDERS[1]

CORINNE JEFFERY, BRIGADIER (RETIRED) DICK LAMBE, and COLONEL (RETIRED) JOHN BEARFOOT

1. INTRODUCTION

Work on the training of higher-level commanders began in April 1994, at a time of changing perceptions concerning the military threat facing the United Kingdom. The United Kingdom was no longer confronted with a coordinated threat on land, at sea, and in the air from a monolithic Warsaw Pact led by the Soviet Union. As various nation–states formed and changed configuration, the strategic focus moved from interstate to intrastate conflict. Moreover, the use of force in these intrastate conflicts gained a legitimacy that would have been unthinkable in conflict resolution just 10 years earlier. This shift resulted in an increased number of peace support operations of various types and sizes. The majority of these operations necessitated,

---

[1] British Crown Copyright 1999. Published with the permission of the Defence Evaluation and Research Agency on behalf of the Controller of HMSO. The opinions expressed in this research article are those of the authors and do not reflect the official opinion or policy of either the United Kingdom Ministry of Defence or the Defence Evaluation and Research Agency.

CORINNE JEFFERY, BRIGADIER (RETIRED) DICK LAMBE, and COLONEL (RETIRED) JOHN BEARFOOT • Defence Evaluation and Research Agency, Fort Halstead, Kent, United Kingdom, TN14 7BP

The Human in Command: Exploring the Modern Military Experience, edited by McCann and Pigeau, Kluwer Academic/Plenum Publishers, New York, 2000.

at a minimum, a joint response[2] from the United Kingdom; many required the United Kingdom to act as part of a coalition. Joint, coalition (often called combined), and multinational operations therefore became increasingly important and occurred more frequently. The Defence Cost Studies (United Kingdom, 1994) recognized this situation; as a result, a Permanent Joint Headquarters (PJHQ) and a Joint Services Command and Staff College (JSCSC) were created. The formation of these organizations has emphasized the need to ensure that appropriate training and education are available for those participating in joint, coalition, and multinational operations. Since the training of commanders had hitherto largely been carried out on a single-service basis, no formal career structure was in place to groom U.K. officers specifically for joint, coalition, and multinational command, and there was therefore no requirement for the coordination of career management, advancement, and training.

The challenge for the military is to provide relevant, cost-effective training that prepares senior commanders for the complex conditions of contemporary and future operations. Therefore, the individual services would need to understand the requirements for joint service, so that officers with the potential for success at the senior command level can be identified and receive the requisite training.

The work on determining the training needs of higher-level commanders described in this chapter was funded by the United Kingdom Ministry of Defence (UK MoD) Corporate Research Programme into the Human Sciences and forms part of a Technology Thrust Initiative (TTI) into Future Command. The research was supported by a group of stakeholders from the United Kingdom armed forces and was undertaken by the Land Systems Sector of the Defence Evaluation and Research Agency (DERA), an agency of the UK MoD.

2. AIM AND SCOPE

The aims of the work were (a) to define the training needs of joint commanders (JCs), joint force commanders (JFCs), and their staffs; and (b) to identify ways to meet those training needs. The JC is the three-star or four-star officer designated as the military strategic commander by the chiefs of staff, with ultimate responsibility for operations. The JFC is a two-star formation commander who functions primarily at the operational level of conflict and sometimes at the tactical level.

The project's initial scope was to do the following:

- Define the range of duties and activities undertaken by JCs, JFCs, and their staffs, taking into account how those duties and activities may change in future operations.

- Produce an Operational Task and Performance Requirement (OTPR).[3]

---

[2] A joint response includes more than one branch of a country's armed forces: in this case, the British Army, the Royal Air Force (RAF), and the Royal Navy (RN).

[3] This document identifies and defines the operational tasks and skills required by JCs and JFCs; defines the process associated with undertaking the tasks; and maps the skills, experience, knowledge, and characteristics required for each task.

- Define the training requirements for joint commanders and joint force commanders.

- Identify how these training requirements could best be met.

- Consider such issues as the sequencing of training as part of a senior commander's career progression, the need for refresher training and special pre-operational training, and the need for individual and team training.

This scope subsequently widened to enable the DERA team to study the routes by which senior commanders in the three services attain higher command. The ultimate intent was to determine how to enlarge the overall pool of qualified and trained officers eligible for joint command.

3. DATA CAPTURE PROCESS

An empirical process for capturing data on the training needs for joint command was employed. First, a team of three senior subject matter experts (SSMEs) was assembled, with one SSME representing each of the three services. This team compiled a baseline set of requirements for higher command in a joint environment. This initial work provided the basis for structuring a program of interviews with currently serving officers who had experience in and/or responsibility for joint operations. Other relevant material was gathered by a variety of routes, including an information and literature search, visits, a training needs analysis (TNA), and limited historical analysis.

Two separate series of interviews were conducted. The first series confirmed and advanced the original baseline; the second provided information about several outstanding issues. An office call was then made on each service's chief of staff. The SSME team provided access to the military echelon. In all, 47 officers were surveyed in 59 interviews. The initial interviews confirmed the expectation that experienced commanders might have trouble providing enough interview time to allow the researchers to capture the breadth and depth of information needed for the training analysis. It was also found (again, as expected) that senior commanders are unaccustomed to expressing requirements for skills and knowledge in the objective terms needed for training purposes. Subsequent interviews were therefore structured to focus on the main problems associated with joint command. Interviewees described their operational experiences, often anecdotally; elements of these descriptions were later categorized as either tasks, skills, or knowledge.

The study's TNA element used a "process by situation" model rather than the better-known "hierarchical" model. In outline, the "process by situation" model considers (a) the situations in which the JC and JFC operate; (b) the job components and tasks required of the JC and JFC; and (c) the processes by which and within which the JC and JFC operate. This model was selected because it is more flexible than the hierarchical model, but it is emphasized that no existing model could fully cope with the wide range of skills, knowledge, and experience required at the levels of command being studied. A significant proportion of the assessment of many of the skills is based on subjective judgment, and commanders at the highest level tend to base decisions on a mix of (a) definable skills and knowledge, (b) analysis, and (c) intuition. The SSMEs' opinions concerning the job and the tasks therefore constituted an essential element in the analysis.

A limited amount of historical analysis was also undertaken, particularly regarding command and leadership skills. This analysis demonstrated the impossibility of developing a comprehensive list of the characteristics that all commanders must possess: history has shown that all commanders are different. But it was possible to isolate a number of characteristics without which a commander is unlikely to succeed.

4. ANALYSIS

Figure 1 illustrates the two main areas of analysis (the double-bordered boxes in the figure) and the resulting products (the single-bordered boxes).

4.1. Analysis of the Training Requirements

The training requirements for JCs, JFCs, and their staffs were derived in two steps. First, their respective roles and responsibilities were identified. Then an analysis was conducted to determine what a person requires in order to satisfactorily discharge those roles and responsibilities: that is, what tasks, subtasks, characteristics, knowledge, qualities, and command skills does he or she need? It was assumed that the most legitimate source of such information was the set of individuals who have (or have previously had) the responsibility for and/or experience of joint operations.

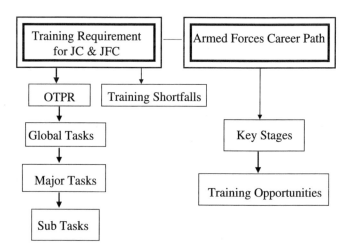

FIGURE 1. Initial analysis.

4.2. Operational Task and Performance Requirement (OTPR)

Data capture and initial analysis provided the basis for defining an Operational Task and Performance Requirement (OTPR) for each job position. (See Figure 2 for an example.) The OTPR identifies the operational tasks and skills required by JCs and JFCs. Global tasks, which reflect the cyclical process applicable to most jobs and domains, comprise skills, experience, knowledge, and characteristics. Each global task is linked to the major tasks, subtasks, skills, experience, knowledge, and characteristics required for its achievement. In all, 8 global tasks, 14 major tasks, and 77 subtasks were identified as fundamental to a JC's or JFC's professional obligations.

The initial analysis also identified areas where training could be improved—that is, areas in which senior commanders indicated that they could have been better prepared before being appointed to joint command. Section 5, "Results," discusses these training shortfalls in detail.

4.3. Analysis of the Current Career Path in Each Service

While the operational tasks and skills required by JCs and JFCs were possible to define, there was less consensus on how to gain, improve, develop, or teach these

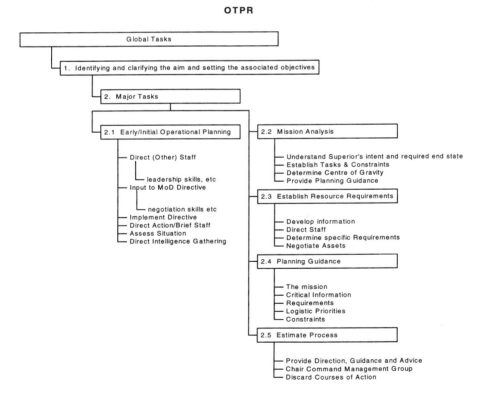

FIGURE 2. Example Operational Task and Performance Requirement.

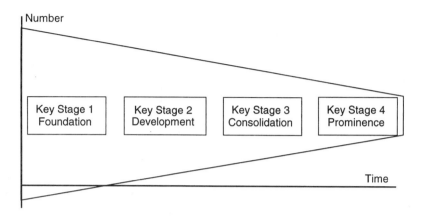

FIGURE 3. Key stages in the career path.

skills. Finding a discernible and logical training route that would lead progressively to the JFC level and then to the JC level—and that would also have some commonality across the services—was difficult. The next stage of the analysis therefore focused on the current career path in each service, in order to identify the many factors that determine the services' career structures and potential training opportunities.[4] Each training opportunity was analyzed, and the necessary tasks, subtasks, knowledge, qualities, and command skills were identified.

The first step in characterizing the desirable career path across services involved identifying several exceptional officers from each service. By consensus, these officers were considered to be contenders for unwavering earliest advancement (that is, spending the minimum amount of time possible at each rank) to at least a one-star and probably a two-star command position. Their individual career paths were analyzed; then a career path representing the amalgamation of those in the sample was created. The merged career progression was divided, on the basis of age and rank achieved (within the rules governing that service), into four essential "key" stages: foundation, development, consolidation, and prominence. It was assumed that in order to pass from one key stage to the next, an individual must attain specific competencies. The key stages allowed the sequencing of training as part of a commander's overall career progression to be considered. Figure 3 illustrates the concept diagrammatically, showing the relative number of officers across the key stages (on the vertical axis) and the relative time spent in each stage (on the horizontal axis). The characteristics of the four key stages are described below.

- *Key Stage 1—Foundation:* The specialized education, experience, and training of a JC or JFC candidate must be underpinned by a foundation phase that extends from entering a service until being put in command of a single-service unit. Historically, officers have received little exposure to detailed joint doctrine and training during this period, except when a specific post or unit required such exposure. (Amalgamating the single-service staff colleges into

---

[4] For the purposes of this analysis, training opportunities were defined as military postings, appointments, operations, exercises, and courses.

the JSCSC has helped rectify this deficiency.) During the foundation stage, the individual services identify officers with high potential for becoming a JC or JFC. The services then have that potential confirmed by formal assessment at the JSCSC. The foundation stage for a suitable candidate typically culminates with a high-profile posting to the Ministry of Defence, to the joint staff (that is, the Joint Force Headquarters [JFHQ]), or to a major single-service headquarters. The comparative ages and ranks for this stage are as follows:

RN	Cadet to Commander	Age 35
Army	Cadet to Lieutenant Colonel	Age 37
RAF	Cadet to Wing Commander	Age 36

- *Key Stage 2—Development:* In the development stage, candidates are typically offered either (a) command of a single-service unit or (b) a demanding staff appointment (for example, a posting as an exchange or liaison officer or as an attaché). A high-potential officer would probably benefit from international experience (for example, in NATO [the North Atlantic Treaty Organization] or the United Nations) at this point in his or her career path. During this stage, the officer can put into practice his or her accumulated theory of operational command and professional leadership expertise. The comparative ages and ranks for this stage are as follows:

RN	Commander to Captain	Age 40
Army	Lieutenant Colonel to Brigadier	Age 43
RAF	Wing Commander to Group Captain	Age 40

- *Key Stage 3—Consolidation:* The consolidation stage of training and development amalgamates and blends the candidate's accumulated command and staff experience. It involves a significant graduation from operational commander to strategic thinker. After successfully completing the HCSC (the Higher Command and Staff Course), a candidate will normally be offered either a single-service or a joint-service operational command appointment. A demanding joint-service staff or director-level appointment in the Ministry of Defence typically follows. Candidates who exhibit high performance levels in these positions are then selected for an important operational command post, a step that is almost certainly necessary for progression to a JFC appointment. This post bestows membership in the Joint Command Group, which comprises the two-star commanders of designated operational combat formations (originally two, and now three, from each service, and including a Royal Marine). Although an appointment to this Group does not guarantee progression within the joint realm, the Group— which consists of the most able officers from each service—does form the pool from which JC and JFC appointees are selected. The comparative ages and ranks for this stage are as follows:

RN	Captain to Rear Admiral	Age 46
Army	Brigadier to Major General	Age 47
RAF	Group Captain to Air Vice Marshal	Age 46

- *Key Stage 4—Prominence:* The prominence stage represents the culmination of an armed forces career. Only the most talented officers reach this stage. Here, their command skills, political/military staff ability, and strategic knowledge are blended with an astute grasp of and sensitivity to national and international issues. This combination, along with knowledge of government procedures and mechanisms, produces officers who can provide the consummate military advice to Cabinet.

4.4. Defining the Structured Career Path for JCs and JFCs

In the next phase of the work, the OTPR was translated into a new training regime that would work within the key-stages framework to produce well-prepared senior commanders. Complete assessment of all possible mixes of training opportunities would have been a complex, multidimensional job requiring extensive SME effort. A prototype tool was therefore developed to support the analysis by reducing the manual effort required and ensuring that the data and information were studied without bias. A number of training mixes were then compared to the OTPR to (a) determine which combination provides the best overall training regime and (b) highlight any new or additional training requirements. Figure 4 illustrates this final analysis process.

5. RESULTS

Training and knowledge in several important areas were identified as possibilities for improvement. These included media training and awareness, negotiation skills,

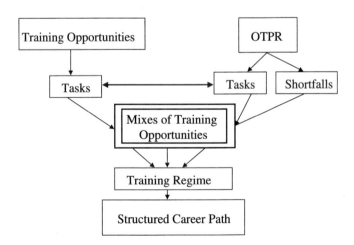

FIGURE 4. Comparison of OTPR with training opportunities.

intelligence/information warfare, rules of engagement (ROEs), nongovernmental organizations (NGOs), other governmental departments (OGDs), logistics (particularly for sustainment and recovery), and the relevance and application of emerging technology. The recommended career structure for joint commanders that is detailed in Section 6, "Recommendations for Training of Higher-Level Commanders," addresses these shortfalls, ensuring that future JCs and JFCs receive the optimum mixture of education, experience, and training—thereby fully developing the skills needed for discharging their responsibilities.

A number of new training possibilities were identified. For example, it was recommended that two joint update briefing sessions be programmed during Key Stage 2: one before the officer assumes unit command and the other before the officer takes on a staff appointment. These training sessions, which would be at least two years apart, would include media awareness, ROEs, NGOs, OGDs, emerging technology, and negotiation techniques. Before an officer assumes the two-star appointment in Key Stage 3, a senior officer's briefing should be provided, in order to facilitate the step change—that is, the significant change—in responsibilities and to update the candidate on media awareness, the political/military dimension (embracing ROEs and OGDs), NGOs, information superiority (including psychological warfare), special forces and intelligence assets, logistics, and finance and budgets. The individual will need another update in Key Stage 4, through a senior officer's briefing and a seminar session incorporating a high-level wargame.

This study identified the requirement for a structured approach to joint services career development, which should include additional training in a number of areas previously identified. Furthermore, the study identified that any training regime should be progressive, in order to support the step changes involved when exercising joint command at the tactical, operational, and strategic levels.

6. RECOMMENDATIONS FOR TRAINING OF HIGHER-LEVEL COMMANDERS

A structured career path for joint command was recommended. By improving the training in the areas identified, this career path would ensure that future JCs and JFCs receive the optimum mixture of education, experience, and training—and thus fully develop the skills needed for discharging their responsibilities. Each key stage provides the opportunity to apply the skills and knowledge at the relevant command level. The following recommendations were made concerning the joint career structure and path:

- Introduce new training in the form of mandatory update briefings and courses for operational commanders.

- Confirm the value of current training opportunities, such as attendance at the Advanced Staff Course and HCSC.

- Recognize the importance of joint appointments.

- Recognize the value of international posts, such as those of a senior staff officer within NATO or the United Nations, for broadening a senior commander's view.

- Develop and introduce a method for assessing a senior commander's potential to exercise joint command. Training can then be targeted at those officers who will benefit most from it and who will be most able to fill senior joint appointments.

- Recognize the benefits of refresher training and special pre-operational training.

7. ASSESSING PERFORMANCE AND POTENTIAL

This study identified a major issue regarding the assessment of commanders' performance and potential. Comments on individual performance currently form part of the armed forces annual assessment report. But this assessment is subjective and is often based on past performance. Yet our previous research determined that a step change in performance is required when moving from each senior rank to the next. Assessments based on past performance therefore possess only a limited ability to predict an individual's true potential for success. A more objective assessment of an individual's potential would provide a better picture of his or her overall capability, along with insight into his or her strengths and weaknesses. Furthermore, the need to evaluate the operational effectiveness and capability of forces is increasing—driven by the requirement to sustain operational readiness and to support the procurement of increasingly complex and expensive operational systems. Both individual and collective performance must be assessed in order to evaluate operational effectiveness, force capability, and the state of readiness. But since opportunities to exercise command at the highest levels are diminishing, identifying individuals with the potential for success at the senior command level is becoming increasingly important.

DERA Fort Halstead has therefore undertaken a study investigating the issue of potential for senior command. The *Oxford English Dictionary* defines potential as the "capacity for use or development," but in the context of DERA's study, the term has a more specific meaning—the ability to undertake the intellectual, moral, physical, and leadership challenges of senior command. The current study's aims are twofold. First, the study aims to identify the competencies[5] that will be required for senior command in the future and to outline possible criteria for measuring those competencies. Second, the study aims to validate these competencies and develop an assessment methodology.

Many of the competencies required to be a successful commander at any level are demonstrated by the majority of good officers. This latest work therefore focuses on identifying which competencies make the difference at the senior command

---

[5] The term *competency* is defined here as "an ability, expressed in terms of behaviour, which is causally related to effective or superior performance in a job" ("Directory of Competencies," 1996).

Table 1. Essential Competencies for Senior Commanders

Interpersonal skills	Cognitive skills	Qualities
Oral communications	Innovation	Resolve/determination/single-mindedness
Guidance	Intuition	Self-assurance (confidence)
Direction	Mental agility	Ability to command respect
Teamworking	Lateral thinking	Physical and moral courage
	Vision	Integrity
	Initiative	Self-control/discipline
	Reasoning/clarity of thought	Robustness
	Evaluation of information	Common sense
	Judgment	
	Decision making/decisiveness	

level. Competencies that fit into this category have been termed *essential*, and they encompass both skills and qualities (see Table 1). The skills are a mix of interpersonal and cognitive. The interpersonal skills are oral communications, guidance, direction, and teamworking. The cognitive skills are innovation, intuition, mental agility, lateral thinking, vision, initiative, reasoning/clarity of thought, evaluation of information, judgment, and decision making/decisiveness. The qualities are resolve/determination/single-mindedness, self-assurance (confidence), the ability to command respect, physical and moral courage, integrity, self-control/discipline, robustness, and common sense.

Identification of the optimum mix of competencies for command is desirable, but the relative contribution made by each competency toward effective command is currently unknown. Some evidence suggests, though, that cognitive skills may contribute the most toward effectiveness at senior command levels (Lewis, 1996; Lewis & Jacobs, 1992). The appropriate mix also depends on the requirements of the military situation. It would therefore be logical to select the individual with the best combination of skills that match the operational need. Yet for the majority of military operations, such an approach would prove impracticable. For example, the commander cannot be selected independently of tasking the formation: each assigned unit comes complete with a commander who is already in charge of it.

The successful measurement of the necessary competencies also depends heavily on defining suitable, observable, and quantifiable criteria. A combination of psychometric tests, interviews, mentors, computerized decision support tools, and stress vignettes (which set specific tasks within a context) will be required to support the assessment of individuals. But this research will not identify benchmark standards—that is, the level of effectiveness that an individual must attain in order to qualify for further development and training. Setting the benchmark must remain a military prerogative.

Finally, the need to introduce a common annual assessment for those serving in joint or combined appointments should be emphasized. Also, the criteria for being promoted to a position that might lead to selection as JC or JFC should be more coincident across the services to ensure a uniform quality of candidates. The combination of common assessment reports and coordinated selection criteria for formally evaluated training would significantly raise overall military standards. The Joint Command Group would therefore be open only to those who have been trained, qualified, and assessed at common, agreed-upon standards.

8. CONCLUSIONS

This chapter describes research conducted by the United Kingdom's Defence Evaluation Research Agency to define the training needs of joint commanders, joint force commanders, and their staffs and to identify how those needs could best be met. The work highlighted areas where knowledge and training could be improved, including media training and awareness and the relevance and application of emerging technology. In addition, recommendations have been made for the structure of a joint career path for higher-level commanders. The results of this work have been presented to the United Kingdom chiefs of staff, who have implemented an action plan for training future higher-level commanders under a joint three-star officer.

9. REFERENCES

Directory of Competencies for Managers. (1996). In *Foresight* (Version 1.10) [Computer program]. Bath, U.K.: Selby MillSmith.

Lewis, P. M. (1996). *Conceptual capacity and officer effectiveness* (Report ARI-RN-96-26). Alexandria, VA: U.S. Army Research Institute for the Behavioral and Social Sciences, Research and Advanced Concepts Office.

Lewis, P., & Jacobs, T. O. (1992). Individual difference in strategic leadership capacity: A constructive/developmental view. In R. L. Phillips & J. G. Hunt (Eds.), *Strategic leadership: A multiorganizational-level perspective*. Westport, CT: Quorum Books.

United Kingdom. (1994). *Training* (Defence Cost Review Study 12A). London, U.K.: Ministry of Defence.

CHAPTER 25

RELATIVE EFFICACY OF AN OPEN VERSUS A RESTRICTED COMMUNICATION STRUCTURE FOR COMMAND AND CONTROL DECISION MAKING
An Experimental Study

MARY OMODEI, ALEXANDER WEARING,
and JIM McLENNAN

1. INTRODUCTION

Modern information and communications technologies have revolutionized command, control, communication, and intelligence (C^3I) practices for military decision making. In principle, these technologies give commanders direct, immediate,

MARY OMODEI • *School of Psychological Science, La Trobe University, Melbourne, Australia 3083*
ALEXANDER WEARING • *Department of Psychology, University of Melbourne, Melbourne, Australia 3052   JIM McLENNAN* • *Swinburne Computer–Human Interaction Laboratory, Swinburne University of Technology, Melbourne, Australia 3122*

The Human in Command: Exploring the Modern Military Experience,
edited by McCann and Pigeau, Kluwer Academic/Plenum Publishers, New York, 2000.

real-time access to all operational staff. And lower-ranked staff have similarly direct and immediate access to their superior officers. But the implications of advances in technology for C³I structures and procedures have been identified as concerns for defence forces (Brehmer, 1992). Despite the apparent acceptance of the importance of psychological processes in effective decision making in dynamic, uncertain environments, there has been relatively little systematic investigation of human decision-making processes in complex command and control environments. Therefore, there is little guidance on how to make the best use of advances in C³I-relevant technologies for decision support. A particular concern is the nature of decision making in situations where subordinates (a) detect what they believe are erroneous or ineffective commands from a superior, and (b) believe that they have information that would assist their superior. To explore this issue, we conducted an experimental investigation of the relative effectiveness of an *open* versus a *restricted* communication structure and of how the team members' personality characteristics mediate decision-making performance in these two environments.

The lack of available information on the basic psychological processes involved in C³I can be attributed to the lack of adequate methodologies for capturing data in field settings and for representing these settings in a laboratory so that concepts and hypothesized relationships can be subjected to experimental testing. But recent advances in video-camera and computer technology have made it possible to record command and control incidents from the participants' perspective as the incidents actually occur. From such recordings, we can then create experimental environments that adequately simulate such incidents. These advances in data collection and task representation allow us to systematically collect key psychological data from the field, identify possible relationships in those data, and then explore the relationships in the laboratory to distinguish spurious from real causal effects. Our research program has made extensive use of head-mounted video cameras to record decision situations. This footage cues decision makers to recall, after the fact, salient aspects of their incident management (Omodei, Wearing, & McLennan, 1997). Findings obtained with such field-based methodology have both informed and been informed by our laboratory-based research using computer-networked command and control simulations. This chapter outlines one of our recent laboratory-based experiments and illustrates the utility of computer-simulated microworlds for studying command and control issues.

Command and control structures for decision making are not unique to military contexts. Important real-world decision-making problems are rarely handled by one person alone, because (a) there is too much information for one person to process, (b) there is a political requirement that responsibility be shared, or (c) the stakes are too high to allow one person to have exclusive control. In these multiperson decision-making structures—as in military command and control—information, resources, roles, and responsibilities are differentially distributed across team members. Typically the structure is configured as an "information and influence hierarchy" under the overall direction of one person (for example, a theatre commander in the military). Real-world examples of such decision environments include aviation operations (for instance, air traffic control, mechanical failure), emergency services (for instance, fire, police, medical, rescue), medical procedures (for instance, surgery, resuscitation), and industrial operations (for instance, emergency shutdown, product recall). The limited research on human decision making in these notionally different task environments suggests that they have a common underlying structure, at least with respect to their psychological demands (Shattuck & Woods, this volume, Chapter 19). This observation suggests that findings obtained in nonmilitary contexts (both naturally occurring and simulated) can be used for both theory building and theory testing in military contexts.

Like the military, most emergency services enforce formal hierarchical command, control, and communication (C^3) structures in which a superior officer possesses overall decision-making responsibility. But informal reports suggest that relaxing the restricted communication structure typically associated with a hierarchical command structure (in which subordinates cannot question instructions) into a more open communication structure (in which subordinates can challenge some aspects of command in a given incident) may lead to more effective incident management. A key distinction here is between *command* structure and *communication* structure. Whereas command structure refers to "who can legitimately tell whom what to do," communication structure refers to "who can talk to whom about what."

While one person may retain ultimate responsibility and authority for decision making, subordinates can provide critical redundancy, especially under conditions of high time pressure and high information load (Orasanu et al., 1998). In addition to performing their individually tasked roles, subordinates can support both each other and their superior(s) by detecting errors or emerging problems and by intervening to prevent situations from deteriorating (Helmreich & Foushee, 1993; Weick, 1990). Of course, in order for subordinates to be able to perform such a critical function, they need to be aware—at least to some extent—of their superior's overall intent (Pigeau & McCann, this volume, Chapter 12). Furthermore, particularly with regard to military command and control structures, deliberate steps may need to be taken in order to make it acceptable for subordinates to disagree (Lewis, Butler, Challans, Craig, & Smidt, this volume, Chapter 10). But recent observations of team decision-making processes have challenged the simplistic assumption that the more open the communication, the better the decision outcome. In fact, aviation accident reports examined by Rodvold, Orasanu, Murray, Tyzzer, and Eastman (1998) led these authors to attribute several accidents to the overly assertive behaviour of subordinates who had been trained in assertiveness skills.

Such observations derive exclusively from retrospective analyses of known accidents (which are relatively rare events); hence, the general conclusions are weakened by a failure to take the low base rate into account. More seriously, such retrospective studies do not take into account the many potential disasters that are averted because a junior officer immediately does what he or she has been commanded to do—despite personal doubts about the order's wisdom—rather than waste precious seconds debating the decision with a superior. To date, there has been no systematic experimental investigation of the relative superiority of open versus restricted communication structures in C^3I. But several attempts have been made to investigate general issues relating to team structure under controlled laboratory conditions. Two independent groups of researchers—Brehmer and Svenmark (1994) and Wang, Luh, Serfaty, and Kleinman (1991)—used quite dissimilar computer-simulated decision tasks to study team communication. Both found that a centralized (limited) communication structure resulted in more effective team performance compared to a fully interconnected communication structure. Although interesting in themselves, these findings cannot be readily generalized to hierarchically organized command and control settings. Neither study explicitly differentiated among roles regarding who could give orders to whom. As an extension to this work, therefore, we investigated the relative efficacy of a *restricted* versus an *open* communication structure while keeping constant (a) the degree of *centralization* of these two *communication* structures and (b) the *rigidity* of the *command* structure. Both communication structures we examined were fully centralized in the sense that all communications had to be routed via the commander; and in both cases the command structure was fully hierarchical—subordinates were required to obey all orders given by their superiors. Thus, the two centralized communication structures differed solely in the extent to which subordinates were permitted to offer criticisms or suggestions to someone higher in the chain of command.

An alternative approach to investigating command and control effectiveness has focused on individual differences in superior/subordinate personality characteristics. It has been claimed that "need for control," "trust," and "assertiveness" of *both* superiors and subordinates together contribute to an optimal interpersonal climate on the flight deck of commercial jet aircraft (Helmreich & Foushee, 1993); in prehospital trauma management and among surgical and anesthesiology teams (Gaba, Howard, & Fish, 1994); in fire service operations (McLennan, Omodei, Rich, & Wearing, 1997); and in nuclear power plant operations and offshore oil installation management (Flin, 1997). In her review of the literature on leader personality in C^2 settings, Flin indicates that "self-confidence" and "decisiveness" are generally regarded as characteristics of good leaders.[1] There is also evidence to suggest that leaders who exhibit a more "intuitive"—but not "impulsive"—style of decision making are perceived by others (including their subordinates) to be better leaders (Jeffery, Lambe, & Bearfoot, this volume, Chapter 24). These observations are consistent with recent theoretical models of decision making in complex, uncertain, and time-pressured environments—environments in which, it is argued, quick and intuitive recognitional strategies characterize the decision making of experts (Klein, 1993).

Our study's design allowed us to investigate the possibility that specific personality characteristics might be differentially important under a restricted versus an open communication structure. The behaviours of interest were those exhibited by subordinates, but we investigated the role played by the personality characteristics of both superiors and their subordinates.[2]

---

[1] Reflecting the lack of attention to subordinate characteristics, the studies Flin reviews do not include any assessment of subordinates.

[2] We agree with the position advocated by Hollander (1993) that any discussion of "leadership" characteristics would be incomplete without a parallel discussion of "followership" characteristics.

1.1. The Study

The study described in this chapter experimentally investigated team decision-making effectiveness under two conditions: (a) a restricted communication condition, in which subordinates were not permitted to offer any suggestions or challenges to the commander; and (b) an open communication condition, in which subordinates were permitted to offer suggestions or challenges to the commander. We used a between-subjects design, and gave instructions to each team concerning how subordinates and their commanders could communicate (thus setting up which condition that team operated under). To ensure that the specific command and control task we selected for the study actually elicited high-level decision-making processes in both superiors and subordinates, we considered it necessary to demonstrate that the overall decision-making effectiveness in the task was, at least in part, associated with high levels of cognitive functioning in team members. We therefore selected two nonredundant aspects of cognitive functioning—"information processing speed" and "field independence"—as indicative of decision-making performance under dynamic uncertainty and time pressure. Finally, we also assessed the following personality attributes of all participants: "need for control," "assertiveness," "trust," "self-confidence," "decisive decision style," "intuitive decision style," and "impulsive decision style."

We hypothesized that the following results would obtain:

- Greater decision-making effectiveness would occur with an open communication structure than with a restricted communication structure.

- Greater decision-making effectiveness would occur with increasing levels of *superiors'* "information processing speed," "field independence," "self-confidence," and "decisive decision style" (linear hypotheses).

- Greater decision-making effectiveness would occur with moderate levels of *superiors'* "need for control," "assertiveness," "trust," "intuitive decision style," and "impulsive decision style" (curvilinear hypotheses).

- Greater decision-making effectiveness would occur with increasing levels of *subordinates'* "information processing speed," "field independence," "self-confidence," and "decisive decision style" (linear hypotheses).

- Greater decision-making effectiveness would occur with moderate levels of *subordinates'* "need for control," "assertiveness," "trust," "intuitive decision style," and "impulsive decision style" (curvilinear hypotheses).

2. METHOD

2.1. *Networked Fire Chief*: The Command and Control Task Environment

For this study, we used *Networked Fire Chief* (Omodei & Wearing, 1998), a networked extension of the *Fire Chief* (Omodei & Wearing, 1995) microworld generation program, to create a command and control scenario in which teams of subjects fought simulated forest fires. *Networked Fire Chief* allows for the creation of detailed forest landscapes that vary in composition, in flammability characteristics, and in economic, environmental, and esthetic value. Within the simulation, fire incidents can be initiated and spread according to various user-defined models of fire behaviour. Teams of subjects try to control the spread of these simulated fires by dispatching fire trucks and helicopters to drop water on the fires, to refill with water at specified dam locations, and to establish firebreaks.

Networked Fire Chief permits the implementation of specific command and communication structures by allowing customization of individual computer stations within a group of linked computer stations. Each station can be customized with respect to (a) what information the station's operator can access about the simulated scenario, (b) what actions its operator can take in the simulated scenario, and (c) what other stations its operator can communicate with.

The study scenario incorporated five computer stations. The Incident Controller station, assigned to the team leader, presented a map of the total landscape area under the team's control. The other four team members each controlled one of the four Sector Controller stations; each such station presented one quadrant (sector) of the total area at a larger resolution. On average, 26 fires broke out during a 20-minute trial for which 20 firefighting appliances were provided. An average of 10 forecast changes in wind strength and/or direction occurred during a trial. The Incident Controller station allowed its operator to move firefighting appliances across sectors to the approximate area of a fire incident, but not to initiate any firefighting. Those operating the Sector Controller stations, on the other hand, could directly control the fires' spread by commanding simulated appliance crews to patrol for and extinguish fires in a 1 km (0.6-mile) radius (two landscape segments as portrayed on the computer screen). But the Sector Controller station operators could not reallocate firefighting resources. Sound-isolating aviation headsets conveyed communications between stations. The person occupying the Incident Controller role could communicate with each of the Sector Controllers, but the latter could not communicate with each other or overhear communications between the Incident Controller and the other Sector Controllers (thus simulating a fully centralized communication structure).

2.2. Measures and Instruments

Overall decision-making effectiveness was assessed according to the value of the landscape saved from destruction by fire. (The *Networked Fire Chief* program automatically calculated this measure, taking into account the relative priority weights assigned to the different landscape types.) Because unattended fires develop exponentially, we used a reflex logarithmic transformation of the amount of landscape saved as an index of decision-making effectiveness. To make the interpretation of results easier, these scores were standardized and further inverted, so that a higher score represented greater decision-making effectiveness. A leader's decision-making effectiveness was assessed as the amount of landscape saved over all four sectors. An individual subordinate's decision-making effectiveness was assessed as the amount of landscape saved in his or her own particular sector.

The "information processing speed" component of cognitive functioning was measured using the Digit Symbol subtest from the Multidimensional Aptitude Battery (Jackson, 1984); "field independence" was assessed with the Group Embedded Figures Test (Witkin, Oltman, Raskin, & Karp, 1971).

Personality characteristics were assessed using the following instruments:

- "need for control": the Need for Control Scale (Burger, 1992)

- "trust": the Global Interpersonal Mistrust–Trust Scale (Omodei & McLennan, in press)

- "assertiveness": the Probability of Being Assertive Scale (Gambrill & Richey, 1988)

- "self-confidence": the Self Mastery Scale (Pearlin & Schooler, 1978)

- "decisive decision style," "intuitive decision style," and "impulsive decision style": Decision Style Scales (Scott & Bruce, 1995)

Additional information was collected from the participants after they completed the experimental trials to help us interpret study findings with respect to the relative superiority of an open versus a restricted communication structure. These measures included the following:

a. the extent to which subordinates were able to make suggestions and raise questions,

b. the extent to which subordinates in fact did so,

c. the extent to which subordinates' suggestions and questions were expected to be helpful,

d. subordinates' estimates of the number of leader errors,

e. the participant's perceived workload,

f. the extent to which incident controllers felt in control of the situation,

g. the extent to which incident controllers felt self-confident, and

h. the participant's estimate of his or her personal performance.

2.3. Procedure

This study's participants—all undergraduate psychology students—formed 28 five-person teams. (Subjects were randomly allocated either to the Incident Controller role or to one of the four Sector Controller roles.) The teams received three hours of training and practice on the forest-fire simulation and in their respective roles over a two-week period before data collection. This training was followed one week later by an experimental session comprising one 20-minute practice trial and two 20-minute experimental trials. The scenarios used for the two experimental trials had different landscape and fire incident settings of approximately equal difficulty. The order of presentation was varied to allow us to (a) check that the participants achieved an adequate level of task mastery and (b) assess the reliability of the performance indicator (that is, the weighted percentage of the landscape saved from fire).

Two research assistants, themselves *Fire Chief* experts, observed the teams throughout the study and provided qualitative descriptions of the characteristics that seemed to distinguish better from weaker teams.

3. RESULTS AND DISCUSSION

3.1. Reliability in Measurement of Decision-Making Effectiveness

Scores on decision-making effectiveness (using the reflex logarithmic transformation outlined above) were found to be normally distributed both for leaders ($N = 28$) and for subordinates ($N = 112$). Analysis of variance indicated that subjects had achieved an adequate level of task mastery and that the two trial settings were equivalent in difficulty level. The intercorrelation among decision-making effectiveness (performance) scores across the two experimental trials indicates a high degree of reliability both for leaders ($r = .75$, $N = 26$) and for subordinates ($r = .70$, $N = 104$). Trial 1 performance data were lost for two of the teams, so subsequent analyses are reported for Trial 2 data only.

3.2. Team Performance Differences across Restricted versus Open Communication Structures

The results did *not* support the hypothesis that an open communication structure would have a performance advantage over a restricted communication structure. Both for overall team performance (leader) and for individual sector performance (subordinate), the differences between communication conditions were negligible (see Table 1).

3.2.1. Strength of the Manipulation of Degree of Openness in Communication Structure

The lack of difference in decision-making performance between the restricted and the open communication structures raises the possibility that we actually failed to achieve an adequate difference between the two groups in the degree of openness of their communication structures (that is, that the experimental manipulation was not strong enough). But participants' responses to items that sought information about their experience and evaluations of the task scenarios (Table 1) indicated

Table 1.   Mean Scores for Decision Performance and for Experience of the Task across Restricted and Open Communication Structures

	Leader		Subordinate	
	Restricted ($n = 14$)	Open ($n = 14$)	Restricted ($n = 56$)	Open ($n = 56$)
Performance				
Standardized performance score (amount of forest saved) ($X = 0, SD = 1$)	0.03	−0.03	0.00	0.00
Experience of Task[a]				
Subordinates able to make suggestions *not at all/very much*	3.69	7.21*	3.84	7.77*
Subordinates willing to make suggestions *not at all/very much*	—	7.36	—	7.52
Subordinates able to question *not at all/very much*	2.31	5.93*	3.05	6.60*
Subordinates willing to question *not at all/very much*	—	5.86	—	5.93
Expectation of subordinates' suggestions being helpful *make worse/very helpful*	7.23	7.50	7.23	7.69
Expectation of subordinates' questions being helpful *make worse/very helpful*	5.92	5.50	5.61	6.20
Subordinate estimates of leader bad decisions *not at all/a great deal*	—	—	4.00	2.93*
Perceived workload *very light/very heavy*	7.00	6.50	6.10	6.40
Felt in control of the situation *not at all/a great deal*	6.80	6.60	7.10	7.10
Felt self-confident *not at all/a great deal*	6.70	5.90	7.10	6.90
Appraised performance *very poorly/very well*	6.70	7.10	6.20	6.50

[a] All items used 9-point scales.
* Significant difference between means for restricted versus open communication structures.

substantial differences between the restricted and the open communication conditions, for both leaders and subordinates alike, with respect to how free they thought subordinates were to make suggestions and ask questions. Furthermore, in the open condition (where subordinates were permitted to make suggestions and ask questions), both leaders and subordinates rated the subordinates as having in fact been willing to do so. These results suggest that the experimental manipulation did alter the task architecture appreciably. The trained observers also reported a large difference between the two conditions in subordinates' attempts to influence their leaders' decision behaviour.

3.2.2. Potential Expectancy Effects

Although leaders and subordinates both expected that suggestions and questioning from subordinates would improve performance, there were no significant differences in these expectations across the two communication conditions. Furthermore, subordinates judged the leader to have made more bad decisions in the restricted condition than in the open condition. Since there were no mean differences in actual performance across conditions, this pattern suggests that participants' expectations were not realized and that therefore the null results cannot be attributed to expectancy effects. It is also noteworthy that there were no mean differences in perceived workload, feeling of control over the situation, feeling of self-confidence, or team performance appraisals across the two communication conditions (restricted versus open) or across the two roles (leader versus subordinate).

3.2.3. Interpreting the Findings

The following explanations (which are not mutually exclusive) might account for the lack of an overall difference in performance across these markedly different experimental conditions:

    a. there are in fact no sizable effects;

    b. for each subject, there are multiple effects in both directions that cancel each other out; and/or

    c. some subjects consistently perform better under a restricted condition, whereas other subjects consistently perform better under a more open condition.

The data provide evidence for both (b) and (c). Replays of subjects' simulation trials, inspection of subjects' own postincident reports, and comments by trained observers suggest that any advantages achieved by early error detection and correction and by pooling of team experience in the open condition were offset by several disadvantages. Communications from subordinates (a) limited the available communication time in which the leader could issue explicit instructions; (b) intruded on the leader's information processing (needed for developing and maintaining situation awareness, and for forming strategies); and (c) disrupted subordinates' cognitive processing (needed for implementing the leader's instructions). Thus, any advantages obtained with an open communication structure were cancelled out, at least when time pressure was high, by erosion of the time available to both leaders and subordinates for assessing the situation, generating an intention, selecting and communicating actions, and implementing those actions. In an open communication structure, additional disadvantages derive from specific threats to team coordination that are attributable to distorted authority relationships among team members. The trained observers' comments suggest that the greatest threats to team stability in the open communication condition stemmed from (a) subordinates who attempted to take over the leadership role with respect to their own sector, demanding a disproportionately large share of the limited firefighting resources; and (b) leaders who proved unable and/or unwilling to manage the inherent ambiguity in conflicting input received from subordinates.

3.3. Personality Characteristics and Decision-Making Effectiveness

We also examined the study data for evidence of systematic individual differences in team members' suitability for the alternative communication structures. Two personality characteristics appear pertinent—namely, "need for control" and "intuitive decision style." But before presenting and discussing these results in detail, we present data that bear on the hypothesized main effects for various personality characteristics on command and control decision performance.

3.3.1. Linear Contributions of Leader and Subordinate Characteristics to Performance

Since there were no significant interactions between leader and subordinate characteristics for any of the study variables (discussed further below), Table 2 reports correlations between scores on personality characteristics and overall decision performance separately for leaders and for subordinates. No pair of personality characteristics intercorrelated at a level greater than 0.4. Therefore, correlations between any one personality measure and performance can be interpreted relatively independently.

As shown in Table 2, the only leader personality characteristic that had a main (linear) effect on overall decision performance was the leader's "need for control." The hypothesized linear relationships for leader "interpersonal trust," "assertiveness," "self-confidence," "decisive decision style," "intuitive decision style," and "impulsive decision style" were not obtained. This pattern of findings suggests that in conditions where a leader must rely totally on subordinates' actions, the leader's ability to maintain a coordinated team is in part associated with a strong need to control. It may well be the case that better team leaders successfully regulate both the cognitive and affective demands that others place on them and the cognitive and affective demands that they, in turn, place on their subordinates.

For subordinates, on the other hand, only the personality characteristic "interpersonal trust" was found to be related to decision performance—and that relationship was in the *opposite* direction to that predicted: that is, low-trusting subordinates actually outperformed their more trusting peers. This result suggests that more trusting individuals might have been more complacent in cooperating with a leader's instructions. Perhaps trusting individuals (a) were not motivated to pay as much attention to the quality of decisions passed to them, taking on trust their leaders' motivations to do well; and (b) were unconcerned about possible negative evaluations by their leaders (or other subordinates) of their own sector's performance. This finding might appear somewhat counterintuitive, given the

Table 2. Correlations between Individual Differences in Personality Characteristics and Team Performance

	Leader (Total Team Score)			Subordinate (Sector Score)		
	Total $(N = 28)$	Restricted $(n = 14)$	Open $(n = 14)$	Total $(N = 112)$	Restricted $(n = 56)$	Open $(n = 56)$
Personality Characteristic						
Need for control	33*	−08[a]	77[a],*	04	08	00
Interpersonal trust	11	06	16	−20*	−26*	−14
Assertiveness	08	−15	30	−02	10	−13
Self-confidence	15	−06	36*	02	09	04
Decisive decision style	17	34*	06	−08	−06	−10
Intuitive decision style	08	−38[b]	45[b]	−06	−02	−10
Impulsive decision style	−07	16	−22	02	15	−10
Cognitive Functioning						
Information processing speed	30	19	54*	24*	33*	14
Field independence	38*	40*	50*	26	34	20
Experience of Task						
Felt in control of the situation *not at all/a great deal*	43*	46	41*	36*	26*	43*
Felt self-confident *not at all/a great deal*	43*	40*	48*	17*	14	19

Note. Decimal points have been omitted from all coefficients.
[a,b] Significant interaction with degree of openness in communication structure.
* Significant at 5 percent level or greater.

widespread acceptance of the central role played by mutual trust in maintaining morale and cohesion in military units. What these findings suggest is that in the specific context of a command and control team, people must earn trust; they don't receive it automatically according to some characteristic level of trustfulness in the other person. Furthermore, the study implemented a fully hierarchical command structure: subordinates were instructed to obey all commands. It is possible that characteristic levels of trustfulness may be advantageous in more devolved command structures (Penrose, this volume, Chapter 11; Pigeau & McCann, this volume, Chapter 12).

3.3.2. Curvilinear Effects of Personality on Performance

To assess possible curvilinear effects of personality characteristics on decision-making effectiveness, we entered each standardized personality score (as a z score) and its square as predictors into the regression equation. The regression coefficient for the quadratic component was taken as a measure of the curvilinear effect. We conducted separate analyses for leaders and for subordinates. Only leader "impulsive decision style" was found to be associated with a significant curvilinear effect ($b = -.64$, $p < .001$), with moderate levels of impulsiveness being preferable to extreme levels. The scatterplot of performance scores against "impulsive decision style" scores revealed that there were no outliers and that the curvilinear relationship held in both the restricted and the open communication conditions. We found no other curvilinear trends.

3.3.3. Interactions between Leader and Subordinate Personality in Effects on Own-Sector Performance

Although we had formulated no specific hypotheses concerning interactions between subordinate and leader personality characteristics in effects on decision-making effectiveness, we took advantage of the opportunity to explore the possibility of such effects. But none were detected.

3.3.4. Interactions between Leader and Subordinate Personality in Effects on Other-Sector Performance

We examined the possibility that a subordinate's personality characteristics might lead to changes in other subordinates' decision-making effectiveness (either directly or in interaction with the corresponding characteristic in the team leader). For example, a subordinate's behaviour could, in principle, lead to a decrement in performance in the remaining sectors (such as would occur if one subordinate managed to influence his or her superior to allocate him or her a disproportionately large number of resources). Again, no such effects were detected.

3.3.5. Interactions between Personality Characteristics and Communication Condition in Effects on Performance

We assessed the possibility of linear interactions between personality characteristics and communication condition in their effects on decision-making effectiveness, by entering the following predictors into the regression equation: condition (as a z score), personality score (as a z score), and the product of these two standardized variables. Once again, we ran separate analyses for leaders and for subordinates. Note that for leaders, our sample size of 28 provides low power for detecting interactions.

No significant interaction effects with the communication structure's degree of openness were detected for subordinate personality characteristics. But we did find significant interaction effects with the degree of openness of the communication structure for leader "need for control" and "intuitive decision style." Leader "need for control" (Figure 1) was unrelated to performance under a restricted communication structure; but under an open communication structure, leaders high in "need for control" significantly outperformed those low in need for control. The most plausible interpretation of this finding is that leaders who are low in need for control, when placed in an open communication structure, are unwilling or unable to coordinate firefighting activity over all sectors in the face of subordinates who demand a disproportionate share of both their time and the available firefighting resources.

A leader's "intuitive decision style" limited performance in a restricted communication structure but was conducive to high performance in an open

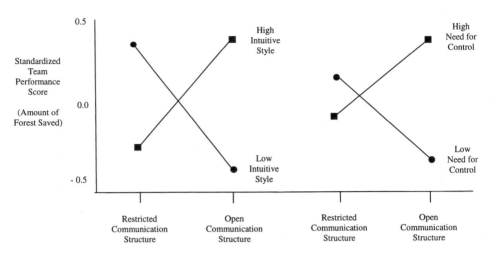

FIGURE 1. Mean team performance by leader "need for control" and "intuitive decision style," against degree of openness of communication structure.

communication structure (Figure 1). This result suggests that intuitive decision making is a relatively high-risk/high-payoff decision strategy: the advantages of fast, relatively automatic, intuitive decision-making are counterbalanced by the increased possibility of substantial, high-cost errors. In a restricted communication structure, such errors will go unchecked. But subordinates in an open communication structure can alert a leader to such errors, thereby providing a source of critical redundancy (Orasanu et al., 1998).

3.4. Control-Related Personality Characteristics, Control-Related Task Experiences, and Decision-Making Effectiveness

3.4.1. Relationship between Control-Related Task Experiences and Decision-Making Performance

Table 2 shows, not surprisingly, that those who felt most in control of the situation and most self-confident performed better, regardless of communication structure.

3.4.2. Relationship between Control-Related Personality Characteristics and Control-Related Task Experiences

Regardless of communication structure, there were no substantial relationships between subordinates' "need for control" and "self-confidence" (measured as personality characteristics) and task-related sense of control or self-confidence (as shown in Table 3). For leaders in the open communication structure *only*, "need for control" (but not "self-confidence") was significantly related to task-related levels of both feeling in control and feeling self-confident. These findings are consistent

Table 3. Correlations between Control-Related Personality Characteristics and Control-Related Task Experiences

	Leader			Subordinate		
	Total (N = 28)	Restricted (n = 14)	Open (n = 14)	Total (N = 112)	Restricted (n = 56)	Open (n = 56)
			Experience of Task Felt in control of the situation *not at all/a great deal*			
Personality Characteristic						
Need for control	36*	05*	66[a]*	14	08	19
Self-confidence	04	–13	17	–02	–10	05
			Felt self-confident *not at all/a great deal*			
Need for control	41*	24	52*	22	22	22
Self-confidence	07	00	07	14	11	19

Note. Decimal points have been omitted from all coefficients.
[a] Significant interaction with degree of openness in communication structure.
* Significant at 5 percent level or greater.

with those outlined above with respect to the observed degradation in the performance of leaders who were low in "need for control" under an open communication structure. The findings also strengthen the conclusion that leaders who are characteristically low in "need for control" are unwilling or unable to maintain sufficient actual control (and hence coordination) in those situations in which subordinates are able to exert some measure of control over them.

3.5. Individual Differences in Cognitive Functioning and Decision-Making Effectiveness

The extent to which the experimental task requires high-level cognitive functioning by participants (that is, the extent to which the task is cognitively demanding) is of interest for two reasons. First, it serves to illustrate that we have in fact created a task that has adequate external validity with respect to command and control decision making. Second, it allows for an examination of possible differences in the cognitive demands imposed by alternative communication structures.

Scores on the two measures of cognitive functioning—"information processing speed" and "field independence"—intercorrelated only moderately ($r = .38$), indicating some empirical overlap, but not sufficient to conclude that there is no useful conceptual distinction between the two. Table 2 shows the independent contributions of leader and subordinate "information processing speed" and "field independence" scores to task performance. Both cognitive-functioning measures correlated significantly with performance. Since the leader had total command authority, it is not surprising that the correlations for leaders' intellectual functioning tended to be somewhat higher than the corresponding correlations for subordinates. In comparing the relative importance of cognitive-functioning levels across degree of openness in communication structure, we found two trends (although neither was statistically significant): (a) leaders' "information processing speed" and "field independence" were more critical under an open communication structure (suggesting that communications from subordinates represent an additional information processing demand and an additional distraction); and (b) subordinates' "information processing speed" was more critical under a restricted communication structure.

4. GENERAL DISCUSSION

The findings are significant for two reasons. First, they contribute to our theoretical understanding of how people make decisions in complex distributed systems. Second, they bear on how best to select and train people who will need to manage time-critical command and control incidents, and how to implement command and control communication structures that optimize overall decision outcomes.

With respect to the degree of openness in the communication structure, we found no differences between an environment in which no suggestions or questions were allowed from subordinates and one in which suggestions and questions were unrestricted. What remains to be demonstrated, given the above-mentioned disadvantages of a fully open communication structure, is the possibility that the optimal communication structure for decision making might reside in the middle ground. A potentially useful structure might permit a *limited* degree of subordinate input—for example, by allowing subordinates to offer suggestions or challenges only when their superior makes a clearly identifiable error or oversight. More generally, what might fruitfully be explored in both field and experimental contexts is the potential advantage of implementing formal structures and procedures that legitimize and even encourage subordinate assertiveness.

Taking a somewhat different approach to the potential disadvantages of open communication, one might ask not so much *when* it is appropriate for a subordinate to be assertive, but *how* to be effectively assertive. For example, Fischer and Orasanu (1997) suggest that many aviation accidents can be attributed to subordinates' use of "indirect" (for example, "Should we consider checking for ice?") rather than "direct" (for example, "We should check for ice.") linguistic constructions when challenging superiors' decisions.

Our findings regarding personality characteristics give some evidence that the prevailing degree of openness in communications should be taken into account in selecting and training leaders for optimal performance. More specifically, in fully open systems, leaders could be encouraged to exercise tight control but also to rely on their intuitive reactions, in the knowledge that subordinates will feel able to challenge any errors they might make in doing so.

Note that the findings were obtained using a fully centralized *communication* structure and a fully hierarchical *command* structure (subordinates were constrained to follow all orders from the superior). The extent to which the study findings might generalize to more open communication structures and to environments in which subordinates have more local decision-making autonomy remains to be examined. But there are no a priori grounds for expecting that the findings would not so generalize.

5. ACKNOWLEDGMENTS

The networking of the *Fire Chief* program was funded by the Information Technology Division of Australia's Defence Science and Technology Organisation. Support was also provided by a grant from the Australian Research Council. The authors wish to acknowledge the contribution made by Jeremy Manton and John Hansen of the Defence Science and Technology Organisation. Significant contributions were also made by Peter Taranto, who took primary responsibility for the programming of *Networked Fire Chief*, and by Glenn Elliott, James Balmford, Irene Bobevski, and Debbie Fooks, who took primary responsibility for designing the firefighting scenarios and for implementing the study.

6. REFERENCES

Brehmer, B. (1992). Dynamic decision making: human control of complex systems. *Acta Psychologica, 81*(3), 211–241.
Brehmer, B., & Svenmark, P. (1994). Distributed decision making in dynamic environments: Timescales and architectures of decision making. In J. P. Caverni, M. Bar-Hillel, F. H. Barron, and H. Jungermann (Eds.), *Contributions to decision making research* (pp. 147–165). Amsterdam: North-Holland/Elsevier.
Burger, J. M. (1992). *Desire for control: Personality, social and clinical perspectives.* New York: Plenum Press.
Fischer, U., & Orasanu, J. (1997). *How to challenge the captain's actions.* Paper presented at the Ninth International Symposium on Aviation Psychology, Columbus, OH.
Flin, R. (1997). *Sitting in the hot seat.* Chichester, U.K.: Wiley.
Gaba, D., Howard, S., & Fish, K. (1994). *Crisis management in anaesthesiology.* New York: Churchill-Livingstone.
Gambrill, E., & Richey, C. (1988). The Gambrill and Richey Assertion Inventory. In A. Kidman (Ed.), *From thought to action: A self help manual* (pp. 92–94). St. Leonards, Australia: Biochemical and General Consulting Service.
Helmreich, R. L., & Foushee, H. C. (1993). Why resource management? In E. L. Weiner, G. B. Kanke, & R. L. Helmreich (Eds.), *Cockpit resource management* (pp. 3–45). San Diego, CA: Academic Press.
Hollander, E. P. (1993). Legitimacy, power and influence: A perspective on relational features of leadership. In M. M. Chemers & R. Ayman (Eds.), *Leadership theory and research: Perspectives and directions* (pp. 29–48). San Diego, CA: Academic Press.
Jackson, D. N. (1984). *Multidimensional Aptitude Battery.* Port Huron, MI: Sigma Assessment Systems.
Klein, G. A. (1993). A recognition-primed decision (RPD) model of rapid decision making. In G. A. Klein, J. Orasanu, R. Calderwood, & C. E. Zsambok (Eds.), *Decision making in action: Models and methods* (pp. 138–147). Norwood, NJ: Ablex.
McLennan, J. P., Omodei, M. M., Rich, D., & Wearing, A. J. (1997). Helmet-mounted video applications for fire officer training and operations. *Journal of the Fire Service College, 3,* 63–74.
Omodei, M. M., & McLennan, J. P. (in press). Conceptualising and measuring interpersonal mistrust–trust. *Journal of Social Psychology.*

Omodei, M. M., & Wearing, A. J. (1995). The *Fire Chief* microworld generating program: An illustration of computer-simulated microworlds as an experimental paradigm for studying complex decision-making behavior. *Behavior Research Methods, Instruments and Computers, 27*, 303–316.

Omodei, M. M., & Wearing, A. J. (1998). *Networked Fire Chief* (Version 1.0) [Computer program]. Melbourne, Australia: La Trobe University.

Omodei, M. M., Wearing, A. J., & McLennan, J. P. (1997). Head-mounted video recording: A methodology for studying naturalistic decision making. In R. Flin, M. Strub, E. Salas, & L. Martin (Eds.), *Decision making under stress: Emerging themes and applications* (pp. 137–146). Aldershot, U.K.: Ashgate.

Orasanu, J., Fischer, U., McDonnell, L., Davison, J., Haars, K., Villeda, E., & VanAken, C. (1998). How do flight crews detect and prevent errors?: Findings from a flight simulation study. In *Proceedings of the Human Factors and Ergonomics Society Forty-Second Annual Meeting*. Santa Monica, CA: Human Factors and Ergonomics Society.

Pearlin, L. I., & Schooler, C. (1978). The structure of coping. *Journal of Health and Social Behaviour, 19*, 2–21.

Rodvold, M. A., Orasanu, J., Murray, L., Tyzzer, L. K., & Eastman, J. (1998). *Has CRM succeeded too well?: Assertiveness on the flight deck*. Unpublished manuscript, NASA Ames Research Center, Moffet Field, CA.

Scott, S. S., & Bruce, R. A. (1995). Decision-making style: The development and assessment of a new measure. *Educational and Psychological Measurement, 55*, 818–831.

Wang, W. P., Luh, P. B., Serfaty, D., & Kleinman, D. L. (1991). Hierarchical team coordination: Effects of team structure. In *Proceedings of the Symposium on Command and Control Research* (pp. 2041–2047). Washington, DC: National Defense University.

Weick, K. E. (1990). The vulnerable system: An analysis of the Tenerife air disaster. *Journal of Management, 16*, 571–593.

Witkin, H. A., Oltman, P. K., Raskin, E., & Karp, S. A. (1971). *Manual for the Embedded Figures Tests*. Palo Alto, CA: Consulting Psychologists Press.

CHAPTER 26

RESEARCH CHALLENGES FOR THE HUMAN IN COMMAND[1]

CAROL McCANN and ROSS PIGEAU[2]

1. INTRODUCTION

As the chapters in this book attest, command is a rich and intricate tapestry of concepts, skills, and behaviour, demanding that military personnel of all ranks invent novel solutions to unique problems, often under extremely stressful environmental, physical, and emotional conditions. Time and again, the authors in this book have intimated (and indeed often stated) that the human alone shoulders the responsibility for achieving the mission: it is the commander's duty to conceive new tactics, to negotiate with belligerents, to manage resources, to monitor morale, to decide, to motivate, to reflect, to act—in short, to creatively express his or her will in the

---

[1] All references in this chapter to numbered chapters are to chapters in this volume. For example, a sentence that mentions "Pigeau and McCann (Chapter 12)" (or, in parentheses, "Pigeau & McCann, Chapter 12") with no date refers to the chapter by those authors in this volume (page numbers accompany any direct quotes): to follow up on such citations, see this volume's Table of Contents. But a citation with a date—typically formatted either "McCann and Pigeau (1999)" or "(McCann & Pigeau, 1999)"—refers to work published elsewhere: to follow up on such citations, see Section 8, "References," at the end of this chapter.

[2] We thank all the workshop participants for their contributions to the ideas summarized in this chapter. We have made every attempt to capture both the substance and the subtlety of participants' positions, while adding original material to round out the discussion and to create a coherent argument. Errors of omission, misinterpretation, or simply poor expression in this chapter are attributable solely to its two authors.

CAROL McCANN and ROSS PIGEAU • *Defence and Civil Institute of Environmental Medicine, 1133 Sheppard Avenue West, Toronto, Ontario, Canada M3M 3B9*

The Human in Command: Exploring the Modern Military Experience, edited by McCann and Pigeau, Kluwer Academic/Plenum Publishers, New York, 2000.

accomplishment of the mission.[3] Although technology—the modern siren that promises Western society speed, efficiency, and force multiplication—can certainly facilitate command, technology can also hinder it. Technology can encourage unrealistic expectations, spawn unforeseen consequences, or simply fail to work. Effective command and control (C^2) depends on human command, not technological control.

As we stated in Chapter 1, "The Human in Command: A Brief Introduction," militaries routinely deal with the direst human conflicts. They witness profound misery, they challenge Nature ceaselessly, and they confront aggressors—all the while striving to uphold their countries' moral and ethical values. Their task must at times seem daunting. Similarly, scientific attempts to understand human behaviour can be equally daunting: humans are, after all, extremely complex organisms. For both militaries and scientists, it is the desire to resolve human conflict, the hope that the human condition can be improved, that fuels the effort. We assert that the military and the research communities must not isolate themselves from each other in their efforts to understand and deal with human behaviour and conflict. The problems are too complex, and the stakes are too high. It is therefore imperative that the military endorse the importance and value of command research. It is equally imperative that the scientific community respond with theories, models, and research paradigms that are directly applicable to the military and their efforts. Each can profit from the other.

This final chapter attempts to merge command's scientific and military domains. We summarize here the many research topics and issues raised at the NATO (North Atlantic Treaty Organization) Human in Command Workshop—during both the formal paper sessions and the evening discussion periods. At that meeting, several participants pointed out that the commander of 2025 will join the service within the next five years. It is urgent, therefore, that scientific research provide militaries with knowledge that will help them equip this commander with the necessary physical, intellectual, emotional, and interpersonal skills to accomplish any mission, safely and effectively.

In order to merge the two domains (that is, science and the military), we must extend our view of command. We need to place command in a larger context—one that has implications for the entire military organization as well as for the individual officer. To facilitate this task and to assist our survey of command research issues, Figure 1 provides a tentative framework for anchoring our discussion. Central to this framework is the military organization itself, wherein command resides (see the large pyramid in Figure 1). The illustration ignores the specific internal structure of any particular military, focusing instead on the characteristics common to them all. For example, all militaries have a supporting component and an operational component, and all are structured hierarchically (thus, the top of the pyramid in Figure 1 represents more senior levels, whereas the base represents entry-level ranks). Furthermore, militaries never operate in isolation. They operate within at least two different contexts, each comprising several communities with which commanders must

---

[3] Indeed, elsewhere (McCann & Pigeau, 1999) we have proposed that command be officially redefined as *"the creative expression of human will necessary to accomplish the mission"* (p. 479; italics in original).

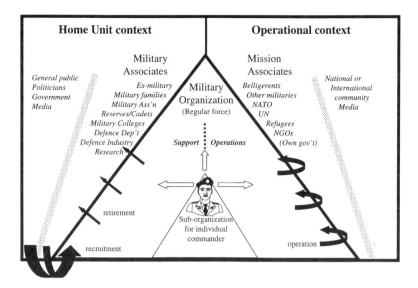

FIGURE 1. The contexts for command.

interact. The *home unit* context (shown on Figure 1's left side) comprises the communities from which the military gets its resources and those to which it is accountable. The *operational* context (on Figure 1's right side) comprises the communities with which the military must interact and coordinate during operations. Militaries must recognize and be responsive to the communities in both contexts. In fact, the amount of authority that an individual commander wields is to some extent related to the number of communities that the commander must deal with as part of his or her overall responsibilities. Very junior ranks typically concern themselves only with the military organization, whereas senior officers regularly deal with many groups outside their own organization.

We will use the framework in Figure 1 to structure our discussion of the myriad challenges facing the human in command—and thereby also address the relevant research issues. We will first describe the communities that flank a military organization's support and operational sides. Then we will explore the circumstances under which command interacts with these external communities. By the chapter's end, many command-related research questions will have surfaced.

2. THE HOME UNIT CONTEXT

Militaries are large institutions with unique characteristics not normally found in other organizations. Militaries embody a nation's ultimate expression of power and influence, either offensively or defensively. During extreme conflict or war, governments can task militaries to use lethal force against adversaries for the purpose of attaining strategic objectives. Militaries are thereby given the discretion to send their personnel into harm's way, with the full knowledge that those personnel may incur the ultimate liability.[4] This prerogative demands that militaries have strong organizational, social, legal, and cultural mechanisms for ensuring that they wield their power properly. Consequently, militaries almost always train, educate, and develop their own members: for example, they do not recruit, as full members, intermediate or senior officers either from other militaries or from the private sector. Since no nation can afford a military whose members are not committed to that nation's ideals and values, militaries must have their own (legislated) judiciary system for enforcing behaviour. Their codes of conduct must meet standards that are higher than those demanded of the nonmilitary general public. These unique organizational characteristics—extreme force, long-term professional commitment, a legal system that is separate from the country's civil legal system—greatly influence militaries' traditions, modes of operating, support structures, and command requirements. It is critical that appropriate attitudes and behaviours be established among military members well before exposing those members to the rigours of operational missions; otherwise, stress and confusion will quickly destroy discipline and morale. The home unit context of military life is therefore vitally important, since this is where military culture is formed and maintained.

We define the term *home unit* in its broadest sense, to include not only the military bases that house personnel and supplies in order to maintain operational readiness, but also the community of military associates (see Figure 1's left side) whose purpose is to provide extended and continuous support to the organization. For the most part, these associates are civilian organizations that sit between the general public and the military itself. The biggest and most influential such organization is a nation's department or ministry of defence. Other institutions in this category include defence contractors, professional associations (such as regimental, historical, or veterans' associations), military colleges and universities, and defence scientists. Retired military members, families of military personnel, veterans, members of reserves, and cadets round out the "associates" group. Outside the boundaries of these extramilitary communities, but still part of the home unit context, are the public at large, the politicians, the elected government, and the media.

The communities in a military's home unit context anchor that military in the national interest. They fund the military's operations, provide it with a personnel pool, and assign its tasks. And it is to these communities that the military must justify its existence, extol its successes, and account for its failures. The relationship between a military and these communities is characterized by dynamic interdependence. For example, politics and public perception greatly affect the way that a military conducts its business, both in peacetime and during times of hostilities. In the late 1980s, the Cold War's end precipitated debate over the military's changing role—particularly whether militaries should be involved in "other people's wars" (Capstick, Chapter 7, p. 83). In Canada, this dilemma has resulted in ambivalence about the country's military participation in U.N. peace support operations: the Canadian public takes pride in humanitarian activity, but has little tolerance for any

---

[4] *Ultimate liability* is a military euphemism for dying for one's country. Although individuals in other professions (for example, police, firefighters, and so on) often die in the line of duty, such individuals cannot be *ordered* to put their lives at risk.

casualties that may result. Public support for such operations can therefore be fickle, short-term, and greatly influenced by media coverage. For any military, the home unit context renders command decision making neither simple nor straightforward; to negotiate these requirements effectively, commanders must possess a cultural awareness, a political sensitivity, and a degree of tact that may run counter to traditional military problem-solving approaches.

The home unit context can affect military organizations at the systemic level—for example, it can influence military members' long-term attitudes toward their profession, as reflected in the vocational-versus-occupational tension that Capstick (Chapter 7) discusses. Since military service is no longer compulsory in many nations, there is a trend toward employing a longer-serving force. This trend is reshaping both recruitment strategies and career management. As a byproduct of this trend, military members now expect "reasonable" postings, opportunities for career advancement, better working conditions during operational deployments, and more equitable human rights. But militaries that allow these attitudes to go unchecked could find themselves populated by occupational soldiers (that is, people who take a 9-to-5 approach to their jobs) rather than by vocational soldiers (that is, individuals who view military service as a calling). What is the correct mixture? And what implications does this mixture have for management and leadership? Another systemic problem is the degree to which a military should reflect the cultural population of the nation it serves. How important is it to preserve military traditions, which provide necessary internal social stability, in the face of societal pressures to integrate the two genders and to accommodate multiple ethnic backgrounds? We believe that the potential command consequences of such "nonoperational" issues may prove more far-reaching than most technological innovations.

Finally, in today's climate of fiscal restraint and financial responsibility, many modern militaries face radically reduced budgets. Such constraints not only affect when and whether new equipment is developed and purchased (and, indeed, when and whether existing equipment is maintained), but also seriously limit opportunities for field training (Labbé, Chapter 9). Of the many factors that affect success in command, planning, training, and discipline are clearly among the most critical. Without the resources necessary for conducting realistic exercises, command's capabilities are severely hamstrung.

All of these factors—funding, support groups, politics, professionalism, recruitment, career management, media relations, and many more—are aspects of military life's home unit context. Besides providing novel human challenges for command, all are pivotal for achieving the high levels of readiness that militaries must demonstrate in order to conduct operations successfully.

3. THE OPERATIONAL CONTEXT

Militaries exist in order to act: more specifically, they exist in order to act on their governments' will. But over the past 15 years, the global and national contexts within which today's militaries find themselves have changed considerably. Indeed, change itself is now a pervasive aspect of military life, posing a significant challenge for command. The effects of change are especially evident in the operational context: today's militaries must often undertake operations that differ completely from those that militaries trained for during the Cold War period. Peace support and humanitarian missions are examples of such *operations other than war* (*OOTW*). They are becoming more frequent, and they demand a new set of command capabilities, such as negotiating skills, linguistic facility, and cultural awareness (Dallaire, Chapter 4). OOTW require mature and sophisticated approaches to problem solving, because the solutions they require are often more complex and more subtle than those that prove successful in classical warfare. It is not uncommon for OOTW missions to be poorly defined, to have shifting objectives, and to require complex rules of engagement. Furthermore, commanders and troops are sometimes placed in distressingly frustrating situations where they can do little more than observe a slaughter or witness the slow degeneration of civilian life (because they have been ordered only to monitor the situation and are forbidden to interfere). Finally, because modern societies show increasing resistance to incurring casualties in other people's wars, commanders have great difficulty finding the correct balance between force protection and military intervention. All of these factors conspire to make OOTW extremely demanding—organizationally, politically, morally, and personally.

Although militaries have always conducted missions that are situated geographically outside their home nation,[5] the number of international communities with which they must now interact is becoming bewildering large (see the "Mission Associates" section on Figure 1's right side). These communities include belligerents; other militaries (such as coalition members); NATO; the United Nations; nongovernmental organizations (NGOs); and civilian refugees. They form the myriad of players in OOTW, each with its own priorities and agenda. The number of organizations in the operational context makes collaboration difficult and reduces the likelihood of producing a coherent action plan. Everts, for example, describes the "inconceivable complexity of maneuvering between the conflicting interests of the belligerents, the enclave's inhabitants, and the national and international organizations" (Chapter 6, p. 77) in the context of operations in Srebrenica. The isolated location of some operational deployments, the poor communications, and the sheer number of military agencies involved can contribute to a sense of ambiguity in, or even a disconnection from, the chain of command (Everts, Chapter 6). Sometimes, though, the problem is the reverse: tactical decisions are made at the political or strategic level without sufficient information about or understanding of the real ground situation. Some commanders have noted that this tendency to micromanage missions seems to be on the rise (Cherrie, Chapter 3). Add to this the challenge of forging effective military teams among coalition forces, especially when each coalition member may have widely differing capabilities, assumptions, and cultural backgrounds (Dallaire, Chapter 4), and one begins to appreciate the complexity of operational command. Finally, the media's ubiquitous presence means that theatre commanders must be ever cognisant of the possible repercussions of

---

[5] Some military operations (for example, disaster assistance, or providing aid to a civil power) do take place within national boundaries, but they are the exception. The context for such operations has not been included in Figure 1.

having their decisions widely publicized. There is probably no greater inducement to conservatism than the knowledge that your decisions are being televised, replayed, and critiqued in front of an information-hungry audience.

In summary, the modern military mission's operational context, with all its ambiguities and complexities, demands a much higher level of command competency than was necessary in past decades. Militaries must anticipate, prepare for, and train to this competency level. Human science can help them achieve that goal.

4. COMMAND CAPABILITIES AND THEIR DEVELOPMENT

Thus far, we have briefly described the two contexts within which military organizations exist; we have sampled some of the challenges facing command in each context; and we have noted that modern commanders need quite a broad range of capabilities. But what, specifically, *are* those capabilities, and are they transferable from one context to the other (for example, do the same qualities that make a good leader in the home unit context also make a good leader in an operational context)? Also, what capabilities besides the "classical" command skills (such as leadership, integrity, and responsibility) are necessary for contemporary military operations: for example, might mental agility, creativity, and diplomacy be required? In addressing these questions, militaries have a responsibility to be as self-reflective (and honest) as possible. They must be able to enumerate those capabilities that are critical for modern command. For its part, the research community has a responsibility to understand the nature of these capabilities and to help the military develop methods for instilling them in its commanders. The workshop participants identified a number of these capabilities, which we have grouped into four categories: intellectual, emotional, interpersonal, and team-related.

Intellectual capability refers to cognitive skills, including information gathering, situation assessment, problem solving, and decision making. Although these skills have been valued by the military community and studied by the research community for years, we question how thoroughly they have been incorporated into training and evaluation. Ironically, this problem could benefit from the application of another intellectual capability that is important for command: the ability to think creatively and adapt to new ideas. It is well known that militaries value their traditions. While good reasons exist for doing so (for example, traditions ensure stability, and stability helps reduce stress in demanding operational situations), these traditions can also stifle creativity and inhibit risk-taking. Modern militaries' operational contexts demand novel solutions that can be implemented quickly. Although arriving at such solutions is often difficult, they may be more easily discovered by employing metacognition—that is, the ability to think about thinking, to understand one's own intellectual capabilities and direct them explicitly toward a solution. Metacognition allows the decision maker to step outside the problem's boundaries, to view the problem (and the resources for solving it) in a different light. Of all the intellectual skills necessary for command, metacognition is the least studied— although we would argue that it may be the capability most often used by successful commanders, particularly senior ones.

If intellectual capability is the most easily identified and most easily justified requirement for command, *emotional capability* is without doubt the least acknowledged and the least researched. Yet emotional fitness is unquestionably essential for command effectiveness. Resolve, resiliency, adaptability, patience, an ability to keep things in perspective, and even a sense of humour are key personality characteristics for maintaining motivation and propagating the will to achieve. Emotional capability is intimately related to how individuals respond to stress. To make a decision in comfortable surroundings is one thing. To make decisions when sleep-deprived, when cold and wet, when missing your family, and when unsure whether your presence is making any difference to the conflict at hand is quite another. Militaries need to (a) understand how individuals cope with stress, (b) know how to plan for its effects, (c) have strategies in place for predeployment training of both members and their families, and (d) objectively assess and treat individuals who are suffering from stress in-theatre.

The third category of command capabilities is *interpersonal skills*. Such skills are crucial because they form the base for a core command function—namely, leadership. Cherrie (Chapter 3) and other workshop participants highlighted several attributes of good leaders: visibility and presence, approachability, the ability to motivate and inspire, the ability to assess subordinates' capabilities and limitations, the ability to communicate verbally and nonverbally. Interpersonal competency is especially important for OOTW, where cultural awareness, negotiation skills, and linguistic proficiency are now becoming mandatory. Just as militaries must cultivate their commanders' emotional capabilities, militaries must also improve their understanding and development of their commanders' interpersonal capabilities.

Finally, and closely tied to interpersonal skills, are *team-building capabilities*—the ability to form effective teams and foster coordinated group effort. To be successful as a team builder, a commander must be able to recognize and select team members based on the correct mixture of competencies; to instill supportive attitudes (such as respect) among them; to establish trust, confidence, and cohesion; and to correctly distribute authority and responsibility among team members. Militaries must ask themselves whether their traditional organizational structures, which are based on warfighting philosophies, promote the type of teamwork skills that may be necessary for complex missions in OOTW.

With these four general classes of capabilities in mind, we are now in a position to explore how they are developed in potential commanders as these individuals traverse the military organization in the course of their careers. In short, we will be describing how commanders gain experience, authority, and responsibility, both in the home unit context and in the operational context. This description will prove important when we propose key research areas in Section 5, "Research Issues in Command."

Potential commanders, who are recruited either from the civilian population or via military colleges (the bottom left corner of Figure 1), enter the military organization as very junior members with little responsibility. At this point, they possess quite limited knowledge and understanding both of the operational context (sometimes based on prevailing romantic notions of combat) and of the home unit context. Although they receive much training and development during the first year after recruitment (largely involving physical skills), this period is directed mainly toward indoctrinating the new member into the military culture. The traditions of the service (for example, air, land, or sea), the unit (for example, squad, wing, or regiment), and the force in general are impressed onto the individual, who is inculcated with the values and ethos of military life. Later, after more specialized training, these individuals become members of a unit that is operationally deployed (that is, they move to the right side of the military triangle in Figure 1). Since their tasks at this point are usually very focused, they have only limited exposure to the mission's context, a limitation that is reflected graphically in Figure 1 by the narrow width of the operational context at that level.

From then on, the typical military career consists of a series of cycles between support and operational postings, with the (potential) commander gaining experience, responsibility, and increased rank. Some retire from the military along the way, while some eventually head small subgroups of military subordinates (for example, a company or squadron), establishing relationships with those subordinates as well as with other commanders at the same level. As they undertake, for example, staff work in the defence department, or assignments in training organizations or with the reserves, their view of and relationships with the communities in the home unit context broaden. Their view of the operational context is extended when they are deployed as commanders with broader mandates and more responsibility, requiring increasing interaction with NATO, NGOs, and other militaries. In this way, commanders move, during their careers, up the levels of rank and responsibility in the military. Their areas of influence in both the home unit context and the operational context gradually increase, while at the same time the complexity of the domains and relationships that they deal with also grows. Their intellectual, emotional, interpersonal, and team capabilities become more relevant and important as they increase in rank.

Senior commanders have direct authority over their subordinates; just as importantly, they have a varying degree of influence over the communities that flank the military organization. At the same time, those communities significantly influence command. Commanders in the operational context, for example, must deal with the activities of the belligerents or NGOs as well as with the political decisions (or indecision) of NATO or the United Nations. Such a commander is influenced by the state of his or her own family—whether they are being adequately cared for during the commander's deployment. Such commanders must interpret the department's decisions, interact with the media, and be concerned with public relations. Thus an increasing part of the business of command involves managing what happens *outside* the military organization, especially on its boundaries.

In summary, then, command issues concern not only how individual commanders perform their tasks, but also how the military institution as a whole approaches developing and supporting command capability—through selection, education, training, career management, appropriate organizational structures, and so on. As an institution, the military must consider its interactions with the communities on its boundaries. On the home unit side, it must ensure that military families are supported; that defence contractors are well managed; that military colleges produce young officers with the potential for command; and that the public correctly perceives the military's effort, values, and commitment. On the operational side, it must ensure that it properly equips and supports its personnel; effectively manages their leave and pay during operational deployments; and adapts to new kinds of operations, such OOTW.

Militaries are large organizations with complex, strategically important tasks; thus their commanders must possess a range of capabilities exceeding those of most professions. In short, command is a gold mine for scientific study—so much so, in fact, that it is difficult to know where to start. Section 5, "Research Issues in Command," attempts to list the more pressing research questions facing command.

5. RESEARCH ISSUES IN COMMAND

Our framework for discussing the military, its contexts, and the command capabilities needed for successfully carrying out missions now puts us in a position to outline the research issues facing command. We hope that the previous sections, and indeed the previous chapters in this book, have convinced the reader that those in the profession of arms confront unique and difficult challenges. They must tackle problems that most organizations have neither the capability nor the will to undertake.

In their deliberations, workshop participants agreed that the following items are among the most important aspects of command that currently require study. Although elements of some of these topics (for example, corporate and political leadership, and normative decision making) have been investigated at universities and in private industry, they also need to be researched in the military context, by experts who understand the domain.

5.1. Leadership

Underlying many of the workshop's presentations and discussions was the critical issue of leadership. While there is no question that leadership has always been important in military operations, the contexts (both home unit and operational) in which commanders lead have been changing. According to Capstick, "[t]he challenge for commanders and leaders in peace support operations is to adapt the classic leadership theories and principles to the realities of today's soldiers and operational context" (Chapter 7, p. 89). For example, building an effective coalition force, the norm in today's operations, requires the welding of military personnel who come from different cultures and who have varying abilities and expectations. Military leaders can find themselves caught between their political masters, their allies, the United Nations, and the belligerents, with only an ill-defined mandate—and sometimes with no mandate at all. Dallaire (Chapter 4), Capstick (Chapter 7), and Everts (Chapter 6) each allude to the difficulty of assessing risk to troops against (sometimes meagre) benefits to the operation. In OOTW, how can commanders motivate subordinates to carry out tedious and difficult tasks when there is no direct threat to them or their nation? At the other end of the spectrum, how can commanders make cool-headed judgments regarding what tasks must be done and then inspire their troops to complete them when death is very much at hand (Cherrie,

Chapter 3; Lane, Chapter 5)? And finally, what leadership skills are necessary for making sound moral judgments—moral in the context of a foreign culture—on the spot and in the glare of the media? The doctrinal framework for leadership presented by Lewis, Butler, Challans, Craig, and Smidt (Chapter 10) usefully delineates and categorizes the values, attributes, and skills considered essential for U.S. Army leaders. This work needs to be extended and validated.

The situational issues described above place huge demands on military leaders. They need to have confidence in themselves, their principles, and their values, while simultaneously maintaining a global, historical perspective. They need interpersonal and communication skills to conduct sensitive negotiations and to interact with the media and with NGOs. But more importantly, as leaders, they need to establish and maintain common intent among their subordinates. Several participants, both military and academic (see Cherrie, Chapter 3, p. 23; Connor, Chapter 8; and Crabbe, Chapter 2, p. 13), noted this crucial aspect of command. When a commander's intent is clear, unity of effort and coordination of action are facilitated, even when events do not unfold according to plan. Common intent across members of a military organization or team can be established through explicit, public communication (for example, by presenting orders verbally and in person) or through more subtle, implicit mechanisms—for example, during training or informal social gatherings (Pigeau & McCann, Chapter 12, offer a fuller description of explicit and implicit intent). Shattuck and Woods (Chapter 19) provide evidence that communicating intent between brigade and battalion commanders is more difficult and, in general, less successful than was previously assumed. Establishing and propagating intent, especially during rapidly changing situations, is therefore considered a key research area in the study of leadership.

5.2. Teamwork

We began our discussion with leadership because it plays such a significant role in other military activities, particularly team building. Indeed, some argue (Bennis, 1999) that excellence in leadership seems to correlate with a leader's ability to choose and retain highly competent staff members who work well together. Certainly a commander's staff can contribute enormously to his or her overall effectiveness. Team building is required not only at the local level (that is, at the commander's staff level) but also at the mission level, where the commander must forge productive relationships between many players, including coalition nations, politicians, and NGOs. This suggests two important research areas in teamwork: (a) methods that leaders can use to identify and select individual members and then to organize them into effective teams; and (b) the potential effects of cultural diversity and social differences on team building. Such research can help raise awareness of leadership issues, and possibly serve as a basis for training in leadership skills.

Apart from their importance to leadership, teams and teamwork are fundamental to the success of military operations. Whether the team is a small air unit on board a frigate or a multinational coalition, as in the Gulf War, team members should share a common understanding of the problem, a common concept for solving it, and a common motivation to achieve success. Lane, describing the team-building process in the Falklands War context, comments that "[t]he more [the team members] trust the leader, the more they give without having something explicitly demanded of them" (Chapter 5, p. 52). Thus, trust and mutual respect play an important role in team building and in a team's functioning. These factors seem even more crucial today, with militaries increasingly attempting to implement the doctrine of mission command, under which subordinate commanders are told the mission objectives and are given latitude for accomplishing them. As Vogelaar and Kramer (Chapter 15) observe, success in mission command demands that three kinds of mutual trust be established: (a) trust by superior commanders that their subordinates will act in accordance with the superior's intentions; (b) an awareness by commanders of how others at the same level in the hierarchy will react in a situation; and (c) trust by subordinate commanders in their superior commander's decision-making capability, integrity, and support.

Many workshop participants who identified team building and teamwork as an issue for research focused on the concept of cohesion as one whose role in a team's functioning and operational effectiveness deserves particular attention. Intuitively, cohesiveness seems to be a basic characteristic of good teams. But the notion of cohesion goes well beyond the simple idea that team members must like each other—in fact, they may not. Instead, cohesion is established by communicating intent, creating a shared vision, and carefully coordinating action. That said, there is little scientific knowledge for how these acts are actually accomplished. Murphy and Farley (Chapter 21) describe work that represents a start in this direction.

Although a degree of cohesion is certainly desirable for effective teamwork, having teams that are too cohesive can produce negative consequences. Such teams tend to create boundaries between themselves and others—as, for example, Winslow (Chapter 20) points out in describing the Canadian Airborne Regiment. These boundaries encourage an "us-versus-them" attitude that can lead to very dangerous behaviour—for example, where the team's needs outweigh the organization's needs. Thus the issue of cohesion is not nearly as straightforward as it may first appear.

Research in team building should therefore address such issues as team organizational structure, the appropriate mixture of team members, balanced team cohesion, and the leadership qualities needed for attaining and implementing desirable team qualities.

5.3. Decision Making

Effective command requires that correct decisions be made in a timely manner. In order to do so, commanders must possess considerable proficiency in military problem solving—a skill that in turn depends on (a) developing complex and highly interconnected cognitive structures; (b) acquiring such skills as logical and spatial reasoning, memory management, and efficient attention allocation; (c) being creative in one's approaches and solutions to problems; and (d) being able to track and understand one's own capabilities, limitations, and biases (that is, metacognition). Workshop participants recommended that the ways in which commanders attain, develop, and ultimately use these cognitive skills be flagged as an important area for research.

Unlike some of the other areas, decision making has a relatively long and distinguished history as a research topic. But its research history has been dominated by problems for which a single solution was considered correct—and, by association, for which there existed only one correct method for arriving at this solution. Furthermore, the problem situations that have been used in laboratory studies have not been dynamic and time-dependent, as they are in real-life command and control (Brehmer, Chapter 16). These factors have limited the generalizability of research results.

Fallesen (Chapter 13) presents evidence that commanders use different approaches in planning an operation depending on whether the situation is familiar and whether the stakes are high. Interestingly, these approaches typically do not involve formal analysis, nor do they involve concurrent option comparison (the method recommended in current doctrine). Rather, expertise is the determining factor for choosing a decision-making strategy—an expertise gained mainly through experience. But today's militaries face problems that differ radically from those they encountered in the past, making it more difficult for commanders to attain sufficient expertise through experience. Research has a clear role here. By investigating alternative decision-making methods and by devising ways to test these methods, scientists may be able to help commanders attain the needed degree of expertise via training. We are not suggesting that the existing (formal) methods for making decisions are wrong or are not useful—only that research is needed in order to better understand the circumstances under which formal versus informal approaches to reasoning are appropriate, particularly for those military situations involving high levels of complexity, uncertainty, time stress, and tension. Also important will be the continued development of appropriate experimental environments, such as microworlds, for studying the continuous dynamic decision-making tasks that characterize command and control (see Brehmer, Chapter 16; also Omodei, Wearing, & McLennan, Chapter 25).

Consensus was strong among participants that creativity in military problem solving is an issue of utmost importance. As one workshop participant, Canadian Lieutenant-Colonel Wayne Pickering, put in during a discussion period, "In the certain-to-be-uncertain missions that we will face in the future, I think it's absolutely essential that we have senior commanders who are creative." Creativity is that most elusive of cognitive skills—one for which, by definition, no formulaic or algorithmic approaches exist. Although there is a significant amount of literature on creativity, mainly from the business management field, much of it is anecdotal. The literature that is based on scientific research seems too sterile to generalize to military situations—although successful attempts have been made to summarize and teach this work (see Fallesen, Chapter 13). Therefore, a concerted attempt to study creativity in military scenarios should be encouraged, followed by an aggressive training program aimed at fostering its practice.

Unfortunately, even if the research community successfully discovers creativity's underlying principles, organizational and cultural obstacles may interfere with its use in military environments. Like most large organizations, military organizations tend to be conservative. Ideas that are too radical—that imply a degree of organizational risk—tend to be suppressed, or, at the very least, not encouraged. In fact, some workshop participants suggested that military organizations often weed out creative individuals early on, or stifle creativity and instill conformity by the time an individual reaches the senior command level. Crabbe, in describing the negative reaction to his innovative use of initiative during a training exercise in Alaska (Chapter 2, pp. 12–13) supports these observations. Labbé endorses the importance of encouraging both officers and noncommissioned officers to "think outside the mold" (Chapter 9, p. 123) and of providing them with opportunities (as well as time) to develop innovative ideas. These observations on creativity suggest that research should concentrate on answering at least three questions: Exactly what constitutes creativity in military environments, and how can it be measured and assessed in an individual? How can creative decision making be successfully taught, once understood? And how can military organizations, as hierarchically structured, stability-seeking cultures, encourage innovative thinking and risk-taking? The answers to these questions could go a long way toward solving many of the problems militaries face in OOTW.

Not all problems, of course, need creative solutions. The military domain is, thankfully, not totally chaotic. The predictable aspects of the environment have allowed the development of sophisticated surveillance, information, and weapons systems for warfare. Increased versatility, maneuverability, durability, and speed have produced vastly more complex physical and information spaces for military operations. High-capacity, relatively low-cost digital systems now allow militaries to rapidly capture, sort, link, and present huge quantities of information. But this boon for military capability is also a potential bane for commanders. Digital technology collects and stores far more information than any individual can assimilate. Furthermore, it often displays this information so poorly that the relevant portions are missed. Hence, the military investment in digital information technology is at risk of being ineffectual (or, worse, dangerous) because no commensurate investment has been made in human science. To remedy this situation, computer-based decision support systems must satisfy at least three basic requirements: (a) deliver only relevant, contextual information suited to the problem; (b) structure and present this information in a manner that allows the user to integrate it quickly and easily; and (c) provide intuitive and flexible utilities for querying databases when information is suspect or missing. Workshop participants felt that immediate research effort should be expended on the second function—namely, structuring and presenting information in ways that are consistent with user models. This difficult problem will need to draw on research in two areas of psychology. The first area examines how decision makers themselves structure and process information: that is, the schemas or scripts underlying the mental models that people hold when tracking an unfolding situation; the cognitive procedures and heuristics for organizing and integrating information—in short, the "cognitive economies" that humans use during problem solving. The second area explores the extent to which these cognitive economies differ among individuals.

Interestingly, even if solutions to the above problems are found, higher-level problems may then present themselves. For example, what is the appropriate level of trust that commanders should place in computer-based decision aids? Should this trust be different than that placed in information provided by other humans?

Another potential problem concerns the secondary effects that new technology may have on operations. Several workshop participants from military backgrounds (for example, Crabbe, Chapter 2; Labbé, Chapter 9) noted that digitization and information technologies may lure commanders back into their headquarters (where the bulk of the information resides) and away from the battlefield, where their presence is critical for influencing the battle. Finally, while no one questions the value of computer-based technologies for providing cognitive support to command, there is concern that technology not be permitted to take over the jobs of planning and of making decisions. Commanders, after all, are not simply decision makers; they are sentient members of organizations who must also take responsibility for those decisions.

5.4. Values and Attitudes

If decision making is the cornerstone of the command edifice, then values and attitudes are its foundation. Most military problems have multiple correct solutions. But some solutions are more acceptable than others. What guides decision makers— be they leaders or members of teams—in choosing solutions are the values and attitudes of the military organization itself.

Several military contributors to the workshop described attitudes that influence command, either positively or negatively. Crabbe (Chapter 2) highlights resoluteness—a characteristic that cannot be taught easily—as paramount for command. Cherrie notes with some dismay the lack of a "caring" (Chapter 3, p. 20) attitude toward subordinates on the part of many senior commanders. Capstick points out the risk of allowing junior leaders to adopt "the exaggerated macho style made popular in American movies and thus convey a rogue image that is incompatible with the principles of peace support operations—and, in fact, would be dangerous in war" (Chapter 7, p. 87). It is important, therefore, to be able to identify the values and attitudes that are critical for command and to understand the role that they play in leadership development and decision making.

Workshop participants stressed the importance of selecting and developing military members (and potential commanders) who reflect the values of the nation they serve. As Canada's Somalia Inquiry (Canada 1997), along with similar investigations in other countries, demonstrated, the public has little tolerance for military attitudes and behaviours that it considers inappropriate. But in ethnically diverse countries, where there may be a range of (possibly incompatible) values, selecting members who reflect appropriate military values can pose a challenge. Furthermore, militaries are under constant pressure to conform to changing public attitudes, as reflected in new government policies regarding, for example, gender integration and the inclusion of visible minorities. The diversity of values and attitudes in the general population poses serious challenges for modern militaries. Not only is it difficult to achieve a uniform code of values and attitudes to guide correct decision making, but team cohesion and cooperation—that is, the establishment of common intent (see Pigeau & McCann, Chapter 12)—are also more difficult to achieve. But a culturally diverse military force offers clear benefits, especially for establishing credibility in different international theatres.

Thus, achieving the right degree of diversity in a military force is an important research issue. As we mentioned in the introduction to this chapter, military organizations are unique because they must recruit, train, and educate their entire workforce. Most new members enlist directly through recruitment centres, while a smaller number enter as officer cadets through military colleges or from university officer-training programs. And the majority of these recruits are young people, between the ages of 18 and 24. Only rarely do people enter military service later in life. Militaries are therefore limited to recruiting from a subset of the larger population—a subset whose members may still be caught up in the nonconformist attitudes typical of young adults. The challenge is either to recruit members with the appropriate organizational values—commitment, self-discipline, work ethic, acceptance of responsibility, and so on—or to instill those values in the new recruits. Failure to do so will result in systemic social problems like those Capstick describes, where some members view soldiering as an occupation while others prefer the more aggressive image of the "[r]ogue [w]arrior" (Chapter 7, p. 87).

5.5. Handling Stress

Maintaining motivation, another important aspect of leadership, is especially difficult in uncertain situations that offer limited scope for action, as described in Everts's account of the Dutch peace support operation in Srebrenica (Chapter 6). And restoring motivation when a key team member is killed in action (Cherrie, Chapter 3) is particularly challenging for leaders. Both cases involve human response to stress: chronic stress in Dutchbat's case and acute stress in the case involving a team member's death. Workshop participants saw stress and stress management as topics in dire need of research (a) to assess the type and severity of stress associated with military operations, (b) to develop monitoring systems or checklists that will help commanders identify stress-related problems, and (c) to recommend and test stress interventions. The results of this research would then lead to guidelines for commanders in the field—guidelines that are "flexible enough to allow a commander to respond to the stresses and strains of each operation," allowing commanders to "pull soldiers out, let them vent their frustration under controlled conditions, and then bring them back according to the tempo, the nature, and the demands of the mission" (Dallaire, Chapter 4, p. 48). It is also important to systematically identify the various factors that contribute to stress in different operational deployments, as Breakwell (Chapter 23) does in the case of senior U.K. commanders. It may be possible to reduce or eliminate some of these factors. In other cases, training to resist a specific combat stressor may be the answer. Research can help militaries determine the optimal approach for stress resistance training—for example, Laberg, Eid, Johnsen, Eriksen, & Zachariassen's investigations of resisting interrogation (Chapter 22).

Although other professions (for example, firefighting and police work) can also be said to have a home unit context and an operational context, few professions experience the sharp dichotomy between the two contexts that is common in the military. One week a commander's team can be under fire in a remote part of the world, witnessing horrific events, and the next week they can be back home with their families and friends attending their children's soccer matches. The enormous psychological contrast between these situations can make recovery—whether of a "normal" lifestyle or of a state of readiness for the next operation—difficult. Very little research has been done on postdeployment support for returning military personnel and on the psychological aspects of their reintegration into their home unit situation.

Another aspect of postdeployment support concerns recovering operational effectiveness, at both the individual level and the unit level. How long do individuals take, psychologically, to return to a state of readiness, and what is the recovery curve's shape? What are the advantages and disadvantages of keeping units together through many deployments? Should commanders regularly re-evaluate subordinates' skills during operations and potentially reassign certain subordinates to different duties to ease the effects of stress and reduce the possibility of burnout?

At a higher level, militaries need to know how they, as organizations, are responding to the pressure of multiple deployments. They need assistance in finding ways to capitalize on their operational experiences. After all, organizations are not immune to stress. Cutbacks, personnel reductions, equipment rust-out, poor media relations, inadequate leadership—all can lead to low morale, attrition, poor motivation, extended sick leave, and so on. Militaries need mechanisms for understanding their own behaviour, for gauging the health of their own culture. Often, this function is given to military centres for "lessons learned," where strategies for "telling the story" are implemented. But during discussion sessions, some workshop participants commented that although operational lessons are identified and recorded (often in great detail), military organizations rarely *learn* from those lessons. Research methods are needed for studying how militaries can exploit lessons learned from previous operations—how they can create, maintain, and use "organizational (or corporate) memory."

5.6. Training Policy and Methods

One organizational responsibility of military command involves determining what training and education military members need in order to function successfully in a range of operational missions. Research can assist in establishing both training policy and training methods. What, for example, is the correct balance between training for warfighting and training for peace support operations? How can this balance be improved with a more comprehensive training program for joint commanders (for example, see Jeffery, Lambe, & Bearfoot, Chapter 24)? What is the psychological cost of learning warfighting skills and then being deployed on operations with very restrictive rules of engagement?

Research could also facilitate the development of approaches, methods, and measures for unique training programs, as exemplified by Paris, Johnston, and Reeves (Chapter 18) for team training, or by Mirabella, Siebold, and Love (Chapter 17) for multiforce training. Particularly urgent is the need to train for skills unique to OOTW, such as cultural awareness, communicating with the media, and negotiating.

Many training programs struggle with the cost of conducting full-scale exercises. For instance, shortages in equipment for training are common, the expense of moving personnel and equipment to the field can be prohibitive, and concerns over the environmental impact of field training are greater than ever. Simulation-based training is therefore becoming increasingly popular as an alternative to field training for mission preparation. Simulations offer better control over training protocols, provide greater opportunities for measuring performance, and allow trainees to play out scenarios whose consequences would be unacceptable in field training. Predeployment simulations can be extremely useful for visualizing a mission's dynamic components and for rehearsing aspects of a plan to gain a feel for time and distance interactions.

But there are valid questions about the degree to which simulation training generalizes to real-world situations. In order to function, simulations must bound both the problem space and the response space. Does this inevitable restriction make them less suitable for training nonstandard (that is, creative) approaches to problem solving? And if so, even though warfighting simulations are becoming quite common, can effective simulators be constructed for OOTW? Can simulations be used to teach negotiation skills, conflict resolution, humanitarian mine-clearing, disaster relief, cultural awareness, aggressive posturing, and so on? These are intriguing and important research questions.

5.7. Organizational Structures

Many of our research recommendations have implications for the role of military organizations. Research is required on the most appropriate organizational structures for handling the full spectrum of operations that militaries now encounter—from training and disaster relief operations, which are carried out in peacetime settings, through various types of operations other than war, to limited or full-scale war using traditional combat methods. Different types of operations may require different kinds of organizational structures—a fact that in turn has implications for command authority. For instance, with the increasing pace of battle and the increased lethality of battlefield weapons in full-scale combat (for example, a soldier with a laser designator and a radio set can now guide weapons of mass destruction directly to targets), battlespace dynamics are being altered. This shift may well necessitate a corresponding change in the structure of military organizations, including a devolution of authority to allow lower-level commanders to react, to be innovative and creative, and to take advantage of vulnerabilities in the enemy's disposition. As Persson, Nyce, and Eriksson (Chapter 14) point out in discussing autonomy, military organizations face an important issue that also confronts many other organizations: the degree of centralization versus decentralization in the organizational structure. The doctrine of mission command, for example, suggests a more decentralized structure than has been typical for command and control in the past. But as Vogelaar and Kramer's investigations (Chapter 15) conclude, such a structure may not be appropriate or possible in all instances. Specifically, research should address the factors that affect the optimal choice of organizational structure, as well as the relationship between structure and establishing intent.

Several workshop participants voiced particular concern regarding the best structures for operations other than war (OOTW): for example, is the traditional chain of command, which is highly effective for warfighting, the right instrument for OOTW? During a discussion session, one workshop participant proposed an alternative: a structure comprising generals working at the operational level and lieutenants and NCOs at the decision-making level, with those between acting as coordinators. Such a radically different structure would have profound implications for the roles, relationships, and training of military members. Penrose's account of the results of implementing a devolved self-directed teams structure in the Australian Federal Police (Chapter 11) documents the difficulties associated with organizational change and suggests that new structures, though potentially beneficial (for example, more flexible), risk upsetting strong, long-established, often tacit relationships and assumptions. An equally important research topic is the appropriate force structure and balance for coalition operations, in which coalition members come from different nations and thus may hold widely differing assumptions about their roles and expected contributions.

6. FOSTERING RESEARCH ON COMMAND

We began this chapter by describing the military domain as situated within two contexts—the home unit context and the operational contexts. Then we highlighted several problem areas that human science research could help solve. We must now make an embarrassing disclosure: few of the research issues that we have identified are particularly new. In the military arena, most of these issues are perennials, arising year after year. Some do reflect changing global politics and technological advances, but by and large, today's principal command challenges correspond fairly closely with yesterday's. Leadership, decision making, stress and coping, teamwork, training, organizational structure—all go back decades.

Why, then, has there not been a long and productive relationship between militaries and the social sciences?[6] In fact, the two domains have had a relationship—but only to a degree. Psychologists, sociologists, historians, and human factors engineers have indeed contributed to solving military problems for years, but the scale of the social scientists' involvement has been pitifully small. For example, McCann and Pigeau (1996) remark that in Canada, human factors research in command and control (C^2) has amounted to less than 3 percent of the nation's entire C^2 research program. The real reason for the lack of relationship between scientists and militaries is more complicated. Consider the following discussion-session remarks, made by a Canadian military participant at the workshop who offered three reasons for commanders' reticence about working with scientists.

> First, [commanders] tend to be conservative, because of the consequences of their actions: they have the lives of a lot of young people under their care. As a result, they tend to be a little suspicious of science, because it offers great change. Second, com-

---

[6] At this point, we adopt the term *social science* rather than *human science* to include psychologists, sociologists, historians, political scientists, and anthropologists.

manders are not used to being questioned on their fundamental beliefs. Scientists tend
to question all of us on our fundamental beliefs. [Third], commanders have egos—and
that's not a bad thing, because when all else fails, it may be your ego that's the only
thing that will carry you through a disaster. But again, scientists tend to deflate commanders' egos. Now, if scientists can figure out how to get to commanders and
overcome those problems, then the relationship will be greatly improved. (Lieutenant-
Colonel Wayne Pickering)

Commanders, it seems, are human. They have the same foibles and are susceptible
to the same conflicts as the rest of humanity—particularly person-versus-self conflicts (see Chapter 1, "The Human in Command: A Brief Introduction"). But militaries are changing. Sober self-reflection is taking place. Militaries are admitting to
human problems and soliciting social scientists' help in solving those problems.

Unfortunately, social scientists have responded slowly to military requests,
citing inadequate funding, immature scientific paradigms, inadequate domain
knowledge, and poor access to military populations as obstacles to proceeding.
Social scientists, it seems, are human too—capable of rationalizing with the best of
them. Because both communities deserve better, profitable avenues for collaboration must be found.

We will first discuss how militaries can facilitate social science research. Then,
in turn, we will recommend ways that social scientists can make their research more
relevant and more accessible to militaries.

6.1. Military Initiatives

Militaries can encourage and support social science research and development in
several ways. First and most simply, workshop participants suggested that senior military leaders strongly and publicly endorse the value of social science research into
command. Junior military members sometimes acquire the perception that admitting weakness is a crime—and one that's worse than the original weakness itself.[7]
Public endorsement would thus send a positive message that senior leadership is
concerned about the emotional, intellectual, and interpersonal well-being of all
military personnel. Indeed, many of this book's chapters represent just such
endorsements.

Endorsement is necessary, but it is not sufficient to bring about the desired
improvements. It must be backed up by policies and programs that encourage
members to collaborate with research scientists. Such a shift will in turn require a
significant attitudinal change within the military, because social science research
differs fundamentally from other forms of research. Sensor or weapon research can
occur off-site, in isolated laboratories, without disrupting military personnel's day-
to-day work. But most social science research cannot be conducted that way, since
the objects of study are the personnel themselves. Although some fundamental
research can be conducted in government and university laboratories using civilian
experimental subjects, applied research always eventually needs to be conducted
inside the military organization. Militaries will therefore need to open their work

---

[7] Interestingly, such perceptions extend only to *human* or personnel problems. Few military members
hesitate to seek external help for equipment problems.

environments (their bases, their exercises, and their workplaces)—and perhaps, on occasion, even their homes—to social scientists. Truly productive collaboration will involve encouraging an attitude of openness and inclusiveness and establishing a long-term relationship of trust.

These suggestions are only the tip of the iceberg, though. Many of the problems and research issues addressed by this book's contributors involve deeply ingrained social, cultural, and doctrinal issues that will have significant implications for militaries. Military organizations themselves will therefore need to be open to new research ideas; to explore alternative methods of accomplishing tasks; to participate in the development of scientific hypotheses; and to support data collection during training, exercises, and even operations. Addressing the problems will demand long-term commitment.

And as is true for most military operations, success is not guaranteed. By its very nature, all research is risk-intensive. Social science research is even more so. After all, few physical scientists worry about having a chemical reaction talk back to them. Nor are they overly concerned about keeping the data from radioisotope studies confidential. Because they study humans (and teams of humans), social scientists require difficult-to-implement experimental procedures and controls. Fortunately, the potential gains in military knowledge more than offset the risks of failure.

6.2. Social Science Initiatives

The single most important initiative that social science can undertake to foster collaboration with militaries involves making its products more accessible to them. The product of social science is not equipment (for example, radar systems, munitions, and propellants). It is *knowledge*—knowledge that guides, triggers change, instills confidence, increases effectiveness, contributes to operational success. Social science knowledge increases self-awareness, both individually and organizationally. We maintain that awareness of the human condition is perhaps the most important capability that command can develop. Self-knowledge, for instance, greatly reduces the likelihood of succumbing to an adversary's attempted manipulation.

But we also assert that social scientists must go well beyond simply producing knowledge concerning human behaviour: they must communicate that knowledge to those who need it. Researchers who want their work to have an effect cannot merely publish their studies' results in erudite scientific journals, although publication in such a venue is certainly necessary for establishing scientific credibility. They must also publish their findings in military journals that are geared for the intelligent lay reader. They must take every opportunity to present their theories and results to interested military audiences, from the most junior to the most senior levels. And they must be available to advise the military concerning doctrine, strategic human resources, and personnel policy. In short, the social sciences must become an indispensable resource to militaries, no different from military intelligence or logistical support.

Social scientists must remember that the military does not exist solely to provide them with the means to do research. Militaries have more legitimate and more important claims to existence. For a research program on command to be successful, a significant level of trust must be established between the two partners (the military and the scientists), but the burden of responsibility for establishing this trust resides solely with the research community. That community must prove that it is capable of responsible, fair, realistic, productive, and professional behaviour. According to one workshop participant, social scientists must be willing to "get down in the dirt" if they want access to military personnel. Simply dropping off boxes of questionnaires to field units will not endear social scientists to the military community.

We believe that social science can benefit militaries as much by raising the awareness of human issues within the military environment as by discovering the principles behind human behaviour. Ideally, then, militaries should institute education programs for developing their own social science professionals. Military colleges should offer undergraduate and graduate programs in psychology, sociology, history, and so on, taught by military professors who conduct their own active research programs in these areas. These colleges should be associated with other military and civilian academic institutions around the world, and they should establish on-site research facilities in the military environment itself.

7. CONCLUSION

At the Human in Command Workshop, senior military officers with varied operational experience got the chance to interact with social scientists from various disciplines. The workshop's organizers aimed to expose each community to the other's successes and challenges. This book's chapters speak to the importance of human issues in command—issues that scientists have under-researched and militaries have overlooked. Some authors offer impassioned testimonials to command's hardships and rewards; others present sound empirical findings, showing the value of social science research.

In this final chapter, we've tried to summarize the workshop participants' views and opinions. We described the military context, seeking to do justice to its remarkably complex, demanding, and fluid nature. We also outlined the pressing command issues requiring research, attempting to explain their scope and interrelationship. On reflection, we believe that we've successfully attained some of those goals, while perhaps falling short of the mark on others. Nevertheless, we think we've accomplished our overall intent: to raise awareness of human issues in command within the military, the research community, and the general reading audience.

But awareness will only go so far. Without commitment, awareness is futile. In our opinion, there is a deep-set reason for what we see as a lack of commitment to the human in command. A philosophical and theoretical vacuum in command and control has long existed, both in the military and in the research community. Foster (1988) observed this problem explicitly, and little progress has occurred since. As a result, militaries and scientists have been left to struggle blindly on their own, buffeted by new trends in technology or new concepts of operation. We believe that the germ of a new philosophy exists in the contributions to this book. This philosophy takes as its fundamental axiom that only humans command—that only human competency, authority, and responsibility can achieve and give direction to command. Therefore it is imperative that a coherent and consistent approach to C^2 be developed and then adopted by both communities. We offer this book as the first step toward achieving that goal.

8. REFERENCES

Bennis, W. (1999). The end of leadership. In *Selected Proceedings of the 1998 Annual Meeting: Leaders and Scholars Association* [On-line]. Available http://academy.umd.edu

Canada. (1997). *Dishonoured legacy: The lessons of the Somalia affair—Report of the Commission of Inquiry into the Deployment of Canadian Forces to Somalia*. Ottawa: Commission of Inquiry into the Deployment of Canadian Forces to Somalia [Somalia Inquiry].

Foster, G. D. (1988). Contemporary C^2 theory and research: The failed quest for a philosophy of command. *Defense Analysis, 4* (3), 201–228.

McCann, C., & Pigeau, R. (1996). Taking command of C^2. In *Proceedings of the Second International Command and Control Research and Technology Symposium* (pp. 531–546). Washington, DC: National Defense University.

McCann, C., & Pigeau, R. (1999). Clarifying the concepts of control and command. In *Proceedings of the 1999 Command and Control Research and Technology Symposium* (pp. 475–490). Newport, RI: Naval Warfare College.

THE CONTRIBUTORS

Note: In this section, titles (for example, Colonel) reflect contributors' situations as we go to press, whereas the chapter title pages reflect chapter authors' situations at the time of the NATO Human in Command Workshop. Occasionally (as in the case of a promotion), a contributor's title in this section will be different from that shown on the associated chapter title page.

Colonel (Retired) John **Bearfoot** now provides support for research into the development of the British Army's training and simulation program. He previously spent 30 years in the British Army, where he specialized in training.

Professor Glynis M. **Breakwell** is Professor of Psychology and Director of the Centre for Defence Psychology at the United Kingdom's University of Surrey. Her research interests include leadership and identity processes in team and intergroup conflict, and risk communication.

Professor Berndt **Brehmer** is Professor of Command and Control Decision Making at the Swedish National Defence College, where he investigates issues in dynamic and distributed decision making.

Lieutenant Colonel Cranson A. **Butler** is a career infantry army officer and project manager who is currently chief of the annual training in the Training Directorate, First U.S. Army, Fort Gillem, Georgia. His interests include team building and leading change, as they apply to leadership behaviours.

Colonel M. D. **Capstick** is a Canadian Army officer. He commanded the Canadian Battalion Group and Sector 3 (Nicosia) in the U.N. Force in Cyprus (1992–1993) and the Canadian contingent of NATO's Stabilization Force in Bosnia–Herzegovina (1997–1998).

Lieutenant Colonel Timothy **Challans** is an infantry officer in the U.S. Army and one of the original co-authors of its new leadership doctrine. He is now an assistant professor of philosophy at the United States Military Academy in West Point, New York.

Brigadier General (Retired) Stanley **Cherrie** served with the U.S. Army in Vietnam, the Gulf, and Bosnia, retiring as U.S. assistant deputy chief of staff for training. He is now a senior military analyst supporting the Army's development of a new constructive simulation (WARSIM 2000) at Fort Leavenworth, Kansas.

Lieutenant Colonel (Retired) William M. **Connor** is writing the U.S. Army's command and control field manual at the Command and General Staff College, Fort Leavenworth, Kansas. He commanded armoured cavalry units in combat in Vietnam.

Lieutenant-General R. R. **Crabbe** retired in 1998 as Canada's deputy chief of the defence staff, after serving in the Canadian Army for almost 20 years. He was the deputy force commander of the United Nations Protection Force (UNPROFOR) in the former Republic of Yugoslavia, for which the government of France awarded him that country's gold medal for national defence.

Lieutenant Colonel Donald M. **Craig** has served in a variety of U.S. Army command and staff positions in the continental United States and in Germany. He is currently chief of the Leader Development Office, Center for Army Leadership, Fort Leavenworth, Kansas.

Lieutenant-General R. A. Dallaire commanded the United Nations Observer Mission in Uganda and Rwanda (UNOMUR) and the United Nations Assistance Mission for Rwanda (UNAMIR). Recently he has been appointed special advisor for officer professional development to the Canadian chief of the defence staff.

Jarle **Eid** is an associate professor in psychology at the Royal Norwegian Naval Academy, with an adjunct position at Norway's University of Bergen. He performs research in military units in Norway to investigate leadership and how people cope with stressful events.

Lieutenant Commander Bård S. **Eriksen** is currently serving in the Royal Norwegian Navy. His research on interrogation was carried out to fulfill part of the requirements for the Royal Norwegian Naval Academy, Part Two (Staff College I).

Dr. Henrik **Eriksson** is an associate professor in the Department of Computer and Information Science, Linköping University, Sweden. His research areas include knowledge-based systems, knowledge acquisition, command and control systems, and medical informatics.

Colonel drs. Peer L. E. M. **Everts** is a professional army officer with vast experience in peace operations and command and staff functions. His current interests include leadership and military culture.

Dr. Jon J. **Fallesen** is a research psychologist who studies soldier and leader performance and cognition to improve commander training and leader development for the U.S. Army.

Major Kelly M. J. **Farley** is a military psychologist on the Canadian Forces Land Staff. His areas of interest include morale, cohesion, confidence in leadership, and hostage survival.

Corinne **Jeffery** is a human factors scientist who is studying simulation, training, and command theory in support of the United Kingdom's armed services.

Major-General M. K. **Jeffery** commands the 1st Canadian Division of the Canadian Land Force. His previous military responsibilities have included several command, instructor, and staff positions in Canada; he also commanded the Canadian contingent of the U.N. Transition Assistance Group (UNTAG) in Namibia.

Dr. Bjørn Helge **Johnsen** is an associate professor in psychology at Norway's University of Bergen, with an adjunct position at the Royal Norwegian Naval Academy. His main research interests are cognitive neuroscience and military psychology.

Dr. Joan Hall **Johnston** is a U.S. Navy senior naval research psychologist responsible for conducting exploratory and advanced research in tactical decision-making, team training, and advanced training technologies.

Drs. E.-H. **Kramer** is a social psychologist in the social sciences department at the Royal Netherlands Military Academy. His research interests include leadership, dilemmas, and organizational design.

Colonel J. Serge **Labbé** is an infantry officer who has served as both chief of staff and deputy commander for 1st Canadian Division. He is currently the deputy assistant chief of staff for operations, plans, and policy at NATO's Joint Headquarters SOUTHEAST, in Izmir, Turkey.

Dr. Jon Christian **Laberg** is a professor in psychology at Norway's University of Bergen, with an adjunct position at the Royal Norwegian Naval Academy. His research interests are in clinical and military psychology.

Brigadier (Retired) Dick **Lambe** began working with the United Kingdom's Defence Evaluation and Research Agency to support research into command theory and training after a successful career in the British Army. He is now the Principal of the Bangladesh Armed Services Defence College.

Commander (Retired) Richard A. **Lane** is a maritime command and control scientist who is researching C^2 and sensor/effector requirements, including decision support systems, for future U.K. maritime command systems.

Colonel (Retired) John P. **Lewis** held multiple general staff and command positions through the brigade level in the U.S. Army. He served as director for the Center for Army Leadership, providing the direction and guidance to bring to completion the U.S. Army's new leadership doctrine (published in July 1999).

Lieutenant Colonel (Retired) James F. **Love** has extensive experience in multiservice and joint-service training research and development, as well as military expertise. As an artillery officer, he served in a variety of command and staff positions. He also wrote the initial version of U.S. Joint Publication 3-0, *Doctrine for Joint Operations* (Washington, DC: Joint Chiefs of Staff).

Carol **McCann** is a human factors scientist who is researching command theory, trust, and teamwork with the Research and Development Branch of the Canadian Department of National Defence.

Dr. Jim **McLennan** is a senior research fellow at the Swinburne Computer–Human Interaction Laboratory, Swinburne University of Technology, Australia.

Dr. Angelo **Mirabella** is an experimental psychologist currently studying how battlefield digitization will change training requirements for soldiers and leaders going into the twenty-first century.

Lieutenant Colonel Peter J. **Murphy** is a military psychologist in the Australian Defence Force. He is currently the staff officer for human performance within the Land Operations Division of the Defence Science and Technology Organisation in Adelaide, Australia.

Dr. James M. **Nyce**, a cultural anthropologist, has studied how information technologies, particularly those in higher education and medicine, emerge and are used in workplaces and organizations.

Dr. Mary **Omodei** conducts research in the School of Psychological Science at Australia's La Trobe University, where she studies complex time-sensitive decision making in simulated and natural environments.

Dr. Carol **Paris**, a naval research psychologist with the U.S. Navy, is responsible for conducting exploratory and advanced research in tactical decision making, performance measurement, and technologies for future naval platforms.

Commander Jeff **Penrose** is the director of the Management of Serious Crime Program, Australian Federal Police. His interests include the practical application of command theory, police practice, and teamwork.

Lieutenant Colonel Per-Arne **Persson** is researching command theory and information systems for support of command and is currently completing his Ph.D. at Sweden's Linköping University.

Dr. Ross **Pigeau** is an experimental psychologist who heads the Command Group at Canada's Defence and Civil Institute of Environmental Medicine (DCIEM). His research interests include command theory, sleep deprivation, and the philosophy of science.

Darian **Reeves** is a research analyst who has developed training and display technologies, performance measurement methodologies, and software for handheld devices used by U.S. Naval Afloat Training Groups.

Lieutenant Colonel Lawrence G. **Shattuck**, Ph.D., is an associate professor at the United States Military Academy, West Point, New York. He employs cognitive systems engineering methodologies to investigate military command and control issues.

Dr. Guy L. **Siebold** is a social psychologist with extensive experience conducting research in his focal areas of training, leadership, cohesion, and motivation.

Lieutenant Colonel Jonathan J. **Smidt** is an aviator with both an operations and an academic background. He is currently managing editor for *Military Review*, the U.S. Army Command and General Staff College journal.

Dr. A. L. W. **Vogelaar**, a social psychologist, heads the social sciences department of Social Sciences at the Royal Netherlands Military Academy. His research interests include leadership, the responsibilities of commanders, trust, and stress.

Professor Alexander **Wearing** is with the psychology department at the University of Melbourne, where he investigates complex problem solving and decision making.

Dr. Donna **Winslow** is a Canadian anthropologist whose research interests include, among other topics, military culture, cultural interoperability, ethical decision making for military leaders, and the analysis of peace operations as complex cultural encounters.

Dr. David D. **Woods** is a professor at the Ohio State University and co-founder of its Institute for Ergonomics. His research interests include investigating complex cognitive systems in a variety of domains, including aviation, medicine, and nuclear power.

Lieutenant Commander Kenneth K. **Zachariassen** is a member of the Royal Norwegian Navy. He has a background in military intelligence.

INDEX

"*n*" and a number following a page number indicates that the term may be found in a footnote on the page indicated.